GEORGIE FAME
There's nothing else to do

By Uli Twelker

*For my friend, Small Faces & fellow Fame Devon Rees! Enjoy Georgie's capers, and there's enough about Marriott, Mac & Mods in here, too.
Best
Uli Twelker, Gütersloh 20/12/2016*

This softbound edition published by
www.VelocePress.com
San Antonio, Texas 78230, U.S.A.

© Veloce Enterprises Inc.
Printed in the U.S.A.
ISBN 978-1-58-850129-5

First edition published 2014 by Uli Twelker Publishing
33 Heckenweg, D-33330 Gütersloh Germany

© Uli Twelker

The right of Uli Twelker to be identified as author of this work is asserted by him in accordance with the Copyright, Designs and Patents Act 1988.

No part of this book may be reproduced, stored in a retrieval system or transmitted, in any form or by any means without prior permission in writing of the publisher, nor be otherwise circulated in any form of binding or cover other than that in which it is published and without a similar condition including this condition being imposed on the subsequent purchaser. Any translations are only legal by permission of the author.

Front cover illustration by Johannes Saurer, Moisburg, Germany
Back cover photographs by Wolfgang Wotke, Gütersloh, Germany
Layout: Thomas Auer, Innsbruck, Austria, www.buchsatz.com
Printing: Czech Republic

ISBN 978-3-00-046731-8

Author's Note

Ever since I started working on this biog in bits and pieces – weekends, holidays, sabbaticals – roughly about 2005, with research going back many many more years, Georgie Fame has been working on his own biography – with the help of Ben Sidran, his congenial, pleasant and knowledgeable American counterpart in all things Jazzy R&B. Therefore, while Fame was always forthcoming, friendly and willing to answer my questions, my book could never have been on Georgie's priority list at any given time. However, when the man learnt that I was finally going ahead in earnest, he expressed his liberal attitude – "You can write what you want!" – but at the same time, most obviously, wished I would "write things down correctly".

This, needless to say, was also my priority. And so I sent him a late draft of my work in progress during late 2013 – with most of the text written, edited and corrected, but with some interview and source material still missing. Georgie was most engaged in reading through it all and offering corrections in a number of long and thorough telephone conversations. Where things I had written turned out not to be true, factually or as far as my interpretations were concerned, I put them right or, in some cases, simply took them out. In other incidents, the artist's views made me reconsider. For instance, with regard to *Tell Me Something – The Songs of Mose Allison*, I had been more critical of some of its aspects, but listening again, toned these down. In other cases, like Georgie's controversial Reggae album *Closing The Gap*, I retained my positive excitement where, for the creator, things had turned out a lot less than desirable.

Also, some source material was deemed dubious by the man who, to his entire credit, lived through it all, while this author had been either too young, not present at the proceedings, or indeed both! Whenever I chose to leave this material in, I decided to do so in order to add some peculiar zeitgeist color – always in danger of clashing with the protagonist's present day memories – or to include some other voices of GF companions who happen(ed) to view things differently. All this has been undertaken with the principle of utmost respect for the man, his dedication to music and his stunning, beautiful, massive as well as massively underrated body of work. Where the clashes of opinion were obvious, I have now added an addendum which gives room for Georgie's own thoughts. No doubt, Fame's own book will soon put things in a different perspective entirely. Till then, hats off to Fame's views!

When GF phoned me not too long ago, he said, "I just never like to read about myself, but I am aware what you're trying to do with this book, and I appreciate it…" So there.

Uli Twelker

Contents

Foreword by Bill Wyman ... 10

Prelude ... 11

Introduction – Georgie Fame & His Music: There's Nothing Else To Do ... 13

1: "Like a little lamb that's lost in wood"? Never! – Childhood & Teenage Years ... 15
R & B – Rhythm & Butlins ... 18
Power & Wilde, Fury & Fame – the Larry Parnes touring stable ... 22
Fame Fired – for expanding on Rock'n'Roll & Jazz! ... 32

2: "Get On The Right Track, Baby!" – The Flamingo Years ... 36
The Flamingo Story ... 37
"Move It On Over" – The Blue Flames take charge ... 39
Enter The Hammond ... 43
Niimoi "Speedy" Acquaye – the conga wizard ... 49
Eddie "Tan Tan" Thornton ... 50
Enter the performing G.I.s ... 51
Regulars at the Flamingo ... 52
Lucky Gordon, Christine Keeler & The Profumo Scandal ... 56
Ska rivals jazzy R&B ... 61
Blue Flames play Blue Beat – but Georgie remains "stumm" ... 64
The Pirate Station that was started because of Georgie – Radio Caroline ... 66
The legendary live album – Rhythm and Blues at the Flamingo ... 68
Rhythm And Blues at the Flamingo – track by track ... 71
Rhythm & Blue Beat – the first studio EP ... 75
Dawn Yawn – The Flamingo legend continues ... 76
The Blue Flames – a merry-go-round talent factory ... 82
"All About My Girl" – A little glimpse into the private price of Fame ... 89
"Do It The Hard Way" – Gigging 10 dates a week ... 89
(Not) All Quiet On The Studio Front – Single misses & Fame At Last ... 91
The first studio album – Fame At Last ... 92
The first Number One – "Yeh Yeh"! ... 95
Red Neck Blues – No Atlantic Crossover ... 100
"Get Away" with Sweet Things – Fame & Flames' Golden Year of 1966 ... 103
The Sweet Things album – track by track ... 105
The second number one – "Get Away"! ... 109
The End Of The Sixties Blue Flames ... 110
The End of The Flamingo Club ... 112
The first Georgie Fame Big Band Album – Sound Venture ... 113
Sound Venture – track by track ... 116

3: Going Solo – The CBS Jazz & Lounge Years 122
"Point Of No Return" – Columbia cash in on Fame's CBS headlines 124
"Knock On Wood" – The solo deal which allowed Pop and R&B 125
More Jazz in Sound Venture mode – The Two Faces Of Fame 129
The Two Faces Of Fame – track by track 130
 "Fame? Who's Fame?" – The Count Basie Connection 133
A Man And His Music – back to the West End 136
How to dread a sure smash – Georgie ties in with "Bonnie & Clyde" movie 139
More than a nostalgic 1930s pastiche – The Third Face Of Fame 143
The Third Face Of Fame – track by track 144
"Side By Side" – Count Basie Revisited 148
"Am I Wasting My Time" – How (not) to follow-up to "Bonnie & Clyde" 150
"For Your Pleasure" – Fame Swinging All Over The World 152
R&B takes preference over lush strings: Seventh Son 154
Seventh Son – track by track 155
"Lush Vibes" – the lounge album Georgie Does His Thing With Strings 159
Georgie Does His Thing With Strings – track by track 159
Entertaining Mr Sloane – Georgie's soundtrack work 163
The Georgie Fame Band that toured the UK – and America: Shorty! 163
Shorty ft. Georgie Fame – track by track 166
Going Home – The Second Keith Mansfield Project 169

4: (Almost) All Our Own Work – The Georgie Fame & Alan Price Years 173
The Price of Fame – TV boasted the night club stars 175
The duet album: Fame & Price/Price & Fame Together 178
"Time I Moved On" – mutual gigs but separate paths 182
"Leaving The City Behind" – Georgie moves his big love and family to the country 187
All Me Own Work – The Reprise album with entirely self-penned songs 189
All Me Own Work – track by track 191
Back to the small Blue Flames – Fame, Holland, Odgers & Bennett 195

5: The Island Years – The Okie Blue Flames and The Big Band Flames 199
The Georgie Fame album – an overlooked masterpiece from 1974 200
"Call Up The Devil" – The Large Blue Flames 203
The Ali Shuffle 206
More Island Sessions in Nashville 207
The Island drought – Singles but no further albums 209
The Daylight album – catalogue number, 20 tracks and no release 210
Daylight – the possible selection track by track 211
Back on the global live circuit 213
Fame For a Price – The Session Man in the 60s and 70s 215
Mississippi Mud in the Thames Valley – Fame plays for Muddy Waters 216
High time for a new album – Right Now! 219

6: The Pye Years – From Stevie Wonder To Hoagy Carmichael — 219
Right Now! – Track-by-Track — 220
Interpreting Elvis – Costello's title track for That's What Friends Are For — 223
That's What Friends Are For – track by track — 225
Closing The Gap – The Reggae album 15 years after the Ska Blue Flames — 227
Closing The Gap – track by track — 228
Back to Jazz – In Hoagland 1981 with Annie Ross and Hoagy Carmichael — 231
Hoagy Carmichael (1900–1981) — 231
Annie Ross (b. 1930) — 232
In Hoagland 1981 – track by track — 234
The Heroes album — 240

7: Dynamite Brass & Dynamite Friends – From Stockholm to Sydney — 242
In Goodmansland – Fame combines his love of Sweden and Big Bands — 244
In Goodmansland – track by track: — 245
"Saturday Night Fish Fry" – Party Flames in the New Romantic 1980s — 248
My Favourite Songs – track by track — 251
Georgie Fame's Brother-in-Charms – Steve Gray — 253
Singer The Musical – Fame's fab lyrics & Steve Gray's great melodies — 254
Singer The Musical – track by track — 256
My Second Home – More Musical Adventures in Sweden — 260
Georgie Fame, Lena Ericsson, Lasse Samuelsson – track by track — 261
"New York Afternoon" – A new sound door opens — 263
The Aussie Blue Flames – Touring and recording "down under" — 264
No Worries – track by track — 265
After Hoagland and Goodmansland – Bakerland: A Portrait of Chet — 268
A Portrait of Chet – Georgie Fame/Ellen Helmus Sextet, track by track — 269

8: The longest-serving band in Fame history: The Vintage 1990 Blue Flames — 272
Guy Barker – "Bugler" Extraordinaire — 272
Alan Skidmore – still in the Blue Flames — 277
"Aaaaaaa-Anthony Kerr" – Wizard on the Vibraphone — 278
James and Tristan Powell join their father's band — 282
"Brother Tristan on guitar" — 284
"Brother James on the drums" — 286
"Working For The Van" – The Van Morrison Connection — 290
Cool Cat Blues – The first Ben Sidran directed album — 295

9: The Go Jazz Years – "The Blues And Him" — 295
Cool Cat Blues – Track by Track — 297
Go Jazz All-Stars Live in Japan – A "pitch black studio" and enthusiastic crowds — 300
Georgie On My Mind – Live In Zagreb hot on the heels of Japan — 301
The Blues And Me – The second Ben Sidran produced album — 304

Three Line Whip – The Family Trio as the Blue Flames nucleus ... 309
Three Line Whip – the family album ... 311
Three Line Whip – Track by Track ... 313
Geoff Gascoyne – the ace bass player who followed the incredible Brian Odgers ... 318
Tristan Powell, engineer and record producer ... 319

10: "Chat as much as you like" – The Ronnie Scott's Club live residencies ... 322
The Story of Ronnie Scott and his Club ... 323
Ronnie Scott – portrait glimpses of the man and the club ... 329
"Jeannine" – Ronnie Scott's Club live specials over the years ... 330
How Long Has This Been Going On – The Morrison & Fame Ronnie Scott's album ... 333
Ronnie Scott's Club and the first Blue Flames live album for 33 years ... 337
Name Droppin': Live At Ronnie Scott's – track by track ... 338
How can this burning band have been ill? – Walking Wounded ... 339
Walking Wounded: Live At Ronnie Scott's Part 2 – track by track ... 340
Tell Me Something: ... 344
Tell Me Something: The Songs of Mose Allison – Track by Track ... 345

11: "Strike Up The Band" – More Big Band adventures ... 348
City Life – track by track ... 349
The Danish Radio Big Band ... 352
Endangered Species: Danish Radio Big Band/Georgie Fame track by track ... 353
Sweden & Denmark, where else in Scandinavia? "S/S Norway"! ... 355
The 55th Birthday Big Band ... 358
"Brass Damage" – continued Big Band bashes ... 360

12: Working For A Stone: The Bill Wyman's Rhythm Kings membership ... 367
Struttin' Our Stuff + Anyway The Wind Blows + Groovin' = 1 Fame album ... 369
"I'm A Qualified Rhythm King" – touring with Bill Wyman ... 371
Double Bill & Just For A Thrill – the 2nd Fame Rhythm Kings "album" ... 373
Two out of a thousand gigs – Osnabrück and Düsseldorf ... 376

13: Poet In New York – adventures in the new millennium ... 379
Poet In New York – track by track ... 382
The first Blue Flames studio album for seven years – Relationships ... 385
Relationships – Track by Track ... 387
On the heels of Relationships – the Blue Flames album Charlestons ... 390
The last Blue Flame (so far) – Alec Dankworth ... 396
"Closing Another Gap" – The Imaginary Swing Album ... 398
Touring with the Blue Flames – More adventures on stage ... 401
Touring with the Blue Flames – Adventures off stage ... 405
Sessions in the new millennium – Georgie much in demand ... 408
TV in the new millennium – Georgie and The Birth of Cool ... 409

14: The Last Blue Flames	412
Tone Wheels 'A' Turnin' – track by track	413
Singer Reloaded: the Fame/Gray/Bell Musical back on stage – and record	421
"Keep It Simple": The acoustic trio album Lost In A Lover's Dream	423
Lost In A Lover's Dream – Track by Track	425
Friday Night Is Music Night – Honouring Georgie's 70th at Cheltenham	428
Anthems For a Band Leader	431
Anthems For A Great Singer	437
"There's nothing else to do" – Clive on Georgie	439
"Lost In A Collector's Dream" – Possible Future Releases	440
The World Wide Star or The World Wide Friend	442
Acknowledgements	444
Interviewees A-Z	446
Discography	447
Bibliography (Selections)	474
Index	480
About The Author	492
Addendum & Photo Credits	493

"Mac's Selfie": Ian McLagan and Georgie Fame at the Royal Albert Hall, October 25th, 2009, 40 years after their last encounter.

Foreword by Bill Wyman (Rolling Stones & Bill Wyman's Rhythm Kings)

Uli Twelker's book on Georgie Fame

Georgie Fame

From the day I first saw Georgie at the Flamingo Jazz Club in early 1963, to the final day he played with my Rhythm Kings last autumn, he has been an inspiration.

He inadvertently introduced me to Mose Allison in those early times, for which I am forever grateful.

Our 15 years together in the Rhythm Kings was something special, and apart from his masterful singing and playing, the little pieces of history he would recite before a song, or in private, always intrigued me

I hope this book will introduce more music lovers to Georgie's awesome talents.

– Bill Wyman

Prelude

In 1981, West London precincts and building sites sported the poster slogan "Georgie Fame – The Godfather of British R&B!" For those who contemplated a wry smile at the time: Georgie Fame deserves that particularly huge claim to fame by a million miles. By 1981, he had at least shared the Godfather tag for a full twenty years – with both Alexis Korner and John Mayall. While Alexis would swing easy with the infant Rolling Stones, future Manfred Mann Paul Jones and the complete Graham Bond Trio featuring Jack Bruce and Peter "Ginger" Baker, while Mayall "educated", or rather employed, Eric Clapton, Peter Green and Mick Taylor, Georgie Fame had exquisite musical ambassadors of his own. Guitarists John McLaughlin and Colin Green, prime drummers Red Reece, Phil Seamen, Jon Hiseman and Mitch Mitchell, the best reed players in town from Glenn Hughes via Johnny Marshall to Tubby Hayes – and legends sealed to Blue Flames history like conga man "Speedy" Acquaye and trumpet ace Eddie "Tan Tan" Thornton. There were literally legions of other "name musicians" – they all passed through his forever changing trademark, "Georgie Fame & The Blue Flames". One of those guys has actually managed to stay with him (on and off) for more than four and a half decades now: saxophone player Alan "El Skid" Skidmore.

As early as 1962, Georgie Fame was one of the first British piano players to master the Hammond organ – a powerful new alternative to those Mickey Mouse "Red River Rock" Farfisa keyboards or those rather tame Lowrey organs. Georgie was also the pioneer in putting some really soulful, sophisticated Rhythm into the Blues where before there had been either Mississippi twelve bar mutterings or Trad Jazz, Swing and Bebop disciples. In fact, for the sake of his then mainly Afro-American audiences in London's Soho district, Air Force G.I.s as well as West Indian immigrants, Fame had made sure he would use several grooves, rhythms, beats: Jump Jive, Funk, Brazilian Sambas and, uniquely, Ska, preceding the whole 2-Tone movement of The Specials and Madness et al by almost twenty years. In typical modesty, Fame may have called Zoot Money's Big Roll Band the best R&B outfit in Sixties Britain, but Zoot himself shut him up on stage at the Forum in Kentish Town during Georgie's 55th Birthday Concert on June 26th, 1998: "No, he had the best!"

A fine bandleader and influential Hammond hero and prime R&B singer, Georgie had only been twenty-one when he sank his substantial "Yeh Yeh" royalties into a Big Band concept LP, *Sound Venture*. A year after its release in 1966, the legendary US

band leader and pianist Count Basie saw Fame's potential as a prime jazz singer, and asked him to accompany him on UK tours, an honour Fame has held with pride and humility ever since. Georgie "I'm still learning" Fame has always honed his craft of ballad singing, swinging, hollering and sophisticated Vocalese – giving words to famous instrumental, mainly horn solos – to such perfection that he may be the world's leading, if unsung, Jazz mastersinger. The French certainly thought so when they gave him the *Prix Billie Holiday* for his album *Poet in New York* in 2000. Likewise, the BBC honoured him with a big radio Gala in 2013 at the *Cheltenham Jazz Festival* – for 50 years in business.

Georgie Fame: poet and composer, singer and player; appearing with his two sons, his ongoing Blue Flames as well as Van Morrison, Bill Wyman's Rhythm Kings and several Big Bands all over the world. Overdue as well as continuing – here's his story!

Georgie Fame & His Music: There's Nothing Else To Do

Whether you are looking at a "Rockin' Chair", a "Jazz Bar Stool" or a "Blues Café Couch", Georgie Fame certainly manages to sit in between all the imaginable musical chairs. Who the hell in this business could claim to have been successful in such numerous styles? On top of his early influences of Jamaican Blue Beat, Latin and Rock'n'Roll, there were soon also Blues, Cool Jazz, Modern Jazz, Big Band Swing, Reggae, Soul, Middle of the Road pop, Jazz Ballads, Vocalese and Music Hall!

Who else, apart from Georgie Fame, manages to play two consecutive nights in venues as contrasting as a pub and a theatre? And who else would present such different music? He would deliver Flamingo-days R&B plus "Humpty Dumpty" in Ska-style, clad in a pilot's overall at "The Half Moon" in London's leafy Thames suburb Putney, and then croon sophisticated Benny Goodman Swing – smartly dressed in a white dinner jacket at London's Ealing Theatre! We are talking about the autumn of 1983; these days Georgie appears tastefully elegant wherever he performs.

Who else can feel at home with the Count Basie Big Band (1967) as well as with the Reggae Philharmonic Orchestra (1980)? Georgie Fame has been the Godfather of British ballrooms, bars and backstreets, and in venues of all sizes worldwide, in bold crossover style for more than 50 years, his Afro-American and West Indian fans helpfully starting the ball of street credibility rolling by spreading the word among their communities, picked up by Thames Valley white boys.

My first – and addictive – live encounter with Georgie Fame was a November 1975 appearance at the London University College with the Blue Flames, a reunion of sorts as he had been a familiar TV friend for eight years via *Beat Club* and *Beat Beat Beat* in my home of Germany. Now, I was incurably hooked to his unique mixture of humour and sophistication, light touch and intensive feeling, and have remained so ever since!

It took me another seven years until I talked to Fame for the first time, at a low key charity concert in North London in 1982. He was decidedly friendly and talkative, although we had never met before. A year later, during the summer of 1983, Georgie Fame & The Blue Flames played a rousing open air concert at Battersea Park, which had the crowd wailing to Louis Jordan's "Saturday Night Fish Fry" from his old Soho days, the always fitting "Funny How Time Slips Away", a truly intensive, and inevitable, reading of "Sitting In The Park" for the fans on the Battersea grass, a happily Reggae-fied "Humpty Dumpty", a positively wild "Zulu" celebrating the sunhine; "Yeh Yeh" and the soft-funky "Daylight" bookending an impressive career overview. Georgie was in a really boisterous, carefree mood, chatting away between sets and raving happily about the imminent release of his latest LP *My Favourite Songs!*, featuring Zoot Money, Andy Fairweather Low and his then current Blue Flames with Steve Gregory, as well as the re-release of his legendary, then 20-year old live album *Rhythm & Blues at the Flamingo*.

Then one day in 1994, I met with Georgie Fame for my first real interview. We did some 'sitting in the park' around the Oetkerhalle in my home town, the East-Westfalian Teutoburger Forest city of Bielefeld, an hour's drive from Hannover. There, he appeared with the WDR Big Band – "one of the best radio Jazz orchestras in Europe" – and Madeline Bell. I had just hoped for some nice anecdotes to spice up a little *GoodTimes* magazine portrait. I did get those anecdotes – and charmingly told too – but little could I anticipate that Fame would treat me to such exciting insights like the proceedings of song writing, the how's and where's of (then) thirty-plus years in recording activities, and modest, nonchalant name-dropping which – just as he had managed to make me feel at ease – made me realize I was talking to a legend.

This was followed by many more of such conversations, in both lavish and lacklustre backstage areas, lounges, gardens and bars. I can only marvel at the patience, and commitment, of the man – to his musical destiny, his band members, and a fellow who planned a book about him. Would I ever finish it? "Maybe posthumously", he grinned one day. All I know is that Georgie Fame is Britain's premier Jazz singer and Hammond player; that the man is probably the best living Jazz vocalist in the world right now; and that – however colourful his whole life up till now turns out to be portrayed by himself, what we have at this point is a unique stage character and his stunning body of work.

So overwhelming in fact that the acknowledgement you hold in your hands is only the tip of the wonderland. Georgie could do with a dozen books. Gotta start somewhere!

Uli Twelker, August 2014

Chapter 1

"Like a little lamb that's lost in wood"? Never! – Childhood & Teenage Years

The above quote, "I'm like a little lamb that is lost in wood", is from George Gerswhin's "Someone To Watch Over Me". Many balladeers have added their dramatic versions to this classic over the years, but Fame, a fine ballad singer himself, would go for a completely different approach in 1968 – a laconic talking style in his broad Lancashire accent; more about that later.

What is crucial here is that his "reading", this interpretation in the local vernacular says so much about the little boy who he would always be able to find a place for in his persona. Even at 71 – when he shouts "All aboard?!" in the middle of a sax solo, for instance – he is still the little lad from the cotton town up North, Leigh, Lancashire, now Greater Manchester and only nine and a half miles west of the Manchester city centre – eight miles southeast of Wigan.

In the last thirty years, hailing from "up North" suddenly did not seem as much of a problem as it had been before. Quite the contrary: Bands like Oasis from Manchester, or Wet Wet Wet from Glasgow, Scotland, were in for high praise in the 1990s, and – if only for a minority – were treated as a positive curiosity. This had been entirely different half a century before, when the young Clive Powell started out. With the exception of those "Fab Four" – The Beatles from the port of Liverpool – being from "up North" meant that you were treated as a little bit backward.

That, for instance, was how The Hollies felt when they came to London after having toured Lancashire.* That is also how The Alan Price Combo out of Newcastle-upon-Tyne, soon to morph into another Sixties legend, The Animals, experienced attitudes towards them. They included Clive Powell's future stage partner Alan Price, who would later manage to cultivate his Geordie boy heritage, developing into a singer/songwriter of some repute, not least in his "Jarrow Song" of 1973, which portrayed an October 1936 protest march against unemployment from the North Eastern town of Jarrow to London, to make the North East felt. And that is certainly how young the Clive Powell felt as a youngster in the cotton mill town of Leigh, Lancashire: proud of his roots.

If you look at the cover of Georgie Fame's 1971 solo album, *Going Home*, you will spot a black and white photograph of a steep road with cobblestones. "It is supposed to be Leigh in Lancashire, my hometown, but it isn't", Georgie says, "The designer

---
* This was portrayed in the Hollies song "Dolphin Days" in 2009, about bringing The Dolphins' Tony Hicks, Bernie Calvert & Bobby Elliott together with Ricky & Dane, i.e. Allan Clarke & Graham Nash.

just took a liberty there. It is just some Northern industrial town. We didn't have these hilly streets in Leigh", which is only 50 feet above sea level.

On the back of the LP sleeve, a similar scene appears in colour. Still only 28 years old and already a veteran of the British music scene, Georgie rides his bike like a young boy. As a "wee lad", Georgie Fame – born Clive Powell in Leigh on 26th June 1943 – used to play on the cobblestones of Cotton Street in this small town situated north-west of Manchester.

It was in these streets that he discovered his love of rhythm – playing castanets by using pieces of slate from derelict buildings. Many British people know Leigh as a name to be reckoned with in the English Rugby League. Young Clive as well as Old Georgie have always been fans of Leigh Rugby Football Club, which in 1995 was re-named Leigh Centurions.

Cotton Street was a more than appropriate name for the family's address, because many youngsters would see their most likely future in one of the cotton mills of the area, or face the alternative of coal mining – a looming reminder, the Parsonage Colliery overlooked the terraced houses of young Clive's neighbourhood. Clive was the younger one of two children, born when his sister was eight years old.

"I suppose it starts with an old photograph of this kid in short pants entering a talent contest in Middleton Towers in Morecambe", Fame would reminisce with the once well-known Deejay Alan Freeman,[1] and indeed one such snapshot appears on the cover of his 2001 album *Relationships*. "I couldn't have been more than six when I went in for this contest – and I won. The neighbours were knocked out. Where we lived it was a real *Coronation Street*", he continued, referring to the Granada TV soap, set in Manchester, which has been running since 1960, "gas lamps, the lot. We were rough and ready kids."

There was an early knack for rhythm, too: "I used to play the bones – you know, the minstrel kick. As kids we used to hang around the derelict sites and get slates off roofs and slice them up into these clickety-clickety bones. Later on, when I could afford it, I went into a music shop and got a pair of professional bones. My uncle taught me the rhythms and movements to 'Roll a Silver Dollar', and my aunt taught me how to dance", something the older Georgie clearly relishes on stage until today. "Among the lot of them I picked up basic rhythms – in fact, they were forced upon me."

On the one hand, he had a solid musical upbringing, starting with religious music. Just like quite a few of his school mates, Clive got his first taste of music performance

1. See Addendum

by singing in church, and at musical evenings in the church hall across the street. "I was never a member of the church choir", he told me, "but sat in the congregation. I learnt those hymns by going to church every week". He attended the church congregation when he was only just six years old. Independent of his Christian upbringing, it was those sounds he loved.

Clive would consequently develop a love of experimenting with different harmonies, entering a local singing competition. He was also musically prolific and gifted enough to teach himself to play the harmonica, and work the piano that was always in the front room on a trial and error basis. His parents heard him blow around and tinkle away all the time, whereas he received (and wanted) only a fairly limited amount of formal tuition on the piano, something he regretted: "I had piano lessons when I was seven but I didn't have the patience to practise," he told Freeman. "My people said 'You'll regret it when you're older'. And I do."

But even as a child, music seemed limited to a pastime activity. Very early in life, Clive Powell saw his father James Powell senior, a pub piano player and accordionist by night with a hobby dance band, deeply involved, or rather stuck, in the textile industry of his home turf, Leigh.

Leigh, the little town which had about 46.000 inhabitants in 1943, had been living from dairy farming before many households turned to cotton spinning and weaving towards the end of the 16th century. A true cottage industry took hold. Should you ever see Georgie Fame wear cord jeans – the fustian cloth, a sort of rough corduroy, was first woven in Leigh and sold to Manchester textile tycoons.

Then it was a Leigh citizen, Thomas High (1718–1803), a local reed-maker and manufacturer who invented the famous carding machine "Spinning Jenny" and a water-powered spinning frame in the 1760s. But just like Georgie Fame's records have often been pirated over the years, Thomas High's ground-breaking inventions were allegedly stolen by entrepreneur Sir Richard Arkwright (1732–1792), who made tons of money with patents that rightfully belonged to Thomas High.

Quite an impressive silk industry developed during the Industrial Revolution, and during the 19th century, this turned into a large cotton business when cotton mills started around the 1830s and several of the silk mills duly changed over to cotton in the years following 1870.

Consequently, during the 1930s, Powell's father found himself in the tradition of the cotton spinners. The night-time musician may have dreamt of working as a professional musician, but going without a day job just "wasn't done" in those days.

Clive's mother "died when I was nine: my real mother, whom I loved dearly", he confessed to Freeman – a fate which he had in common with his future musical partner Alan Price.

"There were just my sister and me. She was sixteen at the time. For nearly a year after my mother died, we had to do everything in the house while my father was at work. I'd go down on my knees and polish the lino and all that. Then my father married again …"

Powell was always imitating the sounds he heard from the radio. Via his parents' and school mates' record collections, Clive listened to Elvis Presley, Bill Haley and the Skiffle craze of Lonnie Donegan – like many other kids at the time. But he especially admired the sound and the fury of the ferocious piano pounding of those particular Southern US gentlemen by the names of Little Richard and Jerry Lee Lewis, who represented the raucous, uninhibited side of dirty Rock'n'Roll, combined with precisely those Gospel flavours which had always touched him so deeply.

His other, even more intensively adored, idol was the more subdued, wailing but wise New Orleans troubadour Antoine "Fats" Domino, who is a Hurricane Katrina survivor – and still singing and playing at 86. Clive admired the seemingly lazy but simultaneously sophisticated good-time piano style that Fats commanded, and told Alan Freeman that he "played in a little band we had and was more interested in Fats than anybody else – his maturity showed in his music and the way he felt." The chubby New Orleans Ninth Ward musician had been recording as early as Dec.10, 1949, starting with the autobiographical and self-deprecating "(They Call Me) The Fat Man" and moving on to smash hits like "Blueberry Hill" and "Hello Josephine". These were often lavishly orchestrated by big band leader Dave Bartholomew, who, 93 and counting in 2014, is still active in the music scene and, incidentally, would collaborate with Alan Price in the mid-1980s. A few years on, Clive would dedicate the EP *Fats For Fame* to him.

Watching Clive Powell's/Georgie Fame's stage antics over the years, those early heroes certainly left their impact throughout – neither the wild men (Little Richard and Jerry Lee) nor the wise man (Fats) being far apart or far away whenever Fame is working an audience. But then he loved them all – and not least that other wild man with Gospel and Country roots, New Orleans' Lloyd Price, whose "Lawdy Miss Clawdy" was still in Fame's repertoire in 2014.

R & B – Rhythm & Butlins

In 1957, still only fourteen years old, Clive Powell, the little Skiffle-rambling and rock-and-rolling piano boy joined a school band, The Dominoes. It was going to be a short experience, but the young teenager felt the bug of the stage intensively enough to practise his piano ever more passionately. The Dominoes played dance halls and pubs – like his father did. Powell told the BBC "My dad played, and virtually every house practically, in the days before television, had a piano in the front room, so there was always home entertainment. My sister played, she is eight years older than me, and she went through all the theory of grade six. And I picked up tunes. My dad was playing tunes of the day, pop songs of the day, 'Mr Sandman', songs from the First World War, stuff like that. But then with the Rock'n'Roll explosion, I think it was Jerry Lee Lewis, Fats Domino, Little Richard and, most importantly, Humphrey Lyttelton's recording of 'Bad Penny Blues' which had a wonderful Boogie Woogie piano by Johnny Parker on the recording. They were the catalysts."

Soon Clive experienced some wild Rock'n'Roll parties: "I started playing with a semi-professional band and we used to get gigs in the working men's clubs around town. This meant I'd get home about eleven or eleven-thirty. They thought I would be home at nine and I got a whacking." Then one night, young Clive returned home at about a quarter to one in the morning. The street lamps had been turned off: "I'd had a few warnings, but I love playing with the band and I was enjoying the company of old people at this dance and I suppose I just forgot."

Clive knocked on the front door of his home, and after repeating the exercise a few times, gave up. Literally shaking from the cold, he sat in the outside toilet and spent the night there. "I sat there until seven in the morning", he recalled, "when they all got up for work. And by that time a bit of hate had started to set in."

Soon enough, Clive felt a deep longing to play his music professionally and, what's more, outside of the confines of his provincial locale, if at all possible!

But for the moment he relented. Duly following his father's professional and musical footsteps, when he left Leigh Central County Secondary School at the age of fifteen young Clive started an apprenticeship as a weaver, while continuing to moonlight with the Dominoes: "Faced with the choice of working in a coalmine or a cotton factory, I chose that latter."

But the youthful Clive Powell's move away from the cotton factory was about to happen once the first summer vacation as an apprentice came his way. He spent his vacation at the Butlin's Holiday Camp – a lovely old-fashioned family resort still going in 2014 with "camps" in Bognor Regis, Minehead and Skegness – this one in Pwllheli in South Wales, in the summer of 1959. There, he was persuaded by his friends to take part in a Butlin's talent competition, "doing my Jerry Lee Lewis-Fats Domino thing and knock everybody out! I got through to the final – beating, incidentally, the Texans, a Liverpool group with Ringo Starr on drums." Getting through to the finals did not mean victory yet, but Georgie was in no doubt about his chances: "and I would have won it, too! But I withdrew before the finals, so Ringo Starr won it."

So why did our man withdraw? "As soon as I came off the stage, Rory Blackwell, whose band had the summer residency, offered me a job – and I took it!" Well, not right away.

The typical daydream which Clive Powell shared with many other aspiring young musicians was about to come true – standing in for the guy you are just admiring on stage. In Clive's case, it was the pianist of the quite popular resident Butlin's band, Rory Blackwell & The Blackjacks. Clive: "By this time, I could sing a few numbers at the piano on my own and word got round the camp, 'He's a good lad!' So I was offered a job by Rory Blackwell, whose band had a residency there with his band", he told Alan Freeman; a job where he would be playing *and* singing. "Rory drove me home after the week's holiday and I brought him into our house. But my parents didn't want to know. We argued all day and in the end I decided I wanted to leave. I was desperate."

What to do? Clive thought hard – Blackwell's offer sounded marvellous, although it would mean the end of his apprenticeship at the cotton mill. He saw himself run away from home – and must have imagined the shame and indignity of being picked up by an officer like some truant on a Teddy Boys picnic. So why not enquire about what he had let himself in for? He actually called on the local police department and said "I'm sixteen and I've been offered a job working as a musician. If I go away, can you bring me back?" The answer was more sensible and much more down-to-earth than he had expected: "If you lead a decent life and you're not committing crimes you can stay away as long as you like'."

Weren't these the kind of the "Pennies From Heaven" he needed, the sure sign? Clive might have had some re-assurance, but he didn't have the heart: "All the same, I didn't do it." He said goodbye to Rory Blackwell with the words "I'm sorry, Rory. I've decided to swallow it." Blackwell shrugged his shoulders and handed over his business card with his telephone number and uttered the fateful "If you change your mind, call me." So what exactly did he run away from at that moment?

Rory "Shakes" Blackwell, born on the 22nd June 1933 and thus ten years Clive's senior, was a singing drummer cum songwriter and held the World Drum Marathon record at the time. He was the leader of The Blackjacks, whose ranks the young pianist was now about to join. The Blackjacks had been noted as the first British Rock'n'Roll band in 1956 (before Cliff Richard & The Drifters/Shadows), and Blackwell had come to a certain amount of media fame by starring in the film *Rock You Sinners* in 1957 with Jackie Collins. The fact that his records and stage act featured US hit adaptations like the Larry Williams' Earl Palmer-powered "Bony Moronie" and Jerry Lee Lewis's "Great Balls Of Fire" suited Powell's preferences. Incidentally, Blackwell had managed to record "Bye Bye Love" in 1957, as early as the Everly Brothers - who obviously had the bigger hit with it.

Rory Blackwell: what a CV to have in mind on an early Monday morning back at the cotton mill. To make matters even more painful, every workmate there seemed to have heard about the discussions back home, some ventilating sour grapes and calling it a "palaver", others patting Clive's shoulders and reminding him this could be his big chance.

But to use the vocabulary of his big Butlin's "break", there was literally "no contest":

At exactly that moment – he had been in the cotton trade for a year – Clive decided that he had had enough after all and decided to hand in his notice. As Clive told Alan Freeman, "The next day I went up to the manager and said 'Can I leave on Friday?'

If Georgie Fame's life is ever going to be dramatized as a biopic movie of the Ray Charles type, the following scene is likely to be included: Father Powell met his son at the gates of the cotton mill and demanded an explanation to his completely unreasonable notice. Clive's increasingly late nights of gigging, in spite of his day job, had been frowned upon at home, but apart from the discussion with Blackwell, there had been no previous warnings via a good old family conference. Powell junior was shaken, but not stirred – he was going to pursue his dream, and he was going to leave the provinces, the cotton mills and his amateur status behind.

Fame: "And that was it. I was on my own. I went to Butlin's for Rory and I met a redcoat from Glasgow called Rene." The two of them soon became friends, "We had an affair at the camp", and the young lady showed fortune telling qualities when one night, she urged him to decline going to a nearby party outside the holiday camp. Georgie heeded her advice, stayed at Butlin's, and sure enough, Rory Blackwell had a car accident, actually being taken to a clinic.

Fame remembers well what followed at the next gig: "Rory was not able to perform to the best of his abilities, so he got the sack. The entertainment manager fired him. And we got the sack with him." Big Rory Blackwell being out of work was bad enough, but the pro would fall back on his feet a lot easier than the band, especially a young lad who had started his "career" about seven minutes ago – well, three weeks is nothing either. The cotton mill was no option, coming home was certainly out of the question – the humiliation would have crushed harder souls than Georgie's. So there was no alternative than following Rory Blackwell to London.

Just as a lot of Clive's Stateside black counterparts had moved away from the cotton fields of the American Deep South once they heard that in northern towns like Chicago and Detroit, the grass was greener and the grind of earning one's keep apparently less grueling – Powell moved in the opposite geographical direction, south, but had a similar motive of musical dedication. This was culminated by an urgent need to branch out to find an audience.

Blackwell had offered the young Clive the job of his singing pianist – and promised fame (pun not yet intended) and fortune in London. First that turned out to be the old Strava Ballroom in Islington, above which Blackwell had rented two rooms where Clive could move in.

The band had to play "for the door"; they received a percentage from the entrance fee takings, which were almost non-existent, "most nights there were about four people in there." Privately, things turned out to be just as bleak. Clive's girl, Rene, had accompanied him to London, "but", as he recalls, "only for a couple of weeks. It wasn't a long relationship." Rene confessed that she had to travel back to her native Scotland, because there were family problems. Clive remembered that "I saw her off at the station and she told me 'You'll be all right. You'll make it.' Poor Rene. We never met again after that. I walked away from the station feeling pretty low."

So the world of glitzy showbiz actually spelt junk food on a far from regular basis, and sleeping upstairs in the pub or on friends' floors and couches rather than some half-decent accommodation. Powell would have endured this new kind of apprenticeship, but after a mere four weeks in Islington, the Blackjacks called it a day. (It was to be an amusing coincidence that Rory Blackwell – whose own career continued for decades – would spend the 1980s as manager of the "Welcome Family Holiday Park, Dawlish Warren" in Devon. It is the very same lovely corner of England where the Fame-Powell family would reside for many years.)

It was now September 1959, and Powell was still only sixteen years old. Was his minimal career plan off once again? Not quite: "Rory got me a gig at an East End pub called The Essex Arms, because he felt guilty after the incident with the car crash. No pay. We used to send the hat round for the bread. On a good night I'd make maybe fifteen bob [shillings]. I was back on the fish and chips. I needed to sleep in that pub, too." – It was situated in Canning Town, near Silvertown Bridge.

He persevered though – and just about survived as the "imported" Cockney pub pianist until Rory Blackwell managed to help even more. He arranged a meeting with theatre maestro, *"Oliver!"*-impresario and Steve Marriott talent-spotter Lionel Bart, who heard Clive play. As Bart told Pete Frame, he remembers the encounter like this: "Clive came back to my place, and stood there playing Jerry Lee numbers on this little upright piano I had – a great big smile on his face. I always called him Bertie Beamer, for years and years, because of his wide, non-stop smile."

Lionel Bart duly arranged an audition with an acquainted concert promoter of his: "Of course, I duly lumbered him, because I sent him to see Larry Parnes. I used to send them all to Larry."

Lo and behold, the man they called "Parnes, Shillings & Pence" turned out to be co-operative. Georgie: "I had never met Larry Parnes before."

Power & Wilde, Fury & Fame – the Larry Parnes touring stable

Larry Parnes was a former women's clothing salesman who, at 27, had become to loathe the fashion business which he felt was tedious for him. Instead, he was immensely proud of his acquaintance – some say relationship – with America's soft crooner Johnny Ray. Parnes had gathered experience in the theatre with his partner, publicist John Kennedy, a New Zealander, who organized the photo studio of *Record Mirror* magazine, and was still (in)famous for a publicity prank unheard of in post-war Britain: for the touring play, *The House of Shame*, Kennedy and Parnes, who had invested heavily, persuaded two actresses to do some street PR clad in provocative "lingerie", streetwalker gear.

Next, John Kennedy joined both studio manager Roy Turvey and concert agent Geoff Wright in running the fortunes of the singing guitarist Thomas "Tommy" William Hicks from Bermondsey, South London (b. 1936). Thomas decided to rename himself Tommy Steele and proceeded to become England's answer to Elvis Presley; he could hardly have foreseen that he started a trend that Larry Parnes would make his very own.

Another idea he would make his very own was the plan to let teenage wonders tour the country together. As Pete Frame points out in his *The Restless Generation*, this

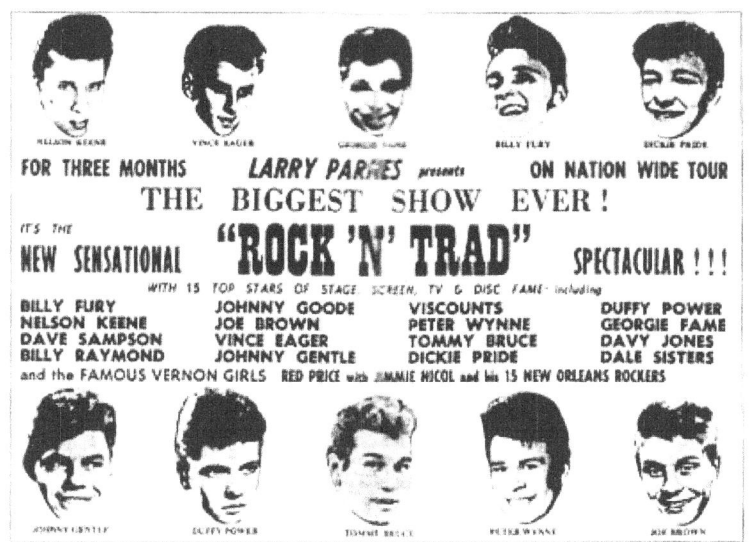

scheme started life in the famous London 2i's coffee bar in Old Compton Street – we will travel that road again. There young pop fans like Cliff Richard, Tony Sheridan and Joe Brown used to hang out: "Although Larry Parnes is later given credit for creating the all-teenage Rock'n'Roll package show, the idea is formulated and test-flown by 2i's coffee bar owner Paul Lincoln at the Romford Odeon, where he launches his discovery Terry Dene."

The event where Clive Powell was to report for an interview, the *Big Beat Show*, was presented by the now renowned concert and popular music impresario Larry Parnes at the "Lewisham Gaumont" theatre on Sunday, 20th September 1959.

There was a first encounter with the touring stable minutes later, with Clive sent out onto the stage at *The Marty Wilde Show* – a 'spectacular' starring the rocking father of a star in the Eighties, Kim Wilde. He found a lonely piano waiting there, and made the most of being thrown in at the deep end – by singing and playing a number by his idol Jerry Lee Lewis.

Fame to Frame: "Colin [Green] was playing guitar for Larry Parnes. When I walked on to do my audition, the band was already on stage. There was no formal audition, no rehearsal. The band was onstage, so I just went on and we did 'High School Confidential'." Powell passed the undeclared audition. Parnes liked him to get his hair bleached blonde "to get on the scene" like Heinz from the Tornados, while according to Pete Frame, "Bobby Woodman and Tex Makins, who had just been elbowed from Billy Fury's band [not for the last time], [had] turned up [in Rory Blackwell's flat] hoping to get something going with Rory, but nothing came of it and they left … but not before persuading Powell to let them bleach his hair."

Whatever, Parnes wanted to officially hire Powell as his urgently needed pianist. But before Clive could play even one note under the close tutelage of the London svengali, Larry Parnes took his chance of re-christening Clive – as he had done with other clients.

The young Powell could not have heard young guitarist Joe Brown's résumé on the man: "Larry Parnes had a talent for two things, making money and making up names", Brown pointed out in his memoir *Brown Sauce*.

Probably sensing that a certain "Harry Webb" of The Drifters would never have made it under his dire family moniker, Parnes and his partner John Kennedy started to equip their rock-and-rolling contractors with exciting show-biz pseudonyms. The way George Melly described it, "they laid down a system of naming their discoveries which was as rigid as that adopted by Mr Bumble in *Oliver*": for instance, a certain Roy Taylor (b. 1940) had been signed in March 1958 as "Vince Eager", a full month before young Harry Webb changed his name to "Cliff Richard" only in April.

"Marty Wilde" had once been Reginald Leonard Smith from Blackheath, and soon the more bluesy West London groover Ray Howard (1941–2014) from Fulham was duly renamed "Duffy Power" and would grow out of Parnes Pop and Rock'n'Roll to Blues with Alexis Korner. John Askew (b. 1938) became "Johnny Gentle" and would tour Scotland with the Beatles.

Young Clive Powell emerged from Parnes' re-christening session as "Clive Wells", and was immediately faced with the question "Can you play tomorrow night?" Well, Clive couldn't, due to a previous commitment. Up in Leigh, he still played with a local band called Ronnie Carr & The Blu Set at the time. They would gather some fame by backing the first tours of Screaming "I Put A Spell On You" Jay Hawkins in the UK, (and Georgie would meet Ronnie and his wife again in 1966 while playing at the Manchester Odeon).

Larry Parnes shrugged this gig information off with the request to call him. When he did, the secretary neither recognized a Clive Powell nor a Clive Wells."

"Clive Wells", which Parnes had given our man and forgotten all about weeks later, was definitely passé. He then came up with "Lance Fortune", in a complete blackout move: Larry had given that name to one of his other star contenders. Chris Morris, a school pupil from Birkenhead, had auditioned for Parnes at the 2is coffee bar, and it was *him* who had transformed into Lance Fortune. How could he "forget"?

Well, Morris had become Lance Fortune, but he had not become a Parnes performer, signing instead with a competing agency called the George Cooper Organization. If that made Parnes angry, he was almost heart attack material when Morris-Fortune scored a hit single with the song "Be Mine" soon after.

So, after Lional Bart's Bertie Beamer, Clive Wells and Lance Fortune, what about the fourth and final attempt to rename the piano phenomenon Clive Powell?

Clive Powell: "Larry sort of came along to me and said 'I've got a new name for you. You remind me of Wee Georgie Wood – and I think you're gonna be famous: I'm gonna call you Georgie Fame! And I'm gonna give you the opening spot on the show. You're no longer just a backing piano player. Now you're a singer in your own right.'"

Fame instead of Fortune, okay, maybe, but who was Georgie Wood? He was a person of short statue – a pantomime and music hall personality, a role model for Randy Newman's "Short People" who was only four feet and five inches tall. So where was the link to Powell? On the other hand, Clive Powell sounded very much like Duffy Power, who had been hired previously.

"So back in 1959, I was saddled with the name Georgie Fame by the impresario Larry Parnes. It was very much against my will, but when I protested "What's wrong with my real name?" he said, 'If you don't use my name, I won't use you in my show' – and I needed the gig." This became a gig that would soon entail more and more of Georgie's own solo spots: During the Parnes package tours, 'Georgie Fame' would officially have his first chance as a singing artist.

Was the name change really inevitable? Difficult to confirm or deny this with hindsight, but: There were at least two contenders on the Larry Parnes Circus who did not give in to the threat of "christening or crucifying": the two extraordinary singing guitarists Tony Sheridan (having served Vince Eager & The Vagabonds and Vince Taylor & The Playboys as well as The Beat Boys) and Joe Brown with his "Bruvvers" – he called everybody "Bruv" the Cockney way.

Anthony Esmond Sheridan McGinnity (1940–2013) carried his stage name in his real passport-stated identity, and his guitar skills saw him work for Parnes and others in spite of stubbornness and an overall lack of discipline and punctuality.

But apart from sticking to his name, his antics soon began to displease Larry Parnes decidedly, so he took according steps. As Alan Clayson writes in *Ringo Starr: Straight Man or Joker?*: "However, though nineteen-year-old Sheridan – a guitarist-singer of unusual flair – created a ripple with four numbers before 1959's *Oh Boy!*-cameras, an invitation to do likewise on a *Boy Meets Girls* [by producer Jack Good] headlined by Gene Vincent was cancelled when, in his own publicist's words [in a Polydor press release 1962], Sheridan 'went haywire' (failing to be on time, arriving without his guitar, etc). Television was, therefore, closed to him, and only on sufferance did Larry Parnes allow Sheridan just under ten minutes on an all-British supporting bill – Billy Fury, Joe Brown (from the *Boy Meets Girls* house band), and Georgie Fame – to Vincent and Eddie Cochran, an Oklahoman Elvis then in the British Top Thirty for the fourth time, on a round Britain package tour, beginning on Elvis' birthday – 8 January 1960.

"Sheridan was not only a phenomenal guitarist but a great singer too", Fame told Pete Frame, "on that tour, he was doing 'You'll Never Walk Alone' and I remember, [...], it used to bring the house down every night."

The other singing guitarist who kept his name was Joe Brown (b. 1941), who grew up in East London's borough of Plaistow. Brown faced the same fate when he joined the Parnes pack. He described the scene in *Brown Sauce*, as it could have happened to Georgie, but as he pointed out, Joe then proceeded to treat the whole threat as cheap comedy:

"'To start with', he said the next day, 'you need a new name. You can't walk around with a name like Joe Brown.' – 'Why not?' I asked. 'Hundreds of other people do.' – 'My point exactly', he said, stabbing a finger at me. 'You need something that rolls off the tongue.' Holy Harry, I thought. He wants to call me dribble [...]

"Suddenly he shot forward in his chair and rested his hands on the desk, looking straight at me. 'Twitch', he said. I duly obliged. 'What's the matter with your face?' he asked in alarm. 'Nothing', I said, 'I just twitched'. – 'No, no, no, no, no. You don't understand. That's what we'll call you. Twitch. Elmer Twitch.' – I gaped at him. 'I think

I'd prefer Dribble', I said. He ignored me. 'And of course you'll have a group. We'll call them The Fidgets. Elmer Twitch and The Fidgets. I can see it. I like it.'

I stood up to leave. He got the message. 'I suppose', he said, 'we could always leave it as Joe Brown.'"

Brown soon branched out. His *Boy Meets Girls* TV house band became synonymous with his road and recording band The Bruvvers, and similar to Georgie, he had millstone hits like "A Picture Of You". Brown also appeared in stage and film Musicals, like *What A Crazy World* in 1963, again with Marty Wilde, or *Charlie Girl*. Like Fame with Steve Gray, Joe Brown would go on to write his own Musical with Roger Cook, *Don't You Rock Me Daddio*, in 2006. Georgie's musical "family tree" is a jungle of Amazonian dimensions, as for instance celebrated songwriter Cook was in the group Blue Mink with Georgie's future Musical partner in *Singer*, Madeline Bell. Joe Brown, again like Georgie, still performs as of 2014. As this author was happy to witness during April of that year on consecutive nights, both appear in top form.

So there – could Georgie have taken Joe Brown's risk? Certainly not then, as he was completely unknown, as Parnes was well aware. Then again, you never know what these things are good for. Who wants to be confused with Jazz pianist and Thelonious Monk friend Bud Powell for the rest of his life, even if he died in 1966 at only 41? Why should a Clive Powell be on the same poster as Duffy Power? Georgie Fame it was, and Georgie Fame was – is and always will be – legend.

Towards the end of September 1959, young Powell-Fame was finally playing for the Larry Parnes band that was to play countless package tours all over Britain. Fame: "My first gig on that first tour was at the 'Quinton Essoldo' in Birmingham. There had been a gap after the audition, a week or two weeks", but now they were on!" Powell performed as a "Lancashire Lad" mixture of Fats Domino and Jerry Lee Lewis, backing, amongst others, Marty Wilde, Jess Conrad, Tony Sheridan, Terry Dene, Duffy Power, and the very first of the Parnes-christened lads, Vince Eager.

The vintage Vince Eager gets portrayed by Parnes guitarist Joe Brown as "Six feet four of gold lame suit, he sang in a high voice with a strong fast vibrato that put you in mind of someone sawing up aluminium. He said it was just his gimmick. Yes, the gimmick was all-important whether you were at Butlin's or in the Southend Odeon".

Vince Eager is still around in 2014. He recently gathered some ex-cohorts for old and new favourites on the good-hearted, fun-induced collection *788 Years of Rock'n'Roll*, including Georgie's latter day Rhythm Kings partner Albert Lee on guitar, but many other Parnes pals like Marty Wilde, Clem Cattini on drums, Tex Makins on bass and his old guitarist Colin Green: "Yeah, Vince called me up and asked if I would play on an album. He called Tex as well, and we got together and that's that. It was a little studio in Wiltshire in the southwest of England, and we recorded some tracks. Clem Cattini came down. Vince works quite a lot, actually. He's not been well, but he came out. I don't know if Vince tried to get hold of him [Georgie Fame], but I think he would have done. He can be quite difficult to get hold of."

Dickie Pride (1941–1969) was another "star". The singer, a certain Richard Charles Kneller from Surrey, had attended the School Of Church Music in Croydon – but instead of becoming an opera singer as suggested, he had joined a skiffle group, The Semi-Tones, before fellow vocalist Russ Conway decided to recommend him to Larry Parnes. He was only 16 then, and doing Little Richard so well got him the nickname "The Sheik Of Shake", an honour he had to share with the Liverpudlian performer Karl Terry, who rocked the Cavern Club with his Cruisers (and still does in 2014.)

Pride, often with guitarist Albert Lee in tow, had only enjoyed one Top 40 success in England, "Primrose Hill", but TV producer Jack Good gave him a chance on his *Wham! Rock'n'Roll* show. An album of Tin Pan Alley standards, *Pride Without Prejudice*, failed. Although both Billy Fury and Joe Brown remembered Dickie as the most talented of the "Parnes Package", his career nose-dived, and the heroin-using Pride died from an overdose of sleeping pills.

Fury and Brown's verdict was confirmed by future Fame band member Mick Eve in Colin Harper's John McLaughlin biog *Bathed In Lightning*: "Dickie Pride, he was marvellous, best one I ever worked with I think. He was an enthusiast. We'd finish a gig and he'd be 'Oh, let's come round your house', and he'd come round, we'd have a cup of coffee, have a smoke, a bit of chat, and then we'd start listening to [trumpeter] Clifford Brown solos …"

On the Parnes tour bus, Dickie had inspired the young Georgie on the tour coach with his love of barbershop-high-harmony singing and turned him on to the American vocal group The Four Freshmen, whose Hoagy Carmichael adoptions pleased him no end, as revealed in a BBC program in 1999, where an older Clive was deejaying.

Pride's other love was going to become Georgie's love, too, as Mick Eve picks up the coffee & chat story, "[…] and start inventing words to all the [Clifford Brown] solos. In fact, that was the last of my Clifford Brown collection, when he was really ill – I let him walk off with all the Clifford Brown albums I had, cos he was determined to write lyrics to every solo Clifford Brown ever did. It would have been quite a job of work – but he would have been capable, that was the thing. He wasn't bullshitting. He could do it. Jon Hendricks, King Pleasure, Annie Ross – those people could do it. And Dickie was one of those." And Georgie Fame was one of those, too, as we shall see.

By January 1960, Georgie Fame got in the support slot of a British tour of visiting US-musicians. Again as part of the Larry Parnes organization, Powell was now a regular member of Colin Green's Beat Boys.

Colin Green (b. 1941), who would continue to play with Georgie on and off for years to come, got into music like this: "My aunt went to a church service with me every Sunday morning, and she played the piano. My dad was killed in 1946, and his sister is actually still alive. She's 102 [in 2013]. She actually started my interest in music.

"The guitar became kind of a little bit popular, and it turned out that my father had played the guitar. My aunt suddenly produced this guitar, and I knew this was exactly right. I took no lessons of any description. I kind of instinctively knew how to play it. It is an absolute gift. People asked how I did what I did, and I can't answer that. But I soon found myself after a while – I was out working especially with others, that I've got no real background – I don't know what I know. So I went back and learned and filled in some of the holes. It was one of the reasons I started teaching: because I thought if I've got to tell somebody else, that will identify quite quickly what I do and what I don't know. So I was the benefactor from my teaching. I still am. I still learn all the time."

As a step to becoming a full-on pro, young Colin was able to buy his first top-of-the-range guitar, a Burns, in January 1959, after his aunt had lent him the money for it.

Green's first professional engagements had led him to recording with Glen Stuart and The Clansmen, also in 1959: "I was working with various people, with Clive among them, like for Eddie Calvert, the trumpet player. The original line-up for that had been guitar, piano, bass and drums. The pianist left and we replaced him with another guitar player. So we had a two-guitars-bass-drums line-up, which was sort of the thing at that time. That guitar player was working for Glen Stuart. That was how I got to be on that particular recording, "Weeping Willow" [recorded at London's Lansdowne Studios for Pye, with the B-side "Delia Darling"]. The first incarnation of Colin Green's Beat Boys featured Alan Leclaire on piano, Bobby Woodman on drums and, long-term, bass player Ted "Tex" Makins – an incredibly experienced musician.

The young man (b. 1940) had started his Johnny Makins Skiffle Group three years previously with the adventurously named Johnny d'Avensac on guitar, both of them moonlighting for the Zodiac Jazz Band, before they both found employment in the Rick Richards Skiffle Group, by which time the man with the French roots retired.

Richards, a.k.a. Rick Hardy, soon took Tex Makins into the Worried Men, who had the distinction of once sporting Adam Faith as their lead singer, and in whose ranks two future Shadows drummers combined their rhythmic prowess with Tex – namely ex-Vipers striker Tony Meehan and Brian Bennett, the latter destined to become a member of Georgie Fame's band much later. When Tex finally arrived in the Parnes stable with Alan Leclaire and Bobby Woodman, the Beat Boys would be called the Vince Eager Band – but instead of Colin Green, their guitarists had been Joe Moretti and Big Jim Sullivan, who in turn would come back into the picture. Also during 1958, Vince Taylor asked Makins, Meehan and Tony Sheridan to be his band. What goes around …

It was a slightly different Beat Boys – Colin Green, Bobby Woodman, Tex Makins and Georgie Fame, who accompanied Billy Fury and Marty Wilde at the Royal Albert Hall for the *New Musical Express* Pop Poll, in September 1959.

Apart from Fury, Wilde and Parnes, the young Beat Boys around Fame and Green also accompanied Duffy Power, who remembered their acquaintance very well, a year before his death in 2014, but does not recall a special rapport with Georgie:

"Well, I wouldn't say that, but we knew one another, shared rooms together. I remember one tour, where I think he introduced me to the wrong woman at one time. That's the only thing that has any strength about it. Apart from that we used to cover for people on this thing called *Rock'n'Trad Spectacular* [1961], which was a big show that involved Jack Good, and that Larry Parnes put on [featuring Billy Fury as its headliner, plus Joe Brown, Johnny Gentle and, of course, Georgie Fame]. A lot of the acts used to fall out with colds or something, and it was an eighteen piece band – and we used to cover for them. So we did quite a lot of that show.

"But Georgie introduced me to a girl, or woman, who really bowed me up [Lee "Lady Lee" Middleton]. She was going with everyone really, behind my back, including Billy Fury, who she ended up living with. So it was a strain, because I put a lot of hope in her. She said she was a singer and she had a manager, but it wasn't like that at all. I don't want to hold a grudge against him [Georgie], but I always remember that he took me there. He was part of

the clubs and stuff and I kept going back there. That was where my life turned, really. She later married Kenny Everett, the comedian."

Duffy elaborates on that in another interview with Colin Harper: "I was on this big tour with Larry Parnes. I came out of the office on Oxford Street one day, and Georgie Fame was standing on the pavement. I was driving. I had a car at that time – it was 1960, [although] I hadn't passed my test then. I gave him a lift, to Fulham, and we ended up with a couple of birds smoking reefers, which was quite new then. I never saw him round there again – but I never left for nine months. I moved out of home, my mum and dad went nuts, and later it turned out this girl was a singer, as I thought, but also a kind of high-class prostitute. So that really did me in."

According to Duffy Power[2] reminiscing in 2013, he was also responsible for introducing Georgie to the music of Mose Allison, something that Fame folklore puts firmly into the post-Parnes era: "Yeah, I did, I played him Mose Allison. Long before he started doing that voice, I turned him onto Mose Allison. He never owned up to that, he never said that I did. He would never mention Mose Allison anyway. He really ripped his voice off, didn't he? I remember that I played it to him first. One thing I got from other women that I mixed with was superb Jazz & Blues records, mad Jazz singers which I liked."

That girl singer had recommended Allison to Duffy in the first place, and another tip was an early Flamingo visitor: She "introduced me to Billie Holliday", Power told Harper, "Mose Allison, Jesse Fuller, loads of people. She started totally my interest in Folk-Blues. I stayed with her for a while, but I was in a terrible state. I was still doing my Rock act, but that needs plenty of enthusiasm, and I was very, very miserable."

Come the new decade, and Colin Green, Fame, Tex Makins as well as their new drummer Red Reece – the man whose exemplary swing and infectious groove Georgie would rave about for decades to come – had become experienced road musicians.

In 1960, Green and Makins also made up The Quiet Three with drummer Jimmy Nicol –[3] and again worked for Larry Parnes' rocker Eager, as Vince Eager's Quiet Three.

But what a "gig" the next one for the Beat Boys turned out to be. Georgie remembers: "Back in 1960, Larry Parnes brought over the great American Rock'n'Rollers Gene

2. & 3. See Addendum

Vincent and Eddie Cochran. I was a sixteen-year-old piano player on that tour. And there was another band on the tour called Nero and the Gladiators."

For the young pianist Fame, the sojourn had an immediate educating effect: "The first time we ever got to hear of Ray Charles", he told his BBC Radio audience in 1999 during a series of six episodes with his Blue Flames, "was on the Eddie Cochran/Gene Vincent tour in 1960 when we were called into a rehearsal room to decide which musicians in the Larry Parnes pool would back Eddie Cochran and Gene Vincent. Then we turned up at the little place in Gerrard Street, Soho – and there was Eddie Cochran, sitting on a stool with his Gretsch guitar and his leather waistcoat and trousers. And he asked the assembled musicians if anybody had heard of Ray Charles.

"And I don't think anybody put their hands up, and Eddie started to play that opening lick on 'What'd I Say", which Ray Charles played on the Wurlitzer electric piano. At that time, we didn't know what a Wurlitzer electric piano was. We thought it was some kind of new guitar sound. But Eddie played it of course on his guitar – and a whole new world opened up!"

It opened up for many more Britons, too, Fame reminds us, in that "On that fateful tour, Eddie Cochran was singularly responsible in introducing the masses of Great Britain to the music of Ray Charles" – a fact that he stresses till this very day whenever he is about to dive into "I Got A Woman" during his shows, because Ray Charles was as much a revelation to Clive as it was for "the masses of his country".

Georgie never fails to mention why that tour was fateful, although the vast majority of his fans are well aware of the tragedy: "Eddie Cochran was tragically killed in a car accident after we just finished a week at the Bristol Hippodrome." The car had actually been a taxi, driven by a pro driver with the unlikely name George Martin. Its wreck had been found by a young police cadet, Dave Harman, who later re-christened himself the Parnes way and became Dave Dee, leading his band Dozy, Beaky, Mick & Tich through many hits, including one with at least lyrical Fame appeal: "Last Night In Soho". Gene Vincent's bad leg got even worse through the accident, but Cochran's co-songwriter Sharon Sheeley survived just like the non-Fab-Four-related George Martin.

Cochran's assisting British guitarist Tony Sheridan could easily have been killed in this accident, too – after all he had been offered a seat in the car that was going to take the US giants back to London, killing Cochran and crippling Vincent! But Sheridan's haywire attitude saved his life. Sources differ as to whether Tony was being late as usual or just not bothered about riding with the rockers. Whatever, he continued to play, tried his luck in Germany, taught the Beatles how to "make show" in Hamburg, watched them explode (while befriending Fame in the process) and stayed in Germany all his life, except for a spell in Vietnam, acting as tonic for the troops, going white-haired within weeks and returning to Northern Germany for good.

More than a decade after Beatlemania, Sheridan would start ambitious projects like working with the Liverpool Symphony Orchestra in 1975 and recording with the real Elvis' backing band, but his antics and anti-social behavior always put a lid on real career moves. Tony appeared together with Georgie decades later, in 2004, for a jubilee of the German band the Street Doctors, played the 50th anniversary of the Star-Club, and died less than a year later, seen off by Reeperbahn Royalty and old fans in Hamburg's "Michel" church in a coffin painted by his daughter.

As for Eddie Cochran being an "Oklahoman Elvis", Sheridan's opinion of Cochran had run higher by far: "Eddie Cochran was real and I was a copy. He was a very good guitarist and he was into all sorts of things, which influenced his music. He might suddenly do something differently, and that is when innovation can happen." Georgie Fame would sign such praise.

According to Pete Frame, whose opinion of the often "psychotic" Rock'n'Roller Gene Vincent was highly critical, Eddie Cochran "was a sweetheart. Not only a gentleman with a warm personality and a great sense of humour but also a masterful guitarist, who was happy to sit around teaching licks and tricks to his travelling companions – including Big Jim Sullivan, Joe Brown, Colin Green and Tony Sheridan, all of whom benefitted from his instruction, all of whom took his advice and replaced their third string with a thinner gauge second string, allowing them to bend the notes. He put Georgie Fame in the direction of Ray Charles and Soul music …"

After the fateful 1960 tour, Fame had his first contact with a recording studio as well. He debuted putting his playing piano on tape on the "Pistol Packing Mama" single by the other tour star, swinging, "psychic" Rockabilly hero Gene Vincent, including the single B-side ballad, "Weeping Willow". Colin Green: "It was myself and Georgie and Red Reece and Billy McVay, the saxophone player, who is better known as Ray McVay, the bandleader. And a guy called Vince Cooze was the [double] bass player. Why that was at the particular time, I don't know. For Georgie it was a first, I had recorded the Glen Stuart single."

It was during these Larry Parnes extravaganzas that Georgie, while still coming to terms with the decision of making music his life's calling and income, met a Manchester saxophonist, four years his senior, who had his own solution to the question of professional musicianship.

Fame: "Well, the best example I can think of is Art Themen. He is one of our best saxophone players. I first met Art in 1960, when I was working with Larry Parnes, and we did a summer season in Blackpool, and Joe Brown was topping the bill. We did matinees at the Queen's Theatre in Blackpool, and in the evening, the theatre was taken by a residency by George Formby. There were two saxophone players in the band, they weren't from London. There was a saxophone player from Liverpool, I can't remember his name [it was probably Brian "Sax" Jones from the Undertakers] and there was Art Themen. It was coming 1960. I was seventeen years old and Art was probably about the same age. He was in medical school, but he was playing the saxophone. And he did the summer season. But Art Themen went on to do his medical studies and he became one of our leading orthopedic surgeons in the United Kingdom, and also one of our best Jazz and uniquely-sounding tenor saxophone players. So Art Themen is probably the best example I can think of having parallel careers, both equally successful and applaudable."

Art Themen, who would later, in 1969, work for Georgie's band, too, remembers the Blackpool encounter equally well, the difference being that the sax man recounts the meeting as a member of the band Nero and the Gladiators: "Our meeting happened for the first time in Blackpool. We were both very much teenagers. He [Georgie] was up-and-coming. I suppose I was a keen amateur, a saxophone player from Manchester, which is close to Blackpool. We met through this agent called Larry Parnes, who got together a group of five or six young good-looking singers of popular music, including Georgie. And the backing band was called Nero and the Gladiators, with Mike O'Neill. Apparently, they used to play in togas, like the Romans. But by the time we did this show, I'm glad to say I wasn't dressed in a toga, but anyway I was part of Nero and the Gladiators. He [Mike] was from Warrington and had a rather English sort of humour which I'm sure you wouldn't be able to get over in the book, because in the North, you would pronounce 'Nero' like 'Neero' – so that was always a kind of humorous thing, the way Mike said that. He was a great guy."

Mike O'Neill (1938–2013), who had started in Vince Taylor's band, had started as just another member of the stars-backing Cabin Boys in Larry Parnes' stable together with guitarist Colin Green. They backed Colin Hicks, Tommy Steele's younger brother, for instance on an Italian tour on the strength of their single "Giddy Up A Ding-Dong". Hicks' version of that old Freddie Bell & The Bell Boys chestnut from *Rock Around The Clock* appeared in *Europa di Notte*, and the craze was set again.

Prior to coming back from Italy, where Hicks opted to stay, O'Neill bought some gladiator film gear, from a movie set in Rome (while a few years later, no doubt, he could have scored that in Chris Farlowe's shops in Islington and Notting Hill). Boots Slade, Colin Green and Mike started Nero and the Gladiators, a band who appeared in Roman costumes in their stage act: The Gladiators loved to sing that the Romans used to dig that crazy Rock'n'Roll in their number "That's A Long Time Ago". But they mostly played Duane Eddy/Ventures/Shadows type instrumentals like "Boots" and, of course, "In the Hall of The Mountain King". Mike and his men would not stick to their togas for very long, though. They were part of the Parnes tour with Eddie Cochran and Gene Vincent.

O'Neill would also go on to play in The John Barry Seven, the Ivy League and Tony Colton & The Crawdaddies. Some years later, with Tony Colton, he was to start the underrated supergroup Heads, Hands & Feet. They featured the future Chas'n'Dave comedy rocker/pianist Chas Hodges, as well as Chris Farlowe's lightning speed guitarist Albert Lee. The band would record several underrated albums and provide the backing for Jerry Lee Lewis' all-star double LP *The Session* in 1973. Albert Lee relocated to Los Angeles in 1974, backing Emmylou Harris and the Everly Brothers amongst others. In spite of still living in Santa Monica, Lee has been Georgie Fame's colleague in Bill Wyman's Rhythm Kings since 1997.

Fame Fired – for expanding on Rock'n'Roll & Jazz!

Following gigs for Marty Wilde and the roster of Parnes singers on the package tours and the "fateful tour", Powell, Green, Makins & Reece worked for a singer called Clay Nicholls, now called The Blueflames.

Larry Parnes had seen the four Beat Boys/Blueflames/Blue Flames rehearse with Nicholls, and that gave him the idea that Billy Fury should have his own band. And why not simply nick that name in the process?! Quite a bold move, but then the name was hardly copyright protected, as Nicholls' previous band had also been called The Blue Flames, and at one time drummer Clem Cattini, guitarist Joe Brown and Clive's home front Lancashire friend Mike O'Neill had been members.

By the summer of 1961, Fame and his friends had permanently joined Billy Fury as his exclusive backing combo The Blue Flames: Fury had looked at all the available musicians in the stable and found Green, Makins & Reece just the ticket, with Fame on piano. He had of course worked with them before sporadically during tours from 1959.

Saxophonist Mick Eve, who also worked with the Parnes circus and would later join Georgie, remembers: "We would go out and back various Rock'n'Roll singers. Some of them in this country were very musicianly, and we enjoyed backing them. So I did Rock'n'Roll type gigs and came across people like Tex Makins, who was part of Marty Wilde & The Wildcats – this other guy always liked to use him if he could get him. We stayed in touch with these people, and they finished up being in the Blue Flames for Billy Fury. Georgie was part of the four of them who backed Billy Fury."

They usually played two 20-minute-sets per night backing his ballads and light Rock' n'Roll style. This still mostly happened on the Larry Parnes promoted package tours with people like Peter Jay & The Jaywalkers, Eden Kane (the brother of Peter "Where Do You Go To, My Lovely" Sarstedt) or Joe Brown.

Georgie Fame and his boys weren't the only disciples when it came to playing Rock the light way but loving the music of Ray Charles and Eddie Cochran. Over in Paris, France, the teenage star Johnny Hallyday made the headlines. He had started out as an Edith Piaf fan, and his new claim to fame was bringing the Rock'n'Roll craze to France. His first album, *Hello Johnny*, had only been released in 1960.

Johnny Hallyday enjoyed a massive impact but was at pains to stay ahead of the trends. Now, towards the end of 1961, Hallyday was already in the process of recording his fourth album, changing from Vogue to Philips, *Salut Les Copains!*, which is French for something like "hey buddies".

For this task, Hallyday hired Georgie as his Rock'n'Roll piano player, along with a bunch of his colleagues. There were the other Parnes pals and Marty Wilde Wildcats, Joe Moretti on lead guitar and Big Jim Sullivan on rhythm guitar (both Future Blue Flames) with Brian "Licorice" Locking on bass. Andy White, who would go on to take Ringo Starr's Abbey Road stool for "Love Me Do" in 1962, was on drums, and Jean Tosan played the saxophone.

From September 5th to 12th, 1961, they convened at the Studio Fontana, also called Philips Studio, in Stanhope House, at Stanhope Place near Marble Arch, London, which had an 8-input German Neumann valve system then, rebuilt for stereo in 1958. Georgie performed as the piano player on the recording of eight songs for the album: "Nous Quand On S'embrace", "Toi Qui Regrettes", "Viens Danser Le Twist", "Let's Twist Again" (which topped mean European charts but not the UK's), "Douce Violenvce", "Tu Peux La Prendre", "Avec Une Poignée De Terre" and "Il Faut Saisir Sa Chance".

Georgie could certainly use the studio money, because towards the end of that year 1961, Billy Fury sacked The Blue Flames for "refusing to stick to simple Rock'n'Roll piano". Were they crossing over to Rhythm & Jazz even back in 1961? Georgie remembered the incident – chatting in 1994:

"Yeah, because what happened was: We did a concert with Billy Fury as The Blue Flames – Billy Fury & The Blue Flames in the Olympia Theatre in Paris, with Chubby Checker, and The Shadows without Cliff Richard. And at the sound check, there was nobody in the theatre. Billy Fury wasn't there. Of course, he was great, Billy was a nice kind. We were just messing around trying to play a couple of Ray Charles tunes that Eddie Cochran had played: Because we were on that tour with Eddie – and through Eddie Cochran we had begun to listen to Ray Charles: He sang 'What'd I Say', and he recorded 'Hallelujah I Love Her So' also that time. We had never heard of Ray Charles until Eddie Cochran came along. So, at the sound check in Paris, we weren't playing one of Billy Fury's tunes, we were just playing 'What'd I Say' or Percy Faith's 'In A Summer Place'.

"We were just doing something else because Billy wasn't there. His road manager Hal Carter came running down the aisle in the theatre, he'd been sitting at the back with Larry Parnes, and said 'It's not rocking, it's not rocking!' We were quite rude to him. So therefore, after that concert, we were given the sack!"

Getting all worked up about a number like "What'd I Say" in particular seems pretty awkward even for the day and age of late 1961. Earlier that same year, even the – compared to Billy Fury – equally soft and civilized Rock'n'Roller Cliff Richard had got his cords around the Ray Charles tune, for his album *Listen To Cliff*. But maybe that's exactly what got Fury's gander up.

Watching from the wings, so to speak, Parnes' sax man Mick Eve could understand the boys ever so well: "I never liked Billy Fury as a Rock singer, he wasn't as good as a lot of the others, I didn't think, but he had this musical thing – an underlying taste for Rhythm & Blues, Ray Charles and things like that. And I guess we were all waking up to that at this point."

Reminiscing about his period with the Larry Parnes "Circus" and then Fury, Georgie's memories turned positive later, as he told Pete Frame: "I have to say that the two years I spent with the Parnes stable was the best learning experience I could have had. When I joined, I could only play in a couple of keys, in a very limited style, and I was only busking it for much of the time – but working with so many different singers, and with musicians who were as keen to progress as I was, gave me a very solid footing in the business."

Billy Fury went and assembled his new band The Tornados. Fame found out that in spite of getting a little bored with Fury's watered-down British version of Rock'n'Roll, his love of Ray Charles, King Pleasure and Louis Prima was an acquired taste – meaning that "gigs were impossible to come by". So that was a time when – no engagements, no money down – "at the end of 1961, we were out of work for a while, and one of my oldest friends, Mike O'Neill, who had this band Nero and the Gladiators", rescued Fame, the ties that bound being their origins from Leigh, Lancashire.

Georgie reminisced with *Rave* reporter Dick Tatham how Mike O'Neill came to the rescue: "'Look, mate. I know things are tough. Now, we've got this flat in Soho, just a couple of rooms. You're welcome to doss down there. Most nights you will have to kip on a mattress on the floor – or in a chair. But it'll be better than a park bench'."

Fame: "Mike put me up. He let me sleep in his flat in Old Compton Street in Soho for several weeks at the time when Billy Fury gave me the sack in 1961." Actually, the flat was used by the whole Nero & The Gladiators

band, and when they had left to do a gig, "I was walking the streets until they got back."

"He had a great record collection and I listened to Mike's records all the time during this out-of-work period: I would sit listening to King Pleasure, James Brown, Mose Allison and others and say 'Man, this is it for me!'[4] It would never be enough just to listen to it!" There was the dream to produce these sounds himself, and also, how else was he supposed to spend his time, anyway? There was no money to even buy decent food, let alone the funds to lead even the most basic social life. The only friend, apart from Mike O'Neill, was the future Moody Blues, Move and T. Rex manager Tony Secunda (1940–1995), who would faithfully call round from time to time and suggest a mutual meal of fish and chips or a hamburger. Secunda later discovered Chrissie Hynde.

But music continued to be the great healer for Fame, and his lonely times at the O'Neill flat proved as re-assuring as they were fruitful. Georgie: "Mike had a terrific influence on my Jazz education. It was among that pile of records I first heard Chet Baker. Mike really is responsible for me being where I am now." And in the liner notes to *A Portrait Of Chet* 28 years later, Georgie would continue that "Chet Baker's Riverside album *It Could Happen To You* was played constantly and Mike wrote lyrics to some of Chet's solos. I followed his lead" – so the seed was sown.

4. See Addendum

"Get On The Right Track, Baby!" – The Flamingo Years

Georgie, who was as skint as he was desperate for musical engagements, got another valuable connection from "landlord" Mike O'Neill, who showed his young Lancastrian friend the way to a renowned venue that was situated virtually next door to the Jazz education flat: "More importantly, Mike took me round the corner to a Jazz club in Wardour Street – and introduced me to the guy that was running the place, who later became my manager, his name was Rik Gunnell. And that club was called the Flamingo. Among other things, Mike introduced me to the Flamingo 'All-nighter'."

Out-of-work piano man Georgie Fame saw this opportunity, seized his chance and contacted his band buddies, who he had stayed in touch with. He played them the sounds and songs he had heard up in the O'Neill apartment, and the others, Green, Reece & Makins, definitely liked what they heard, just as Georgie appreciated them: "I learned a lot from Colin, because Colin was the best musician in the band. I just felt that we were all in the same wash together, all learning at the same time, trying to do whatever we wanted to do. I just got lumbered with the mantle of having to be the band leader. Whoever is the bandleader has to be the bandleader and then has to make all the other decisions which allow the musicians to concentrate on their playing."

Before the pre-Flames Billy Fury days, of course, it was Green who had been the Beat Boys' bandleader, although "it wasn't much of a change really, because we were still playing the same style of things – the only difference being that I didn't sing at that time, and Clive did. That was the logical step, if you like. He was singing and I wasn't. We were on equal musical terms. I don't think we were equal on financial terms."

Georgie swiftly slotted into assuming the Blue Flames' leadership. Slowly but surely, "and thanks to my old friend Mike O'Neill", he landed the band a residency in one of Soho's trendiest jazz basements, the Flamingo Club, quite an achievement for a Rock'n'Roll orientated group: "It was March 1962 when we started the residency in the Flamingo Club in Soho. I was only eighteen. We stayed for over three years."

Initially, O'Neill had put them in touch with tenor saxophonist Alan Watson. Al was the leader of the Flamingo house band. He told the newly formed Blue Flames he would try and find a niche for them – and he kept his promise. First, they replaced him for an afternoon session – a lucky break: the sax twister Al Watson – who called himself "Earl Watson" because he loved US sax star Earl Bostic – urgently needed a replacement because he and his regular and gorgeously named Fabulous Twisters had a better paid previous booking for a Sunday afternoon TV show.

As Georgie once told *Rave*'s Dick Tatham: "This was it: our big break. I began to feel after only eight bars or so that we were going to get by. We did that – and more. I could sense the voltage stepping up in the audience. Finally, we came away from the Flamingo feeling high – and with the feeling of more bookings."

As for the exuberant atmosphere, Colin Green confirms that "it was terrific. On reflection, it was a little bit frightening, simply because there were a lot of very, very drunk or high G.I.s, quite a lot of high atmosphere. And there was a single entrance and exit for the club – there's never been a fire in there: goodness knows what would have happened, nothing like an emergency exit. Everybody kept well out of there. But the musical atmosphere was fantastic."

The first gig they played was on a Sunday afternoon – for those punters who couldn't face the grind of real life after the All-nighters an offer they wouldn't refuse: not the hottest spot, but it was a start. Based on that lucky double booking, Fame & Flames worked the place into such a state that Watson kept them instead of the double-dealing Fabulous Twisters: Al Watson & The Blue Flames they were called some nights.

Georgie would never ever forget all the help and inspiration which he got from Mike O'Neill. The two Lancastrians remained life-long friends, sharing their talent of writing lyrics for Chet Baker's trumpet solos and other lyric-creations for instrumentals.

Back in 1961, and the formerly Jerry-Lee, Cochran & Charles fed Blue Flames had landed their new sound in the Mecca of Modern Jazz, as a little history lesson will make clear.

The Flamingo Story

In order to re-live the colossal standing which the Flamingo Club had accumulated since its inauguration a decade earlier, and the traditions which Georgie Fame & The Blue Flames were about to add to, and alter, it is best to take a closer look at an era when the "teenager" was still considered an American phenomenon, and Jazz was a sort of music that was frowned upon by the man in pipes and slippers mode, at least if it wasn't "Trad", the Dixieland kind.

Music historians may still find traces of the Swinging Sixties' London today. They can take a guided tour of Abbey Road Studios, likely to encounter swearing taxi drivers when they use the zebra crossing the way Georgie's friends John, Paul, George and Ringo did. They can also still watch gigs in one of the old 60s clubs, like that little basement in No. 100, Oxford Street – which got started as the Feldman Swing Club in 1942 and has been simply called the "100 Club" since the current owner's father took it over in 1964.

South of Oxford Street is where the district of Soho begins, the quarter that suffered from cholera in 1854 because of a sewage contaminated public water pump. It was these jolly, coloured and dangerous streets and alleys which had housed London's erotically inclined money-making for well over 200 years, with its little "establishments" and numerous prostitutes openly on the pavement – at least until the 1959 Streets Offences Act, but hundreds of strip clubs remained. Gerrard Street was the main path through

Chinatown, and Frith Street became synonymous with the influx of Italian immigrants, and of course what they brought was – coffee bars.

Unheard of by Northern Europeans, the espresso coffee machine had been patented as early as 1938, and now the craze had come to London in the 1950s. The "Bar Italia" had been first in 1949, then Gina Lollobrigida opened "The Moka" in 29 Frith Street in 1953. Then there was the already mentioned "2i's Coffee Bar" in 59 Old Compton Street, where many of our protagonists had hung out and performed. Other espresso handouts with live music were the Heaven & Hell in Old Compton Street and the Top Ten in Berwick Street.

Right there in the heart of Soho, there is the still famous Ronnie Scott's Club, which has been in Frith Street for ages after it started out in Gerrard Street round the corner. There, in the heart of Soho, was the home of the Flamingo Club when Georgie Fame and The Blue Flames started to play there. Unfortunately, it is part of an Irish pub chain now, and with a ton of irony, its name is – wait for it – *O'Neill's*!

The young London East End-born entrepreneur and semi-pro nightclub pianist Jeffrey Sonny Krugerkoff, or Jeff Kruger (1931–2014), the son of hairdressers Sam and Tillie Kruger, felt the motivation for his own Jazz Club back in August 1952. He wanted an outlet for Jazz enthusiasts who, at the time, would hardly be able to find their favourite music on BBC Radio's "Light Programme". On top of that, he wanted the musicians, and ladies for that matter, to feel more comfortable than in a dubious upstairs pub room. As he said in a radio interview:

"In or around 1952, I was dating some of the loveliest girls I could find, and I wanted to hear Jazz in a lovely surrounding. Club 51 smelt like walking into the basement of a pub. [The] Feldman Club in Oxford Street was dingy. You didn't feel proud of walking in there with a nice young lady. I decided there and then, somehow I wanted to open a club where dress code applied and with the best music available. I knew I had to charge prices unacceptable in those days, but I believed that an audience was there. It turned out to be absolutely correct."

In the 'souterrain' basement of the Madison Hotel in Coventry Street near Piccadilly Circus, Kruger began to organize his first concerts, formal affairs still, where the male guests would be expected to wear a tie, and the ladies wore nice dresses – jeans were still something strictly out of US movies. Right from the beginning, there was a lot of variety: Kenny Graham and his Afro Cubists had got together again for the opening night, and their unusual style could be called Latin Bebop.

Soon, Kruger moved beneath the "Mapleton Restaurant" at Leicester Square. There were appearances by first class British Jazz giants like The Tony Crombie Quartet, The Johnny Dankworth Seven, and even some internationally acclaimed American stars, for instance Sarah Vaughan on her first tour of England, and Billie Holiday in 1954. He told Spencer Leigh that Holiday was the most unhappy person he had ever met, "in control of her voice, which was marvellous, but not of herself."

After several changes of venues, for instance to the "Pigalle" Restaurant near Piccadilly Circus, Kruger established his "Flamingo Club" in the heart of Chinatown in 1957: the address was 33–37 Wardour Street, between two shoe shops, one of which was then displaced by a – you guessed it – Chinese restaurant.

Wardour Street, named in the 18th century after architect Sir Archibald Wardour (now how about that for a song?) was sufficiently atmospheric for some Jazz connotations. It had actually once been shown as a "thoroughfare" on Fairthorne and Newcourt's map between 1642 and 1647. Subsequently it had been a one way street from Leicester Square to Oxford Street, and while – in the 19th century – it was a street where you bought shoddy furniture, it became the administrational home of the British film industry in the 1930s. It was the address of the equally famous Marquee Club. But while the Marquee catered for Traditional, Dixieland-flavoured Jazz at the time, Kruger offered several kinds of Modern Jazz.

On the first night in Soho, 7th April 1957, The Tony Kinsey Quartet played there with Joe Harriott (1928–1973) on alto sax, a master who bridged the gap from Bebop to Free Jazz and had moved from Jamaica to London in 1951. Also on the bill were The Jazz Couriers, who featured Tubby Hayes (1935–1973) and Ronnie Scott (1927–1996), two real tenor saxophone enigmas. Both would play with Georgie Fame later – on his revered but also criticized Big Band masterpiece, *Sound Venture*.

Interesting for Georgie – had he known it at the time – was that Jeff Kruger had been the first to book Chet Baker for a British tour. A US trumpeter in England? This was like a brutal burglar in Harrods as far as the Musicians' Union was concerned, and they told both Kruger and Baker that they risked HMP, "Her Majesty's pleasure" if Young Chet didn't stick to singing but picked up his bugle.

Joe Harriott and Ronnie Scott had been with Tony Crombie before in the late 1940s, so they were already much admired characters at the club. In fact, Ronnie Scott, Tony Crombie and also Johnny Dankworth had all led their own respective Big Bands in the early 1950s, whose size did not make commercial sense anymore – that's why they got together in smaller units.

The Johnny Burch Quartet sported saxophonist Dick Heckstall-Smith, drummer Peter "Ginger" Baker and bass player Jack Bruce. Those three were active in Alexis Korner's Blues Incorporated as well, and would also soon become the cornerstone of the Graham Bond Trio: They had done trio spots inside the Alexis Show, until one day Bond simply signed them off the Blues Incorporated roster to go freelance – leaving Bruce & Baker dazed and confused.

The great range of styles continued: the star of the Tony Kinsey Quartet was now another sax master, baritone man Ronnie Ross, the man who was to become David Bowie's saxophone tutor when the young dude was still called Davy Jones and had arts and crafts lessons from Peter Frampton's father. By 1959, Ronnie Scott had opened his own "Ronnie Scott's Jazz Club", just a few blocks down – but more of that venue later.

"Move It On Over" – The Blue Flames take charge

Who could put it better than the British Jazz connoisseur and charmer George Melly in his Sixties book *Revolt Into Style: The Pop Arts In Britain*: "Georgie Fame was king here. He used organ and saxes, Modern Jazz musicians; the Flamingo had been a Modern Jazz club, just as the Marquee had been a Traditional Jazz club, and, like children who reject their parents and yet betray their origins in everything they do and say, the Marquee Blues and the Flamingo 'Soul' reflected this." And it happened like this:

With the Sixties having just started, the Flamingo Club wasted no time in allowing Rock'n'Roll to creep in, too, by hiring Jerry Lee Lewis into the trendy cellar, soon to be followed by his ardent fan, Fame. By this time, Jeffrey Kruger had passed the running of the club to his father, Sam Kruger, and started to get involved with the Jazz label Ember Records, which also catered for a range of styles from R&B via Country to Soul and even Rockabilly, with artists like Roy Young, Matt Munro and John Barry, as well as The Platters or Sonny Terry & Brownie McGhee.

As far as the Flamingo Club was concerned, Jeffrey Kruger was now acting mostly as the landlord, having lost active interest in the venue because, in his view, Modern Jazz musicians tended to just stand on the bandstand, no poetry in motion, instead of entertaining the crowd with jokes, inspiring moves and a willingness to communicate. On the other hand, he had a snobbish attitude towards non-Jazz musicians, including Georgie.

What a pity that he did not appreciate the phenomenon of Georgie Fame mixing Jazz and fun, then – all his doubts would have vanished, all his problems been solved. Once Fame came, he watched in awe at how he and The Blue Flames became synonymous with the Flamingo and raised its popularity level to a thing of legend.

Also, Kruger junior helped the Flamingo in other ways, not least by introducing players like the future Blue Flames drummer Tony Crombie – who he had lured into playing Rock'n'Roll – and his long-serving quartet to television producers. One of his themes with Bill LeSage can be heard in the TV series *The Man From Interpol*. Also, Kruger would get *Jazz at the Flamingo* onto BBC radio.

In May 1962, very shortly after getting their feet in the tiny door of the place, the Blue Flames got more slots in the Flamingo. Weekends at the Flamingo were extra special. Regular shows ran until about eleven o'clock. Then, from midnight, Kruger had leased the Flamingo Club out as The All-nighters Club, to the managing pair of Rik Gunnell, an ex-bouncer and boxer, and his brother John, men, they said, who "mixed with the kind of people who would bury you under the M1 motorway if you looked at them the wrong way."

These two German expatriates were alleged to sport dubious links to the Kray Twins – those famous brothers Ronnie and Reggie who "cultivated" organized crime from London's East End during the 1950s and 1960s and adored their status as West End night-club owners, hob-nobbing with Diana Dors or Frank Sinatra.

With their partner Tony Harris, the Gunnells eventually took over completely. The three started the legendary "Twist Sessions" – and of course the "Flamingo All-Niters"! Such an "All-nighter" lasted until six in the morning, with Johnny Gunnell acting as compère – and this type of event had previously run at the "Mapleton" in Leicester Square.

The Gunnell Brothers developed their club, and a roster of numerous R&B artists in fine style, and in order to keep up appearances, you didn't have to walk far in Soho, as Sixties apprentice Archie Bland observed about a fine boutique on the corner of Wardour Street and Shaftesbury Avenue: "In the 1960s that building was a high-class menswear shop called Krantz Ltd, and I was a junior salesman there from 1966 to 1968. I used to serve the actors, the rich and famous and the strippers. Two of the best customers were Ricky Gunnell and John Gunnell, who were Georgie Fame's and Chris Farlowe's agents. They were very generous men, and I used to get a £10 tip to take the bags to the car."

Regular club customer Val O'Leary, who married Savoy Brown Blues Band founder John O'Leary, is quoted by Harry Shapiro with a revealing account of the Flamingo's vibes: "The club atmosphere then was superb. I started going out to the Jazz clubs and suddenly this 'new music' appeared called R&B and everybody was raving over Rhythm & Blues. The first time I ever went to the Flamingo, the air was so thick with marihuana, you could get high just walking in there. You didn't really need to take anything if you didn't want to – you could get high on the atmosphere."

As Georgie accounts vividly, "now we got the Friday and Saturday nights, and then we started the 'All-nighters'. Later, Gunnell leased the place for extra nights, Tuesdays and Thursdays. That was when the Rolling Stones played there once – it was on a Tuesday or a Wednesday".

For those too young to have witnessed a phenomenon like the All-Nighters, one has to take it from the horse's mouth, and the most elaborate mouth there must be author John Pidgeon, writer of *Rod Stewart and the Changing Faces*, who can be found elaborating freely about the club on the website *rocksbackpages.com*:

"Outside the Flamingo, the audience from the evening session, over at eleven, has gone. Everyone waiting now is here for the midnight hour. The white-knuckle ride of a rush from the pills has smoothed into a surge of euphoria so intensely exhilarating it nearly takes my breath away …"! Well, "rush from the pills", no wonder Townshend, Daltrey, Moon and Entwistle would get ideas as soon as they were old enough! "Inside, the lights are dim, and the heat, under the false ceiling, ferocious."

Round the same time, their sax player Al "Earl" Watson, the afore mentioned Earl Bostic fan who got them their spot in the first place, fell into trouble with Rik Gunnell. Georgie: "Earl Watson tried to fire us, and Gunnell fired him instead". So Watson "left" the Blue Flames for The Migil Five. Georgie wasted no time and re-shuffled the band – getting new members into his quartet regularly from now on.

Watson was quickly replaced: "We needed a sax player, so Mick Eve came in, almost a year after we had started at the Flamingo." Mick was an experienced Jazz tenor saxophonist who had become semi-pro on leaving the army – just like, for instance, John Mayall up in Manchester before he came to London: "I had to do military service at eighteen, so I was a couple of years older than a lot of the people I was playing with when I got out of the military. But I had been playing in a band during that time and made up my mind that once I was out I wanted to play the saxophone. So it was the things that were open to us, our musical tastes tended to be towards the jazzier side of Blues, if you will. Jimmy Witherspoon and people like that were an inspiration."

Mick Eve had been playing with Brian Auger as well as fellow sax man Glenn Hughes, not to be confused with the Trapeze and Deep Purple bass man of the same name. Jazz-Hughes would become a member of the Blue Flames later on. That way, Mick Eve had been a Flamingo Club regular, and as mentioned, he had also been a Larry Parnes man, having backed Dickie Pride.

One of Mick Eve's pre-Flames endeavours, apart from his ever fluctuating Mick Eve Sextet, had been the Billy Woods Band. It was his first contact with the Jump Jive music, Louis Jordan style, which Georgie had come to appreciate.

Mick Eve in 2012: "I met the Blue Flames in this decent sized pub in the West End called the Flamingo. I had been working there with a line-up, working with the Rock'n'Roll backing musicians which did include Brian Auger, and did include John McLaughlin, only as a casual thing, when they needed a support act. They realized that we had been playing to black American servicemen dotted around the UK, and *they* enlightened us by making us listen to their jukebox. They could hear what we were doing but went 'Yeah, you wanna hear Horace Silver' or whatever it was, and they'd put on something that would open our ears."

"The Blue Flames had a similar leaning really towards that kind of music. When I heard them playing in the Flamingo the very first time they were down there, he [Georgie] was just playing upright piano, and guitar, drums and bass were there. It was lovely, but the owner of the club said 'Well, why don't you play the saxophone with them?' And that was how we then started doing it on a regular basis four or five nights a week. We were playing a lot, and there is no better training for a young twenty-year-old or somebody only in their teens, you know. It made you play, so it just developed from there."

Dick Heckstall-Smith, the saxophonist in the groups of Johnny Burch, Alexis Korner and Graham Bond, was similarly impressed at spotting the "men in their teens" – Fame & McLaughlin – at the Flamingo: "And I'm coming down the stairs into this venue which was absolutely packed with black American servicemen. You wouldn't find a white there. They were there because of what the music was: Georgie and the Blue Flames. And one part of the Blue Flames was their guitar player ... this guitar stuff John was playing those days when he was 18 – I was absolutely lifted by the boots ..."

Georgie shared Heckstall-Smith's enthusiasm for McLaughlin, while he felt restricted with his available keyboard situation, as he told Duncan Heining in *Record Collector*: "John was playing hard Bebop at the time but he fitted in just fantastically. When John was in the band, I didn't even have a Hammond organ. I was playing piano. Rik Gunnell had to rent an upright piano for our sets at the Flamingo because the Kruger brothers, who [still] owned the club, wouldn't let me play the club [baby grand] piano because that was reserved for Jazz musicians. Brian Dee, Johnny Burch, Brian Auger – they were all the frequent piano players at the All-nighters and Bill LeSage [of the Johnny Dankworth Seven] when he wasn't playing vibes. – I've got photographs of me sitting at the old upright facing the wall with John McLaughlin with a Gretsch guitar with my back to the back and I'm singing and playing because they wouldn't let me play the baby grand."

Enter The Hammond

Mick Eve had found the dependency on pianos in pubs and clubs an absolute drag even before the Blue Flames times, when his own sextet had a similar line-up. As Mick told Colin Harper, "It'd usually be one sax, trumpet, guitar, bass, drums and keyboards. But the keyboard thing was a problem. Sometimes we'd travel up and we'd have Brian Auger sitting in the dressing room or the bar all night, can't play a note because the piano wasn't in tune. One of the trumpet players I worked with was Eddie Thornton [who would become a Blue Flame soon] – he kept on at me about, 'Oh, you gotta listen to the Jimmy Smith records – this is the answer [a Hammond organ], it'll always be in tune.' Very shortly after, both John [McLaughlin] and I joined the Blue Flames and, again, it was out of tune bloody pianos, anywhere you went!" By the time Eddie would follow suit – first as a guest during the autumn of 1963 – the problem had long been solved!

"Until the Mods came in, the Flamingo was a black club", Georgie recalled, "it was full of West Indians, pimps and prostitutes – and great American GIs, stationed over here in the US Air Force. They would come in from their bases for the weekend. They brought records with them, saying 'Have you heard these? They even lent me their own records so that I could hear for myself. One of them, Carl Smith, gave me 'Green Onions' by Booker T & the M.G.s."

Over a very brief period, a trio of borrowed singles would change Georgie's sense of sound: Richard "Groove" Holmes' and Gene Ammons' "Groovin' With Jug", Jimmy Smith's "Midnight Special". Whatever Georgie and his boys liked, it was in the set in no time at all!

As Fame reminisces, "I was one of the first to buy a Hammond organ in England. The first person to buy a Hammond organ was Graham Bond, who was a saxophone player, a Jazz saxophone player, who came down to the Flamingo, sitting in with my band, sitting in with the Johnny Burch Quartet, who played with Alexis Korner and later formed his own band, The Graham Bond Organisation, and bought a Hammond. And I think two weeks later, I bought mine, at the end of 1962. So apart from Graham, I think I was the first. It was the sound. I was playing piano in the band, in the Flamingo Club. They wouldn't let me play the grand piano, or the baby grand piano, because that was reserved for Jazz musicians. So we had to rent an upright piano, which I played. And I heard Richard 'Groove' Holmes, Jimmy Smith, Booker T. and the MGs, all in the space of maybe one week, and I went out and I bought my own Hammond organ!

"And then all the groups started buying them. We had the wrong models. We had the small Spinet models, L 100. And then I up-dated mine to an M 1 or 2, I think, which was still a Spinet. Doesn't have the big keyboard, doesn't have the big sound that the great organists had that you listened to. And then at the beginning of 1966, or at the end of 1965, I bought my A 100, which is a full-sized Hammond. And I still use it on tour. That gives you the sound, like the B3 with the speakers, it's a real Hammond sound! I still take her on the road along with two Leslie speaker cabinets, and she will undoubtedly outlive me."

Georgie tends to call his Hammond organ a "she", like a Captain addresses his beloved ship, and while as a mere observer it is easy to sympathise anyway, the fact that this author has seen the A100 model in action regularly since October 1975 makes for absolute solidarity in terms of this affection.

"But we all played the little ones, and you can't get the right sound out of them. I think Steve Winwood probably got the best sound out of all from the small Hammond. But Steve doesn't play the little one any more, he has go two or three big ones in his house. We just used Leslies [those famous rotating speakers] for them, that *is* the combination: The Hammond organ and the Leslie cabinet, that is the magic combination. That's what is on stage there. Don Leslie invented the Leslie. And when Hammond Organ heard about it, they tried to put him out of business, they tried to kill his business, because Hammond made their own speakers. But they didn't compare to the Leslie, and Jimmy Smith put the two together. And in the end, when Hammond realized they couldn't win the battle, and they couldn't put Don Leslie out of business, they bought his business, and made him part of the Hammond business."

Taking the Hammond Story into the present era, Georgie continues: "Now the whole Hammond thing is owned by Suzuki in Japan. And they make digital B-3s, which Joey de Francesco plays. And he makes it sound good, but I can't make it sound good for me, so I play the old one and will continue to do so. For me, they lost the sound. They lost their magical sound in 1972: They did it for commercial reasons. They wanted to stay in the market, and the market was going transistorized, and they thought they had to move with the market. They didn't realize what they had! And they could easily manufacture them again. They have the technology to make them like they did before.

"It is like an old Volkswagen. You can still get the parts. If you have a Beetle, of which most of them may still be made in Brazil, I know. But if you have an old 1500 Beetle Volkswagen, which is the best one, you can still get the parts to make it good. And it's the same with the Hammond organ. You can still get the valves and the necessary equipment if anything goes wrong. You need a Hammond engineer that knows exactly how the thing works.

"Now that's the problem: Who is going to be a Hammond engineer in ten years time? I don't know if there's any youngsters who are learning this technology. There is a great Hammond organ engineer in England, who I have used for thirty or more years. And Steve Winwood uses him. Me and Steve have the same Hammond organ engineer, called Clive Bosch. Now when he stops working, I don't think he has an apprentice. He doesn't have an apprentice. So I don't know who is going to take over."

"But fortunately, these instruments are made so well. Nothing goes wrong with them if you treat them carefully. I call my engineer at least twice a year, and he refuses to come out. He says 'No, there's nothing wrong with it'. I say 'Come and check it out! Once a year, just look at it, check the valves.' And he comes, reluctantly! He just looks at it, ta ta ta, thirty minutes later he's gone. As long as he takes care of it. Cause they weren't built to be taken on the road. They were built to be put in your front room, or in your church. It's heavy, but if you want the sound, you have to be prepared to carry it. Two men can do it, if it's split. So long as there's engineers around to fix it and if they do their homework, it will be ok."

Indirectly, Georgie is responsible for his mate Brian Auger starting to play Hammond as well, something the prolific Jazz pianist never wanted. But during one immensely hot weekend, a holidaying Fame had become so severely sunburnt on a Cornwall beach that he had to be treated in hospital, and Auger had had to dep for him. Harper: "Shrewdly, Brian Auger relied on his own resources and kept his independence, although it involved a little effort."

With regard to the first of these purchases, the Hammond Spinet L100, Mick Eve deserves credit as the key Blue Flame in this case. As Georgie pointed out, "Mick Eve had joined us on tenor saxophone and effectively became the band 'straw boss', organizing rehearsals and dates outside the club as well as introducing new players." Eve not only frequently "motivated" the band to get a grip on all those new songs they had heard on the borrowed records, but he also made them put their hard earned Sterling into the band kitty – and this was where, in November 1962, the money for the Hammond investment came from. As Eve told Pete Frame in 1993, "it didn't really have much effect on the repertoire – we used to do things like James Brown's 'Night Train' on the piano, but we now had a much fuller sound and it was more in tune, because most of the pianos at gigs were useless. Gigs were now much nicer."

Well, according to Colin Harper, the "purchase" was backed by none other than his manager: "Georgie Fame had committed himself to Rik Gunnell (who by the end of 1964 was running a booming R&B agency as well as managing the Blue Flames) by allowing the latter to buy him a Hammond", but Georgie's memory is usually precise.

The Hammond effect on the repertoire *was* considerable, too. Georgie told Val Wilmer at the time that he did indeed learn more about Jazz singers than he had already detected in Mike O'Neill's collection, naming Oscar Brown and King Pleasure, Eric Morris, Rufus Thomas – and Prince Buster, with whom he undertook his first recording project on the Hammond organ, playing on Buster's album *Soul Of Africa*.

True to Fame's growing reputation as a "musician's musician", the recent switch to the organ had been watched ardently by soon famous contenders, like Ian McLagan: "I went there a couple of times before I was in the Small Faces days, never went there with Ronnie [Lane] and Steve [Marriott] or Kenney [Jones]. I was in a different band, The Muleskinners. Georgie was someone I idolized. I thought he was fantastic! He was very Mod, and he played a great Hammond. In fact, the Hammond that I bought – the first one, which is now in Kenney's house – I got that because I realized that the B3 which I wanted, was too much and too heavy. The L 100 was good enough, and it was small enough. It was still expensive, but that's what he played, so I got that. I've got a photograph of me and Clive, of me and Georgie Fame at the Albert Hall when the Faces played there a couple of years ago. He was sitting at his Hammond, and I said 'Would you mind if we had a picture taken with a 'selfie'. We sat there at the Hammond, and he said it had been 40 years, and I said yeah, it's ridiculous. I never had a photo taken with him before."

Another contender was the future organist in Chris Farlowe & The Thunderbirds, former Wes Minster Five member Dave Greenslade: In Martyn Hanson's *Playing The*

Band, he recalls their audition, walking over from the Scene Club in Ham Yard: "We went on stage and Georgie's Hammond organ was there, which he allowed me to use. It was the first time I had ever played one – he even showed me around the instrument. It was really good of Georgie to do that."

The Blue Flames continued to play a mixture of classic Rock'n'Roll – Chuck Berry, Little Richard and Jerry Lee Lewis style – but also the jazzy Ray Charles, King Pleasure and James Brown type Soul. What was his never clearly told secret, his magic instinct? Georgie never acted as a copy-cat, not even when he chose the State of Mississippi's Mose Allison and his voice as a role model. Whether he tackled a James Brown Harlem number, a tea-room ditty like "Eso Beso" or Fats Domino's cozy N'Awlins groove, he never tried to impersonate these heroes. And neither did you necessarily want to hear the originals. You liked the way that Georgie did them, with enough understanding of the culture he adored, but also filtered through a musical character all his own, a "Middle Class White Boy" just like Mose. And what's more, he listened to his band mates.

Eve: "We all contributed towards what material we should do as well. That was a nice part of it. Everyone's input counted. The drummer had lovely ideas: he would hear a record in somebody's house, and find out the name of it. Georgie Fame himself had a great repertoire that he'd listened to – for a young man I couldn't believe what he'd heard. So he was capable of reproducing this vocally, and playing enough organ to cover it as well. Copying stuff wasn't as easy in those days. You couldn't just rattle off the CD for someone, or put it in a computer. You had to make the effort to stick it on a tape recorder, silly things like that. But then, we got this repertoire together, really, just by listening to Ray Charles, Mose Allison – Fats Domino we would always listen to, Little Richard, and mix it all up together. Then you get this early sound that we got, I suppose."

Georgie reminisced about this in 2012 in a contemplative chat: "I still love Fats Domino as much as I did when I was fourteen years old! And I still play Fats Domino tunes on my gigs. Why not? And I am still learning about Jazz every time I perform. I'm still having my education continued, it has never stopped."

This was a time when only a minority of the British Flamingo visitors would know about the originals, because the singles the Blue Flames learnt from were often rare American imports, and the radio programmers, with the honorable exception of Radio Luxembourg, had not tuned into hip music yet. So they kind of had to trust in Georgie & Co. in coming up with faithful, authentic versions – or even better ones?

Georgie picked up the bait in the same chat: "You are entering a kind of political territory here, because the original Rock'n'Roll was Black American Rhythm & Blues. And the white population of America took the Black Man's music and called it Rock'n'Roll and commercialized it, and introduced it to the white people, including me. And the media feeds you this big mesh. Now it takes quite a while for you to realize – "Wait a minute, I can go and re-source this." There was no internet in those days. So if the media told you this was happening – "Elvis Presley is the King of Rock'n'Roll!" – you accept that.

"It's only later when you speak to other musicians, and you travel a bit, and then you maybe go to find certain record shops that have the real thing, you learn where it came from. Joe Turner, Joe Turner wrote 'Shake, Rattle & Roll'. But we didn't hear Joe Turner. We heard Bill Haley, because the White establishment fed it to us that way, and the Black establishment didn't have the means to do so. And B. B. King very graciously says that. He thanks bands like the Rolling Stones and the Beatles for actually taking the Black Man's music back to America and introducing it to the whole population. So that is political."

Guitarist Colin Green got itchy feet around the early summer of 1962, having been offered more regular gigs and higher fees by trumpet troopers The Eddie Calvert Band: "I think I just wanted to branch out and do further things musically. And Calvert was a huge name. He was a very, very good man and a fine musician. I learnt an awful lot from him. It was just a change, and a part of growing up I think, and of widening the perspective. We did night clubs as well, but it was a different type of audience, much more show biz and much more disciplined. When I got the job, it was extremely well paid, so it was a good career move. I was given 50 pieces of music, and he said 'Right, we'll start on Monday', and I would do any of these from memory. So I had to learn the sheets by the following Monday." Colin confirmed it was as rigid as Frank Zappa was later reputed to be, but better than going through the motions with something you already knew.

Colin Green's successor Joe Moretti – who had also been part of the Larry Parnes clan and was therefore well-known to Georgie – hailed from Scotland. Glaswegian Joseph Edward Moretti, an Irish/Scottish/Italian kid from the Docklands, was a young Rock'n'Roll crazy who had met Alex Harvey during a kind of "Glasgow's Tommy Steele" competition. The winning Harvey got Joe into his Kansas City Band, and after deserting to the Rikki Barnes All Stars, Moretti went to London to become a pro, like so many before and after him.

At the inevitable 2i's coffee bar he met and swopped chops with drummer Brian Bennett and Tony Sheridan – according to the Ipswich Hank Marvin, Roger Clarke-Johnson, "the two i's stood for the two Italians who ran the tiny little musicians' grotto and whose names ended with I".[5] That way, he met Colin Hicks, who as we heard not only happened to be the real Tommy Steele's brother but also got a vacancy in his Cabin Boys – so there was Joe, together with Jimmy Nicol and Tony Belcher. Come Christmas 1958, Joe had backed up Vince Eager, thereby meeting Blue Flame Tex Makins.

Very soon though, Joe fell in with Vince Taylor & The Playboys, where he succeeded Tony Sheridan, and turned out to be the crucial ace in the band, using his considerable Rock'n'Roll chops – for which Taylor nicknamed him "Scotty" after Presley's guitarist Scotty Moore – on Taylor's BBC-ruined, failed hit single "Brand New Cadillac". The tired and emotionless record executives, whose lack of humour and imagination Georgie would come to suffer in good time, banned the great little 45 because of their commercial connotations. Had you actually tried to purchase one of those American cruisers round London – it wasn't even on sale in the UK at the time!

Moretti wrote even more magic music history by playing the iconic axe in Nero & The Gladiators, and also tried his luck with Country music in Johnny Duncan and His Blue Grass Boys, replacing their Denny Wright. Just like Colin Green at

5. See Adendum

another time, Joe also worked for Eddie Calvert & The Wise Guys, playing Schlager-type instrumental tunes, and in 1960, he joined Johnny Kidd & the Pirates, by which time he had honed his fat guitar sound by buying Tony Sheridan's Grimshaw guitar and creating all the decisive licks and solos on "Shakin' All Over". What about regular axe-wielding Pirate Alan Caddy? Too nervous for the studio. And what about Mick Green, Van Morrison's favourite Pirate? He only joined after the event.

Anyway, Moretti never went on tour with Johnny Kidd, but had become a mate of Georgie's in the Parnes coach-flying circus by backing Gene Vincent in the Cabin Boys, out of which piano player Mike O'Neill formed his Roman toga combo Nero and the Gladiators, including Joe.

And Joe shared a number one hit on his CV with Georgie, on Johnny Hallyday's single smash "Viens Danser Le Twist" from the Philips sessions. With the Gladiators, Moretti was cheated out of another chance for a chart smash when the band's "In The Hall Of The Mountain King" got a BBC ban on the heels of the unforgotten "Cadillac" snub. What was it this time, auntie? It was throwing dirt on the reputation of classical composer Edward Grieg, of course. Very soon, Keith Emerson or Jon Lord would get away with "ruining" classical music themes, and Welsh chainsaw riff rocker Dave Edmunds could even "destroy" Khachaturian's "Sabre Dance" without the Soviets interfering with a Radio Moscow ban – but O'Neill's Gladiators got banned, reason enough for Joe to defect from one Leigh Lancashire lad to another.

Moretti didn't stay long with Georgie and the Blue Flames either, though – he had started to get numerous studio session engagements. For the moment, he was replaced by a mate of Mick Eve's who was going to share guitar duties with him years later on Donovan's "Mellow Yellow" single (1966): "I suggested John McLaughlin to give the line-up more stability", Eve told Pete Frame.

John McLaughlin – a sensitive player and eternal searcher for the perfect chords and sounds, whose childhood guitar hero was Django Reinhardt – had been with Alexis Korner's group, as well as with other bands like – hold it – The Marzipan Twisters, or Big Pete Deutcher and his Professors of Ragtime. Judging by the sounds of their hilarious names, these troupes were certainly Flamingo fun compatible. But John had also been with Brian Auger's band.

McLaughlin came over as a highly talented guitarist, like Moretti, but he stood at the completely opposite end of the stylistic spectrum: John would not touch Rock'n'Roll music with a sissy-bar, refused to nick Jimmy Reed licks or Chuck Berry clichés, and famously, he served as Jimmy Page's classical guitar tutor: "How to steal Bert Jansch and get away with it?" John McLaughlin's days in the Blue Flames were going to be last for nine month – he would leave in spring 1963, and soon joined the Hammond-competing Graham Bond Organisation, spelt with an "s", yes, and often advertized as the Graham Bond ORGANisation, to stress the Hammond. According to Bond biographer Harry Shapiro, John "McLaughlin felt this new group was 'musically higher, stronger, more involved and challenging than what I'd done up to then."

Georgie had often played "opposite" Graham Bond and his rhythm section of Jack Bruce and Peter "Ginger" Baker before that trio went out on his own: They had been part of the Johnny Burch Octet *and* Alexis Korner's Blues Incorporated, as had John McLaughlin's successor Dick Heckstall-Smith, by the way.

By 1963, the Graham Bond Quartet – Bond, Bruce, Baker & John McLaughlin – had not only recorded some great material with singer and harmonica ace Duffy Power. The five of them had also been on a package tour together – which also featured Duffy's former Larry Parnes partners Marty Wilde and Joe Brown, as well as Susan Maughan and Rolf Harris.

For a while after John McLaughlin left, Fame did not employ a regular guitarist Mick Eve: "There was a changeover period: Early on, by the time we had the Hammond organ, and no more out-of-tune pianos to worry about, suddenly, when John McLaughlin was leaving, he couldn't get Joe Moretti back and he couldn't get Colin Green back, and he said 'Well, I think we'll do it without (a guitar)'."

Niimoi "Speedy" Acquaye – the conga wizard

Instead, the addition of another member proved most significant – an African percussionist. "One of the first people I met down at the Flamingo Club was a man by the name of Niimoi "Speedy" Acquaye. He was from Ghana, and he walked into the band room with his conga drum. I wouldn't tell you what was inside it, but he got the gig!"

Acquaye (1931–1991) was born on the African Gold Coast, which was later renamed Accra. He played a little drum which he received from his parents even before he attended school from the age of twelve. When he was sixteen, he accompanied his parents on a steamer to Britain, after a short spell in the Ghanaian army at such a young age. The ship was the famous *Empire Windrush*, which in an ironic twist of fate had been a German, Hamburg "Blohm & Voss" built ship called the *Monte Rosa*. It had done pre-war cruises for top Nazis before it became a troopship and now served to join the races together rather than running a racist course (although, as landlord monster Rachman would show, the world is never black & white, or rather brown and white).

Niimoi's first artistic engagement was the Robinson Crusoe related pantomime "Man Friday" in Nottingham. He had arrived in London by 1951 and was assisted by his cousin Uncle Ben. Around Archer Street in Soho, they would wait for a chance to get an evening entertainment engagement, working as fire eaters, actors, or even better as dancers or drummers. Drumming became his great love, and he had the chance to join Flamingo Club musicians' circle, working with fellow drummer Phil Seamen and sax players Tubby Hayes and Ronnie Scott.

Mick Eve has only slightly different memories: "We brought along Speedy, the conga drummer. And he was like a little cabaret act, and when we had a long night, we knew that at the start of the second set, you could leave him alone for about ten minutes. He would go out and entertain people. Not fire-eating exactly – he had experience in that – but he'd do all kind of nonsense as well as playing a whole lot of percussion and get the crowd all join in with chants. He was quite a character, Speedy, and he's no longer with us. His first ever job in England when he got here was to be "Man Friday", in a Robinson Crusoe pantomime, up in Leeds. Then he came down to London and would always be about in whatever Jazz situation was going on, or semi Jazz, and we would all come across him. Speedy was never in the band at that point. But once we didn't have a guitarist, the idea was that the extra wages that would have gone onto the guitarist, we'd give to Speedy. It wasn't necessarily a revolutionary musical step, he did an interesting thing with the conga drum obviously, but we were always playing a little thing like Mongo Santamaria with a Cuban influence at that point as well."

For Georgie Fame, getting Speedy into his Blue Flames seemed like a gift from heaven. With eager interest and passion, he soaked up all he could learn and feel about African music. He may have been the singer, band leader and Hammond hero, but he made Acquaye the very special star of the band, and he never got tired of singing his praises: "Speedy introduced me to West African music, which I love dearly, and a song of mine is dedicated to Niimoi". It was "Zulu", which appeared much later on *Right Now!* in 1979, and the lyrics went like this: "An upstairs room in Prince's Square, along the Moscow Road, Alexis lived round the Korner [pun probably intended] – at the time we didn't know!"

Georgie would also have all the patience in the world for Speedy's meticulous stage preparations, waiting for him to change the skins of his African drums or tuning up for ages seemed to come with Niimoi's genius. A few months after Speedy Acquaye joined the band, original bass man Tex Makins left the Blue Flames to join Johnny Halliday. He was replaced by Boots Slade from Nero and the Gladiators, so all was kept in the family.

As Georgie told John Pidgeon in a 1972 interview, Acquaye's arrival was part of a step-by-step enlargement of the Blue Flames: "Speedy started coming down almost every weekend and playing with us all night, then John Marshall, who's a baritone player, started coming down and having a blow. Graham Bond used to come in and play, all kinds of people used to come in and play. At this time Ronnie Jones was on the [US Air Force] base at High Wycombe and he used to come down and sing. Geno Washington was on a base somewhere else [Bentwaters], he used to come down and sing. And it started stomping. Eddie Thornton was working at the Blue Angel night club playing calypsos and soft music, and in his break he used to come running over to the All-nighter in his evening suit and play trumpet with us. Then we had trumpet, baritone, tenor. The word got round and we started going out doing gigs. We used to do about five gigs at the Flamingo, and every Friday and Saturday we'd go out and do a base and, no matter where it was, come back to the All-nighter."

Eddie "Tan Tan" Thornton

Eddie Thornton (b. 1932) came from Spanish Town in Jamaica and had been with the first group ever to get broadcast on Jamaican radio playing live – The Roy Coulton Band. It featured one of the original members of The Skatalites, Don Drummond, on trombone. During the 1950s, Eddie, forever better known under his funny nickname

"Tan Tan", and the Roy Coulton Band toured worldwide. Looking around on this multi-faceted planet, Thornton found himself immigrating into the West Indian friendly metropolis of London, UK, – by some accounts, Count Suckle first felt differently – where he soon felt at home in the heart of the community, Soho, not least because of the proximity of the Flamingo Club.

One of the first bands he joined in London was the Mick Eve Sextet, which featured John McLaughlin on guitar, and as we have heard, Mick had sung the praises of the "always in tune" Hammond organ before the G.I.s were in Georgie's ear. As Eve told author John Pidgeon in 1972, "Eddie Thornton was working at the 'Blue Angel' night club, playing Calypsos and soft music, and in his break he used to come running over to the All-nighter in his evening suit and play trumpet with us." He played for Georgie, on and off, until 1980, would record for The Beatles, The Small Faces and perform with Aswad, Boney M. and Chris Farlowe's family R&B band protégés Kitty, Daisy and Lewis. There will be more from Tan Tan.

Enter the performing G.I.s

For several soldiers, handing out singles onto the stage was not enough. They jumped up themselves: "A lot of great American G.I.s used to get up and sing with the band – people like Ronnie Jones." The soon-to-be ex-service man Ronnie Jones would join Mick Eve in his own The Night-Timers (sometimes also The Nightimers, and once featuring the Blue Flames' ex-guitarist Joe Moretti) as would "the most famous one of all" – William Francis "Geno" Washington with his Ram Jam Band, who had been stationed at the US base of Bentwaters near Ipswich. Washington, a gutsy Soul singer, stage and movie actor, hypnotist and children's book author, is also still active in 2014 with an ever-revolving Ram Jam Band line-up. His live album *Hand Clappin, Foot Stompin, Funky-Butt ... Live!* came two years after *R&B at the Flamingo* and stayed in the UK charts for 38 weeks.

Geno Washington, still belting it out after all these years, remains fond of those days, as he told this author in 2010:

"They are all friends of mine from the Flamingo Club. Alan Price, when I was still in the Air Force, he was in The Animals. So I used to sing with the Animals on the weekends. So that's how I know him very well, and all the other Animals, they are friends of mine. And then Georgie Fame – I know Georgie from the Flamingo Club. I used to go down there, and in the city were Georgie Fame, Zoot Money, Chris Farlowe, and all those guys that became big, John Mayall, he had all those famous guitarists with them, Eric Clapton, Jeff Beck.[6] So I got to know all them from the Flamingo Club – a club specializing in Jazz, Blues and Soul: We brought the Soul into it! The Gunnell Brothers there were my managers also. All those groups who played in the Flamingo were managed by the Gunnell Brothers."

Geno's family ties also helped to bring some unlikely fans into the clubs like the Flamingo: "Herman's Hermits lead singer Peter Noone is my brother-in-law. He is married to my wife Frenchie's sister. And he is a good friend of the Beach Boys. So he

6. See Addendum

mentioned my name – did they ever hear of me? – and they went "Yeah, every time we tour England, every time we got a day off, we make our way to see Geno Washington and The Ram Jam Band!"

As Fame pointed out in the liner notes of his 2009 album *Tone Wheels 'A' Turnin'*. "Of the many G.I. 'Brothers' that were based in the UK, (and the All-Nighter before it was put off limits in 1963–64), only three are still in touch, Ronnie Jones of High Wycombe and Geno Washington of Bentwaters, who both stayed in Europe having successful singing careers and Kunle Mwanga (Wethersfield). Kunle remains a very successful figure in the Jazz fraternity in the USA, and I'm very grateful to him for his contribution herein [Mwanga wrote the liner notes for the 2009 album *Tone Wheels 'A' Turnin'*]. Perhaps more poignantly, for when he was [still known as] George Conley, a G.I. in London 1962, he introduced me to the work of Eddie Jefferson."

A kind of part-time singer with the Blue Flames, Ronnie "Psycho" Gordon had come to Britain as part of what used to be called the "Windrush" generation – West Indians from the colonies with British passports who, initially, boarded the *HMS Empire Windrush* in 1948 for Tilbury Docks on English motherland shores, just like Speedy Acquaye. What could they expect from the centre of the Empire – London? Wages that would have put John Lee Hooker's brothers and sisters to shame down in the Deep South of the United States – slave wages.

Ronnie Gordon came to London's Tottenham suburb via Southampton, on one of the last such ships, the *Irpinia*, in 1957 – having toasted his 20th birthday during the voyage. Like all of his forerunners he brought a love of music with him. His very first musical memories are of Duke Ellington tunes, and then he joined talent competitions in cinemas where R&B American style ruled, soon turned into Ska the way Kingston bands played it – and that's how he met Laurel Aitken, one of the first Ska/Reggae performers which were turned into gold by Island producer Chris Blackwell, a London-Kingston commuter who had been born as part of the white "aristocracy" of Jamaica.

Those sounds were what Ronnie Gordon soon heard in Tottenham, too. In the "El Rio" club in Notting Hill, he met future Blue Flame Mick Eve, who had been in the RAF Hertfordshire and also loved these Caribbean sounds. And that's how he ended up gigging and recording with the Blue Flames and, of course, Georgie on the organ.

There was also Herbie Goins (b. 1939), the man originally out of Ocala, Florida, who had never been stationed in England, but as a young G.I. went to Germany with the US Army. He later joined a band by Eric Delaney and came to England, landing the lead singer slot in Alexis Korner's Blues Incorporated, before he followed Ronnie Jones as the Night Timers front man.

Regulars at the Flamingo

Soon, the regulars at the Flamingo Club would also include: the two "Fathers of White Blues", John Mayall with his Bluesbreakers and Alexis Korner's Blues Incorporated; Chris Farlowe & The Thunderbirds; The Spencer Davis Group with the young British

Hammond hero, multi-instrumentalist, prime composer, powerful lead singer and one-off Ray Charles impersonator, Steve Winwood; plus The Monarchs and then Them, both featuring the young Belfast Cowboy Van Morrison – so by the time that Fame's future boss arrived at the premises, the Flames were well established there.

Georgie's soon to be agent Ruby Bard, who was then the manageress of Jazz acts like Kenny Ball and the Temperance Seven, points out in Johnny Rogan's *Van Morrison – No Surrender* that the Monarchs "weren't an easy band to deal with – they were a right bunch of tearaways." In spite of that verdict, Ruby Bard had arranged an audition at the time when Georgie Fame & The Blue Flames had slotted well into their residency: "I dealt with a German promoter who booked a few of my Jazz bands, and he decided to take the Monarchs following an audition. It was good experience for any young group to play Germany. They'd have to develop their set in order to survive.

Georgie was well aware of the chances and temptations of playing Germany between Hamburg's Reeperbahn and Wiesbaden's G.U. club dozen, but he was ever so busy where he was, as he remembered in 2009:

By that time "I played London and all over England. But we had the residency in the Flamingo Club in London. Five nights a week we played in the Flamingo, and we also played in other places. We would play in American Air Force bases, or a Rhythm & Blues club outside London on a Friday in the evening. And then we would pack the wagon and we would drive back to London and then we would play in the Flamingo from midnight until six o'clock in the morning. And we would do the same thing on a Saturday.

"And then we would play a Sunday afternoon in the Flamingo, for people that couldn't get home. And then on the Sunday evening, we would play in another club in London. And then on Sunday night from midnight to six a.m. we'd play in a West Indian Rhythm & Blues club, full of Jamaicans. So that is seven gigs in three days. And we did this regularly. At one point, we were doing ten jobs a week for a long time – for almost a year. We were young, we had the stamina, and we had the enthusiasm. And the public was growing with us at the same time. That is how it happened", so how can you go to Germany?

Geno Washington, Chris Farlowe, John Mayall, Ronnie Jones and Spencer Davis were now all managed by the Gunnell Brothers, as were PJ Proby and The Steampacket with Brian Auger, Long John Baldry, Rod Stewart and Julie Driscoll. Towards the end of the year 1964, Rik Gunnell's R&B agency was unrivaled in Europe. By that time, he also managed Elkie Brooks, Zoot Money, The Cheynes, Tony Knight's Chessmen and many more.

In his chronicle *Ready, Steady, Go! Swinging London and the invention of Cool*, Shawn Levy summarizes the R&B trend and its setters and their venues in a nutshell:

"The movement had formed and risen in London clubs and suburban halls that had recently converted from temples of traditional Jazz into meccas of R&B and the Blues – places like the Flamingo, the Marquee, the Piccadilly, the Ealing Club and the Crawdaddy, where white boys like Alexis Korner, Graham Bond, Zoot Money, Chris Barber and the indefatigable Georgie Fame could be heard a-wailin' and a-moanin' and a-bangin' out imitations – often stirring – of American originals that only a handful of Brits had, prior to the early '60s, taken note of."

The Rolling Stones were part of the Flamingo Story, too, as Bill Wyman remembered in *Stone Alone*. They had played their last gig at the Ricky Tick Club with drummer Tony Chapman: "We seemed all set for an uneventful gig at The Ricky Tick Club at Windsor [where Georgie would be secretly taped during a gig in 1965] the next week. It was a good night: the American service men in the audience understood the Chicago Rhythm-and-Blues music we were trying to emulate. But as we were packing up the equipment after the show, the boys told Tony Chapman he was fired. He was furious. Pulling me aside, 'Come on, Bill, let's go and start a new band.' I replied that I was quite happy with the Stones. He left us there, red-faced and angry", and proceeded to start a second edition of the group The Preachers with Peter Frampton – yet another Bill Wyman protégé and some-time Billy Wyman's Rhythm Kings member in the 1990s.

The Stones took on Charlie Watts, who had been an admirer of Jazz and R&B and Georgie via visits to the Flamingo with his friend David Green, a Ronnie Scott's Club house band bass player at the mere age of 18. As Alan Clayson writes, "It was flattery of a kind that Watts and Green were accepted not as suburban striplings barely old enough to quaff a Cherryade on the premises, but as just two of the crowd when they first ventured into a Flamingo All-nighter. The headlining act was Georgie Fame & The Blue Flames – anticipating 'Jazz-Rock' by a decade – but Charlie was more captivated by the jazzier supporting quintet …"

Wyman quotes Watts as saying "'I was into Modern Jazz, but I had a theory that R&B was going to be a big part of the scene and I wanted to be in it' […] And so the Stones – Mick, Keith, Brian, Charlie, Stu and me – first played together on 14 January 1963, at the Flamingo, Soho."

Wyman elaborates that "there were two jewels in the crown for the Stones to aspire to among the Soho Jazz haunts. The Flamingo Jazz club at 33 Wardour Street was the London hangout for the 'Cool Jazz' set, and we were presented by the promoters as 'original R&B starring the Rolling Stones and guest'. Our gig on 14 January 1963 marked the debut of our 'new' line-up: Jones, Richards, Jagger, Stewart, Wyman and Watts. But the Jazz crowd received us coldly. We were too Rock'n'Roll for the large contingent of blacks in the audience who had as their idol Georgie Fame, a regular performer. He was an incredibly good pianist and vocalist and reasonably friendly, compared with most of the Jazz fraternity. Later he told us that he would stand at the bar, so cool, watching us and thinking: 'Who are these young upstarts?'

"The other citadel was the Marquee, run by John Gee and Harold Pendleton [and Chris Barber]. They never liked us, viewing us as a dangerous threat to the Jazz status quo. The feeling was entirely mutual. We regarded them and kindred spirits as music snobs determined to sabotage our progress. What was odd about Pendleton's attitude to us was that his partner in the National Jazz Federation was Chris Barber, that true progressive in music and great champion of the Blues music." This would soon apply to Pendleton as well, as the first *National Jazz Festival* which he started in Richmond in 1961 and would soon (1964) be re-named the *National Jazz & Blues Festival*. It moved to Windsor, Sunbury and Plumpton and finally located to Reading, revamped again in 1971 as the *National Jazz, Blues and Rock Festival* and in time became the famous Rock friendly *Reading Festival*.

And yes, Georgie was to become a regular there.

Back to the The Marquee: the club would soon veer towards the more harmonica-fuelled, Chicago line of Blues, catering mainly for white students of black music, contrary to the Flamingo which continued to nurture Jazz, R&B and Soul for their predominantly black customers.

So the two clubs were quite different, as bass player and arranger John Paul Jones confirmed, quoted in the first part of Rolling Stones manager Andrew Loog Oldham's autobiography, *Stoned*: "The Flamingo was just funkier and jazzier – the scene [at the Marquee] was all white Pop ... and it was pills ... whereas with Jazz and Rhythm & Blues everybody was smoking, so you had two different cultures. Pop musicians hadn't come across smoke, apart from Billy Fury ... The Flamingo was extremely seedy, hot and sweaty, but a brilliant vibe. The music was great, everyone was into black R&B and some Jazz ... Brian Auger was down there, Sonny Rollins, Roland Kirk [US visitors checking out the Flamingo via their residencies at the nearby Ronnie Scott's Club], Geno Washington, Duffy Power, Dickie Pride, Cyril Green, Georgie Fame, Alexis Korner. Basically they were all Jazzers who played R&B. [It] was why the Stones and the Yardbirds didn't fit in ... We were into Otis Redding and the Mar-Keys, they were all into Chuck Berry and the Chess people, Blues twirts really. As a musical scene they just didn't rate, really."

Privately, Marquee man Mick Jagger would hang out with Flamingo friend Georgie, as Bill Wyman noted: "... at home, he was frequenting Soho's Sods Club with friends like Eric Clapton, Georgie Fame and Dave Davies of the Kinks.

In *Kink: An Autobiography*, Dave points out that "in Soho, I liked to go to the Whiskey à Go Go or the Flamingo, where Georgie Fame and the Blue Flames would often be in residence. I got to know Georgie well; he was a nice guy who knew how to enjoy himself."

These were harmless times, or so it seemed. You queued up in anticipation of a great night with live music, facing a rather tiny entrance area. But inside, the place was quite spacious. You found yourself in a dark room with walls painted in red, not quite the fashion yet in the early Sixties. You had bench seats all around the venue, the only place to sit or stand once you couldn't get a table. The place certainly seemed always full, and sweaty as well, because everybody was dancing. If you wanted a drink, the cellar that housed 400 people, but was often squeezing in up to 600 punters, only had overpriced Coca-Cola. In order to get some rum with it, you had to know or bribe the barkeeper – sometimes the notorious Stones manager and Fame press agent Andrew Loog Oldham would do the honours. And you soon developed a nose for Ganja. Still, it was all about the music, and while a DJ was certainly employed, too, this meant live music ruled, which Georgie Fame soon found out about. "At first I was a bit frightened going there. As soon as I worked in the Flamingo, I felt perfectly okay and safe."

As Georgie told *Mojo* in 1996, "the Flamingo wasn't a fashionable place, it was just a real happening scene. We were probably the hub, though we didn't realize it. All we were interested in was playing" – as he once said, "There's nothing else to do" – and furthering ourselves. We were absolutely knackered, but exhilarated because we'd been playing all day, all night. The Flamingo was the closest one could have been to playing in an American club. We developed the music because we had first-hand access to it. We were living the life."

In London, Fame & The Flames had always loved the Scene Club on top of the Flamingo. The journalist and future record producer Guy Stevens (Mott The Hoople) lamented in the *Record Mirror* edition of 20th July, 1963, that every little Liverpudlian group was billed as R&B in those days, pointing out that Georgie Fame was the real thing:

"A man who plays and sings the Blues in his own way, Georgie Fame, backed with the Blue Flames, is currently packing them in on Friday nights at London's "Scene" Club, which is now becoming known as the centre of Rhythm & Blues in this country. A quiet, sincere musician, Georgie had this to say about the situation.

"There are many kinds of Blues, and it's entirely a question of whether you *have* the Blues or not. The Beatles may not exactly play like Chuck Berry, but they are singing their own type of Blues. Most of the present-day Blues singers are, of course, coloured, because of the environment and society they were born into, but many white musicians are capable of feeling and singing the Blues.' And Georgie does just that, Born 20 years ago … he manages to create a sound that you would only expect from a coloured artist … Georgie's Jazz-based Blues singing shows a variety of influences, all of which have combined and moulded with his own feeling for the Blues to produce a unique and fascinating sound."

Apart from numbers which would later feature on *Rhythm and Blues at the Flamingo*, Guy Stevens mentions a few others at the time – adding to our complete picture of the man's 1963 repertoire: "Numbers featured in his stage act include 'All About My Girl', and a Jimmy McGriff organ original, 'Sticks and Stones'.

"Georgie's style has been compared by many with that of Ray Charles, and he admits a tremendous admiration and respect for that artist, and was knocked out when he saw him on his tour earlier this year. Although a basic similarity exists, Georgie's own style has now developed beyond plagiarisation.

"A quiet, inward person off-stage, when performing [Georgie] completely loses himself in his music, and finds expression and meaning in singing the Blues. He lists his own personal favourites as Ray Charles, King Pleasure, Oscar Brown jr, Mose Allison, Jimmy Witherspoon, and Sam Cooke, and likes dancing to Chuck Berry and Fats Domino. But his tastes are always changing, maturing, and as he himself says, 'you can find the best Blues in every little corner, anywhere, and you should never stop looking for them.'"

Lucky Gordon, Christine Keeler & The Profumo Scandal

Admittedly, it wasn't all about the music: The Flamingo Club became one of the prime stages in the infamous "Profumo Affair". But it started musically enough, with one of the protanonists, Lucky Gordon, being brought along by a part-time Blue Flame, his brother Ronnie "Psycho" Gordon, one of the "performing G.I.s".

For the club, it started like this:

On October 27th, 1962, just a few months after Fame & Flames had started their residency the club, there was a tough fight between two guests, with Georgie and the band grooving along nicely: "Don't shoot me, I'm only the piano ... – no, wait, the organ player!" The Jamaican drug dealer and hobby Jazz singer Aloysius "Lucky" Gordon, and Johnny Edgecombe, a Jazz promoter, pimp and jewel thief from Antigua, got into some vicious knife-wrangling down at the Flamingo – an event significant enough for "Lucky Gordon" to be incorporated into the song "Flamingo All-nighter" by Georgie Fame in the next millennium.

Both Lucky Gordon and Edgecombe were lovers of the VIP model, escort girl and Flamingo regular Christine Keeler, and Edgecombe had actually moved into her flat in Sheffield Terrace in Kensington during September. Both guys were extremely dangerous. Freshly abandoned, Lucky Gordon – whose idea of sex was "With the knife in one hand, he had me" (Keeler) – had held Christine hostage for two days, after he had attacked her with an axe, which was not very gentlemen-like even in Flamingo terms. Anyway, that night in the Flamingo, Edgecombe was going to slash Gordon's face so badly that he had to be treated in hospital.

Christine Keeler did not seem to realize that the great R&B, Jazz and Soul entertainer who rocked the Flamingo Club with his Blues Flames during many given nights –including this fateful one – was Georgie Fame. She certainly didn't do any name-dropping in her book *The Truth At Last – My Story*: In the account of her life and – inevitably – the Profumo affair and her attempts to get away from it, Keeler mentions the Flamingo Club only in its late-night disguise, as an All-nighters club in Soho's Wardour Street, where she was attempting a distraction from her sorrows and smoked with her acquaintance Paul Mann. She points out that she had not had any marijuana since her trips downtown with Stephen Ward, a certain black lady, and Lucky Gordon. Her decision to return to what she called "black clubs" – although a trendy thing to do inside the Chelsea scene – had been made on the spot, when they sat around her apartment, as they were the only establishments open at that time of the night. So they were on their way.

A few nights later – "I didn't much care about anything" – Keeler finds herself at the Flamingo Club again, and describes the events which moved the whole world from her own more and more fuming, helpless perspective. "Yet again, I felt lost, abandoned. Johnnie [Edgecombe] and I went to the All Nighters Club – I was in angry with life and didn't care about Lucky Gordon, or the consequences of meeting him.

"What a stupid woman."

As Keeler continues that Lucky had been there, just as he often was. She found him drinking and smoking with his mates, crazy-eyed. She reported that no sooner had he spotted her and Johnnie, Gordon wandered over and grabbed a chair as a weapon. "Lucky chased me through the club. I got lost in the crowded dance floor and Johnnie caught up with Lucky. Girls were screaming while the men stood back and enjoyed the macho show." Apparently, Lucky Gordon headed for the exit. Johnnie was up behind him, and then the security bouncers were blocking Gordon's escape.

"Johnnie seemed to stroll towards Lucky and the whipped out a knife. It was all over in a second. The knife flashed and then Lucky's face was pouring with blood." Keeler reported that Gordon moved his hands towards his face and cried with pain and anger. He had a tremendous, frightening cut down the side of his face. Keeler writes of blood running into his eyes, blocking his eyesight and that he had screamed there would be prison for Johnnie.

Once in hospital, seventeen stitches were needed for Gordon, and a jealous Lucky sent these stitches to Christine Keeler: she would get two in her lovely face for each and every one of his. She bought a Luger pistol, and both Keeler and Edgecombe went underground for fear of the gruesome Gordon. Edgecombe pleaded with Christine to find him a capable solicitor before he could show up at a police station, but Keeler was having none of that. She would give evidence against him as the vicious slasher.

What nerve: Even in hiding, Christine Keeler's lover Johnny Edgecombe was too edgy to leave other women alone, and when Keeler found him with one in December, she walked out on him, finding refuge in a flat that belonged to the "society osteopath" Dr Stephen Ward, the man who had introduced Keeler to Lucky Gordon in the first place, and the witness who, in Keeler's book talks about Prince Philip enjoying visits in London night clubs with David, the Marquess of Milford Haven.

In the apartment, her good friend and escort mate Mandy Rice-Davis stayed, and would smooth her edgy nerves. But "Johnny Too Bad" Edgecombe had followed in a taxi, and he figured (quite rightly) that his beloved Christine stayed in the flat – and fired seven shots at Ward's door lock.

So who was this Profumo then? Well, just a not too crucially important politician really. All the above scuffles had been topped one year previously – in 1961 – in a glorious country mansion in Cliveden in the area of Maidenhead. It was at a party thrown by Lord Astor when Dr Stephen Ward introduced Christine Keeler – who apparently was "twisting round the pool", or rather in it – to the British Secretary of State for War, John Dennis "Jack" Profumo, who also proudly held the title of 5th Baron of Profumo of the Kingdom of Sardinia. How does an osteopath get invited to such peerage? Well, the Lord's bad back was treated with a rather ingenious combination of chiropractic and sex-practic: Christine Keeler's mate Mandy Rice-Davies was to lie on his back, which probably signalled the start of the wellness movement.

With John Profumo, Keeler started some kind of affair while simultaneously – busy girl – "servicing" a certain Yevgeny Eugene Ivanov, who was a naval attaché at the Soviet Embassy in London. Sharing a lady with a Russian in "The Spy Who Loved Me" style did not go down too well in the heyday of the Cold War.

Who could elaborate on this better than John O'Farrell in his sarcastic but concise *An Utterly Exasperated History of Modern Britain*:

"John Profumo was a minor member of the British government, not even inside the cabinet. At the beginning of 1963, the only reason the British public might have been vaguely aware of him was that he was the husband of one of the greatest show-business names of the day. Valerie Hobson was the star of countless wholesome and jolly films and most recently leading lady in *The King and I*."

The British public might very well have become more aware of John Profumo shortly before the balls got rolling if, in 1962, plot-paranoid Prime Minister Macmillan would have got rid of him too among seven cabinet members and nine junior ministers during his so-called "Night of long knives". By the way, we do not know whether The Troggs sang "Night Of The Long Grass" four years later to rub it all in!

The affair had leaked, and it was to topple John Profumo, although the minister felt protected by "Parliamentary privilege". O'Farrell: "Profumo was advised by the cabinet secretary to end the relationship, which he promptly did after only four weeks. 'Hmmm', thought the minister, 'what's the best way to end this illicit and potentially explosive affair? I know. I'll give her a handwritten note. That definitely won't resurface later to incriminate me." It did, of course.

Meanwhile, gossip around the country had slowly, then rapidly increased, assuming that the Secretary of State for War had been coordinating hostess dates with a Soviet agent. So, Profumo saw himself under growing expectations to deny this frivolous assumption. In March 1963, he addressed the House of Commons with his version. It showed a remarkable lack of instinct – in making everybody believe that seeing Miss Keeler had been a wholly platonic, hmm, affair. O'Farrell's comment was: "Today, that would be taken to mean, 'Oh, so he was obviously sleeping with her then.'"

Keeler reprints the entire Profumo statement to the House of Commons in her book, but remains laconic about the upheavals: The way she saw it, the Macmillan administration was "under siege from the Labour Party and the press. We were starting to hear about 'thirteen years of Tory misrule' and how familiar is that?" Allegedly, it had all been just a rumour because few people knew for sure Profumo and Keeler had had sex. "Or that I had also slept with Eugene."

This did not harm Profumo in the long run: His loving wife Val stayed with him, he humbly cleaned toilets for the East London Toynbee Hall charity in East London, and in 1975, Profumo received a CBE for this. He never talked about this affair until he died.

But all this, not surprisingly, did endanger the British government: Prime Minister Harold Macmillan narrowly escaped a Parliamentary vote, but resigned soon after, in October 1963, due to misdiagnosed prostate cancer. Still, this threat at least prevented big headlines that his resignation had been caused primarily by the Profumo scandal.

Macmillan's fate notwithstanding, the worst hit victim of the scandal was Stephen Ward. His social life came to light when Christine Keeler was called to court in a trial which had nothing to do with Profumo, but the "spy girl" rumour stuck. In the end, Ward was prosecuted for living off "immoral earnings". Had he really been Christine Keeler's pimp? He denied this. Some doubted it, believing he was Keeler's true friend.

He was for a while, and Keeler is clear in her verdict, believing that the pimp thing was a front to get Ward out of the spy scandal: "That such charges were even brought was one of the great miscarriages of British justice, something that many legal experts as well as scholars of the time now recognize. Stephen never lived off women like a pimp. He never did that. The charges were just a weapon."

To cut a long story at least a little bit shorter – which was duly adapted in films like *Scandal* and a theatre play, *A Letter of Resignation* – Ward was tragically found dead before getting sentenced. Murdered by secret agents? The official verdict was suicide, what else?

But Keeler backs this one and names proof, claiming that the prescription had been for Nembutal, the drug which Ward took to take his own life, "after writing some notes, one of which said: 'It is really more than I can stand, the horror, day after day at the court and in the streets. I am sorry to disappoint the vultures.'

Keeler continues that she was so desperate through all this that she developed a form of asthma in the process and was not able to breathe.

"I was devastated by it all. I couldn't breathe properly. It was a sort of asthma but so acute I thought I would die."

There is no tragedy which an Englishman can't see the funny side of, and sure enough a satirical LP was released, *Fool Britannia*, which featured Peter Sellers, the much later *Denver Clan* star Joan Collins and Anthony Newley. The latter's record company, good old Decca, had got cold feet about releasing hot stuff like this, but the Flamingo's own Jeff Kruger stepped in with his Ember label and scored big time. Another release about the affair, "Christine", by Joyce Blair a.k.a. "Miss X" got a Radio Luxembourg and BBC ban, which guaranteed another chart entry, of course.

It seems a pity that Stephen Ward didn't live to see the *Scandal* movie from 1988, developed and directed by author and record/film producer Joe Boyd, who led the early careers of Pink Floyd and Fairport Convention. In *White Bicycles: Making Music in the 1960s*, Boyd shares the observation that "our film helped England re-write a bit of its own history: the movie's success placed Ward and Keeler in the role of victims or the Establishment rather than the irresponsible upstarts the press had made them out to be at the time."

Stephen Ward, according to Boyd, as a lover of the liberating lure of those days, concludes, was "someone for whom the Sixties came too late to undo the damage inflicted by aristocratic snobbery and cruelty."

To top the film, there is even an Andrew Lloyd Webber way of looking at the whole caboodle, *Stephen Ward The Musical*. And if the dear readership is more documentaty inclined, there is the wonderwul *nickelinthemachine.com* for lots of insider's facts and photos.

Christine Keeler herself got nine months at, as Georgie would say, "Her Majesty's Pleasure", for lying about being threatened again by Lucky Gordon, and, unsurprisingly, Lucky went inside anyway.

But true to Blue Beat folklore, Lucky Gordon enjoyed a second career, long after his three years' "time" behind bars, using his considerable gourmet skills – as a cook for Island Recording Studios in Notting Hill, and then as the tour chef for Island star Bob Marley and his Wailers during the era of the *Kaya* album, 1977/1978. And should you ever hear a cover version of "Heaven Knows I'm Miserable Now" by ACT, that's Lucky himself supplying the "Skank" vocals. There is also a re-mix of "Moments In Love" by The Art Of Noise which features Gordon. Not quite the same as being a part-time Blue Flame like his brother Ronnie "Psycho" Gordon then, but he made a new album in 2012.

When all this came to a head, guitarist Colin Green wasn't in the band anymore, but during his time, these things certainly went beyond his radar: "I think we were blissfully unaware of that [the Profumo affair]."

Due to knife-thrashing scuffles like this, the Flamingo Club soon got "off limits" for members of the US Forces – some presumed it was quite a welcome excuse for getting rid of Afro-Americans, and dark-skinned customers in general, in an era which wasn't as racially unbiased as Commonwealth conduct would lead one to believe. If that was the case, then West Indians chose not to notice – increasingly, they just loved their Flamingo.

His involvement in the "scene" around all this pandemonium led to Fame being quoted as calling Keeler a prostitute, something he denies convincingly. "How and why would I call Christine Keeler a prostitute? How was I to know, and also it would have been none of my business! Of course, I had always said that the Flamingo 'was full of West Indians, pimps and prostitutes', but that was it! The quote in question appeared in the liner notes of the Ace Records compilation *Mod Classics* and was written up by one Dean Rudland, who in turn blamed the magazine *Record Collector*."

Whether you will ever decide to read on in Christine Keeler's book or the numerous other accounts, the point is to imagine it all to the soundtrack of Georgie Fame and the Blue Flames – will you ever listen to the crowd roar in the background of *Rhythm And Blues At The Flamingo* again without thinking of Christine, Lucky and Johnnie?

Ska rivals jazzy R&B

More and more, the Flamingo Club, which had initially attracted mainly Afro-American Air Force personnel, became a home from home for a lot of West Indian immigrants, too. Just like the US G.I.s stationed around Greater London, they couldn't care less about Beat, Pop, "Trad Jazz" or Vaudeville ballads in other clubs around town. So where the American soldiers had got more R&B and Soul, the Jamaicans now got Ska, often called Blue Beat with regard to the London record label of the same name, the calypso makers Melodisc subsidiary Blue Beat Records. Georgie: "Thanks to the West Indian contingent, I got to hear and play a lot of Ska, as it was called then."

As Jeffrey Kruger said in a radio interview, "We were the only club that allowed the West Indian immigrants to come in. They were banned from most places and had their own kind of music, which eventually went from Blue Beat, as they called it, to Ska. It was the first time that immigrants and Whites were able to mix together with no problem, and the common denominator was music."

Georgie didn't take to new, edgy the club atmosphere like a fish to water, as he admitted, twelve years after, to Chris Welch in Melody Maker, August 1974: "I was terrified at first. There were terrific fights between the US airmen and Africans and the West Indians. If ever there was any trouble, we stopped and went straight into 'Jumpin'

With Symphony Sid'. There would be bottles flying everywhere [so Georgie could have played 'Saturday Night Fish Fry' by Louis Jordan as well], and it was supposed to cool them down. It was also supposed to stop the customers who wanted to hear the band from leaving. But it got terrible and after a while, it was put off limits to the GIs. Then all the white kids who had been too scared to come before, heard about it, and next week, the place was packed with Mods …"

Although live music was always the heart and soul of the Flamingo Club, there was one sensation whose impact is hard to grasp in today's world of mega P.A.s and finely tuned arena monitoring: the colossal "sound-system" of Kingston disc-jockey Count Suckle. His real name was Wilbert Augustus Campbell, (b. August 12th, 1931 as one of thirteen children). He came over to Britain with two more secret stowaway mates in tow, "Duke Vin" (Vincent Forbes) and "The Tickler" (aka Lenny Fry), but when the captain discovered them, they had been in the open ocean for too long.

Shocked by foul, rainy drizzle, frowns by the Whites and far too civilized music, they found themselves in West London's Notting Hill, where they had to camp in Rachman-style dumps. With no suitable dance halls in sight, the Count and the Duke assembled their own huge mobile sound systems – with speakers bigger than cinema gear – and became the sensation of private parties within the British Afro-Caribbean community. Did the Notting Hill neighbours and the local policemen "on the beat" like it? You bet.

One of their gadgets: speeding singles up to make them more attractive to jive to. As soon as the first Ska and Blue Beat records arrived from Jamaica towards the late 1950s, a new craze was taking shape: Suckle & Vin's jet-plane-loud sound system "clashes". These were popularity matches – who had the rarest and most hilarious records?

It is the stuff of legend that Duke Vin beat Count Suckle in a 1956 "clash" at Lambeth Town Hall. Vin claimed he never lost a clash, but Count Suckle was acting against the lines of a Louis Jordan song: "I run my mouth *and* my business, brother!" When the Count secured a stint at the Flamingo Club to work his sound systems after the live bands had appeared, so many punters stood in line to get in that a traffic jam ensued.

Suckle was a true entertainer, and served as DJ and "the selector" of his records in one person. Proud of his huge and rare record collection, according to Georgie "the best record collection of anybody I have ever met in my life, he was no mean dancer when he got the chance to – he was a fantastic dancer! He used to get direct imports from Memphis and the Caribbean … all the old Blue Beat stuff was being played in the clubs where we played." When Georgie met him, Count Suckle had showcased lots of singles that had never been heard on British shores for many years.

The Count had started at Blues parties, held a residency at the Roaring Twenties Club in the soon trendy "togs"-flogging Carnaby Street (No. 50), and which had actually been opened with a performance by Georgie Fame and the Blue Flames: "We played there a lot, a Carnaby Street nightspot which, in addition to Afro-Caribbeans, attracted the cream of the white Sixties counter-culture. It became an epi centre of Swinging London, before Carnaby Street became the fashion street that it was. We opened it, and played there for months and months and months. It was run by a fantastic Jamaican disc jockey by the name of Count Suckle. That was where I heard [like he did in the Flamingo before] some wonderful recordings. Some of them were Jazz things, a lot of Blue Beat, all that stuff, but really, fantastic dance stuff."

Georgie Fame and the Blue Flames did not only open the Roaring Twenties, and the Scene Club, but also the Ram Jam Club in the more and more Jamaican Brixton area.

The Rolling Stones, The Who and The Animals were curious to listen and nick some licks. Suckle remembered that a 17-year-old Mick Jagger used to ask if he could borrow some new singles which the Count had on mail order from a Tennessee record shop. As quoted in the British *Telegraph*, "The club also attracted politicians: 'Profumo would come, always at about 5am, with Christine Keeler and Mandy Rice-Davies.'"

For Mick Eve, the Roaring Twenties and Count Suckle's discs were also a revelation, as he told Pete Frame: "He had a marvelous collection, and we would borrow records off him to copy. That was an amazing place; I've never known anywhere like that. Rougher than the Flamingo – fights there all the time, the police used to leave it alone, but it would be full of drug dealers, hookers, pimps, gangsters, villains. We'd go there on a Sunday night, when the Flamingo was shut."

Soon, the Count started his own "Count Suckle Cue Club", which later became "Q Club" in 1962, not far away from The Flamingo on 5a Praed Street in Paddington. (It ran from 1960 to 1980), and punters were still asking: "Where does the Count get those records from?" Punters of the kind that made regulars blush: Stevie Wonder, The Four Tops, and the Commodores were seen in the "Q" before it shut down its gates, sensing that Suckle had seen the sign of the times: Soul.

Just like the Americans, the Jamaican expatriates had soon sussed out – you brought your favourite singles along, and they would find their way into the band repertoire, for the following weekend even, if you were lucky. Made immortal by the 2008 documentary film, *Count Suckle and the Birth of Ska*, directed by Gus Berger, Vin died in 2012, and Suckle passed away May 19, 2014, at the age of 82.

Consequently – taking the shrewdness and eclecticism of Suckle & Vin to heart, Georgie now combined New Orleans Rock, Calypso, Rhythm & Jazz à la Mose Allison and Phil Upchurch (he would get the chance to play with both, much later on) – and Blue Beat, which was what they used to call Madness-type Ska, the forerunner of Reggae, in early Sixties' Jamaica and Great Britain.

The first time Georgie lugged his bulky Hammond into the recording studio was in the name of Ska as well – for none other than his Jamaican hero Prince Buster. On the other side of Baker Street, there were the premises of the old Advision Studios, and it was here that Fame lent his organ sounds to Buster's *Soul Of Africa* album. Another studio cat was legendary trombonist Rico Rodriguez.

As Georgie told Duncan Heining, "I knew Rico because I was very involved with the West Indian community at the time because half of the punters down the Flamingo were West Indian and Count Suckle, the great disc jockey, had his own club in Carnaby Street called the Roaring Twenties, which was a real West Indian club. We were very much part of that community. Prince Buster always swears he told me how to play Blue Beat but I'll take that with a pinch of salt because I was well into the scene before I played with him." Fame would meet both Rico and Buster again over the years, most notably for his 2005 BBC television special *The Birth Of Cool*, when Rico came up and played "Humpty Dumpty". The two of them also collaborated with them on "Madness" and "Enjoy Yourself" during one of Jools Holland's *Later* spectaculars.

Rico remembers the first encounter very well, as found on several net sites: "Yeah, when I come to England I was looking for Laurel Aitken, he had a label called *Blue Beat* label. Then I saw Laurel, so Laurel gave me all the sessions, yunno. I was getting work for Laurel. My first 3 or 4 years in England was quite OK because I was getting sessions and then after 4 years I was getting work for Prince Buster, when he came to England, 'cause he was working on the *Blue Beat* Label as well. Those were the two things that kept me going yunno. As well as Georgie Fame, a keyboard player from Liverpool [oh well] he had a band in Carnegie Street, in the West End. I used to go there in the nights, I used to play. So the manager of the club, he gave me money 'cause he liked how I play. I used to play Don Drummond music and Skatalites music, and it was new to them. So me and Georgie Fame become very good friends, yunno. When you come to England you not steady. I was like a wanderer. So after I left Georgie Fame Band I play with many other bands."

Blue Beat/Ska was also most certainly to the fore when it came to the first recording chances for The Blue Flames.

On "Baby Baby (Don't You Worry)", the Blue Flames, including a non-singing Fame on Hammond organ were used as a backing group for singer Perry Ford & The Sapphires harmless twist workout: nice, but not a stand-out. This 1962 Decca single was backed by "Prince of Fools", another dance crazy number – maybe the Hully Gully – which sported crooner Ford and his girlish Sapphires in a chorus not unlike the A-side.

Decca had been the second largest record label in the world before World War II, presenting artists like Al Jolson, Bing Crosby, and later Bill Haley. They started the manufacture of 10" and 12" LPs in 1949 and 7" singles in 1950, while British Decca had just made crucial early 60s misjudgements: first refusing to release "Tell Laura I Love Her" by Ray Peterson and leaving it to Ricky Valance of competitor EMI. Then old Decca famously refused to sign the Beatles, which were also caught by EMI. Rolling Stones to the rescue! But couldn't they be the right "major" for Georgie Fame?

Blue Flames play Blue Beat – but Georgie remains "stumm"

In the summer of 1963, the Blue Flames were involved in four further single releases by the Rhythm & Blues label R&B Discs Limited. "R&B", incidentally, could be read as short for rhythmic and bluesy music just as well as for the two proprietors, Rita and Benny Eisen, who were based in Stoke-Newington and organized several independent music labels at the time, King (UK), Ska Beat, and now this new logo with blue lettering on a white background. Truly R&B obsessed, Rita & Benny were always on the prowl for new, promising acts, and they enjoyed Georgie Fame & The Blue Flames a lot, at the Flamingo Club as well as the "Roaring 20's" in Carnaby Street. Impressed by what they saw and heard, they approached Georgie and his band about recording prospects.

Fame and his Flames were naturally delighted about getting such a chance again, but immediately Flamingo & Fame agent Rik Gunnell stepped in. His verdict: Georgie's shouting and caressing voice, which had wooed Rita & Benny in the first place, was to be a no-go area in the recording studio. Fame wouldn't be allowed by Gunnell to sing on record before a major deal had been secured.

Rik Gunnell had, for a while, been negotiating with the majors at the time: EMI, the "Baby Baby" label Decca, Philips, Pye and Oriole. Those "Power Five" companies included a lot of sub-labels that seemed to spell variety. EMI, for example, had the comedy and Beatles moniker Parlophone, Columbia Records (as a sub-EMI successor to the Columbia Graphophone Company, not CBS) and HMV; Philips had Fontana, for the Flamingo players The Spencer Davis Group; and Decca sported Brunswick and Coral. So it was instrumentals only, Booker T style, for the band, and sax man Mick Eve remembered it vaguely when he was interviewed in 2002 by Nick Rossi:

"Rita and Benny came to us on a gig with the Blue Flames and asked us if we'd come and do a session. The first one must have been backing the popular duo Clive & Gloria, although I don't remember much about them. We did two instrumentals on that session and they asked us back to do another session with Georgie singing. But Rik Gunnell intervened and said that Fame mustn't sing a note, because he was about to negotiate a record deal, so Rita and Benny had to swallow it."

So they duly did two instrumental singles, first "J.A. Blues", a Blue Beat instrumental with a soft off-beat, lead melody provided by the saxophones, as if imagining good old Billy Vaughan in Kingston Town, with a great sax solo thrown in. It was backed by "Orange Street", Rhythm'n'Swing with Georgie's hot Hammond and his saxophone players taking turns, Mick Eve supplying the first solo, and it is probably Peter Coe on the second one, as he depped (later to join permanently) for Johnny Marshall in July and August 1963, when these recordings were made, before the first live album.

For the second instrumental "Stop Right There", the trumpet comes to the fore. It is absolute happy-go-lucky middle-of-the-road stuff, but it sounds catchy and easy-going with great bass lines – a sign of the times and proof of Georgie Fame's willingness to appeal to a wide range of punters with his music. Again, a great saxophone solo lifts things out of the ordinary. The flip-side, "Rick's Tune" is another Blue Beat workout – as a departure from its predecessor, "J.A. Blues", the lead melody is shared by tenor sax and trumpet this time, the "bugler" being a recent welcome Blue Flames guest, Eddie "Tan Tan" Thornton, who would join the Blue Flames permanently in January 1964.

Around the same time, the single "Shake Some Time"/"Comin' Home" appeared, and it featured Ronnie "Psycho" Gordon as a lead singer, the already mentioned brother of "Lucky" Gordon, the Profumo protagonist.

"Shake Some Time" had a straight, driving 4/4 rhythm, with Red Reece's bass drum accentuating the groove surprisingly high up in the mix, framing Fame's organ sounds and delivering a highly effective backing for Gordon's easy and natural vocal delivery. The single is a rare item, but the A-side is available via Georgie's *Live at the Ricky Tick*, which was belatedly released as an R&B Records LP in 2014.

Mick Eve takes up the following events with regard to Georgie and Gordon's recordings: "I said, 'Well, listen, I will bring a friend of mine that works at the post office. I'll get him round from work and he'll sing a couple of tunes.' This is a guy called Ronnie Gordon. So he brought in two tunes that we did, so we did four titles on the second session. That was the early Blue Beat. I don't have any of them. I had one of them, but I gave it to the bass player that took over from Tex [Makins], Boots Slade. He said he wanted to use it for promotion. And of course that's the last I saw of it. No musical masterpiece, but it's a bit of history."

Gordon only cut that one Flames single, and then joined a group called Red Bludd's Bluesicians, who featured yet another Hammond player who could "do the Booker T.": Jon Lord. He worked at Ford's in Dagenham – like the Dagenham native Sandie Shaw – and then became a kind of singing postman in Mount Pleasant for three decades, until he retired from delivering the Royal Mail in 2001.

Purchasing a keyboard, he got lessons and was soon fit enough for pub gigs with none other than old Mick Eve, and his activities have culminated in an actual studio album in 2012, *Lucky Gordon Speaks His Mind*, on the Barefoot label. Apart from the Specials tune "A Message To You, Rudy", it features that old Blue Flames Single "Shake some Time" under the new title of "Slip Your Shoes Off Baby", and he delivers "Pork Pie Hat" in true Jamaican style. A lot of it sounds Jazz-influenced, too – no wonder, as the Constitution Band (named after the London club they used to play) that Mick Eve assembled for the (ad)venture, actually features members of his 70s Jazz-Funk outfit Gonzales, including some Blue Flames members.

The Pirate Station that was started because of Georgie – Radio Caroline

It was around this time that the ex-manager of Alexis Korner's Blues Incorporated, who now acted as Georgie's co-manager and record promo agent, made himself felt on the scene. He was an Irishman called Ronan O'Rahilly, who doubled as a film producer, had an actor's studio in London also ran the "Scene" Club in Soho.

A lover of Rhythm & Blues music via his American mother, O'Rahilly always had brilliant ideas – apparently, he was responsible for persuading Graham Bond to lift his trio with Ginger Baker and Jack Bruce out of Alexisis Korner's Blues Incorporated. O'Rahilly was also the quiet man in the background when the Blue Flames' Mick Eve started the Nightimers with Ronnie Jones.

He had the other brilliant idea of somehow breaking the monopoly that BBC radio held on the British airways. He could not get any interest, let alone airplay for an unreleased Georgie Fame single which our man had recorded for his JA music label, an independent operation, which was a novelty at the time.

O'Rahilly told Tom Lodge, "Yeah, I was running the Scene Club. I used to have the Rolling Stones appear there before they were known. That's how they got started. At that time I found this young organ player, great Blues music. 'Ok Georgie', I said to him, 'we'll try and get you a recording contract'. So we recorded the song Yeh Yeh, but all the record companies said his music was too 'black'."

As Georgie pointed out in his 1999 BBC radio series quite openly, you could say that "In the days before Radio Caroline, there wasn't much for us on the radio, really."

The BBC would only play records by the big four: EMI, Decca, Philips and Pye. Their monopoly was re-enforced by the *Wireless Telegraphy Act*, totally ridiculous by today's standards, whereby even listening to the – perfectly legal – *Radio Luxembourg* which operated from the Grand Dutchy of Luxembourg, was supposed to be an offence if you lived on British soil. But after the BBC, even the independent *Radio Luxembourg* refused to play Fame – their programmes had all been sponsored by those four British labels; or rather "sponsored", as in "Payola", as they would have said in America.

O'Rahilly bought an ancient Danish ferry, the *Fredericia*, in early 1964, renamed it *RV Caroline*. He soon equipped it with transmitting gear, which was easier for him than for most, because his parents owned the private Irish port of Greenore, complete with a shipyard. *Radio Caroline*, named after President Kennedy's little daughter, "I was flying to Dallas Texas to buy the transmitter and I was reading this magazine, *Time* or *Life* or something. There was this picture of President Kennedy chasing his daughter around the Oval Office, and the caption read 'Caroline holds up government.' 'That's it!' I said. 'Caroline! Yes, that's it!'"

Next, he started a test programme on the 27th March, anchored some three miles off the coast of Felixstowe. The government hated it, and O'Rahilly remembers laughable accusations, for instance by the British politician Tony Wedgwood Benn, who had claimed *Radio Caroline* had disturbed other ships' rescue signals. Who could have known that many of the DJs on *Radio Caroline* would become famous for ages, including Dave Lee Travis, Tommy Vance, Simon Dee, Tony Blackburn or Johnnie Walker, most of whom later defected to BBC Radio 1?

While the story of *Radio Caroline* and pirate radios in general, including their brutal but fruitless crushing by the British Government on August 14th, 1967, has often been told in hilarious detail, including the infectious movie *Radio Rock Revolution*, Georgie Fame has a special place in its legend and legacy via the fact that this particular station was started because of *his* records.

Georgie got a chance for a very special celebration of those heady pirate radio days. In the summer of 2014, from August 6th to the 8th, he went on the *Pirate Radio Beat Boat Cruise*, "celebrating the 50th Anniversary of pirate radio and the *Birth of British Beat & R'n'B* boom on the classic ocean liner Marco Polo", with three nights at sea and two days ashore in Antwerp and Amsterdam, together with Eddie Floyd and The Rhythm Kings.

The legendary live album – Rhythm and Blues at the Flamingo

It was not easy to get the major companies curious, not to mention seriously interested in Fame and the Flames' particular mix of party philosophy, serious Jazz, Mississippi tinged Blues and the Soul of the Harlem clubs on the other side of the Atlantic.

Georgie remembered how difficult it was talking to Duncan Heining in 2009, and also sketched his idiosyncratic way out of the rut: "We knew we had a scene and the band was sounding okay, so let's do it. So, we did our own independent production and sold it to EMI. We then got a deal for five years with EMI. But the executives had no idea what was going on down the street."

Calling their shamelessly ecstatic party programme "Rockhouse", those Fame & Flames raves, celebrated in Georgie's famous, loud, chequered Madras jacket, were immortalized on the legendary, historic, loose, atmospheric live album *Rhythm and Blues at the Flamingo*, recorded in September 1963 and released in early 1964.

The concert LP got financed by Rik Gunnell, who leased it to EMI's Columbia record label. Georgie's manager had been thinking as hard about marketing Fame as Pirate O'Rahilly, and what's more, he had also invested heavily before any deal was done. As he told *New Musical Express* in 1964, and his words echoed Fame's:

"We have had a lot of trouble over the last few months recording Georgie's debut on disc. It is not as if it was difficult to put him on disc, because demand for Georgie is fantastic and the club is constantly being inundated with queries about his first record. The trouble has been presenting Georgie in the right way. We have tried many things at great expense, in fact altogether, I have had ten records made by Georgie. Then we hit the nail on the head when Ian Samwell came to see me."

Ian Samwell became the producer of the debut album, and it was engineered by Glyn Johns. Both characters played a significant part for Fame as well as British music in general and deserve a closer look at this point.

The South London musician and producer Ian "Sammy" Samwell (1937 – 2003) had composed his claim to fame, "Move It", for Cliff Richard, as well as the follow-up single "High Class Baby". Writing also for Joe Brown and Georgie's short-time girl friend and sun studio companion Elkie Brooks, Ian Samwell also played guitar in the pre-Shadows UK group The Drifters, and he also produced the instrumental group Sounds Incorporated.

Sounds Incorporated – later shortened to Sounds Inc. – had backed Georgie Fame's faves Little Richard, Jerry Lee Lewis and also Gene Vincent and Sam Cooke or Brenda Lee in England and had hits with "The Spartans" and "Spanish Harlem" on EMI-Columbia. Their version of the "William Tell Overture" reached # 2 in Australia. They also played in the music film *Live It Up!* They worked as Cilla Black's backing group, too, from 1964, and they had strong Beatles connections – getting support slots with the boys all over the globe, including New York's Shea Stadium in 1965. Additionally, their three horn players were invited to play on "Good Morning, Good Morning" on the Beatles album *Sgt Pepper's Lonely Hearts Club Band*.

Four years before *Rhythm and Blues at the Flamingo*, in 1959, Samwell had written "Say You Love Me Too", significant because it was the first British song covered by an

American act, in this case The Isley Brothers. Apart from this pedigree, what made him street credible and interesting for Georgie Fame was his reputation as a Mod disc jockey. Samwell had run/fronted dance sessions with his own disc collection at the Lyceum Ballroom in London as early as the summer of 1961, soon entertaining thousands of Mod fans at the venue – in what was probably the first discotheque in the world – as well as in the Orchid Ballroom in Purley. In the 1970s, Samwell went on to produce the band Hummingbird, a prolific studio funk group that would feature Fame's future Blue Flame Bernie Holland on guitar.

As Samwell told NME in 1963 how the idea for the kind of recording took shape: "I was round at Georgie's flat one day, listening to some of the demo records he had made, and to me the whole trouble seemed to be that no one as yet had managed to record Georgie in the way he performs – live and exciting. [But] the trouble I think was to try not to disturb his activities while performing." Well, whether you can call it disturbing, but – let's wait and see.

Glyn Johns (born 1942 in Epsom, Surrey) had originally been a singer in a band called The Presidents and had issued some singles for Pye and Immediate, but he soon became a record engineer as an apprentice for Kinks and Who producer Shel Talmy.[7] Glyn Johns, endearingly called "Glynnis" by John Lennon, later worked with everybody from The Rolling Stones via Bob Dylan, Eric Clapton and The Eagles, famously re-mixing The Beatles' *Get Back/Let It Be* album and doing more work for Georgie Fame over the years. Johns also re-vitalized the career of one-time Blue Flame Andy Fairweather Low by producing and engineering his 2006 comeback album *Sweet Soulful Music*, and he also engineered the 2014 collection by Georgie's Hammond pal, ex Small Face Ian McLagan and the Bump Band, *United States*.

Legendary as it would become, *Rhythm and Blues at the Flamingo* was dogged by some pretty problematic, well disturbing, mishaps. For a start, there were no congas on the recording, although the fans, and certainly Georgie Fame himself, considered these big African drums to be an integral part of the Blue Flames' sound. Instead, the band had to opt for the rather unusual use of bongos.

The quite apparently joyful party mood also betrays another gruesome slip on the actual night. During the first run-through, which was meant to be the proper gig, there was a mistake in the microphone set-up – "I'm sorry, one of the tracks is down", Georgie remembered Glyn Johns shrugging his shoulders – so the whole thing had to be done again, harking back to all that initial enthusiasm.

Finally, much of the repertoire on show here had not been shaped by the performing guitarist Big Jim Sullivan – although his competence and verve has never been in any doubt – but either by the recently departed John McLaughlin or by a line-up which did actually sound really good without a guitar part. But Ian Samwell put his foot down – an axe was indispensable in the era of guitar bands.

As Ian Samwell told Fame expert Nick Rossi, "For the album we put microphones above the audience, so that the excitement would be there. And we invited a lot of regulars, just to let them know what was going on. Clive was more likely to play on a weekend. It was a pretty noisy crowd. They were very excited; they were going to be

7. See Addendum

on record, so to speak. The only thing that I changed about it all was to bring in Big Jim Sullivan as the guitarist." [8]

So the guitarist had really been Samwell's idea: "Yes, they didn't have a guitar, but felt they needed something to hold down the rhythm; not that they had a bad rhythm section at all: Red Reece on the drums and Speedy Acquaye." [9]

But as Fame recalled to Duncan Heining, "The band sounded fine. We had an organ, two saxophones, bass and drums and on conga drums Speedy Acquaye (sic). The only guitarist I could think of was Jim Sullivan, who I knew from the Larry Parnes days. He was a great guitar player but not for that band at that time. It was all-electrified and a bit heavy for us because we were getting like, 'Hey, man, we're getting cool here!' (Laughing). Speedy, meanwhile, was detained at Her Majesty's Pleasure on a little trumped up charge. So Timmy Thomas, who was a frequent visitor down the Flamingo, came in and played bongos!"

Still, *Rhythm and Blues at the Flamingo* was the nearest Fame and his Flames ever came to capturing those magic nights at the Flamingo Club in 33, Wardour Street on wax. The set list can be called eclectic in the real, most positive sense of the word, using some Mississippi Blues as well as Jamaican Blue Beat, Calypso, also pure US-Pop, and Soul directly from New York's Harlem district. Fame was adept and comfortable in all these styles, and this very diversity would turn out to be a blueprint for more than half a century in music without a proper career plan. Where many performers tend to "use", even exploit other artists' influences, Fame adapts them or, if at all possible, promotes their work and works hard at their friendship, on and off stage.

At the same time, the still young Fame found his natural role model in the frequently mentioned and praised Mississippi "Middle Class White Boy" Mose Allison, who felt a strong connection to black R&B but would actually turn the tag *Middle Class White Boy* self-deprecatingly into an album title for Discovery Records in 1982. Critics have had a go at Fame's obsession with Allison for ages, but while a young Ray Charles had copied Nat King Cole and Charles Brown to an extent where he would positively impersonate them – famously criticized by his producer Ahmet Ertegun – it wasn't simply Fame just mimicking Mose: the Southern man simply happened to sing exactly like Georgie wanted to. Spot the gradual graduation on their collaboration *Tell Me Something* in 1996.

Born in 1927 in Tippo, Mississippi, the philosophy graduate from Louisiana State University Mose Allison had started to play trumpet and piano at an early age and was renowned for his elegant playing and laconic vocal style with often sarcastic, precisely observed lyrics. Working from out of New York City since 1956, he had been meeting Fame hero Phil Woods amongst others. His debut LP was *Back Country Suite* in 1957. Allison was only allowed to release an all-vocal album in 1963. Fame is in good company loving the man: Flamingo men John Mayall, Pete Townshend & The Who, The Rolling Stones, Van Morrison, Jimi Hendrix and later J.J. Cale adored the wise man, and he is one of many who interpreted his reading of Willie Dixon's "Seventh Son", plus of course the BritBlues standard "Parchman Farm" about life in a prison camp in the American Deep South. Allison has famously played residences in London's Soho district into the 2000s, including Ronnie Scott's Club and the Pizza Express.

8. & 9. See Addendum

Rhythm And Blues at the Flamingo – track by track

"Night Train" was often Fame's introductory instrumental – while he was announced by co-manager Johnny Gunnell – and clearly inspired by the manner in which James Brown used to work then, although the Harlem Shuffler tended to use "Night Train" as the final number in his 'Apollo' shows from 1961, not as the opener. Fame did not apply Brown's breakneck speed, but was eager to throw this thing directly towards his American G.I.s audience, based at those air bases closest to London. You could hear Fame shouting out "Atlanta, Georgia", "Washington D.C." and "All aboard?" just like Godfather Brown, before launching into this lively Funk thing which gives an opportunity to all the Blue Flames to take their solos: Big Jim Sullivan, the two sax players, Mick Eve on tenor and Johnny Marshall on baritone, bass player Boots Slade and Red Reece on drums. As Eve had pointed out, the number had already been in the repertoire when Fame still played piano instead of organ.

The song's origins go back much further than James Brown: Duke Ellington's saxophonist Johnnie Hodges recorded the memorable theme as early as 1941 (actually with a small combo that used Ellington on piano) and called it "That's The Blues, Old Man", and his boss, The Duke, applied this to his more elaborate composition "Happy-Go-Lucky Local", which was one of four movements in his Jazz symphony *Deep South Suite* in 1946. One of his tenor saxophonists was Jimmie Forrest, and he made good use of the tune when he did it in November 1951 as "Night Train". Rather than stealing it, though, he created the attractive stop-start breaks in the middle which Georgie made such good use of. (Ah, the Fifties – in our age of copyright catastrophes, the fact that neither Ellington nor Hodges ever sued Forrest for stealing their main claim says a lot about the comparatively relaxed business vibes of the times.) [10]

The horns launch straight into an infections Swing riff: Fame knew "Let The Good Times Roll" via his idol, Louis Jordan, who had presented this hard-hitting Swing as a single in 1946 with his Tympani Five, credited to his then-wife Fleecy Moore. Then of course, Georgie heard "Roll" again via the much credited Ray Charles. Short and sweet, the Blue Flames really have fun here and infect all aboard.

"Do The Dog", with front man Georgie Fame getting announced one more time by club manager Johnny Gunnell, full of pill-popping panache, served as an excuse for some more energetic dancing – with Georgie shouting out just that one order – or wait, he subsequently asked the audience to "do the hound dog", "the bulldog", or "any

10. See Addendum

kind of dog". More highlights of the piece are Big Jim Sullivan's guitar solo and Fame's own Hammond work. John Lennon expressed his enthusiasm of the number in the *Melody Maker*, and it became the first single on which Georgie Fame's voice could be heard. It did not chart, though.

Less than a third of the Flamingo audience were white. Still, the Blue Flames were well advised to include more conventional standards of the day, "Eso Beso" being one of them. Originally called "Eso Beso (That Song)", it had been a Top 20 success in the USA and Germany for Paul Anka – perfect material for doing the Calypso on the Flamingo dance floor. They also did wonderfully silly things like "Speedy Gonzales". Cliff Richard would record "Eso Beso" two years after Georgie for his May 1966 album *Kinda Latin*.

Oscar Brown Junior's adaptation of "Work Song" was next: The 1960 composition by cornetist Nat Adderley – brother of Julian 'Cannonball' Adderley – had originally come out as an instrumental track on the similarly called *Work Song* album, with the legendary Louis Hayes (b. 1937) on drums. Hayes continued to work with many of Fame's heroes like Dexter Gordon and John Coltrane, and would play for Georgie four decades later on the celebrated *Poet in New York*. Oscar Brown Jr. (1926–2005) from Chicago, the Jazzer who consequently sacrificed fame for politically sound Civil Rights campaigns, had put words to "Work Song" the following year, as presented on his *Sin And Soul ... and then some*. While Georgie could have decided to give this example of Mississippi history a more laid back treatment, Mose Allison style, he chose to let the adrenalin flow here with some great swing again, before there are compère Gunnell's calls for "Coke and hot dogs, spend your money, please!"

"Parchman Farm" is a song whose vibe Mose Allison picked up from the black Delta Blues man Bukka White, who wrote and sang his "Parchman Farm Blues" from bitter prison farm experience in 1940. Fame certainly added the archetypal Hammond organ theme to Mose's piano arrangement, and this cannot be separated from the number anymore, a true sign of a classic in its own right. It's no surprise that on Georgie's next live album named after his band *Shorty* in 1970, he repeated the exercise to great effect and satisfaction. Among the many versions that Mose Allison and possibly Georgie Fame inspired were Paul Jones singing it with the Manfred Mann group in 1965 for a BBC radio broadcast, with John Mayall recording it later the same year for *Bluesbreakers with Eric Clapton*.

"You Can't Sit Down", written by, amongst others, Jazz guitarist Phil Upchurch, is a Booker T. tested Twist, at almost five minutes the longest number of the show – an instrumental full of exciting breaks where all the Blue Flames again get a chance to fill the gaps with their solo ideas. (Phil Upchurch would become label mate for Georgie Fame a quarter of a century later, on Ben Sidran's American Go Jazz label.)

There was Soul for Greater London's Mod alumni, which American G.I.s liked just as much as the Jazz which they increasingly got from the Blue Flames. But for the growing number of the West Indian Flamingo punters, consisting of West Indian Londoners, it had to be early, fast Reggae, i.e. Ska – or, as they used to call it, Blue Beat, hence "Humpty Dumpty", seemingly kids stuff, but in fact one of the most popular rhymes of the English language. As a tune, it's performed here with an off-beat, which had been a big 1961 hit for Trench Town vocalist Eric "Monty" Morris, the original lead singer in the Skatalites. Morris as well as the group (which reformed in 1983) recorded several singles for Prince Buster. For Georgie Fame's own taste in music, this was just as well – he always had a soft spot for it. A studio version of the song was also on his EP release, *Rhythm & Blue Beat.*

For adults: "Humpty Dumpty's 17th century meaning had been brandy boiled with ale, and later stood for a clumsy, fat person. (The French had their "Boule Boule" rhyme, and today's Georgie would sure love the Swedish-Norwegian equivalent: "Lille Trille", whereas the Germans went for the heavy on the tongue "Runtzelken Puntzelken" – now there's a song waiting …). Pantomime, stage and literary references abound, not least it was used in Robert Penn Warren's Pulitzer prized *All the King's Men.*

Back to the US contingent: Smokey Robinson & The Miracles' Soul stomper "Shop Around" was the first Motown million seller and hit the US charts at # 2, reaching Number 1 in the American R&B listings during February 1961. For quite a while, it was a popular live staple and also became the B-side of "Do The Dog".

Sonny Boy Williamson's "Baby Please Don't Go" was another reminder of Georgie's eclectic tastes as well as those of his role model of the time, Mose Allison, who had been Fame's introduction to this song via Mike O'Neill's record collection: Chicago based performers like Sonny Boy Williamson, or Big Joe Williams, who pioneered the song in 1935 as Joe Williams & The Washboard Blues Singers and re-recorded in 1941, certainly catered for a different fan base than the flashy, Detroit based Soul crooner Smokey Robinson.

But again, Fame and his Flames made this transition work with absolute ease. The song floated around much in those days and was also presented by The Animals, and also Van Morrison's early group Them. Consequently, Morrison later featured it with different bands.

It's a timeless standard, which together with "Work Song", "Parchman Farm" and "Night Train" became the *Rhythm And Blues at the Flamingo* EP, so punters with less money could buy four club favourites without shelling out for a complete album. This four song collection was so successful that contrary to the single, it reached # 8 in the UK charts.

Glyn Johns recorded more numbers during the *Rhythm and Blues at the Flamingo* performance, but, at the time, they were not included in the original LP. "Parker's Mood" does not sound unlike the famous "Moody's Mood For Love" on the album follow-up *Fame At Last.* Both songs were written by the pioneer of 'Vocalese' – putting Jazz lyrics to instrumental solos – Eddie Jefferson from Pittsburgh, Pennsylvania, who had impressed Georgie early on. (Jefferson would get killed outside of a Jazz Club in Detroit in 1979. He was 60 years of age.)

Here, Georgie's "Parker's Mood" is a very slow Swing with great Vocalese phrasing that was originally sung by Eddie Jefferson's Vocalese partner King Pleasure (1922–1981) – his real name was Clarence Banks. As a young Bebop fan, he moved to New York in

1945 and had adapted these Jefferson musings about Charlie Parker, one year before that bass genius died in 1955, making his version a hit. Georgie handles the thoughts about deciding whether or not to 'go to Kansas City' really sensitively. Johnny Marshall sounds great on alto sax.

"Money" (Bradford/Gordy) had become quite popular not only via the Tamla Motown craze, but also through the omnipresent Beatles cover version – but Georgie gives it a much faster treatment, his Hammond organ became greatly enhanced by a great groove provided by ace drummer Red Reece, Tommy Thomas on congas and Boots Slade on bass. This was also released only later – like "Parker's Mood", it appeared on the box set *The In-Crowd*. The studio version of "Money" (also to be found on those two releases) is much more conventional, mainly due to a rather straight if effective drum beat and the congas getting a more restrained part than the bongos during the *Rhythm and Blues at the Flamingo* proceedings.

The reason why even this complete set list was only a little part of the Blue Flames' huge repertoire was not only the punters' demands – the band loved to listen to new records virtually as a way of life. Mick Eve: "And then social life, or whatever term there was for it, was really spent hanging out with people who had lovely record collections with stuff that we didn't know existed. They were hard to buy in those days. There was one little shop in Lyall Street that specialized in Rhythm & Blues records. You would see all sorts of people in there, who in later life went 'Oh, you remember the shop in Lyall Street, that's where I first heard Muddy Waters' or whatever'. It was all full of hope and optimism then, at the start of the Sixties. You thought the music world was gonna change. But how wrong we were, you know? You just hope – you live in hope."

As you could easily hear on *Rhythm and Blues at the Flamingo*, The Blue Flames, with all their knowledge of ten Rock-Ola jukeboxes' worth of material, were never in danger of becoming a living juke-box themselves. Mick Eve confirms: "I think the Blue Flames – possibly because of Georgie Fame himself, who even as a seventeen year old – had a sense of direction he was going to stick to, whereas with the other line-ups that went round backing different Rock'n'Roll singers before that, we tended to do a bit of everything, which is not really the answer. We were going down to the Flamingo – and the interval music would purely be a little record player in the dressing room that they put a microphone in front of – and they would all be listening to *Ray Charles at Newport* or whatever it was at the time, or a popular thing like a James Brown thing, when they first started coming out. So you were surrounded by it, and the Blue Flames had more of a sense of direction."

The sound and the atmosphere of that album would have repercussions for many decades to come. One of the most loving, if quirky, tributes came from the Danish Mod group Route 66. Fake stylus on vinyl sounds and all, their Hammond Swing number "It Ain't Nice" recreated the sound of Fame & Flames, with the help of producer Matthew Fisher, who was no stranger to skilful Hammond work himself via his many years in Procol Harum, having supplied the famous "Whiter Shade Of Pale" sounds. The one time Route 66 band member Claes Johanson pointed out in the liner notes to their sole, eponymous 1984 album *Route 66* that "'It Ain't Nice' was supposed to emulate the sound of Georgie Fame's *Rhythm And Blues At The Flamingo*, (which had just then been re-released on RSO Records at the time).

Matthew Fisher had actually gone to that club and seen Fame many times, so he became extremely enthusiastic as we started adding bits and pieces like a live audience, the characteristic announcer, and even crackles "to make it all sound like the original vinyl album we were using for reference." The announcer was of course John Gunnell, as usual calling out the band, here as 'Grover Jones & The Night Swingers', and telling the audience "The bars is open. We got lots of expensive Coca-Cola and coffee. All we ask is: spend money!" – rather a nice one, that spoof got Gunnell down to a T.

Rhythm & Blue Beat – the first studio EP

For Georgie's first EP collection – the popular 60s format of four numbers on a 7-inch record with a picture sleeve – Fame also chose the magic word "Rhythm", in order to create some continuity after the Flamingo live album. In April 1964, he cut four tracks in the style that had become ever more popular in the club.

The contract enabled Fame to play more Bluebeat, but now his voice was part of the deal, too, at long last. Five numbers were recorded for the EP, of which Prince Buster's "Black Head Chinaman" remained unreleased until it appeared on the box set *The In-Crowd* in 1998.

Rhythm & Blue Beat (EMI-Columbia, re-issued as *Blue Beat* by RSO in 1980). It was credited as "Georgie Fame & The Blue Flames (trumpet – Eddie Thornton)". "Tan Tan" Thornton, as he loved to be called, was just a – potentially frequent – guest with the band at that time, for the simple reason that he had a six-days-a-week nightclub engagement that was too lucrative to leave.

Here on *Rhythm & Blue Beat*, the Blue Flames covered Prince Buster's "Madness", an infectious, fast Reggae tune, which had originally been released in 1963 by The Prince Buster All-Stars.

Buster, a.k.a. Cecil Bustamente Campbell, born 1938 in Kingston's Orange Street, is seen as the most influential of the Ska, pre-Reggae era. He carries the title OD, Order of Disctinction, a Jamaican honour. One year after "Madness", he would record "Al Capone" and chart with it in the UK in 1967. He took part in the 1972 movie *The Harder They Come* in 1972 in a DJ cameo role, and had a late chart success with "Whine & Grine" in 1998.

15 years after Georgie's recording, "Madness" was to become the band-christening and defining title track for the band of the same name. Those Nutty Boys Madness with singer Suggs & Co. from London's Camden Town a.k.a. Norton Folgate not only chose the name, but made the title their first single. Two further decades on from Madness' chart success with "Madness", Prince Buster, Suggs and Georgie Fame could be seen performing the song in 2008 on the TV programme *Later With Jools Holland*, the piano-pounding presenter looking just as happy as the threesome and trombonist Rico, swiftly combining the song "Madness" with Prince Buster's "Enjoy Yourself".

Another track was the 1956 "Tom Hark Goes Blue Beat" by Olias Lerole and his Zig-Zag-Jive-Flutes, but copyrighted by Rupert Bopape, and had been a massive international hit, covered in 1958 by the Ted Heath Orchestra and in 1963 by Bert Kaempfert. The original "Tom Hark" had come out as a Kwela instrumental with chat recorded in South Africa for the EMI label. It had featured a certain Aaron Jack Lerole on penny whistle. Tom Hark was a police lookout.

Fame then gave that old children's song "Humpty Dumpty" the Jamaican treatment, following Eric 'Monty' Morris. The final track was "One Whole Year, Baby", in which Georgie repeats the months of the year many times over, cause all that time he had believed the girl in question loved him just like he had loved her: "January, February, March, April, May, June, July, August, September, October, November, December" – at that speed a welcome tongue twister for English-learning kids all over the world and all those adults for whom it is never too late for a happy childhood. Interestingly, the Blue Beat touch was a Fame & Flames idea here, as the 1955 original by Earl Curry & His Orchestra had sported Big Band arrangement. (Jimmy Nicol & The Shubdubs also did a version, and Tommy Quickly & The Remo Four up in Liverpool used to play it as well around that time, in 1964. And much later, in 1991, Desmond "Israelites" Dekker would do his own reading of the song, confirming its popularity.)

While the *Rhythm & Blue Beat* EP did not make the charts yet, Georgie did reach a more than respectable #8 with the live follow-up, a four-track excerpt of *Rhythm and Blues at the Flamingo*.

Dawn Yawn – The Flamingo legend continues

Georgie Fame & The Blue Flames now played the Flamingo five nights a week. John Mayall and his Bluesbreakers had recently started to fill the support slot for them. Setting up, often in transit from another gig, was always a sweaty and stressful endeavour: "Sometimes the jazz group, some great jazz player like Don Rendell or Tubby Hayes would be on", Georgie told *Mojo* writer Spencer Bright in 1996, "and we would slap the organ on stage while they were playing, say 'Hi guys, how you doing?' Then we'd retire to the little rat-infested dressing room or go to the bar." Ah – the old Flamingo.

The sets which The Blue Flames played at the Flamingo All-Nighters usually started at approximately one in the morning, and another one at four thirty. In between, what could you do but go to an all-night café Fame mentioned in his song "Flamingo All-Nighter". Most of the time, this would be "Yollie's Cafe" in Tisbury Court, which wasn't exactly trendy London – romantically run down more with hindsight than through the eyes of a Blue Flame between 1964 and 1965.

If Georgie and the band members were too tired even for a coffee break, they would revert to their nearby shared flats, which could be in Soho as well as in Notting Hill down Oxford Street and the Uxbridge Road towards the west. Their flats also used to be let by Peter Rachman, the Bayswater and Notting Hill rent-a-hole "slumlord", a Polish-Jewish concentration camp survivor who was the dirty landlord in the Profumo

Affair, owning the luxury apartment in which escort girls Christine Keeler and Mandy Rice-Davis pleased acquaintances, and who used Keeler for sex and as a poisoning-preventing food taster. His atrocious treatment of often poor tenants by partitioning flats into ever smaller units and even dividing rooms so that two dumps would share only one – statutory – window, would soon lead to the expression "Rachmanism" in the Oxford English Dictionary, for lack of a single alternative expression. Sometimes, as Fame related to journalist Spencer Bright in 1996, Rachman simply moved all their belongings, locked the apartment in question and left a note stuck to the door, telling them where they lived next, all in a period of a single, if long drawn out All-nighter.

Christine Keeler confirms this in her memoir *The Truth At Last – My Story*: "Peter charged enormous rents for the properties and if there were problems the utilities would be switched off or the drains blocked. He had contacts in the Tory government including one minister, Eric Marples, who tipped him off about property – Peter owned land on which sections of the M6 motorway now run."

It's all part of the general atmosphere in London's club land: Keeler's boy friend Johnny Edgecombe worked his drug juke joint from one of Rachman's properties. Keeler had a relationship with both, and while she claims that "When I was with him I didn't know the extent of his empire or exactly how he ran it", she describes in great detail his background of surviving the war, or his Nazi-induced fear of starvation, and elaborates on their relationship: "All the time I was with him we had sex at least once a day – after lunch. He called it his 'afternoon nap'."

She would also describe how the system of mini-flats which Georgie also rented had been worked out: "One of the girls Peter had met turned him onto the property market. Girls wanted flats and the respectable-looking Peter could rent them and then sub-let them to the girls. Immigration from the West Indies was high and landlords did not want to rent to black people. But they would to Peter who turned the properties into lucrative sub-let properties – he was making tens of thousands of pounds a year by the time I met him. I never knew about the terror tactics with tenants who didn't pay rent or were difficult. I knew there were 'assistants' for I fell in love with one of them."

Fame and his Flames may have been tired after their frequent and wild Friday and Saturday All-nighter marathons. Exhaustion led to a "Dawn Yawn", as Georgie would call it on his big band number on the *Sound Venture* album which he started to record around the end of 1964: "The Club has closed, you're so tired, all night long you've really been blowing. No cabs, they're all hired, wonder where people are going …" It was no surprise that you couldn't get a taxi – night owls used them to get to Victoria Station and have a shower, or hang out in all night cafés. In Fleet Street – and then start a new club round! These were youngsters who just couldn't get enough of it all, survivors fuelled by Purple Hearts who were then entertained by the Flames with a Sunday afternoon show, which would then of course be followed by a club gig elsewhere. Brian Auger remembers that Flamingo manager Rik Gunnell once let him have a glimpse at the Blue Flames' "pill bill" for one week – astounding!

But the pills didn't always work, did they? *New Record Mirror* had reported on 27th July 1963: "Georgie Fame Car Smash": "Georgie Fame and the Blue Flames, featuring in NRM last week, were in the news again last Saturday. They were driving in a Jaguar along the Watford By-pass to an engagement at a U.S. Air Force base when they collided with another car. Both cars were smashed, but only the occupants of the other car were hurt. Georgie and the Blue Flames missed their base date, but go to the All-night Session at the Flamingo Club, London, in time to go on at 12.30."

Also, more and more Mods infiltrated the Flamingo Club, arriving on their immaculately tended Vespas – and clad in the best that nearby fashion Mecca Carnaby Street had to offer, soft-woolen mohair sweaters and Ben Sherman shirts, their "chicks" in Mary Quant's miniskirts, to virtually take over the Flamingo Club. In the process, R&B remained as hip as the customer elite – apart from Mod disciples The Who and The Small Faces, several Beatles and Rolling Stones members still loved to hang out in this establishment:

And even the Rolling Stones were still far from able to match the competition the Blue Flames put up. Bill Wyman remembered that "they looked down on us because we weren't jazzy enough for the surroundings, while you" – he was talking to Fame himself on BBC Radio in 1999 – "always had a soft spot for us." To which Georgie, who had always been watching the Stones from the Flamingo bar initially – replied: "A very soft spot!"

Jazzy enough or not, such thoughts would not enter the mind of Beatle Ringo Starr, who tended to venture into London after "a hard day's night". He would be dancing late-night to Count Suckle's singles, enjoying the erotic dance moves of West Indian dance floor buddies.

As Alan Clayson found out, "Slumming it, he might troop over to Wardour Street's Flamingo, the Marquee or Crazy Elephant to mingle amongst Mods up too late to pester anyone for autographs. Instead, they'd be grooving to Zoot Money's Big Roll Band, Chris Farlowe, the Spencer Davus Group, the Graham Bond Organization or, less often since his Number One with 'Yeah Yeah' (sic), Georgie Fame. All these would back visiting black Americans such as Dionne Warwick, Stevie Wonder or Rufus Thomas. If touted as the Swinging Club of Swinging London, the Flamingo wasn't the Harlem Apollo but it was the nearest to it Ringo was ever likely to experience as, in the States, 'We really can't get out. It's too much of a problem."

One reason why Ringo and the other Beatles wouldn't have this problem in London was simple: sometimes bands played just for them. As Night-Timer Ronnie Jones stated to Colin Harper, at the Scene Club – managed by Radio Caroline/Fame/Nightimers agent Ronan O'Rahilly – the Nightimers sometimes just played for the Fab Four and their small entourage.

How great it really was to come down to the Flamingo is continued in a truly inimitable way by John Pidgeon, again, on *www.rocksbackpages*: "Inside, the lights are dim, and the heat, under the false ceiling, ferocious, Tony Clarke's 'Ain't Love Good, Ain't Love Proud' [July 1964] comes over the PA, or James Brown's 'Papa's Got A Brand New Bag' [July 1965, and pretty soon covered by Georgie], which I hear for the first time on the stairs to the basement, and inevitably before the night is over, since it is a favourite of John Gunnell's, Lord Kitchener's priapic 'Dr Kitch' [also swiftly covered by Fame]. Gunnell, who runs the club with his older brother Rik, introduces the acts and, between the sets, plays records from the band room beside the stage, spicing his MC's patter with a crude parody of Jamaican patois, which nevertheless amuses, rather than offends, the West Indians in the audience. There are always two bands on, each playing two alternate sets, with Zoot Money's Big Roll Band or Chris Farlowe & The Thunderbirds or Ronnie Jones and the Nightimers opening, and Georgie Fame and the Blue Flames closing the session. The All-nighter is unmissable.

"From midnight to six we dance and fidget and talk nonsense, start to feel not so great, swallow more pills and feel great again, and suddenly we're outside in the cold, cold light. Those six hours can flash by so fast, I once ask on my way out why the bands haven't done two sets tonight. 'What're you on, son? Here, you sure you're old enough to be in this joint?' I wasn't.

"We have a wash at Charing Cross station, a coffee in the Strand, occasionally shop for Blue Beat records at a stall in Petticoat Lane, anything to put off the return to the real world and the inevitable come-down. Some hardcore Flamingo fans even go back for more. There's a Sunday afternoon session, where John Gunnell, easing his way through the day with a bottle of Scotch, heckles the bands he's booked. In theory, and in amphetamine-powered defiance of fatigue, you can attend six sessions between Friday and Sunday."

Guitarist Colin Green, who had re-joined the band in autumn 1964, enjoyed the vibes in the Flamingo in spite of the tremendous work load: "We were working an awful lot, doing four or five gigs over the weekend. And by the time we got to the Flamingo, we would have already done an out-of-town gig on a Saturday night. We would arrive around half past twelve, get down and get in and play – do the All-nighters. We didn't think anything of it, really, because that was what we did, and it was good to be in there. Good to be so busy and to be playing the music that we wanted to play, with confidence. We were part of the changes that occurred – only we didn't realize it at the time. We were just doing our thing, and it was really nice that other people liked it as well. "

Soon, there were more changes: Georgie Fame and the Blue Flames increasingly played engagements outside of the club. Mick Eve: "We just all agreed we couldn't play in the same venue five times a week: at one point it was Monday, Thursday, Friday All-Nighter, Saturday All-Nighter and Sunday afternoons. Now a lot of the time the same staff, apart from anyone else, would get fed up with hearing the same songs, so we would always pick up on 'Oh, there's a record in the charts this week, that's quite nice'. It was Carol King singing "It Might As Well Rain Until September". It's still a good song."

One venue of particular significance for the Blue Flames, and many other Flamingo regulars as well, was the "Bluesville Club" in Ipswich, way up north east, but within easy reach via the pre-motorway days cross-country lane A12. The "Bluesville" had started out as a Jazz club in the 1950s. During the winter months, the proprietors, Nanda and Ron Lesley, used the St. Matthews Baths Hall, where they had put a "bouncing floor" over the swimming pool. In the summer, the club was able to move to the Ipswich Manor Ballroom. The London Marquee Club founder and "landlord" Harold Pendleton was an early friend, as were Alexis Korner and Cyril Davies, long before the club changed from Jazz to Rhythm & Blues during 1962. That link came about because the Lesleys actually ran a similar venue in London, and could book their acts in the capital for a Monday in the provinces. They were also busy as promoters in Colchester, Sheffield and Aylesbury.

Georgie Fame and the Blue Flames were regular favourites there, just like Long John Baldry and the Hoochie Coochie Men – the band he had formed out of the Cyril Davis All Stars when the big harmonica genius had passed away. Roger Clarke-Johnson is a witness who remembers it all well. The legendary Cornwall guitarist, bass-player, singer and long-time Ipswich resident was then active in The Night Sect, who apart from the Bluesville Club regularly played London's "Beat City" in Shaftesbury Avenue and The Scene Club in Great Windmill Street.

"True, there was only the M1 motorway in those days, but you could get to and from London ever so easily, because the A12 had always been a trunk road, and so Ipswich was never out of reach. Of course Georgie and his band were often knackered when they set up for their Monday, but they were always spot-on. The thing that first impressed me about Herr Powell was his great version of 'Gimme That Wine' – 'beat my head out of shape but leave my grape!' – it was epic!"

With The Flames branching out, there had to be a replacement guaranteeing a similar amount of fun, fan adulation, freaky sounds and fantastic stage presence. Relief arrived via Alexis Korner's cohort George Bruno "Zoot" Money, who – having re-located from Bournemouth to London with his Big Roll Band – worshipped similar R&B and Soul idols and interpreted them with a lot of originality, "open to Jazz influences" as well as madness, not least by jumping off stage during his highlight number "Barefootin'" (Zoot Money would share the song with Fame on the latter's *My Favourite Songs* in 1983) and throwing about shoes he had taken from the Flamingo visitors. With a name like that, by the way, many must have wondered whether the man had been christened by Fame's old svengali, Larry Parnes. But no, George got his a.k.a. Zoot from loving saxophonist Zoot Sims, and Money is actually his proper surname.

Zoot Money would in time also play the "Bluesville" in Ipswich, by the way, and according to Nanda Lesley's memories for the Ipswich Star, "he was a wild man, he would do such crazy things at the gigs as climb up the curtains!"

But more importantly, he remembers his Flamingo times with Georgie Fame very well: "During that time, the attitude as far as I was concerned about the bands that I was interested in, we all have this same informed friendly competition. Now it's 'kill them before they kill us!' We shared ideas in fact: no sooner had you listened to something by Georgie and vice versa, and he may not have heard the version that I was playing an adaptation from, we would both want to know, who was that, what was that, where did you get this, to broaden our knowledge of music and to get to appreciate other stuff that might be similar that we had never heard of.

"For instance, I wasn't turned on to Mose Allison by Georgie, but there was no doubt that through hearing him interpret Allison, he exactly fired up my curiosity, my record game! In terms of direct competition, yes, friendly competition – it was just when I first came to London, he was obviously in the Flamingo. It was all going very well with him, but it was becoming obvious that his manager and the agency had to get him out to make more money elsewhere, because he was becoming popular, and they were demanding money for him elsewhere, bigger money."

"So the Flamingo couldn't really survive without some kind of a resident, reliable set of bands where the same 'kind of music' – and I use that in parenthesis there – can be played. And where people can come down and they know that they would hear those kinds of influences being played. And there were a lot of bands trying to do it, and some of them were very successful, too." Zoot added: "I can remember Tony Knight's Chessmen were very good at it [i.e. that certain 'kind of music']. (Their Johnny Almond played his sax for Zoot Money's Big Roll Band later.) "The guitarist went on to form Vinegar Joe": Pete Gage, one-time husband of Elkie Brooks, and many times playing for one of Geno Washington's Ram Jam Bands."

Zoot Money continues: "But at the time, everyone was doing a great job at reproducing black music, Soul music. I presume because we had a broader concept of music, a broader appreciation, going through Jazz, Rhythm & Blues, Blues etc., similarly to what Clive was doing and appreciating, that's the connection he came down to see. He thought: 'Ooh, taking over from me, eh?' No, I just wanted to play down there. I just wanted to be in the same arena as guys like Georgie, playing to people that I knew would appreciate what's going down. Whereas it could have been a 'How dare you come up here?', he was grateful that somebody would take on the residency, or wanted to play at the residency for peanuts, night in, night out, while he went out and made a real living, as it were."

Georgie confirmed the appreciation in 1999, talking to his guest Zoot Money during one episode in his BBC Radio programme: "I always thought that your band – Big Roll Band – was the best British band of that era. And when you did come to London, we were starting to be on the verge of breaking out of the Flamingo."

Zoot Money confirmed this aspect then: "I remember that five different bands were vying for the position, doing gigs for free down there, which went down very well with the girls!"

But Zoot also took the compliment with a pinch of salt: "But he was always jealous. He always wanted to do at least one or two at the Flamingo eventually, so that he could keep his hand in. Because that was home! And it became home for us."

One benefit of Money's Big Roll Band was its stable line-up, as Georgie admitted. "Your band had a regular personnel, I mean my band would change personnel weekly. It was a very tight band, captured on that lovely album [*Zoot!*] *Live at Klooks Kleek* [the Zoot equivalent of *Rhythm and Blues at the Flamingo*]. My old LP of that isn't playable anymore."

One love that Fame & Money definitely had in common was the raving through the Friday and Saturday nights, although they were both busy as hell. Zoot again: "The All-Nighters, yeah: well, not many people wanted, or would do as many as we did. For the band there were thirteen, fourteen gigs in one week. I got a date sheet saying that – that includes afternoons and radio shows in the morning, afternoon gigs at the Gowler's House, which Clive would remember with great fondness."

"At the Gowler's House, which is the American Forces' place where Clive would hang out in West London near Queensway – which was great on a Sunday afternoon – it was all happening. Of course, there were afternoon and evening and nighttime sessions that had to be filled in at the Flamingo.-

"And at the weekend, the evening and the All-nighter had to be done by somebody – of course, if we were only just in town or Ipswich, we would get back for the All-Nighter.

"Both Clive and I would really enjoy the All-Nighters. All bets were off: You could try new stuff, you could really get into your day – and if somebody didn't feel up to soloing standard, then somebody else took that many more solos, you know. It was not a big problem."

Fame: "It was a great place to play, a midnight to 6am thing on Fridays and Saturdays, and the clientele at the Flamingo was really fantastic – a lot of West Indians, pimps and prostitutes, late night people. People that worked in other clubs till three o'clock in the morning, and then they'd come down to the Flamingo till six o'clock, till we stopped playing."

Competing bands were ardently watched first hand by Chris Farlowe & Thunderbirds guitarist Albert Lee, as he told Colin Harper: "I guess there was a healthy rivalry [among the Flamingo bands]. It was mix and match really – we'd sit in with each other, different bands. It was a friendly atmosphere. Eric [Clapton] was down there, too with John Mayall and he'd sit in with Farlowe, and so on. So we all knew each other around that time – a lot of good players. Andy Summers was playing down there regularly with Zoot Money. If the Night-Timers were on, Chris might sit in with them … and the same goes with Georgie Fame – Chris used to get up with Georgie Fame occasionally. I only did that once, I think. Colin Green couldn't make a gig so I played a club with Georgie. It was good fun – a bit of a challenge. I didn't know what to expect. Now, I wonder why I was so nervous, really, because I work with Georgie all the time in Bill Wyman's band. I feel so grateful that I was living in London, so I was able to just get on a train and be in the West End in 25 minutes. I mean, that was where everything was going on."

The Blue Flames – a merry-go-round talent factory

Georgie Fame was far too much of a seriously funny party cheerleader to be called something straight-facedly serious like the "Father of White Blues", like John Mayall, who shared this accolade with Alexis Korner, Georgie Fame's competitor at the Soho "Roundhouse" (and at the "Flamingo", too). But, just like these Thames Delta Daddies' backing groups, John Mayall's Bluesbreakers and Alexis Korner's Blues Incorporated, the Fame-led Blue Flames had become a similarly seminal third British R&B talent factory – see Prelude –, augmented towards a seven-piece band with congas courtesy of Speedy Acquaye, and sax players Johnny Marshall and Mick Eve. These came in shortly after their Soho residency had started, with guitar legends John McLaughlin, Joe Moretti and one-off Big Jim Sullivan coming and going along the way.

The line-up had changed as quickly as it produced legends, and casualties! Scotsman Joe Moretti (1938–2012) went on to play with Tom Jones – playing on his "It's Not Unusual". He also graced Flamingo regular Chris Farlowe's number one "Out Of Time", tracked with Marianne Faithfull, Alma Cogan and Petula Clark's *These Are My Songs*. In Germany, he worked with Vienna crooner Peter Alexander, who covered Engelbert Humperdinck material, for instance "The Last Waltz" became "Der letzte Walzer". Moretti, Sullivan and McLaughlin deserve several books of their own, but let's mention a few crucial contributions. Joe backed the deserted Hollies lead-singer Allan Clarke on *My Real Name Is 'Arold*, joined Clarke's friend Phil Everly for "There's Nothing Too Good For My Baby" and even performed on the Bay City Rollers' "Saturday Night". Fame's life-long friend and occasional singing partner Madeline Bell invited Moretti to tour with her in Swaziland and other African regions, moving to Johannesburg in 1981, as a tax exile and refugee.

As far as famous sessions and numerous non-credited studio appearances were concerned, Big Jim Sullivan, (1941–2012), who came from Uxbridge near West London, was certainly Moretti's equal. Familiar to Georgie via services for Billy Fury and Marty Wilde as well as the Johnny Hallyday sessions, Big Jim was hired for *Rhythm and Blues at the Flamingo*, would go on and play on The Blue Flames' next album *Fame At Last* and would be moving on to play for Shirley Bassey and Petula Clark, but also quite anonymously in bands like The Searchers and The Kinks, before spending many years in Las Vegas with Tom Jones later on in his career.

At the "Parnes Circus", Big Jim had learnt his trade together with Blue Flames guitarist Colin Green of course, who remembers his friend fondly: "Jim and I started our career in the music business together." They toured together on many shows where, along with drummer Brian Bennett – another future Blue Flames member – they would practice duets on the long train journeys between concerts: "In the early days, we studied together whilst on tour. I those days we travelled a lot by train and passed the time with music studies. We later always said that we (Jim, Brian Bennett and myself) studied at the British Rail School of Music! When *R&B at the Flamingo* was made, I was with Eddie Calvert – Georgie asked Jim to play [sic]", well, Johns and Samwell insisted.

Ritchie Blackmore and Steve Howe from Yes were two famous students of Big Jim Sullivan. After engagements for Tom Jones and a friendship with Elvis Presley, Sullivan worked solidly for the James Last Band between 1978 and 1987, partly together with Georgie's good friend and singing partner Madeline Bell. About working with Fame partner Van Morrison later in life, Sullivan once said: "I came to realize that money can't make a decent human being out of you. Here is a man worth 50 million pounds and is as unhappy a person as I have ever seen. He is so unhappy that he treats everybody as if he had bought them and they belonged to him to do what he likes with them. My stay with Van was very short lived and the lesson learned from him will stay with me for a long time."

Eventually, the original guitarist Colin Green returned, after having been away from the band for two and a half years. According to Pete Frame, Green "had been playing a summer season in Blackpool; Georgie, up there for a gig, talked him into joining again."

After his spell with the Blue Flames, John McLaughlin didn't stay with Graham Bond for long and worked for Brian Auger. According to a remark by producer Ian Samwell many years after the end of the Sixties, Mc Laughlin could also have been the guitarist on the *Fame At Last* album before he rejoined the Georgie Fame Band for gigs during 1967 and 1968: "John McLaughlin is a good bet. He was the best session player in town, and he lived just down the street from me", he is quoted in Colin Harper's *Bathed In Lightning* which came out in 2014.

McLaughlin moved to America in 1969 to join Tony Williams' Lifetime. Hitting it really big by playing on Miles Davis's *In A Silent Way* album, he had done sessions from The Rolling Stones to Larry Coryell. McLaughlin soon became Mahavishnu John McLaughlin and formed his legendary Mahavishnu Orchestra, playing with Carlos Santana along the way and becoming "the best guitarist alive" according to Jeff Beck.

On the bass front, original Blue Flame Ted "Tex" Makins had returned from France shortly after the recording of *Rhythm and Blues at the Flamingo*, whereupon Boots Slade left for The Alan Price Set – where he was bound to run into Georgie again. Makins stayed for almost two and a half years, through many line-ups, and left for The Sidewinders at the end of 1965. He was followed by veteran Cliff Barton, who had been with The Cyril Davies All-Stars, Long John Baldry & The Hoochie Coochie Men and also Alan Price. After six months, Cliff left and heeded Alexis Korner's call into Free At Last. His successor was the omnipresent Ricky Brown from Screaming Lord Sutch & The Savages and Cyril Davis & The All Stars. He also played for the Rolling Stones when Bill Wyman couldn't make it, and had been in Speampacket. Before he rejoined Georgie Fame in 1967, and as late as 1999, Brown was a member, with his old drumming friend Carlo, of The Carlo Little All Stars.

As far as drummers were concerned, Fame had been lucky so far in holding on to Red Reece all the way. According to Rolling Stones drummer Charlie Watts, Red Reece had been the first drummer he had ever seen who could play Rock'n'Roll "properly. He used to play like black rhythm and blues players, so I used to love watching him play. He had a great sound." After almost three years in the Blue Flames, drummer Red Reece left them in the lurch more and more often towards the end of 1963, to be replaced by his colleagues Tommy Frost or, alternatively Roy Mills when his health wouldn't allow him to play.

He eventually quit the music business around 1967, after playing on several Duffy Power demos, later released on *Innovations*, recorded in late 1965/early 1966, and rejoining the Georgie Fame Band only weeks after The Blue Flames had been disbanded. Baritone sax man Johnny Marshall, according to Pete Frame, sang his praises, "Red was fabulous – to this day, I have never known another drummer who had his qualities", and Colin Green also has equally high praise for his old Beat Boys & Blue Flames drummer.

Mick Eve remembers Reece very well, also following his fate in years to come: "Certainly, the fact of Red (Reece) not being able to turn up and play the drums anymore, he hardly had the strength to lift up drum sticks. He played good when he did, and I got him out of a rehab home just for one night, and took him out to the gig in the

Eighties, a pub in Fulham that always put on music. He couldn't believe how loud it all was. Doing all the motions on the bar like drumming with his fingers and spot on – always a lovely sense of timing, he hadn't lost that. But he couldn't believe they were putting a microphone on a bass drum – "what's that?" We never had that in those days – we were lucky to have one mike for Fame to sing through and if we were luckier, a second mike so that the two saxes would get round. People had to listen really, because if you were at the back in some of these halls, I don't know how they ever heard the little P.A.s that were out there."

Georgie had his own take on Reece, as he revealed to Duncan Heining: "Red Reece started to mess himself up after about a year down the Flamingo, when Phil (Seamen) became a feature. We all looked after Phil at one time or another in our lives. Red unfortunately went down the wrong path. If you look at the Blue Flames for the three year period at the Flamingo, there were more drummers in and out of that band than any other band. I still bump into friends of drummers, who say 'My mate was in the Blue Flames'. I can remember most of the drummers but …"

Reece was eventually followed by Tex Makins' and Colin Green's Quiet Three partner, Jimmy Nicol, the "Humpty Dumpty" covering man who would then famously stand in for Ringo Starr as a part-time Beatle, establishing one of the many instances the Beatles and Flames career would mingle.[11] So how had the Fabs come across the Blue Flame?

Alan Clayson writes that Brian Epstein needed someone "who looked like a Beatle, but an outcast", and their producer Georgie Martin knew Jimmy Nicol from the Beatles cover album *This Is Merseybeat*. And he goes on, "The Beatles would remember that Terry Heneberry, producer of both their 1963 radio series, *Pop Go The Beatles*, and the Rabin Band's forgotten *Go Man Go Show* three years before, had thought highly of Nicol, too. From the Liverpudlians' own circle, so did Tommy Quickly after Jimmy had drummed on one of his Pye singles – and Georgie Fame in whose Blue Flames Jimmy was presently working. Moreover, he'd also made a couple of singles with his own now dispersed outfit, the Shubdubs, who'd each adopted a severe moptop."

There may be a lesson about cause and effect here, because Georgie remembered, sitting in a bar after a Blue Flames gig at the Gronau Jazz Festival in May 2012, that as Jimmy Nicol & The Shubdubs, they had also operated after the Beatles sojourn.

Anyway, over to Clayson again, "That strange Wednesday, 24-year-old Nicol was stirred from an after-lunch nap in his Barnes living room by a ring from George Martin. No, it wasn't another session job – well, not the kind he might have expected. Could he be at Studio Two by three o'clock to rehearse with the Beatles? Behind Ringo's famous Ludwig kit, Jimmy ran through several items with them over two hours with curt tuition mainly from John and George, and 'no music script but that didn't matter. I already knew the numbers from *Beatlemania*.'

"Reeling with disbelief at this amazing assignment, he telephoned an understanding Georgie Fame and dashed home to pack for Denmark."

Did Jimmy Nicol have a "chip on his shoulder" when he was invited to return to the Blue Flames fold? After all, as Clayson reports with glee, "Back with the Blue Flames, Nicol would be signing as many autograph books as Georgie Fame. As further barom-

---

11. See Addendum

eter of his unlooked for fame, he was contracted to regroup the Shubdubs to take the place of the Dave Clark Five for a Blackpool summer season after Clark developed a stomach ulcer."

What about the rumour of Beatles manager Brian Epstein having blacklisted him, for rubbing in his Beatles fame too much?

Fame in 2012: "He didn't really have chip on his shoulder, no. He came back from the Beatles tour when he depped for Ringo, when they took him out of the band, and he went out on the road. He came back, and obviously from working with the Blue Flames down at the Flamingo to being in stadiums with the Beatles, he came back and wanted to form his own band. That's what it was – he wanted to make a success on the strength of the fact that he had been on the road with the Beatles. He came back and said 'I want to start my own band!'

"And we all said 'Good luck!' It became Jimmy Nicol & The Shubdubs, playing some kind of Blue Beat stuff, and I didn't know that story about Brian Epstein blacklisting him. It might be true. I don't know why Brian would do that, maybe because he was cashing in on The Beatles too much. I know that he went to live in Mexico years later and was known as "El Quinto Beatle". But nothing ever happened with that. But he was a good drummer." [12]

Towards the end of the year, the strain of working non-stop began to show more and more, and the band began to crumble at the edges, as ex-Blue Flame Mick Eve could not help noticing: "It was all kind of one by one by one. First of all, [manager] Rik [Gunnell] broke the other saxophone player's jaw, Johnny Marshall. So he couldn't play, and [Glenn Hughes] was the one I had been working with before, so I brought him along. And then the bass player [Tex Makins] was thinking about going back to work with Johnny Hallyday again. And Red [Reece], the drummer, was in no state. Until a few years ago, he believed that he had got the sack, but he hadn't. He just didn't bother to come, you know. It was a Sunday afternoon. I remember going round, the last time that I saw him in that previous life, as it were. He was in a terrible state: it was three o'clock in the afternoon, and he thought it was three o'clock in the morning. And so we had to drag him out and get him down to the Flamingo. At that point, we started using other drummers – two or three, all sitting in at different times. [Phil Seamen] was tremendous. He was the only one who was capable of replacing Red, really. He was uncanny – again, in a terrible state. You would think 'How can he play like this?' But he would, and my God, he would make you play as well."

During the summer of 1964, and only serving his steady job there for two months, The Blue Flames would present one of the most revered drummers in Britain – admired in the entire Jazz world: Phil Seamen (1926–1972). Seamen had been drumming for eleven years before Georgie Fame was even born. The young Clive must have heard him on the radio with the Joe Loss Orchestra towards the end of the 1940s. Then Seamen worked with Joe Harriott, Tubby Hayes, Ronnie Scott's Orchestra and dozens of legends, and was with Alexis Korner's Blues Incorporated by the time he met Georgie. An incredibly sharp drummer and even sharper storyteller, Phil Seamen was also

12. See Addendum

"Mr Unreliable" due to his alcohol and heroin use, which in 1957 had spoiled his chances of going the USA with Ronnie Scott. Even during his brief stint in the Blue Flames, his young colleague Micky Waller, 20 at the time – the future Jeff Beck Group and Rod Stewart drummer who some say never had his own kit – was always on stand-by, as he told Pete Frame:

"[Phil Seamen] used to stand at the side of the stage hurling abuse at me".

For the young future Stones drummer Charlie Watts, Seamen had always been *the* master to admire the most. As he told *Rhythm* magazine in 2001, Phil was "the best drummer in England. He used to play timpani style – very unusual in those days – but he played with his fingers like a real timpanist. In those days, he was the nearest thing we had to Philly Joe Jones or somebody like that. I learnt to play by watching Phil Seamen play a bass drum or Red Reece, in Georgie Fame's band, play a back beat."

By August 1964, the mad genius had left the Blue Flames again, even though he then continued to dep from time to time. One of the key musicians in Seamen's own band had been Georgie Fame's 1990s arranger and writing partner Steve Gray. Seamen worked for the Dick Morrissey Quartet, and later made the headlines as part of his ex-student Ginger Baker's Air Force, but he also, like everyone else, did numerous sessions, famously applying restrained discipline on Cilla Black's "Anyone Who Had A Heart".

In order to grasp how Seamen chose to function as a top-notch drummer, someone who has lived with him is probably the best choice of information. Saxophonist Dick Heckstall-Smith let him live in his home in the early Sixties, and he was told first-hand "how he got 'on' (hooked) in the first place. He *decided* to, all in the space of half an hour, in the compartment of a train on the way to Manchester.

"Apparently, he was working very, very hard at the time – in the Fifties it was – and he was on his way to do a radio show, followed by a gig with that other Jazz legend, Ronnie Scott. Alone in his compartment and extremely short of sleep, he faced his problem. Up till then he'd been using heroin and cocaine, though very carefully, and he wasn't yet addicted. His physical symptoms were telling him two opposite things. If he used drugs today, he would be addicted for the rest of his (shortened) life. If he didn't use the drugs, he wouldn't be able to do justice to the gig – he would, by his standards, be a bad drummer. He had a really bad half-hour, and by the end of it, he had decided. He was going to be as good a drummer as it was possible for him to be, for whatever time remained to him. He went off to the toilet with his works and shot up … The clarity of this story, and the clarity of the decision, increased my respect for Phil enormously."

Seamen's Blue Flames successor from September 1964 was fellow veteran Bill Eyden (1930–2004), who worked with the legendary Jazz Couriers at Ronnie Scott's Jazz Club, playing with Ronnie and sax player Tubby Hayes for more than twenty years. After leaving the Flames in December 1965, Bill Eyden remained there in the resident Ronnie Scott Trio with Stan Tracey until 1969. Many radio buffs knew Eyden via his appearances on "The Goon Show" with the Ray Ellington Quartet. Eyden had also played for Long John Baldry, Harry South and Fame friend Dick Morrissey – in whose band he also replaced Phil Seamen, by the way. Bill's claim to fame remains his last minute early 1967 addition to the session line up of Procol Harum for "A Whiter Shade Of Pale", a fairly down-to-earth pattern, Georgie pointed out in 2012, "that my little granddaughter could have played."

Tenor saxophonist Mick Eve had been joined for the summer of 1962 by tenor, bass clarinet and clarinet man Tony Coe, then 28, who came from Humphrey Lyttelton and was soon to join the Johnny Dankworth Orchestra, shortly after opting out of an offer to join Count Basie's Big Band. He later worked for Stan Tracey and the Kenny Clarke-Francy Boland Big Band, also Dizzy Gillespie, and worked in sessions for John Martyn and The Hollies.

Coe was succeeded by baritone man Johnny Marshall, who was about to return after the days of this band and had special significance for Georgie's artistic development.

In July 1964, Mick Eve had gone to start the R&B & Soul Blue Flames competitors The Night-Timers, getting US singer Ronnie Jones in there from Alexis Korner's group, and reuniting with one-time Blue Flame Joe Moretti. In the Night-Timers, he also met up with John McLaughlin again, as well as John Baldwyn a.k.a. John Paul Jones, the bass player, session man and producer, who would join Led Zeppelin four years later. John Paul Jones would go on to produce Georgie's good friend Madeline Bell's album *Comin' Atcha* in 1973.

Eve: "At that point I thought 'There is no future in this music, it's better to do something else'. And I liked all the venues we had been playing. They were nice places to go and work at. I didn't see the need to move on to theatres or anything like that. It was just the way the scene appeared at the time. All the happy, young people that we wanted to play to were going to the Eel Pie Island, the Ricky Tick Club, and all these other places I could still work at with a new line-up, if I found the right singer. And to me first of all [who] could sing, Ronnie Jones was the obvious one."

Quite possibly, when Eve changed over to The Nightimers with Ronnie Jones, the sheer load of the working schedule could not have been as hectic as it was with Georgie:

"Probably not – only because we didn't do the All-nighters now: If we were playing in Stoke-on-Trent on a Saturday night, we might then go on and play in Manchester until two in the morning, so we were still doing a bit of that: doubles, late-nighters as well as the evenings. Then, a little bit later, a club called the Tube Club came along, which replaced The Roaring Twenties really, and we would – again – turn up at two in the morning, and he would pay us to play a set until four o'clock or something. So we were doubling, but yeah, there were a lot more gigs – we would play Tuesday, Wednesday, Thursday. What a luxury, but we didn't realize and thought this would go on forever."

Mick Eve would later serve in the Funk band Gonzales which always sported several other 70s Blue Flames members, like Steve Gregory on tenor sax and flute, and Buddy Beadle on baritone, soprano sax and flute, plus Chris Mercer from the Night-Timers and Chris Farlowe's band. Apart from their own top notch albums like the Abbey Road production *Gonzalez* (1974) and *Our Only Weapon Is Our Music* (1975). Gonzales showed true crossover guts by providing the horns for The Tremeloes' *Don't Let The Music Die* (also 1975), which Dave Munden & Co released under the pseudonym Space first, in order not to shock the Sixties hits clientele. (This was due to Mick Eve's sideline as a concert promoter – at the time he worked for The Trems' "Starlight" agency, and in the 1980s would score gigs for Steve Marriott's Packet Of Three.)

Eve was replaced by the longest running tenor sax man in the band, Peter Coe, who, joined by Glenn Hughes in November of that year, 1964, stayed right until the end. Coe, an art school man from Cambridge, had served in dance bands, including gigs at US bases in his area, and he came in time for playing on two of Georgie's biggest hits ever. Through the connection, he was to meet and join the Beatles for one night at Abbey Road in 1966. Baritone sax man Hughes was not so lucky, as we shall see.

But of course, running a hot band with a lot of fluctuations was never without hassle, as Fame's mate Zoot Money observed: "To be fair, he did have quite a few personnel changes, which is something I found out later. That really upset him: the fact that he had to keep getting new people in, not necessarily because they had the right feel, but because they were available, or they were reliable. Some were and some weren't. So he had to keep being the big bandleader and crack the whip, whereas when you look at my band – we were a bit more like a group really, other than a band as such."

"All About My Girl" – A little glimpse into the private price of Fame

Mancunian singer Elkie Brooks was a regular in the Flamingo, and mentions the club and Georgie in her autobiography *Finding My Voice*, claiming that "I fell in love with the Flamingo, and it quickly became my reason for returning to London time and time again. It reminded me of performing at the American air bases that were alive with Rhythm & Blues [...] Brooks remembered that she never actually worked at the Flamingo, but got the chance to do a number of jam sessions – apart from Georgie and the Flames these happened with Chris Farlowe's Thunderbirds as well as John Mayall's Bluesbreakers.

Brooks reveals that "Georgie's band was my favourite. He wasn't what you'd call a schooled musician but he had great feel and I have to say I'd never heard a white man play like that before. His music was a fantastic fusion of R&B and Jazz; it was incredible. My love of Georgie's music and our jamming sessions soon blossomed. To be honest, I fell in love with his playing more than him [...]" But she still took him up North to meet his parents, while knowing full well that Georgie "was living with a half English, half Spanish woman called Carmen. To be blunt, I think I was just a little something on the side for him. He and Carmen were a team and over the course of the six months that Georgie and I saw each other I was never able to persuade him to give her up."

When a date at Fame's flat in North London fell through because Georgie "had to go and do some gigs", he and Brooks parted, but not before Elkie revealed that "Georgie introduced me to drugs, albeit only weed." Trying to forget Fame by hanging out at The Scene Club instead of the Flamingo, Brooks promptly met and dated another keyboard player – Alan Price, the man who played with their resident band, The Animals. And guess what? "[...] Like my relationship with Georgie, as fast as I fell for him, he seemed to lose interest in me. Looking back on it now, I think Alan only went out with me because I knew Georgie and he really wanted to meet him. It wasn't long after I'd introduced them that Alan seemed to cool off things with me. My instincts were right because he and Georgie formed quite a successful partnership and made two albums together."

Elkie's instincts may have been right, but whether her sense of chronology was as precise, remains doubtful. Alan Price left the Animals in 1965, and the first television collaboration between Georgie and Alan happened in 1969.

"Do It The Hard Way" – Gigging 10 dates a week

The Beatles might well have sung "Eight Days A Week" in those days in portraying their career moves, but for Fame & Flames it felt like they were working even harder:

Not content with the Flamingo or the equally renowned Scene Club in the Capital, Georgie Fame & The Blue Flames soon played up to 10 dates per week, that's 40 gigs a month: "It was fun and it was hard work as well. For a period of about eight or nine months, we were working ten gigs in seven days! It was fun. We could play like six or seven sets a night without repeating ourselves." Fame will frequently add that pill-popping played its part – not only The Who took "Purple Hearts", which contained amphetamines. London Mods would all have them ready anytime, and Georgie and his band were no exception. Also, just like famous Flamingo visitor Paul McCartney, Fame loved "African weed" as well as the next pro.

Far from taking their popularity for granted, Fame was always on the lookout for new sounds. Just as Eddie Cochran had introduced him to Ray Charles during the Billy-Fury-days, he was now into US Jazz singers like King Pleasure and Eddie Jefferson via recommendations from G.I.s., while having digs in the Notting Hill area had made him more and more knowledgeable about everything that Jamaican Blue Beat had to offer.

But the American G.I. soldiers' path to Georgie Fame & The Blue Flames in Soho's Flamingo was not a one way street. Often enough, the band would flock to them, in US air bases like Alconbury or Chicksands in East Anglia. Those were the days before band coaches or even roomy vans: the Blue Flames would have to squeeze into a Bedford "Dormobile", hovering in sections where their equipment would have left some space. In those American air bases, a strict class system applied, so one musical set was performed at the Airmen's Club, and then another series of songs at the officer's mess of the NCOs (non-commissioned officers). Fame and Flames liked the fact that local girls had been invited, after all there was no language barrier in the United Kingdom, the officers' and soldiers' wives wouldn't be crowded out so much by the men, and the guys, including the musicians, would feel all the better because of it. Their breaks would be enjoyed with great meals, not to mention tax-free whiskeys and smoking materials of all kinds. Playing these air bases did as much for advertising the Fame & Flames residency at Soho's Flamingo Club as mere word of mouth, and so quite a few G.I.s who found their way into the club had previously seen Georgie and his group in their barracks.

Apart from these fruitful exchanges between the Flamingo and the Air Force, there were the countless appearances in clubs all over London and the South of England. They should all have a blinking G.F. button on a Google map: Fame's beloved "Ricky Tick" Club, for instance – now the title of a Georgie Fame live LP! – which was situated in a completely derelict council house near the Queen's Windsor Castle. There were many return performances at the "Roaring Twenties" establishment in Carnaby Street, where Jamaican Deejay Count Suckle still called the shots.

There were regular Flames games at the "Klooks Kleek", a Rhythm & Blues and Jazz club situated in the Railway Hotel in West Hampstead named after drummer Kenny Clark's Savoy Records album *Klook's Clique* from 1956, which Georgie and band visited 22 times. Opened via a gig by tenor saxman Don Rendell in January 1961 – who held the Jazz musicians' record of playing there twenty times – this was where Graham Bond (39 gigs there), John Mayall and his Bluesbreakers (33), Zoot Money and his Big Roll Band (34) as well as Alvin Lee's band Ten Years After would record their live albums: *Live At Klooks Kleek* (Bond 1964), *John Mayall Plays John Mayall Recorded Live At Klooks Kleek!* (1964/1965), *Zoot!* (1966) and TYA's *Undead* (1967) respectively. Luminaries like "Little" Stevie Wonder, Jimmy McGriff and Family swung and rocked the place, as did Fame's horn players Tubby Hayes and Dick Morrissey, who managed seven times each, before Keef Hartley and his band played the final gig there with Miller Anderson.

Soon, Fame & Flames toured all over the United Kingdom, with two roadies helping them along with all the gear that had to go into the Dormobile.

London's club and bar land beyond the Flamingo, especially around Fame's then home in the Notting Hill Gate neighbourhood, was also described by Joe Boyd in *White Biclycles*: "The area was still recovering from years of Peter Rachman's slumlordship, and the race riots of 1958. The side streets of Westbourne Park Road, later home to 'Trustafarians', media types, artists, musicians, and the odd record-producer (and more recently colonized by stockbrokers), were full of after-hour shebeens [from Irish síbín, illicit whiskey] and ganja dens, the kind of places Stephen Ward had taken Christine Keeler to take Lucky Gordon a few years earlier."

It was also a time of experimentation, as Georgie reminisced on air for the BBC: "The BBC did the first tests with stereo recording for broadcast at the Camden Theatre in Camden Town, Mornington Crescent, which was in those days a BBC theatre, and it was the Rolling Stones and me and my band. And we played about twenty minutes apiece. It went out as a test stereo broadcast when nobody had stereo radios. I remember seeing like two vocal mics on the same stand. My good friend Bill Wyman has the tapes, he has collected everything."

The BBC show in question was, in fact, Georgie's first radio broadcast on March 19th, 1964, produced by Ian Grant, which featured the Stones and an introduction by compère Long John Baldry, who also contributed a number with The Blue Flames.

The Blue Flames, Mick Eve, Johnny Marshall, Tex Makins, Red Reece and Speedy Acquaye, played their rousing set as follows: "Night Train", "Bright Lights Big City", "Walking The Dog", "Do Re Me", "Let The Sun Shine In" and finally "You're Breaking My Heart" with a vocal performance by Long John Baldry.

(Not) All Quiet On The Studio Front – Single misses & Fame At Last

After "Do The Dog" and "Shop Around" had been lifted from *Rhythm and Blues at the Flamingo,* it was time for the first Columbia studio single. "Do-Re-Mi" is typical of what Sixties people called "groovy": a great 4/4 beat, a roaring Hammond organ, catchy sax responses and a simplistic love call: "Do-re-mi-fa-so-la-ti – forget about the do(ugh) and think about me me!" It was written by the New Orleans veteran singer and guitarist Earl King (1934–2003), who often worked with Fats Domino's orchestra leader Dave Bartholomew, with whose wife, Pearl Bartholomew, Earl wrote "I Hear You Knocking" and Elvis' "One Night".[13] King is noted for numbers like "Trick Bag", which was recorded by Jimi Hendrix, The Meters and Robert Palmer. King originally wrote "Do-ReMi" for Lee "Working In A Coalmine" Dorsey.

It was the B-side of "Green Onions", that iconic Booker T single written by Booker, Steve Cropper, Al Jackson and Lewie Steinberg, which prompted Fame's Hammond fame at live gigs and would re-appear on the next album.

The second studio single "Bend A Little" by Fred Jay and Reggie Oberecht, rocked at a more relaxed pace. Jay was a veteran Jewish Austrian lyric writer and ukulele player, who fled to France from the Nazis and later immigrated to New York, hitting for Chuck Willis with "What Am I Living For" in 1958, covered by Conway Twitty. Eight years after Georgie's hit, he had the German mega seller "Es fährt ein Zug nach Nirgendwo" (There Goes A Train To Nowhere) with and for singer Christian Anders. He also wrote "Mr Paul McCartney" for the Berlin singer Marianne Rosenberg. The girls' backing vocals may take matters a little too happy-go-lucky for the mean Mod, but Georgie's solo makes up for any missing street credibility.

On the flip-side, "I'm In Love With You" by R. Barrett, there was the lazy 6/8 Blues pattern that Fats Domino and Dave Bartholomew have always loved so much, succeeding in getting Domino expert Fame hooked along the way, sports trumpet and guitar licks courtesy of the occasionally jamming and guesting Edward "Eddie Tan Tan" Thornton and a returned Colin Green. And, as so often in those days, the ladies' choir is never far off. Both titles have instrumental backing by Birmingham pianist Earl Guest (b. 1930) and his orchestra instead of the Blue Flames.

The first studio album – Fame At Last

After the chart success of the EP *Rhythm & Blue Beat* (#8), and the live LP from the Flamingo, it was the first studio album in particular, bearing the cheeky but absolutely fitting title *Fame At Last*, which was to make or break the alleged novelty chart topper. Would it satisfy fans of the groovy *Rhythm and Blues at the Flamingo*, or would producer Ian Samwell go for something more polished in order to woo the mainstream audiences?

Samwell as well as Fame probably knew they didn't have to. *Fame At Last*, while sounding absolutely spot-on, continued the exciting Hammond & Horns based Blue Flames sound, adding girls where suitable, but it didn't mess with a trademark that was less

13. See Addendum

a formula than an organic necessity. The album, with a cover that sported an American looking Jazz design, soon charted in the United Kingdom and went up to #15 in October 1964, which was about to kick-start the following small discs' maximum attention: a dozen of Fame's 45s would make the "hit-parade"!

"Get On The Right Track Baby", to this day, often serves as the perfect opener for Georgie's shows, and it was the perfect vehicle to start his first studio album off. Written by Titus Turner (1933–1984), an R&B artist from Atlanta, Georgia, it had been covered by Ray Charles in 1960, who recorded Turner's "Sticks And Stones" as well. Titus Turner also composed Little Willie John's success "All Around The World", covered as "Grits Ain't Groceries" by Little Milton, while Fame's friend John Lennon toyed with Turner's "Leave My Kitten Alone" during the early Beatles sessions. The "Right Track" shuffle comes over as a perfect vehicle for Hammond organ wailing and heavy Leslie rotation, lovely brass arrangements and an exemplary cooperation of drums and congas carried by fluent bass lines.

"Let The Sun Shine In" ups the tempo even further. This wild dance number had been supplied by New York songsmith Teddy Randazzo (1935–2003), who had his writing partners Bobby Weinstein and Billy Barberis in his internationally active band at the time between the Copacabana and Las Vegas. It is not to be confused with the same title from the *Hair* Musical. Fame and producer Ian Samwell employ a sharp female vocal backing here, a first for Georgie which works out well. His Hammond solo is short but full of vigour, great breaks enhance the excitement even further.

"The Monkey Time" could have been lifted straight from the Flamingo Club, pushing the popular Monkey Dance. You crouched like a fighter, knees bent and fists closed and then you turn left and raise your right arm – welcome to the Flamingo Zoo. The song was written by Chicago legend Curtis Mayfield (1942–1999) for his Impressions, but had become a hit in 1963 for yet another American R&B singer, Major Lance (1939–1994), who many remember via his "Um Um Um Um Um Um" success and later fame as a Northern Soul star. Both "Sun Shine" and "Monkey Time" have rhythm guitar parts which could have been played by either Big Jim Sullivan or John McLaughlin, as Colin Green cannot recall having played on any *At Last* tracks.

"All About My Girl" was an instrumental supplied by the often Fame-quoted Jimmy McGriff, a true Hammond organ feast where Georgie really lets loose, ably assisted by Mick Eve on saxophone, both of them taking turns during the breakneck breaks.

"The Point Of No Return", just like "Get On The Right Track, Baby", is still very much part of the Fame road shows. It was written by the Brill Building assembly line hit-makers lyricist Gerry Goffin and singing composer Carol King – "in spite of its title it happened before their divorce" (in 1968), as Georgie often likes to point out grinningly – and really, the song is convincing as a plea for eternally unbreakable love. Georgie found the song on a late period Louis Jordan single released on Ray Charles' *Tangerine* label, and he follows Jordan's reading even more closely than the Gene McDaniels 1962 original. Potentially sentimental as a ballad, perhaps, but Fame followed Gene McDaniels' 1962 original by giving it an exquisitely catchy groove and those cleverly executed breaks in the chorus. Elvis Costello, oft-quoted Fame fan and *Sound Venture* endorser, liked this tune enough to cover it on his 1988 album *Spike*.[14]

"Gimme That Wine" contained the hilariously autobiographical Blue Flames line "'Cos I can't get loose without my juice", the perfect working musician's slogan. The talking verses are reminiscent of "Saturday Night Fish Fry", describing crazy scenes like a clothes-hiding wife, a car accident and a late night robbery by bandits, all rendered for the punch line of saving the wine bottle! Its author was Fame's major influence Jon Hendricks, the "Yeh Yeh" lyricist, who had recorded this number on several albums, most notably *The Hottest New Group In Jazz* as part of Lambert, Hendricks & Ross.

"Pink Champagne" by Jimmy Liggins, the American bandleader – with his Drops of Joy – and R&B guitarist (1922–1983) convinces as a call & response Swing number where Fame's "Champagne" shouts are echoed by cleverly arranged saxophones. Like Georgie's idol, Cassius "Ali" Clay, Liggins had been a boxer as "Kid Zulu", and his 1948 "Cadillac Boogie" was probably the first Rock'n'Roll record, as it influenced the official virgin R'n'R "Rocket 88".

"Monkeying Around" was Booker T. territory for Georgie, having been written and sung by Memphis Soul artist William Bell together with the Booker T. & The MGs guitarist Steve Cropper. Those two are now more famous for writing "Born Under A Bad Sign", which Albert King as well as Cream would make famous a mere three years after this album. Fame had certainly grasped the growing popularity of Soul, with his James Brown impersonations on *Rhythm And Blues At The Flamingo*. He could now build on that set, with another great example to follow which, like "Monkeying", could have had Big Jim Sullivan or John McLaughlin on guitar.

"Pride & Joy" had been a big Tamla Motown hit in the previous year, in spring 1963, as performed by Marvin Gaye together with the vocal backing of Martha & The Vandellas – the girls hit with "Heat Wave" soon after. Marvin Gaye co-wrote "Pride & Joy" with Norman "Papa Was A Rolling Stone" Whitfield and his producer William "Micky" Stevenson, and dedicated it to his girl friend Anna Gordy, 18 years older than him, Motown boss Berry Gordy's sister, and Mrs Gaye by the time *Fame At Last* came out. Georgie uses that infectious sax theme to the full and has his girl troupe emulate the Vandellas really well. (Twenty years after this song, Stevie Ray Vaughan would strike with a number of the same title – but his Texan "Pride & Joy" had nothing to do with Gaye & Fame's ode to Anna.)

14. See Addendum

"Green Onions" had been the mentioned September 1962 single by Booker T. & the MGs which Fame was given at the Flamingo Club and took as his inspiration to "buy a Hammond organ the next day". It was written by the whole Memphis based quartet for their Stax Records single: Booker T Jones, Steve Cropper, Al Jackson and bass player Lewis Steinberg, who preceded Donald "Duck" Dunn. Described as done in chromatic minor with a 5th chord by Ken Stephenson in *What to Listen for in Rock: A Stylistic Analysis*, it is quite an achievement by Georgie Fame that his version with the Blue Flames is often seen on a par with, or even superior, to the Booker T. original, and it was hardly a surprise that it became his own first studio single prior to this album.

"I Love The Life I Live" formed the "Be positive" cry by Chicago's Chess Records legend Willie Dixon that Fame had so loved in the big bass man's repertoire and especially in Mose Allison's reading. And once again, he manages to transfer a true night club atmosphere reminiscent of the Flamingo All-Nighters onto the record. A hot Hammond mixed with an ultra cool vocal delivery and "in the pocket" groove, which was never better than in this recording.

How many times has Georgie performed "Moody's Mood For Love"? It seems custom-made for him, although so many people have performed it over the years. The number started life as an instrumental, recorded by sax master James Moody (1925–2010) from Savannah, Georgia, who had been playing in a 'negro band' in the US Air Force, because the camps were segregated at the time. Fed up with racism, he worked in Europe after discharge, and had been invited to record "12 sides" for Metronome in Sweden in 1949.

"In The Mood For Love" was one, and it was a first take, becoming a hit in 1952 on the licensing Prestige Records. Those famous notes you hear at the beginning, they were not part of a conscious creative process. Moody was just trying out the alto sax – he normally played tenor. These notes turned into the familiar "There I go, there I go, there I go" for Georgie and dozens of others when Eddie Jefferson wrote words to the tune, and King Pleasure had the hit. Louis Armstrong, Nat King Cole, Frank Sinatra, Sam Cooke, Smokey Robinson, Fats Domino, James Taylor and Cliff Richard were amongst the many male singers who loved and recorded the number.

All these often fantastic versions had female competition via Georgie's friends Annie Ross and Blossom Dearie, as well as Brenda Lee, Shirley Horn, Sarah Vaughan, Julie London, Aretha Franklin, Sheena Easton or, in the 21st century, by the contrasting characters Barbara Streisand and Amy Winehouse. Finally, one of the FFFs, Fame's firm favourites, must be the version on *The Cosby Show*, sung by sitcom star Bill Cosby himself, who can count Georgie as an ardent fan.

The first Number One – "Yeh Yeh"!

After some relatively modest selling singles and EPs, the studio album *Fame AT Last* had consolidated Fame's standing in the record world on top of his live reputation. But it was an obscure song which Georgie "found on the streets of Soho" – on a US concert LP by the vocal trio of Lambert, Hendricks & Bavan – and arranged as his very own number.

Fame explains more: "I discovered 'Yeh Yeh' just by buying Jon Hendricks' latest live LP, *Lambert, Hendricks & Bavan: Live at Newport '63*." This would be in his fave record shop in Old Compton Street, *Ray's Records*.

Fame remembers it all so well: "I was a great Jon Hendricks fan by then and I heard this track and thought it might be good for the band. So we rehearsed it and played it up and down the country in all the clubs. And when it came to record the next single: 'Why don't we record that?'"

As always, success has multiple mothers and fathers, while the flop is an orphan, and the way Georgie told it to British journalist Paolo Hewitt, we get a somehow different account:

"The original of 'Yeh Yeh' was by Mongo Santamaría [well, Georgie would elaborate on that soon]. It was an instrumental. Jon wrote the lyrics for it and in 1963 recorded an album with his band. We added it to the repertoire and when we played it in the clubs, we realized it was getting a much better response to it than the other things. So when we went in the studio, Ruby Barr, our agent, God bless her, said 'You should do that "Yeh Yeh", because it don't half go down well.'"

"We were at Pye Studios [ATV House Cumberland Place in London] for half an hour, so we set the gear up and we did two tracks – we did a Johnny Burch track, 'Preach and Teach', and we did 'Yeh Yeh'. Then we packed up the gear and left. A month later we found out it was selling thirty thousand copies a day!"

Jon Hendricks and Annie Ross were already Georgie Fame's all-time idols by then, with both of whom he would record in the future.

Hendricks (b. 1921) was – and is – the Newark, Ohio bred New York based "Poet Laureate of Jazz" according to pianist and author Leonard Feather. Son of a pastor with 14 brothers and sisters, Hendricks started singing at seven. A dedicated teenage drummer, the "local celebrity in Toledo" (Hendricks) went beyond offers by Fats Waller and Ted Lewis, but soon collaborated with stride pianist Art Tatum, who also hailed from Toledo.

Jon was already 36 years old when he teamed up as lyricist with Bostonian singer Dave Lambert (1917–1966), who is said to have brought singing into the Modern Jazz world in a parallel move with Ella Fitzgerald.

Soon making friends, Dave and Jon came to fame as the founders of the Manhattan Transfer-inspiring vocal trio Lambert, Hendricks & Ross. The two writers had put lyrics to Count Basie numbers and thrilled audiences with their Vocalese and Scat singing, and quite by accident found their perfect partner in Annie Ross, a Scottish girl brought up in New York City from age four, who had worked with King Pleasure as a teenager; more about her later.

Hendricks revealed in a 1968 interview with Les Tomkins which appeared in the liner notes to *Sing A Song For Basie* that they had survived a starving period in New York not unlike the one Georgie Fame had experienced down and out in London: "The way we were organized was really quite accidental. We had no intention of having a regular vocal group; we were just doing that one album, *Sing A Song Of Basie* [from which Georgie would use "Every Day I Have The Blues", "Little Pony" and "Jumpin' At The Woodside" in good time].

"We had 13 singers, but they didn't work out so we hired Annie and we multi-tracked. Annie started hanging out at Dave Lambert's, where I was living. She was making pretty good money, working on the Patrice Munsel TV show on ABC in the States. Dave and I were starving."

When one day they collected their last cents, they realized that album was Number 13, and soon the sensation was rolling big style, until Annie Ross opted out because she was ailing from drug addiction, and was replaced short term by Canadian Jazz singer Annie Marie Moss, which gave the trio an absurd name change to Lambert, Hendricks & Moss.

The singer and actress Yolande Bavan (b. 1942 in Ceylon, today's Sri Lanka), had followed Ross & Moss, and shortly after, she appeared on that live LP *Live At Newport '63*. Bavan proceeded to make two more concert albums with Lambert & Hendricks. She left the trio abruptly in 1964 with Lambert, who got killed in a Connecticut car crash in 1966. Yolande Bavan appeared in musicals (*Snow White & The Seven Dwarfs*) and films (*Cosmopolitan*), while music fans may have heard her featured on the Weather Report album *I Sing The Body Electric* in 1972.

Jon Hendricks moved to London for five years from 1968 to 1973, later settled in Mill Valley near San Francisco and from 2000 has been back in Toledo, teaching there as a Distinguished Professor of Jazz Studies, and he was also the first American Jazz performer to read at the Paris Sorbonne.

"Yeh Yeh" shot to Number 1 in Britain in December 1964, kicking the Beatles and their smash "I Feel Fine" off the pole position as 1965 took momentum, and reached a very respectable #21 in the USA, making Georgie Fame & The Blue Flames a household name internationally. Peter Coe remembers, as quoted from Pete Frame, that when Colin Green came back into the band, "the first thing we did was go down to Great Newport Street and rehearse "Yeh Yeh". We had been playing it around the clubs, but we thrashed out a version which we thought was suitable for a single."

For years, Georgie has been refining the art of recounting the history of detecting this "Yeh Yeh" composition, and the ensuing international adventures of The Blue Flames, in his legendary, and eagerly lapped up, between-numbers-banter on stages all over the world, and no doubt spoken with him like the Fame's Prayer:

"That song, this composition originally was an instrumental by two musicians from Mongo Santamaria's orchestra, a very fine Afro-Cuban band based in New York City. Rogers Grant, the piano player, and the baritone saxophonist Pat Patrick were the ones who composed that melody. And Mongo recorded it as an instrumental, real slow he played it. The great Jon Hendricks, master jazz lyricist of all time, one of my mentors – probably my main mentor, along with Mose Allison, but that's another story – Jon Hendricks put lyrics to this tune, then took on a 400-mile drive from a 4th of July gig that hadn't ended until five a.m. to Newport. There, Jon did the first recording – vocal recording – live at the Newport Jazz Festival in 1963, and he was accompanied by Coleman Hawkins on the tenor saxophone, and Clark Terry, sorry, (usually repeated in high-pitched falsetto), 'Clark Terry' (frequent laughter, chuckles in the audience) on the trumpet. And me, as a student of Jon Hendricks, I just went out and bought Jon Hendricks' latest album, and that was on it, that number was on it. It gave me my first top pop hit, but its origins were in Afro-Cuban Jazz!"

Even after all this encyclopaedic enlightenment, you still don't get to hear the song in that instant at a typical Fame concert, because there is more to tell about its impact in Sweden. Fame has frequently been known to say "You will all be familiar with the story by now, but I am going to tell you anyway." So you will read it, too – watch out for Swedish adventures in the later chapter "Dynamite Friends & Dynamite Brass".

The "record-buying public" outside of London may have been forgiven for thinking that here was a young star – still only 21 after all – who had made it big on the quick with "Yeh Yeh". Yet the way Georgie summed up the road to real record success to raving *Rave* reporter Dave Tatham makes it clear that this path was a long and winding one indeed. Thinking back to the summer of 1965, he reminisced that "we all realized that we still needed a big hit disc to get us properly known all over the country. But it was so long coming. I had begun to wonder if we would *ever* get it. My regular appearances at the Flamingo fronting my own group started around July 1962. But it wasn't till September 1963 that my first Columbia single – "Do The Dog" – came out. And it wasn't till the December 1964 that "Yeh Yeh" gave us the out-and-out smash. Sure, we felt great when we got it. There was one special reason. When our previous discs hadn't hit the Ten, people had said 'Why not water it down, Georgie? Go for a more commercial sound.' But we did nothing of the sort. We make the kind of music that gives us a hundred percent excitement to play. Now it seems more and more fans get *their* kind of excitement from listening to it. Like I said, I've waited three years for this to happen. And if ever a wait has been worthwhile, this one has!"

"Yeh Yeh" was also on another Jon Hendricks album in 1965, *Recorded in Person at the Trident*, which had been recorded that same year in Sausalito, California with local musicians.

The B-side of "Yeh Yeh" was a clever Johnny Burch composition in 6/4-time called "Preach And Teach", which – like the massive A-side hit – is still a regular feature in Fame's live sets. The London pianist and composer Johnny Burch (1932–2006) had toured Germany with Graham Bond. Both his quartet and his octet in the Sixties were full of horn blowers from the Fame universe: Dick Heckstall-Smith, Peter King, Ray Warleigh and, later, Dick Morrissey. "Preach And Teach" was also recorded by Buddy Rich, and got another re-shuffle by Georgie himself for his 2003 album *Charlestons*.

Georgie took his complete Blue Flames on to *Ready Steady Go*, the recently DVD-honoured *ITV* music programme, and presented "Yeh Yeh" there, including a rousing, prolonged tenor sax solo by recent purchase Peter Coe.

"And", as Fame remembers well, "I actually recorded my hit version of "Yeh Yeh" in Deutsch – to sell more records in Deutschland. It sold more records in Deutschland because I recorded it in London in Deutsch, [although a lot of fans still wanted the original version]. That's corporate politics for you. That's what it was. They did the same thing in Italy. But if you look at the movies: Every film you see in Deutschland, especially on television – it doesn't matter if it's Clint Eastwood, or Dustin Hoffman, they dub it in Deutsch. Usually with a guy that doesn't sound anything like the original voice. So the fact that I was singing "Yeh Yeh" in Deutsch, even though the accent may not have been good, or perfect, at least it was me singing in Deutsch, not some guy that they put the voice on, the voice over."

„Yeh Yeh": „Komm' ich am Abend von meiner Arbeit nach Haus, klingelt mein Baby, oh Baby gehen wir aus" [he sings it in German]. It doesn't swing so much, but if the records sell, that's ok. But I didn't get the invitation to play here.

In spite of that, the band was confident enough to tackle any challenge now. Fame in 2009: "The Beatles played in Hamburg for how many years, two years? And they had to play five, six sets a night. And we were doing the same thing in Soho. And we had so much material! We did not play the same song twice in one night, even if we were doing three jobs.

"We weren't invited to do any tours of the [European] continent until after "Yeh Yeh" was a hit. The first invitation we had to play outside England when "Yeh Yeh" was a hit, was in Sweden. Georgie Fame & The Blue Flames went to Sweden, and Denmark."

All this success with singles, albums and tours did by not make Fame go over the top: "We carried on doing what we were doing. We could now afford a couple of road managers and maybe travel by train sometimes." Georgie's second hit "In The Meantime", charted in the UK at #22 in March 1965, and managed another placing in the US, although only at a modest #97. This was also written by fellow London Jazzer Johnny "Preach & Teach" Burch, "who in the meantime was able to get himself a nice house in Kent thanks to the "Yeh Yeh"-B-side royalties", as Georgie often relates in his shows.

For his next single, Fame boldly picked two of his own compositions, "Like We Used To Be", backed by "It Ain't Right", which made the Top Forty in England at a modest #33. "Like It Used To Be" already showed Georgie's affection for dance floor safe Soul material, where he takes precise, attractive turns with his brass section, building up to a rousing chorus twice, only to let loose on his Hammond for a short and wild solo before returning to the next verse. A decade later, Georgie would re-vamp the song during one of his many Island sessions, applying a faster rhythm and different yet equally attractive horn arrangement.

"It Ain't Right" is a slow swinging Blues ballad, which like its singles partner belies Fame's belief that he was not really quite ready to work as a composer. The US, incidentally, chose "Blue Monday" as the B-side, and Holland followed suit, even changing the "airplay order" and making "Blue Monday" the main contender.

The 1964-recorded "Yeh Yeh" and subsequent 1965 singles were produced by Tony Palmer, who also guided the sessions for an excellent composer's debut of Blue Flames trumpeter Eddie "Tan Tan" Thornton, called "Tan Tan's Tune", an incredibly swinging and sophisticated instrumental number with a great theme and rousing solo. With Palmer, the Blue Flames also tackled Jimmy McGriff's "Soul Stomp" in an exemplary, hot version. Both tracks should have impressed as album material, but remained in the vaults until 1998, when they were resurrected for the Boxed Set *The In-Crowd*.

There were no LP releases by Georgie Fame during 1965, but this kind of gap was not as significant in the Sixties as it would become during the 1970s. There was a regular turnout of singles, and what's more, two EP releases of new material serviced a format that was still very popular, and amounted to the same sizeable output that other artists put on an LP with recent singles.

Fats For Fame was a loving, and long overdue, tribute of Georgie's to his teenage hero Fats Domino, and the cover shot shows him looking at a series of Fats LPs on his piano's sheet music stand. "No No", not to be confused with Domino's "No No Baby" from 1951, was the flipside of "Sick And Tired", on Fats' 1958 Imperial single.

Fame recorded both sides for his EP, joyfully celebrating Fats' happy-go-lucky style with the Blue Flames for the Boogie and the Rock'n'Roll choices.

He added Fats' 1956 hit "Blue Monday", which his partner Dave Bartholomew had originally written for Smiley Lewis. Also from Fats Domino's 1956 record repertoire, "So Long", based on trioles like "Blue Monday", had been the B-side of "When My Dreamboat Comes Home", (which Georgie recorded too, although much later, in 1992, for his album with the BBC Big Band *City Life*.) *Fats For Fame* charted at a respectable #15 in England, thus keeping him in the top league of EMI Columbia artists.

The second EP, *Move It On Over*, did not chart, but was a welcome excerpt from the live repertoire, the title track a homage to Ray Charles' reading of the Hank Williams tune. "Rockin' Pneumonia and The Boogie Woogie Flu", Rufus Thomas' "Walking The Dog" and "High Heel Sneekers" were also standard repertoire, but who did these numbers better than the high octane Blue Flames?

Subsequently, John Mayall's very catchy love stomper "Something" was also a minor UK Top Thirty hit at # 23 in October 1965, backed by the wild, breakneck speed and Hammond-heavy Booker T. & The MGs instrumental "Outrage". When interviewed in 2001 about writing for other artists, John Mayall spontaneously replied "I never actually did". The Blues veteran was surprised when this author reminded him of "Something" – yeah, that was indeed an exception from the rule: "We shared the same management, the Rik Gunnell Agency. Rik ran the Flamingo at the time, and he managed both Georgie and myself. In those days, I was busy writing songs in order to sell my compositions to other people, so I sent this one to Georgie when he was looking for something [pun intended?] for a single, and he went and recorded it straight away. My original is kept in mid tempo, and he made a fast version out of it, which was interesting for me to hear. But that must have been the only song of mine that was covered."

Georgie Fame generally remembers the Mid Sixties with affection: "The Sixties in London – it was a very vibrant period. There were a lot of bands around. There were a lot of places to play. There was a lot of social life, a lot of activity! I mean three or four years of that period in my life I never got out of bed before two o'clock in the afternoon, I had been up till six or seven in the morning – not necessarily partying but working!" A lot of energy, and also kind of a legend in his own life time: in 1965 typical quotes were, for instance, "No 1 R&B Singer", "Britain's Most Promising Singer" and "Top Male Jazz Singer".

Red Neck Blues – No Atlantic Crossover

In true British Commonwealth style, in 1965 the Blue Flames band was as racially mixed as the repertoire, a fact that hardly raised an eyebrow in The Flamingo Club, or indeed any other European venue by now. But this did not seem to go down too well at all in the still segregated Southern US home of all things Blues & Rock. Recordings for the American TV-show *Hullaballoo* had to be produced back in the United Kingdom, because Georgie's long-standing trumpeter and conga player were both Afro-Britons: Eddie Thornton and Speedy Acquaye. Apart from obvious management incompetence, Fame's insistence to bring this "integrated band" was responsible for the cancellation of a projected American tour. Different, separate hotels would have had to be booked, and some venues in the Southern States would have cancelled completely.

Fame remembers how the US tour fell through: "We were rather disappointed because we were playing American music – Black American music, and after 'Yeh Yeh' was a worldwide hit, I thought that we ought to go to America, and play." Instead of touring the States, Georgie Fame & The Blue Flames were invited to join – as a hot British act well prepared via "Pride & Joy" in their set! – the March 1965 *The Tamla Motown Show – Motor Town Revue* with the Supremes, Martha & The Vandellas and Stevie Wonder for 42 British gigs – twenty-one dates with two shows per night! The promoters Harold Davison and Arthur Howes presented the Motown Package with the heading "From Hitsville USA".

Georgie Fame and The Blue Flames were representing the only British stars invited for this unique Soul showcase, an incredible honour indeed, while some insiders also claimed that this friendly invitation may have been issued in order to boost ticket sales of an endeavour that wasn't as popular yet as it was going to be only one year later.

Fame's old pal from Leigh days and one time Beat Boys member, Ronnie Carr, recalls the occasion well on his website *lankybeat.com*:

"Together with a distracted June Carr, Georgie Fame & The Blue Flames played live when he was guest band on the Motown Show Tour in 1965 -1966. Here at rehearsals at the Odeon, Manchester, we met the full show parade: Smokey Robinson & The Miracles – Dianna [sic] Ross & The Supremes – Martha & The Vandellas and Stevie Wonder; and the whole squad. Now that was a night to remember. This was the tour which was poorly attended as they were not very well known then. Absolutely brilliant. I'm so glad that they all went on to the stardom they deserved."

Martha Reeves fondly remembered on NPR Radio how she first came to Europe: "I was there before the Motown Revue, before Dusty Springfield used her influence to get all of us there. But we toured with Georgie Fame, when his hit record "I Say Yeh, Yeh" (sic) was riding the charts. And he allowed me to come over. I was – I didn't have the Vandellas – I had to go on my own. And I toured with Georgie Fame, 40 one-nighters. It was just wonderful, the reception to our music. But when the Motown Revue went over because of Dusty Springfield and the *Ready Steady Go!* special, we were so – we got the same reception that The Beatles got in New York. It was wonderful to make the exchange. We used to have to exchange artists. When an English act came to America, we'd have to send an American act to England. And when we arrived, there was – they stopped Heathrow Airport. They had flowers and banners from the Tamla Motown Appreciation Society. Thanks to Dave Godin, God rest his soul, we were very well-received. So I remember it very well."

Subsequently, the Blue Flames went down a storm at the "5th National Jazz & Blues Festival" in Richmond, with another triumph waiting in September in London's Royal Albert Hall: "Pop From Britain" saw Georgie Fame and The Blue Flames together with Cliff Bennett & The Rebel Rousers and The Moody Blues.

There were other prestigious occasions, and at one of them, Georgie met up with Van Morrison again. By the time Van led his band Them, the two would meet frequently at the Flamingo, and also at other spectacular events, like the Poll Winners' "parade" of the *New Musical Express*. Rogan again:

"The promising chart progress of 'Here Comes The Night' was crowned by an appearance at the most important and star-studded UK pop shows of the Sixties. On Sunday, 11 April the New Musical Express preented its annual Poll Winners' Concert at the Empire Pool, Wembley, where 10,000 spectators could enjoy, for as little as seven shillings and sixpence [about 35 pence in decimal when it was about three dollars to the pound] a line-up that brought together the Beatles, the Rolling Stones, the Kinks, the Animals, the Moody Blues, Freddy & The Dreamers, Wayne Fontana & The Mindbenders, the Rockin' Berries, The Seekers, The Ivy League, Georgie Fame & The Blue Flames and Sounds Incorporated."

It was still 1965, and it had been one hell of a ride so far for Georgie: "The Flamingo wasn't a fashionable place. It was just a real happening scene. We were probably the hub, though we didn't realize it. All we were interested in was playing and furthering ourselves. We were absolutely knackered, but exhilarated because we'd been playing all day, all night. The Flamingo was the closest one could have been to playing in an American club, We developed the music because we had first-hand access to it. We were living the life."

Georgie summarized all these crazy events of his roller coaster ride once again while he was still active there – or had them described – in the 1965 edition of the *Radio Luxembourg Annual*. What a hell of a ride it had been – so far:

"One night a friend [obviously Mike O'Neill] took me down to the Flamingo Club in London. It was scary in there, full of happy coloured people having a ball with some swinging Rhythm-and-Blues band … One Sunday, I arrived there to find they were short of a band. 'Let me have a go', I asked. We grabbed a group together and went down a bomb! In fact, Rik Gunnell, who owns the club [in 1965] and later became my manager, was so impressed he took me on permanently … With the Blue Flames, I began to build a following for our Rhythm-and-Blues and Jazz … From one night a week we progressed to doing all-night sessions on Fridays. I was mad because I could never make up the sleep I lost, but, somehow, it soon didn't matter. Then we got the Saturday and Monday dates and I began to learn about the music I was playing … American GIs would come to the club and bring me records by people like Mose Allison and Oscar Brown Jr. I was learning all the time. Georgie Fame & The Blue Flames were swinging like mad."

"Get Away" with Sweet Things – Fame & Flames' Golden Year of 1966

1966 promised to be just as hot and hasty as the previous year for Georgie and his band. Fame, meanwhile, had switched producers – leaving first Ian Samwell and then Tony Palmer for the Argentinian born Dennis "Denny" Cordell (1943–1995). Since 1964, Cordell had worked for Chris Blackwell's Island Records and had become independent after producing the Moody Blues album *The Magnificent Moodies* (although their hit "Go Now" had been supervised by Alex Wharton). Cordell helped to initiate the indie label type subsidiaries Deram for Decca and Regal Zonophone for EMI, and worked with bands like The Move and Procol Harum, the latter just getting started from the ashes of The Paramounts.

Georgie Fame and producer Denny Cordell had struck an immediate chord and worked together very well on the next Blue Flames LP, *Sweet Things*, which came out in May 1966, again on EMI-Columbia, as well as the prestigious Big Band project which Georgie had started.

The *Sweet Things* album was a further move into the world of Soul, the music of the Industrial north of the US, especially Detroit – no doubt inspired by the Motown Revue – as much as those hot Southern music meccas like Memphis and New Orleans. Not only did Otis Redding mingle with Chris Farlowe & The Thunderbirds and tour the UK with Herbie Goins and the Night-Timers in tow – featuring ex-Flame Mick Eve on sax – but the whole nation seemed to dance along to Soul grooves like "The Midnight Hour", with all groups except for Georgie's sporting a front man. As journalist Tyler pointed out, sarcastically referring to Fame as suffering from "organ neck", he didn't seem to bother to step out of the shadow of his Hammond. Well, the man soon would – but his ardent fans didn't like it too much.

Georgie had enough self-esteem to run his own course, and a March 1966 "Group's group" poll in one of the music papers showed that his "name-dropping" considered two heroes who sat behind their organs during gigs: His winners were Stevie Winwood on vocals and Alan Price on keyboards, joined by Jack Bruce on bass and the Hollies – and formerly Dolphins' and The Fentones' – great drummer Bobby Elliott, a prolific Jazz sticksman whose fills and grooves would make many of his groups' tracks extra special.

With no further Powell/Fame compositions to the fore this time around, Georgie's successful Soul leanings were solidified with a great Blue Flames line-up of guitarist Colin Green, the horn section of Glenn Hughes on baritone sax, tenor and flute, Peter Coe on alto and tenor and Eddie "Tan Tan" Thornton on trumpet again. The rhythm section was made up of Cliff Barton on bass, Speedy Acquaye on congas and by new drummer John "Mitch" Mitchell.

Mitchell (1947–2008) had started out as a child actor, like so many colleagues of the Sixties. Mickey Dolenz of The Monkees fame for instance – who would tour with Mitch Mitchell in 1967 in his next band, The Jimi Hendrix Experience – played in the US-TV series *Circus Boy*; Phil Collins from Genesis was Steve Marriott's successor in the British children's television adaptation of Enid Blyton's *Famous Five*; while Mitchell had been the mischievous schoolboy in the *Jennings* TV serial, whose

1948 radio beginnings Georgie had surely listened to back in Leigh long before Mitch joined.

But Little John Mitchell wanted to live in the world of music. He was interested in tap dancing, like so many Afro-American drummers, and he was soon searching for a link to the pros, in Jim Marshall's music shop in his London suburb of Hanwell/Ealing (Jim was indeed *the* Marshall dealer with the huge stacks). He was just 13 when he played for Pete Nelson & The Travellers, and still only 15, he joined Frankie Reid & The Casuals, changed to Johnny Harris & The Shades before landing a bigger gig with Mod masters The Riot Squad, who were masterminded by Larry Page of Kinks & Troggs fame (and who, with Mitchell long gone, would sport David Bowie in their ranks).

Mitch would dep for the chaotic drummer Viv Prince in The Pretty Things during a tour if Australasia as well as play with The Who – while those fellow Mods, pre Keith Moon, were contemplating a replacement for their rhythm boy Doug Sandom. By December 1965, Mitchell replaced Georgie Fame's Blue Flames drummer Bill "Whiter Shade Of Pale" Eyden, without ever having been asked in officially.

Mitchell's style had now become extremely flexible and adaptable through all his engagements, but his first love had always been Jazz, influenced as he was by American idols Max Roach, Elvin Jones and Joe Morello, and he especially adored the Swing department exemplified by Eric Delaney or, in fact, his predecessor Phil Seamen. His Jazz grip, holding his left, snare-directed stick between his middle and ring finger, certainly hinted that way. Talking in his biog *The Hendrix Experience*, he added, "I already loved Earl Palmer [1924–2008, the man behind Little Richard, Fats Domino and hundreds of others], Benny Benjamin [1925–1969, a.k.a. "Papa Zita", who played on all Motown stuff from early Stevie Wonder to the Temptations] and Al Jackson [junior, 1935–1975, the Booker T drummer and Stax Records sessioneer]".

One of the first gigs that "Mitch" played with Georgie Fame & The Blue Flames, in fact only his second sojourn as a new Flame, happened on December 18th 1965 at the popular "California (Pool) Ballroom" in Dunstable's Whipsnade Road and was described with panache in the *Dunstable Gazette*:

"Georgie Fame and the Blue Flames stopped the dancing at the California Ballroom on Saturday. The biggest cheer of the night was for a solo by ex "Riot Squad" drummer John Mitchell. It was only his second night with the band.

"Georgie told the '*Gazette*' that John had fitted in remarkably well and that once they had worked out the musical arrangements 'things would really move.' Another of the evening's highlights was a wonderful piece of guitar work by Colin Green on the Jimmy Reed number 'Rock Me Baby'.

"Georgie showed his vocal talent in an arrangement of 'Don't Get Scared' [by Stan Getz and Lars Gullin]. This was an excellent piece of Jazz singing. His whisper-smooth voice and rubber bottom lip wound their way round some intricate phrasing which was reminiscent of Anita O'Day's. This top rate band – if you want a label, call them Jazz Rhythm and Blues – did a very professional job and were warmly appreciated by the Dunstable audience. The line-up: Georgie Fame – organ; Peter Coe – alto, tenor saxes, flute; Tex Makin [sic], bass guitar; Speedy Acquaye, conga drum; John Mitchell, drums;

Glen Hughes, baritone sax; Eddie Thornton, trumpet." *Dunstable Gazette* Dec. 1965.

The following summer, Georgie and the Blue Flames were booked to play Cliff Bennett & The Rebel Rousers' familiar hunting ground and almost second home, the Star-Club in the vicinity of Hamburg's Reeperbahn in July 1966. R&B and Soul singer Bennett was the lucky guy who had a song custom-made for him by his Beatle friend Paul McCartney: "Got To Get You Into My Life".

When you looked at the neon-lit display of the Star-Club on the boulevard Grosse Freiheit, the massive number of stars that had graced the stage was like a Who's Who of Fame's past, and dreams, too. His early heroes Jerry Lee Lewis and Fats Domino had appeared here, as had Ray Charles and Gene Vincent. Tony Sheridan, Georgie's mate from many Larry Parnes tours – including the one with Eddie Cochran – had been a Hamburg resident for years and had educated the Beatles into a tight unit. Forever as gifted as he was unreliable, his legendary sloppiness had prevented him from joining Cochran on that fateful car journey via Chippenham – and saved his life.

Georgie doesn't remember much from that 1966 gig – "Did I play the Star-Club?" – but in 2012, he was heartily invited back, for one of two 50-year jubilee celebrations, held in Hamburg's air-conditioned circus tent "Fliegende Bauten" (flying buildings), which unfortunately clashed with Fame's other commitments.

The Sweet Things album – track by track

The title track of the new, imminent album, "Sweet Thing", started things off with, clever, highly danceable Easy Soul. The catchy number, which had been written by Ivy Joe Hunter (b. 1940, not to be confused with Ivory Joe Hunter) and Mickey Stevenson, had not been a hit for the Detroit Soul veterans The Spinners when it came out in 1964 as their first Tamla Motown single. Georgie employs neither lead singer Bobby Smith's high-pitched vocals nor their backing choir, but manages to make the number his very own. Producer Denny Cordell manages to show the horns and the Hammond in the best possible sound accordingly, and drummer Mitch Mitchell shows how he can apply his Jazz chops to some great Soul grooves. The number was done by The Supremes and by Marvin Gaye, too.

The Spinners were called the Detroit Spinners in England at the time, because over there, the mixed race Liverpool folk group of the same name had made the rounds since their 1957 debut at the Cavern Club. (For trivia hunters: Alan Price liked their folk cover of "The Blaydon Races" so much that he included it in his 1983 album *Geordie Roots and Branches*.) The "Motown Spinners" was another aka in the UK, because the band, which was formed towards the end of the 1950s, had been bought up by the giant Soul label together with their original record company "Tri-Phi".

From Tamla Motown, Detroit, to Stax Records, Memphis: "See Saw" had been a 1965 Atlantic Records US hit for Don Covay, once the ex driver of the Little Richard Revue, who wrote the thing with Booker T guitarist Steve Cropper. Covay had been in the

Doo-Wop group The Rainbows with Marvin Gaye and Billy "Sitting In The Park" Stewart, and had a thrilling thing in common with Georgie – employing a member of the Jimi Hendrix Experience. For Fame, it was Mitch Mitchell right here; for Don Covay it was Hendrix himself, on "Mercy Mercy"! The Blue Flames take care of speeding the number up compared to the original.

You can imagine the Flamingo crowd dancing like mad to ex boxer Lee "Kid Chocolate" Dorsey's fast-paced "Ride Your Pony". Fame had covered his "Do Re Mi" before. "Ride Your Pony" had been composed by New Orleans R&B pioneer Naomi Neville a.k.a. Allen R. Toussaint, the man who had brought Covay down from Oregon to Louisiana once. Fame's Hammond organ rarely sounded dirtier than on this number, and he can really let rip with hard edged soul singing, too.

Respite from the dance floor came next, with the Willie Nelson ballad "Funny How Time Slips Away", which is still featured in Fame's live repertoire today, and which was refined three times in the studio between 1966 and 1979, with this version maybe still the most charming, not least because of the horn arrangement led by Eddie Thornton on trumpet. Ever since Nelson wrote the song in 1961, it had been everywhere, debuted by Billy Walker even before Willie Nelson's LP debut.

The song was covered by Fame's 1965 tour companions The Supremes as well as Arthur "Anna" Alexander and Billy Joe Royal on his album *Down in the Boondocks*. Four years after Georgie, Elvis Presley would tackle it as well, and by his own accounts, for instance during his annual Ronnie Scotts Club concerts, he pointed out that he had not even heard Willie Nelson's own interpretation at the time, but had encountered the song via Joe Hinton, a Southern States contemporary of Bobby Bland and Junior Parker whose sophisticated Gospel/Soul certainly appealed to Fame.

The mood remains contemplative for "Sitting In The Park". Afro-American Soul crooner Billy Stewart (1937–1970), a Fats Domino lookalike who had released "A Fat Boy Can Cry" accordingly, charted with "Park" in the US in 1965, but still, this fine ballad has always been identified with Fame in the UK and the rest of Europe. Fame and Cordell's great arrangement benefits from Glenn Hughes' imaginative flute work and Mitch Mitchell's subtly paced tom fills, and, like "Funny How Time Slips Away", would get a renewed studio treatment in 1978. Columbia released it as a single towards the end of the year, after the break-up of the Blue Flames, and it reached a respectable number 12 in the UK charts.

A return to the pleasures of Jamaican music follows – with Lord Kitchener's "parental guidance" Calypso "Dr Kitch". Lord Kitchener's real name was Aldwyn Roberts (1922–2000). He was a kind of father figure for many of the West Indian UK immigrants, and consequently for the Flamingo club audience. Kitchener had written "Cricket, Lovely Cricket" when Georgie was only seven years old. The singer from Trinidad had released the funny number in 1963 as a single on Jump Up, a subsidiary label of Island Records. It became a big hit in Mod clubs. All this makes "Dr Kitch" quite an inspired if risqué choice for Fame, with "doctor's injection" lyrics like "I push it in, she pull it out". The number was pretty obviously perfect for being covered by someone like Judge Dread, too. This Brixton Ska singer and ex Trojan Records debt collector owed so much to Prince Buster and numerous BBC Radio bans.

As Georgie pointed out during his performances at Ronnie Scott's Club in London during April 2013, he got a BBC ban himself for "Dr Kitch", but for all the wrong reasons: "The programmers heard 'I push it in, I push it out', and they immediately thought it was about drugs!" Not too surprising perhaps, in the light of the impact that particular kind of needle had for some of the Blue Flames. Anyway, this ban was topped by a "no no" from Imperial in the USA, who did not release it at all, including the current American single "Getaway" on the album instead, and making it the album title in the process.

"My Girl", written by Smokey Robinson and his fellow Miracles member Ronald White, had been done by Motown giants The Temptations in 1964, becoming a number one a year later. At the time of Georgie & The Blue Flames' cover, The Rolling Stones had also covered the famous number in September 1966, but they only released it on their *Flowers* album a year after *Sweet Things*. Fame easily does this number justice, on a par with Temptations singer David Ruffin. The Flames really revel in it, with Colin Green playing the ascending notes in the guitar intro over the C chord as a perfect example for the pentatonic scale that helped to make the song so famous. Georgie's version owes more to the Otis Redding reading of the number. Maybe this is one reason why the song does also not appear on the US *Getaway* album on Imperial Records. Instead, the British "Getaway" single B-side, the Hammond showcase "El Bandido", is added to the setlist.

Georgie Fame was certainly quick when it came to adapting suitable material right off the current scene. "Music Talk" by Stevie Wonder, Clarence Paul and Ted Hull, had just come out on Wonder's popular fifth album *Uptight – Everything's Alright*. Fame immediately saw the track's potential, with lyrics edging his partners on, like "soon you'll hear the trumpet begin to blow" for Thornton, and "I think the drummer has found a new groove" for Mitchell. If any British group could dare to take up the Funk Brothers – those then still anonymous Motown studio cats, among them bass legend James Jamerson and Richard "Pistol" Allen – it was certainly The Blue Flames. Fame loved this album quite a lot, covering its title track "Uptight" on his later 1980 Pye Reggae album *Closing The Gap*.

"Music Talk", incidentally, was heavily sampled. During recent years, for instance, it was used by: The Beatnuts on "World's Famous Intro" (*Intoxicated Demons* EP on

Relativity, 1993); by Pete Rock and C.L. Smooth on their "Wig Out" (*Mecca & The Soul Brother*, Liberty 1992); and by the Dark Sun Riders on "Magnificent Son" (*Seeds of Evolution*, Island 1995). But the most prominent adaptation happened via The Chemical Brothers, who quoted it on "Playground For a Wedgeless Firm" (*Exit Planet Dust*, Freestyle Dust, 1995). Enjoy it on *www.whosampled.com*.

"The In-Crowd" by Billy Page, with an arrangement by his brother, the famous Gene Page, had managed #13 in America when sung by Dobie Gray, and only #25 in the UK. But it reached the US Top Five as a jazzy Ramsey Lewis instrumental, and as such was used by British radio personality Jimmy Savile, and consequently it became interesting for Georgie, as a perfect vehicle for his Hammond organ and his prolific brass section – a true calling card that also served as the title for a big Verve Records 3-CD-boxed Fame *The In-Crowd* retrospective in 1998.

"The World Is Round" was an R&B staple by Mississippi and Memphis legend Rufus Thomas (1917–2001), the "Rabbit Foot Minstrels" entertainer who answered Big Mama Thornton's "Hound Dog" with "Bear Cat" [surely Big Mama T wrote 'Hound Dog'] and many more dog-related singles, and issued this single in 1965 on Stax Records. He was often backed by Georgie's idols, Booker T & The MGs, thus perfect for Fame and his Blue Flames, who sail through it as if it had been written with them in mind, with Speedy Acquaye adding extra panache to Cliff Barton and Mitch Mitchell's disciplined groove.

Sam Cooke's "The Whole World's Shaking" with its fanfare-like horn riff, is another certified dance number for the Blue Flames. It had been Cooke's follow up to the popular "Shake" single, which those other Mod stars, The Small Faces, had covered with tremendous energy.

"Last Night" is a rousing 1961 instrumental, the longest number on the album, written by members of the legendary Memphis group The Mar-Keys, Charles "Packy" Axton, Chips Moman, Jerry Lee "Smoochie" Smith, Floyd Newman and Gil Caple. The Mar-Keys were Steve Cropper and Duck Dunn's pre Booker T. Stax Soul band. Just perfect for the final outburst of an LP, just as it is always fitting for ending a wild gig, which is often how Georgie in all the clubs around the "Smoke", the rest of the country and beyond. The breaks introduced yet another musician's solo, like in "Tell them what I said, Pete" for saxophonist Peter Coe, getting some great Hammond sounds in, shouting out snippets from other songs like "Nowhere To Run" by the Motown touring mates Martha & The Vandellas, or recalling carousing problems like "Early in the morning and I can't get right, and she said where'd you go last night". He even had the horns recite "(I Can't Get No) Satisfaction" by the Flames-loving Rolling Stones. The wild and still precise Blue Flames version certainly packs more punch than the already brilliant Mar-Keys original. The American suits at Fame's US label Imperial liked this treatment of the song enough to make it a B-side for "Funny How Time Slips Away", though they edited it slightly.

There was at least one other recording made for the album, "Sweet Talk" by an unknown composer: a pleasant Swing with big brass, deft Hammond touches, Mitch in great form and a short but poignant sax solo, of which only an acetate exists.

Sweet Things, Georgie Fame & The Blues Flames' third album, rushed to Number 6 in the British Album Charts. Soon after, Georgie was visited by his idol Jon Hendricks for jam sessions, recording for an up-coming album project with The Harry South Big Band as well as some serious Jazz talk.

The second number one – "Get Away"!

Initially, Georgie's next composition "Get Away" wasn't even meant as a genuine single release. Fame wrote it as a TV and radio advert: "In 1966, we got a telephone call from an ad agency, representing National Benzole Petrol. They wanted a piece of music, to be written as a commercial, that they could give away as a floppy disc to anybody that went in and bought four gallons of their petrol, and they were paying handsomely for this commission."

"And me and the band were actually in a television studio in Bristol, waiting our turn to do something. Now, then I realized that the studio had been booked in London at 10 o'clock the next morning, for this song that I hadn't thought about. And I picked up the guitar and sort of strummed along in the dressing room. And I think I thought of Bo Diddley. I just did a fairly crude impersonation of Bo Diddley – he deserves some of the royalties, really.

"We drove back to London and I stayed up all night and I wrote up some lyrics and I went into the studio at 10 o'clock the next morning, and did it. It was The Blue Flames. I wrote it so quickly and in fact it was all recorded so fast that I didn't even have time to teach the guitar player the tune, so I had to play the guitar on the original recording myself." He didn't actually, because his faithful guitar player was at hand, Colin Green: "Well, I did play on the record, that's right. And Georgie played the guitar on it, that's right, too. I played tambourine, but it wasn't a question of having no time, he just wanted to play it. I'd have played happily."

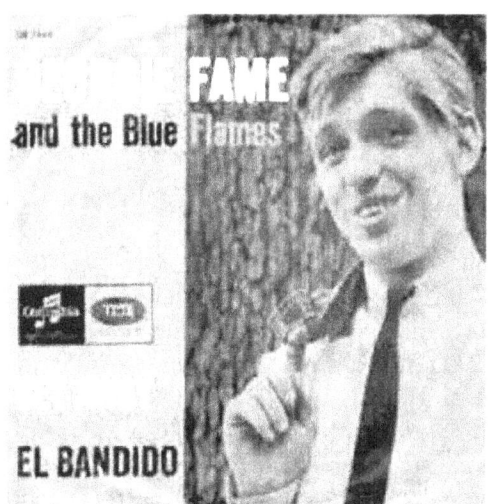

"But then we were listening to the playback – these guys from the ad agency and National Benzole and the management and the rest of the staff, they were all huddled in the back. And my producer Denny Cordell – bless him – came over, sidled up to me as we were listening to the playback, and he said 'You know, man, this is really good! This is actually very commercial, and it doesn't mention anything about petrol!'

"So anyway, we put it out as a single, and then the BBC played it, and it went to number one. So the BBC gave National Benzole Petrol thousands and thousands of pounds for free advertising before they realized what was happening. So it worked both ways. The petrol company got the kick out of it and all the publicity that they wanted, and because it didn't mention the actual name of the product, the BBC played it, and it was a huge success! It was just a one-off commercial wrangler. So in the end, we got paid twice, and quite handsomely, too!"

"Getaway" was finally Fame's first self-composed pole position, while he and The Blue Flames excited the audience at yet another huge open air event: The "6th Annual Jazz & Blues Festival" at Windsor.

The End Of The Sixties Blue Flames

Possibly as a result of this Jon Hendricks visit, and also lured by the dollar signs in manager Rik Gunnell's eyes, Fame announced his intention to disband the Blue Flames and record with Big Bands and orchestras, a move that Fame's friend "Long" John Baldry followed almost at the same time, albeit for the time being towards much more cabaret orientated waters.

But Fame's manager Rik Gunnell was not a Brian Epstein, who could be advised by his client to do the "dirty work" for him – Georgie had to pass the news himself while in Gunnell's office in Gerrard Street. And the fact that drummer Mitch Mitchell shared a flat with Georgie did not make the crucial talk any easier.

Georgie told Paolo Hewitt, "I broke up the band in the office at Gerrard Street … Everybody was okay about it but Mitch was really pissed off. So there was me and Mitch left in the office and Mitch was crying."

As if mirroring the fact that Mitchell was in tears at the decision, soon *Melody Maker* ran the big front page headline "Georgie Fame snuffs Flames", choosing a photograph of a shrugging Fame holding a ciggie to rub it all in.

The competing *Record Mirror* had covered the big break-up in mid-September – while only a few days before, The Blue Flames had played their last ever British date at the Ricky Tick Club in Windsor on September 17th, bowing out at the Gala du Disque in Amsterdam on October 2nd.

The tears though, had actually dried within minutes: A short while later on that same afternoon, in mid-sobbing so to speak, the phone rang in the Gunnell office, with Chas Chandler on the phone – one-time Animals bass player and lately a dedicated talent scout. He had scored big in New York City, bringing home a flash and fab and flabbergasting guitarist, Seattle native James Marshall Hendrix – who everybody called Jimi. Jimi was auditioning and jamming, and wouldn't the boys love to come along? "We're looking for a good drummer for him", Chandler had enquired, "know anybody decent who is free, Clive?"

Clive had one sitting on the office sofa, of course, who dearly needed Ray Davies' song advice "Stop Your Sobbing". Spontaneously, they ambled over to the club – Ken Colyer's Jazz Club, and both Georgie and his just-fired Flame Mitch jammed with

Hendrix. The way Mitch whizzed over the provided drums and cymbals got him the job, while some sources claim that a coin was flipped in order to decide between Mitch and John Mayall drummer Aynsley Dunbar. Mitchell joined the Jimi Hendrix Experience officially on October 5th, a mere three days after the final Blue Flames gig in Amsterdam.

Roger Clarke-Johnson from Ipswich, then a regular in *Blaises* night club, "which was just behind the *Royal Albert Hall*, with his own band, saw Hendrix even before the encounter with Mitchell." There was this very shy and extremely polite young black man with shortly cropped hair and a typical, conventional blue blazer graced by yellow 'golden' brass buttons. Then he got on stage, and he was just phonemenally good. And on drums with that resident band was Genesis' first drummer incidentally, Chris Stewart. When we drove back to Blaises, 'Hey Joe' was on the radio." Hendrix himself would be billed at *Blaises* on 21st December, 1966.

About two months later, Mitchell was to combine his acting and drumming skills for a very special extra-curricular task: play on some Hollies studio tracks. How come? In January 1967, Hollies drummer Bobby Elliott – Georgie's 1966 favourite, remember – was stuck in a Hamburg hospital with a split appendix, and the Hollies were booked in Abbey Road Studios to record their album *Evolution*. The revolving rhythm kings Clem Cattini of Tornados fame and Mitch Mitchell of Fame fame were told to "groove like Elliott" – many fans didn't realize at the time that Bobby wasn't part of the procedures at all.

Apart from The Jimi Hendrix Experience, Mitchell never ever forgot the Blue Flames Experience, as Georgie's son James Powell would experience some decades later.

Contrary to Mitch Mitchell, the break-up was a relief for Colin Green: "The honest truth about that – there were so many drugs going on: two of the band died, Cliff Barton and Glenn Hughes."

Cliff Barton had gone to Alexis Korner and then joined the Denny Laine Band, which Denny had started after leaving the Moody Blues. He also did sessions for Jimmy Page with Jeff Beck and Donovan. But on May 16th, 1968, the West Ealing man died at the West Middlesex Hospital in London. Unfortunately, his heroin addiction had led him to develop septicaemia, and after five days in the clinic, he passed away at just 24.

Georgie had had to let Hughes go because of his weak health, he had the same heroin problem as Barton, and he died only weeks after the break-up, on October 28th, 1966, in a house fire in his Shepherds Bush abode, a fate that reminds this author of the death, a quarter of a century later, of Small Face veteran Steve Marriott in April 1991, shortly after dreams of a Humble Pie reunion of sorts with Peter Frampton seemed to have faded. (Here, the cocktail had been cocaine, valium and alcohol.)

"And", as Colin Green continues, "I was drinking quite heavily. And I got home one night, and there was a call for me from Switzerland, saying "Would you like to come and work in Switzerland", and I just thought "Lovely! Mountains, nice place get away from this!" And that's exactly what I did – and that was that. I worked for Bob Azzam. He had a huge hit with a song called "Mustapha" (in French). And how that came about: the very first person who I had gone to as a [guitar tutor] was Micky Jones, who eventually had a group called Foreigner. He at that time was playing for Johnny Halliday. And Azzam, who worked an awful lot in Paris, was looking for a guitar player, and Micky recommended me. I was not falling out with Georgie at all. It was just a decision to go other ways. In fact, I lived in Switzerland for nearly two years, and Georgie came over to Switzerland on a couple of occasions. Each time he called me, and I met up and got to eat with him in Zurich and in Val."

Peter Coe (1930–2009) spent a year as Polydor Records' Big Band contractor, then became an illustrator and designer as his day job and proceeded to win three BBC Big Band competitions between 1975 and 1981. (You could only win twice, but Coe called his band Ceeporte Big Band in a cheeky anagram coup).

The End of The Flamingo Club

In The Flamingo and many other clubs, more and more of the idolized role models turned up in person: Wilson Pickett and Otis Redding were able to point out person to person what a Soul sensation sounds like. Redding bonded with local lad and Fame pal Chris Farlowe: "I will never forget that! He was down there, listening! He came into London to do a gig, and in those days everybody went down to the Flamingo Club, because it was a great atmosphere. You could have a drink down there, there was food, and of course you could listen to some great bands. I remember one day we were playing down there and Otis just turned up and sat down and listened to me and the band. He came into my dressing room at the end. And he just said he thought I was a very good singer, and would I do a TV show with him? And I did it! That TV show was in London." And then Redding died in a plane crash: "I was called by his manager. I couldn't really believe it – it was a very sad time. No doubt, if Otis Redding had lived, I would have done some recording with him. A missed chance, and that is the story of my life. But I am not complaining."

With people like Pickett and Redding roaming Europe, the scene got more crammed for British Soul, and at the same time, "Clubland" changed considerably, no doubt causing concern about new avenues to explore.

Six months after the demise of the Blue Flames, the All-nighters ceased to exist. And pretty soon, the natural enemy of the live club raised its ugly head: the discotheque. So the management tried to face that record-spinning competition by offering the more progressively orientated club, the Pink Flamingo, where Cream played, for instance, and from 1969, you could go to the Flamingo At The Temple, where Atomic Rooster, Van Der Graaf Generator or Barclay James Harvest performed.

Up on the first floor, there was the more Progressive Rock orientated "WAG Club" (The Whisky-A-Go-Go) from 1981 to 2001 – the final end of an era, which was immortalized by Georgie Fame in the song "Flamingo All-nighter" and which even name-checks the affair around Christine Keeler and Lucky Gordon.

"When I was a young man in 1962, London was buzzing, I was buzzing, too!
Flamingo All-Nighter was where we played.
We were living and learning, and getting paid.
It started off round midnight, lots of happy feet.
Now and then a big fight, turning up the heat!
Rik Gunnell, Al Watson, and Mike O'Neill
Zoot Money, Big Roll Band, no better deal
Good Ganja, sweet Bourbon, and a Purple Heart.
No egos, no hassles, just playing our part."

The credited Rik Gunnell soon operated Bee Gees manager Robert Stigwood's offices in the United States, namely in New York and Los Angeles. From the mid-Seventies, he returned to Austria, running a night club for "après-ski" punters in Kitzbühel, which he presided over until his death in 2007.

Flamingo founder Jeffrey Kruger departed to new pastures, monitoring US artists on tour in Europe, for instance Marvin Gaye, Johnny Cash and Gladys Knight. His path crossed with Ex-Blue-Flame Mitch Mitchell when he was involved in a Jimi Hendrix soundtrack album, *Experience*, and he was the UK earner behind singer Glen Campbell's success. Jumping at his chance when the suits in the London headquarters of Capitol Records told him "You can have the cowboy", Krüger saw "By The Time I Get To Phoenix" and "Wichita Lineman" chart and pave the way for nationwide tours which he promoted. Those slow numbers, meanwhile, seemed like stuff which CBS might soon choose for their new balladeer Georgie Fame. As for "By The Time I Get To Phoenix", they did – as we shall see!

But such a move was not what our man had in mind for himself: From summer 1966, Georgie Fame's real aspirations still leant more and more towards Jazz. His new album was *Sound Venture*, an eclectic yet truly breath-taking Jazz collection which had been recorded over more than a year, starting as early as 1964, when his live audiences bopped but his singles still flopped, with the renowned Harry South Big Band. But the young professional had run out of money in the process of putting up his own limited funds to hire his dream team of the British "Jazz Cream", and the project had been put on hold. Yet when Georgie's "Yeh Yeh" shot to Number 1, he had the welcome Sterling to finish his heartfelt and ambitious LP: "I got interested in Jazz, and I wanted to sing with a big band. So I sunk the royalties that I got out of 'Yeh Yeh' into producing the Big Band album with Harry South, with all of Britain's finest Jazz musicians at the time. It was a wonderful experience again. It hit the album charts at a very respectable #5 in October 1966, which is very rare indeed for a jazz album."

The first Georgie Fame Big Band Album – Sound Venture

If you trundle through some music encyclopedias, there is still the popular belief that Georgie Fame, the revered star of the "Flamingo All-nighter", disbanded his guaranteed-to-party combo The Blue Flames in order to become a 'serious' Jazz interpreter. As if the fun had gone out the window with his impending big band album *Sound Venture*. For Georgie, the real, creative fun had started with this attractively orchestrated venture, much as he soon regretted the loss of his Flamingo comrades.

The popular Harry South Big Band included saxophone buffs like Ronnie Scott, the famous club-owner who started Bebop in England in the 1940s and established Soho's premier Jazz club which is still going strong today. He brought along Tubby Hayes, his tenor sax partner from the Jazz Couriers, vintage 1957. Hayes had played in New York, led his own Big Bands and would lead the brass section on rock band Family's legendary debut album *Music in A Doll's House* one year after *Sound Venture*. "He got himself a heroin problem", was Georgie's later statement on a great talent lost way too early in 1973 at only 38, during a final, fatal heart operation.

Dick Morrissey (1940–2000), the renowned reeds player who was to achieve stardom in the influential Jazz-Rock bands If three years on, was a veteran of the London Jazz scene, having played regularly at the Marquee, Ronnie Scott's and the Barnes Bull's Head, his first solo album having appeared in 1961. He would work with Georgie again, like the equally admired Ray Warleigh (b. 1938), an Australian flautist and saxophonist who came to the UK when he was 22 and played with lots of Georgie's friends, like Alexis Korner, Ronnie Scott, Tubby Hayes and John Mayall, but also worked with a range of artists from Marianne Faithful to Scott Walker.

Alan Branscombe (1936–1986) was a tenor saxophonist but also an adept pianist and vibes player, who had worked with Tubby Hayes and was with *Sound Venture* pianist Stan Tracey at the time of recording. Jackie Sharp, Ray Wilcox also played Sax.

Trumpets abounded likewise: Kenny Wheeler (b. 1930) from Canada had worked with Johnny Dankworth and Blue Flame John McLaughlin – not least on the legendary Windmill Tilter tribute to Don Quixote – and impressed audiences at the *5th Annual British Jazz and Blues Festival* as part of the Eric Burdon & The Animals Big Band in the year before *Sound Venture*. Ken would share the stage with Georgie Fame all of 47 years later at the Herts Jazz Festival 2013 in Welwyn Garden City.

Jimmy Deuchar (1930–1993) was another guy in the Tubby Hayes/Ronnie Scott club circuit. Like Hayes, Deuchar had toured Germany with orchestra leader Kurt Edelhagen and returned to him shortly after finishing Sound Venture. Jimmy famously worked for the Kenny Clarke-Francy Boland Big Band and was also a member of the BBC Big Band.

Ian Hamer (1932–2006) had led The Six Sounds with Harry South, which became the Ian Hamer Sextet, featuring *Venture* venturers Morrissey, Branscombe, Bill Eyden and Humphrey Lyttelton's trombonist Keith Christie (1935–1980), as well as future Blue Flame Alan Skidmore.

Wheeler, Deuchar and Hamer were joined on trumpet by Bert Courtley and Tony Fisher. Keith Christie's trombone parts complemented by Ken Goldie: Phew, what a band!

Stan Tracey provided piano parts, and as sessions had been running throughout those last one and a half years between late 1964 and early 1966, some of Georgie Fame's Blue Flames had been integrated as well: Colin Green on guitar; both Bill Eyden and Phil Seamen on drums; Phil Bates on bass. Colin: "It was a little bit intimidating with all those heavy Jazz guys there. But it was a great experience. Harry South was lovely, a lovely man. It was Harry who did all the arrangements."

Scanning the results of the Melody Maker Readers poll of 1966, published on 18th February, 1967, you realize that Georgie managed to hire the cream of the nation's Jazz talent for his hard-earned "Yeh Yeh" royalty money: Tubby Hayes was *Musician of the Year* and top performer on tenor sax, flute and vibes (he would achieve this again in the following year), Harry South was named best arranger, and Stan Tracey was prime composer and pianist, Phil Seamen again became the champion drummer. And Kenny Wheeler's time would come in 1968.

But as Georgie reminisced, these champions of sophistication weren't necessarily the coolest of cats when it came to covering new ground – even less likely if the guy calling the shots might have the stamina and the Sterling, but not (yet) the status:

44 years after the event, Fame still vividly recalls it all: "It was 1964. I was interested in trying to sing with a Big Band, and I was introduced to a British Jazz piano player and arranger called Harry South, who had his own Big Band, which maybe only played four times a year, but it contained all the best British Jazz musicians at the time. Yeah, Harry South.

"There was the saxophone player in my band, a very good baritone saxophone player, called Johnny Marshall. He had played with good British dance bands, Jazz bands, and he recommended Harry South to me, when I expressed the opinion that I would like to sing in a Jazz orchestra, because Jon Hendricks, one of my mentors, who did the lyrics to "Yeh Yeh" and also the first vocal recording of "Yeh Yeh", was a fantastic inspiration. I had heard him sing with the Count Basie Orchestra.

"So that was the direction I wanted to go. So I met Harry South. In fact I went to a Jazz club in London that still exist – a pub by the river [Thames] in Barnes called *The Bull's Head* – and Harry South was a member of the Dick Morrissey Quartet, which was one of the best British Jazz groups. Morrissey was a fantastic tenor saxophone player. I think they were playing with Jimmy Witherspoon.

"And I went on a bus and I met Harry South. I told him of my interest, and we agreed to do some things. Eventually we made a recording called *Sound Venture*. The recordings were started in 1964/65, and we did four tracks. Then I had to wait until "Yeh Yeh" was a hit and I had the money to pay for the rest of the recording.

"The album came out in 1966. It went in the Pop charts, because I was selling a lot of records at the time, and this was a Jazz album with a Big Band, and it went in the Pop charts, number five. And Elvis Costello has said publicly that it was one of the most important albums for him as a young person. So that was when I got interested singing with Big Bands."

One wonders whether Fame ever asked himself whether he could interest an audience in his new sojourn.

"I did tread a rather delicate path at that time, because of my interest in Jazz. When I started to sing with a Big Band, some of my traditional fans thought that I was deserting my Rhythm & Blues roots to move into Jazz, and some of the older Jazz fans thought I was too young to be on the same bandstand as the Jazz musicians. But if you look at all the great Jazz players, Clifford Brown played in a Rhythm & Blues band before he became the Jazz star that he was before he sadly died. And the band he played in, in Philadelphia, was called Chris Powell & The Blue Flames, and my real name is Clive Powell, and my band is The Blue Flames. So there is a coincidence.

"John Coltrane used to work the bar in Philadelphia, playing 'Booting-Doopah-Doopah-Doo' saxophone. Dizzy Gillespie played Rhythm & Blues, Sonny Rollins was inspired by Louis Jordan. Louis Jordan was Sonny Rollins's first influence as a saxophone player. All these great Jazz artists started with it – Rhythm & Blues is the mother of Jazz. So it is a natural progression. So these idiots in the Sixties were categorizing everything, and said 'You can only do this, you can't do that, and this!'

"There is a Harry South arrangement for a tune by James Brown, 'Papa's Got A Brand New Bag'. I insisted, because I was paying for this recording *Sound Venture*, which contained a lot of good Jazz tunes and a lot of material by Jon Hendricks, that we record "Papa's Got A Brand New Bag". And some of the musicians in the band at the time were not happy, playing this Rhythm & Blues, this Funk, because they were Jazz musicians. So I was treading a delicate path at the time. Now everybody is doing it. This is before these crossover bands, Jazz-Funk."

Sound Venture – track by track

Fame started off tenderly with "Many Happy Returns", his own catchy melody in a 6/8 rhythm, a romance for the wee hours in true Early Sinatra-style, taking turns with banks of horns and reeds, with saxophones taking care of the romance and trumpets adding drama.

"Down For The Count" lives up to its title, because here the young musical director really swings free and easy. And if he was shivering with nerves in front of all those hardened pros, this certain edge only adds to the overall impact of his rendition. It starts with the small combo, based on Colin Green's groovy chords, but soon the whole Big Band starts wailing in, leaving space for a bass line here and a drum break there. What a timeless, concentrated rendition.

"It's For Love The Petals Fall", which was also sung by Karla Bonoff, bows to another of Fame's strong qualities, the love of Latin styles. This slow Rumba evokes dreams of Cuban beaches, three decades before Ry Cooder could make the famous claim for this kind of style on his All-Star smashes of the *Buena Vista Social Club*.

"I Am Missing You" presents more lovesick thoughts, a slower Swing – still faster than anything on Frank Sinatra's *In The Wee Small Hours*, mind you – which Georgie again wrote himself, and really seemed to feel at home in. Contrary to what he sings about, he never misses his cue here!

Willie Nelson's "Funny How Time Slips Away" has stayed in the Flames sets for a long time. It is interesting to note how he rearranged it over the years. *Sound Venture* saw his second, much more elaborate "cinemascope" saxophone and stuffed trumpet heavy but very effective version developing from the first, smaller Blue Flames club band reading on *Sweet Things*. Some lines get spoken here, to great effect.

His own Seventies Blue Flames tackled the song for a third time 23 years after this lavish version: for the 1979 Pye album *Right Now!*, the brass and woodwind would be slightly rearranged, but Ray Warleigh is again on flute and sax, still stunning after all these years.

"Lil' Pony" shows what Fame had learnt from his mentor Jon Hendricks – it was on *Sing A Song For Basie* by Lambert, Hendricks & Ross – and from Jazz trumpeter and arranger Neil Hefti (1922–2008), the Nebraskan *Batman* composer. An early Charlie Barnet collaborator, he had delivered the sophisticated pony charts for Count Basie. Jon Hendricks had not only written the lyrics to "Yeh Yeh", but, along with Mike O'Neill, introduced Georgie to the pleasures of making up words himself where before a trumpet or sax solo had spoken to the listener. Just as Hendricks had served as the unofficial advisor for *Sound Venture*, Fame and producer Ben Sidran invited Hendricks into the studios for a re-recording a quarter of a century after this, included in Fame's 1991 Go Jazz album *Cool Cat Blues*. This breakneck speed reading has the benefit of an obvious joy of delving into a freshly detected art form – swinging damn fast and mastering the most sophisticated tongue twisters.

"Lovey Dovey", written by Memphis Edward "Eddie" Curtis jr. with Atlantic boss Ahmet Ertegun, presents some of Eddie's "advice" on how to pay compliments to women, wrapped in a relaxed Swing mood. The singer seems totally at ease as far as the audiences 'indoors' are concerned, not audibly in awe of the assembled studio talent that waited for cues and cash. Telling ladies you loved their peaches probably just about passed in the pre-women's lib days, but was rendered tongue in cheek anyway, whereas loving the way father slammed the back door may be timeless. (Another line from the song was quoted in Steve Miller's "The Joker", who gave Curtis a co-credit.)

The Clovers had a US R&B chart # 2 with this number, and Georgie was in further good company – he will surely have heard covers by Clyde McPhatter, Buddy Knox, Dick Dale and The Coasters. Subsequent readings came from the duet of Otis Redding and Carla Thomas, with Texan shouter Delbert McClinton following in 1976. Georgie had already been aware of Eddie Curtis via his other famous custom-made composition for Ray Charles, "It Should Have Been Me".

"Lil' Darling", like the Little Pony, came courtesy of composer and arranger Neil Hefti, and later Jon Hendricks again. This number also belonged to Hefti's custom-made Count Basie nuggets. The crucial difference to "Little Pony" is its slow reading, which has to be exactly right to achieve the suitable soothing effect. The Jon Hendricks penned lyric version was recorded by Lambert, Hendricks and Ross in 1958 – and Count Basie's orchestra was part of those sessions, too. The Blue Flames had already issued another version where Georgie's Hammond reigned instead of the bar piano, romantic reeds and big brass in action here.

With "Three Blind Mice", like on "Humpty Dumpty" before, our man proves that you can adapt childrens' songs to exotic rhythms – these mice made kids swing hard – and looked for mice – years before Fame got into BBC television programmes for youngsters with Alan Price. Inspiration for this treatment of the ancient nursery rhyme came via Nat King Cole and Lambert, Hendricks and Bavan, and there had been a Calypso version in the 1962 *James Bond Dr No* movie, delivered by Art Blakey & his Jazz Messengers, sung in a Jamaican accent not unlike Fame's own, with the mice roaming all over Kingston Town for a change.

Some crucial career history is drawn out for Georgie's own "Dawn Yawn". It succeeds in showing off all the bravado and hipness of the mid-1960s – reminiscing about leaving the Flamingo Club in Soho early in the morning, "the cats all high" when "today becomes tomorrow". Not a yawn is in sight when you groove along to this sophisticated tune. Georgie picked this song of his own pen to represent *Sound Venture* in his 1990 compilation *The First Thirty Years*, and it is indeed a gem.

Fame's Flamingo cohort Dick Heckstall-Smith, the sax player extraordinaire working in Alexis Korner's Blues Incorprated, the Graham Bond Organization and later for Georgie, was good company in one of those "dawn yawns", as he revealed in *Blowing The Blues*: "Blues Inc. did a lot of work round Christmas '62, but I was still doing a stint at the Flamingo whenever possible, followed by an all-nighter at the now defunct Roaring Twenties in Carnaby Street with Georgie Fame. It was a *long* long all-nighter, and afterwards Georgie and I set off back to my place at 11 Miranda Road, Archway, on one of the first tubes of Christmas Day. As we emerged from the Northern Line into the daylight, we found that it had been snowing – three or four inches of it. The world looked utterly magical: new, white and beautiful. Georgie and I were the first humans on a brand-new Earth; ours were the very first footsteps. And we were bound for *bed*, dog-tired and happy. As we turned the corner into Miranda Road, Georgie stopped and carefully wrote 'Merry Christmas' with his finger in the virgin whiteness on the rear window of a parked Volks. I wonder whose it was."

The energy level is held for more Swing time fun, with the dangerously speedy "Feed Me", leading into a finale which is also a kind of departure.

As is folklore now, American GIs had given Georgie some serious Bronx Funk by then, and Fame leads the Harry South Big Band through James Brown's "Papa's Got A Brand New Bag". Elvis Costello – in his *Mojo* essay about *Sound Venture* featured below in excerpts – may have complained of the brass section playing 'from the charts', i.e. in a formal way. But for this then 14-year-old author, as I recall well, the Fame version made more sense than Brown's, because it combined familiar Jazz elements with New Soul. He never went over the top, while still more than retaining all the necessary adrenalin.

Again, there was at least one other track recorded at the time which did not make it onto the album: "Funky Mama" by John Patton took shape around October/November

1966. With its prominence of the Hammond organ, guitar and brass, it was more in vein with the *Sweet Things* album, but while a great little tune, would have seemed out of place on the Big Band LP, and didn't really suit the next LP in 1967 either.

The record shot into the British album Top Ten, peaking at No. 5 and making the album Georgie Fame's best seller of all time after its predecessor *Sweet Things*. Not a bad feat for a 22-year old, acting thoughtful and bold at a period in his life when most of his generation had not even left university. Georgie, though, had passed his master's degree with flying colours via the release of *Sound Venture*. It presented a tremendous achievement which stands tall to this day.

Few have put praise for *Sweet Things* and disdain for *Sound Venture* in more direct terms than George Melly. Again in *Revolt Into Style*, he compares Fame's Soul and Jazz leanings like this: "The fashions ebbed and flowed. Straight R and B didn't last long. 'Soul' supplanted it, but the trouble with Soul was that whereas it seemed to come naturally to American Negroes, it was very difficult to make it sound convincing if you were white and British. Georgie Fame got close to it for a time but, faced with popularity, withdrew into a rather pretentious Jazz-inflected shell that pleased nobody."

In complete contrast to Melly's misery, the already mentioned Costello, then a young 12-year-old boy by the name of Declan MacManus, and the son of lounge singer Ross MacManus – who had a hit with "Hey, Patsy Girl" in 1966 – learnt to love Georgie Fame in general and *Sound Venture* in particular, as he pointed out in an article for *Mojo* magazine "Last Year A Record Changed My Life":

"In 1966, I was twelve and already a big Georgie Fame fan. I'd got 'Yeh Yeh' and 'Getaway' and 'In The Meantime' and I loved the *Fame At Last* EP. I saved up for a few weeks to buy *Sound Venture*. I went to this store in Richmond to buy it - the same place I bought my first guitar. It was such a hip record. Apart from anything else it had such a great title! And Georgie plays killer organ. I'd been used to the sound of the big band but this was different. There was no strict dance tempo and it wasn't smooth like Joe Loss - this was a swinging band and the line-up was a who's who of the jazz scene."

Costello reminisced that the album had a tremendous influence on him because the numbers covered such a wide range of styles from Willie Nelson to James Brown. He credits Georgie as one of the first Rhythm & Blues guys in Britain to have featured Brown. Young Elvis contrasts Fame's impeccable taste with "Brian Matthew four hours a week on the radio", but then puts the Brown-thing in perspective, not liking "Papa's Got A Brand New Bag" too much because "it sounds really clunky, like they're reading it off a chart, not like James Brown's horn prayers at all."

The former Declan McManus also has praise for Fame's own numbers: the melodic "Many Happy Returns", the All-nighters hangover "Dawn Yawn" and the ballad sensitivities of "Lil' Darlin", not forgetting "Three Blind Mice" which was on Lambert, Hendrix & Bavan live album. He praises Fame's voice as "very smooth with no vibrato, like a tenor sax, a lovely sound. Apart from Zoot Money, nobody else in this country was doing what Georgie was doing. I saw him on TV recently at the Montreux Jazz Festival and a lot of those songs were still in his set."

"I know every note on that record and every detail about it. Dave Redfern took the photos, Chris Welch wrote the sleeve notes and I could even tell you where the sleeve was printed!...Costello observes quite correctly that Georgie Fame never really got his due respect in the Sixties history books and films, a notion he shares with Bill Wyman, and he puts it down to featuring guitars for rhythm rather than axe hero material, remembering a Flames performance with Joe Loss and his father where he forgot to mention to Georgie the impact *Sound Venture* had on him.

Well, he might have "in the meantime" while inviting Georgie and the Blue Flames to the Royal Albert Hall for the Blues Fest of October 2014.

"I've still got my original copy of *Sound Venture*. When I was a young man short of money I sold most of my records, including my Small Faces singles, but I kept *Sgt Pepper*, *Revolver* - and *Sound Venture*. I couldn't sell it and I still play it. I have jags of playing vinyl and it still sounds good. I'm on a crusade to get it reissued..."

Fame was proud – he relished the first-rate Jazz musicians on his ongoing album production *Sound Venture*. And in a famous move, he was able to help out an even more famous fellow when the need for a great brass section arose. Paul McCartney had given his great Soul composition "Got To Get You Into My Life" to the hard working Rhythm & Blues as well as Soul act Cliff Bennett & The Rebel Rousers, whom he knew from mutual Hamburg days in the Star-Club. Now McCartney wanted to cut a version with the Beatles, as an ingredient for their work in progress, *Revolver*, and how could they top the Rebel Rousers' rousing performance? They needed a Jazz horn section!

Fame was able to help because parallel to the recording of his band album *Sweet Things*, he was busy completing *Sound Venture*.

According to the scholarly Beatles-track-by-track analysis *Revolution In The Head* by Ian MacDonald, Paul McCartney had spotted Georgie in the "Bag O'Nails" night club in Soho's Kingly Street on a night out with Jane Asher on the 6th April 1966. Fame picks up the story: "Paul McCartney called me and said to me 'Georgie, you know some Jazz musicians, don't you?!' I said 'Yeah'. 'Can you get me four – couple of saxophones and two trumpet players, and send them to Abbey Road tomorrow?' I said 'You want Jazz musicians?' He said 'Yeah'. So I called Ronnie Scott. And it was Ronnie on saxophone, Alan Branscombe on the saxophone [according to this author's sources also Peter Coe], Ian Hamer on trumpet, and my own Jamaican trumpet player Eddie Thornton. I went round to the (Abbey Road) studio, and they were doing 'Got To Get You Into My Life', and I think they also played 'Lady Madonna'". Actually, on that Fab Four tribute to Fame's first hero Fats Domino, Ronnie Scott and Bill Povey served on tenor saxes, while Harry Klein and Bill Jackman were on baritone saxes, in February 1968, according to MacDonald. Fame again: "I walked in just to see if it was okay, if he was happy with the Jazz musicians that I got him."

So there it was, the third and final studio album for EMI-Columbia, *Sound Venture*. Neither that Big Band treasure nor the more band-orientated albums *Fame At Last* and *Sweet Things* have ever been officially re-released in any format, while *Rhythm & Blues At The Flamingo* at least re-appeared on vinyl in 1983. That left Eastern European bootleggers to do the job for them. They will not be named here, but suffice to say that Georgie is sure that he was paid royalties by them from time to time down the line. What he has to say on the matter, he revealed to Duncan Heining:

"Look at the sleeve. It [*Sound Venture*] was a Rik Gunnell production and Rik was smart and hung on to the rights to all those recordings. I should own them – he used my money.

"Rik was a funny guy. He bought me a silver Jaguar for my birthday in 1965. I woke up on the 26th June and outside the flat was this brand new S type Jaguar. 'Happy Birthday, son'. Of course, it was my money he was using. It didn't come out of his pocket (laughing). But that's part and parcel of the thing."

The Blue Flames 1964 in happier times, from the left Eddie Thornton, Speedy Acquaye, Red Reece, G. F. biting the hi-hat, Mick Eve, Tex Makins

Chapter 3

Going Solo –
The CBS Jazz & Lounge Years

Only days after playing his last gig with The Blue Flames in Amsterdam, Holland on October 1st, 1966 Fame would put his Big Band activities on tour with ten quickly hired seasoned studio cats, many of them from the Harry South sessions, covering sixteen concerts all over the United Kingdom for the promotion of his album *Sound Venture* before nostalgia for the Flamingo Flames could set in.

But in his parallel universe, the artist born as Clive Powell also prepared to assemble his personal musicians – to go on tour as his new Georgie Fame Band. Almost visibly reneging on his decision to disband the celebrated Flamingo Club combo, he found yet another outfit of similar proportions and personnel, albeit without using the legendary Blue Flames moniker.

Fame surely remembered that when he disbanded the Flames, there was an overall sigh of regret by his musicians and followers alike, although a lot of fans certainly must have appreciated his ambitious Big Band plans as well. What had changed?

Apparently, nothing much, apart from a severe "attitude": a massive million pound sterling chip on manager Rik Gunnell's shoulder. Georgie remembered the autumn of the big changes 18 years later, reminiscing in 1994: "At that time – it was certainly after 'Get Away' and before 'The Ballad of Bonnie and Clyde'. I think it was the end of 1966, maybe beginning of '67 [September 1966 actually]. Mitch Mitchell was the drummer at the time, I remember – anyway, at that time, my manager was building up his business, because he had the best agency for Rhythm & Blues bands in London. All the bands in the agency were working all the time.

"And *then* he decided he wanted to become an executive, and that's why he didn't want the band, because the personnel was always changing, all the time. It was difficult to keep it together but it was good. So I said okay, and he negotiated a new contract with CBS Records, which meant I became more of a solo artist, which was a good experience for me." But why immediately start another six-piece band? And why not call it The Blue Flames again?

Georgie: "Because I missed the band, and I wanted a band! And it was my manager's idea to break up the band, because he thought *he* could make more money, if we didn't have to keep paying the band and if I became more of a solo artist." Of course, he was still talking about Rik Gunnell of Flamingo fame.

"So I said 'I want my own band. I want to put the band together again, 'cause I'm just part of a band and I want to play with them'. But then he said – I don't know how these executive type people who don't play anything justify their existence; they always think they have to come up with these ideas – he said 'Well, don't call it "The Blue Flames", because it's not "The Blue Flames"!' – 'But', I said, 'we're going to play Blue Flames music!' But he said 'If you call it The Blue Flames, everybody will think it's just an old band, and times are changing'. This bullshit! So it just became Georgie Fame & his Band. Jon Hiseman was on drums [later in the year] in that band we're talking about."

Trumpeter Eddie "Tan Tan" Thornton was again part of the Georgie Fame Band procedures, while he was also busy recording with The Small Faces at the Olympic Studios in Barnes, with *R&B at the Flamingo* engineer Glyn Johns at the knobs.

In 2014, Georgie's Hammond organ pal Ian "Mac" McLagan remembers with a huge grin how Tan Tan's famous stutter arose – especially when he had had a few ganja tokes with Speedy Acquaye, who he used to bring along for smoking:

"Ronnie Lane wrote 'Eddie's Dreaming' as a tribute to trumpeter Eddie 'Tan Tan' Thornton. He played with Georgie Fame, and he had a stutter. In the studio with us, he was a little high, and when the horns were recorded, he rambled on, but couldn't get anything out: 'I g-g-got to t-t-tell ya …!' We left all that on the tapes, but over the years, the engineers had cut that out. It killed the joke, 'Eddie's Dreaming', and now [with the 2014 remix for the *Here Come The Nice* box], Eddie's stutter is on one of the two versions. I met Eddie recently when he played in Japan with Billy Bragg. He always wanted the Small Faces to eat enough healthy spinach. These days I actually do that.

Tan Tan was joined by baritone saxophonist Johnny Marshall and bass player Rik Brown. Red Reece almost immediately re-joined; then another Blue Flame drummer took over – Hughie Flint, who after his Blue Flames stint had been with fellow Flamingo colleague John Mayall's Bluesbreakers, and had featured on their renowned *Bluesbreakers with Eric Clapton* LP, the legendary "Beano" album, together with future Blue Flame Alan Skidmore. We will come to his story presently. All this meant, of course, was that line-up changes continued to happen just like they had before in the Flames – but now only his name would be up there, so it seemed of less consequence.

Even for his "small" band, Fame opted for two further brass and woodwind players in trombonist Derek Wadsworth plus tenor sax blower and flute player Lyn Dobson. Yorkshire man Wadsworth, a partner from up north (1939–2008) had worked for Dusty Springfield, was soon to work for the Rolling Stones in the studio on *Their Satanaic Majesty's Request*, and went on to work with Jon Hiseman's Jazz-Rockers Colosseum and Neil Ardley as well as Cat Stevens and Alan Price (for his *Between Today And Yesterday* and the soundtrack of *Alfie Darling* 1975), surely a gigantic find for Georgie.

Lyn Dobson, a colleague of Tan Tan during the Small Faces sessions, had played the famous flute solo in Manfred Mann's "Pretty Flamingo", and apart from work with Georgie, he would get claims to fame in the Keef Hartley Band and Jazzrock pioneers Soft Machine.

Just like the famous and unforgotten Blue Flames before them, the Georgie Fame Band were ready by December 7th – the previous November 12th deadline had proved too hectic – and they played yet another twice nightly Package Tour featuring the Gunnell brothers' stable mates Chris Farlowe & The Thunderbirds as well as The Animals.

For Fame, the ambivalence about "growing" as a solo artist instead of keeping with the success formula of his non-stop-partying Blue Flames was certainly understandable. He thrived on the bandstand, a star in an all-star band. But at the same time, *Sound Venture* had shown that he could elegantly step into the limelight, leave the Hammond organ aside for a moment, and become the focus, sure of himself – quite rightly so – and leading his audience to pastures new. The theory that Georgie became stilted with ballad material and pop could never be held true. Over those legendary Flamingo years he had become much too versatile and thoroughly experienced to be type-cast as a swinging party clown. His own ballads would prove this too, much later in his career.

"Point Of No Return" – Columbia cash in on Fame's CBS headlines

In December 1966, Georgie's last Columbia single "Sitting In The Park" had rushed to Number 12 in the UK charts, months after he had left the label. This was followed by the label's only to be expected Greatest Hits collection, *Hall Of Fame*, although a dozen hits had not really been forthcoming. (In a similar move, Decca Records had released the Small Faces' *From The Beginning* LP at the same time, because those young Flamingo Club devotees and Mod contenders had by then moved to Andrew Loog Oldham's Immediate label.)

Hall Of Fame consisted of eight A-sides that had charted, including of course "Yeh Yeh", "Getaway", "Sunny" and "Sitting In The Park". John Mayall's "Something" appeared with its B-side, Booker T's "Outrage". That left five album tracks, with only one each from *Sweet Things* (the title track) and *Sound Venture* ("Lil' Darling"), but three from *Fame At Last*: "Get On The Right Track, Baby", "Point Of No Return" and "Let The Sunshine In". The *Hall Of Fame* – contrary to Fame's last two studio albums, charted just outside the Top 10 at number 12, but stayed in the charts for an impressive eighteen weeks.

A look at the composers' credits on *Hall Of Fame* showed that just two out of 14 tracks were Fame creations, Powell products. The remaining dozen was well chosen, but certainly in the Pop world, the Beatles, Hollies, Kinks, Donovan & Dylan had just presented completely self-written albums. Georgie saw it quite differently for his circles, looking back in 2009, and he has a point, too:

"We were all doing covers – we were covering the originals from America. The reason that my version of "Sunny" was a hit – when was that, 1967? [That's when *Hall Of Fame* came out] 1966? [That's when the single was released] – was because we heard the Bobby Hebb version, the original version, and we recorded it before his version came out, was released in England. That's the way the procedure was in those days.

"My producer at the time, Denny Cordell, who had immaculate taste in music – he used to listen to great Chicago Soul singers including Billy Stewart, Little Milton, all those guys. And we did dig their records, and we do. We were still learning our trade, and we needed the source to help us to develop.

"The reason the Beatles, Lennon and McCartney started to write their own original material based on the original music that they heard in America. And if you listen to the early Beatles records, and the Rolling Stones' records, there's a lot of covers of original American artists. It's like I said before, you have to start somewhere. You can't just wake up and be a genius, an original genius. You have to have the inspiration from somewhere. And if you're lucky and talented enough, then the original influences that you have, like in my case, of people like Mose Allison, Fats Domino and Jerry Lee Lewis, Ray Charles, Chet Baker, Jon Hendricks, King Pleasure and great Jazz instrumentalists. My sound and my attitude and my approach to performing and creating is a mixture of all those influences."

Also in December 1966, Georgie could be seen previewing his show "Fame In '67" in London's Brian Epstein owned "Saville Theatre". As support acts for "Fame in '67", Beatles manager Epstein booked Folk lady Julie Felix and a personally-invited young contender – Cat Stevens. The talented song smith, soon-to-be categorized in a new breed of 'singer-songwriters', had just charted with "I Love My Dog", a release whose impact Fame confirmed in the press: "I rather like that Cat Stevens thing. The words don't mean much, but it's good as a record. If this guy is handled carefully, he'll have a bigger hit still next time." "Fame in '67" ran successfully until the end of January, 1967.

The Columbia hits notwithstanding, Fame was now a CBS artist, and represented his new "major label" in February at the MIDEM Convention in Cannes on the French Riviera. The sojourn continued with both a concert and a TV Special in Paris.

Sound Venture continued to stay in the charts in 1967 and became the tenth best-selling UK Jazz LP of that year, and Georgie then took the complete Harry South Orchestra to London's Royal Festival Hall. This would make up one half of Georgie's follow-up album; but before that, it was time for some singles.

"Knock On Wood" – The solo deal which allowed Pop and R&B

If CBS Records saw Georgie Fame as an "English Andy Williams", as Fame claimed, they certainly acted accordingly by giving him a qualified welcome to underline that status. Apart from the hefty advance that Fame mentioned, they expressed quite a lot of respect by giving his single releases a special emblem – a custom-made logo displaying "Fame In '67 On CBS". Collectors can spot that feature on his hits "Because I Love You" and, of course, later on "The Ballad of Bonnie and Clyde". Also, listening to Fame's last two, pre

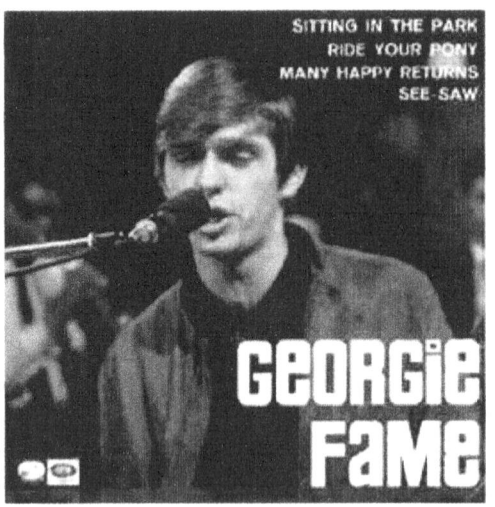

solo career singles on EMI-Columbia, "Sunny" and "Sitting In The Park", the suggestion that these can also be seen as Andy Williams territory more than Blues or Soul isn't a million miles off the mark.

The CBS contract gained momentum at last with their first release in March 1967, parallel to Columbia's "Sitting In The Park" which was still selling well. They surely made Georgie hit #15 in the charts, a respectable Top 20 placing, with two of his own numbers, "Because I Love You", a catchy love song that made proficient use of his brass section, and the wonderfully laconic "Bidin' My Time ('Cos I Love You)" on the flipside, which would have done the Blue Flames line-up proud. So Fame was given free reign with his compositions. And he seemed to wear the crooner tag quite well, which means successfully, but not harmonically; he was having his doubts with the A-side: "I like the tune, but the performance wasn't great. We were going to re-record it two weeks after the original session with added tuba and vibes, but CBS was in a hurry to release it. After all, I had been with them for three months without putting out a record."

The "we" implied Georgie's always full-on and successful cooperation with producer Denny Cordell (1943–1995), who also worked with The Moody Blues and Joe Cocker and was just enjoying a world-wide hit with Procol Harum's "A Whiter Shade Of Pale", "borrowing" Blue Flames ex-drummer Bill Eyden for that studio recording – a fact Georgie still frequently makes fun of whenever he applies the "Pale" intro to his Hammond because the drum pattern is ever so simple, especially for a player regularly faced with the demands of Jazz.

But for the next single, here was the crunch: if the CBS men in suits had really stuck to the easy-going crooner tag entirely, how come Georgie Fame was allowed to experiment with R&B singles in other territories? ("Markets" would mean applying a term certainly not used as nonchalantly then as it is today). Fame recorded the Stax Soul classic "Knock

On Wood", which he would later share with original shouter Eddie Floyd on a joint European tour as members of Bill Wyman's Rhythm Kings, watching Floyd permanently under headphones, busy listening to world-wide covers of – you got it – "Knock On Wood"!

He coupled the Stax Soul classic with a lovely composition by the Lovin' Spoonful's John Sebastian, "Didn't Want To Have To Do It", which received some airplay as a UK promo single, suiting Georgie's laconic style to a T, as if it had been custom-made for him by the New Yorker bard and songwriter.

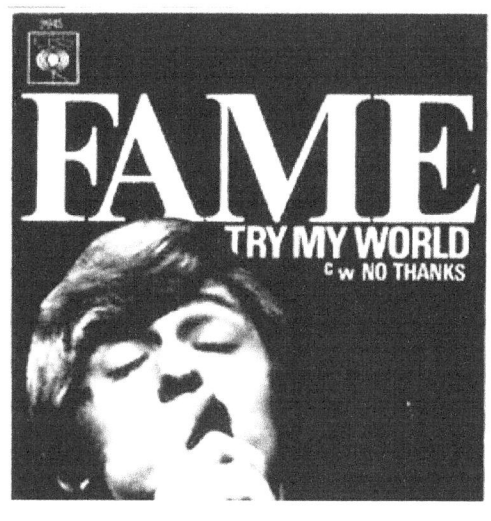

Fame was able to secure proper releases by coupling "Knock On Wood" with another Soul hit, this time from the Motown stable, in Junior Walker's "Roadrunner". While there was no official British single release in England, *Knock On Wood* would also headline the last ever EP Fame knocked out, hitting a fantastic #2 in the listings. So, in spite of this sensational success, CBS, like many other major labels, didn't see any future in that format, which continued to thrive in France.

Georgie then released a single whose weird combination caused widespread, if mild amusement, not because these good songs had comedy character or were inadequate, but because the pairing of the titles had such a funny effect:

"Try My World" – "No Thanks". It sounded as if the flipside was meant as a rather rude reaction to the main number. Taken on their own, both songs were fine compositions and performances, but Georgie explained the pairing well when he performed the flip side "No Thanks" during a stint at the "Gyllene Cirkeln" Club in Stockholm in late 1967, which was shown on TV: "This one was originally the B-side of a single I released not so long ago, and it was an enormous flop. The A-side was called "Try My World" and the B-side didn't have a title. But it was such a contrast from the A-side we just called it "No Thanks".

"Try My World" had been written by Fame with the renowned New York poet and performer Fran Landesman (1927–2011), who had been born Frances Deitsch and enjoyed the early "Beat" scene in New York's bohemian Greenwich Village. There, she met and married Jay Landesman, the editor of the trendy magazine *Neurotica* which featured Beat legends like Jack "On The Road" Kerouac and the notorious Allen Ginsberg.

Fran Landesman had started writing lyrics inspired by the "Crystal Bar" which her husband and her brother-in-law had opened in St. Louis, Missouri, and she had worked with Bob Dorough, the American Bebop and Cool Jazz pianist, composer and Vocalese singer. Dorough had lived in Paris from 1954 to 1955, recording with Georgie Fame adoring vocalist Blossom Dearie during that time. He returned to the United States and released his first album, *Devil May Care*, in 1956. (The title song "Devil May Care" was covered by many artists, including Jamie Cullum). The LP contained a version of "Yardbird Suite" with lyrics by Dorough over the famous Charlie Parker song.

Fran christened one of her sons Miles Davis, so where's the connection? Miles liked the album, so when Columbia asked Miles to record a Christmas song in 1962, Davis asked the Fran Landesman-inspired Dorough for lyrics and singing duties. The result was a downbeat tune called "Blue Xmas," released on Columbia's Jingle Bell Jazz compilation. Dorough also deserves a credit because he wrote the Georgie Fame stage number "Comin' Home Baby" with his bassist friend Ben Tucker. It was a Top 40 hit for Mel Tormé in 1962, earning Tormé two Grammy nominations.

Anyway, Fran Landesman and her husband Jay moved to London in 1964 to work with several musicians, including Dudley Moore and Georgie.

The song "Try My World" itself is an easy flowing, dreamy affair set with attractive harp, piano and trumpet touches, the Hammond and guitar nicely assisting the bass & drums engine room. The subdued guitar is supplied by Georgie's old Flamingo Blue Flame, John McLaughlin, who also stayed for the B-side.

The Rhythm & Blues number "No Thanks" was written with Tony Colton, who had supplied "Red Number 9" for Georgie with Ray Smith and was soon to form Heads, Hands & Feet with Albert Lee from Chris Farlowe's Thunderbirds. The single reached a rather mild #29 placing on the UK charts, and the question whether – again – the Blue Flames type B-side should have headlined is beside the point. Plenty of airplay would have enabled the audience to choose.

Listening to Georgie's Top 20 hit "Because I Love You", his No. 2 EP "Knock On Wood" and his up-coming *The Two Faces Of Fame* album, fans would see a real star on all fronts. But they could also ask "Is he Pop, is he Soul or is he Jazz"? Fame had the answer for *Melody Maker* Magazine: "I feel a closer affinity to Jazz than Pop – as Pop. The Pop side of Jazz is Rhythm & Blues. But Pop also has its own thing, such as The Beatles' songs. They have taken Pop about as far as Charlie Parker took Jazz. On the Rhythm & Blues scene, though, there is a natural transition from Pop to Jazz. I think people somehow resent musicians who start out in Jazz and then come back to Pop. I have done it the other way round. I'm heading towards Jazz and this is probably the reason that people accept me, it's a natural growth."

Fame was also heading for Brazil, again as a kind of ambassador of Pop, but on the Copacabana, this is as near to Latin Jazz as you can get. At the "Rio de Janeiro Song Festival", he sang "Celebration", a real beach number with a lively brass section and an unforgettable chorus line. It was here that he first made the acquaintance of Swedish Pop and Jazz singer Sylvia Vrethammar.

"Celebration" was composed by the "Puppet On A String" hit creators Bill Martin and Phil Coulter, and got issued as a single in 1967 in Brazil, with "Try My World" as the B-side. It was also included in the Argentinean Georgie Fame LP *La Balada de Bonnie & Clyde* (CBS 8851). "Celebration" seemed custom-made for a Latin song contest, and that could have been the reason why it was never issued outside Latin America.

More Jazz in Sound Venture mode – The Two Faces Of Fame

Soon, it was time, in early 1967, to produce a follow-up to the runaway Big Band album success with EMI-Columbia, *Sound Venture*. It seemed that in a diplomatic move, Fame was given the chance to show that both of his chosen sojourns, the club compatible quintet or sextet, and the Big Band, were valuable paths to follow, whether it was live or in the studio. The fact was, though, that for *The Two Faces Of Fame*, the recordings of the live show had just not been good enough to meet the CBS standards of High Fidelity, and neither did they please Fame much, and so he duly filled the gaps:

For most of the studio side of his two-faced new album, Georgie chose an entirely different quartet: there was saxophonist Peter King – not to be confused with the equally sax-blowing but eleven years older Pete King who ran Ronnie Scott's Jazz Club together with its founder and owner; Gordon Beck appeared on piano; Jeff Clyne was on bass; and Tony Oxley served on drums (Tony for some reason gets called "Terry" on the sleeve). In one of the episodes of his own radio programme series for BBC 2, Georgie invited Peter King and reminisced: "I first met you in one of the old Marquee Clubs. I think the one on Oxford Street, in the early Sixties."

Peter King "had started out on alto saxophone in 1957, but then switched to tenor sax in 1963 to get away from the "Bird" [Charlie Parker] influence, and then changed back to the alto at the end of the Sixties, playing both instruments for a while." This swap of instruments explains Georgie's surprise when it came to their mutual LP sessions in 1967:

"The first recordings that we did together were some extra tracks that we needed because for the album that we planned at the Royal Festival Hall, the sound recording was so bad. So we had to do some extra tracks and I called you up, and I thought you were going to turn up with an alto, but you walked in with a tenor." Anyway, the recording that ensued was atmospheric and high calibre.

The Two Faces Of Fame succeeded as intended – a collection which truly showed Georgie's "two ends of the market": One side presenting Fame with the Blue Flames-like Georgie Fame Band and then with The Harry South Big Band; one side conceived with a little Jazz studio combo put together especially for the occasion. Again, if you look at the *Melody Maker* Readers' Poll for 1967, published on February 24th, 1968, Georgie was able to grab a lot of the champions for this venture following *Sound Venture*: Tubby Hayes, like the previous year, was named in four categories – as musician of the year and top player in the sections flute, tenor sax and vibes. Tony Coe was second on clarinet, fourth on tenor sax and sixth on the alto, Jeff Clyne was double bass governour, Harry South was top Big Band personality – and if Ronnie Scott didn't score so much that year, he had won in many of the MM lists all through the 1950s, so what the hell.

But you could read Fame's double vision, his "two faces", in a different way on top of the three line-ups, as the concert and studio creation aspects of his work: The first six tracks – the A-side of the vinyl record – were cut live in the Royal Festival Hall on the 18th March, 1967, with the complete show documented as a colour film by a BBC television crew for a future screening – whereas the remaining five numbers on the flip side had been laid down in London's CBS studios. The album was produced again by Denny Cordell, with whom Fame had gelled so very well during the making of Sweet Things, and who had shared production credits on Sound Venture.

The LP was housed in a "split screen" sleeve that showed Georgie in a light blue pin-striped suit for the Royal Festival Hall and in a light brown roll-neck sweater and matching leather jacket for club dates, based on photographs that were created by the renowned Dezo Hoffman. (For "pic spotters": The chess pattern in the background of the leather jacket portrait proves that another photo from the series was used for Georgie's Starline budget release *Fame Again!*).

The Two Faces of Fame came out in July 1967 and quickly managed a UK chart placing of #22, staying in the listings for fifteen weeks.

The Two Faces Of Fame – track by track

For "Greenback Dollar Bill" – an old Louis Prima showcase by Reynold Richards – Georgie's Hammond organ was back for a swing exercise in Ray Charles style, not unlike "It Should Have Been Me", featuring Johnny Scott on "congo drums" (as it was put on the back sleeve). It was the congas of course, whose integral sound had been supplied for years by Jamaican rhythm ace Niimoi "Speedy" Acquaye. The African drums nicely offset the finger-snipping rhythm supplied by Brown & Flint, the brass section's lines and accents perfectly rendering this old-school Flamingo Fame, with the man himself not only singing well but also squeaking in falsetto! So all the ingredients are intact, but this still feels a bit like taking a freaky fringe play to the palladium. Soho sounds don't sound the same in an open-university course, do they?

"Things Ain't What They Used To Be" by Ellington & Persons still swings, but in a comparatively slow, easy, relaxed mood, with Georgie's trademark cat miaowing appearing in between (yes, he already did that in those days), but it could never distract him from some serious organ wailing, which in turn, the horn cats take up and converse with adequately. After the last lines of Rik Brown's bass, Georgie states in his on-stage banter that "Things ain't what they used to be – I'm not. There are several more faces of Fame, but I'm not likely to show them in public."

"River's Invitation", written by Percy Mayfield, a kind of smooth Rhythm & Blues artist favoured by Ray Charles for his composition "Hit The Road Jack", is a straight shuffle, again, with typical conga off-beats, for which Fame abandons the organ for some guitar work, which he once debuted for "Get Away". The number is over too soon, there is a feeling that groove could have gone on for several minutes.

In Milt Jackson and John Lewis's "Bluesology", it is Big Band time after just three small group snippets, and before you can marvel at the wonderful Harry South musicians, Georgie presents us with a prime example of his sophisticated Vocalese, which he learnt from his favourite New York trio, Lambert, Hendricks & Ross, albeit at a fairly easy-going speed. He had created the vocals together with Mike O'Neill, but these would only be credited on later albums, like *Live At Montreux Jazz Festival* with the Hudik Big Band.

Effortlessly wailing, the one-time Blue Flames members Eddie Thornton, Johnny Marshall, Tony Coe and Lyn Dobson are joined by more *Sound Venture* horns: Ronnie Scott, Tubby Hayes and Dick Morrissey on tenors, plus Harry Klein on baritone sax, Alan Branscombe on alto sax, Keith Christie, Chris Smith and Gib Wallace on trombones, trumpeters Greg Bowen, Ian Hamer, Kenny Wheeler, Les Condon and Derek Watkins – all of them household names in British Jazz. Big Band bass was provided by Phil Bates, who, with Lyn Dobson, and Jon Hiseman on drums, presented "Bluesology" at a much faster pace during a Jazz Festival in Prague later that year.

In "Don't Try" by Shakespeare & Salmon, "Don't try claiming insurance on your heart" was certainly not Georgie's whole comment. But this remains all the listener is getting on disc before this slow Swing starts. It is about the tongue in cheek wisdom of never taking your loving partner for granted. She (or he) may be in danger of going with somebody else. After the tongue twister of "Bluesology", Georgie is back at the Hammond organ, doing his beloved bit of letting the chords wail for a long time.

"Keep Your Big Mouth Shut" was provided by Fame's friend Jon Hendricks, and it is a humorous re-write of Willie Dixon's Swing "It Should Have Been Me", mentioning an old Blue Flames drummer:

"One day as I was lounging with me feet above the floor, I spied Phil Seamen, knocking at my door", using anecdotes about keeping secrets, name-checking "Miles" and a "free-loading" Zoot Money in for a drink which has Fame hide his gin bottle before feigning joy in seeing the fellow aficionado and inviting him in, or causing a punch-up on the dance floor due to playing the prime party animal. The brass accents are a treat again here. Instead of using Georgie's new road group and the Harry South Big Band for an entire concert LP, this is all they could salvage from the Royal Festival Hall apparently.

"You're Driving Me Crazy" is a 1930 Musical comedy composition for the film *Smiles* created by Walter Donaldson. Apart from Guy Lombardo, Rudy Valée & His Connecticut Yankees as well as Louis Armstrong, long-time Fame champions like Peggy Lee and Chet Baker recorded the song, and there is even a sexy cartoon version from 1931 featuring the world famous Betty Boop. The outrageous Temperance Seven had a number 1 hit with this in 1961, produced by George Martin. Hughie Flint's clever but still relaxed drum fills lead into another Vocalese Swing, which was really set to become Georgie Fame's art form of choice. Using lyrics for Chet Baker's solo written by his friend Mike O'Neill, Georgie would later "follow his lead" and write his own poetry for Chet's trumpet passages. With Lyn Dobson taking over for some great tenor work, followed by a stunning piano solo by Gordon Beck. Georgie would revisit this song on *Portrait of Chet* all of 22 years later.

"C'est La Vie" by E.R. White and Maxwell Wolfson had been made popular by US jazz singer Dick Haymes. It clearly shows that late night bar music has always been one of Fame's strengths. This presents a lament on the detours and mysteries of who loves who during the "wee small hours" way past midnight. It leaves the main work to Jeff Clyne's cleverly meandering bass, but the icing on the cake becomes Peter King's melancholic tenor sax. Georgie's phrasing, once the singer takes over again, remains immaculate.

For "El Pussycat", written by arranger, composer and flute as well as sax player Bobby Capers, Georgie Fame is back at his Hammond, presenting the only studio track supplied by his new Georgie Fame Band. The quintet is joined by Johnny Scott on congas again for one of those typical Sixties style dance instrumentals which you will invariably find on Mod compilations like the *Hammond Heroes* series. This was ample proof that the old chestnuts for a Flamingo Club comeback were still intact.

"It Could Happen To You", composed by Jimmy Van Heusen and written by Johnny Burke, is the second song in a trilogy of life-long favourites. A 1944 standard first presented by Dorothy Lamour in the Paramount Musical movie *And The Angels Sing*, had been interpreted by, amongst others, Nat King Cole. Chet Baker even called his 1958 Riverside album *It Could Happen To You*. Georgie included a new arrangement of it on *Portrait of Chet* in 1989, using the same Vocalese lyric for Baker's trumpet solo by Mike O'Neill which he applies here. It is one of those numbers that can easily become cheesy in the larynxes of lesser mortals and but is handled here with care and ease from ballad to swing sections, with an admirable knack for not just sounding sweet, but also a slight bit hurt in the process, Beck, King, Clyne & Oxley assisting with due subtlety.

It is interesting to note that on this studio recording, Georgie was just as meticulous in pronouncing the end consonant "t" in 1967 as he was in 2012 when he re-recorded the song once again for *Lost In A Lover's Dream*".

In the Richard Rogers & Lorenz Hart number "Do It The Hard Way" from the same Chet Baker album, things lighten up for more fast Swing with the quartet and another Vocalese performance of O'Neill's lyrics makes a welcome return: clever sequencing assuring that this particular Fame strength does not get into the dangerous waters of sounding contrived or academic. The rhythm section is really cooking here, setting the perfect foil for Peter King and Gordon Beck. They are once again displaying their endless creativity on their respective instruments, the tenor sax and the piano. This completes a trio of songs re-shuffled in 1989 for *Portrait of Chet*.

It is interesting to note that three of Georgie's studio choices were numbers that were to remain with the man for much of his career, interpreted in Big Band situations, as well as being ever more perfected in all sorts of different settings, whether it was a small studio in the Netherlands or a prestige recording in New York City. Delivering the perfect reading of a composition is what many producers thrive for in literally "cutting" a rendition from as many takes as were physically possible for their client. Jazz doesn't work like that, and Georgie Fame certainly doesn't work that way.

His renditions are note-perfect, sensitively felt and carefully arranged each and every single time. That does not mean he won't try and get a subtly different angle, a completely fresh arrangement or a slight change in singing a tune. With a voice that doesn't just refuse to age but gets even better with the passing of years, multiple versions never seem to imply a man lacking in material –tremendous choices always being available – but, rather, bear witness to the welcome tradition of keeping a song alive. Should there remain some difficulties in deciding on the "really definite reading" then be that as it may. You don't have to decide, ever; but if you did, you could well come to a different conclusion every time that you decide to give the man's music your attention.

"Fame? Who's Fame?" – The Count Basie Connection

Taking the complete Harry South Big Band into the Royal Festival Hall was now well documented on the album, and "that led directly really to the tour with Basie". Basie, of course, was none other than that great American Jazz legend they all called the "Count" – William Allen Basie from New Jersey, leader of The Count Basie Orchestra, then 64. Fame: "I thought that I could cover both ends of the market. So we sent the album (not *Two Faces of Fame* yet, but *Sound Venture*) to Basie's manager, and they liked the idea, so we did a tour".

The Count and his agent certainly loved what they heard, but they also had to solve a dilemma, as Georgie explained in 2009: "You know, the great Joe Williams, the young Joe Williams who sang with Count Basie for many years, actually not that many years at the time – for me it seemed like a long time – but he became a solo artist in the Mid-Sixties. And Basie had other singers in the band. At the time of the tour I did, he didn't have a singer":

Their original choice of vocalist for a European tour, Tony Bennett, couldn't make it because of ill health, so Fame's enthusiasm and availability came in very useful.

On the other hand, Big Basie was willing to play along – literally – with Georgie's *Sound Venture* repertoire – which spoke volumes about Fame's adept choice of material.

This was where Fame met his life-long friend Richard B. Boone (1930–1999), a trombonist from Little Rock, Arkansas who had worked in Los Angeles with Dexter Gordon and became a member of the Count Basie Orchestra in 1966 after working behind Della Reese. Georgie regularly met Boone in Copenhagen, where the latter lived from 1970. He enjoyed Richard's gigs in Scandinavian Jazz clubs, and saw him become a member of the Danish Radio Big Band in 1973. They also had a mutual mate in the Copenhagen resident Bob Rockwell, a Ben Sidran cohort and Danish Blue Flame with whom they both worked.

The Georgie Fame/Count Basie Orchestra tour started with a performance in the Royal Albert Hall in May 1967: "A delighted Fame faced his curious and dedicated audience. While some critics had a rather academic go at the project by calling it under-rehearsed, most of the 7000 people in the audience realized that here was a historically significant event simply to be relished and enjoyed instead of analyzing what could have been in a more perfect world. *Melody Maker* was on the punters' side by realizing that 'it was a dream come true' for Georgie Fame, the day he starred in a major orchestra concert with the Count Basie Orchestra. Here was a young English singer and successful Pop artist swinging along with one of the world's most famous and respected Jazz orchestras.

"And as Georgie said when he stepped on stage for his first number with the Count at The Royal Albert Hall, London, on Thursday last week: 'Welcome to my dreams'.

The concert was a logical climax of Georgie's Jazz leanings since he first broke away from the world of Rock'n'Roll backing quartet and began singing Jazz and Blues with the old Blue Flames at The Flamingo.

"Amazing how Fame's very recent band, with a couple of its members still actively involved in his repertoire, can become "the old Blue Flames" in a very short time" – the *Melody Maker* certainly felt the pulse of having to be hip. The report continues:

"He first tangibly expressed his desire to mix the dual ideas of Pop and Jazz with appearances and recordings with the Harry South Orchestra. A few years ago, such a teaming would have been unthinkable, and it's a tribute to Georgie's enthusiasm and talent that the once vast gulf between Jazz and popular music is being narrowed.

"For a first time venture, and in view of the limited rehearsal time available and the natural combinations of nerves and suspicions, the concert can be judged a success, and certainly the packed audience responded with warm applause."

"Count Basie played the first half … then came Georgie for the second set using Bill Eyden on drums and Harry South on piano. The Basie band cut cleanly through Harry's arrangements which they had rehearsed for a bare two hours that afternoon at Ronnie Scott's Club. Most of the material was that used on Georgie's album with South called *Sound Venture*, opening with a bouncy 'Lovey Dovey'. Then came 'It Could Happen To You', a nice ballad, and a roaring 'Three Blind Mice', with lyrics by Georgie's mate, Jon Hendricks. After initial nerves, Fame's voice came through more confidently on 'Don't Try', and he had the chance to sit down and play some Hammond organ as well. Next came 'Keep Your Big Mouth Shut', 'Feed Me', 'Missing You', 'Dawn Yawn', a scat vocal on 'Bluesology', then Count Basie returned to the piano. 'L'il Pony' was the final flag waver, as they say in Big Band parlance, taken far too fast for comfort, but it was still an exciting sound.

"The major drawback of the evening was the appalling acoustics of the Albert Hall, which are ideal for massed pipe bands, but not for a Jazz rhythm section. From my position at the back of the stalls, every rim shot or brass flare was echoed off the walls and roof.

"After the show, the Count and Georgie were swamped with press and photographers in the artist's bar. Georgie said, 'I woke up yesterday morning with a cold and a sore throat – and I never have sore throats normally. Basie was knocked out and we're talking about doing something together in the autumn. There are no plans for an LP at the moment, no matter what anybody says. But if there are plans made there will be no bother, because I have got over the initial audition. I got to know all of the band beforehand because I know that a lot of them thought I was just a Pop star planted on Basie. They were saying 'Fame? Who's Fame?' At the rehearsal Harry Edison [trumpet player] was lovely. He had expected to be given Pop charts, but he looked at them and said, 'Fame, you've got a whole lot of music here, baby!'"

Having "got over the initial audition", and also having survived the debut in the face of hectic rehearsals – all this would pay off handsomely even without a projected album. The Count's orchestra and Georgie reconvened in October for two big Jazz festivals in Warsaw and Prague. During the summer months of 1967, Fame crossed the Atlantic in Basie's direction. He managed to get the support slot for a Gene Pitney tour. The tough terms were playing clubs with a US pick-up band, but at least it was a foot in the American door for Georgie.

Another American heard Georgie play Ronnie Scott's Club in the new capital of Pop and all things hip, London. Enamoured with the dynamic, energetic and also still quite innovative atmosphere of "Swinging London", the Irish-Scottish-Norwegian US Jazz lady Blossom Dearie – 19 years Georgie Fame's senior – appreciated and simply loved our man's stage presence and stylistic versatility. So she wrote him a tribute song about him. She confessed "I'm impressed, my ears are blessed" and boldly called the whole thing "Sweet Georgie Fame". Like Georgie, Ms Dearie regularly played Ronnie Scott's Jazz Club in London's Soho and was of like mind.

Fame: "I'd met her in Ronnie Scott's Club, and I went away and came back a week later, and she was still playing in the club. I thought 'Well, I'm going to listen'. And I sat down in front of the stage, and she sang this song, which she had written in the previous week." The protagonist was stunned – so much so in fact that it took him almost two years to come up with a musical reply – see "Blossom" on *Seventh Son* in 1969.

Listening to Georgie Fame live between 2000 and 2014, one often wondered why he would suddenly leap into an almost church-like organ version of the Bee Gees ballad "Words". The answer goes back to this "Sweet Georgie Fame" autumn of 1967:

With Georgie at the height of his commercial and artistic power and popularity in the recording and concert world, it certainly wouldn't be long before the film industry also took note. He was certainly rubbing shoulders with the Beatles, who had two successful movies on their CV, directed by Richard Lester, and were in the process of filming their own mock documentary cum hippie comedy, *Magical Mystery Tour*. United Artists wanted to make a cinema film called *The Mini-Mob*, with shooting to begin on the 18th of September. Its music had been contracted to be composed by the Bee Gees: Barry, Robin and Maurice Gibb.

In *Tales Of The Brothers Gibb*, Georgie Fame reminisces about the music for the projected film: "I think they did write about half a dozen tunes. At that time it was considered a good move to try and get into movies. I always liked their harmonizing, their vocals, and Barry Gibb's written a lot of good tunes. It wasn't my kind of music, but I admired them, especially the high voices. They had a very distinctive sound which is important if you want to make inroads. You could always tell the BeeGees apart from anybody else because of their individual sound."

The *Tales* authors point out that "Georgie Fame had a starring role in the Robert Amran directed film [as Georgie Hart; the other main actors were Rosemary Nicols as Charlotte and John Clive as Joe], but it never actually gained [a British] release. 'It might not have been good enough!' he speculated.

"I don't know whether it was edited, I never saw a completed version of it. It was all rather embarrassing – most of it was shot by the river at Maidenhead, I think. We were meant to be kidnapped on a boat."

The film *The Mini Affair* did get a release in the United States, too, titled *The Mini Mob* over there and getting substantial promotional backing. There were leaflets around referring to the original title, wondering "Can the country that survived the Vikings, the Romans [hey, Nero and the Gladiators!], Napoleon, two World Wars, and the Great Train Robbery, survive ... The Mini Affair?"

While the title track was supplied by session cats, Georgie Fame himself was hired to sing the B-side "Words", in an arrangement not unlike his later *Georgie Does His Thing With Strings* album, which at that time was, of course, the Bee Gees signature sound as well. When the project was shelved, the Gibb Brothers issued the song as their own single at the turn of 1967 into 1968, almost simultaneously to Fame's looming gangster single, "The Ballad of Bonnie and Clyde". What a pity he didn't cover the song in his *Strings* album, but there you go.

A Man And His Music – back to the West End

While 1966 had closed for Georgie with a show called "*The Sound of '67*", the new presentation was called "*A Man and His Music*", and it was showcased from Christmas 1967 until the end of January 1968 at the Mayfair Theatre in London.

Fame remembers: "I was invited to do a short season at the Mayfair Theatre. I still got the programme. The plan was to do the first half to concentrate on the Jazz side of things – I think Jon Hiseman might have been playing drums by that time. So I decided to put a kind of Jazz quartet together for the first, and then the second half was more of a Blue Flames kind of set, and I asked Jon to be part of it – he might have been part of both, I can't remember. I specifically got him to do the first half, because it was going to be a Jazz quartet. I was asked to do a special evening which went on for a couple of weeks. It was a small theatre, a nice theatre, and we decided to do whatever the gamut of my bloody career or talents were up to that point. And my Jazz interest was increasing all the time, so I decided to do the first set with some of the Chet Baker things, and other Jazz things. In the band were surely John McLaughlin and I think Jon Hiseman. Maybe Lyn Dobson [true] and I can't remember who played the bass. But I have the programme, I would have to look."

Jon Hiseman, who had joined the Georgie Fame Band in the summer of 1967 when had he left the Graham Bond Organisation after one year, remembers their time together at the Mayfair with affection and amusement, in Martyn Hanson's book *Playing The Band*:

"Georgie loved to hear us jamming and told the band to play heavy Jazz for the first twenty minutes – then he would come on to: 'Ladies and gentlemen, the star of our show – Georgie Fame!'" As far as Hiseman remembers, Georgie had tremendous fun watching the band from the side of the stage, surely more fun in fact than his manager Rik Gunnell, for whom fun must have spelt a relapse into the keenly chaotic days of the Blue Flames.

Hiseman picks it up: "After a few nights […], Rik Gunnell turned up and was horrified. But he got his own back by screwing us on the fee for the residency."

Jon was renowned in Jazz circles for having "declared war" on the hi-hat and for playing with two bass drums like Ginger Baker, and joined Georgie via Colin Richardson of the Rik Gunnell agency, well aware that our man was probably looking for a more "funky" drummer. But Jon had his own recollection corrected by a true visual and sonic revelation, as he told me when we chatted in 2011:

"Tell him I think fondly of the times we did. He is wonderful, and the interesting thing is – about two years ago a man sent me a DVD from America which was actually the broadcast from the Prague Jazz Festival in 1967. This is a jazz group! I don't remember this at all. I was so shocked – I thought I was going to see the Blue Flames, and out comes this quartet and plays – I couldn't believe it. I was so young, and so thin – I put two stone on since '67. I can't believe how good the quality of the DVD is – Georgie must have seen this, too, I guess. I say in the book I was not the right drummer for Georgie, but I enjoyed it and I learnt a lot", adding in his memoirs that "I found that Georgie Fame required a much more conventional drummer and I had to apply myself to simplicity for the first time, but I don't really think my style ever fitted. It was good discipline though …"

"Simplicity" became the key word when apart from the Warsaw festival, they played in a factory canteen outside of the capital. When their gear van had not arrived on time, it might have been okay for Georgie to use the house piano, and Lyn Dobson carried his instruments anyway. But for Jon to rattle a matchbox in front of a microphone like one of today's plastic "chicken shakes" was more basic than the inventive pro could have imagined.

Jon certainly enjoyed the "perks" that came with joining a prominent, well-reputed band. Martyn Hanson writes in Jon's book that when he left by plane in October 1967 to play in Fame's band, along with Lyn Dobson and Rik Brown at the "Jazz Jamboree" in Warsaw and also the "Jazzoveho Festivalu" in Prague, he had the feeling of having "arrived" in terms of being treated with respect, and the DVD showed him that reed player Dobson, bass player Brown and Hiseman himself were allowed long solos Jazz style instead of Georgie Fame's Soul sound which he was known for, and still mixed with the Jazz songs from his last two albums *Sound Venture* and *The Two Faces Of Fame*.

Hiseman further explains in his book that "while I enjoyed the relative sanity of working with Georgie, I wasn't really a Funk player and didn't have enough control then – I was more used to floating and shading. Not actually owning any Funk records and after so many years of unfettered improvisation, poor acoustics and very little studio experience, my timing, by today's standards, was suspect."

Just as Hiseman had learnt a lot from Fame, and Fame had learnt a lot from guitarist Colin Green, Georgie also has a soft spot for John McLaughlin and was glad to hire him again, as he told me when I interviewed him for Colin Harper's excellent McLaughlin biography *Bathed In Lightning*: "He had even been a Jazz player when he joined the Blue Flames. He was incredible. He was in the band in 1962/63. Well, he just got better! John [McLaughlin] was still in London, and he also played rhythm guitar on my recording of "Sunny" in the studio. I did learn a lot from him. Just playing, chords, melody – cause he was way ahead of his time. When he was playing in my band, I always thought perhaps that that was restricting for him, because it was kind of too simple for him. But he was glad to do the gig, and it was great when he got back. That time we weren't recording anyway, we were just gigging. And then he joined Graham Bond."

The *New Musical Express* ran a most positive review: 'Georgie Fame proved that his versatility is equal to his virtuosity as he played to a capacity audience of (mostly) adults. He kept away from old favourites and played lesser-known but more sophisticated Jazz numbers. In the first half, tunes like 'It Could Happen To You', 'Stockholm Sweetenin' and 'Do It The Hard Way' were enjoyable and well-performed by Georgie's nine-piece band. The second half was livelier, with numbers such as 'Hide The Bacon, The Rabbi's Watching' in which Fame pummeled the organ, extracting its lifeblood; 'A Waiting Time', which was only surpassed by 'The Ballad Of Bonnie And Clyde', quite fantastic, except that the off-stage record of the Tommy guns got stuck! Friday showed a rapidly maturing and ever-developing talent and a spectrum, in fact, of musical entertainment."

Watching the incident with the stuck machine-gun tape on YouTube today would be a priceless, hilarious joy which Fame himself would highly appreciate. Making it public knowledge would have re-connected Georgie from the middle of the road to the underworld of the Flamingo and Scene vibes.

But then, where do you re-connect? By now, there was Georgie the R&B and Ska cat from Soho, the whippersnapper turned serious Jazz singer, and the pop star gangster gimmick singer. Fame himself remembered this often discussed predicament much later for the BBC, in 2013. Realizing that a number of fans surely loved their Georgie Fame in all of those incarnations and re-inventions, he nevertheless mused "Some people around me got the feeling that I alienated quite a few people by switching direction. I know for a fact that I alienated myself with some of the old Jazz elite by trying to involve myself in the world of Jazz because they looked at me as a young whippersnapper [a word GF uses a lot more than this writer applies it in this chronicle] and Rock'n'Roller who had no right being there. And then my more kind of Pop fans were thinking I was deserting them for the world of Jazz. But I didn't see it like that. I always looked at it as part of my musical education."

While Fame was trying to embrace the "suit or cardigan" Jazz audience, most favourably without estranging his Mod/R&B or Pop audience, his successor of the Flamingo Club residencies, Zoot Money, went the completely opposite way – he turned "leftfield" heading for the "Kaftan" clad audience. Disbanding his Big Roll Band, Money re-emerged without the brass section, keeping guitarist Andy Summers (formerly Somers) and drummer Colin Allen with bass player Pat Donaldson for the hippie quartet Dantalian's Chariot. Could Georgie have gone that way?

If you think that our "sound venturer" would rather have been seen dead than wearing a kaftan, take a look at his TV appearance for "Seventh Son" just two years on. As far as the politics of disc making is concerned, Fame had the last laugh of the two former All-nighters competitors: While Zoot Money and his Dantalian's Chariot single "Madman Running Through The Fields" is quite rightly regarded as a Flower Power hymn of prime significance, it did not grace the charts, and the subsequent album *Chariot Rising* was initially scrapped, only appearing 28 years later (!) in 1995 on the Tenth Planet label.

By the end of 1967, Zoot Money had returned to Rhythm & Blues via running Eric Burdon's New Animals as their musical director, and drummer Colin Allen became a sort of fortnight's "Blue Flame" by joining the Georgie Fame Band, as he told the *Record Collector*'s Nick James in 2010: "As for myself, I had no plans. Shortly afterwards, I went to Sweden for two weeks with Georgie Fame, then to Spain for a short holiday. On the day I returned, I got a call from John Mayall. The rest is history."

It is also part of history that Mayall not only once sold a song to Georgie – "Something" – but in hiring Colin Allen sported his third Fame drummer in a row after Hughie Flint and Jon Hiseman, (and after sacking Allen and the rest of the Bluesbreakers went without a drummer for a while.)

How to dread a sure smash – Georgie ties in with "Bonnie & Clyde" movie

The next single, 'The Ballad of Bonnie and Clyde', was such a "smash-on-demand" project that Fame had anticipated it could only be instantly popular. Here is the story: Mitch Murray (b. 1940) is renowned as an experienced, seen-it-all songwriting buff who had wanted to serve The Beatles with their first number one, "How Do You Do It". John Lennon hated it, so Gerry & The Pacemakers picked it up, scoring their pole position.

One year later, Murray wrote the instructive *How To Write A Hit Song* (which did actually seem to work for Sting), and today works as a successful humorous speech writer and comedian author. He worked together with another seasoned and street-wise pro, songwriter and record producer Peter Callander (1939–2014), whom he met in 1966. By that time, Callander had already scored hits, not least Cilla Black's "A Fool Am I", which one of Abba's front ladies, Agneta Fältskog, covered for her 2005 return to fame, *My Colouring Book*.

There was a real assembly line of Murray/Callandar chart hits during the 1960s and 1970s. The Tremeloes used their party patent "Even The Bad Times Are Good", and now Georgie was another treasured customer (prior to the Vanity Fair band hitting hard with "Hitchin' A Ride", and before the two even started their Bus Stop label for the group Paper Lace, but that is, as they say, another story.)

Contrary to many an incidental supporter's belief, this song had never been part of whatever director's cut of the famous Hollywood movie featuring Faye Dunaway and Warren Beatty. It was simply Murray & Callander's clever Tinsel Town tie-in, which Georgie Fame was initially reluctant to cut in the first place, in spite of, or no – more likely and perversely *because* of a hunch that "this would be my third number one hit" after "Yeh Yeh" and "Getaway". For many years, Georgie was just as reluctant to perform this number live, sometimes brushing off requests for it, but he often relented when got the chance to use the inventive and imaginative arrangement commissioned by the Count Basie Orchestra.

This was the first recording session for a long time not to be supervised by Denny Cordell, but by Mike Smith. Producer Mike (Michael Robert) Smith (1935–2011) is not to be confused with yet another British musician of the same name, i.e. Mike (Michael George) Smith (1943–2008), who served as lead singer of The Dave Clark Five, and who worked with Manfred Mann's Mike d'Abo in the 1970s and produced a duo album, *Smith & d'Abo*. Our Mike Smith shares the notoriety of turning down the Beatles for Decca in 1962, together with A&R man Dick Rowe – though in all fairness the Fab Four demo in question, which earned the attention of George Martin and survives as *The Silver Beatles*, was a beat & ballads mix which The Tremeloes, who got the Decca duo's thumbs-up instead, could have rattled off just as easily.

Georgie Fame's Smith had engineered and produced Mantovani and Vera Lynn, and the former Fame boss Billy Fury's "Halfway To Paradise". He would move on to Marmalade and Love Affair. Smith remembered that "when I took the tape into the studio to overdub the sound effects, I discovered an electrical fault. We had clicks all through the rhythm track. We had to add a new rhythm track and to this day, Georgie doesn't believe what we did. It was an outstanding record and the sound effects were wonderful."

For Fame as the main "actor" in the *Bonnie & Clyde* ballad coup, the actual circumstances of the recording resembled the hectic surroundings of the 1966 "Get Away" single in more than one respect. In order to take part in the session with the booked studio musicians, Georgie had to leave his band of Lyn Dobson, Rik Brown and Jon Hiseman up in the north of England, cruising somewhere on the chicken-in-a-basket cabaret circuit. Mike Smith may well have had good reasons to round up his pros in London for the venture, but for Hiseman and the others it seemed rather ironic that – while being left out of the adventures of recording this thriller tie-in – they had to mime to the song on TV as soon as it catapulted itself into the world's hit parades, with Jon having the extra task of providing the Kalashnikov sounds on his snare drum during live-gigs.

The record was not only a British number one single during the Christmas period 1967/1968. It was also a world-wide smash, with singles being released overseas in Australia, Canada, Brazil and the USA (where it made #7), and in European countries like Denmark, Norway and Finland, Germany, France, Spain, Portugal and Italy. There, they released two different, attractive picture sleeves singles, each of them with only one side sung in Italian: "The Ballad of Bonnie and Clyde" with an Italian version of "Try

My World" on the B-side, "Nel Tuo Mondo", then the other way round: "La Ballata Di Bonnie E Clyde"/"Try My World".

Fame: "From a business point-of-view, they were absolutely right. It proved to be true. I had to record 'The Ballad of Bonnie and Clyde' in Italian, because the Italian record company, CBS, said "If you do this in Italian, we'll sell many more records." And they're only interested in selling records. So I did it. "Questa la sole di due si ciama du Bonnie e Clyde".

For Argentina, the cover read "La Balada De Bonnie Y Clyde", and its B-side was called "Cuidado Con El Perro" (Beware Of The Dog). The unusual thing noted in Buenos Aires' record shops was another attractive picture sleeve (which was not standard packaging policy either in the UK and Argentina) and its 33 rpm LP speed.

As it was, the number fired the imagination of many an admirer and brought Fame a lot of fame and fans and friends, not least an eleven year-old Guy Barker, who would tell Georgie – and this author – all about his obsession with the record, Georgie's voice and all the machine-gun pandemonium years later.

Fame himself had had his doubts about recording this novelty song. But did he feel that the criticism matched the outcry towards Flamingo "Brother" Long John Baldry at the time, when the lanky crooner apparently "left" R&B in order to serve housewives – and house husbands, undoubtedly – with his ballad "Let The Heartaches Begin"?

Fame categorically denied this: "No, not at all. But John Baldry is much more steeped into Traditional Blues, if you like, than I ever was. So when we worked down at the Flamingo Club, which was essentially a black club, full of black American G.I.s and West Indians and Africans, we veered more towards that kind of Urban American thing. Although, I mean, Mose Allison was a rural American Blues singer. John for me was always more into Lightnin' Hopkins and John Lee Hooker, Jimmy Reed, stuff like that, but he is right in a way: trends come and go. That's why Jazz and Blues are

Georgie performing in the German *Beat Club*, March 1968.

very popular at the moment with the younger generation – it goes round and round in cycles. What he might be referring to is the way that the Rhythm & Blues thing as we knew it had changed. Of course, we were all lucky to have hit records, but, I mean, even John's record, 'Mexico', had nothing to do with the Blues.

"And I didn't want to record 'Bonnie and Clyde', because it wasn't aesthetically the material that I would record, anyway. But because of political pressures from my manager and the record company, I recorded it, and it was the biggest selling single I had, but musically it wasn't the kind of thing that I would ever consider. Although – having said that – I have a wonderful Big Band arrangement of it which I use all the time. [It would first be released on his CD Georgie Fame with the Danish Radio Big Band *Endangered Species*.]

"That arrangement was written for the Count Basie Orchestra, and it swings like hell. When I toured with Basie in 1967 and 1968 – when "Bonnie and Clyde" was a hit, that arrangement was done specifically for the Basie Band, so I don't mind doing it like that! I went to New York to meet the band and rehearse with them, and Chico O'Farrell was the staff arranger at the time. I gave him a copy of my recording of 'Bonnie and Clyde' and said, 'Please, see if you can find a way to write an arrangement for Basie's band, as if they were playing it for the first time. It's a very corny song, but if you can find a way to make it swing, please do.' He did it, and wrote this wonderful arrangement, which I have been singing ever since."

Apart from numerous TV appearances in the UK, Georgie got a chance to present "The Ballad of Bonnie and Clyde" on German television, as a guest of the highly acclaimed *Beat Club* series of the small Radio Bremen station which was a must for Deutsche teenagers on Saturday afternoons, often dutifully recorded open mic onto reel-to-reel recorders, with the whole family told to keep it quiet for the "racket". With Georgie appearing there on 9th March, most of the songs were more on the romantic side, with the Moody Blues presenting "Nights In White Satin" and Sharon Tandy revealing her version of the Beatles' "Fool On The Hill". The Fabs themselves sent in a video tape of "Lady Madonna", with the racket side covered by future Blue Flame Andy Fairweather Low's Amen Corner's pumping out "Bend Me Shape Me" and Dave Dee & Co whipping out "The Legend of Xanadu" – seven years after young police cadet Dave Harman-Dee was the first witness at Eddie Cochran's car accident …

The B-side of "The Ballad of Bonnie and Clyde", "Beware Of The Dog", continued the great tradition of Fame instrumentals, this time harking back to the Detroit Soul with a Motown-thing that made the most of the sharp brass section that played so nostalgically on the A-side.

More than a nostalgic 1930s pastiche – The Third Face Of Fame

For the follow-up to *The Two Faces Of Fame*, January 1968's sessions for the cleverly derived album title *The Third Face Of Fame*, Georgie Fame was backed by selected ex Blue Flames, like Bill Eyden, John McLaughlin, Tony Coe, John Marshall and Phil Bates, as well as The Harry South Orchestra – among them Ian Hamer, Les Condon, the two Dereks, Derek Healey and Derek Watkins (three if you count arranger Derek Wadsworth), plus another "trumpet royale" with the wonderfully named Albert Hall.

Ronnie Scott, Harry Klein and Cyril Reubens complemented Marshall's sax work; Terry Smith came in on second guitar. Another rhythm man was Ronnie Scott's Club house drummer Tony Oxley, who had also drummed in the Tubby Hayes Orchestra and had just helped deliver the amazing Don Quichote concept Jazz album *Windmill Tilter* in March 1968, created by Fame's flugelhorn catch, Canadian Kenny Wheeler, together with the Johnny Dankworth Orchestra, who also featured the *Third Face* guys Coe, Condon and McLaughlin – the London Jazz carousel in full swing.

It was Fame's debut in "true stereo" no less – and in an original concept that had been dreamt up by his new producer Mike Smith. As the single "The Ballad of Bonnie and Clyde" had recently been so exceptionally successful, why not stay in the same musical environment for a complete set of songs?!

Were they again in danger of being accused of selling out, as they apparently had been with the smash single? Georgie Fame and Mike Smith, rather than jumping on a real or imagined bandwagon like The New Vaudeville Band's chart successes with "Winchester Cathedral" or "Finchley Central", had been intent on creating an album in the mood of the 1930s, an undertaking that Fame certainly possessed enough credibility of his own for. He had always been curious as far as musical genres were concerned, embracing Fats Domino's New Orleans Rock'n'Roll as much as West Indian Ska, or the jazzy Rhythm & Blues of one Ray Charles as presented to him by a UK-touring

Eddie Cochran on "that tragic tour in 1962". But in the end it was this sheer versatility that won out – Blues became just as much part of the menu as Jazz, Comedy and sing-along tunes – while the overall atmosphere remained nostalgic.

The LP sleeve was graced by the then familiar, but sadly out-of-fashion service of detailed liner notes. For all their fanfare and often quirky display of hip and hilarious language use, these often contributed immediate insight, atmosphere and – in the long run – a welcome time warp. *Third Fame* "compère" Nigel Hunter, for instance, a *Disc* magazine writer and Beatles aficionado, contrasted the album's style with the early 1968 Rock revival: "Whereas King Rock seems to have been lurking in partial exile in one of his foreign embassies during the intervening years, King Fame went from strength to strength in this time, rising above all labels and pigeon-hole classifications except those marked 'Talent' and 'Originality'.

There is some insight into the album's planning "while the star was moving around in the States, and could only be reached telephonically (in Mike [Smith]'s words) 'every other Shrove Tuesday'". His liner notes summarize the album thus: "*The Third Face Of Fame* has many pleasant expressions, Jazz, whimsical, self-deprecating humour, sentimentality and Blues. It proves again that, whether King Rock has revived or not, King Fame is firmly fixed and secure on his individual throne."

Clocking in at 32:48, *The Third Face Of Fame* album seemed rather short and sweet when compared to its predecessor *The Two Faces Of Fame*, which had been seven minutes longer while it equally presented eleven tracks.

The Third Face Of Fame – track by track

"The Ballad of Bonnie and Clyde" of course, the smash single, had to open the album, and with its theme and arrangement – overseen by short-term Georgie Fame Band member Derek Wadsworth – it fitted the bill of the Tempting Thirties perfectly. The studio crew used only trombone player John Marshall from the trusted Harry South team, coupled with Morris Platt. Otherwise it was veteran Arthur Greenslade on piano, who famously arranged "Goldfinger" for Shirley Bassey and also worked for Chris Farlowe. George Kish played guitar, Ernie Shear was on banjo, Greg Bowen and Bobby Haughey were on trumpets. Drums got thumped by Hayden Jackson, who wrote "Francis & Day's Drum Tutor" and who these days plays in the "progressive post-rock" band The Allusionists. Quite unusually, there were both an electric bass guitar, supplied by Ronnie Seabrooke, and a double bass, played by Frank Clarke, who had done Beatles sessions in the past. Memories of the *Flamingo* album – the backing track had to be recorded twice due to a technical hitch.

Lennon McCartney's "When I'm Sixty-Four", a number from the Beatles album *Sgt Pepper's Lonely Hearts Club Band*, had been Music Hall anyway in its original Beatles arrangement with soprano and bass clarinets provided by George Martin. And Fame – who had furnished the Fab Four with his own Blue Flames related Soul horn section for "Got You Get You Into My Life" in 1966, simply went the whole hog with this Harry South arrangement, taking the pace a little more slowly and making the horn section a little more old-fashioned still, Vaudeville style. George Martin and McCartney will have approved: Fame was making a point that this context was where the number had really belonged all along.

It could also be seen as marking a very special anniversary: The year before, May 15th, 1967, had turned out to become a very special date for Georgie's good friend Paul McCartney. He had attended a posh dinner party thrown by Brian Epstein, the Beatles' manager, to celebrate the fact that their album *Sgt Pepper's Lonely Hearts Club Band* had been completed after four months of grueling studio work. Dinner over, adrenalin was still flowing for Paul "When I'm Sixty-Four" Paul, and he drove to one of his favourite nighttime hand-outs in the West End, Soho's 9, Kingly Street, home of the Bag O'Nails nighclub. Georgie Fame was scheduled to play there with his band, as McCartney told biographer Barry Miles for *Many Years From Now*:

"The night I met Linda, I was in the Bag O'Nails watching Georgie Fame and the Blue Flames [sic] play a great set. Speedy [Acquaye] was banging away. She was there with the Animals, who she knew from photographing them in New York. They were sitting a couple of alcoves down, near the stage. The band had finished and they got up to either leave or go for a drink or a pee or something, and she passed our table. I was near the edge and stood up just as she was passing, blocking her exit, and so I said, 'Oh, sorry. Hi. How are you? How're you doing?' I introduced myself, and said, 'We're going on to another club after this, would you like to join us?'

"That was my big pulling line! Well, I'd never used it before, of course, but it worked this time! It was a fairly slim chance but it worked. She said, 'Yes, okay, we'll go on. How shall we do it?' I forget how we did it. 'You come in our car' or whatever, and we all went on, the people I was with and the Animals, we went on to the Speakeasy", all of this to the soundtrack of the Georgie Fame Band.

Only a few months on, Mike Smith would sniff the hit potential of yet another Lennon/McCartney tune – 97 percent Macca really – "Obladi Oblada". As the Beatles would not release it as a British single (an EMI/Odeon single got to number one in Germany), Smith created a UK pole position for The Marmalade – for a song that McCartney nicked from the Blue Flames' Speedy Acquaye apparently. Georgie: "This was simply one of Speedy's slogans down in the Flamingo – he would just go "Obladi-oblada life goes on" all the time, and Paul must simply have picked it up!" Other sources say that the slogan had its origin with another conga player, Paul's Nigerian friend Jimmy Scott-Emuakpor.

"Ask Me Nice" by Mose Allison, with great breaks and an avalanche of reeds and brass, ranks with the best of the *Sound Venture* LP in terms of Harry South's breathtaking Big Band Jazz arrangement here: six saxophones worked in by that album's Ronnie Scott and ex-Blue Flame Tony Coe. Trombonist John Marshall had also been on *The Two Faces of Fame*.

In the same mood came "Exactly Like You", written by poet and school teacher Dorothy Fields and American composer Jimmy McHugh for Lew Leslie's *International Revue* (which also contained their smash "On The Sunny Side Of The Street"). It is a concise and precise fast swinger, complete with sharp horn section accents and a rousing Deep South rhythm section line-up of Gordon Beck (p), Phil Bates (b), Bill Eyden (dr) and Terry Smith sharing guitar duties with the returned Blue Flame John McLaughlin. We get the third track running which was arranged courtesy of Harry South.Once popularized by Lionel Hampton, a range of stars from Benny Goodman to Diana Krall relished recording the tune.

"Someone To Watch Over Me" – as noted in the first chapter – was a lovely link that Georgie created between his love of George Gershwin and the 'Great American Songbook' on one side and his connection to his Lancashire heritage. The arrangement was provided by fellow Northerner Derek Wadsworth, Fame's one-time trombone player, with a wonderfully restrained reed section. Georgie "declaims a touching 'Someone To Watch Over Me' in an accent that will be appreciated in Leigh", noted liner notes writer Nigel Hunter on the album sleeve, and could have mentioned the tribute-to-Wes-Montgomery guitar solo which was probably thumb-picked by John McLaughlin.

Epic US picked this track for a 1969 Georgie Fame single, backed by the Swing Waltz "For Your Pleasure".

"Blue Prelude", a number from 1933 by Gordon Jenkins and Joe Bishop, and regrettably clocking in at a mere 1.55, sounds like the Roaring Twenties thanks to a another retro-arrangement by Derek Wadsworth. In spite of its sophisticated syncopations, this qualifies as a Charleston, the lustfully erotic dance rhythm celebrated in the bars from London and New York to Berlin which was to become the title of a Georgie Fame album in 2003. It had previously been done by Judy Garland in 1957 and later by Nina Simone.

Back to Swing on side 2 of the original LP with "Bullets Laverne" by Norman Greenbaum and B. Kane. When you hear the Broadway Musical type attack the Harry South Big Band applies here thanks to his own arrangement, it is hard to believe that the song was written by the American performer Norman "Spirit In The Sky" Greenbaum, who released his version under the moniker 'Dr Wests's Medicine Show and Junk Band' – a name which Georgie must have loved. As a single release, it was backed by another album track,"St James Infirmary".

"This Is Always" by Harry Warren and Mack Gordon had been performed by the Harry James Orchestra, Frank Sinatra, Cab Calloway and, crucially, by Chet Baker, so it is a natural for the Georgie Fame ballad catalogue, performed ever so sensitively and with brisk attention to detail by arranger Derek Wadsworth as well as Georgie's own sensitive reading, who nevertheless has a tongue-in-cheek moment with some cat calls and kisses here.

The jolly marching rhythm of "Side By Side", a Harry M. Woods tune with lyrics by Gus Kahn dating from 1927, had become popular via a Gene Krupa recording featuring Anita O'Day, but Fame certainly knew the version by The Duke Ellington Orchestra with vocals by saxophonist Johnny Hodges from 1958. Travelling along without having a barrel of money certainly fit Georgie's preferences at the end of the day. The effective harmony singing (Hunter: "He duets appropriately with himself") sounds like harmonizing with Alan Price. For movie train spotters: The catchy tune was also featured in two cinema films, *Richie Rich* and *The Adventures of Rocky and Bullwinkle*.

In complete contrast, the traditional American New Orleans Jazz funeral tune "St. James Infirmary", gets a deep, agitated reading by Fame, proving again that he would take his Jazz as seriously as the fun he would otherwise willingly be providing for his fans. This does not prevent him from applying the notorious cat sounds in his phrasing that he uses to this day.

The famous number was first popularized on record in 1927 on Vocalion by Fess Williams and his Royal Flush Orchestra, under the title "Gambler Blues (St. James Infirmary)". The lyrics were penned by one Joe Primrose a.k.a. Irving Mills. But the melody of this goes way, way back – it could actually have been composed by the Scottish bagpipes player Mac Crimmon in the 16th century. It was later applied to a ballad called "The Unfortunate Rake" or The Unfortunate Lass". The storyline was about dying from a veneral disease on the stairs of St. James' Hospital (sinful enough to spark off frequent bans and also moralizing versions). Right in the centre of the red light district of Storyville, which Fame's future friend Dr John would relive in his music, St. James Methodist church had been offering first and as well as, albeit primitive, hospital facilities.

There is a catch, though, which works in Georgie's favour: The lyrics had been in use before Storyville was taking shape, so the song could be about the St. James workhouse in London's Poland Street, which had been started by the Parish of St. James as early as 1728 – amongst other services letting street women give birth there.

Kid Ory, King Oliver, Cab Calloway, Blind Willie McTell and Louis Armstrong recorded it in the States, among countless others. Nearer to Georgie's world were organist Jimmy Smith, British Hammond competitor Graham Bond and, also in 1968, the Animals. Many more excellent versions of "St. James Infirmary" were recorded, for instance by Bobby Bland, Allen Toussaint, Lou Rawls (1966 LP *Live!*), Joe Cocker (1972 LP *Joe Cocker*) and Van Morrison (2003 CD *What's Wrong With This Picture?*)

Fame closed the album with Donovan Leitch's "Mellow Yellow", the song which apparently was about smoking dried banana skins for hallucinogenic effects, a legend started by Country Joe McDonald in 1966 which has since proved to be nonsense. As in "When I'm Sixty-Four", the popular Scottish Folk bard's Music Hall touches – and especially the strip club type brass interlude of the original Donovan single – were consequently enhanced by Georgie in Count Basie style, which again gave the impression that this song was custom-made for Georgie's and Mike Smith's original 1930s concept, and certainly suited his talents. Paul McCartney is also a direct link between "When I'm Sixty-Four", which he had written and performed of course, and "Mellow

Yellow", which is not only in the same mood but also graced with Paul's backing vocals in the original Donovan recording – with guitar parts supplied by ex-Blue Flame John McLaughlin. (In the 2006 BGO double-reissue of *Two Faces* and *Third Fame*, John Tobler can't resist mentioning "Mellow Yellow" in his new liner notes, "which [Donovan producer] Micky Most told me he thought at first was about a sexual banana-shaped vibrator …")

Neither this sixth Fame album *The Third Face Of Fame*, released in April 1968, nor his next single "Bullets Laverne"/"St. James Infirmary" charted, while an undeterred Fame kept touring hard, swung like hell and rocked on in spite of it. Speculating that these records were not of its time would be off the mark, because the huge music industry of Britain and America was certainly big enough for several mainstream sections – Frank Sinatra, Tom Jones or Tony Bennett used lavish orchestral arrangements and jazzy material all the time, and in a year when The Scaffold hit the charts at #1 with "Lily The Pink", comedy couldn't have been completely wrong, could it?

Also, just like the previous year, music was moving backwards and forwards at the same time in 1968. The Beatles' had combined Music Hall and Psych on their "Penny Lane"/"Strawberry Fields Forever" single, only to be toppled by the arch romantic "Release Me" by Engelbert Humperdinck. Now, their double White Album *The Beatles* contained more Vaudeville à la "Honey Pie" next to avant-garde ramblings like "Revolution No. 9" and the Heavy Metal onslaughts of "Helter Skelter". Georgie was well-advised to stay within credible territory, and if that meant R&B and Jazz to be joined by some nostalgic material, that certainly did not hurt his credibility, except for the increasingly opinionated taste police of the music press.

"Side By Side" – Count Basie Revisited

After touring through February 1968, Fame gave notice to the members of The Georgie Fame Band. He flew around in Europe, to appear in TV programmes and perform "The Ballad of Bonnie & Clyde" to a playback. It is interesting to note that the other British colleagues he encountered there exemplified the two directions the Rhythm & Blues legends of the early Sixties had taken: Stevie Winwood had abandoned The Spencer Davis Group in order to follow the Progressive trail with Traffic; whereas the Manfred Mann band, Mike d'Abo having replaced Paul Jones, were clearly on a Pop path with their catchy version of Dylan's "The Mighty Quinn".

Georgie now hankered between Pop and Jazz, and only a year later Manfred Mann would opt for Jazz with Manfred Mann's Chapter Three. Who could foresee that both Mann as well as Georgie Fame would re-consider again soon for rockier paths?

And then, Fame reunited with The Count Basie Orchestra. This time, after the haphazard coupling of the previous year, they were going to tackle proceedings long-term, with proper rehearsals, for which Georgie took the trouble of flying all the way to Boston, Massachusetts. It was there that Basie's arranger Chico O'Farrell supplied Fame and the Count's cats with his famous arrangement of "The Ballad Of Bonnie and

Clyde" which Georgie still uses today, and has employed with the BBC Big Band, the German WDR and NDR outfits, the Dutch Metropole Orchestra, Don Lusher's Big Band and half a dozen Swedish and Danish orchestras, too.

The tour, this time, was to take in Great Britain and Europe during April and May 1968. It went down a storm in the UK, documented in the BBC TV spectacular *Together: Count Basie and Georgie Fame*, which was screened on the 12th May. Six songs from *The Two Faces Of Fame, The Third Face Of Fame* and earlier albums featured Georgie, while seven instrumentals, including "Shiny Stockings" from Basie's 1955 album *April In Paris*, concentrated on the orchestra itself. Everyone agreed that Fame, initially tense, compèred and performed brilliantly. On the continent though, as Georgie told *Goldmine* magazine in 1982, "some of the European audiences didn't take too kindly to a young whippersnapper like me singing up front with the band, but in England it was very successful". Quite ridiculous, as Fame was 25 at the time – as old as, say, Frank Sinatra when he was fronting Big Bands all the time. Two years earlier, though, not every critic in the UK had been kind when it came to judging Georgie's progression to *Sound Venture*.

Georgie continues about the Zeitgeist of 1968, and it sounds familiar: "At that time – although the musicians were great – I was slightly frowned upon by the established Jazz community who saw me as a threat from Rock'n'Roll land. And a lot of Rock'n'Roll fans accused me of deserting the cause – how dare he further his career and improve himself as a musician! So I was caught in the middle of a crossfire. Didn't bother me. Never has, never will."

So there he was again – discussing the old dichotomy between Pop/Rock and Jazz, Rhythm & Blues and Jazz, Rock'n'Roll and Jazz, the pure love of putting musicians in pigeon holes – including the love of some musicians to stay on those rather than "not being bothered".

Instead of feeling bothered, Georgie had a lot of fun, most of all with his special guests Annie Ross and Jon Hendricks. Both of them Vocalese buffs in their own right, those two had impressed him as part of the New York trio Lambert, Hendricks & Ross, whose repertoire nuggets were included in the Fame-Basie set during the tour. The concert review on the London show in *Melody Maker* was certainly glowing, while repeating some alleged received wisdoms which seem quite exaggerated with hindsight:

"Georgie's singing style is a mixture of various influences, ranging from Mose Allison to Jon Hendricks, but he is still the only European singer I can think of who could live with the Basie band – and live with it he did! Remembering the dreadful fiasco of The Royal Albert Hall concert last year, Saturday night was a hundred percent improvement."

At this point, it may have been too early to think of a follow-up to *The Third Face of Fame*. Maybe a studio-collaboration with the Count Basie Orchestra would have been welcomed in 1968. A mutual Fame & Basie album would certainly have had the autumn cum Christmas market "in the pocket" but, although it was on the horizon, in the end nothing came of the plans.

But there was to be another live TV documentation when Fame met Count Basie for their mutual concert at the Berlin Jazz Festival on the 9th November, again with Annie Ross and Jon Hendricks and their beloved Lambert Hendricks & Ross material. Thirty-five minutes of their Berlin appearance, 55 minutes of their earlier London showcase – the perfect DVD, were the BBC and the SFB (Sender Freies Berlin) to do their homework.

Another artist excited by the prospects of Vocalese singing was Georgie's old Flamingo friend Van Morrison when he recorded his album *Astral Weeks*, as his biographer Johnny Rogan points out:

"The only performer Morrison ever name-checked as an influence was King Pleasure, the champion of Vocalese – the method of fitting lyrics to well-known Jazz solos. With the 1952 album *King Pleasure Sings*, a generation of listeners, including Van Morrison, had been introduced to the art of Vocalese, which later featured in the work of many performers from Annie Ross through to Georgie Fame and Al Jarreau."

Rogan is right in name-checking, but "later featured in the work" certainly does not apply to Fame: His Vocalese art had featured on *The Two Faces of Fame* in 1967, while *Astral Weeks* had been recorded on 25th September and 15th October 1968.

"Am I Wasting My Time" – How (not) to follow-up to "Bonnie & Clyde"

Prophetic words: Certainly, Georgie Fame the solo artist himself was now being handled more lucratively than ever. Was Georgie wasting his time by having signed a literally big deal with the new British branch of American giant CBS records? Whatever the answer, there had to be thoughts for a follow-up to that big gangster 'chart-topper'. CBS and Fame had chosen to make the parent album *The Third Face Of Fame* versatile, albeit not geared to a Rock audience, and they stuck to that notion by sticking to conventional instrumentation of small combo, brass and strings rather than the wild guitar sounds of the day, or the more laid back West Coast sound now beginning to prevail in the USA.

Fame saw this critically, because he still had the urge for Rhythm & Blues, but also wooed the Jazz community: "By the time I recorded the single 'By The Time I Get To Phoenix', I was under contract to CBS Records. I had already recorded 'The Ballad of Bonnie and Clyde', which was another huge hit (UK #1 in December 1967), and that's when I entered my 'Middle of the Road' period! I think CBS Europe saw me as the sort of 'English Andy Williams'. I had done a few Jazz things – *and* I was still rocking! But it was that 'grey area' after the Rhythm & Blues thing faded. In the late Sixties – apart from the Flower Power thing – the rest of it was terribly 'Middle-of-the-Roady', and I went through about three years of that."

One has to see this remark of Georgie's in perspective, because for a long time, during the 1970s almost through the 1990s, some key players and major critics from the Rock aristocracy, as well as many new music trends and fashions, had made the term "Easy Listening" something of a dirty word. Music encyclopedia compilers and record store managers alike punished the more pleasant, relaxed artists by relegating them to this section of their book or store; Georgie Fame's name would not often feature in Jazz books, nor often be found in Jazz departments, until a few years ago.

Instead, he would find his records (and later his CDs) on the "Easy Listening" shelves. There, he got thrown in with Alan Price, who was also apparently too polished for Rock, with Neil Sedaka – too old to rock and roll, in spite of recording with 10cc? –, and Andy Williams: there we are! The same could be said of TV queen Cilla Black – with whom, incidentally, Fame was to perform before long. All that did not prevent him from mixing pleasant ballads and easy-sing-along numbers with some serious and sophisticatedly performed Jazz material during those five CBS years, some of which he is still performing at the time of writing.

Presenting a further novelty number, as a follow-up to "The Ballad of Bonnie & Clyde", would have been out of the question. This would have further typecast a tremendously multi-faceted artist. Instead, a ballad did not seem like a bad idea. The Oklahoma born composer, and Californian resident, Jimmy Webb (b. 1946) had impressed recently with his work "MacArthur Park", originally performed on record by British actor Richard Harris and covered by Fame's Soho club colleague Long John Baldry, following his own runaway success with the equally dramatic "Let The Heartaches Begin".

CBS and Georgie chose Jimmy Webb's "By The Time I Get To Phoenix", which had first appeared on Johnny Rivers' album *Changes* – Rivers' version received a first of several Grammy awards a year later. Quite an inspired choice then, elaborately arranged with strings and some imaginative brush work. This was a kind of taster for the aforementioned album project of Fame's in a year's time, *Georgie Does His Thing With Strings*.

"Phoenix" was coupled with one of Fame's own compositions, "For Your Pleasure", for which one of the backing singers, Madeline Bell, has a story: "We have known each other since the 'Flamingo'. I was in London at that time. In those days, there were quite a few music clubs in London, so you could go from one to another, you know. There were loads of clubs for live music. I sang that ['For Your Pleasure'] to him on the night of *Singer* [in Amsterdam on May 25th, 2012], on stage when we finished 'The Nearness Of You'. As he got up, he said 'Thank you Baby' and I just said 'For your pleasure'. I did the backing vocal on his version. That's when I first heard it, because he recorded it. And if you got a copy of him singing it – that is me, Kay Garner and Lesley Duncan doing the backing vocals. I went into the studio afterwards and I said I wanted to do that song."

The single, released in the UK, Denmark, France, Argentina and Chile, and which came in a strange additional British DJ edition backed by Simon & Garfunkel's "Sounds of Silence", did not chart. For the American/Canadian market – and followed by other countries in the process – Georgie and his advisors/managers opted for the Johnny Dankworth composition "Hideaway", a contemplative Latin Rumba, written by one of the most renowned British Big Band leaders, husband of Jazz singer Dame Cleo Laine, whose son Alec Dankworth would join the Blue Flames in 2003. Dankworth had been commissioned to write the song for the Richard Burton/Elizabeth Taylor cinema film *Boom*.

The tune's B-side was another composition by the "Bonnie & Clyde" team Murray & Callander, "Kentucky Child", a mid-tempo Charleston, New Vaudeville Band style, and if Fame should have wanted another chart smash badly, he might have opted for this as the A-side. The fact that he did not makes accusations of becoming pure Pop rather sour grapes.

Instead, Fame performed both numbers in Italian, thereby probably pleasing some of Frank Sinatra's Sicilian buddies no end: "Kentucky"/"La Donna Che Sogno". The Spanish called the single "Chica De Kentucky"/"Escondite", but buyers got the English versions.

Fame continued to record during the spring of 1969, spending two months with sessions comprising the Keith Mansfield Orchestra for future release. One of the emerging tracks, the pleasant and romantic ballad, string driven thing called "Peaceful", was coupled with the hardly exposed "Hideaway" and promptly got to #16 in the charts.

For some custom-made inroads to the American market, CBS got Bob Dylan's long-time producer Bob Johnston on a plane to London. Dylan was about to top the British album charts with *Nashville Skyline*. Johnston and Fame picked two songs from the folk poet's previous, 1967 album *John Wesley Harding*, "Down Along The Cove" and "I'll Be Your Baby Tonight". The A-side elaborates on the original 12-bar Blues with the kind of female Gospel choir that Dylan would later use during his new-born Christian days, while in "I'll Be Your Baby Tonight", Fame attempted to sing the great melody nonchalantly – very much in contrast to the Hollies version that had just come out on *The Hollies Sing Dylan*, or the gorgeous Reggae-fied reading by UB40 with Robert Palmer years later. Anyway, it did not chart.

"For Your Pleasure" – Fame Swinging All Over The World

Fame hardly had time to muse about the politics of planting hits. Having dissolved his band in February 1968 when "Bonny & Clyde" hit seriously, he was touring non-stop with pick-up bands and orchestras, showing his face in a solo capacity on TV programmes all over the world as well. With hindsight, he told Melody Maker in 1970: "Just before *Bonnie & Clyde* sidetracked me into cabaret, I had a great new band with Jon Hiseman, but that hit turned me into a solo artist." So he hadn't forgotten, but keeping a band on a retainer was a move that must have seemed like burning money to Rik Gunnell.

With engagements in Sweden, Austria, Portugal and Italy in Europe, and an overseas return to Rio de Janeiro's renowned International Song Festival, Fame would hardly have had time for American tours to promote the Bob Dylan inspired single "I'll Be Your Baby Tonight" in the event of a hit, but in spite of missing out on the US with Georgie, drummer Jon Hiseman soon went stateside with John Mayall, before he started his own Colosseum with future Fame Band member Dick Heckstall-Smith on sax plus the Flamingo many-nighters Chris Farlowe and Hammond colleague Dave Greenslade: "My idea was a fusion of Jazz and Rock, but I knew that instrumental music had a small audience, so I also wanted to do what Graham Bond, Georgie Fame and John Mayall were doing with vocals", he says in *Playing the Band*.

Both Fame and Mayall remained dear to Hiseman's heart, but could also be coolly put in perspective, as he told *Sounds* three years after on April 3, 1971: "The time I spent with John [Mayall] and Georgie [Fame], I learnt a lot, but they were unproductive times because I didn't feel that I was getting anywhere [...] I am sure that most of the credit for Colosseum and what it stands for today must go to Graham Bond and Chris Farlowe and the Thunderbirds and Georgie Fame and the Blue Flames [although it wasn't them anymore at the time] and to John [Mayall] for hammering round the country with relatively little success for long years playing nothing but good music. Heads must bow because their sacrifice has been greater than mine has ever been ..."

So had Georgie felt that those times on the road had been unproductive? Was he tired of the sacrifices? The chance of (world) wide television coverage was certainly too good to miss, and lest we forget, the road was not the well-oiled industry it would soon become. Before long, Georgie would resume his touring activities anyway, and with renewed gusto, but there would soon be TV appearances which showed much of the funny, the creative, the positive side of cabaret.

During 1968, Georgie had got an invitation to an episode in the television series *Lulu's Back In Town* from the eponymous Scottish R&B shouter. The "Shout" hit singer coupled Fame with Alan Price, and this combination proved so successful that it had serious implications for both singers/keyboard wizards. Fame and Price turned up dressed absolutely formally with coat tails and white cravats, hired for a special slapstick piano number where Georgie started tinkling the ebonies and ivories like a madman, only to be rather violently prevented from more attack by the "attacking" Geordie man. Fisticuffs broke loose, the piano stool broke in two pieces, and here the studio audience's laughter was not pre-recorded, but genuine.

Apparently, and not surprisingly, both Fame and Price had admired one another for quite a while. Alan Price, not a stranger to being criticized, be it for deserting the Animals when they needed a stable line-up, or hi-jacking the credits for the "Traditional/Arranged" tag of "House of The Rising Sun", felt a definite kinship when Georgie was lauded with snide remarks as the young wisecrack who had hired the Ronnie-Scott-led Jazz elite for his Big Band album *Sound Venture*, and who was continuing to use adept Jazzers in his band line-ups, just as Alan himself was with his own outfit.

In return, "the Ronnie Scott led Jazz elite" had such a fine reputation that they found themselves hired in the most unlikely environments, for instance in the vain campaign to rescue the Mod kings The Small Faces from disbanding, who had recorded a 6-weeks-at-number-1 album in *Ogdens' Nut Gone Flake* in 1968 but did not seem to be able to re-enact it on stage. As Roland Schmitt and this author pointed out in *Happy Boys Happy!*: "There were half-hearted attempts. The band had at least chosen the *Ogdens'* numbers 'Song Of A Baker' and 'Rollin' Over' for the stage set, and even hired guest musicians. Ronnie [Lane]: 'There was the half-arsed attempt to present Georgie Fame's brass section. [Ronnie Scott, Johnny Marshall and Tony Coe on saxes, Les Condon, Ian Hamer and Derek Healey on trumpets plus Morris Platt, trombone, documented on the album *The Autumn Stone*]. So we got into it alright, but this turned out to be so bloody expensive, and people were still screaming, so we gave that up."

(The strategy did not prevent the disbanding of The Small Faces, but it was their deserted leader, Alexis Korner prodigy Steve Marriott who remembered the Fame-led reed & brass university when he hired flute player Lyn Dobson for Humble Pie's debut album *As Safe As Yesterday Is*. The Marriott-free Faces, as a trio armed with Rod Stewart and Ronnie Wood, remembered the Fame bugler Harry Beckett for their single "Had Me A Real Good Time".)

On 17th January 1969, Georgie Fame was back at the Albert Hall, but in quite different company: with Blues Rock legends Ten Years After and Alan Price's Barnes neighbour Roger Chapman with his progressive band Family. This was not a bad pairing, though, because both had shown R&B and Jazz leanings previously: witness Alvin Lee's version of "At The Woodchopper's Ball" on the TYA live album *Undead* and Roger Chapman's "Old Songs – New Songs" on the then most popular Family album *Music In A Doll's House*. The fact that Ten Years After ventured into heavy Blues Rock and Family married Folk with Psychedelia only showed that concert bills were not as codified as they would become in the near future. Still, watching these once jazzy Rock bands perform did not faze Fame for the moment: he was in for pursuing his course and cause, melting horn sections and punchy rhythms – no wailing guitar solos for him.

Archivists claim there were three TV specials with Georgie: two custom-made with Fame as the main star by Radio-Television-Belge in Brussels, and one for Austrian TV ORF which was used for Vienna's claim in the Montreux International Festival. Wiped, all of them, as would be the case with many BBC programmes of the era. Still, not all the attics between Antwerp and Salzburg have yet been searched for bootleg video copies.

R&B takes preference over lush strings: Seventh Son

Following the lavish, and often openly quaint and nostalgic arrangements on *The Third Face Of Fame* (called *Anni Rugenti* in Italy), Fame had gone one step further – and recorded an album accompanied by strings. Such a move is lauded in this day and age – one thinks of Amy McDonald's 2011 orchestral version of her album *A Curious Thing* or Paul Carrack's critically acclaimed violin-soaked effort *A Different Hat*. But then, purists as well as "style policing" Flamingo revisionists were out to get the man formerly known as Clive Powell, and Georgie put the album on hold in order to record a further collection with a troupe of hand-picked, fine Jazz musicians. As a renewed attempt, if only subconsciously, at some street credibility, this didn't really make sense: the 15 strong big band line-up resembled his highly ambitious but still frowned upon *Sound Venture* setting.

For the *Seventh Son* album, there was Blue Flame Colin Green again on acoustic and electric guitar. As a tried and tested sideman, he arranged the whole album with Georgie, coming up with great ideas along the way. He had Harvey Burns on drums, a renowned session player who had worked for Al Stewart and was in Cat Stevens' services for *Mona Bone Jakon* that same year. He would stay on for the band project *Shorty*. Brian Odgers had already been hailed as a legendary double-bass master. Now equally adept on electric bass, he would serve Georgie Fame up until the 1990s.

Frank Ricotti on vibraphone had also worked as a much in-demand studio man, who would go on to rattle tambourines and cabbassas for part-time Rhythm King Peter Frampton, and Mark Knopfler. He also played tuned percussion for Fame's future band mate Van Morrison as well as Blood, Sweat & Tears. Certainly, Georgie did not have to hide behind that particular US band, with regard to his own horn-soaked *Seventh Son* achievement. Pete Aherne also worked on percussion, playing when Frank Ricotti was busy elsewhere.

Still, for Georgie it must have seemed like a breath of fresh air, with four of his own compositions in, numbers by his old mentor Mike O'Neill and many lyrics supplied by his favourite poet of the time, Jeff Ryan. The album was recorded from June until the autumn of 1969 and released on November 18th by CBS. At the production helm, Georgie wanted his TV partner Alan Price, who turned out to be spot on in realizing Fame's strengths.

Seventh Son – track by track

The Willie Dixon standard "Seventh Son" had been a favourite with many American and British R&B artists, not least Georgie's role model Mose Allison and the Hamburg Star-Club favourites The Remo Four, led by Tony Ashton. Its theme – the ability of second sight and looking into the future – seemed too good to miss in the context of Rock'n'Roll mysticism. And why leave all the voodoo to Dr John?

But Georgie Fame had apparently outgrown the old Flamingo Club habit of imaginatively recording a standard of his own stage show honed for years for the sake of the dance crowd, in the most effective groove. Instead, he and Colin Green had a surprise for this venture: they chose a clever 7/4 time signature, honoring the "Seven" in the title. This still didn't detract from an incredible drive. Plus, they double-tracked Fame's voice to great effect and let the whole big brass section off the leash in fine style!

In complete contrast to Georgie and his big combo, the Climax Blues Band created a completely laid-back, dead slow version which thrived on the bass vocals of sax man Colin Cooper and the tenor voice of guitarist Peter Haycock, both sadly gone now.

A British chart placing of #25 wasn't sensational, but any Top 30 listing is proof that a number is recognized by the public to some extent. Still, this successful realization of a great idea was in good company with the equally odd 5/4 count of Blind Faith's "Do What You Like" where Georgie's Flamingo friend Steve Winwood played Hammond, and is not simply a nostalgic nod to "Take Five" – thus deserving a much wider acceptance. Jethro Tull's 'Living In The Past', a big hit the same year, was also in 5/4, as was part of the Pentangle's minor UK hit/BBC TV theme song 'Light Flight' – another part being in 7/4: must have been a trend in 1969 …

"Blossom" by one of Fame's prime lyricists, Jeffrey Alexander Ryan and Georgie (credited as Clive Powell) is a Swing Waltz which alternates nicely between a Jazz trio feel and the luxurious icing on that cake by the big brass section. As previously sketched, this was a kind of heartfelt obligation by Georgie to repay a compliment made to him two years previously by American Jazz chanteuse Blossom Dearie with the song "Sweet Georgie Fame". He would re-visit the song 44 years later (!) with an acoustic version for the trio album *Lost In A Lover's Dream*.

Still, a public compliment in song always tends to put you on the spot, as, for instance, US guitarist Roy Buchanan would find out in 1975 when Jeff Beck created the unforgettable "Cause We've Ended As Lovers" on *Blow By Blow*. It seems much better to be the first one in than having to come up with a reply like "My Friend Jeff", or, in this case, "Blossom". Fame of course is probably the prime mover when it comes to portraying personalities: boxer Cassius Clay in "The Ali Shuffle"; Alex Higgins In "The Hurricane"; or the BBC 2 Radio legend Terry Wogan in "Wogan's Air", which Fame presented with a nod and a wink to live audiences as early as 1983, but only recorded in 2002. Georgie is certainly the champion in creative *Name Dropping*.

"Inside Story", again by Jeff Ryan and Clive Powell himself presents some pulsating yet melancholy friendly Rock patterns by Brian Odgers' electric bass and Harvey Burns' charged but relaxed groove, sparse electric piano and well placed horn accents drive this tale of being alone in the big metropolis, wondering when the pain of watching people inside will stop.

"Am I Wasting My Time?" was written by Mike O'Neill of Nero and the Gladiators. O'Neill and his group are still regularly quoted by Fame to this day. He genuinely likes this Sixties combo: apart from owing so much to their leader O'Neill, who put him up in 1962 when Georgie was "between engagements", erstwhile Gladiators Boots Slade and Colin Green both became Blue Flames. This Swing is not a million miles away from "The Ballad of Bonnie and Clyde" or indeed other 1930s reminiscences on *The Third Face Of Fame*. It was a nice touch to change the rhythm to straight 4/4 near the fade-out. Like so many of Fame's album tracks, this was presented in his TV shows with Alan Price.

"Is It Really The Same?" was based on a composition by Keith Jarrett which the young pianist recorded in 1966 with the Charles Lloyd Quartet, and got supplied with lyrics by Mike O'Neill. It presents one more driving groove, an urgent Swing with a Blue Flames feel and Georgie back on the Hammond organ. Great breaks are filled by Harvey Burns, an inspired sax solo and a subtle yet song-defining guitar riff by Colin Green.

"Somebody Stole My Thunder" by Jeff Ryan and James Lacy remains one of the best dance floor items ever supplied by Fame. Its significance also became clear as CBS later made it into the accompanying single, backed by Fame's recent title song for a film soundtrack, *Entertaining Mr Sloane*. It got some praise in the press:

Record Mirror wrote about their "Star Single" of the week, "Somebody Stole My Thunder"/"Entertaining Me Sloane" on June 6th, 1970, showing the bearded, long-haired entertainer beside it: "It's a track from the *Seventh Son* album, but no matter. Well, not much matter." Apparently, the custom of lifting Singles tracks from an album instead of presenting brand new material had not been fully accepted in the British record world, the writing on the wall in terms of the superiority of the album, at a time when "download" was a term for lorry drivers or – good morning America – truck drivers.

The review continues: "Georgie wrote this surefire number and the Alan Price production drives like the proverbial clappers. Fast paced, with beautiful, incisive brass figures, hard-swinging drumming and Georgie driving his considerable weight and authority on the whole proceedings. For sure one of our most consistent, if restless, musicians – this is part-Pop, part-Modern Jazz, part-orchestral. One of Georgie's best performances; which puts it in a phrase how good it is. – Chart Cert."

An urgent guitar riff and also funky rhythm work by Colin Green make this pure Soul and a welcome follow-up to the James Brown leanings Georgie had successfully attempted in "Papa's Got A Brand New Bag", complete with a great interlude before a final onslaught, where the horns get into their own again. Nobody stole Georgie Fame's thunder yet! This became the title track of a latter-day double LP and CD, *Somebody Stole My Thunder*, which Fame himself hails as much more representative than any of the many cheapo hits collections.

Georgie's "Ho Ho Ho" comes out as a rather forlorn Christmas story about "Missus Claus" knocking on Mr Powell's door, who "was eager to be willing". The "Jingle Bells" quotes on xylophone are a little corny, and the early fadeout makes this a bit undecided.

"Bird In A World Of People", again composed by Mike O'Neill – is fine melancholic Jazz with sophisticated time signatures, another hint back to the *Sound Venture* album, and a clever citation of "Confirmation", which genre buffs quickly recognized as Charlie Parker generated. Peter King is on sax. It certainly reminds us of "The Woodshed" on *The Blues And Me* and 1995's Ronnie Scott's Club live document *Walking Wounded*. At six and a half minutes running-time, this is a tour de force with hot-blooded swing, painful regret – the central achievement of the album. Georgie's voice is in absolutely top form, and doesn't need any fiddling on the soundboard.

Lyrically, the Powell composition "Fully Booked" serves as some kind of tongue-in-cheek predecessor to the famous "Mambo No. 5", with its name-dropping of all the ladies at Georgie Fame's "disposal", which the family man had obvious fun at rendering. This was the B-side of the "Seventh Son" single. Apparently, neither Fame nor his partner Jeff Ryan had got round to deciding on a melody for this praise of backstage and front-of-stage ladies, and so Georgie simply narrated the tale of his startling effect on the female fan base – a stylistic choice which made the twinkle-twinkle nature of his pursuits more casual, those spoken words also serving as a hint at what was to come in the completely self-penned album *All Me Own Work* at the end of 1972 on the Warner Bros label.

"Vino Tequila" is another composition by Jeff Ryan and James Lacy. With only the highly accomplished guitar accompaniment by Colin Green's acoustic picking, this sad ballad – sung in Spanish! – presents a lovesick Georgie, once again showing a sheer versatility which is usually reserved, in people's imagination, to the Beatles, those four fellow Northerners Fame often "hung out" with "in" clubs like the Bag O'Nails.

The tie-in launch of the single of the same name, "Seventh Son"/"Fully Booked" – on November 28th – caused quite a stir, resulting in #35 in *Record Mirror* charts, a January rating of #10 at Radio Luxembourg, and #30 in the *NME*.

Fame certainly did his thing promoting the single – appearing in a hilarious hooded gown during the Alan Price television show *Monster Music Mash* on BBC-2 TV on November 11th, 1969.

Four days after the album's release, Georgie's "Seventh Son" was performed again in the BBC Television Centre with the TV Pop girl dance troupe, Pan's People, on *The Price Of Fame,* his joint BBC2 television programme in eight episodes with Alan Price. What better way to promote the new album?

With plans to take this whole bunch of studio musician "cats" on the road at the start of the New Year 1970, Fame stayed in London for the Christmas festivities. Boxing Day as well as the following December 27th had been pencilled in for a second Georgie Fame spot on the Portuguese television show *Zip Zip*.

According to this author's Portuguese Fame "correspondent" António Alfaiate, "*Zip Zip*"was a weekly chat show, with musicians as guests, which was on the air for seven months between May 26th, 1969 and December 29th, 1969. Georgie had been on the programme in October 1969. One of his songs came as a pleasant surprise, because it was a Brazilian number that he sang in Portuguese, 'A Mulher da Gente' (composed by Grande Otelo). It was the second time that Georgie was on Portuguese TV in 1969.

"The first appearance was on January 1st on the programme *Variedades. Zip Zip* was maybe the first "window" of liberty on a television then very much controlled by the government. The series was recorded every Saturday at a theatre in front an audience and was broadcast the next Monday after difficult negotiations with the authorities.

Scheduled to be recorded in Lisbon, the presentation was postponed for three months, for which the Georgie Fame Fanclub Newsletter claimed "certain censorship problems on the show – as you know, it's mainly a 'chat' programme", which is in line with Alfaiate's observations. Since the programme ended on the 29th December 1969, the planned second presence of Georgie never happened.

As far as the fan club was concerned, Fame reminisced for the BBC in 2013 and mentioned "Jackie Tibbs, who later became Mrs Jackie Herman, was the fan club secretary. [Pianist/singer/prcussionist] Cab Kay's daughter Terry was also in the office – they had their own office in Old Compton Street. I think Paul McCartney kept his going until most recently." You received a newsletter about every month, for about a shilling, in those simple days before the internet. Georgie: "It was a little bit like Facebook, what you had for dinner last week."

"Lush Vibes" – the lounge album Georgie Does His Thing With Strings

As mentioned, Fame had recorded this album before *Seventh Son*. Like his 1968 album, *The Third Face Of Fame*, it was produced by Mike Smith, but instead of using Big Band arrangements, Fame and Smith worked with the Keith Mansfield Orchestra.

It was led by composer/arranger Keith Mansfield, born in 1941 and thus two years Georgie's senior. At the time, Mansfield had had recent chart success by providing the hit – and the crucial as well as critically dividing orchestral backing – for Love Affair's "Everlasting Love". Other accolades were for arranging "Reflections Of My Life" by Marmalade and for producing the album *Dusty ... Definitely* in 1968. Mansfield had also worked with the Jazz musician Maynard Furguson and is married to singer Salena Jones, who shares her experience of appearing at Ronnie Scott's Jazz Club – and working with the Count Basie Orchestra – with Georgie. Using Art Themen on saxophone in the studio is another factor they had in common.

Keith Mansfield was also renowned for the theme music of *Grandstand* on BBC and for his "Funky Fanfare" trailer music, used as recently as 2012. It was once meant for the 1960s TV series *Astro Daters* and was lately sampled by Danger Mouse and MF DOOM as DangerDoom for the number "Old School" featuring Talib K. Last but not least, Mansfield was respected for a lot of work in UK library music, a genre in which Fame's later working partner Steve Gray also thrived.

Georgie had not been too happy about being asked to record this album, and he still remembered his frustration in 2009 when he talked about it to Duncan Heining:

"They can't resist meddling – the non-players, the advisers, the so-called managers that don't actually play and don't sweat, and their adrenaline doesn't flow when you're actually creating this stuff. They can't resist meddling to justify their existence and their percentage ... Mike Smith was a very good in-house producer at CBS but it wasn't where I was coming from. I was thrown into an alien regime. I did a strings album that wasn't bad. At least it gave me the chance to sing some ballads but then again Mike Smith chose 70% of the repertoire and a lot of those tunes were tunes I would never consider singing. I managed to get 'Everything Happens To Me' and a couple of other nice tunes but most of it was selected for me. We used to have these discussions that verged on arguments – 'What do you want me to sing that for? Well, this is what the company wants you to do blah blah.'"

As will be seen, some of those choices were also made by some of the top Pop, Jazz, Soul and Blues singers of the time, so Fame was not exactly out in the artistically deprived MOR desert.

Georgie Does His Thing With Strings – track by track

"And I Love Her" by Lennon & McCartney is introduced via a single cornet. This very contemplative Rumba number was performed live by Paul McCartney in the early, pre-recording Beatles repertoire. After that, it was only done once in 1964 for a BBC

Top Gear show. Written mainly by Paul, John Lennon claimed to have contributed the commercial middle-eight section at producer George Martin's request.

Fame may have complained of being "given" songs to record, but he was actually in excellent Jazz company in covering this song: Esther Phillips, Julie London, Shirley Horn and Rita Lee were the ladies, Ramsey Lewis and Roland Kirk as well as Chet Atkins had supplied instrumental versions, and there were also takers form the Reggae and Soul world with the Wailers and the Detroit Emeralds using this song. What's more, two years after Fame the R&B veteran Bobby Womack contributed his take – crucial enough for Georgie as he was to cover the man's "Daylight" six years later.

"Maybe In The Spring Again" by James Lacey and Georgie's lyricist partner Jeffrey Alexander Ryan gets a Swing waltz arrangement. Underlined by Harvey Burns's relaxed brush work, the strings' background is nicely offset by flute and piano touches, as Georgie hopes for spring time, getting his love back to him – a rather short performance that could have benefitted from another verse and more soloing.

"In The Wee Small Hours (Of The Morning)" comes from Frank Sinatra's concept album of the same name, about his Ava Gardner relationship troubles. The 1955 ballad itself, by David Mann and Bob Hilliard, has been in the repertoires of Count Basie, and recently of Jamie Cullum. The pace is slowed down to a truly melancholic mood here, which is then picked up by brushes and piano, only to give in to the loneliness encompassed by cornet – strings assisting in true Hollywood style. Lying awake with sad thoughts really does become imaginable here.

"What's New" is the world famous standard from 1939, composed by Bob Haggart as "I'm Free", with lyrics provided by Johnny Burke. Popularized by Frank Sinatra, it later became the title track for one of Linda Ronstadt's albums in her lounge Jazz series. As John Scheinfeld points out in his Fame biography, Ronstadt received praise where Georgie had to meet frowns and scepticism with these lush, moody tunes, although it must be said that he tackles this memorable composition with more understatement than Linda's dramatic lament.

"Woe Is Me" by P. Smythe and Jeffrey Alexander Ryan is another slow Swing which Fame liked enough to include it in his first CD compilation in 1990: *The First Thirty Years*. Lost love in spring time is the subject. "The winter weather which together we ignored is worse now there's no central heating" is unintentionally funny in the context of well performed sadness.

Singing about how "A House Is Not A Home" when "no one is there to hold you tight and no one there that you can kiss good night" – slowly the projected feeling of irrevocable loss takes on the dimensions of Frank Sinatra's 1950s Capitol albums, the almost unbearable melancholy here taken off a little bit by the rhythm guitar towards the end. Composed by Burt Bacharach and written by his lyricist Hal David for Dionne Warwick and the film of the same name, this has some great acoustic guitar work.

Again, credibility for choosing such a number lies in the fact that giants like Stevie Wonder, Luther Vandross, Ronald Isley of the Isley Brothers and Dusty Springfield made sure they included it in their repertoire.

Dusty also picked Herb Alpert's "This Guy's In Love With You", as did B.J. Thomas and Sacha Distel and Motown man Jimmy Ruffin in those days, while Georgie may well have worried that tear jerker Des O'Connor was also fond of it. Here, Fame's Jazz combo is thankfully in the front seat for this swingy number, which Georgie paces up compared to the original. Allowing the strings in only after the first verse, he and his band mates are moving things along.

The fact that Fame chose Herb Alpert's 1968 #1 smash which surely millions already owned as a single record shows that his love for a tune like this Burt Bacharach & Hal David classic must have come first and foremost – above and beyond the calls of commercial considerations. A few subdued drum fills loosen the proceedings up again towards the end.

"Girl Talk" by Neil Hefti and Julie London's husband Bobby "Route 66" Troup works as a 6/8 mid-tempo Blues that lightens up the mood by relating young ladies' gossip, "the weaker sex, the speaker's ex" being a cute play on words because it calls for an obvious but nice and naughty spoonerism. When he talks about "dishing the dirt" he gives us a tiny bit of that by including a laid back electric guitar solo. Betty Carter, Julie London and Tony Bennett had also laid their vocals on this number. So again, Georgie seemed in good and tasteful company here.

"Who's Kissing You Blues" by Georgie himself and Jeffrey Alexander Ryan comes on as another slow Swing – a consequent move as Fame is getting back into lovesick mode: "Lost in the snow, no place to go" reminding us of the central heating problem. But Georgie must have noticed that himself, as he accelerates the pace with piano, bass & brushed drums and some relaxed but more adventurous phrasing.

"Everything Happens To Me" by Matt Dennis and George Adair and first recorded by Sinatra with the Tommy Dorsey Orchestra in 1940, and later with the Hollywood String Quartet, is extra special because a considerable part is sung a cappella before strings and the bar trio assist Georgie in telling us about his ongoing bad luck: "I've gone and mortgaged all my castles in the air". Such a move is hardly surprising, and he's telling us why, "Your answer was goodbye, there was even postage due". The phrasing at the end is a daring little teaser which Georgie still uses live today. A small-group re-arrangement of this favourite Stan Getz, Charlie Parker and Chet Baker tune appeared on Georgie's 1989 *A Potrait of Chet* with the Ellen Helmus Quintet. This was actually one of the songs Georgie himself picked for the album, while producer Mike Smith had decided on the bulk of its repertoire.

"Guess Who I Saw Today" works really well as a love-gone-sour-soap. What starts as a harmonious hour after the office, "Can I fix you a Martini?" turns into a dramatic revelation: 'Georgie' as the protagonist comes home to his partner and tells her that he had found a lovely new French café – and there in the darkness, "Guess who I saw today? I saw you!" There is no ending here, a fact that only enhances the tension, very well performed with the punchline only revealed in the last second. Again, this song works as a male-female or a female-male drama. Of the many vocalists who tried their skills with this Murray Grand and Elisse Boyd Musical composition from 1952 (for *New Faces of 1952*), Janis Siegel of Manhattan Transfer fame (a true

Jon Hendricks disciple like Georgie) succeeded with a fine, sensitive version on her 2001 album *I Wish You Love*. Only a direct comparison to the Fame version lets her appear to sing a touch too beautifully, while our own man, albeit impeccable in tone, manages to add the crucial nonchalance that is necessary to point out that the atrocious breach of confidence of the two-timing has hardly sunk in.

In "Need Your Love So Bad", the trump card gets saved for the finale. Written in 1955 by Little Willie John's older brother Mertis John junior, Peter Green had pioneered the use of strings in British Blues with Fleetwood Mac using this very tune. But Georgie wisely decided not to use their arrangement or sound picture, instead opting for a lighter approach with a slightly more up-tempo reading. Again, this version seems far too short for the listener to really get into it.

The album cover is amongst the most eye-catching in the Fame catalogue. Clad in a smart, dark-brown suit with an open blue shirt and facing the camera in a dreamy notion, Georgie is surrounded by three lavishly posing, naked girls, who manage to remain "decent" by hiding their lovely assets behind violins and a cello. While this design concept put Fame in the Easy Listening bracket, fans must have seen beyond this, only to find a worthwhile achievement which still works fine today.

In their *New albums by the panel* section of February 14th, 1970, Valentine's Day as a fitting date for a young lovers' album, *Record Mirror* let Georgie Fame headline above Judith Durham, Arlo Guthrie, The Box Tops and Gary Puckett and the Union Gap, Pearls Before Swine, The Fifth Avenue Band as well as Paul Siebel. The magazine presented the headline "Super smooth George swings with strings", listed all the tracks and wrote: "Though released surprisingly quickly after Georgie's *Seventh Son* album, this offers yet another facet of his talent. Plucked away from his earthy Blues roots [well, with the exception of "Need Your Love So Bad"] Georgie is equally happy singing smoothly along with [the] Keith Mansfield Orchestra on Bacharach/David numbers 'A House Is Not A Home' and 'This Guy's In Love With You'.

"As well as some good old standards there's a particularly interesting composition by J. Lacey and Jeff Alexander Ryan, 'Maybe In The Spring Again', with a touch of Swing, and Georgie's own 'Who's Kissing You Blues'. Woeful ballads, tender love songs, they're all there on an easy-listening album and a worthy addition to a collection. A novelty sleeve, with naked ladies and strategically placed string instruments, and listen for the inevitable send-up humour at the end. – VM"

Entertaining Mr Sloane – Georgie's soundtrack work

Around the time of recording *Georgie Does His Things With Strings*, Fame got the commission to write a film score for a movie with Anglo-Amalgamated Film Distributors Ltd., *Entertaining Mr Sloane*. This mysterious, dark work by London film director Douglas Hickox (1929–1988) was the second adaptation of the theatre play of the same name by Joe Orton – ITV in Britain had produced and screened an earlier version in July 1968. Hickox hired name actors Peter McEnery, Alan Webb and Harry Andrews – for his black comedy about a mysterious woman, Kath (played by Beryl Reid), in the London suburbs who seduces a young man, who in turn gets eyed by her brother, and shares a dark secret with the father. The film was also released in America in July 1970.

There was no soundtrack LP from the album, but as mentioned Georgie used the title track, which he wrote and sang, as the B-side of his 1970 single "Somebody Stole My Thunder", which he lifted from the *Seventh Son* album from late 1969. For die-heart fans, the movie is now available as a DVD.

Colin Green remembers collaborating on the creation of this film music: "He got the contract and basically said 'We'll write the score', which meant he and I did it. We disappeared then to his cottage in the country and basically wrote notes for the score and wrote most of the incidental music. I don't think the soundtrack came out on an album. It was the first film project I was involved in writing. I had been playing on some."

The Georgie Fame Band that toured the UK – and America: Shorty!

Tenor Saxophonist Alan Skidmore (b. 21st April 1942 in London) was one of the key members in Georgie Fame's new band. Perfectly suited for Georgie's purpose, he had toured with comedian Tony Hancock as a 16-year-old, and had worked as a member of Ronnie Scott's select group. With Alan Skidmore, Georgie had acquired some real London Jazz aristocrat.

Alan Skidmore's father, Richard James "Jimmy" Skidmore (1916–1998), also excelled as a tenor saxophonist and was well-known and respected for his work with Jazz mainstream master and radio personality Humphrey Lyttelton. More significant for Fame, Skidmore junior had played the Flamingo club, together with Brian Auger, and also Alexis Korner. Skid was also a member of Ronnie Scott's Group, so he played in both London clubs that are quite inseparable from Georgie's career. He had also, for instance, worked on Brian Bennett's *Change Of Direction* album in 1967, the versatile Shadows drummer and producer would join the Blue Flames in 1972. Another example is pianist Stan Tracey's band Seven Ages of Man, where Skidmore played with Blue Flame Peter King and incidentally met more of the studio crew on Fame's *Seventh Son*, among them fellow tenor man Tony Coe, vibraphonist Frank Ricotti, trumpeter Derek Watkins and trombone man Chris Pyne.

Jimmy Skidmore's son Alan appreciated the sounds he grew up with, but soon he became an ardent admirer of John Coltrane, an influence you could hear during his first *NDR Jazz Workshop* in Hamburg, 1967, and on his 1969 solo debut LP *Once Upon A Time*. And he also dearly loved Miles Davis. Skidmore junior had famously supplied the smoky sax solo on John Mayall's *Bluesbreakers with Eric Clapton "Beano"* album track "Have You Heard":

"I wasn't actually on the road with John Mayall and Eric Clapton. I just did three albums with them – the *"Beano"* album and another couple [*A Hard Road, Bare Wires*]. But who I was on the road with for quite a long time was Alexis Korner, which is a university, being at university, really, learning to play a slow Blues in E major." With regard to "Have You Heard", Skidmore added rather shyly: "Michael Brecker once told me that this track got him on the path to picking up the saxophone" – how much more praise can you get?

Skidmore first met Fame "at The Flamingo, in the days when – as Clive talks about on the gigs – there was Dick Heckstall-Smith and the bass player was Jack Bruce, and then Ginger Baker, until Alexis Korner pinched them. I was coming in and I was around at that time."

Jazz aficionado "Skid" soon had his own in-service-training as far as the Blues was concerned: "That was just slightly early. Although I was playing, I hadn't quite got into that. But I was forced, kicked into it by being asked to do the John Mayall recordings and joining Alexis Korner's band for a few years of touring. So that did the trick. It's like I have said to other people in the past: 'If you can't play the Blues, you may as well give up!', because that's the most important thing that you have got to play. That affects everything else that you play. It's the basis. But then we didn't really work much together, I don't think, before about 1968. I was with Alexis Korner for quite a long time.

"Being with Alexis Korner is being at university, really, learning to play a slow Blues in E major. There is a fantastic story about Miles [Davis], you know that one? There was somebody. I can't remember who it was, doing a trumpet workshop in New York, for trumpet students, and Miles decides to go along: check it out, see what's happening. The guy sees Miles come in the door, at the back of the place. Miles comes in, stands there, just to check out things. Then the guy asks the students a question: 'If a piece of music is written in the key of E major concept – where does that put the trumpet? – Mr Davis, would you like to tell us?' So Miles says 'Back in the fucking case!' Obviously, that puts the B flat instruments out of it, into F sharp. But then, getting back to that, I had to play Blues in E major concept for quite a few years with Alexis Korner, along with Chris Pyne on trombone."

Skidmore joined the soon to be renamed Georgie Fame Band at the end of 1969: "I don't think I had to do an audition, as far as I can remember, no. We are talking about a long time ago, and I have to reach into the grey matter. We did a few gigs together in this country. It seemed to come around very quickly."

Then the plan of a US sojourn was suddenly in the air. Skidmore: "I can remember being somewhere in Bond Street, in an office or something with him, organizing this tour of the States, with a band they didn't know what to call it. Just 'Georgie Fame?' – I said 'Why don't we call it Shorty?'

"So that was my idea: 'Don't go Shorty' comes around by being in Germany where, instead of saying 'Dankeschön', I started saying "Don't go short." And it turned from that "Don't go short" into "Don't go Shorty", and then it became "Shorty". So it developed, and we ended up as being *Shorty featuring Georgie Fame*."

For Fame's guitarist, Colin Green, the idea of a Shorty US tour was too little, too late – certainly a case of a lost opportunity: "It was a real shame that we couldn't have gone to America at the time when the band was hot. I was always told that we didn't do that because we were an integrated band, and this didn't go down too well. But I don't know whether that was the actual reason or whether we just didn't hit it there, because he had the hit there subsequently with "The Ballad of Bonnie and Clyde", and he got saddled with that as an image. So they wouldn't take him really seriously as a Blues man. Then, in 1970, the name Shorty was applied, definitely, to try and get away from that image and kind of build a new career, if you like. It was quite a bold move. We only went once, so I don't know how well that worked."

Apart from Alan Skidmore and Colin Green, the band featured members from the 15-strong group Fame had had on the road in the autumn of 1969 in order to promote his *Seventh Son* album. There was Brian Odgers, for whom 'Skid' still had a lot of praise in 2012: "Brian Odgers, who was the bass guitarist, although originally a very fine double bass player – he was tremendous, a lovely man, fantastic. He was doing so many sessions a day. He decided to take up the bass guitar, and he did very well. But I'm afraid he has since packed it in altogether. Sadly he is not playing anymore. There is a really good recording with John McLaughlin, *Extrapolation*, that is with Brian Odgers on bass: Tony Oxley, John McLaughlin and Brian Odgers."

Georgie Fame confirms Skidmore's view in Colin Harper's John McLaughlin biog *Bathed In Lightning*: "I don't think that at that time he [McLaughlin] had done the album with John Surman, and with Brian Odgers, *Extrapolation*, a great, revolutionary album in 1969, because I didn't meet Brian Odgers until 1969/70 when we started working together. And he had just done that album. I haven't seen him for several years. He was very close with Alan Skidmore, and Skid hasn't heard from him for year or two. He [Odgers] lost interest in playing I think, a pity cause he was a fantastic musician."

The drums were still played by Harvey Burns. The first foreign dates by the new band were in Sydney, Australia. In one of the city's biggest clubs, they managed to draw big audiences for three weeks. In the meantime, Fame's manager Rik Gunnell "was the US representative for the Robert Stigwood Organization in America, and that gave me the idea of touring over there", as Georgie recalls.

"And then we toured the States", Skidmore reminisces, "in June 1970 on a Pan Am aero plane, from Heathrow to Los Angeles, across the top in one go. There weren't many people. There were about twelve people on the aircraft, and six of them were the band! There wasn't much left in the booze cabinet at the end of the trip. We did a couple of weeks at the 'Whisky-A-Go-Go' club on Sunset Strip. The funny thing was: we arrived, and we checked into this very nice Hyatt on the corner of 79th Street and Sunset Strip" – the hotel that was immortalized by Steve Marriott in the contemporary, 1971 Humble Pie song "79th And Sunset".

Alan Skidmore: "That is the one. I wandered down the road, a couple of blocks, and saw a bar. And when I walked in, the first person that I saw was the bass player I had been working with for some years before with Alexis Korner – a very nice guy by the name of Danny Thompson. He was in the pub – he was the first guy I saw. You are 7000 miles away from home. You go and find a bar. You want a beer, and you bump into an old mate. We were on tour for a good few weeks. It must have been four or five weeks – we did San Francisco: we played in this place called Fillmore West for a week or so. We played a club in New York, then in Chicago. I've done a few tours of the States, with Georgie and with other people. Washington and Philadelphia may have been with someone else. I can't really understand why the man isn't a huge success in the States, in his own right, anyway! He should be. He is one of the greatest singers that I've ever heard in my life. He is just phenomenal!"

Just before the tour, the single that had been extracted from the *Seventh Son* album, "Somebody Stole My Thunder", a track which has been on countless compilations ever since, went down a storm in a long "American" live version which was a real concert cornerstone.

The album for the tour, albeit recorded in the UK before the event, was quite obviously called *Shorty ft. Georgie Fame* and, in terms of adventure friendly repertoire, was certainly on a par with *Rhythm & Blues at the Flamingo* and an improvement on the partly live *The Two Faces of Fame*. The sound is as clear as it is 'in your face' – and you can imagine not only the US Hippie community take notice of an outfit that can rock hard and swing like there's no tomorrow.

Shorty ft. Georgie Fame – track by track

Fame's own "Oliver's Gone" makes use of the bandleader's love of changing rhythms. Colin Green introduces a rocky theme a little bit like Robbie Robertson leads into The Band's "The Weight" – Georgie was going to meet him six years later at Shangri-La Studios in L.A. while recording the shelved *Daylight* for Island Records. Changing into a Swing section shows that the *Shorty* Flames have by no means relinquished the Fame trademarks of a jazzy sound.

"Bluesology" had been backed by the Harry South Orchestra back in 1967 – here, Fame's Hammond leads into the Milt Jackson tune at a breakneck pace, 120 beats per minute instead of the comfortable 96 on *The Two Faces Of Fame*. "Alan Skidmore on the saxophone", Georgie is just about able to announce at the end, having mastered the tongue twister lyrics in true 'try this at home and get hurt' manner.

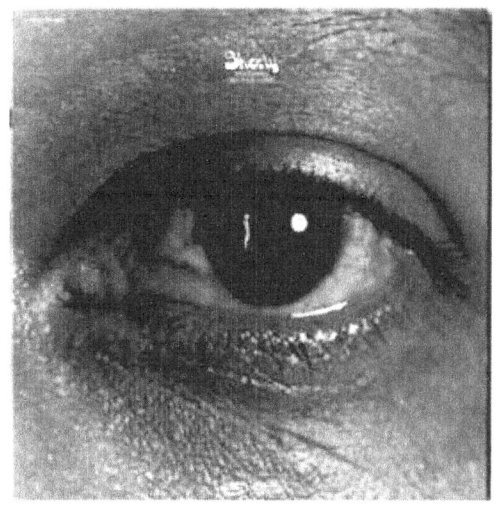

"Saskatchewan Sunrise" by Jeffrey Alexander Ryan and R. Jones follows at a more relaxed pace, and is a number to be treasured as it suits Georgie's laconic singing talents so well. He seems utterly at ease here, and can be heard oozing the same quality that he himself loved about, say, J.J. Cale.

"Parchman Farm" had been a live staple since the Flamingo Club days; this finger-snapping, urgent as well as cool reading of the Mose Allison could be the best that Fame, or any other artist, has ever put on record. The rhythm section swings like hell once again, and the way Fame's Hammond and Green's funky guitar work around Alan Skidmore's sax wailings is exemplary, especially as Brian Odgers lays down an elegant bass line to die for – all this for more than seven minutes of pure enjoyment and ecstasy.

Mike O'Neill's "Is It Really The Same" stays rather close to the arrangement on the *Seventh Son* album, pushing the hypnotic riff forward for another great Alan Skidmore chance to wail, and sounding even more coherent than on the studio recording.

When Fame decided to apply a 7/4 rhythm for the title track "Seventh Son", the Willie Dixon composition's percussion work sounded a bit technical and cold on the actual studio recording, in spite of striking a successful chord with audiences everywhere. Once again, the live reading leaves a more organic impression, maybe due to the percussive introduction being cleverly picked on electric guitar by Colin Green instead of the more obvious cowbell. Great Hammond work by Georgie himself – the only thing missing is the harmony singing by Alan Price. The ad-libbing towards the second section and the clever natural fadeout are also great treats.

"Somebody Stole My Thunder", as mentioned, has dated ever so well in its studio incarnation, remaining a Northern Soul classic, but if anything, this live workout recreates all its crucial ingredients – and rectifies its only flaw, being too short. The Shorty boys go in for a repeat rendition that is not only welcome but entirely natural.

More mellow tones for "Inside Story" about the city lights and city angst, as always moved along and dynamically developed by Harvey Burns delightful groove with bass drum and snare patterns to really write home about.

"Fully Booked", again from *Seventh Son*, got an almost complete overhaul – a twelve minute Blues medley marathon that starts out as Mose Allison's "One Room Country Shack" which shows the band's capacities to great effect again. The rhythm and the character of the studio recording is only picked up in the second half, relegating the first version to a mere sketch for this successful blast, Georgie's catcalls included.

The album only came out in the US, on Epic Records, and contained liner notes by by Blossom Dearie, including the lyrics to her song "Sweet Georgie Fame".

Although Fame & Green, Skidmore, Odgers & Burns had apparently enjoyed the tour, it had not been financially viable at all: "I lost 10,000 quid with it", Georgie remembers with a shrug, "and that was a hell of a lot of money then" – about 110,000 Deutschmarks for instance. "When I met Alan Skidmore at Ronnie Scott's about that", he muses, "Skid said 'Great, let's do another one!'"

Another tour was offered, actually, and a trip which had a lot of prestige – supporting John Mayall. Having disbanded his Bluesbreakers in the meantime, Mayall had scored big with a drummer-less *The Turning Point* and was very popular in the United States, where he now lived as a resident of the very Laurel Canyon that had graced his 1969 Decca album *Blues From Laurel Canyon*. But Fame shied away from the financial risks, and when he flew back to the USA, it was for recording purposes only. He finished three tracks at CBS Studios in New York City, of which two songs were selected for his next single: "Fire And Rain" by fast-rising singer-songwriter James Taylor, backed by Roger Nichols and Paul Williams' "Someday Man" from the 1970 Paul Williams album of the same name, which had also been the B-side of The Monkees' "Listen To The Band" single.

Both sides of the single record fitted Fame's character really well. On the one hand the experienced character who has "seen it all" (Taylor once claimed the fire & rain metaphor was about the effects and after-effects of shock therapy in a mental institution) – alternating between composer Taylor's relaxed singing style and a more dramatic, well paced reading when the brass section comes in. Then the "Someday Man" who has all the time in the world – for the US side of his career, no less? – done in an arrangement that takes turns between a straight Country beat and Swing. American CBS opted for the third recorded track for the B-side, which was the comedian Music Hall number "The Movie Star Song" which would not have seemed out of place on Fame's 1930's album *The Third Face Of Fame* and gave the artist an opportunity to pursue one of his favourite pastimes, name-dropping – though here it's not musicians but Hollywood stars he name-checks.

On August 15th, *Record Mirror* made "Fire And Rain"/"Someday Man" another of their *Star Singles*, and the verdict was "My theory is that Georgie is never bad – just variable on standards of excellence. This James Taylor song has him delving into imaginative phrasing, and the piano opening gets it going from the off. It's a plaintive, but fiery song … not instantly spot-on commercially, but the appeal runs deep after a couple of plays. He really does work well on this type of quality material. It's a much simpler formula, very much a one-man scene, but Georgie swings it more than a shade. And the finale is splendid. Chart Cert."

Going Home – The Second Keith Mansfield Project

What CBS wanted was not necessarily as inspirational as the *Shorty* project: another solo album of the more commercial kind, a follow-up to the LP *Georgie Does His Things With Strings*, a somewhat criticized but artistically successful collaboration with the orchestra leader Keith Mansfield. For the new venture *Going Home*, whose tracks had been stockpiled months ago, Mansfield also served as hands-on producer with the assisting Martin Clarke.

This time, the accent was on horns as much as on strings, and executive producer Mike Smith also made sure that choruses received lavish female backing vocals – another point of concern for the Flamingo R&B police as much as for Georgie himself. The choice of material was inspired again, but inspired by an administration that clearly wanted Easy Listening safety: literally, radio mainstream fodder that didn't hurt at breakfast. And while it must be noted that all of Fame's performances are highly professional when it comes to singing them with perfect phrasing, it is not as if fun was really oozing out of these tracks. But the man was under contract, and he would shut up for the time being.

"I Believe In Love" was written by the singers Scott English and Rosetta Hightower. Amongst the violins, trumpets and girls, what remained of Blue Flames traces were a funky rhythm guitar, congas, punchy drumming, and Fender Rhodes electric piano, probably by Georgie himself. With a very pleasant melody and catchy chorus, this was exactly the material that Fame fans feared would put their idol in the bracket of family friendly artist, a lapse that had apparently begun with "The Ballad of Bonnie and Clyde" and continued with "Rosetta". Georgie certainly delivered the song with routine panache. Scott English, who four years before this had written Jeff Beck's lapse into cabaret, "Hi Ho Silver Lining", was to enjoy his own Top 20 chart success during 1972 with his song "Brandy".

"It Won't Hurt To Try It" by K. Allison certainly hurt the critics, reverting as it did to the conventional repertoire of crooners. Nevertheless, it is a commercial ballad done as a slow Swing waltz, Ray Conniff style. This way it could have been on *Georgie Does His Thing With Strings*.

For the title track of the album, Georgie Fame chose a number by the English singer-songwriter Gary Benson. Benson would have his own chart success with "Don't Throw It All Away" four years later [and he was also noted for his songsmith collaborations with the Hollies' lead singer Allan Clarke. Their joint composing led to the 1989 Adopt-a-child-on-ITV Hollies single "Find Me A Family".]

"Going Home" sounds interesting because of its hard-hitting, none too Brazilian Bossa Nova rhythm. "Caught the six o'clock flight from Columbus in Ohio" certainly fitted Georgie's mood and his love of flying, while "Going home to Mama's home cooking" sounds odd for the man who lost his mother early in life. Again, the decisive drumming style saves it from being too smooth.

"Foolish Child" was the first of a couple of compositions supplied by Gary Osbourne, the British songwriter who, seven years after this project, would receive the rare accolade of working with Elton John, succeeding John's custom made poet Bernie Taupin for a while. More strings, but also inspired percussion work and acoustic guitar characterize a romantic song that fades out with a trombone solo.

"Sister Jane" is a composition by the London singer-songwriter and comedian Earl Okin (b.1949), who also wrote for Cilla Black and Helen Shapiro, and who would tour with Paul McCartney & Wings later in the Seventies. "Sister Jane" had just a touch of the Beatles – fitting because Okin's first single had been recorded at Abbey Road – using the violins "Eleanor Rigby" style in the chorus. Okin's "Sister Jane" is the kind of girl who "takes taxis when there's no Jaguar", so this is about a society girl the protagonist has aimed a little too high for, sophisticated as he may be.

Georgie had made a wise choice in tackling Manhattan Pop and Jazz singer/songwriter Kenny Rankin's atmospheric ballad "Peaceful", and releasing it as a single in 1969. He promptly achieved another Top 20 charting (#16). He and Keith Mansfield must have done something right in arranging the song with delicate electric piano and a busy rhythm guitar, because Helen Reddy didn't change too much when she covered the song in 1973, reaching #12 in the US Pop charts (#2 in Adult & Contemporary). "Peaceful" was included in Rankin's 1967 debut album *Mind Dusters* and was also released as a single. Rankin died of cancer in June 2009.

"Happiness" with lyrics by Vicki Pike sounds like Eurovision Song Contest material, although it was supplied by a New Yorker, Teddy Randazzo. He also wrote the big hit "Goin' Out Of My Head" which was covered by Frank Sinatra and The Zombies. "Happiness" is catchy enough, but the way the girls assist Georgie vocally is not really in true Soul style but decidedly middle-of-the-road, pleasant but harmless.

"Children Of My Mind" was the second song Gary Osbourne submitted for *Going Home*, and succeeds as a charming chant about idealistic painters and writers carrying on working in spite of poverty, before the children of their mind become the orphans of their soul – a lovely metaphor. The female choir assists in the refrain but adds some nice call-and response work in the verses as well.

"Lay Me Down", written by producer, trumpeter and keyboard player Phil Pickett,[15] had been on an Irish album by Paddy Maguire, where it featured Fame's colleague Steve Winwood as well as his occasional vocal partner Madeline Bell on backing vocals, helped by Doris Tory, who wrote the Hollies-Hit "Just One Look". Consequently, backing vocals play their crucial part in Georgie's reading as well – which is typical for this collection, anyway. "Lay Me Down" is the first song in the set where piano is complemented by some electric organ, although it doesn't sound much like a Hammond. "Lay me down by that old railroad track, lay me down with the world at my back" may have been too

15. See Addendum

dramatic for a typical Georgie Fame gig, but it would not seem out of place for his later Musical work with *The Singer*.

"Easy Lovin', Easy Livin'" by Valerie Avon and Harold Spiro slows the tempo down for another contemplative ballad. A truly memorable melody carries the track, which has its sentimentality nicely curbed by the applied drum pattern and energetic fills. Interestingly, "Easy Lovin', Easy Livin'" was also recorded by The Troggs, whose Reg Presley had written "Love Is All Around" as his own ballad and world hit. The Londoner Valerie Avon a.k.a. Patricia Valerie Murtah from Willesdon/London (b.1937) had been a member of The Avons during the 1950s and 1960s before she got into songwriting. She and Spiro also wrote for Fame's ex employer Billy Fury ("In Summer"), The Searchers ("Desdemona"), managed a Shadows chart-topper with "Dance On" – and a mere three years after *Going Home* scored big for Olivia Newton-John with the Eurovision Song Contest smash "Long Live Love".

"Pass It Around" by Kenny Young worked as a band track after all. Speedy Acquaye's congas and the bass are very much to the fore, and the electric piano licks by Georgie add enough punch, so there are no strings this time, and none are needed either.

American composer, producer and environmental campaigner Kenny Young is most famous for writing "Under The Boardwalk", which has been recorded by legions of artists ranging from The Rolling Stones to Aaron Neville.

"Stormy" had been written by the later Atlanta Rhythm Section members Buddy Buie and James Barney "J.R." Cobb for Dennis Yost & The Classics IV in 1969. It was not only covered by Santana in 1978 – using the singer of a Flamingo Club cohort of Georgie's: Alex Ligertwood from Brian Auger's band Oblivion Express – but it already sounds a lot like a Santana track here, with Speedy's tropical percussion, strings and brass work arranged effectively and perfectly here. Nevertheless, Carlos Santana would have had a hard time detecting any guitar in the mix.

While critics frowned upon a Pop career move like this in the early Seventies, it was the *Record Mirror* which reviewed Georgie's LP on May 29th, 1971 in a very constructive way:

Going Home (CBS 64350): "The first album to come from Georgie since his contrasting strings and *'Seventh Son'* album, and recorded before the Fame and Price partnership was made official. This album rates as one of his very best, being well produced and with vocals handled particularly well, including nostalgic ballad styled numbers and two noticeably up-tempo tracks 'I Believe In Love' and 'Happiness'. 'I Believe In Love' a Rosetta Hightower and Scott English song would make a good single and has full vocal backing and nice drumming, with Georgie exercising excellent vocal control. Nice guitar backing and strings. With the aid of 'Rosetta' it is hopeful that this album will reach more than the dedicated followers of Fame, and anyone who listens must appreciate the professionalism and care which has gone into it. Grade AA stuff. V.M."

A recent review by Jason Ankeny on the *AllMusic* website also sounds convincingly and deservedly positive: "*Going Home* boasts a maturity and subtlety often missing from Georgie Fame's previous LPs. Its simple approach strips away some of the more gimmicky elements of his earlier efforts, emphasizing the increasingly honest soulfulness of

Fame Again! The compilation with *Two Faces of Fame* photo material.

his vocals. Keith Mansfield's thoughtful arrangements likewise eschew excess in favor of a wonderfully mellow sound that perfectly underscores Fame's natural warmth and grace. Electric piano grooves further establish the set's smoky, jazzy atmosphere. Best of all are the songs, each of them covers and impeccably chosen. Kenny Rankin's "Peaceful" proves a particularly evocative selection."

So what about Georgie Fame's goodhearted but also somewhat frustrated accusation that CBS wanted to make him "the British Andy Williams"? If it ever rang true, then it was on this last LP for the corporation. But given the tons of charm he exuded with the top notch material and his experience in getting the most out of each number, this has a period charm and attraction that this writer still holds in awe. Georgie was about to respond with an album that would not accept any outside material whatsoever. It was going to be "all me own work" – *All Me Own Work*!

Chapter 4

(Almost) All Our Own Work – The Georgie Fame & Alan Price Years

Flashback to 1969: The "bad company" of Alvin Lee's Ten Years After and Roger Chapman's Family in London's *Royal Albert Hall* in January seemed to inspire a return to R&B roots in Fame. While his 1969 hit singles had sounded quite relaxed and fairly middle-of-the-road enough for the public, they had their impact on sophisticated fans and colleagues alike:

"Stormy" would be picked up eventually by Santana. And as mentioned, The Climax Blues Band were one of many acts covering Mose Allison's "Seventh Son", which Fame had led to #27 in December 1969. Still, the man refused to be stereotyped: "Seventh Son" might have been serious R&B, especially with the sophisticated 7/4 rhythm arrangement applied by his great 15-piece studio group, but at the same time, he presented the song in a most theatrical, comical way as part of his new television series with "Seventh Son" producer Alan Price, the singing organist who had made his mark as a song-writing force and bandleader.

The two of them had had strong personal ties which went way way back. During his stretch of the long residency at the Flamingo Club in Soho in the second club winter of 1963, Fame had of course been aware of the Animals from Newcastle. During a break in his show, he ambled over to the *Scene Club* to listen in. He remembers Eric Burdon leaping up on a black baby grand piano while he was into John Lee Hooker's 'Big Boss Man'. Price, at the time, was playing a Vox Continental organ. Georgie told reporter Carinthia West of *The Independent* in 1992 that he could even remember their dark three-button Italian suits with black ties, "which was de rigueur for lots of groups at the time. I went and knocked on the band room door to say hello, and said I'd meet Alan the next day at this pub called De Hems in Macclesfield Street [near Mike O'Neill's Gerrard Street], where you could get steak and kidney and oyster pudding, as well as good beer."

Alan Price picked up the story for West: "Anyhow, that night we'd done a bad set and weren't happy, but somebody said Georgie Fame had arrived. We were excited because we knew from the gig pages of *Melody Maker* that Georgie Fame and the Blue Flames were working all the time. That was the thing you aimed for, to be playing all the time.

"When Georgie came into the dressing room he was wearing a black overcoat with a velvet collar – very Mod. I think he had a girl with him called Carmen, but that may have been the next day. He told me he'd enjoyed the band and that we were going to give the scene a kick up the arse. He meant the scene down south." Alan remembered

The Scene didn't have a drink licence: The Animals often went out and bought a small Scotch and Coke; which were duly mixed into their cocktail: "We'd get through five bottles that way. Georgie Fame talked to me as if I were the leader and said to come and meet him at De Hems the next day. [...] Often Clive was playing the All-nighter at the Flamingo until five or six in the morning." After leaving the Animals and founding his own Alan Price Set, he and Georgie met at the *Scotch of St James's*.

Coming from similar Northern backgrounds helped. Sharing almost identical interests in music and sport they found "drinking was a social interest, to say the least – though we'd never get deliberately out of it." One favourite habit was to leave British shores on a whim and hopping over to the other side of the Channel, in order to sample Paris discos "which had more class".

Observing the respective first decade in Georgie Fame's and Alan Price's 1958–1968 careers, both artists' paths reveal quite a few stunning professional parallels, too. Both Northern lads were born only about a year apart, learnt to play the piano very early in life and became ardent Jerry Lee Lewis fans. While the young Powell had led his own Dominoes in Leigh Lancashire, Price gigged around Fairfield, Durham in The Kansas City Five with big bass player Chas Chandler, which became The Alan Price Trio in the Newcastle-upon-Tyne area. In connection with shouter Eric Burdon, this trio progressed into the Alan Price Combo and then The Animals, due to the tag given to their wild stage act. They accompanied John Lee Hooker thirty years before Georgie Fame was to do the same with the Van Morrison Band.

Then Alan Price left the famous band in the turmoil of that traditional song picked up by Dylan: "House Of The Rising Sun". This timeless anthem had become a world #1 in Alan Price's arrangement, but certainly helped by guitarist Hilton Valentine's famous guitar arpeggios. Due to the label credits claiming "Trad./Arr. Price", royalties exclusively belonged to the pianist, the reason for leaving might have been "fear of fighting" more than the stated fear of flying.

Price set up his own Alan Price Set, featuring ex Blue Flames bass player Boots Slade and future Blue Flames saxophonist Steve Gregory. Their version of Screaming Jay Hawkins' "I Put A Spell On You" accomplished a higher chart position than The Animals' version. Price, a solid composer and imaginative lyric writer himself, chose to promote the song-writing of a prime chronicler of American life and strife, Randy Newman, similar to the manner in which Georgie Fame had embraced and "endorsed" Mose Allison, and he had hits with Kaper and Deutsch's "Hi Lili, Hi Lo" and Randy Newman's "Simon Smith And The Amazing Dancing Bear".

Further chart success followed in 1968: His own "The House That Jack Built" showed a similar kind of quirkiness to that which Georgie presented in his 1930s material on *The Third Face Of Fame*; while "Don't Stop The Carnival" mirrored Fame's love of Caribbean culture.

At the end of that high-profile year, the band leader had virtually handed his Alan Price Set over to singer – and ex Zoot Money's Big Roll Band member – Paul Williams, claiming he had proved they were top notch and he wanted to be without that "stressful monster" of a wage-demanding band, which "someone else could take on for a while". Price then briefly reunited with The Animals for a charity gig in Newcastle – forgive and forget. His "Set" though, would be giving up after one mere further single release.

The Price of Fame – TV boasted the night club stars

Apart from joining Decca's "indie" label Deram, the Geordie man took up television work together with Georgie Fame when both were contracted to film a pilot programme for a planned series of shows.

As Georgie told Carinthia West, "We started working together in the early Seventies [sic, 1969]. One evening, we were both on the same bill at Bradford University. We were in the urinal, and that's when we said: 'Let's form a band.' The catalyst was when we appeared on Lulu's live TV show together. We shared a piano, wore rented tails, and sang 'Back in the USSR', the Beatles song – so we had this crazy idea. We got the strings in the orchestra to play the theme from *Dr Zhivago*, while we staged a mock battle and interrupted each others' playing. We ended up rolling on the floor pretending to fight. Word has it that Billy Cotton Jnr. was strolling along the gantry at the time and said 'Give these boys a series.' This became *The Price of Fame*.

For their test debut, Price & Fame managed to hire Delaney & Bonnie featuring Eric Clapton, who had famously just deserted his super group Blind Faith. The show hit it so big that *The Price of Fame* appeared on the BBC2 channel in eight episodes, starting on 20th November, 1969 and running well into 1970. They included part of their bands – for instance Colin Green on guitar and Clive Thacker on drums – and combined them with the *Top of the Pops* dance troupe Pan's People. During the Christmas edition on Christmas Day, December 25, 1969, for instance, they had The Ladybirds and "the fifth Beatle" Billy Preston as guests. The third episode had them present songs by John Lennon & Paul McCartney, with Fame tackling the stomping "You Can't Do That" in a soulful way with a big brass section, Price tenderly crooning "Here, There & Everywhere" with strings and choir, and both had obvious fun delivering "Good Day Sunshine".

Ex-colleague Mick Eve watched these proceedings with a dismissive verdict: "I just didn't like what was going on, funny songs being suggested. I have seen a video since, which convinced me I was right to go, where he had his hair all done strange, and so had Alan Price, and they both looked distinctly uncomfortable. They were not going to be Sam & Dave – that's for sure. It was horrendous, middle-of-the-road kind of music."

Looking at two grand-pianos locked into shape like puzzle pieces, with Fame & Price facing one another and having an adrenalin-soaked go at Jerry Lee Lewis's "Great Balls Of Fire", one wonders if that much obvious fun could have been acted out – to this spectator it surely looks like the real thing. The same goes for accompanying guest star Thelma Houston for "Jumping Jack Flash" and "Zip-A-Dee Doo-Dah", Georgie at the Hammond and Alan on grand piano, both handling backing vocals and obviously relishing those moments. Georgie also got the chance to deliver his then current hit "Seventh Son", barefooting it clad in a most ridiculous bathrobe straight out of a car boot sale, and the very catchy "Am I Wasting My Time?" from the Price-produced parent album *Seventh Son*. The shows were so successful and popular that in 1971, a sequel of further shows was screened.

And rather than putting the long-running friendship between Georgie and Alan to the test with all this work, the collaboration seemed to make it stronger, according to Fame's memories to Miss West: "People often come up and ask me to sing Alan's songs, but it never annoys me. I was waiting to go on and play at a 'Save the Spire' concert for Salisbury cathedral last week. There was a bloke standing next to his wife 10 yards away and I heard him say: 'Where's your bear, then?' He meant Alan's song 'Simon Smith and his Amazing Dancing Bear', but I think it tells how strong the partnership was and the impact it's had on people. We established our professional relationship long after our personal one. Nothing's going to break it."

Also, the live-on-stage Fame encounter with the guesting piano brother Price led to a further collaboration in the recording studio, this time with both partners taking part actively. According to the *Disc* and BBC *Radio 1* reporter Mike Ledgerwood, the seed of working together beyond television studios had been sown on the 17th November 1970, via a Georgie Fame appearance at the London *Revolution* club. On spotting Alan Price in the audience with his lady, they both did "Bring It On Home To Me" by The Animals and the how-many-hints-do-you-need "Let's Work Together", the Wilbert Harrison tune made famous by Canned Heat, led to Price jumping on stage, where they did Buddy Holly songs like "Rave On" and "Oh Boy", but also the Jerry Lee Lewis tune they had performed on two grand pianos for the TV screen in 1969, "Great Balls Of Fire". Following something that *Radio 1* Ledgerwood called "deliberate double booking" at Bradford University, plans were made for a Price & Fame band.

On the 6th February 1971 in *Record Mirror*, the studio and stage collaboration of the two likeable and ever so comparable TV artists became "official", for instance with a Record Mirror headlining "Price-Fame To Tie Up": "It's confirmed… Georgie Fame and Alan Price have joined forces on a permanent basis and have already formed a band. But names of musicians in their group, as yet without a name, will not be revealed before next week.

"Confirmation of their teaming-up follows weeks of rumours. The duo have worked together many times in the past, making their first appearance on a Lulu TV show in 1968, doing a musical/comedy act. Said Georgie, 'For a long time, Alan and I have toyed with the idea of working together full time. But not until now did we feel that the time was right. We both had a lot of musical ground to cover – Alan had his own band as I did and I was determined to tour America, which I did last summer.

"Album Set For May: Alan and Georgie had their own TV series in 1970 and since then, many requests have poured in for a permanent band. The difficulties over recording contracts have been overcome and CBS and Decca have agreed to handle the pair and the resultant recordings on a joint basis. They are due in the studio within the next few days and a single is tentatively set for March and an album for May."

The first time they tried their collective forces in the studio was on the Mike Snow novelty song "Rosetta", which was among the tracks they recorded in March 1971. As a single backed by Alan Price's "John And Mary", it hit the UK charts at #11 – eventually peaking at #7 – in April. The single was promoted on radio and TV programmes, and there were also several concerts around the London circuit.

As pop press princess Penny Valentine wrote in *Sounds* of March 27.1971:

"Rosetta" (CBS), written by Mike Snow and produced by Mike Smith with a great deal of humour, this track started off so peculiarly I thought Alan's vocals had been locked out of the studio and were playing in another room, but it settles down to a rollicking pace with an almost "Olbi Di" feel about the lyrics. I think it could probably drive you mad over a period of time, but it will do very well, I cannot dispute."

Shortly after the release of the single, and with all their TV experience to back them up, Price and Fame finally appeared live in the flesh. Again, *Sounds* was among the weekly mags like *Melody Maker* and *New Musical Express*, when they announced on May 2nd, 1971:

"Alan Price and Georgie Fame make their third concert appearance since they joined forces this Friday (21) at Harrowgate Royal Hall. Zoot Money will also appear on the bill – Zoot will join Alan and Georgie permanently on all future concert appearances. On May 31 they appear at Margate Winter Gardens." Zoot on all gigs did not quite work out, but he certainly remained a very welcome regular for Fame & Price, which for Alan's separate band continues to this day.

But there was also the already announced album waiting to be finished, and the two returned to the "red light district" of the sound-proof walls in the CBS studios.

With their easily blending voices, the two veterans produced a versatile collection called *Fame & Price/Price & Fame Together,* with Blue-Flames-type numbers, Country and Gospel tunes, and could again be seen on BBC TV. Each partner brought one of his own band members – it was Colin Green from Fame's group and Clive Thacker, who had come to Alan Price from Brian Auger & The Trinity. In a rather interesting coincidence of keeping it all in one musical family, Thacker would stay in the Alan Price Band for years and was often found playing on Georgie's idol Mose Allison's London gigs during the Nineties and Noughties.

Shrugging off the various critics, who lamented about his Jazz leanings as much as his mainstream orientation, Fame simply soldiered on: "For me, music is simply a life-long, pleasant learning process!" Judged without bias, it turns out that Georgie has not ignored the Blue Flames format of a six- to seven-piece band here, contrary to his two previous releases, *Georgie Does His Thing With Strings* backed by The Keith Mansfield Orchestra and *Seventh Son* with an augmented, veritable Big Band line-up. While this album resumes the careless Sixties habit of not mentioning the participating musicians – something a Fame album had only lapsed into for *Going Home* – as far as the actual music is concerned, on this record he remains a reliable, always interesting artist, as does partner Price.

The duet album: Fame & Price/Price & Fame Together

The happy-go-lucky Mike Snow number "Rosetta" has long become a kind of symbol for Georgie Fame – and Alan Price – for apparently "selling out" to their cabaret audiences: This is a hippie cliché which conveniently ignores the fact that artists all over the spectrum tried to give people a good time. Composer Mike Snow's real name was Mike Liston, who was in the Ian Samwell produced group The Ferris Wheel, together with Madeline Bell's later husband, ex-Checkmates drummer Barry Reeves. For archivists: Snow went to Nashville two years on, 1973, to work with Dr Hook main man Dennis Locorriere.

"In those days, we were making records as if we were doing gigs", Fame told the BBC in 2013 when asked about its spontaneous live sound: "We probably did [it live]. And not only was it the early Seventies, it was early stereo, where engineers were experimenting in the studio."

"Yellow Man", addresses Chinese racial clichés in a pretty blunt way, obviously going on about eating rice and being extremely tight-fisted, but just about subtle enough to prevent it from being too obvious. This was by no means considered politically correct in that day and age, but then this is highly ironical Randy Newman material which raised a storm once he described "Short People" – and we can guess how much fun Price & Fame had with it, especially as Pricey always had been an ardent fan.

Alan Price's "The Dole Song" is politically outspoken with trade union issues like equal pay, and does not have many Fame traces. The track could be on a regular Price album – especially the working class orientated *Between Today And Yesterday* which he issued in 1973 – with the exception of the "Burn baby burn" harmony singing towards the end.

"Time I Moved On", on the other hand, is a typically romantic, whimsical Georgie Fame composition, playing on his fascination with the contrast between country and city life again. Tenderly played with organ and electric piano offset by Colin Green's acoustic guitar, this could well have succeeded as a single release – with a great finger-clicking fade adding to the overall impact.

A real duet follows – Alan Price's "John And Mary" is a driving, rocky number destined to get a live crowd excited with great dynamics, even borrowing Fleetwood Mac's "Rattlesnake Shake" riff in the process. This is as far away from family entertainment as you can get, a highlight of the album.

Another Price-written song, "Here and Now", is more up-tempo and gets its Rock leanings from energetic piano work and Colin Green's distorted guitar licks and solo, developing a nice groove that becomes a touch middle-of-the-road with its "Sha-la-la-la"-Chorus – innocent fun maybe, but well executed.

Calypso meets Bo Diddley: A second tune by Mike Liston is "Home Is Where The Heart Is", written with his guitarist in The Ferris Wheel, Terry Edmunds. (Incidentally, the guitar spot in that band was soon to be taken over by a certain Bernie Holland, an imminent Blue Flames member.) Apart from the rhythmic delights and a catchy chorus, "Home Is Where The Heart Is" benefits from a sophisticated way of Fame & Price singing "against" each other in a kind of canon.

"Ballad Of Billy Joe" was written by Arkansas Country singer Charlie Rich, before he had his huge hit with "The Most Beautiful Girl" in 1973. Georgie and Alan get rid of the honky-tonk arrangement and instead enjoy more harmony singing – on the foundation of a very prominent bass line courtesy of Brian Odgers, fuzz guitar and a swirling Leslie-driven Hammond solo – this is how Fame & Price must have sounded in a sweaty club away from the chicken-in-a-basket-circuit.[16]

"That's How Strong My Love Is", was a very popular O.V. Wright Gospel meets Memphis Soul tune from 1964, which was written by his publicist-manager Roosevelt Jamison. Here, it is arranged here in a 12-bar Blues tempo, fitting for the duo's delivery with Alan's falsetto complementing Fame's tenor perfectly. A very inspired choice, its cover versions probably known to Fame & Price were by Otis Redding, The In-Crowd and also The Rolling Stones. This song had been released with three-part-harmonies on the 1965 *Hollies* album, and just before *Together* it also appeared by Candi Staton. Finally, the hymn would turn up on Humble Pie's *Eat It* album two years after this version, so Mod brother Steve Marriott obviously rated the tune just as much as Georgie did.

"Blue Condition" is Alan Price's fourth composition on this album, his electric piano riff getting picked up by Colin Green's whaling guitar and soon underlined by economically accented bass and drums driving along some cool R&B. The two-part harmonies quickly turn over to a real delight of a Jazz guitar solo, which Colin ends by those wailing riffs he continues as little accentuations. Hand-clapping ends one of the best tracks those two ever did together.

"I Can't Take Much Longer" by Bonnie Bramlett – who Price & Fame had on the show with husband Delaney featuring Eric Clapton – and Joey Cooper is from the controversial Delaney & Bonnie album *Accept No Substitute* on the Elektra label – controversial because they tried to go with Apple Records in spite of a valid contract.

16. See Addendum

It is a well-executed little Rock number, its choice significant because with Leon Russell and Carl Radle, two Tulsa Oklahoma players appeared on the original who would participate in Georgie Fame's Island recordings a couple of years later.

So really, in spite of the conventional cover shot of Fame & Price that could have advertised cherry pink and apple blossom white, this was fine Rhythm & Blues and singer/songwriter material, with the catchy single thrown in.

"Two At The Price Of One" read the fat print of *Record Mirror*'s 3rd July review of their first (and so far the only one released) album together, starting off with a minor complaint:

"Lack of an album sleeve with our review copy means that the very fine production of this goes un-credited – but is nonetheless commendable. The duo have come up with some good ideas and a nice collection of songs. Includes 'Rosetta' and the B side 'John And Mary'. Randy Newman's 'Yellow Man' with its humorous lyrics and oriental sound [a predecessor to 'Hong Kong Blues' on the In Hoagland 1981 album] comes across well, and ' Home Is Where Your Heart Is' has nice percussion and interesting vocal effect, with Georgie and Alan singing in 'round' style. 'That's How Strong My Love Is' with unusual harmony effect was disconcerting at first, but on further hearings becomes fascinating, as does the distorted vocal handling on Alan Price's 'Blue Condition'.

"As a bonus the pair present their own compositions with solo vocal, Alan choosing a story song with nice organ passage, 'The Dole Song', and Georgie singing wistfully on 'Time I Moved On', which though not so up-tempo, has the pleasant feel of 'Peaceful' [from the recent *Going Home* album of Georgie's]. This is a good collection definitely two for the price of one! – V.M."

On the 7th August 1971, *Record Mirror* wrote under "Fame And Price": "Georgie Fame and Alan Price went into the studios this week to record their follow single up for 'Rosetta'. They will also be appearing on the LP spot of *'Top of the Pops'* to promote their current album 'Georgie Fame And Alan Price Together'.

"The duo appear at the Winter Gardens, Weston Super Mare on Saturday July 31st and the following Monday commence a week's cabaret at the Golden Garden Wythenshawe, before flying to appear in Palma de Majorca's major night club."

In late 1971, a second CBS single materialized, obviously a hit like "Rosetta" demanded: "Follow Me"! This was exactly, or ironically, the very title which appeared. The catchy A-side was composed by Tony Hiller with Colin Frechter, who was the musical director, arranger and keyboard player for the British pop group The Brotherhood of Man. "Follow Me" was recorded by the Abba type vocal quartet on their 1972 LP *"We're The Brotherhood of Man"*. Incidentally, *Strings* and *Going Home* producer Keith Mansfield was the musical director on The Brotherhood of Man recording of "Follow Me".

Tony Hiller had found fame with The Hiller Brothers, and the hit merchant wrote for everyone between Cliff Richard and James Last and is known for "Save Your Kisses For Me", which Brotherhood of Man also made famous.

"Follow Me" was hardly typical for Fame & Price's ambitions, while not out of place with regard to their single predecessor: It applied the same happy-go-lucky rhythm as "Rosetta", complete with the pair taking turns vocally as well as harmonizing. Price's proficient piano work, a great Hammond organ by Fame and even a banjo get thrown in to make it all jolly enough.

The B-side, "Sergeant Jobsworth", written by Georgie, was a humorous tale about Fame going out to a garden market in the early morning to buy flowers for his dearly beloved, only to be stopped by a police sergeant, who actually name-checks Georgie as a guy he knew from television – interestingly mirroring the amusing way Long John Baldry had with anecdotes like the one on "Intro: Conditional Discharge" for "Don't Try To Lay No Boogie Woogie On The King Of Rock'n'Roll" on the album *It Ain't Easy* from the same year. "Sergeant Jobsworth" was arranged as a more dramatic mid-tempo R&B number that showed how well the duo and their band functioned as a serious rock outfit if the CBS people would let them. But apparently they wanted chart action first and foremost, while on stage, Jazz and Blues tunes were effortlessly mingled with new compositions.

"Fame Price Again", Record Mirror headlined on December 11th, 1971, in time for the Christmas Singles market: "Sergeant Jobsworth"/"Follow Me" (CBS 7602): "More directly commercial than 'Rosetta' – and a natural-born hit. There are those who will say that the structure doesn't really stretch the musical abilities of the duo, but it's a fast-paced, catchy, optimistic, bluebirdy sort of song which never lets up. Good hard piano, organ – a production that looks like Top Five to me. – Chart Cert."

A chart cert it certainly wasn't but Georgie remained ever so optimistic, in spite of the relative failure of "Follow Me", whose logistical problems Georgie Fame related to journalist Mabbs via cool and non-frustrated analysis:

"With 'Rosetta' it was just that 'well well well' part that everyone remembered. It was a very commercial song. But although we can enjoy playing 'Follow Me' – it's a good little ditty – we didn't want to record it. CBS thought it would be a hit and we flew down from up north to record it. But though they played the hell out of 'Follow Me' on the radio the official release date was changed twice and then I think it disappeared in the Christmas rush.

"Although it's important to get a catchy single I don't think the next one will be quite as commercial as 'Follow Me'. I've got a couple of numbers floating about that we might consider using."

On television, the pair proved label-compatible by leaning heavily towards the cabaret side of things, with appearances on *The Two Ronnies* and the family orientated *The Morecambe & Wise Show*.

"Time I Moved On" – mutual gigs but separate paths

The first big concert spectacular which Georgie and Alan did was in May 1970 with the Canadian trumpeter and bandleader Maynard Ferguson (1928–2006) and his assorted orchestra. Ferguson had enjoyed musical training from the age of four, attended the French conservatory in Montreal and learned to play the saxes, clarinet, slide trombone and eventually lost his heart to the bugle. He was just 15 years old when he started his first band, and soon played with the legendary Jimmy Dorsey and veterans Charlie Barnet and Stan Kenton. He went out on many US tours until 1967, for instance with Harold Davison's Top Brass. In 1968, he had toured Sweden, South America, Italy and Portugal, and early 1970 had seen his first tour of Australia. With Fame & Price, his Big Band featured Martin Drover on lead trumpet, Chris Pyne from *Seventh Son* on trombone and Fame Band regular Peter King on the alto and flute. The show also featured Soul singer Totlyn Jackson.

A live review of a typical live show of the duo could be found, again in *Record Mirror* in their edition of April 22nd, simply titled "Fame and Price": "Pavilion, Hemel Hempstead. For one of their few appearances in the London area, Georgie Fame and Alan Price attracted an almost capacity audience, but apart from some younger fans collected since their hit success with 'Rosetta', the majority were in their late twenties and beyond.

"The duo have tailored their act to suit their current work circuit and audiences – being largely cabaret – with Alan Price adding some funny quips to his announcements, and everything being kept within an easily digestible format.

"During their act, Fame and Price featured many of their better known hits. 'Simon Smith and his Amazing Dancing Bear', with Alan on electric piano, was supported with a strong drum rhythm by Clive Thacker, and Georgie Fame's 'Yeh Yeh' picked the proceedings up, providing the liveliest point of the evening. On 'The Point Of No Return' with Colin Green a long-standing sideman with Georgie – providing excellent guitar work – the feeling became spontaneous and more exciting. V.M."

By July 1972, Fame & Price had been working together as a live unit for one and a half years – and almost four years if we include their television work ever since the Lulu Show back in 1968.

There was still only a single chart hit, the oft-lamented cabaret ditty 'Rosetta', and so far only one album.

But when *Record Mirror* reporter Mike Hennessey investigated their state of (un)happiness during their rehearsals at the famed *Bag O'Nails* club in London's Kingly Street, the vibes turned out to be decidedly positive: "It was undeniably happy music produced by two north country keyboard men – both exalting in playing together again for the first time in several weeks. Fame and Price, the masters of the sheepish grin, the knowing wink, and that shrewd musicianly philosophy which is more often encountered among the Jazz fraternity than in the Pop field – were rehearsing at the *Bag O'Nails* and picking their way uncertainly through Gilbert O'Sullivan's 'Matrimony'.

Alan Price told the reporter with the Cognac family name that in spite of the follow-up to their hit having stalled, and the fact that solo gigs may have taken place, the duo did have a focus, and a future: "But although we do things on our own, we really dig playing together. And we plan to continue working as a band. The rehearsal really went great today [in the aforementioned *Bag O'Nails Club* in Soho] and I just wish there was somewhere where we could go and start playing again now.

"We don't really care about hits. We just like playing and the people seem to like where we play. I don't really care what the critics or the record companies say."

Asked about the Jazz haven Ronnie Scott's Club as a suitable, classy venue; Price seemed skeptical: "I don't think they could afford us, and anyway, I think they get the right kind of audiences. I did a gig there with the Scaffold [those Liverpool poets with Paul McCartney's brother Mike McGear who put cabaret over the top with ditties like "Lily The Pink"] and I don't think the people would really dig our music." Hennessey concluded that in order to watch Fame & Price, you had to make do with the provinces or television: "You either have to go to somewhere like Stockton-on-Trent, or Southend (Talk of the South, last week in July) or else tune into Sounds for Saturday on BBC TV.

Hennessey chose to call Georgie "Cheshire's cheeriest son" (in spite of his Lancashire roots) and Alan "Newcastle's nicest introvert", but still gets flak for his doubts about the impact of a bona fide Fame & Price success story. Then he explains "the two dedicated talents'" perspective: " ... over the last 18 months, playing two or three gigs a week, the Price Fame outfit has invariably pulled big audiences and sent them home happy. But perhaps most of all it has worked on the individual creative level. Each has drawn strength and inspiration from the other in order to lay down what each considers their best music to date."

At the same time, there was no end in sight for the Fame & Price live collaboration, although none of the two protagonists would agree to getting pinned down to duo status, or else to necessarily composing together, as Georgie made clear to Val Mabbs for the March 25th *Record Mirror*: "I think we're playing too much tennis and golf. Really, we don't feel there's any point in forcing things in that direction if it doesn't just happen.

"At the time of joining up it was the automatic thing to say, and we hoped that a lot of original things would be coming out. Now we find that our writing works out okay as it is."

Apart from the fact that neither Lennon/McCartney nor other composing partnerships in Pop, Rock, or Jazz for that matter, worked together as much as their trademark tags suggested, Fame and Price pointed out at the time that the collaboration did take place in terms of creating suitable arrangements for the numbers written or picked, and that both of them worked closely together in selecting the right musicians for their ever-evolving band, where long-standing guitarist Colin Green seemed to be the only constant player. They must have been aware that continuity could have helped the band identify with the duo's image and sound scape, but Georgie generally shrugged his shoulders and took line-up changes in his stride or as chances.

He told Mabbs, "We have added a new bass player, Dave Markee – I don't think he's played with any 'real' groups before [true: he came directly from Trinity College in London]. He comes from York, and Alan met him through somebody else. He's rehearsed with us and played a couple of gigs". And immediately, Georgie spotted relief for his left Hammond hand in their two-keyboard line-up: "Although we might have to stick to rigid forms in some cases, it's not limited at all. We can rely on each other and allow each other to play with as much freedom as possible. And if I want I can just stop playing and leave it to Alan – that's a tremendous amount of freedom. The only thing is that I play organ more while Alan plays piano, but I'm trying to get him off that, so I can have a play! At least now we have a bass player I don't have to leap about from organ to guitar.

"As for the other band members, "Colin [Green] is still there, and Tolly [Clive Thacker on the drums] is back with us. We had thought about adding something else, like maybe a couple of horns, but finances won't let us do that. We're going out on tour of Britain in April and we'll just use the line-up that we have at the moment."

This is an interesting statement for a performer who was able to afford two or three horn players during much of the Blue Flames' life span between 1963 and 1966, and who continued to use saxophones and trumpet in the Georgie Fame Bands from 1967 up until the *Seventh Son* and *Shorty* periods 1969–1970. Did he *still* regret disbanding the Blue Flames?

When asked this question by this author in 1994, the answer was a definite yes, yet at the time of Price & Fame's second touring year – and the fifth year of the cooperation – Fame told reporter Hennessey: "No I don't at all. In fact it's probably one of the reasons why I don't want a front line again – I don't think I could handle and take that, on a personal basis. Now I have much more freedom."

What's more – he would contradict this statement by going out in 1974, with enough reeds and brass to enact *Sound Venture* in its entirety! The same is true for his partner: The Alan Price Set's hits, "Simone Smith And The Amazing Dancing Bear" or "Don't Stop The Carnival", were unthinkable without Steve Gregory's tenor saxophone, Clive Burrows on baritone and John Walters on trumpet. Perhaps the answer to the puzzle can be found in Alan Price's remark at the time that Ronnie Scott's Club "couldn't afford us."

Georgie Fame's concert collaboration with Alan Price continued on and off. On November 18th 1972, more activities by the duo were reported by *Record Mirror* under "Fame and Price":

"Georgie Fame and Alan Price, who recently completed weekly television appearances on *The Two Ronnies Show*, are to make a live broadcast for Radio One this month. The concert takes place on November 18, from 7.45 when Highway will be appearing, and will be broadcast live from the start of the Fame & Price set, from 9.15. The concert, which is part of the BBC Radio Midland 50th anniversary celebration, will take place in the courtyard of Sudely Castle, Winchcombe, Gloucester, and the broadcast excerpt from the show will last 45 minutes."

Record Mirror of 9th December 1972, next to an announcement of Humble Pie touring with the Blackberries for the first time (with whom, as mentioned, they had recorded the recent Fame & Price track "That's How Strong My Love Is" for their double album *Eat It*) printed "Fame": "Georgie Fame and Alan Price will be performing their first London gig for some time this weekend. They will be appearing for one night only at the Royal Court Theatre on Sunday night."

Their activities continued in 1973, as *Record Mirror* reported on 22nd January: "Fame and Price show": "Georgie Fame and Alan Price make an appearance Royal Court Theatre on January 30, in aid of the Theatre Upstairs. Tickets range from £5 to £1, and are available from the Box Office, Theatre Upstairs, Royal Court Theatre, Sloane Square, London SW 1.

Meanwhile, with their second mutual album remaining in the vaults, both Fame and Price had released their respective solo albums: *All Me Own Work* (which gets reviewed in the next chapter) and *Oh Lucky Man!*

Just as Georgie had shown himself pleased with the results of *All Me Own Work*, which came out on August 18th, 1972, Alan Price praised his tie-in with the projected *Oh Lucky Man!* movie, whose soundtrack and songs were in the can: "I've been writing the music for this Lindsay Anderson film 'Oh Lucky Man' – and I also appear in it with the other guys in the band – Clive Thacker, Colin Green and Dave Markee. We play all the music, and it's the best music I've ever written. Incidentally, the main part in the film belonged to *A Clockwork Orange* star Malcolm McDowell, who had impressed Georgie Fame's son Tristan back in their home in Devon.

While CBS had administered the records of Fame & Price, they were also taken over – if eventually only for a single Single release – by Warner Brothers. Alan Price was the one to mention a second Fame & Price album to journalist Hennessey: "I'm tied up with Warner's in the States and Canada, so that's enough [although both *Oh Lucky Man* and his 1973 album *Between Today And Yesterday* would come out with them in the UK, too]. When we make another album together though ["when", not "if"], I guess it will come out through Warner's here." The reporter added that another album would come out in the autumn most likely, promoted via a full UK tour. There were certainly more gigs to follow, well into the year 1973 actually, and the other single as well, but the album remained eternally "forthcoming".

The recordings for a sophomore LP had certainly garnered some interesting and worthwhile material, as Colin Green remembers, confirming that he played on all of its numbers: "As I recall – and it was a long time ago – there was some good stuff, it was fairly unusual for its day. But there was some original stuff. I don't know the politics behind why it didn't get released, but I thought it was good."

Georgie does not agree: "It was an extension of what we had done with the first album. We were still stuck in that rut, working in the cabaret clubs, without actually evolving musically, which was the original intention of working together. But we got saddled with that Light Entertainment thing. It never came out and Warner's have the tapes. They might not even know that they got it. A lot of these big companies don't even know what they've got in the archive, until someone goes into special projects and starts digging around. I'm not really interested in that. I don't think it was all that inspirational artistically."

While reporter Val Mabbs had related Fame & Price's second album forecast, naming the autumn of 1972 as a likely release date, he had pointed out both of the boys' opinion that touring endlessly would be a "retrograde step", and ended his article with a verdict that many fans, including the then 19-year-old author of this book ("Rosetta" was a sizeable chart success in Germany, and "Follow Me" was available in every ever so provincial record shop, golden years) may have confirmed at the time: "But though they seem happy enough, the potential that they both have has yet to be brought out to the full since the decision to team up was made." How right Mabbs would turn out to be.

At least *Record Mirror* announced the single on February 3rd, 1973. The column was "Mirrorpick – Peter Jones on new singles", the headline was "Georgie and Alan get into commercialism": Georgie Fame and Alan Price: Don't Hit Me When I'm Down; Street Light (Reprise K 14230): "A Fame-penned song with a banjo-backed beat with some falsetto-backed vocal bits which must be regarded as uncharacteristic. But it's a good-natured, bounce-along piece which comes over in a commercial and distinctive style. I like it, but it may take few plays to register widely. Chart Cert."

Other tracks that survive from the album sessions are Alan Price's moody "I'm A Gambler" with an everlasting but skillful and effective drum intro and snappy fills by Clive Thacker, and "What You're Doing I Can Do (aka Hey Baby)". "I'm A Gambler" would finally surface by 1977, in a more straight, energetic and commercial version, on Alan's eponymous *Alan Price* album, while "What You're Doing", which only had a guide vocal in its original take, re-appeared as an album track and culled single under the title of, you guessed it, of "Hey Baby" on Georgie's *All Me Own Work*, albeit with the subtitle "(I'm Getting Ready)". Both original recordings can be heard on the Verve Box Set *The In-Crowd*.

While Price was busy in the film world, Fame, Colin Green and varying band members continued to play gigs on their own. But at the same time, partner Alan was not the only one of the pair to work with Lindsay Anderson. Georgie, as a committed rugby league fanatic and expert, helped the director with the West End theatre play *The Changing Room*, getting Anderson acquainted with the tennis changing rooms on his home turf – in Wigan and Leigh.

Their friendship remained, as Alan Price, once again, told Carinthia West: "Often Clive and I would take the *Golden Arrow*, an old-fashioned train with all the candelabra and the brass, and go to Paris, champagne all the way. We'd go to a bloody good restaurant when we got there and have oysters and more champagne. Sometimes we took girlfriends. It was a nice day out, something to do. Later on, when we did cabaret together, we'd be somewhere like Liverpool and play golf in the morning, table tennis in the afternoon, then go swimming. Golf was a wonderful boon because it kept me out of the boozer and in the open air. We stopped working together in 1973, but people still think we're together."

Mick Eve, by that time "working all over Europe with Herbie Goins and not really there to watch", mused at the time and apparently still does: "I don't know what they were both thinking of at that point. And I think Pricey himself was still mystified why he did it. They had a falling-out on the road I think, they couldn't agree to work with each other."

"Leaving The City Behind" – Georgie moves his big love and family to the country

What about Georgie Fame's personal life? There had always been gossip columns, suggestions about who was inspiring the singing Hammond hero's feelings, but it was only in 1972 that the public became aware that Fame had been hitched seriously, and that this had occurred quite a long time ago at that:

Her name was Nicolette Elaine Katherine Harrison. She was the daughter of a stockbroker, Michael Harrison, and his wife, Baroness Maria Koskull. Via her Latvian born mother – who had first fled to Hamburg, Germany, and then on to England when Hitler's rise was felt as early as 1929 – there was blue blood in the beautiful blonde girl. So, Nicolette moved in the highest circles. The film director Carol Reed was a next-door neighbour at their Argyll House in King's Road, Chelsea, and the multi-talented Peter Ustinov lived further down the road.

Just like a certain young Astrid Kirchherr in Baroness Maria's former home of Hamburg – the blonde lady who shaped the Beatles' early Existentialist mop top look in the more respectable Hanseatic suburbs beyond the seedy, Soho-like "Reeperbahn" – Nicolette went for a "French Beatnik" image, and "hung out", chilled at the "Cubano" coffee shop in London's Brompton Road. Back home, her increasingly close friend Lady Annabel Vane-Tempest-Stewart, who was the daughter of the 8th Marquess of Londonderry, was a regular and welcome guest. Annabel had lost her mother early in life, and saw Nicolette's mother Maria as a kind of stepmother.

Days in coffee shops and cozy evenings at Argyll House aside, Nicolette and Annabel led the lives of young debutantes. In this capacity, they were actually among the very last young ladies ever to be invited to Buckingham Palace by Her Majesty, Queen Elizabeth II. Her Royal Highness was going to stop having official courts in the Palace, as she probably wanted to be in sync with modernity. More importantly, Lady Annabel fancied herself as a bit of a matchmaker. Adoring Nicolette, and adoring her brother 'Alastair' Alexander as well, she saw how these two very attractive youngsters might fall for one another. She succeeded.

So in 1958, and at only eighteen years of age, the young debutante Nicolette married the equally youthful 9th Marquess of Londonderry, 'Alistair' Alexander Charles

Robert Vane-Tempest-Stewart. Marquess Alistair himself had been just eighteen years old when he received his title three years previously. It was the period sixty years pre-William-and-Harry, and so the way the Marquess dealt with life was deemed highly unusual. Running as he did an actual Jazz combo, the Eton Five, was certainly "frowned upon". Having fallen for the stunning Nicolette, the young peer then proceeded to neglect providing her with an engagement ring: typically, a mishap the tabloids would note at the time.

But the couple certainly seemed happy enough, enjoying life in three big estates – one of which, Londonderry House, they sold to the Hilton Hotel chain, but not before throwing a final lavish party. The musical entertainment was provided by two personalities and their bands of some significance to this story: Alexis Korner and Benny Goodman!

Very soon, Nicolette gave birth to two daughters, Lady Sophia in 1959, and Lady Cosima in 1961 – the Cosima Stewart of "Dream Pony" on Georgie's Reprise album *All Me Own Work*.

Little Lady Cosima was three years old when one day, her mother Nicoletta was sitting in Wynard Park, County Durham, the family mansion which her husband, the Marquess, had renovated in the most spectacular way. The phone rang and her sister-in-law, Lady Annabel Goldsmith, was on the line, telling her to switch the television on immediately. Why the hurry? Was there a war on?

As Lady Goldsmith (who is also the mother of Jemima Khan, the one-time Hugh Grant girlfriend) points out in her autobiography, which was published in 2004, *Annabel – An Unconventional Life*: "Three years after Cosima's birth, in 1964, I was at home watching *Top Of The Pops* on television and was so struck with the good looks of the young man whose record had reached the number one slot, that I immediately rang Nico to tell her to switch on the programme. She was just in time to catch the end of Georgie Fame singing 'Yeh Yeh!' and she was star struck. A few years later Georgie and his group, The Blue Flames, were playing concerts in a double bill with the Supremes in the northern provinces, and Alastair invited them all over to Wynard, and it was there that the romance between Nico and Georgie began."

In 1969, the eagerly desired heir to the Londonderry estates and title arrived: Nicoletta gave birth to their son Tristan, who quickly bore the impressive title of James Vane-Tempest-Stewart, Viscount Castlereagh. But it was hardly a year later when Alistair had found out that he was not the heir's father. Tristan was – obviously – Georgie's child. Before long, Fame was blamed with adultery, and the all too predictable scandal followed.

"After Nico and Alistair were divorced in 1971, she and Georgie got married, spending the honeymoon with Jimmy [her husband] and me in Jamaica. On their return they went to live in Maperton in Somerset and Cosima, who was at St Paul's Girls School in London [...] came to live with me at Pelham Cottage."

On 4th March, 1972, *Record Mirror* was hot on the heels of the tabloids and the broadsheets in covering one of the prime show-biz weddings of the year. Their own chosen heading was "Fame dash to wedding": "Making an overnight dash by train from Newcastle, Georgie Fame arrived in London for his wedding to the Marchioness of Londonderry (Nico), last Friday. The wedding took place at Marylebone register office at 11.30 a.m., and the only guests present were John Gunnell from the Robert Stigwood Organisation, and Georgie's father James Powell, publicist Mike Housego, and nanny of the Marchioness' three children, Mavis Young. Even Georgie's partner Alan Price was unaware of the wedding until the news leaked out in the national press.

"Immediately after the wedding, Georgie went to ATV studios to rehearse for 'Saturday Variety' screened last weekend. Fame & Price this week are in the studios recording for their next album and possible single."

At the time of the couple getting into the registration office in Marylebone, Central London on February 25th, 1972, Nicolette and Alistair's son was not Viscount Castlereagh anymore, but had instead become "just" Tristan Powell. That same year, his brother James was born, and the young family's home in Somerset was to become a haven away from the pressures of show biz and also the hectic music club scene in London – town and country becoming an eternal subject for Georgie, both in his choice of songs to interpret and as a recurring theme in creating his own increasingly blooming lyric writing.

Georgie reminisced in 2009: "I moved out of London in 1971. I moved to the countryside because I wanted to start a family and I wanted my children to grow up in a stable, healthy, sane environment, a natural environment. I lived in the south-west of England, in Somerset and Dorset. And I was capable of providing a house and a home for living in that environment. So they had a very nice, healthy upbringing."

Much to the relief of the young family and also their circle of friends, tensions with the past did not last. Nicolette's ex-husband Alistair – who had re-married himself –suggested forgiveness and contact. Before long, he and his new wife, the dancer Doreen Wells, became firm friends of the Powells a.k.a. Fames, and to complete the picture, they had two sons as well, Frederick and Reginald.

All Me Own Work – The Reprise album with entirely self-penned songs

"When Georgie returned from a flying visit to the West Indies at the end of March 1972", *Record Mirror* reported, "he found that Alan Price was using their band for recording and film commitments. […] Luckily, it turned out that Colin Green could make all the dates asked for, whether it was Price solo, Fame alone or Price & Fame together."

Georgie Fame had recognized the signs of the times and cut down on his constant touring in 1972 – "There was not too much demand, anyway".

Instead, he decided to produce an entirely self-penned album. *All Me Own Work* may be unspectacular, in parts experimental, but in retrospect it sounds inspired – another departure for Georgie, who works here with an intimate trio format of Colin Green on guitar, Brian Odgers on bass, and Brian Bennett, the former Shadows drummer, from his ongoing stand-by road band, which for gigs had already been re-named The Blue Flames again. The Shadows had disbanded officially in October 1969, and so Bennett was free for freelance live and studio work.

The trio was complemented by Colosseum's Dick Heckstall-Smith, a Flamingo veteran like Georgie, who still suffered from the aftermath of the great Jazz-Rock sextet's break-up and had just completed his first solo album, which he laconically called *A Story Ended* and which contained abandoned Colosseum material.

In order to understand the making of *All Me Own Work*, it is crucial to put it in the context of the musical climate of those times – the era of both the rise of the singer/songwriter, and the age of Progressive Rock.

Two examples will suffice. The singing pianist Reg Dwight, ex-Bluesology with mentor Long John Baldry and a.k.a. Elton John, had started his meteoric rise with one hundred percent self-written material, albeit helped – like Georgie – by a lyricist, in his case Bernie Taupin. Albums like *Tumbleweed Connection* and *Honky Chateau* showed a stunning, seemingly effortless creativity.

Keith Emerson of The Nice fame – who had employed Alan Skidmore for Nice Records – made his Hammond organ cross the bridge between classical and R&B music and was meanwhile using the instrument as a stage prop that was shaken about and thrashed with a knife – a custom he had started while he was with The V.I.P.s in 1967 – while hoarding banks of synthesisers all around him. Combining this with an actual singer-songwriter, King Crimson's Greg Lake – plus drummer Carl Palmer – and a hit with "Lucky Man" proved no mean feat.

Elsewhere, Georgie's Flamingo Club organ competitor Graham Bond also explored new territory with every release. Albums like *Holy Magick* or *We Put Our Magick On You* with his wife Diane Stewart were mystical, dark affairs, a far cry from the R&B sounds he had executed with Jack Bruce, Ginger Baker and – wait for it – Dick Heckstall-Smith on sax; who was, incidentally, also at hand for *All Me Own Work*.

Apart from this, accusations of "going Cabaret" and releasing family hits like "Rosetta" with Alan Price must have been quite frustrating for Fame. So some experimentation, for part of his first album away from CBS Records, did not come entirely unexpected. Comparing the daring stuff with the tried and tested formulas on the album showed, however, that Georgie was indeed still most comfortable in his jazzy Latin-R&B-Soul triangle, and in that respect had not lost his touch at all.

Fame's own take: "I was encouraged to write my own songs. I think some of them didn't quite work out, but that was why the album was called *All Me Own Work*. There were some interesting songs, I wrote songs like playing balls with my father back in Lancashire and stuff. But it was a transitional period. I was looking for a new direction. I didn't know which direction I was going to go, because everybody said that Rhythm & Blues singing was dead – so you have to start writing your own songs because everybody is doing that, that's where all the money is, blah blah blah! And I had this one record deal with Warner Reprise. And that's how that album came about. I've never sung any of these songs [live]."

All Me Own Work – track by track

"Super Road": Georgie started the album with an acoustic guitar in his hand – the way he had tackled the "Get Away" track for British Petroleum, assisted here by Colin Green's second guitar. Brian Odgers can be enjoyed supplying great double bass lines, and Brian Bennett is assisting on various percussion utensils. The hint at a tropical Calypso groove makes "Super Road" sound a little bit like a Donovan track, all sparse melody, more talking than singing, in loose contemplation. Lyrically, this is a great opener, with Georgie showing real love for poetry, beginning with "I'm a gravel aggravator, a wireless operator – I'm a junkie hater, political debater" and thus showing he saw the signs of the times. "No time to waste, gigging in haste, motorway tea tastes like champagne to me" shows the old Blue Flames trouper as tongue-in-cheek as his claim to be "king of the road", and "playing the jukebox down in the boondocks" again proves his sheer joy at word-play.

"Too Good To Be True" is a romantic love lament which Georgie goes to the piano and, yes, the cembalo for, which apart from The Yardbirds' "Heart Full Of Soul" isn't used too often in contemporary music. Lines like "Saw your face in the crowd, and that's when I found: I swore wouldn't have another taste, wouldn't waste myself too soon", all work well, and the chorus harmonies again sound as if Alan Price had his voice in here, as on the album *Seventh Son*.

The "Train" arrival gets notified by some railway station announcements probably taken from the studio archives, and we get some Booker T chops at last in the intro that sounds like a "Time Is Tight" spoof, but Georgie surely comes into his own, and his "You better hurry" can be taken as a call to the dance floor. Fame shines with great piano chops answered by Colin Green's smart licks, and then overdubs his Hammond organ, while Bennett & Odgers deliver their most agitated and infectious performances of the whole album. This is surely one to resurrect for live gigs in the future, and could have been another single.

"Seven Power" hints at the 7/4 rhythm pattern cleverly applied to this track, something he had successfully tried on "Seventh Son" three years previously. But with a crunchy wah-wah guitar pedal and synthesizer, this is an undeniable stylistic departure for Georgie. Colin Green adds some attractively funky rhythm guitar – a trick Led Zeppelin were employing at roughly the same time with "No Quarter", when they took one of Fame's specialities, James Brown Soul, to 5/4 time, albeit introducing a Soul groove that proves to be as utterly un-danceable as Georgie's "Seven Power" verses – until there is some relief when he gets to the more accessible 4/4 chorus.

"City Hicker" touches on one of Fame's infinite favourite themes, the contrast between the eventful city life and more sedate country dwelling: "John came up from the country on a summer's day, walked the town till he found himself a place to stay … laying his head he wished for a better place soon." The story is about a musician of course: "Played his horn after midnight to keep his chops in shape". The song sounds interesting due to Green's acoustic intro reminiscent of Paul McCartney's "Blackbird". There are his light Country licks, complemented by Fame's piano and, for the second time on this album, the cembalo. The crisp contributions by the rhythm section include some well placed syncopations – and Cliff Bennett's fills continue to impress. This became the single B-side of "Hey Baby (I'm Getting Ready)".

"Narcolepsy" means chronic sleep disorder, which comes as no surprise for employees of the Flamingo Club and other comparable establishments. But for the Blue Flames, the term had a more special meaning, as Georgie explains: "I did write a song for Glenn Hughes, the baritone player in the Blue Flames. He was a fantastic saxophone player. And that song was called 'Narcolepsy'. That is talking about Red Reece and playing with Hughes, because they both unfortunately were involved in heroin. And 'Narcolepsy' is a sleeping sickness, which is a reference to heroin abuse."

The song works well as a piano ballad – "Gone are the days when the nights were long, when Red was around to enjoy our song, now he walks down the street with his head hanging low, shuffles gone to his feel he got no place to go." – Georgie on the piano and synthesizer, Colin Green supplying sharp guitar kicks to a solid rhythm backing with sophisticated Odgers-bass and cowbell overkill. The surprise is an up-tempo chorus, where the band really comes into its own and shows what a live power it must have displayed.

"Passed Me By" showed Fame's desire for experimentation again. Partly nostalgic as a nod to his childhood hero Fats Domino, he displays the "Fat Man"'s typical piano lines but enhances them with a synthesizer theme. Georgie has our legs entangled should we attempt to shake them to this rhythm, because he set this superficially relaxed New Orleans tune in 11/4 time – even trickier than on "Seven Power" because it sounds so relaxed here. Dick Heckstall-Smith, the old Flamingo Club cohort via the Graham Bond Organization – and fresh out of Colosseum by the time of these recordings – adds worthwhile sax work here, serving up his soprano and tenor simultaneously – Heckstall-Smith should have played more during these sessions. Although Georgie never played this one live either, he certainly did not forget about it, because he would revive "Passed Me By" 20 years later on the album *The Blues And Me*.

"Hey Baby (I'm Getting Ready)" is *the* instantly catchy tune on the album, the one that had cried out to become the single release, and it did come out on 7", albeit without any chart success. The influential *Melody Maker* may have stated "Frankly, it's rather disappointing", but that seems a bit too harsh, judging from the danceable rhythm and a chorus that invites the listener to join in immediately. The song had developed out of a track recorded for the aborted second Georgie Fame & Alan Price album, the

Fame composition "What You're Doing I Can Do", with ad-lib lyric-free vocals, but charming nonetheless. It appeared in 1998 on the Verve Boxed Set *The In-Crowd*.

The short song sketch "Dream Pony" is credited to Georgie Fame, Kathryn Ireland and Cosima Stewart, the daughter of Fame's wife, Nicolette, from a first marriage, born in 1961. When the *All Me Own Work* sessions took place, Cosima Stewart was eleven years old. It is possible that it is actually Cosima who is singing on the track. Georgie mentioned Cosima again in other contexts, like the reason he wrote "That Ole Rock'n'Roll" for the *Georgie Fame* Island album 1974 and the inspiration behind "Country Girl" on *Right Now!* in 1978. Fans who have heard the master tapes to the album have reported that there had been a short orchestral section added to the song snippet, but it does not appear on the vinyl version.

All Me Own Work was certainly a stylistic departure from previous albums, and it came over as much more mellow. Colin Green rates the album and concludes, "Yes, I think he was finding his feet very much as a songwriter, and there was quite a bit of autobiographical stuff in that. I like the album, actually. The mellowness was due to both of us – it was just what came out, really, what the songs said. The way the songs were written, they dictated the arrangements pretty much."

So how was this work received by the public? It certainly did not sell well, a fact which does not signify its lack of quality, but rather a certain reservation by an audience which was used to swingy grooves and catchy tunes, whatever the style – or the writer for that matter – happened to be called. The journalist John Pidgeon, familiar with all things Mod due to his work about the Small Faces, wrote a mild review for the *New Musical Express* which is as revelatory as it is sensitive:

"Fame by Fame – and it's not bad: Georgie Fame: '*All Me Own Work*' (Reprise): The title is more than just a neat cliché. As well as singing, playing keyboards, guitars, a synthesizer and (according to the credits) toys (!), Fame wrote all the songs, produced the album, and had a hand in the sleeve design. It was 10 years ago that together with the Blue Flames he first played the all-nighter session at the Flamingo Club in Wardour Street, W.1, where, in what must be one of the most powerful instances of a reciprocal artist-audience relationships ever, he developed his unique style.

"The black GIs there would lay their record collections on him; so he heard performers like Oscar Brown Jr. and the heaviest influence of all, Mose Allison, whose nasal, deadpan delivery still echoes in his singing.

"Today there are new influences as well, though these affect the instrumental elements on the album rather than the vocal style. The range of keyboards has been extended too, and the old familiar organ dominates only one track. Piano, which Fame played before the Flamingo days in Billy Fury's back-up band, prevails, even underpinning other keyboards when they are used.

"Since breaking up the Blue Flames in 1966 he has fronted a variety of outfits without re-establishing a permanent band. For this album he assembled ex-Shadows drummer Brian Bennett, bassist Brian Odgers, and his long-time guitarist Colin Green. This tight and experienced group is augmented on one track by another veteran, Dick Heckstall-Smith, on saxophone.

"Their music, avoiding flash, is always controlled; everyone plays well within his limits. Perhaps Fame's writing doesn't consistently provide material for them to get their teeth into. Only on "Train", driven hard under Georgie's Hammond by Stax-ish bass and drums, "Too Good to Be True", the Fats Domino inspired "Passed Me By" with Heckstall-Smith's honky sax and "Hey Baby (I'm Getting Ready)", do they come near to extending themselves.

"The remaining tracks are a mixture of anecdote and commonplace, inoffensive but not startingly good.

"Fame is a musician, and there is a sense that it's only his long experience of playing other people's songs that has enabled him to write his own. However the fact is that he's not the world's most intuitive songwriter doesn't devalue his musical ability. He shouldn't deprive himself of the chance to play the best material, because when he does he's great.

"To do an album of one's own compositions is a common ambition amongst musicians, and Georgie can rightly feel quite proud of his. But now he's done it, maybe he won't so limit himself again."

So there: This was the day and age of the nasty review – the year when new albums by the then current darlings like Rod Stewart and Marc Bolan had been greeted with the headline "Would you buy a used riff from these gentlemen?" So with a lesser pen and rougher soul, complaints could have stung and stiffened future compositional efforts. As it was, it would be some time until Fame would attempt another completely self-written album. But his already respectable compositions soon got better, even if his artistic "Survival" didn't depend on it.

Meanwhile, the self-composed LP received a considerably better verdict by *Record Mirror*. On September 9th, 1972, they wrote "Fame in his element" about *All Me Own Work* (Reprise 44183): "An appropriate title for this album, which consists entirely of Georgie's own compositions, is produced by him, and even has a cover designed, and autographed, by his own band. It's also his first album since joining Reprise [Records], and it reflects his own personality and musical experimentation to a great degree.

"Certainly some of the lyrics – something that George has admitted to having trouble with – can be faulted: but basically, they have a humour or insight that, if not expounded with the greatest sensitivity, can instill that feeling in the listener. 'Narcolepsy' is particularly notable, reciting the tragic events that surrounded members of the Fame band in the early days, particularly the death of Glynn (sic) Hughes. And the line 'I rode for a time on a lemming train' indicates the realization of the futility of the life that a lot of these excellent musicians got caught up in.

"'Dream Pony', on the other hand, is a simple little child's ditty, sung by the Lady Cosima, the nine-year old daughter of Georgie's wife.

"'Passed Me By', combining synthesizer and piano, would not shame Fats Domino, and there's also some excellent work on the sax by Dick Heckstall-Smith. I'd consider *All Me Own Work* to be one of the better solo albums to emerge from Georgie in recent years, and it's a must for long-term fans as it catalogues well the heights and depths that Georgie has passed through – but doubt it not, here he's in his own element, and happy to be there. V.M." So for once, there is no attempt at analyzing what Georgie could have done to make the demanding public and the critic happy, but he is measured by his own goals and aspirations.

Georgie certainly wanted it this way – create in peace and without pressure, which was why he had not tied himself to a so-many albums per year contract with Warner's, unlike his partner Alan Price. As it was, he was satisfied with the way *Work* had turned out, as he told Mike Hennessy in Record Mirror in July 1972, before the album came out on August 18th: "It's the best thing I've ever done. It's called *All Me Own Work* – for the obvious reason that all the songs on it are mine. It's the first time I've written all the material on an album."

The single which was culled from *All Me Own Work* got praise by the *Record Mirror* on July 22nd, who found "Fame in top form": Hey Baby (I'm Getting Ready); City Hicker (Reprise K 14191): "For me, the single of the week because of its style, class, melody and all-around amiability. Good old-style piano bashing, plus vocal woe-woes, with walking-bass figures. It all stands or falls on Georgie's personality, and there's no shortage of that – performed by anyone else it'd surely droop a bit. Instead it is near vintage Fame. Chart Cert."

The move from the chosen path of Jazz and Jazz Rock albums via the imposed Pop and Ballad collections towards a singer/songwriter LP was consequential and logical. Before long, this was going to be corrected by issuing truly eclectic, versatile works that were nevertheless always easy on the ear. Georgie continued to love Jazz, but he defied categorization by adding Rock'n'Roll, Country Rock, Blues, Soul and Reggae as he pleased. Love of music in favour of an efficient, albeit potentially boring career plan – what more could Fame's widespread appreciation society possibly want?

EMI wasted no time and continued to cash in on a still popular brand name, presenting well-known, tried and tested songs that sounded more commercial than the more daring *All Me Own Work* material which Georgie released on his new label, refined and sophisticated, in order to develop and keep up with trends.

Fame Again! was the casual yet eye-catching title for a mid-price companion to the 1967 *Hall of Fame* which was treated pretty well by the press. As *Record Mirror* wrote on April 8th, 1972 about *Fame Again!* (EMI-Starline): "For those who missed them the first time around, many of the best Fame tracks are available here at budget price. Highlight of a successful career with 'Yeh Yeh', the number one hit sounding as good as ever and 'Getaway' written by Georgie; a chart-topper prior to the break-up of the Blue Flames. Even the earliest single 'I'm In Love With You Baby' and 'Bend A Little' is featured. In contrast there's a taste of Georgie's venture into the world of Big Bands with 'L'il Darlin'. One of an excellent series. V.M." (see cover p. 172)

Back to the small Blue Flames – Fame, Holland, Odgers & Bennett

In order to promote *All Me Own Work*, and parallel to his ongoing gigs and recording dates with Alan Price for the recording of a second duo album, Fame started to assemble a small band, comprising two *Work* players, and one new guy, because "Colin Green had become a session musician", according to Georgie.

Green preferred this, recalling that "I was very heavily into studio work then, so I wasn't missing gigs." The new guy was Bernie Holland.

Bernie Holland had been a drummer for the Cheltenham based Sinners, but soon changed to guitar for the Blues cover band Jam. He accompanied Long John Baldry in the legendary, once 'Elton John endowed' group Bluesology, when he was just nineteen, and had appeared on television with Baldry in 1968 in the US on *The Bobbie Gentry Show*.

Bernie: "The very first job I had was with a band called Bluesology. That was the name of a piece of music, a tune. I can't remember who wrote it. [The number that inspired the band was by Milt Jackson from the Modern Jazz Quartet, the same composition as that which Georgie Fame had put lyrics to.] That was the name of the band that was backing Long John Baldry. The trumpet player with that band lives in Germany, Marc Charig. He actually played cornet, and we also had Elton Dean and Pete Gavin on drums [with a line-up that pianist "Fat" Reg Dwight had already left, who was taking his subsequent stage name "Elton John" from *Elton* Dean and *John* Baldry]. I played with Pete Gavin in another band called Jody Grind."

Holland was a part-time member of Rock hopefuls Patto. He actually founded the progressive Jody Grind, who were named after a Horace Silver number. Apart from their drummer Pete Gavin, they featured pianist Tim Hinkley, a later Alvin Lee cohort. It was through Hinkley that Holland met ex-Blue-Flames drummer Mitch Mitchell: "I was with Mitch, after he had left Georgie Fame, and before I joined Georgie Fame. I actually played with Mitch Mitchell later on in a band called Hinkley's Heroes, some years later. The line-up changed a lot, and Mitch was on drums. He lived with a friend of mine in Fulham, who has taught me how to produce music on a computer: Poli Palmer. He lived with Mitch in a flat in Fulham for some time. Poli was with [the band] Family."

Bernie remembers his pre-Fame times: "In 1970, there was a club, *Blaises*, where people used to go and jam. Various people would come along and play. One night, Hendrix turned up. He just came down to relax, and he got up on stage and played, and I played bass with him, just a jam, just a Blues. This was before I joined Georgie Fame, I started working with Georgie in 1972." Jimi had come back to one of the first venues in London where he ever set foot as a jamming guitarist, as Roger Clarke-Johnson had recalled at the time of Mitch's Experience beginnings.

Holland's many years with Fame started like this: "I'll tell you exactly what happened: I was living in a flat in Hendon, doing all sorts of things, not being in any one band. When I was with Jody Grind, it was a three piece band with Tim Hinkley and Pete Gavin, but we did actually have a horn player sometimes, towards the end. Pete Gavin had left the band to join Heads, Hands & Feet, with Albert Lee and Tony Colton. Tony Colton was the songwriter and lead singer. Tony phoned me up, this was in the autumn of 1972, and he said 'Do you like Georgie Fame?' I said yeah. 'Would you like to play with him?' I said 'Yeah, I'd like to play with Georgie Fame.' – 'He's looking for a guitarist, he wants to get a new band together.'"

"He was getting a four piece band. It was Georgie Fame & The Blue Flames, but it was only a quartet. Tony asked 'Can I give him your phone number?' What happened was, Clive rang me up, 'Has Tony Colton been on the phone to you? I need to come over and see you.' He came over to my flat with a Grundig tape recorder, it was a reel-to-reel. He said 'I'm gonna leave this tape recorder with you for a few days. There is a tape on it. You know how to operate it?' So we had a drink, and he said 'Have a listen to this tape'. He played a couple of things for me and I said 'Yeah, this is great. I am going to enjoy doing this.'"

"I wondered who was going to be in the band, and he went 'I've got a bass player called Brian Odgers'. He doesn't play anymore now, which is a waste, because he is one of the greatest bass players I have ever worked with. I am still in touch with him. He played with John McLaughlin at one time. He is fantastic, a great musician. I don't even want to call him a bass player, he is a fantastic musician, who just happens to play bass guitar. At the time I didn't know who he was. On drums there was a guy called Brian Bennett", the renowned Shadows-drummer of course. Holland: "I am still in touch with Brian today on Facebook. He spends some time in Spain and Portugal. He was on drums."

So after very few and basic rehearsals, the new small Blue Flames started gigging. Holland again: "I remember the first night was in Liverpool, we had two nights in this theatre in Liverpool, with Brian Bennett, Georgie and me. It was a great gig. It really was fantastic, for the first gig. That was a highlight. That was the best line-up I did with him. I'm not saying that everything we did after that went downhill, it didn't. But for me, that was the high of my fulfilment, playing with him, with that quartet. I wish someone had filmed it or recorded it, amazing. People weren't much into that at the time, we didn't have things like YouTube, it was long before that started. So we had this band – it was fantastic, it was just great. Right from the word go it was really happening. I think it's the best band he's ever had. I knew I'd say that – ha ha!"

Apart from the Mitch Mitchell connection, Bernie Holland also seemed an inspired choice because of his contacts to the former Flamingo Club hero and occasional honorary Blue Flame Graham Bond: "I didn't actually work with Graham Bond, I played with him. This was a very strange situation. There was a studio in Central London. I got a phone call inviting me to come to this studio, some friends saying 'Would you like to come? Nobody is getting paid for it.' Do you remember 'happenings'? This was a 'happening' with Graham Bond. He was dressed in these strange purple and red robes and had all these candles and incense burning stuff. I think there were other things being burned as well. We were in the studio all night. Not long after that, I got news he fell in front of a tube train and was killed, unfortunately."

The experiences with the Blue Flames led to more session opportunities, too: "A similar thing happened with Frank Zappa. I played bass with him, another jam session in the Speakeasy Club in London, in Margaret Street. And I knew the drummer at the time, Aynsley Dunbar. He is a friend of mine. 'Frank's coming, Frank Zappa, we're having a drink and we're gonna have a jam. We are going to need someone to play bass.' I said yeah, because I played bass with Georgie Fame sometimes. Georgie had asked me to play bass with him, because he couldn't get a bass player. So I did a few gigs with him on bass."

From 1974, and on top of his work with the Blue Flames, Bernie Holland was a member of the London studio Soul band Hummingbird, which was produced by early Blue Flames soundboard director Ian Samwell. They featured the just-dumped Jeff Beck Group members Bobby Tench, the lead vocalist now also on guitar, wo later joined Humble Pie and then The Alan Price Band, Clive Chaman on bass and Max Middleton on keyboards, with Reg Isadore and then Bernard "Pretty" Purdie as their drummers. Their studio choir included Georgie's lifetime friend Madeline Bell. Bernie Holland's connection to the ex-Jeff Beck Group led to Beck picking up Holland's 1973 composition "Diamond Dust" for his album *Blow By Blow*, which Bernie is justifiably proud of.

One of the most adventurous gigs of the year 1973 took Georgie and his band to the Portuguese Algarve in October. They played in a night club, and there was actually a whole coach load of tourists from the UK who cheered him on. Fame on BBC radio: "It was a nice little bar, I think in Carvoeiro, which was run by an English photographer by the name of Tim Motion. What a memory!"

According to António Alfaiate, "the bar was then called 'Sobe e Desce' (roughly translated as 'Up and Down'). The owner at the time was the Irish photographer and sax player Tim Motion, who had opened the place in 1967. Over the years, a number of excellent musicians played the 'Sobe e Desce': Brian Auger, Cat Stevens, Jon Hendricks, Ronnie Scott, and Jim Mullen. These days, the name of the place is 'Jailhouse'.

That same year 1973, Fame was back in the Algarve, this time only with his drummer Brian Bennett.

Alfaiate again: "They stayed at the 'Hotel Penina' – the very place which was immortalized by the Paul McCartney in a song that he wrote of the same name in December 1968. The Beatles never recorded it, and Paul gave it away to the Portuguese band Jotta Herre, who had been playing at the hotel then and who also proceeded to record it. After them, the Portuguese singer Carlos Mendes has also recorded the song.

"Georgie and Brian Bennett played at the Casino do Alvor, backed by three Portuguese musicians: Mário de Jesus on trumpet, Luís Waddington on guitar and Dany Silva on bass. Silva actually became quite well known as a singer in Portugal and he is still playing today.

"It seems that Georgie and Brian had a barter deal with the hotel there: They would play at the casino and for thir efforts, they were entitled to free food, drink (!) and accomodation at the hotel. Those were the days."

Portuguese radio broadcast the concert they did live on the night of the 4th to the 5th October 1973, and so good bootlegs exist, where you can hear the progress of a true party gig. The repertoire was "Yeh Yeh", "Sunny", "By The Time I Get To Phoenix", "The Point Of No Return", "Dr Kitch", "Happy Time (Tempo Feliz)", "Two Newly Weds", "How Deep Is The Ocean", "The Ballad of Bonnie and Clyde", "Sitting In The Park", and "Last Night".

The "crown jewel" here was "Two Newly Weds", a song with very funny lyrics which, unfortunately, Georgie never recorded officially.

Chapter 5

The Island Years – The Okie Blue Flames and The Big Band Flames

The time certainly seemed right for a return to Rhythm & Blues. In 1974 Chris Blackwell, the British-Jamaican label boss and Bob Marley champion, offered Georgie Fame a lucrative contract with his Island Records, home of recent biggies like Traffic, Free and Jethro Tull – and a big budget to match. Island Records had originally been a Jamaican label, founded by Blackwell in 1959 and named after the Harry Belafonte hit "Island In The Sun". The operation moved to England in 1962 and soon had hits like "My Boy Lolipop" by Millie Jackson.

Top producer Glyn Johns – who apart from engineering *Rhythm And Blues At The Flamingo* eleven years before in September 1963 had worked with The Beatles (mixing the *Let It Be* album during 1969 in a much more subtle way to Phil Spector), The Rolling Stones, The Small Faces, Humble Pie, The Steve Miller Band and The Eagles – led sessions for a traditional as well as up-to-date Blue Flames-album, which came to be simply, and unimaginatively, titled *Georgie Fame*. It was recorded in London and Tulsa, Oklahoma.

J.J. Cale (1938–2013) was also present during the Fame recordings made in his hometown of Tulsa, Oklahoma, the home of Shelter Records. The link to that label comes of little surprise when one remembers that the company, with offices in Los Angeles and Tulsa, had not only been started by Leon *Mad Dogs & Englishmen* Russell (b.1942), but also Georgie Fame's much praised ex-producer Denny Cordell (1943–1995), who before becoming freelance had worked for Chris Blackwell's Island label to which Georgie was now contracted.

Other key players in Tulsa and Nashville, both of them Tulsa-born, were bass man Carl Radle (1942–1980) of Delaney & Bonnie as well as *Mad Dogs & Englishmen* fame, and drummer Jamie Oldaker (b.1951), a young man whose skilful and relaxed groove belied his junior years. Jamie had really come of age via studio work: "I worked for Leon and Cale in Shelter in 1973. Right before that I played with Bob Seger in 1972. I was on the original album with 'Turn The Page' on it. Back in Tulsa I started working for Shelter. Then I went with Eric [Clapton] in 1974. J.J. Cale had been playing around Tulsa in the late Sixties, and he'd come back from L.A. and he'd come in and play and I'd sit in. I'd play around town, and when I worked with Leon, he was in the studio, and hanging around. He'd come and jam with us and play. So it was all that Tulsa thing: Leon, Cale, around the Shelter Records company. Carl Radle (1942–1980), absolutely, I miss him every day!"

The prime guitarists during the sessions were Tommy Triplehorn and Marc Benno. Triplehorne had come to Tulsa via Los Angeles as an ex-member of Gary Lewis & The Playboys. Tommy had joined the singing son of comedian Jerry Lewis in 1965, together with drummer Jimmy Karstein, Carl Radle and song-writing partner Leon Russell, who now employed all of them in Tulsa studios. Marc Benno, a.k.a. Benny Daron, is an inspired Texan guitarist and songwriter (b. July 1947 in Dallas) who had worked with Lightnin' Hopkins and Steve Miller, and who had formed the Asylum Choir with Leon Russell. Five years after his contributions to *Georgie Fame*, Glyn Johns was to produce his album *Lost In Austin*.

As with meeting Georgie Fame in Tulsa, Oldaker says that "Glyn Johns produced that record, I remember. Glyn wanted to come and record there, and Georgie came in. I think it was me, Marc Benno as a guitar player, Tommy Triplehorne, Carl Radle. Dick Simms played keyboards as well, and then I'd drum. It was a fun record to do, I remember; he was really good! He was kind of the English Mose Allison character. He used to drink a lot of Bloody Marys. He makes his Bloody Marys every morning before he went to the studio, while we were making the record, but no ice. He'd just make this big, huge pitcher of Bloody Marys. We all had to drink Bloody Marys, like ten o'clock in the morning. He was a fantastic musician, fantastic to play with, wonderful. I was very young then, anyhow. And I think it all happened pretty quickly when we did the sessions. It was a lot of fun playing *with* him. He was a brilliant leader, and we pretty well did what he wanted. We had fun recording, and it wasn't really a very stressful time.

"He worked just like Cale. Cale was like that. He didn't like to do stuff more than once or twice, maybe once, and go to the next one. We kind of played like it was live. I think we rehearsed: we went to a club, somewhere in Tulsa, before we went into the studio, I remember. We started recording later, but before [that] we'd go to the club and there we could set up the equipment and we could actually play, like we were in a night-club. And then we went to the studio."

The Georgie Fame album – an overlooked masterpiece from 1974

"Everloving Woman" is a delightful exercise in laid back grooves: Jamie Oldaker on his – even then – thirty year old Ludwig drum kit and Carl Dean Radle's elastically rolling bass provide the perfect foil for Georgie's tasteful Fender Rhodes licks in Tulsa, Oklahoma. The guitar was provided by Tommy Triplehorne, wailing in attractive contrast to the song's easy-going nature.

Georgie himself is having a ball by the sounds of it, complementing his silken, relaxed vocals by countless "oohs" and "aahs" to emphasize the feeling of moving in the perfect groove – and if he has one thing in common with Eric Clapton apart from this band, it is his love of J.J. Cale's music, a fact which he proved in 1999, when he forged his own composition "Rhythm King" in a similar kind of pattern. Quite rightly,

Island made this the album's only single, but in spite of frequent airplay in England and Germany, it did not make an impact.

"Don't 'B' Movie Me" is an expression so nonchalant and cool. It must have appealed to Georgie, and he does his composition justice with the words of John Ryan by having a brass section work at full throttle – on stage, this would soon be Bud Beadle, Steve Gregory and Eddie 'Tan Tan' Thornton. Apart from their service in the Blue Flames' ranks, two of those three horns men also worked for the Jazz-Rock ensemble Gonzales, with Tan Tan

a veteran from the Flamingo days. The Flamingo Flames are evoked on this album more than once: "I'm the dude that taught you all" could certainly be true as a reminder to band members as well as a private partner.

In "Donut Man" Fame found one of two Marc Benno compositions that appealed to him, this one on the Texan Blues man's 1972 album *Ambush*. In a folky way, the Texan singer-songwriter sang about a donut man on the corner of 5th and Main, who had a hole in his shirt and shoes, and nothing much to lose. Georgie was in good company covering it, as Rita Coolidge chose the song as well, on her LP *The Lady's Not For Sale*. "Donut Man" again shows Georgie's uncanny knack in selecting songs that have so much Fame in them – they sound like having been written to order. "Donut Man" certainly fits that bill.

"Ozone", another Fame/Ryan composition, is a relaxed slow Swing, with the Carl Radle and Jamie Oldaker rhythm section at their most subdued and utterly comfortable, and Georgie obviously soothingly confident and in his element. Island Records liked this enough to make it, in the US, the B-side of the LP's single, "Everlovin' Woman".

"Leaving The City Behind" sounds autobiographical – as long ago, Fame had left the heady, heavily hedonistic pleasures of "The Smoke" behind in order to raise his family in the rural peace of Devon. An imaginative, sophisticated marching drum pattern by Jamie Oldaker and pleasant Rhodes E-piano form the background for a relaxed reading, with the chorus enhanced by attractive female backing vocals, like everything here of course – uncredited.

The B-side continues with the same topic, by applying the catchy Gallagher & Lyle [17] composition "Country Morning". (That duo had been an integral part of ex (Small) Faces member Ronnie Lane's way of leaving the city behind for Wales: Lane started the Slim Chance band with Gallagher & Lyle, who only too quickly realized their potential, and went their separate ways.) Georgie found this tune on their Glyn Johns produced and engineered album *Seeds*, and it must have fitted his own mood perfectly: "Turn

---

17. See Addendum

the radio on, the J.Y. Show is shining bright" – or if "the country air takes your cares away", nothing much can go wrong. Again, the horn section makes this a true Blue Flames number.

"We Were Always Sweethearts" was a lovely composition by yet another Glyn Johns production customer, singer-songwriter and guitarist William Royce "Boz" Scaggs. Ohio-born but a Dallas Texan like Benno, Boz had presented the song as the starter for his 1971 *Moments*, albeit with a faster, more brass-heavy arrangement than Georgie's relaxed reading, but both versions have a Hammond organ and an easy Funk groove in common. A soft female backing choir is added for Georgie, reminiscent of the *Going Home* album and entirely fitting here. Fame & Scaggs would work together sixteen years after this on the *Cool Cat Blues*, helmed by Ben Sidran, who plays vibraphone on *Moments*, and an acquaintance of Glyn Johns via the Steve Miller Band. This number was left off the US version of *Georgie Fame*.

The second Marc Benno composition on the album, "Hall St. Jive" – in spite of the immaculate quality of "Donut Man" – is the most amusing and Flames-compatible number which Georgie recorded in the entire sessions. A favourite of drummer Jamie Oldaker as well, Fame's ever so humourous rendition, complete with hilarious falsetto backing vocals and an easy Swing plus inventive and deft Hammond touches all add to a performance that is to be treasured and could lift every single Georgie Fame & The Blue Flames gig. A contender for a massive Single hit beyond anything that was released during the Seventies!

"Hall St Jive", like "We Were Always Sweethearts" was left off the *Georgie Fame* LP in America, a most unfortunate move in this author's opinion.

"That Old Rock'n'Roll" has its story in the Fame household, as Georgie remembers: 'My step daughter [Cosima] asked me sometime in 1973, 'Can you play Rock'n'Roll as well?' – I said 'Can I play Rock'n'Roll?' Check Georgie's childhood, and Jerry Lee was his second name – 'and so I sat down at the piano and soon came up with this tune' – for which John Ryan supplied the lyrics again, including the lovely spoken intro "Children have eyes ... until suddenly:" – and then the mayhem begins. Island Records made this the B-side of the LP's single "Everlovin' Woman" in the UK, Germany, Spain and New Zealand, and Georgie revived the tune for his Blue Flames album *My Favourite Songs* in 1983.

"Survival" was the album's finale, and its pièce de resistance, too – a slow 12-bar Blues with lovely saxophone licks, Fame's Hammond organ backing and supplementing licks from electric piano and sparse, wah-wah'ed guitar: "Survival of the planet", John Ryan says, "means, don't spoil a masterpiece, it means every leave's important, all the creatures golden geese, means every natural resource, every one there, means everything is valuable. Hey, some day someone will sure set it right. Why don't we all wait and see – as someone, and not like the best of us, fighting, as long as that someone's – not me!"

As Fame's environmental lament, "Survival" was well ahead of its time. It re-appeared on *Cool Cat Blues* (1990) and *Tone Wheels-A-Turnin'* (2009) and has been revived for live work as recently as 2012.

"Johnny Too Bad" was composed by The Slickers, a Jamaican Rocksteady and Reggae group of the late 1960s and early 1970s. The song was featured on the soundtrack for the 1972 Jimmy Cliff film *The Harder They Come* and, after Georgie had done his version, the legendary Scottish singer-songwriter John Martyn (1948–2009) covered it, adding extra lyrics, initially on his 1980 album *Grace & Danger*, a calling card for Martyn for decades, which makes Georgie's choice all the more appropriate.

"Johnny Too Bad" only appeared on the US version of the album, which incidentally displayed the black & white sleeve illustration with red instead of green lettering, and supplied detailed liner notes – although these also managed to neglect mentioning the line-ups of the recordings. "Tan Tan" Thornton may well have been part of this number, as had drummer Dave Mattacks, whose crisp snare sound is hard to miss on this clever Reggae workout.

There was one further track recorded for the album in Tulsa, which was called "A Different Kind Of Blues". It is a relaxed shuffle where Georgie once again uses his relaxed singing style, and some inspired slide guitar by Tulsa's Tommy Triplehorne.

Lively cover choices – like J.J. Cale's "Everloving Woman" or Gallagher & Lyle's "Country Morning" showed impeccable taste. But in spite of all that and a high-class line-up with many members of the US Rock and Country aristocracy, the album bombed, a fact that Georgie did not know yet when he happily mingled with Eric Clapton and Charlie Watts for Glyn Johns' wedding reception.

The lack of success (of the album, not the Johns' marriage) was most probably due to Island's simplistic, unimaginative cover packaging: There was nothing wrong with the drawing of Georgie's attractive enough head on the record sleeve, but the LP had to find attention without a title, and the cover did not reveal even one of the participating musicians. Was it possible that Island Record's multi millionaire Chris Blackwell could not be bothered to score the rights?

Fame, looking back in 1994: "I think he wanted people to think it was the Blue Flames reformed, but it wasn't: it was Carl Radle on bass, Jamie Oldaker on drums, just before they started working with Eric Clapton, and a guy named Tommy Triplehorne – he was from Tulsa, Oklahoma, too, just like the other guys."

Jamie Oldaker is not sure that Fame's timing is right: "I don't think it was before. I started with Eric in April '74. I'm not sure how [Marc] Benno got in the picture, other than probably he was involved with Leon [Russell] before with Asylum Choir records, back in L.A."

"Call Up The Devil" – The Large Blue Flames

The album's J.J. Cale-type Blues-Rock numbers could have been performed by the Blue Flames Quartet starring Fame, Holland, Odgers & Bennett, but the more elaborate horn arrangements, like on "Don't B-Movie Me", called for a bigger line-up, and that's exactly what happened – to an extent that was hardly predictable for anybody who jumped on that particular bandwagon.

What the public read about first went like this: On August 10th, 1974, *Record Mirror* featured the heading "Blue Flames fire back" and reported that "Georgie Fame and his new Blue Flames debut at the Reading Festival on August 24th." They pointed out that "two original members of the band, Colin Green and Eddie Thornton, have joined the new line-up and several ex-Blue Flames are expected to sit in."

Failing to notice that some band members, including guitarists Colin Green and Bernie Holland, were simply taken over from previous line-ups which were just not called The Blue Flames at the time, they also reported that "former Shadows drummer, Brian Bennett, has also joined the band. Their debutic album, *Survival* (sic) [It would have made sense to call it that, but as it was, *Georgie Fame* contained "Survival" as its piece de resistance], is being released by Island on September 13 and following Reading a major tour of Britain is scheduled."

The intinerary was impressive: During August of 1974, it was Coventry on the 27th, Barbarella's, Birmingham (28th), Leamington (29th) and New Theatre, Cardiff on the 30th. September would see the Key Theatre in Peterborough on the 1st, Civic Hall in Elstree on the 5th, Halifax Civic Theatre on the 6th, Whitworth Civic Hall 8th, Canterbury's Marlowe Theatre with its exemplary acoustics on the 9th, Redcar's Coatham Ball 11th, Scarborough Penthouse 13th, Dunfermline Carnegie Hall on the 14th, Grangemouth Town Hall 15th, Motherwell Civic Hall 16th, London's Lyceum followed on the 18th, the Princess Theatre in Aldershot on the 19th, the Lafayette Club on Slade's home turf in Wolverhampton on the 20th, Belfrey Sutton Coldfield on the 21st, and finally the Civic Theatre in Darlington, 22nd.

Record Mirror, on 13th July 1974 specified details about the line-up: "Fame re-light Flames": "Keyboard magician Georgie Fame has been reunited with the Blue Flames, the band which backed him in the early sixties and saw chart success with Yeh Yeh and Getaway. RRM understands the New Blue Flames is a 10-piece outfit making their debut with Georgie at the Reading Festival next month. The band consists of former Shadows drummer Brian Bennett; Lennox Langton, a Trinidadian, on congas; Brian Odges (sic) on bass; Colin Green, an original Blue Flame, on guitar; Bernie Holland who played with Stomu Yamasht'a on second guitar; Steve Gregory who worked with Alan Price and Alan Skidmore on tenor saxes; Eddie Thornton and session man Henry Lowther on trumpets and Buddy Beadle.

"The New Blue Flames have been rehearsing with Georgie for the past month and an album and single are expected to be released by Island in the near future. Plans are also in hand for a tour." Was the group getting out of hand?

As Fame remembers it in 2013, chatting away in London's Bloomsbury Hotel before another Soho gig in Ronnie Scott's Club, "it really was. I didn't want it any bigger than the old Blue Flames. I meant to reform that band. But I suddenly had Alan Skidmore and Steve Gregory on tenor sax. Buddy Beadle plays alto, and I didn't need two alto saxes either, but Peter King wanted in on it, too. There were even two drummers: apart from Brian Bennett, I also had Mitch Mitchell on that tour. The tour was kind of financed by Chris Blackwell – I would say that it pretty much paid for itself."

This sounded more convivial than his outburst to Duncan Heining in 2009: "The Blue Flames was really just five or six pieces but when a lot of musicians started hearing that this band was being formed, they all wanted to be in it and I foolishly allowed them in – people like Elton Dean and Marc Charig and Stan Sulzman. So, we ended up with far too many – a band of lunatics it was and far too many of them (*laughing*). After that I thought 'No, I just want a little unit that I can control and play the music I want to play."

Bernie Holland picks up those vivid memories: "After that, the band started expanding, people started coming into the band, like Peter King, Alan Skidmore, Steve Gregory, Bud Beadle, Elton Dean played with us. There was a whole load of horn players in."

Colin Green also had a hand in the Mega Flames: "We did reform the Blue Flames to go on tour with quite a big line-up. It lasted for about six months. And I think we did some recording for that, but I can't remember precisely. But that's not like me, so maybe I didn't. When we rehearsed for that tour, we went down to Georgie's place. There were three sax players, two trumpets – it was quite a big line-up, and I offered to write the charts for that. But Clive didn't want any charts. He just wanted everybody to do their thing. So it was quite interesting sometimes.

"But one particular night, everything just worked, it was just magic. But that was one night out of – many! It got to be far too chaotic for my taste. Musically, I like things to be a little bit organized. I like the freedom that that sort of thing can offer, but it's too much – the odds are against you, really, against it being consistently good. There was a lot of drinking going on as well, but I personally think it was just too many egos, and really, Clive should have got hold of it. But if that's what he wanted to do, that's fine. It didn't need that sort of line-up. And you can have loose arrangements, but you should have some order in it."

Colin Green's time with Georgie had come to an amicable end; Green faced a marvellous career on his own, which enhanced his already incredibly versatile CV, including a collaboration spectrum from Shirley Bassey to Alexis Korner with C.C.S., the BeeGees, Bert Kaempfert, plus Rhythm King Martin Taylor and the German-French singer/songwriter Patricia Kaas. Green has a working trio, 3 Play, together with saxophonist Dave Richmond and bass player Mick Allport. Colin also has an album out, *Now & Then*, which features recent and old recordings, some with the late Blue Mink and Georgie Fame studio drummer, Barry Morgan.

And this is how sax master Alan Skidmore, who knew most of the players via his Brotherhood of Breath, recalls the huge project: "If my memory serves me right, there was a tour with a much larger band, which was 1974. It was the whole of the UK: Stan Sultzman, Elton Dean, Mark Charig, Buddy Beadle on baritone saxophone, myself, Eddie "Tan Tan" Thornton, Brian Bennett on drums – and a lot of fun was had by all! I will leave the rest to your imagination. And the tour did encompass Scotland, which was quite memorable – that's all I am going to say. In all there were thirteen of us, and we went all over the country."

Skidmore continues: "After that, I think, there was quite a long gap where I was actually touring a lot in my own right in Germany – I vividly remember the tiny but atmospheric *Bunker Ulmenwall* Jazz club in Bielefeld – Switzerland, and all over Europe.

We kind of parted company for a good while and I was extremely busy, doing what I was doing at that time. It was working for [TV and radio station] WDR in Cologne for five years. I commuted a huge amount of times. I was also at the NDR in Hamburg. I was doing that along with the European Jazz Quintet, and SOH, not SOS, which was just three saxophones – Surman, Osbourne & Skidmore. That was another project."

One seminal shaker was missing from the proceedings, but would return in good time: Speedy Acquaye. He was keeping busy on the road and in all sorts of studios elsewhere, for instance helping The Faces add some colour to their long-suffering album Oh La La, which Rod Stewart seemed to be avoiding at all costs – so Speedy helped with the instrumental "Fly In The Ointment". In *Happy Boys Happy!*, Roland Schmitt and myself describe it as "a dynamic instrumental piece, it spotlights Woody's slide guitar, and features an appearance by guest percussionist Niimoi Speedy Acquaye from Georgie Fame's Blue Flames, whose brass section had toured with The Small Faces; the soho-based Ghana man died in 1993." Georgie helped pay for his Ghana funeral.

Talking about the Small Faces – Fame's fellow Mod and occasional Flamingo visitor Ronnie Lane had left The Faces in the meantime and, just like Georgie, had signed with Island Records. His eponymous Island album *Ronnie Lane's Slim Chance* – why should Ronnie get a proper LP title if Georgie didn't get one – featured the old Fats Domino chestnut on Georgie's *Fats For Fame* EP, "Blue Monday"; Lane obviously had the same taste in good vibes and heroes, and most probably heard Fame's version down in Wardour Street.

The Ali Shuffle

After the modest airplay of the initial Island single "Everlovin' Woman" and the parent album, there was an immediate follow-up with Georgie Fame's witty and chart-friendly homage to his hero Cassius Clay a.k.a. Muhammad Ali, who he had once met in the Flamingo Club. An infectious rhythm, lots of background vocal response, a precise brass section and possibly Speedy Acquaye's best conga and percussion work ever had hit record spelled all over this.

"The Ali Shuffle", which went on for the B-side for "Round Two". As the 1970s were the age of the gimmick single, this should have made the chart lists with a bit more of a promotion campaign than Island Records were ready to fork out for.

This was actually recorded with the big Blue Flames line-up, as Alan Skidmore confirms: "We went into the studio and did some recordings. That was round about the time when Clive wrote a piece dedicated to Muhammad Ali, 'The Ali Shuffle'. The complete line-up is documented at the back of the picture sleeve which Island lavished on potential buyers.

Guitarist Bernie Holland agrees with the attraction of the topic for Fame: "Yeah, Georgie was a great admirer of Muhammad Ali. I think what he liked about Muhammad Ali was that everybody was taking Muhammad Ali seriously, except Muhammad Ali. 'I'm the greatest, I'm the greatest', you know. And in fighting, he is making up a verse about the guy. 'Float like a butterfly, sting like a bee', 'I'm pretty, I'm pretty.

He's ugly'. Some people were getting annoyed with him, 'Who does this guy think he is?' This is what Clive liked about him: Ali knew what he was doing. He knew exactly what he was doing. He knew that this was all a big joke, except for when he was in the ring, boxing. That was no joke at all. Especially for the person he was fighting it was no joke. And Ali was a dancer, and I think Fame liked that as well: a guy couldn't get near him 'cause he was dancing around the ring. He was tiring the other guy out. So that's how 'The Ali Shuffle' was the song he wrote, and we would do that on loads of gigs."

Like the one *Record Mirror* wrote about on April 12th, 1975: Georgie Fame and The Blue Flames/Dingwalls: "Georgie Fame is back on the road again and judging by Tuesday's performance is back on true form.

"Always one of the few true innovatos, Georgie Fame was in his time responsible for breaking a great many musical barriers. Originally a humble pianist in Billy Fury's backing band, he has moved a long way since those days of weekly [daily, more like] appearances at London's Flamingo R + B Club.

"He has lost none of the energy and charm that made him so popular both within and out of the rather restricting confines of pop. This point was well illustrated at Dingwalls by the presence of such varied and notable characters like Roger Chapman, George Melly and Elton Dean, the ex Soft Machinist who now seems to have joined the Blue Flames on a semi permanent basis.

"The music itself is just as varied as it ever was, ranging from Jazz on the opener [Pink] Champagne to 'eavy Rock on For Chrysler's Sake and even managing a bit of Latin style Reggae on Ali Shuffle.

"Ali Shuffle, incidentally was Georgie's last single. Fast and frantic, it was a superb song that made the less illustrious Johnny Wakelin's version look very timid indeed. Ali Shuffle was probably the most overlooked and underrated single to appear last year.

"Georgie Fame is definitely not over the hill and if he can continue making friends the way he did at Dingwalls, then he should do very well over these coming months. Alan Edwards

Record Mirror wrote on December 7th, 1974: Georgie Fame: "Ali Shuffle" (Island 6218): "No prizes for guessing who the Ali of the title refers to … and here, to a jolly little Reggae beat accompanied by lots of jungle drums, is Georgie Fame doing a silly.. Not the most inspiring thing I've ever heard him do, in fact, that coffee ad he does on the box is much better …"

Most British TV viewers knew at the time that the unnamed author referred to Fame's "Maxwell House" instant coffee commercials, following on from Alan Price's "Smarties" sweets adverts two years previously.

More Island Sessions in Nashville

Fame's label mates, The Sutherland Brothers & Quiver featuring singer/ songwriters Iain and pre-"Sailing" Gavin Sutherland apparently left Island Records because the label would not distribute their singles in the US. With Georgie, it was the other way round: no longplayers after the first album for Blackwell, more sessions took place during 1975. After London and Tulsa, Oklahoma, the next stop was Nashville, Tennessee, where Georgie flew with his guitarist Bernie Holland in tow.

Guitarist Bernie Holland: "I went to Nashville with him. What happened was, he phoned me up – he did this with a few of his musicians. He'd take them on a trip. He didn't need to take them. It was almost like a teacher taking you on an educational outing. And he rang me up and said 'Do you want to come to Nashville?' He said 'There's not a lot of money involved, but you'll meet some people, and you will see some of it.' I said 'You bet I will come to Nashville'. Everything was to be laid on for you, plane flights, hotels and everything else."

"He just took me to Nashville. Just the two of us, we just flew over together, from Heathrow to New York and from New York to Nashville. This was in the autumn [of 1975] – it was just a little landing strip then, and we landed near the little hut where they check you out. Obviously, everything had been sorted out. I got out of this airplane, and it was like walking into an oven. I could not believe it, straight away I was soaking wet with sweat, and we got in the car: All the cars were air-conditioned – we went to the studio that was air-conditioned, everywhere was. When I was in Nashville, I met Lee Ritenour and Buddy Emmons. He is the greatest steel guitar player in the world, and I couldn't believe what he was doing. He just laughed and played.

"And J.J. Cale was on the sessions as well, a man of few words. There were two answers you'd get, one was "Yeh", and the other was "No", but an amazing player, with that snaky guitar style, sounds like a snake – where he comes from [Tulsa, Oklahoma], it's Rattlesnake country. It is all about his environment in his music. A J.J. Cale solo is like a second rattlesnake, whirling its way round the desert. He did a great album with Eric Clapton recently.

"People like Clapton and Fame, they're not scared of collaborating, they know their limitations, but they know that within their limitations they can work with anybody, because they are true to what they are doing. You don't have to be Johnny McLaughlin – now he played with Georgie Fame years ago. I was following in the footsteps of Johnny McLaughlin, makes me think sometimes. Georgie Fame was a clearing house for me. Georgie Fame means what he says and he means what he plays.

"I had heard about Nashville, and for a long time, I didn't respect Country music. I thought it was just redneck music. I decided I wanted to go and see *Grand Ole Opry*, and I saw Hank Snow, Marty Robbins and loads of other artistes. I realized these people were telling stories when they were singing the songs. Okay, the song might only have two or three chords in it. It might be very simple and easy to play, but it's not easy to deal with the life they lived. It is not easy to understand experiences.

"When they wrote these songs, they were telling stories about what had happened to them in their life. I thought, 'hang on a minute: before you start condemning this as redneck music, this is an important part of American Folk tradition'. It was a learning curve, and when I heard these guys play, I thought what they are doing is just as well done as anything anybody else is doing. It's all about doing something well.

"I was coming back to the studio, it was just down the road – Nashville is just a main street, all the guitar shops and the *Grand Ole Opry* and everything else – and I came to a pedestrian crossing, and there was this light "Walk" for green and "Don't Walk" for red. The red light was on and I sort of skipped across the road, as there was no car coming, and I heard this voice behind me: 'Freeze! Put your hands up!' – a guy with a gun on me, a sheriff or whatever you call them, a lawman. I said 'I'm sorry, officer, I apologize, sorry if I did anything wrong, I'm not meaning to'. He heard my accent, and he sort of put the gun away, and said 'Where are you from?'

"I said I was from London in England. He said 'What do you do in London England then when the light is red?' I said 'We just walk across the road. Nobody puts a gun on us! If there's no car coming, if it's clear to go, we just run across the road! Maybe you thought I was running away, because I had done something, maybe that's why you put the gun on me.' We started talking and I told him what I was doing, and straight away his whole demeanour changed, "Oh wow, you're a musician!" – after five minutes, we were the best of friends."

The Island drought – Singles but no further albums

1975 was set to become yet another year without any Georgie Fame releases.

A second album was recorded under the direction of Glyn Johns, but somehow, Chris Blackwell did not sanction its release. Judging from some tracks that surfaced later, the album was certainly a worthy follow-up to *Georgie Fame*. Just two examples will make this clear:

"Cool Cat Blues" was Georgie's homage to the man he originally formed his singing style on: Mose Allison. You can see how Mose would have done it, but Georgie doesn't make the mistake of doing a pastiche on the Mississippi vertan. This was a fourteen year old number by the time it would see the light of day eventually on Georgie's 1990 album of the same name. Written with J. Alexander Ryan, this 1975 version swings in an attractively relaxed way as well, but also gets an imaginative string arrangement, prominent "midnight" sax work and outstanding trumpet feature. Once again, it is hard to stomach the knowledge that such a great recording has lain in the vaults for so long.

While recording in London in 1975, Fairport Convention drummer Dave Mattacks, a keenly booked studio cat as well, refined the Jazz-Rock master class "For Chrysler's Sake", an instrumental – which was originally intended for a car advert that the title refers to, in the true Fame tradition of "Getaway" gasoline and "Maxwell House" coffee. "For Chrysler's Sake" is stunning, featuring the most complicated time signatures ever applied by the Blue Flames, and makes full use of a big and nasty brass section in the process.

Their relentless attacks – which they tried out on live gigs too at the time – also serve to bring out Georgie's Hammond organ, before the pace is relieved a little for Alan Skidmore's great sax solo, while Dave Mattacks grooves on the cymbals and gets another of his high-risk breaks down. Delightful – and a piece to make the band they call Chicago run for their lives.

The Daylight album – catalogue number, 20 tracks and no release

This third album project, *Daylight*, was pencilled in by Chris Blackwell for 1976, but in spite of a catalogue number, the LP apparently never reached any shops. So did that ever come out? Fame: "It was never released. The tapes are in Island's possession. There are some good tracks – with Denny Cordell, again. We recorded in California", and he might have added, in Tulsa and back home in London, too.

"On a lot of tracks, we used Booker T. and Steve Cropper and Duck Dunn. Then we did some tracks with Brazilian guys, Raul de Souza, the trombone player. Perhaps it was a little too eclectic. I do have a mix, a tape of the master mix of the proposed album – which Chris (Blackwell) didn't think he should put out at that time. It has never been released as far as I know. But there were a lot of tracks that we did, and it would take a lot of time to go through them to decide which ones were suitable." These tracks were produced by Denny Cordell, the man Georgie trusted since the time of *Sweet Things*.

All these sessions did at least lead to several attractive single releases, two of them in 1976, featuring again the writing team of Fame and J. Alexander Ryan:

"Yes Honestly" was a tender shuffle for the popular LWT television sitcom *Yes Honestly*. But in spite of the constant replay of the tune during its 13 episodes, there were not enough takers in the record stores. Its B-side was, as it says in Ryan's lyrics, a "simple little love song called "Lily", which starts out as a ballad but soon develops into a well-arranged Bossa Nova, prominently featuring Steve Gregory on flute.

"Sweet Perfection" featured an unusual call & response routine between Fame and female singers, starting out as a Waltz but soon reverting to a more conventional 4/4, charming listeners with an immediately unforgettable melody. Georgie remembered the song in late 1985 when he re-recorded it with Swedish producer and arranger Lars "Lasse" Samuelsson and singer Lena Ericsson for a Gospel project which incorporated an album called simply *Georgie Fame, Lena Ericsson, Lasse Samuelson* and a tour through 50 Swedish churches. For that version, the initial Waltz rhythm was left out.

On the single, the song "Sweet Perfection" was backed by the up-tempo "Thanking Heaven", a catchy Soul tune with crisp conga work. Lively brass attacks and sophisticated breaks helped make it a perfect vehicle for the large version of the Blue Flames which had toured in 1974. This was again written by Fame with J. Alexander Ryan.

The *Record Mirror*'s verdict June 19, 1976 was "Misses: Sweet, but not perfect, George": Georgie Fame: 'Sweet Perfection' (Island WIP 6311) A rather low-key song from Mr Fame, much more subdued in pace and delivery than the songs he normally does. Because of that it tends to sound as though it's all on one level, and doesn't excite the senses much."

In 1977, the Bobby Womack composition "Daylight" followed as standard single and – owing to its Disco-fied Soft Funk nature – also as a 12-inch "Maxi Single", credited to producer Denny Cordell, "taken from the forthcoming album "Daylight" ILPS 9487" according to the label printout. Its B-side was a kind of musicians-only instrumental to let the band loose, "Three Legged Mule", with Georgie good-heartedly edging his many wind and brass players on.

On April 16th, 1977, Record Mirror saw "Very Old Boys: Georgie Fame: 'Daylight' (Island WIPS 6384) Sixties rocker returns with a Bobby Womack song. Not a bad effort, but I can't see him become a pop star again at this late date. +++"

The single was presented together with new records by Roger Daltrey, Johnny Cash and Ray Stevens.

Looking at these three single releases, it must be said that the small 45s still possessed much more significance during the 1970s than they did a decade later. It still seems like a case of lost chances that there was hardly any attempt at promoting these records anywhere, and the decision for another long playing record seemed to take forever.

With hindsight, Chris Blackwell could have easily compiled an attractive album from the assembled material, with sixteen tracks remaining unreleased at the time, as the following track-by-track description will make clear. The team might have decided that there was no need for another "Getaway"/"Get Away" just yet, or that the two tricky instrumentals were indeed too eclectic. But with the title track "Daylight" certainly included again, at fourteen choices one would have arrived at a generous running time for a new album.

Alternatively, instead of using the songs as singles, Blackwell should have ended up with two albums for 1975 and 1976, and it has to be repeated: one hell (two hells) of an opportunity missed, and a shameful mismanagement of an incredible artist who never actually complained about this, but must have been utterly disappointed "in private" just the same.

Georgie Fame & Verve Records released many of these tracks as part of a 3-CD Boxed Set *The In-Crowd* in 1998 (for which this author could happily supply some of the original vinyl covers, including the sleeve which Georgie calls "the one with the dirty fingernails": the US Imperial release *Yeh Yeh*, which was *Fame At Last* with the hit but minus two other tracks), while the Japanese issued a carefully compiled double disc called *The Island Years* which apparently featured all the previously issued tracks, including the five issued singles which have been described previously.

Daylight – the possible selection track by track

"Give Him A Hand", set in a drummer's basement, is a slow-moving half-time shuffle with a Gospel choir, off-beat rhythm guitar chugging and Georgie seems ever so relaxed about a "hoo-hah Hendrix" and his Rock'n'Roll band, perfect to groove along to, Jazz Rock leading into a highly polished, brassed-up fast section with Jerry Lee Lewis piano fade-out. Its composer is unknown, and the song may well have been ready for the 1975 release plan.

"The Preacher and The Bear" tells the story of a hunting priest who sets out on a Sunday morning, much against his religion. It is a pure Talking Swing set to an acoustic guitar, in a kind of lazy, ironic-laconic Louis Jordan tradition – not a singing line in sight, but, "Oh, Lordy", a cracker of a story. The understated horn section is a dream. Again, the composer is unknown.

Fame wrote and composed "Do I Love You" himself and tried his hand at the then popular Barry White string-sectioned, soft-funk Philly style, while singing this in his very own manner. The violin arrangement is convincing and gets an even more sophisticated sheen via Dave Mattacks' drumming. Mattacks, called DM in the scene, had defined Folk-Rockers Fairport Convention's rhythm imprint for many years as well as that of the Albion Band and had become a much in-demand session player as well.

"Like We Used To Be" was of course a re-vamp of Georgie's old, self-written 1965 single, done in J.J. Cale style in Nashville, with Bernie Holland and Tommy Triplehorn's guitars, and a nicely flanged horn arrangement, driven by Carl Radle and Jamie Oldaker's engine room. Re-visiting was not only a much-mentioned pleasure of Georgie's, it also would have lured in potential buyers.

"(The Way You) Do The Things You Do", a classic 1964 single by The Temptations, written by Smokey Robinson and Bobby Rogers, comes over here as a very danceable, solid shuffle – Fame must have known (and also played) this Soul piece even during the Flamingo days. His Blue Flames-esque arranging chops have rarely sounded more relaxed and assured than here, including the exemplary brass.

"California Girl" is a Booker T Jones/Eddie Floyd composition which was probably recorded around the same time as Fame's contributions to Eric Clapton's *No Reason To Cry* album. This ballad features Hammond organ as well as synth strings plus a moving tenor sax solo.

"Three-legged Mule" is Fame's own attempt at some kind of Funk Comedy, using a dance rhythm, Hammond and Georgie's attempt at sounding like a horse.

Fame and Ryan were also responsible for the Tulsa recorded comedy tune "Nicotine And Tar", a hillbilly spoof complete with banjo and a lot of relentless smoker's coughs all the way, Jamie Oldaker supplying his (pun hopefully tolerated) 'smoking' snare, hi-hat and bass drum groove. Humour had been key ingredient of a successful Georgie Fame album since the Sixties, and it would have added to the variety of an Island release.

Willie Nelson's "It's Not Supposed To Be That Way" was also laid down in Nashville, in spite of its original Reggae feel. Georgie's Hammond, vibraphone and steel guitar create a dramatic backdrop for the story of a man who cannot accept life's changes after his wife has left him: part of the Nelson concept LP *Phrases And Stages* from 1974, his last album for Atlantic records.

Georgie took over "Hot Stuff" from Jon Hendricks, using a lightning speed pace and great tongue-twisting chops to get its clever lyrics across – getting some respite when an inventive trombone gets going, only to start singing again after a short, easy to miss Hammond interlude: a true piece of art with great rhythm and a bit of Fender Rhodes thrown in.

"Bouden Buck" of unknown origin is another Country tune from Nashville, featuring Buddy Emmons on steel guitar and Fame's own cohort Bernie Holland on lead, with Carl Radle on bass and possibly Willie Hall on drums.

There was also time to re-arrange Georgie's once second number one hit record "Getaway", with pretty similar brass work but a nicely driving snare brush groove and vibraphone which gives this a whole new Okie, J.J. Cale-esque atmosphere.

"Barefootin'" was meant as a good-hearted tribute to Georgie's Flamingo Club blood brother Zoot Money, the brass section down in Los Angeles being "right on the money" (for the inevitable pun). Georgie Fame & Zoot Money would record another version in 1983 for *My Favourite Songs*, but this is the more hard-hitting version and should have been released in spite of not really adding much to the Zoot original.

Another delightful instrumental is added to the canon with a short, fast and elegant Bernie Holland composition, "Bernie's Tune", where the long-time Blue Fames guitarist shares his acoustic solo spot with Raoul de Souza's trombone, as recorded in Los Angeles.

"Call Up The Devil", by Fame & J. Alexander Ryan, uses a Latin groove with Speedy Acquaye's percussive skills and baritone sax to lead into some falsetto singing – highly unusual for Georgie, as is the prominent guitar work. There is such a lot happening in this number, which may confuse at first but gains clarity from repeated listening.

There have been a lot of lacklustre versions of "Sea Of Heartbreak", the Paul Hampton and Hal David standard from 1961 which was famously recorded by Don Gibson and Johnny Cash. But this one possesses a fine Gospel touch with the help of a backing choir that features Lennox Langton and Andy Fairweather Low's great vocals.

The connections to Tulsa, Oklahoma, incidentally, did not end with the various Island sessions, as drummer Jamie Oldaker recalls: "He [Georgie] came back to Tulsa again and played a show there. There was a wedding. Somehow I can't remember who it was that was getting married. But they wanted Georgie Fame to come and play it. It was called the Tulsa Club, it was a country club type place. I don't know what the date was, but it was later, Carl [Radle] had already passed away [so it was after 1980], so Gary Gilmore played bass on that show. It was me, Georgie, Walt Richmond on keyboards [who a quarter of a century later was to play on *Road To Escondido* with Eric and JJ], and Tommy Triplehorne on the guitar. They booked Georgie to play this wedding. So he came in town and we rehearsed and played this wedding." [18]

Back on the global live circuit

And so, while Rock's dinosaurs had a hard time, because Punk had reared its highly hyped head, many skilled musicians detected that a more down-to-earth movement had come on the horizon, namely Pub Rock. Georgie Fame fans had to rely on the ever-reliable round of gigs on that circuit, albeit not only in the UK, but in "club land" all over the world. Georgie and his various Blue Flames incarnations – with Sixties survivors Eddie Thornton and Speedy Acquaye part of the line-up – continued to please, and often delivered the party atmosphere which the brand name had been renowned for ever since the Flamingo Club era.

Consequently, Georgie Fame & The Blue Flames recorded a live album in the London *Caribe Club*, as our man revealed in a TV interview in 1977. Alas, it never saw the light of day.

18. See Addendum

On the drum stool, changes were in sight by 1976. Georgie: "Brian Bennett had so many studio jobs that his time in my band was always only a matter of weeks. His successor was Tony Crombie."

Tony Crombie (1925–1999) was a Forties Big Band and Hard Bop legend: 51 years old at the time of getting hired by Georgie, the drummer had served London clubs already by the time Georgie was born, and played "behind" Duke Ellington on a British tour when Fame was five, helping to start the famous Bebop "Club Eleven" the same year.

Another link to Georgie was that Crombie actually had future orchestra leader Harry South in his own Big Band in 1954 and, when they recorded for Decca, had even featured Fame's idol and future collaborator Annie Ross, later performing on her album *Skylark*. But the Big Band business promised fewer and fewer profits in the mid-1950s, so Crombie as well as sax legend Ronnie Scott had dissolved their orchestras and founded a kind of super group, i.e. a kind of Super Big Band, featuring Stan Tracey on piano, bass player Lennie Bush, trumpeter Les Condon and three saxophone players in Benny Green, Pete King and Derek Humble.

In the summer of 1956, Tony Crombie watched the Bill Haley infused movie *Rock Around The Clock* and soon proved that he could Rock'n'Roll as Tony Crombie and his Rockets, with "disenfranchised Jazzers" (Pete Frame) like Rex Morris on sax and pianist Red Mitchell, who had to play standing up just like Little Richard and Jerry Lee Lewis: "I've tried playing Swing and straight dance numbers", he told a local paper according to Frame, "I've been a martyr long enough [a pro for 16 years] – now I want to eat! That's the great thing about Rock'n'Roll … we get an audience! It's a question of economics: I am merely giving the public what it wants." But the public wanted genuine Rock stars, not elderly Jazzers copying a style, and according to many, their singer Clyde Ray was aping Johnny Ray, who was a poor man's Elvis in the first place.

But Crombie's Rockets group – which had included the Shadows' Jet Harris for a while – reverted to Jazz just two years later. Georgie could hardly get a better man at the time than the one who'd been the Ronnie Scott Club's house drummer accompanying Ella Fitzgerald or Jimmy Witherspoon, and he certainly valued his other skills. Tony Crombie occasionally doubled as a gifted piano player and also was a dab hand at the vibraphone. He composed soundtracks for the 1960 films *The Spider's Web* and *A Tell Tale Heart* (collaborating with Bill Le Sage) the same year he started the band Jazz Inc. – with pianist Stan Tracey again.

Georgie: "Crombie couldn't play Funk styles, but what he could play. He played better than any other drummer. He was a great swinger. His own work had dried up by that time, so he was glad that he could work with me. He was from the previous generation, and when you have got somebody in from a different era, you automatically have some kind of advisor. So you get to learn all the time – I had some great times with him."

Tony Crombie's past in the Flamingo Club had connected him to Georgie's Whisky-A-Go-Go Wardour Street buddy Slim Gaillard, as Bernie Holland can remember clearly: "I had worked with Slim a few years earlier with Tony Crombie, another drummer with Georgie Fame in the mid 1970s. He had lots of drummers – Clive Thacker was a

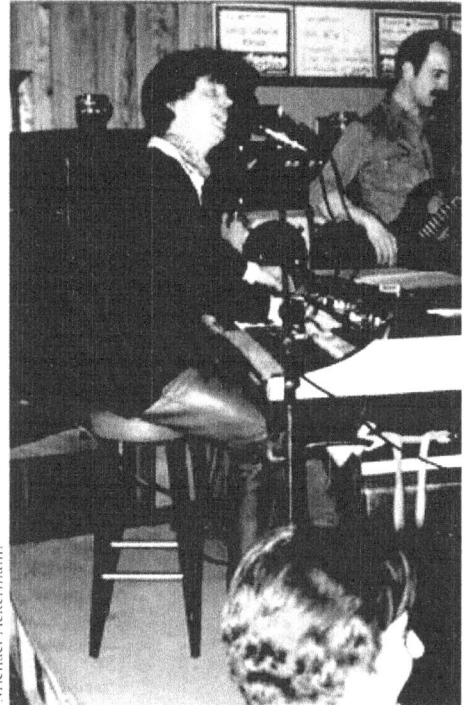 

Blue Flames 18th May 1978 — L to R: Georgie Fame, Brian "Badger" Odgers, Speedy Acquaye, Tony Crombie, Bernie Holland

drummer with Georgie Fame. So was Dave Mattacks, and me — I played drums with him! I taught drums and percussion at a high school.

"There was just one gig I played drums with him. Anyway, Tony Crombie and I share a lot of interests — in art and antiques, paintings and stuff. He rang me up once 'Look, you play bass, don't you?' I said yeah. 'Would you do a bass gig for me? It's a guy called Slim Gaillard. He plays guitar and sings, a real one-off guy.' He told me a little bit of history about Slim Gaillard. There was a double act called "Slim & Slam", Slim Gaillard and Slam Stewart [They had a 1938 hit called "Tutti Frutti" which Little Richard borrowed from.] He was called Slam cause he slapped the bass with the palm of his hand. Slim had this thing called "Vout" [a kind of Vocalese], Jive talk — Fame took a lot of stuff off of him as well. This gig with Tony Crombie, playing bass with him and Slim was great — fantastic."

Fame For a Price — The Session Man in the 60s and 70s

Georgie's session career had started before his own really, when he played on that Gene Vincent single "Pistol Packin' Mama". It was the B-side of "Anna Annabelle" and also the track "Weeping Willow" which was on a Capitol LP called *The Crazy Beat of Gene*

Vincent as early as 1960. As mentioned, he also graced a Johnny Hallyday album.

Sessions for Ska/Blue Beat stars followed soon, where Fame's playing can be heard on the song "Telephone" by Derrick Morgan and a number of Prince Buster tracks, among them "Wash All Your Troubles Away" and "The Lion Roars", Buster singing the latter with a lady called Hazel. On the Prince's album *I Feel The Spirit*, Georgie debuts his Hammond organ on "Beggars Are No Choosers".

Mississippi Mud in the Thames Valley – Fame plays for Muddy Waters

By now a legend in his own right, at the end of 1971, between gigs with Alan Price, Fame was invited to take part in the *London Sessions* for Chicago's Blues godfather McKinley Morganfield a.k.a. Muddy Waters – as "Georgie Fortune" for the obvious contractual reasons. He was in tremendous company for these sessions, primarily because of a most welcome reunion with his 1966 Blue Flames drummer and Jimi Hendrix survivor Mitch Mitchell. Other colleagues at I.B.C. Studios in London were Muddy's guitar partner Sam Lawhorn and a delighted Rory Gallagher, Family and Blind Faith man Ric Grech on bass, Carey Bell Harrington on harmonica. On three tracks, Georgie shared organ and piano duties with Steve Winwood. Rosetta Hightower sang backing vocals, and there was a horn section of trumpeters Ernie Royal and Joe Newman, trombonist Garnett Brown, and on tenor saxophone, a namesake of Fame's performed: Seldon Powell.

Georgie has mixed feelings remembering these recording dates: "Sure, it was an honour to play for Muddy Waters, but I remember he played in the most weird keys, and I had a hard time following him."

"I was called to the session, and everything was in the key of F-sharp or B. And in those days I could only play in three or four keys – C, G and F. And having to play with guitar players, I could play a bit in E and A. And even though they were just Blues things, I couldn't play in those keys decently, if you listen to the recording. He'd put a capo on his guitar.

"Now when I met Muddy Waters like ten, fifteen years later, he went Yeah man, *The London Muddy Waters Sessions*, and I mentioned to him 'Man, that recording session was really terrible. I mean everything was in F-sharp or B. I was very uncomfortable, I'm sorry about that, man – You don't tell a Muddy Waters to put his cap on, tell him 'I can't play in this key!' But he said "Shit, man, you should have said! You should have told me! – I would have moved the capo.'

"But you were so in awe with somebody like Muddy Waters, you didn't dare say 'Hey, man, can you change the key?' So all that strain I had put myself under could have easily been avoided. There you are."

Georgie Fame producer Glyn Johns recruited Fame for several of his own productions, to play some piano and mostly Hammond organ on a number of acclaimed albums. The most lasting experience was their collaboration for two LPs by the ex Amen Corner singing front man – and in those days very much frustrated guitarist cum teenage idol – Andy Fairweather Low. When Georgie appeared on Andy Fairweather Low's mid-Seventies albums *La Booga Rooga* (1975) and *Be Bop'n'Holla* (1976), he had the good fortune of integrating The Blue Flames' then current horn section of Eddie Thornton, Buddy Beadle and Steve Gregory.

Fairweather Low, who had always rated Fame tremendously and had even depped as a stand-in band member for a while, reminisced in 2008: "I became briefly a Blue Flame, for a short period as well, with Georgie Fame, around the time of *Be Bop'n'Holla*, in 1976. Because he played on *Be Bop'n'Holla*, we became really good friends, [and still are really good friends]. And I was and I still am a big fan! I saw him just recently at the Beckham Jazz Festival with a big orchestra, and it was stunning, absolutely stunning." On *Be Bop'n'Holla*, the inner sleeve photographs show how much Georgie Fame must have contributed to the good vibrations of the sessions.

The compliment was to be returned by Georgie when he covered Fairweather Low's Top 20 chart success "Wide-Eyed And Legless" on his *Charlestons* album in 2002. Fairweather Low: "That's a fantastic version, and at the end, when he goes into "Do You Know The Way To San José", I went 'Why didn't I think of that?!' And then Fame went and did another, acoustic version on *Lost In A Lover's Dream* in 2012, accompanied just by guitar and bass."

When Andy Fairweather-Low had his British chart hit (1975 UK #6) with the *La Booga Rooga* single "Wide-Eyed and Legless", Georgie accompanied him to the *Top Of The Pops* TV appearance, returning as a session man to the TV stage where he had often been seen in a frontman's capacity. For those who remember the show, or treasure it on video/DVD – Georgie must have had serious fun – there is hardly a Hollywood or Pinewood Studios actor able to put, on cue, such a wide smile on his face.

Georgie also played on Eric Clapton's *No Reason To Cry* album which the rather worse for wear master guitarist held at The Band's Shangri-La Studios in Los Angeles during 1976. Georgie: "I only played on a couple [of tracks], I think. I didn't expect them to use them. They were just recording at Zuma Beach, you know, at The Band's 'Shangri-La Studios', and I was staying just a couple of miles down the road with Denny Cordell, the producer. The Band were staying up the hill in a hotel. I think I played on 'County Jail', and one other one. But I've got the album: you can hardly hear the organ. I don't think I did any solos, weaving along in the background." Biographer Marc Roberty, in his *Eric Clapton: Day By Day*, only lists Georgie on "Double Trouble".

It was not just the renowned Hammond organ sound and occasional piano that producer Glyn Johns wanted from Georgie. Johns led the sessions for the St. Kitts born,

Birmingham raised singer-songwriter Joan Armatrading, following her final breakthrough with the eponymous third album *Joan Armatrading* in 1976. Johns needed Fame's services for some tasty Fender Rhodes electric piano touches, which the Blue Flame session man supplied with impeccable taste for Armatrading's fourth stroke *Show Some Emotion* (1977).

Chapter 6
The Pye Years – From Stevie Wonder To Hoagy Carmichael

Looking at the sheer amount and rich variety of songs which Georgie Fame recorded during his four years with Island Records, and comparing this impressive body of work to the one lonely album and three single releases that actually hit the shops at the time, one wonders whether this wouldn't have killed the enthusiasm even in an artist who has always loved his work and took every aspect of meticulous creation seriously.

But Fame did not appear to be irritated. He continued to play every gig that came his way, one of the most amusing ones this author has seen taking place in the *100 Club* in London's Oxford Street in October 1978, when "Zulu" truly mesmerized the masses. Fame supplemented his income by writing the music to TV commercials – viewers who had previously seen him perform with Alan Price on interlocking pianos, suddenly watched and heard him present Maxwell House Coffee.

High time for a new album – Right Now!

Come 1978, and Georgie Fame accepted a none-too-lucrative record deal with Pye Records. The label which had once, in collaboration with the French Vogue company, marketed top names like The Kinks, Sandie Shaw or Long John Baldry with immense success, was less dominant in the late 1970s market. Still, running their own studios in London was a useful asset, and Fame made them the scene for his first album in more than four years, *Right Now!*, which appeared at the beginning of 1979. He had written most of the material himself again, as on his neglected *All Me Own Work*, but tried a much more commercial touch here, albeit hitting more towards contented suburban 30+ commuters than an Inner London in-crowd or New Wave conscious youngsters.

Fame arranged the album in connection with the Soft Machine's Karl Jenkins (b. February 1944), a Welshman who had started as an oboist in the National Youth Jazz Orchestra of Wales and had later co-founded the Jazz Fusion band Nucleus. At the time of *Right Now!*, Jenkins had been with Soft Machine for seven years, winning the "British Jazz Album Of The Year" in 1973 for the LP *Six*, and had played on Mike Oldfield's *Tubular Bells* for a BBC transmission that same year. Like Fame, Jenkins was also involved in writing and producing advertising music – De Beers diamonds, for instance – and had won several industry prizes. Karl Jenkins also handled production duties, together with James Parsons. The album was engineered by Pye's house engineer Terry Evennett.

The most remarkable collaboration on the album happened, again, with the aforementioned American jazz lyricist, poet and eccentric performance artist Fran Landesman. Fans and customers of her lyrics included George Shearing, Ella Fitzgerald as well as Shirley Bassey. Georgie must have loved Fran's and her husband Jay's crazy "Fame & Fury & Power"-Parnes style stage names of Fran Fabulous and Stan Stunning, as well as the scandal of a *Desert Island Discs* BBC radio programme in 1996, where Ms Landesman wanted some cannabis as a "luxury item". The lady they called the "Godmother of Hip" during her early Greenwich adventures, was our Godfather of British R&B's contender during the 1980s in Ronnie Scott's Club.

His reliable 1978 Blue Flames line-up of Bernie Holland on guitar, Brian Odgers on bass, Steve Gregory – ex Alan Price Set – on saxophone, Malcolm Griffiths on trombone and Speedy Acquaye on tablas joined assorted studio horn blowers: Henry Lowther, ex John Mayall's Bluesbreakers on trumpet and flugelhorn; and Ray Warleigh from *Sound Venture* times on alto sax, piccolo, alto and bass flutes.

Apart from the Flames, a hardened gang of studio pros were at work around guitarist Alan Parker. On drums, it was Morgan Studios owner Barry Morgan playing on the tracks. Both had been in the Soul Pop group Blue Mink with Georgie's friend Madeline Bell, assisting her with solo work as well like her eponymous 1971 album and enjoying chart success with "Melting Pot" and "Good Morning Freedom".

Together with keyboardist Alan Hawkshaw, they had founded the Themes International Music Ltd library, a leading company for the recording of film archive, incidental, atmospheric "mood" music started in 1970. This was something that Steve Gray, Georgie's friend and writing/studio partner from the 1980s onwards, was also proficient in: check out *Shades Of Gray* by The Steve Gray Orchestra on Vocalion Records.

Fame was in good company here, as the guys had worked with his Blues friend Alexis Korner, too, in the Big Band studio conglomerate C.C.S.

What they recorded for *Right Now!*, was a mixture of pleasant AOR material, blended with fine ballads in "Eros Hotel" and "Too Shy To Say", complemented by welcome, exciting Latin stage favourites like "Ollie's Party", "Zulu", and "Little Samba". This possibly served as a guideline for young talents like Matt Bianco, who would soon copy Fame"s easy Rio approach for a chart-bound remake of "Yeh Yeh".

Right Now! – Track-by-Track

"A Different Dream", also Fame"s first single in two years and a belated follow-up to "Daylight", was written in collaboration with the poet Fran Landesman, who supplied a philosophical contrast to "Country" from the Island *Georgie Fame* album.

She imagined Fame the family man who had retreated to village scenes was looking at city life again, where you "mingle with the crème de la menthe" and where you "must learn to speak the city's language, or baby, you'll be left out in the cold". Judging from his charming stage presence, which was more apparent than ever before, there was no need to worry.

Musically, "A Different Dream" was partly a continuation of the mainstream manner of Fame's CBS years, and also a nod to the Disco generation. This up-tempo combination, complete with Barry White style funk guitar, elaborate string arrangement and lively female vocal backing, made this release very nicely quaint, the perfect radio fodder for BBC Radio 2.

The remake of Willie Nelson's Fame favourite "Funny How Time Slips Away", which Fame had presented both on *Sweet Things* and on his *Sound Venture* Big Band album in 1966, may have seemed a pointless exercise a dozen years after the event at a time when his albums were still widely available, and compilations complemented them.

But the revamped arrangement with particularly effective, jazzy guitar work and lovely reeds render this so pleasant that it makes a welcome return here which fits with the album's overall relaxed atmosphere. There is a little Fender Rhodes instead of a Hammond organ and a very effective brass onslaught in the instrumental passage, for flautist and sax man Ray Warleigh. Warleigh had also worked for Karl Jenkins' Soft Machine. This was his second reading of "Funny How Time Slips Away": Warleigh had previously worked on the recording found on Georgie's *Sound Venture* album in 1966.

Georgie Fame's own "Little Samba" shows off the Latin prowess of his Seventies Flames, with Brian Odgers as always spot-on with his precise bass work, tasteful guitarist Bernie Holland, seen-it-all drummer Barry Morgan and the faithful Speedy Acquaye supplying some great rhythm touches, live and in the studio: "I wrote my composition as a reflection on my trip to Brazil in 1967."

Lush strings and lovely girls are back for another Fame composition, the middle-of-the-road shuffle "I'm In Love With Ya Baby".

Back to the live repertoire of The Blue Flames, "Ollie's Party" – also the single B-side – gets performed in Patois, mock Jamaican slang which Fame has always managed with complete ease, and without embarrassing the West Indian/African section of his band, namely Eddie "Tan Tan" Thornton and Speedy Acquaye, who did not get a credit for playing on this recording, although he is quoted as having played on "Zulu".

One of the highlights of the entire album is the contemplative "Eros Hotel", again based on a poem by Fran Landesman. Harking back to Georgie's ongoing engagements at Ronnie Scott's Club, Fame & Fran describe the Soho Square surroundings, not only meeting up in some seedy establishment, but also "going down to Foyles to buy a book".

Side two of the album begins with "'Cross A Lazy Afternoon", lyrics written by Candida Lycett Green, an Irish born author, nee Candida Betjemen. She married the

Savile Row tailor Rupert Lycett Green, in whose shop "Blades" the Beatles were keen customers and helped make the couple part of an "In-Crowd". Lycett Green has been described as the finest writer on the English countryside with books like "Over The Hills And Far Away" and "Goodbye London", both themes very dear to Georgie Fame's heart. The fact that the lady was dismissed from *Queen* Magazine because of her work in the satirical *Private Eye* must have endeared her to him even more.

With its Disco touches, "'Cross A Lazy Afternoon" was way ahead of its time, it sounds exactly like one of those lush, trendy Stock/Aitken/Waterman productions five years later, and would have fitted the young vocal contender Rick Astley to a T. Interestingly, only a few years down the line and Georgie would join young Astley, Kylie Minogue and even Bananarama – in order to collaborate with that trendy triumvirate.

Very much in contrast to the big production numbers, Fame's "Country Girl" may use strings and flute, but it rests more on the folky ballad style of his Gallagher & Lyle cover "Country Morning" on the *Georgie Fame* Island LP. Lyrically, Fame picks up on the urban/rural contrast which has always fascinated him, living in romantic Dorset but working the metropolises of the world.

Fame has always appreciated the work of Stevie Wonder, a welcome excuse to add some more refined Latin-American touches to this album. "Don't You Worry 'Bout A Thing" from his album *Innervisions*, sounds more conventional than Wonder's original, but ultimately also more sophisticated, with Ray Warleigh's subdued flute and Georgie's relaxed but absolutely assured reading a real gem. Another highlight is the guitar solo by Terry Smith (b. May 1943), the If guitarist and Dick Morrissey co-front man who had been involved with The Walker Brothers, especially Scott Walker, and with soul singer J.J. Jackson, which explains the affinity to this kind of material.

The choice of a second Stevie Wonder composition, the lush "Too Shy To Say" from the album *Fulfillingness First Finale*, fortunately, seems to make the quiet point that the 1969 CBS opus *Georgie Does His Things With Strings* had not been a mistake after all. This melancholic interpretation with full orchestral backing, lovingly arranged by Karl Jenkins, sounds really impressive. Timeless beauty for those who did not come to this recording with set expectations, as will be seen with *Melody Maker* critic Chris Welch.

The Blue Flames' party piece number three, "Zulu", was an audience favourite at the time, with the whole band 'monkeying around' and at the same time making full use of the attractive brass arrangement and well-channelled percussive pandemonium, featuring Blue Flame Speedy Acquaye on his other album contribution to great effect. At some live gigs, "Zulu" could be fifteen minutes long and feature a long instrumental first section, spiked with African chants referring to "Osei", probably to singer and saxophonist Teddy Osei in the band Osibisa. The tune had first been introduced at the "Half Moon" pub in Putney, called "Come In, Mister Smith – Your Time Is Up!"

It is possible to see Fame and Fran Landesman's "Last Song" as a kind of sequel to "Dawn Yawn" off *Sound Venture*, "everybody's partied out" again here on this Fran Landesman assisted ballad, where they have "run out of booze" and "Mary would go but if she can't find her shoes". Georgie's final advice "You don't have to go home, you just have to get out of here" is still used with glee in his live appearances.

Fame had certainly taken fewer risks here than during the collected Island recordings, but his decisions made sense then, and they do make sense after the event as well. No matter how daringly a top innovative session drummer like Dave Mattacks once performed on "For Chrysler's Sake", and how effectively the Tulsa crowd around Eric Clapton's Band accompanied him, the question remains – how useful had that been when it was either never acknowledged in public, or hidden in the vaults by a timid, undecided Chris Blackwell? Here, Georgie stuck to his guns and delivered a quality album, which had to suffer from a low promotional budget but still gave the fans a welcome return to the record racks.

Of the album's protagonists, as mentioned, quite a few comprised The Blue Flames at the time, but at a gig in North Finchley's Jazz and Blues club The Torrington, near Woodside Park, it became clear who was missing: Tony Crombie. During the *Right Now!* sessions, he was probably busy performing with his own band. Crombie died in 1999 at the age of 74, while one of his peers, pianist Stan Tracey, still played on at 87 until his death in December 2013 – and used to have "young" Guy Barker from the Blue Flames on trumpet every now and then: what goes around!

Before the next album, Bernie Holland left the Blue Flames: "I remember the year I finished working with Georgie Fame & The Blue Flames was the year that Margaret Thatcher became Prime Minister, 1979. And the reason why I finished working with him was not because we had fallen out or anything, nothing to do with that at all.

"It was because he had two sons, Tristan and James – Tristan plays guitar and James plays drums – and they came of age. Having him for a father, imagine the music you are surrounded with all the time. As a child you can't help it but play music. So they were the same age as I was when I joined Long John Baldry, they were 18–19, they're good and they're learning, and they've got him as a mentor and a guide. And of course, if you see his record collection, he's got everything that you'd ever want to listen to, to come to appreciate the culture and where he is coming from, musically and historically."

With Tristan being 12 at the time and James all but seven, the writing may not have been on the wall just yet, but there is some prophecy in what Holland describes.

Interpreting Elvis – Costello's title track for That's What Friends Are For

Being back in the category of contemporary album artists after a five year gap certainly gave Georgie Fame the boost to return to the studio before long, and he actually managed a further LP release in that very same year of 1979, albeit on a more modest budget scheme which didn't allow the use of the lavish orchestral backing that he had used on *Right Now!* Still, *That's What Friends Are For*, recorded during August when *Right Now!* had just begun to hit the shops, had a lot going for it, not least having its title track supplied by a Young Turk who had grown up with Georgie's music, had grooved to *Sound Venture* where others had fancied The Who: Elvis Costello.

Fame often shared stages with the cabaret singer Ross MacManus – the "Patsy Girl" crooner who often took his son Declan to watch artists perform at the BBC studios for various radio programmes. So it was an honour when 15 years or so later, Declan MacManus a.k.a. Elvis Costello wrote a song for Fame: the actual title track. As Costello remembered in an article on *Sound Venture* in *Mojo Magazine*, "Georgie was the first person to commission me to write a song for him. I had one knocking about called *That's What Friends Are For*, which was a little bit too swingy for me so I adapted it for him. I'm glad he cut it but I'm sorry I didn't write him a better song. He'd do a great version of 'Almost Blue'."

Georgie repaid Costello's compliment in an interview with German journalist Norman Bender, and also re-assured Costello as to the song's quality: "Cause he's a good songwriter, he's a great singer. His father used to sing in a British dance band, so he grew up listening to dance bands and Big Bands. I was only 21 years old when I started recording the Harry South Big Band thing. I was only 23 years old when I was singing with Basie's orchestra. But it was something I wanted to try to do. I recorded one of his songs. He wrote a song and sent it to Chris Blackwell at Island Records. It was called 'That's What Friends Are For'. And I turned it around and rearranged it, but it's a good song. I like it."

Fame also surprised listeners with a more adventurous, Latin-Funk approach, its highlights being Bill Withers' "A Lovely Day" and a fantastic version of "Sitting In The Park", with a kind of Level-42-type bass line supplied by Brian Odgers. Half of the 10 titles, which made it a shorter album than its predecessor, were written by Fame himself, some with the assistance of Candida Lycett Green again, who had supplied the lyric to "'Cross A Lazy Afternoon" on *Right Now!*.

Studio guitarist Alan Parker, Brian Odgers on bass and drummer Barry Morgan remained from the previous 1978 album sessions, while Blue Flames trumpeter Eddie "Tan Tan" Thornton took turns with Mike Davis. Brian Smith's flute and sax services replaced Ray Warleigh, with Dick Morrissey coming in on tenor sax and Blue Flame Malcolm Griffiths on trombone. This time, Georgie Fame's production partner was Pye Records engineer Terry Evennett, who had worked with a wide roster of artists ranging from Pop people like Brotherhood of Man to British Blues ambassadors Savoy Brown.

Browsing through Georgie Fame record racks at the time, the cover of *That's What Friends Are For* was an immediate eye-catcher. Other than tasteful but conventional portraits of the artist, like *Seventh Son*, or in fact the Pye Records predecessor *Right Now!*, this album reverted to seemingly haphazard, more daringly simple artistry which had not been employed since *Shorty*.

Bold strokes of red colour on white, with *Georgie Fame* scribbled on the front and the album title on the back in black carbon, this was the work of the painter and, not apparent here, linguist, bon vivant and master gardener, Teddy Millington-Drake (1932–1994), who had spent his early childhood in Uruguay, arrived in London in 1940 and was famous for his romantic and melancholic watercolours, but also for abstract works which resembled the *That's What Friends Are For* cover painting and which are still auctioned at considerable prices today.

That's What Friends Are For – track by track

Like "A Different Dream" on *Right Now!*, the new album was ignited with a highly commercial, radio friendly Pop track for the singles market, "Maybe Tomorrow". It was produced by Robbie Patton, "who let me sing it in a pitch that was too high for me, really", as Georgie remembers. Patton, who in 1979 toured with Fleetwood Mac, had his own albums produced by Mac's Christine McVie, had composed the song with Jonathan Cain from The Babys. He later worked with Santana, so Fame certainly had the right instinct to work with a young artist to get back into the charts. But for Georgie, things did not make an impact, maybe because the pleasant enough composition did not have that really great key in Fame's comfort zone. (Robbie Patton actually managed a hit later, with Fleetwood Mac, no less, when he co-wrote their "Hold Me", also with Christine McVie in 1982, reaching #4 in the US).

Bill Withers' "Lovely Day" was a wise choice for Fame. The laconic style of the West Virginia singer who had started recording demos from his L.A. day job on a Douglas Aircraft assembly line, sang in clubs at night and hit it big with "Ain't No Sunshine" in 1972, fitted Fame like a glove. But at the same time, the number, executed here with fine Fender Rhodes work and a disciplined horn section, becomes a true Fame & Flames number.

Withers (b. July1938) had recorded this song for his 1977 *Menagerie* album, and his single reached #7 in the UK in 1978 (US #3), a year before this album, a true sign that Georgie liked and appreciated the song rather than calculating chart success. Sales merits were repeated by Bill Withers himself about a decade later, in 1988, when the Ben Liebrand-twiddled "Lovely Day (Sunshine Mix)" reached #4 in England.

Saxophonist Dick Morrissey used "Lovely Day" in the same year, 1979, for his EMI-Harvest album with Jim Mullen, *Cape Wrath*. Both had been in the Average White Band together and now ran the successful Morrissey Mullen. Their pleasant Easy Listening version became special via keyboardist Max Middleton's imaginative string arrangement. During the sessions for Georgie's album, Mullen played as well, but only on "You".

"L. In L.A." was all Fame's own work, an up-tempo number where he sings about his loathing of that huge metropolis – "L standing for 'ell' as Northern, Lancastrian for 'hell'" – by swiftly brushing on all the clichés of sunny weather, the coast, the freeways and Hollywood, certainly getting homesick watching "a whole lot of people going nowhere together with nothin' to say", knowing he is not alone in that assessment.

"You", one of the album's highlights with its Caribbean Latin-Reggae flavour, was based on lyrics by Candida Lycett Green and presented a completely different line-up: two long-standing Blue Flames members, conga man Speedy Acquaye and tenor saxophonist Steve Gregory, saw their only appearance on this album. They worked together with Dick Morrissey's band partner Jim Mullen on guitar, Ian Hamer on trumpet, and ace drummer Henry Spinetti, who had just joined the Eric Clapton Band and had been working with Fame via the Glyn Johns-led LP sessions with Andy Fairweather Low and Joan Armatrading, a few years before.

With its easy-going yet intensive touches, this could easily be a Glyn Johns production. Thanks to the help of Candida Lycett Green, the song uses some great metaphors, like "You black out the blue in me" and thus creates a love song that comes over honest rather than soppy. The Reggae rhythm, with hindsight, hints at things to come, of which Georgie was most probably unaware.

The Latin touch of "I Don't Care Who I Dance With" – "if the music's good" and "the rhythm is right", Lycett Green reckons he doesn't care too much who he dances with – is given a similar arrangement to Stevie Wonder's "Don't You Worry 'Bout A Thing" on *Right Now!*, creating a nice kind of continuity here, a number which could do with a live re-vamp today.

The title track was Elvis Costello's composition "That's What Friends Are For". "He wrote the song, and sent it to Chris Blackwell at Island Records. I changed it round a bit, but yeah, I could use it", Fame remembers, and certainly, combining brass work with acoustic slide guitar was quite an original idea. Costello never recorded this song officially, but dedicated fans know where to find the original demo of a song that deals with drink and dames rather juicily but sufficiently tongue in cheek.

Georgie's "Don't Hit Me When I'm Down" had been a Fame & Price single in 1973 and presents more Jamaican flavor, with thrilling trumpet by Eddie Thornton. The lyrics deal with the problem of one's lady playing ball as long as her man is successful, but then – in this case, the bloke doesn't lose his humour.

A new version of Billy Stewart's American original and Georgie's 1966 European hit "Sitting In The Park", comes as highly sophisticated fare, based on Brian Odgers' delicious bass line and Barry Morgan's sensitive percussion work.

There is more light Funk via another Bill Withers cover version, this time from his 1976 album *Naked And Warm*: "If I Didn't Mean You Well", which as a single did not chart for Withers (apart from a #88 in the R&B listings). Here, following some fantastic breaks and fills, Georgie's Hammond organ can be heard, which is always ever so welcome.

Georgie's gorgeous song about life on the road, "Cat's Eyes", became the Single B-Side to the opener "Maybe Tomorrow": "Tired as the colour of Mississippi Red", but for once not on his way to a gig, but "keeping his eyes on the cat's eyes", "hope to make it in time" to reach "the good-looking woman taking care of me". In the vein of "That Old Rock'n'Roll", there is a slow beginning and then up-tempo rhythm with Alan Parker's guitar dancing nicely on Steve Gregory's and Dick Morrissey's lively saxophone lines. This is also on *Cool Cat Blues*.

The album came out on Pye records in late 1979, to little fanfare. Like *Right Now!* and a great number of other Fame albums, it was thankfully re-relased in Japan in 2007, in a tasteful digipak sleeve with a booklet containing all the lyrics. With the Japanese custom of writing song titles in their Kanji, Hiragana and Katagana script in phonetic English, "Lovely Day", for instance, came out as "Ravuri Day", a fact that would have amused British comedian and radio personality Kenny Everett (1944–1955) no end in his time – reminding him of Japanese tourist training for crossing the roads: "Rook reft, rook light".

Apart from being all too brief at 36 minutes running time, the album bears repeated listening and should have been made known to a much larger audience. Luckily, Fame at least got a chance to present the album on television when it came out.

Around the time of the release of *That's What Friends Are For*, Fame appeared for the Grampian TV (today's STV – Scottish Television) show *The Entertainers*. Just like Acker Bilk, Shakin' Stevens, The Pasadena Roof Orchestra, old Fame friend Peter Skellern or ex-partner Alan Price between 1977 and 1981, Georgie could celebrate a 25-minute live set in front of a studio audience with his Blue Flames.

This time, the band consisted of old stalwarts trumpeter Eddie Thornton and conga player Speedy Acquaye, Bernie Holland on guitar, Brian Odgers on bass, Tony Crombie on drums, Malcolm Griffiths on trombone and Steve Gregory on sax. He presented a great little set: "Let The Good Times Roll", "Funny How Time Slips Away" – "Yeh Yeh" just introduced as "a song I picked up on the streets in Soho in 1963", no long stories told yet.

The Reggae tune "You" followed as the only track from the new album, before a young looking Georgie left his Hammond organ and almost danced the Chuck Berry duck walk for "Getaway", incorporating some mild James Brown nicked dance steps as well. "Getaway" received a great guitar solo by the soon departing Bernie Holland. Georgie, in a buoyant mood all through, went to the piano and became a little sentimental for his "Eros Hotel" from *Right Now!* What a great heartfelt flute solo by Steve Gregory, and jazzy bass lines from Brian Odgers.

Then it was back to the party mood for "Zulu", started by Speedy Acquaye on his congas. A piano-led fast version of "The Ballad of Bonnie and Clyde" resembled the version on *My Favourite Songs* four years later. Soon, it was all over to the riff of "Last Night", with a quick "Satisfaction" worked in, no time to introduce the band, as director Alan Franchi had probably made the "Kill it now" sign. There you are.

Closing The Gap – The Reggae album 15 years after the Ska Blue Flames

Stylistically, Fame remained inspired – and between all musical chairs. 1980 saw a melodic, tender Reggae album *Closing The Gap*, recorded with the Reggae Philharmonic Orchestra. Georgie felt he had to explain what he meant by "gap" to critics who assumed that there was a bandwagon to be jumped on by veteran Fame. Of course, it was the other way round: "I recorded Blue Beat tunes in the early Sixties with Jamaica's Prince Buster, before the term 'Reggae' was even coined!"

Apparently, Pye Records were in the process of going under at the time, so the label executives were in no position to pay Georgie Fame any advance on the record. Instead, they offered him another album, studio time, rights to the masters and all, as a parting gift.

Fame had been contemplating a Reggae project and chose the quite legendary Lloyd Charmers, who had been born as Lloyd Tyrell in Bob Marley"s Trench Town in Kingston, Jamaica when Georgie was three years old. During the Ska era, he had led the Charmers duo, who had made records for Fame's future pal Prince Buster. Interestingly, after his duo broke up, Charmers worked in a band called The Flames with Alton Ellis.

Charmers had had success with instrumentals like "African Zulu" but was also notorious as an artist who had become known for some daring sounds, e.g. in his song "Birth Control" (recorded as Lloyd Terrell), where amongst some "pussy talk" and erotic sighing, you could hear the bed springs creaking. The song fittingly appeared on an album called *Censored!* and was duly x-rated. Once again, Georgie showed great instincts in picking Charmers – his "Birth Control" melody line had just been nicked by the highly popular UK stars The Specials, for their song "Too Much – Too Young".

A skilled organist and arranger like Georgie himself, Lloyd Charmers often showed impeccable taste, like when he made "Reggae Wonderland", a tropical version of Bert Kaempfert's trumpet-led instrumental smash "Wonderland By Night" from 1959. They both had a soft spot for the Hamburg based sound magician – proved by Georgie collaborating in the Kaempfert tribute album with German pianist *Paul Kuhn meets Bert Kaempfert – Remember When* (2003), where he sang the Kaempfert/Milt Gabler tune for Nat Cole, "L.O.V.E." and "Dankeschön". So there was a meeting of kindred spirits somewhere.

Although repeated listening reveals a fine effort, Fame has often commented that the resulting album, *Closing The Gap*, had tended to almost turn into a Lloyd Charmers solo effort:

"It wasn't a good album. It was a good idea, but the producer wasn't really up to it, Lloyd Charmers. It was more of an ego trip for Lloyd. Nice guy, though. You see, Pye Records were dying at the time. I had a deal with them, so they wanted me to do something like Dub. They didn't know what they were doing and the company was about to close anyway. So they gave me the masters as a parting gift if you like, instead of giving me some money. I would disown it if I could, but I can't."

Closing The Gap – track by track

The choice of material and execution by the Reggae Philharmonic Orchestra, is actually very inspired and hugely charming. The album starts with the Charmers' anthem "Give A Little More", one of four of his own compositions: a plea for humanity and charity and goodwill which easily equals the relevance of Michael Jackson's "We Are The World" without having to come over as pompous. Instead, Charmers and Fame secure a seducing, positively swaying arrangement, getting their point home that the gap between "big wealthy millionaires who cherish their wealth" and "people who work their fingers to the bone" is way too wide.

Charmers actually quotes the bible in his composition, "Don't take what don't belong to thee", (a good-spirited mix of Patois and Olde English), but to these ears stays on this side of sentimentality. An array of trumpets – among them Eddie "Tan Tan" Thornton – does not sound like Georgie's world, but a lovely soprano sax and Charmers own vibraphone touches create a link to Fame's own band. The use of soulful female backing vocals – supplied by The Guardian Angels – certainly constitutes a real departure for Georgie. This was the perfect choice for a single – which again didn't chart.

"Run Away With Me", by contrast, is a straight dance tune, infectious and faster than the introductory song. Gorgeous call and response and interlocking vocals with The Guardian Angels are topped off by pleasant Hammond touches.

The title track on the German release of this album in 1983 – *I Love Jamaica* on Telefunken Records – this begins with Fame's organ, with our man reporting back from Jamaican travels during the bleak British winters, "the rum and the women are fine". The keyboard orchestration is very much of its late-Seventies time, but the general atmosphere is one of exotic romance and works really well. "I Love Jamaica" also became a German single in the same year.

Closing The Gap's climax certainly reached by a new reading of "Eros Hotel", the ballad from the *Right Now!* album. Georgie begins the first verse about a rainy day in London, where he saw her in Soho and they go arm in arm to Foyles to buy a book, freely without any rhythm accompaniment, to the sounds of an oboe, then the Reggae rhythm kicks in for the chorus "Let's go up to the Eros Hotel" – another gap to the world of Fame's songs is closed here.

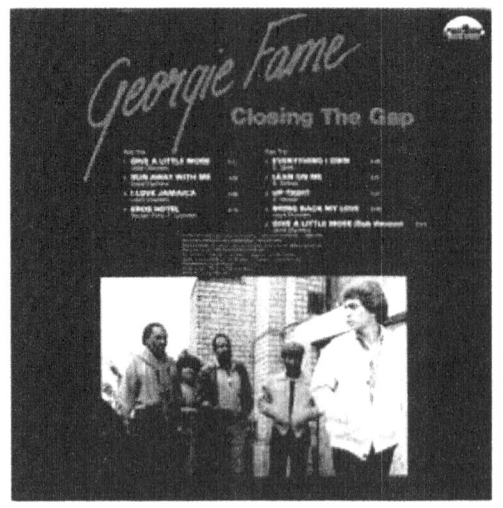

"Everything I Own" had been written by Bread singer David Gates and was a big hit for the American mainstream band, but Lloyd Charmers had re-invented it as a Reggae tune for the man from Kingston's Denham town, Ken Boothe, in 1974. Charmers had his own hit in mind, of course, when he suggested Fame cover it for this album, very catchy and enhanced by The Guardian Angels again, with Georgie firmly back in the BBC Radio 2 vein of some of his CBS albums, and why ever not? – Telefunken made it the German B-side to "I Love Jamaica" in 1983.

Judging from the fact that Fame had chosen two Bill Withers tracks for his *Right Now!* album, the selection of Withers' greatest hit, his US number one "Lean On Me", keeps with the tradition, Georgie singing his responses to The Guardian Angels' calls.

Talking about traditions, choosing Stevie Wonder's "Up Tight" is so right for a wealth of reasons: as often mentioned, Georgie Fame loves Stevie Wonder; his Motown tour buddies The Supremes recorded it; Buddy Rich preferred a Big Band Swing version; and none other than Fame hero Jimmy McGriff also tendered a version.

There is yet another Lloyd Charmers composition, "Bring Back My Love", which links Reggae to a Disco groove very competently, with the producer and bandleader (Charmers, not Fame) throwing in some Beethoven piano quotes in the process. Two years after Rod Stewart's "Do Ya Think I'm Sexy" and the Stones' "Miss You", all this would have needed was tons of airplay – you could certainly not accuse Tyrell-Charmers of missing a trendy beat here. For the finale, he leads Georgie and the band into Dub waters, great electric Jazz piano included – a fine ending to the German album version, and a hint of things to come for the original Pye Records vinyl release:

Here, the opener, "Give A Little More", receives an echo laden Dub treatment as well, with the arrangement intact, but only snippets of the lyrics sung by The Guardian Angels, the melody carried by soprano sax and vibes, that addictive bass line always carrying it all.

Apart from the mentioned Telefunken release in 1983, the album was coupled with a John Holt Reggae album for the Phono-Disc Records double LP *This Is Reggae*, back to back in a single sleeve – a strange hybrid and collector's item. (On the labels, both albums bear the same title, Reggae Stars.) Again, Fame's record was found leaving out the Dub version of "Give A Little More", and interestingly crediting "Uptight" to lyric writers Henry Cosby & Sylvia Moy, while the original release only credits Stevie Wonder, who had supplied the instrumental riff in 1966.

Back to Jazz – In Hoagland 1981 with Annie Ross and Hoagy Carmichael

Even before the Reggae album would see a re-release as *I Love Jamaica* by Decca Germany in 1983, Fame was already "One Step Beyond" musically, as the new Ska champions Madness would put it. He quickly threw himself into yet another recording project. But contractually, he was "One step behind" – i.e. without a recording career, having been left stranded after losing his deal in the wake of Pye Records' imminent demise.

In 1980, Harry South acquaintance John Lambe had the idea to establish an independent record label, a business move which a lot of bands had undertaken, following the obvious examples of the Beatles' Apple Records, Rolling Stones Records and Frank Sinatra's Reprise labels. Most of them, as should be noted with hindsight, enjoyed substantial financial backing and huge distribution from corporations like (in the examples above) EMI, Kinney Music Group and Warner Brothers respectively.

As Georgie remembered in 2009, "A friend of Big Band leader Harry South, John Lambe – quite well-off due to his successful advertising agency – was a big fan of Hoagy Carmichael. He called Harry about an idea for a tribute project – and of course, Harry was all for it: He had nothing going at that particular time, and he badly needed the work. So then Harry called me, and I started gathering ideas, checking all of Hoagy's songs, you know, like 'No, we won't do this one, that one isn't suitable either, but that is a nice one, picking songs that I liked and felt suitable.

"Some numbers seemed to ask for a duet treatment, so I called my good old friend Annie Ross from Lambert, Hendricks & Ross [who divided her time between Los Angeles and London in those days round 1980]. "It all happened incredibly quickly because the budget was so very tight. So we decided to get some musicians together."

Hoagy Carmichael (1900–1981)

Hoagy Carmichael, born in Bloomington, Indiana in November1899, was a contemporary and friend of both Louis Armstrong and Bix Beiderbecke, the latter horn legend a man who boozed himself to death at age 28. Carmichael had persevered with his musical career – in spite of his first choice of studying law to please his family – and in the end published almost 600 songs. The American author and composer Alec Wilder called Hoagy Carmichael "the most talented, inventive, sophisticated and Jazz-oriented of the hundreds of writers composing pop songs in the first half of the 20th century."

The then 79 year-old "Georgia On My Mind" composer and don't-shoot-me-I'm-only-the-piano-player famously starred in Hollywood movies like *To Have And Have Not* (1944), where he presented his "Hong Kong Blues", or *Johnny Angel* (1945), where he showed his romantic side with "Memphis In June". Like Georgie Fame at that time, Carmichael had often collaborated with lyricists, like Johnny Mercer or Paul Francis.

Carmichael had retired to Palm Springs in California when this album, *In Hoagland 1981*, was recorded, but a lot of British Jazz fans remembered his laconic, easy-going style from tours in the late Fifties. In the late 1970s, Carmichael had still appeared on US television from time to time. Chatting to Crystal Gayle about writing "Lazy Bones" in a mere 20 minutes with Johnny Mercer, who had the original idea, it became clear how well his songs suited a female voice, and Gayle in fact proceeded to record her own album of the Indiana-born master's material in *Sings The Heart And Soul Of Hoagy Carmichael* in 1999.

Annie Ross (b. 1930)

Georgie's choice of female partner was the London born Scottish New York expatriate lady who came out of Fame's old Vocalese idols Lambert Hendricks & Ross: Annie Ross. The lady is truly multi-dimensional. She "lives" Blues & ballads, swings like mad, she is the Queen of Vocalese for one thing, and also a composer of repute: Fancy writing a song like "Let's Fly" at age fourteen, and promptly getting it recorded by Johnny Mercer.

Annie Ross (b. July 1930) a.k.a. Annabelle Short, is the daughter of the Scottish Vaudeville artists Jack Short and May Dalziel Short who had gone to Manhattan as a four year old. Where Georgie was a teenage musician, young Annie won her first children's radio contest at the age of five, an MGM contract via Paul Whiteman. Her aunt took her to L.A. soon, and she was still only at the tender age of eight when she sang in *Our Gang Follies of 1938* and *The Little Rascals* – and as a 13 year-old teenager, she appeared in *Presenting Lily Mars* as Judy Garland's sister.

Later there were *Superman III* (1983) or *Throw Mamma From The Train* (1987), and Ms Ross still sang, acted and danced on film sets in the bright lights of California half a century later: Take comparatively recent parts like her cameo by the swimming pool in the 1993 Robert Altman drama comedy *Short Cuts* inspired by Raymond Carver short stories. Annie Ross also enlightened the dim danger zones of those legendary haunting scenes like in the comedy horror movies *Basket Case 2* (1990) and *Basket Case 3: The Progeny* (1991) as Granny Ruth. Her comment in 2012: "Well, they're talking of doing another one. It will be *Basket Case 4*! I talked to the director the other night. He said that he wanted to do a final one."

Just like Georgie, Annabelle Short had left school early to start her singing career, but unlike young Clive, she changed her name to Annie Ross on her own account, starting both her singing career and he life-long commuting between the United States and Europe.

Her crucial mentor was Bob Weinstock of Prestige Records, because he was the "suit" who contracted her to write the words for instrumental Jazz passages, just like King Pleasure had started to do. This was "Twisted", taking up Wardell Gray's saxophone piece from 1949. It appeared on the 1952 collection *King Pleasure Sings/Annie Ross Sings* which influenced Georgie a lot. "Twisted" then got really famous in the Vocalese trio that featured Georgie's great hero Jon Hendricks, the aforementioned Lambert Hendricks & Ross.

Annie Ross is at least four-dimensional when it comes to geography. Scottish born, she has lived lives in New York – where she is still based – Los Angeles, Paris, and – London,

England. It was there that she had left the group during a tour of the UK in 1962 – in order to kick her heroin habit. Since then, she had worked as a London based re-import.

And it was there that she met yet another challenge: Running her own club is something the lady who once replaced Billie Holiday at the *Apollo Theater* was not going to shy away from either. She ran her venue, *Annie's Room*, "ending up as the one who was not getting paid!", but presenting – and paying – stars like Errol Garner, Blossom Dearie, Jon Hendricks of course, and our British Rhythm & Jazz legend Georgie Fame. With Georgie, Annie Ross would share the stages performing with the famous Count Basie Orchestra, and she would now record one of the most swinging, charming albums of the Eighties, *In Hoagland 1981*.

Listening to the concert recordings done down in *Annie's Room* during 1965, released as *Live In London* in 2010, one realizes how many songs in her repertoire were from the "Georgie Fame Songbook":

Cole Porter's "Lil' Darlin'" would appear on *Sound Venture* the year after her performance. Then there was the King Pleasure medley "I'm In The Mood For Love"/"Moody's Mood For Love", Jon Hendricks' "Doodlin'" and the Basie/Hendricks tune "Jumpin' At The Woodside" which Georgie would record several times, 10 years after this album, *In Hoagland 1981*. Then there was "Saturday Night Fish Fry", the Louis Jordan number that was later to appear on *My Favourite Songs* in 1983.

Annie Ross when interviewed in 2012, called in her apartment in the heart of Manhattan, found it perfectly fitting to hear again of these similarities in their repertoire: "You know: when something is good, word gets around and it gets shared, so it was only normal. I mean, in the recording of "Lil' Darlin'" and "Come On Home" and all those things, I had done that with Lambert, Hendricks & Ross. But it was public. If he [Georgie] heard it and liked it and wanted to do it, there was no barrier."

She still had all the time in the world for Fame: "I admire Georgie so much, you know, I would certainly do anything." As to when she met him for the first time, she said, "Well, I can't remember. It was so long ago, it seems like I have always known him." But it didn't happen in *Annie's Room*, "I think it was before that."

About the Hoagy Carmichael project, Annie Ross was able to recall that a television tie-in happened. After Georgie's meeting with the great man at his home in Palm Springs, California, a TV special based on the album was made by Scottish Television and won a gold award at The New York Television Festival: "I remember someone suggested this and then we did a TV show – that coincided with the release of the album."

Ross recalled her first encounter with Hoagy fondly: "I met him when I was a young kid, about fourteen. It was a private party, and he was playing the piano, just kind of tinkling around, and I went up and talked to him. I told him I sang, and I was such a fan of his – and I sang for him and he loved it."

As for the studio sessions, "It was great. We just did it as it was, together with the orchestra. It was very harmonious, to use a pun. And it was fun and we both loved what we were doing. My aunt was a singer, and she recorded with Hoagy: her name was Ella Logan", who famously worked for Frank Sinatra and Louis Armstrong's All Stars.

For her solo parts on the album, Annie Ross was able to choose her own favourites, "of course", and "'I Get Along Without You Very Well' was good."

She is still proud of the rewards she and Jon Hendricks got at New York's Lincoln Center: "In the 'Peter Alan Room' they did one for Jon and I, but they awarded me the *Arts Award* for outstanding [achievements]. Well, it is a lifetime achievement award. 'Music Is Forever' (1995) is the song that I sang for the induction at Lincoln Center, because I wrote it." As for the *Jazz Award*, "that was separate. I got the award without Jon."

At the time of the interview, Annie Ross was still active: "Well, I'm about to make an album, with two guitar players, that's all. Bucky Pizzarelli and John Pizzarelli [b. 1960, whose CV includes James Taylor, Rosemary Clooney and Harry Connick jr.] It will be easy, because we're of the old school. We decide and we do, so I would think it would be over the summer – we will meet on Thursday to decide on the numbers."

There is also Annie's regular gig at the *Metropolitan Room*, round the corner from her apartment, and in 2012, she had been doing it for "about seven or eight years. I have the best band in New York. These are Tardo Hammer [b. 1958] on piano, since 1994 [who had worked with Lionel Hampton and Johnny Griffin] Jimmy Wormworth (b. 1937) on drums [who played for Nelly Lutcher and had already accompanied Lambert, Hendricks and Ross in the early 1960s] and sometimes Bucky Pizzarelli (b. 1926) on guitar." Pizzarelli picked with Dion & The Belmonts, Benny Goodman and, famous accolade, he performed for Ronald Reagan. His New Jersey and Benny Goodman buddy is Warren Vaché, a well-known trumpeter who was born in 1951.

There is now a film documentary of Annie Ross, *No One But Me*.

The musicians on the tribute album *In Hoagland 1981* made up a real dream team of *Sound Venture* proportions, their charts arranged by the *Venture* Big Band leader Harry South together with Fame. The troupe was called the Famous Flamingo Orchestra during the studio proceedings, which took place at Trident, engineered by Steve Short, and Pye Studios with Terry Evenett, where Georgie had cut his last three albums. Accordingly, he used Martin Kershaw on guitar again, as well as Barry Morgan on drums.

Great saxes were supplied by Peter King on the alto and Dick Morrissey on tenor. Both Jazz experts had worked with Georgie before, Peter King, who would become a Blue Flame in the 1990s, on *The Two Faces of Fame* in 1967 and Dick Morrissey on *Sound Venture and Friends*. Morrissey had led the Jazz-Rock pioneers If with *Hoagland* player Jim Mullen on guitar, and they were currently working as Morrissey-Mullen, featuring the If-member and Fame friend Jim Richardson, who based his work on tons of experience with the likes of Chet Baker and Dexter Gordon. He shared bass duties with Darryl Runswick, who in turn worked with Tubby Hayes, as well as *Sound Venture* and *Hoagland* trumpeter Ian Hamer: one big London Jazz family!

Georgie of course supplied piano and Hammond himself. But as he focused on singing much of the time, Fame shared keyboard duties with Geoff Castle (b. 1949), a Londoner and ex-member of the National Youth Jazz Orchestra. He had been in the Graham Collier Septet, played with Nucleus, and according to their leader Ian Carr, had written "his most important composition" in the year of *Hoagland*, Impressions of New York, for the Camden Jazz Week. Working with James Moody was certainly the icing of the cake for Georgie in hiring Geoff for this project.

In Hoagland 1981 – track by track

The proceedings start with the duet "The Old Music Master" – tender Fender Rhodes touches accompany Ms Ross's romantic introduction, but soon Fame takes over with a rousing Boogie rhythm, and soon an imaginative saxophone arrangement is in place for Peter King and Dick Morrissey.

A quirky choir adds further colour to make this 1943 composition with lyrics by Johnny Mercer a great introduction, full of zest and zeal and an indication of the fun that is going to follow. "The Old Music Master" became the B-side for the second single culled from the album. The A-side is the following track:

Seamlessly, the music master leads into the next song with more E-piano and a lovely Jim Richardson bass line. In "Hong Kong Blues", it is Annie Ross who first tells the story of a very unfortunate Memphis man in Hong Kong who "kicked Old Buddha's gong" – which used to be polite slang for being wasted on opium. The protagonist wants to see the Frisco Bay again in this story, which was actually written by Carmichael all on his own. Hoagy famously sang this song in 1943 to Humphrey Bogart and Lauren Bacall in the Hollywood Hemingway adaptation *To Have and Have Not*.

Here, with the line "That's why he says", Annie Ross lets Georgie pick up the rendition. Martin Kershaw's funky guitar patches and the synthesizer solo by Geoff Castle is exactly what Fame had in mind for this recording: "It was my idea!" He might not have chosen such a sound colour during a Ronnie Scott's night, neither in 1981 nor in 2014, but it is certainly fitting here, and it adds to some kind of "outlandish" mood. And thankfully his Hammond organ gets a groovy spot, too, until the line "when he kicked on Buddha's gong" leads into Fame's solo rendition of the next song:

On "Georgia On My Mind", Georgie's Hammond gets nicely set in contrast with piano touches and Dick Morrissey on sax, who would supply the solo as well. Fame's rendition is completely at ease, yet very intensive, and it is obvious how much he has always rated Ray Charles's 1960 signature tune, which many believe the great R&B veteran wrote himself. Stiff competition for Fame in terms of "Georgia On My Mind" also existed from his young friend Stevie Winwood, who had sung the song as a teenager with The Spencer Davis Group in 1965.

Carmichael used lyrics by his student friend Stuart Gorrell from Indiana University. Gorrell's words for Hoagy's fresh party piece were not written with the US State in mind – whose official state song it became in 1979, one year before this recording. Instead, they were dedicated to Hoagy's sister, Georgia Carmichael, at the time. The banker never wrote another song lyric in his life.

"Georgia" leads into the Swing instrumental "One Morning In May" from 1933, where the lovely Harry South-led combo The Famous Flamingo Orchestra really lets loose as if there was a ballroom dance going on, supplying the B-side to "Drip Drop" in the process. But why should they take an instrumental with such wonderful singers around? Georgie remembers a key incident: "We all met at Harry's house, sat round his piano, sampled the possible set list and also decided on the possible keys. It was there and then that Annie made a little mistake that really surprised me, considering all her experience: For the song 'One Morning In May' she decided on a register that was much too low. There is a big difference in performing a song at your leisure sitting on a sofa, or highly strung in a stage or studio situation – so by the time of the recording, it appeared much too low for Annie to sing it satisfactorily. So that is why, in the end, it appears only as an instrumental. There was no time to re-write the score or anything – as all the backing tracks had been done by the time we added the vocal overdubs."

Swing leads into Swing Waltz and "My Resistance Is Low", another duet by Fame & Ross, which Hoagy Carmichael co-wrote with Harold Adamson and played in the movie *The Las Vegas Story* in 1952, after it had been his only UK hit the year before – and a number one at that! A quarter of a century later, it became a chart success (#3) for Peter Sarstedt's brother Clive, who called himself Robin Sarstedt using his second Christian name (Their oldest brother Richard went out as Eden Kane).

Session cat Darryl Runswick offers a great bass line, Georgie lets the organ wail, and the trumpets, courtesy of Chris Pyne and Ian Hamer, get a chance to shine.

"I Get Along Without You Very Well" is an intensively sung and felt solo vocal performance by Annie Ross, who thrives on her declared favourite tune. Jane Brown Thompson's original title from 1938 is called "I Get Along Without You Very Well (Except Sometimes)". It adds the frequently sung line "except sometimes" in order to introduce examples which make it very clear how easily the singer could survive without her lover.

In 1981, Annie Ross surely put all her emotion and discipline into this performance. She was just accompanied by Martin Kershaw on acoustic guitar – a prime lesson in restraint.

The way the lover insists that she is independent but comes over as utterly in love to the listener, this concept could have been the lyrical role model for the band 10CC's "I'm Not In Love", where the statement of independence is also frequently disputed in the verses.

"Oh, I remember it so well", the great Vocalese lady Annie Ross stated with a chuckle about her recording of this song during our interview, police sirens wailing up the skyscrapers in her Manhattan neighbourhood.

"Rockin' Chair" was often performed by Georgie as a softly-swung Swing; here, Hoagy himself presents a short sketch of it in free rhythm. Louis Armstrong and Mildred Bailey had recorded it successfully, and Carmichael's own 1930 recording famously featured Bix Beiderbecke on cornet, Benny Goodman on clarinet, Tommy Dorsey on trombone and Gene Krupa on drums – an early studio supergroup.

Sinatra's version may be the most famous. "Rockin' Chair" became Carmichael's first hit with self-written lyrics, and in spite of his mother's laments like those in "Small Fry" (which will appear later on this album), this one made him leave the law office and become a music pro, trying his luck with writing musicals in Hollywood. So his "calling" came ten years later than in Georgie Fame's own curriculum vitae. Fame himself would sing his version nine years on for *Cool Cat Blues*.

The first single release off the album – not that it got Fame much airplay – was "Drip Drop". Barry Morgan's Charleston intro and Georgie's "Baby's balling, baby's balling" grab the listener's attention, and the quirky "Annie Ross choir" from "The Old Music Master" is back.

But the highlight of this version is the fantastic Vocalese section in the middle, starting with that "big umbrella" – for which Fame received a co-credit in the lyrics section with Ray Gilbert, the man who supplied English words to Carlos Jobim's "Dindi". Energetic bass by regular Blue Flames Jim Richardson and Barry Morgan on drums drive this piece along relentlessly, and this is a welcome pick-me-up after the relative melancholy of the previous three tracks and an indication of the careful sequencing of this album.

The wonderful tone of Peter King's alto saxophone introduces "Stardust" – the ballad most aficionados know by Nat King Cole. Carmichael had originally written it in 1927 as "Star Dust" about a riverboat. Here, Georgie sings the Blues first with Morrissey as his duet partner. It is with the second verse that Annie Ross joins the rendition. Morrissey gets a long tenor sax solo, and he really lets loose. The drama holds the number together perfectly and loops into the next one:

Via a catchy piano bouncing theme, we get a lively shuffle, the true Jazz standard "Up A Lazy River". The brass and reed boys carry the song's joy nicely – and the shuffle soon turns into Ska, Fame's beloved Jamaican jump music from the beginning of his career. Hoagy had written this in 1930, using lyrics by Sidney Arodin, and his hit was covered by thousands, including Acker Bilk, Chris Barber, Louis Prima, Manhattan Transfer and Fame's special lady, Peggy Lee.

Perhaps the most charming of all the duets on this collection is the mock-biographical "Small Fry", about the young carousing Hoagland as a young boy and his worried mother who tells her son that he isn't "the biggest catfish in the sea" and should stick to practising the law instead of dabbling in music. "You were young once", Clive-Hoagy pleads, while his mother, Mrs Carmichael-Ross, concedes "When I was young I was old" and insists "Why don't you stay in shallow water?"

Apart from the gorgeous singing, Ross and Fame obviously enjoy their "acting parts", and whether this was strictly scripted or carefully improvised is almost irrelevant in the face of such a convincing result. Way back in 1938, this was sung by Bing Crosby in the film *Sing You Sinners*, and one of his singing partners was Fred MacMurray, the famous face of *Double Indemnity* – and a familiar face on US, British and German TV in *My Three Sons*. Trivia maybe, but an indicator of how much a song like this means to Fame's cinema going generation.

A Bossa Nova tune is next – this time Georgie & Annie are the old couple in "Two Sleepy People" who are too much in love to say goodnight. This composition by Hoagy Carmichael and lyricist Frank Loesser from 1938 was originally interpreted by Francis Langford and Bob Hope, and then Hope tackled it again with Shirley Ross in the movie *Thanks For The Memory*, so Ross & Fame are surely in impressive company.

Some gorgeous harmony singing seems out to prove how much telepathy and romance there can still be in an old love full of tenderness and, in this case, reminiscences of old times. Interestingly, the guitar and bass accompaniment on this track was later echoed, Bossa Nova and all, by Georgie in his second, 2012 version of "Wide-Eyed And Legless", on his sparse but special album *Lost In A Lover's Dream*. The song seems to regain its relevance for every new generation, as Art Garfunkel, Twiggy and Norah Jones picked "Two Sleepy People" up in their own time.

"Hoagy's Help" serves as a priceless comment of Carmichael himself about how "Rockin' Chair " should be done, complete with an additional line which he did not use in Louis Armstrong's version in the beginning because he thought "it might interfere with the instrumental work". Fame remembers: "While we were recording it, John [Lambe] was writing to Hoagy, corresponding. Hoagy wrote back and there was a kind of connection there! Hoagy even sent a tape over and recorded some speech and little things ["Rocking Chair"] that we put on the album."

The singer's own composition "Hoagland" became a loving tribute by Georgie Fame to his idol. "Now the words and music's done, everybody's had their fun – Hoagland's where I want to be", he claims, and this is absolutely credible.

"There you are" – as Fame concludes at the end – an incredibly heartfelt homage to a great veteran of Jazz.

Georgie: "The collaboration with Hoagy Carmichael himself turned out to be very remarkable. When he heard about our activities and some inquiries, he went into a little studio near his home in Palm Beach and recorded a few suggestions, like some ideas he had not used at the time of writing his songs, because he didn't want them to interfere with Louis Armstrong and his version. He was quite shocked when I visited him in California and presented him with our finished master. He realized that we had incorporated his comments into the final album, and he said 'What have you done?' For the finale, his suggestions about some piano additions led directly into my composition "Hoagland" – he had just not assumed he would be part of the action.

"I gave him the the first pressing of the album so that he could listen to it and hopefully give it the okay, which he did do. He never heard of me – quite rightly, but I went to his house in Palm Springs, we played the LP, I got it on video, we talked a lot about music. What he said was 'It doesn't matter how you sing my songs, boy, because they will always make you sound good!'"

As Fame told journalist Rob Adams in the *Herald Scotland* in 1999, "he [Hoagy] pulled down a bottle of 12-year old Ballantine's and we talked about music. People like

Hoagy were considered old hat – dad's favourite – but sooner or later their stuff hits you, especially when you listen to some of the puerile stuff going round."

Once chatting with Fame in Palm Springs, the 80-year-old icon was delighted and a joint little 1981 theatre tour through the United Kingdom was discussed.

Hoagy had in fact been penciled into appearing in a stage show round the UK, together with Georgie, Annie and most of the cast from the album's "Famous Flamingo Orchestra", like the late, great Dick Morrissey on tenor sax, the "Pied Piper" Peter King on alto sax, trumpet player Ian Hamer and Georgie's regular Blue Flames bassist at the time, Jim "B.B." Richardson and drummer Dave Cutler.

For Fame, the main asset had been that with his trusted colleagues from the Harry South Big Band as well as the augmented Blue Flames, he was able to record once again, this time an album full of lovingly arranged songs by Hoagy Carmichael.

Fame: "I was not really *that* much of a Hoagy Carmichael devotee, but the guy whose idea it was to do this album, who is now dead unfortunately – John Lambe – just loved him. He was a great Hoagy Carmichael fan, and I was happy to go along with the idea of such a tribute album, as I also had a lot of respect for Hoagy's work. But John Lambe didn't know anything about the record business. I had to borrow some money myself to help to complete the production and get the project finished", which at the time ("Here we are in eighty-one!") according to Fame, "sold a lot when it came out, but it was a terrible mess, legally and in production."

Bald Eagle Records, the label it was on, was started as their own joint company. Georgie: "I was a partner in that. There were three partners, and I am one of them. One partner died, so there are two of us left."

Hoagland himself never saw *In Hoagland 1981* in any shop. Sadly, he missed the album's release. And who knows if he would have watched a gig on the projected Fame & Ross tour – having passed away on December 27th, 1981, only a few days before the start of the project.

While some of the Fame & Ross & Flamingo Orchestra tour was cancelled, Fame's label venture *Bald Eagle* went into liquidation. Like losing Pye Records contract before, this was leaving him with the club live circuit – and Big Bands in the UK, Central Europe and Scandinavia, as the survival alternative – plus a few singles projects as well.

Asked in 1994 about the possibility of getting an official re-release of *In Hoagland 1981* on CD, Georgie confirmed that he owned these recordings but did not deem them fit for release yet: "So there are technical things that have to be cleaned up, because a lot of people ask for that album."

The fact that the New York City label DRG have re-released the album twice already as a compact disc, boldly quoting a copyright from Bald Eagle Records on the back, is more than irritating for Georgie, and he pointed out that they don't have his permission – while the thing is still on the market in 2014.

As a kind of afterthought, there was a British TV production: In 1983, the English trumpet player Keith Smith had specialized in touring with his own band "Hefty Jazz" – formed in 1981 – in the context of well-conceived thematic package shows. Smith invited Georgie Fame to headline a UK tour entitled *Stardust Road – An Even-*

ing of Jazz Celebrating the Classic Music of Hoagy Carmichael, which, besides Hefty Jazz, also included the female trio vocal group Sweet Substitute, whose members were Teri Leggett, Angie Masterson and Kate McNab. It was another great opportunity for Georgie to show his vocal qualities with such an excellent repertoire of songs. *Stardust Road*, screened on December 10th, 1983, and part of it was Georgie's rendition of a Hoagy Carmichael tune that was not included on the *Hoagland* album, "Riverboat Shuffle".

The Heroes album

Being without a label had not dried up Fame's creative juices, though. After the Carmichael canon, he was writing songs for a concept album, *Heroes*, about masters of their craft – impressive personalities. He produced the album himself, and intended to include his tribute to Mose Allison on it, the "Cool Cat Blues" which he had already recorded once for Island – and was eventually to release on his *Cool Cat Blues* album eight further years on.

Another track on the album was meant to portray the BBC morning deejay and TV legend Terry Wogan. "Wogan's Air" had to await release until 2003, but it was performed in 1982 as part of a radio special – where "Cool Cat Blues" saw its official debut, too.

"I wrote one for a West Indian cricketer called Vivian Richards." He is Sir Vivian Alexander Richards, KNH (Knight of the Order of National Hero), OBE (Order of the British Empire) an ex-cricketer of the West Indies, born in 1952 in St. Johns, Antigua and Barbuda. ""Dynamite" is a fantastic cricketer who was also a great friend of mine. The idea was to write songs for people who were the best at what they did! I've written a great West Indian kind of feel song for Viv, which actually did come out on the B-side of a dance single I did with Stock/Aitken/Waterman! Not "New York Afternoon", but "Samba", on the other side there is a song called "Willow King", that's my master, and that was for Vivian Richards."

This concept album for "people who were best at what they did" also was to include a song around the life of "a great snooker player: Alex Higgins!" Fame remembered this in 1993: "I did record a single for him, which came out in England, and I own the tapes for that. The idea that I had at the time was to write an album, to write songs dedicated to individuals that I really admired, and those characters didn't necessarily have to be musicians. I did almost complete that album and it is another thing that I could put out. I've got the complete master tapes, good mixes of some of the songs. I wrote this song for Alex Higgins, called 'The Hurricane'".

"The Hurricane"/"Hurricane Part 2" was released as a single in 1982, and just like "Ali Shuffle" eight years previously – which had also been re-recorded for the *Heroes* album – it contained the sequel on the B-side. The main song later appeared on the collection *The First Thirty Years*. Georgie: "I wrote it because I loved him as a snooker player, he was great, also a wonderful entertainer and a very controversial character – a snooker version of Van Morrison if you like!"

"There is also a great piece of music I wrote for the British Royal Air Force Aerobatic Team, 'The Red Arrows Theme'." Like *In Hoagland 1981*, this came out with a credit to the Famous Flamingo Orchestra: "I've written a piece of music which I recorded with my band for them. It's an instrumental, but I do have a text for it, so I might put on my voice and sing it. There was a song I wrote for Ray Charles and a couple of other songs. That was the idea I had at the time but I never completed it."

Chapter 7
Dynamite Brass & Dynamite Friends – From Stockholm to Sydney

The first time Georgie Fame set foot on Swedish soil was in 1966 as part of his runaway success of "Yeh Yeh", as he often recounts with relish on stage before hitting his first world-wide #1: "It got me my first big hit, and the first invitation I had to play outside of the UK, England. At that time, when this song was a hit, in 1965, we went to Sweden for the first job. We flew on a small French type of aircraft called the Caravelle, and as it was a Frogs built plane, it was prone to catch fire. Meanwhile, the aircraft arrived safely in Stockholm.

"Anyway, we looked out of the back window, because we were in economy class. It didn't matter because we were just happy to be on an airplane going someplace. Not like today! And even though we had this #1 hit with 'Yeh Yeh', we were in economy class. It didn't matter. We didn't care. We were happy to be on a plane going somewhere. The airline was SAS, Scandinavian Airline System – at the time it was a global enterprise, not like today, when the less gets said about it, the better.

"The plane landed, we looked out of the window, and we could see dozens and dozens of beautiful, beautiful Swedish girls all standing on top of the airport building, waving and smiling. And we thought 'Yeah, this is it! You have a big hit record. You get a big invitation to play overseas. The world is your oyster. That's what we had been working hard for, for three long years!' We walked off the airplane, and by the time we went onto the tarmac, the welcome committee had gone – the girls had all disappeared. And the reason was that Roger Moore was in first class! And he was just *The Saint* [playing the main part in the popular British 60s TV series]."

From 1966 onwards, Georgie Fame worked in Sweden regularly, and one of the key figures in Georgie's musical Swedish cosmos – one of his best and most enduring friendships, too – was with the Stockholm based trumpeter, flugelhorn player, composer, arranger and bandleader Lars "Lasse" Samuelson, whom he must have missed during his first visit sharing a plane with Roger Moore, *The Saint*. As Samuelson remembers:

"I think I met him the year after. The first time he arrived in Stockholm, it was with his [own] band, The Blue Flames. The next year, he came alone, and he played with the band I had, Dynamite Brass. We did some television programmes, and then we started to work with each other for the shows there. Sometimes, he brought a drummer or another player with him – it was always a little different. But the ground was my band. We played his repertoire, always played his songs. I think I did a lot of the arrangements. I think we did "Getaway", and I did the arrangement for that. At that time, I had a lot of recordings with different Rock artists, so the band was playing with everybody."

There is some great footage of a Swedish television show in 1968 where *Georgie Fame och Dynamite Brass* played live in the famous "Gyllene Cirkeln" ("The Golden Circle") Jazz-Club in Stockholm's ABF Huset (open university house), where from 1962 onwards, a lot of Georgie's heroes and colleagues performed, among them Johnny Griffin, Stanley Turrentine and "Brother" Jack McDuff.

Fame brought Zoot Money's ex Big Roll Band drummer – and future John Mayall man – Colin Allen over to play with him in Dynamite Brass. The octet started a rousing set with "Pink Champagne", which Georgie animatedly sang into two microphones which were gaffa-taped together, with the Shure thing already heavily dented.

Then Fame and the Dynamites went via the Blues "If You're Going To The City" on to "Sitting In The Park" and the B-side of the "enormous" flop "Try My World, "No Thanks", which should really be called "Get Out Of My Woodpile" with regard to its words. Georgie then led the highly motivated outfit into "Parker's Mood" and really worked himself into a frenzy on the organ, sweating quite profusely, before he managed the final number "The Ballad Of Bonnie & Clyde", where he impressively used both arms to let the Hammond do a silent movie soundtrack, emulating all the machine-gun mayhem with his Leslie-d wailing, with young Lasse playing along and then gasping approvingly!

Born on August 4, 1935 in Sundbyberg, trumpeter Lasse Samuelson led his aforementioned Swedish Jazz institution Dynamite Brass, which he had started with his friend Jerry Williams, as well as playing in "Lars Samuelson's Kor och Orchester". His first band had been Sing Song Seven in 1963. Samuelson is also a well-known face on Swedish TV, and subsequently on international television programmes, not least as a conductor of the Eurovision song Contest in 1969, 1975 and 1979. Connoisseurs love his work with the Jazz and Pop singer Siw Malmquist.

Lasse frequently played with other musicians of Georgie Fame's circles, for instance pianist Kjell Öhman – a Hammond man almost exactly Fame's age – born September 3, 1943, whose Organ Grinders formed a long-standing mutual admiration society with Georgie's Blue Flames. Samuelson: "Kjell Öhman is one of the famous piano players here in Sweden. I made a couple of albums with his organ group, The Organ Grinders, as a producer. Georgie liked Kjell's organ playing, the sound that he got from the organ. I think they like each other very much, when they play the organ."

Samuelson produced Organ Grinders albums in 1990 and 1993. His range and influence are astonishing: he worked with the Swedish Radio Jazz Orchestra and even the world's prime party player James Last and his Orchestra, with whom he recorded in 1975. He mixed with international stars ranging from Soul giants like Tina Turner and Arthur Conley to Hollywood legends Sammy Davis Junior and Jerry Lewis, as well as British showbiz personalities of Georgie's age and acquaintance, from noble – Paul Jones – to notorious – P.J. Proby.

The producer is also experienced with a range of divas, female and male – Lena Horn, Ann Murray, Liberace and Elton John. His production credits include Fame idols like Dexter Gordon, Mel Lewis and Thad Jones. He also arranged Lee Hazlewood's last ever album, *Cake Or Death,* in 2006, having produced the man's albums since 1973: "When I worked with Lee Hazlewood, I had left Dynamite Brass and had a Big Band. I think Dynamite Brass stopped working in 1972. They are still working with me [in 2013] when I have some gigs."

If there is one credit Samuelson treasured for working with Georgie – he certainly doesn't need it – it is recording with mutual idol Benny Golson as early as 1964. Fame, Samuelson and Kjell Öhman were also brought together working with the Swedish Sandviken Big Band after a few years' intermission, as Samuelson points out: "I think there had been a stop after 1973, for five or six years. After that, I had a Big Band for television, and he came back and did the gig with us, also with a big orchestra. That was a television series, I think we did 50 programmes; for those I brought Georgie over again. He did an album in England with a Big Band [*Sound Venture*], so he had a lot of arrangements for Big Bands. And he had some arrangements from that period when he played with Count Basie."

Footage survives from a Stockholm club gig in 2003, where Georgie Fame led Lasse Samuelson and the legendary Kjell Öhman through celebrations of his Jazz repertoire. Their rhythm section consisted of drummer Jocke Ekberg and bass man Hans Backenroth, who had worked with Fame before and also have Kenny Barron and Ernie Watts on their CV. Georgie obviously enjoyed introducing the band with the following words:

"The man who is responsible for this evening's event is someone who I met first in 1966, here in Stockholm, with Dynamite Brass in "Gyllene Cirkeln" Sveavägen [naming the club's address]. Here we are, 37 years later, with my oldest Swedish friend – after Hans Vieland, God bless him – Lasse Samuelson!"

With these words, this quintet went through Fame faves like "Jumpin' With Symphony Sid" and "It Could Happen To You".

In Goodmansland – Fame combines his love of Sweden and Big Bands

In spite of all the organizational hang-ups and Old Hoagland 'Hoagy' Carmichael's sad and – all things considered – sudden death, the *In Hoagland 1981* album had added to Georgie Fame's already impeccable Jazz reputation, and in 1983, he was offered a kind of follow-up to the album by the Swedish label Sonet Records. It was to be produced and arranged by a fabulous man from Java, the pianist, arranger and life-long Duke Ellington fanatic Rob Pronk (1928–2012). Pronk worked with the classy Kurt Edelhagen Orchestra in Germany in the 1950s, then led the Netherlands' Metropole Orchestra in the 1960s and was to guest there soon with Georgie, who shared music colleagues like Jerry van Rooyen with Pronk. Dexter Gordon? Don Bias? You name them.

This time, the hero to be honoured was Benny Goodman, often called "The King of Swing", and a man who, apart from his love for this special kind of music as well as a rich range of other styles, shared common ground with Fame in working with a racially integrated band. Georgie's duet partner of choice became Sylvia Vrethammar, who like

Fame has always been able to link Pop and Jazz culture effortlessly with her attractive voice. Georgie had met Sylvia for the first time at the Second International Song Festival in Rio de Janeiro back in October 1967, where Georgie sang "Celebration".

The "Big Band" here was led by Georgie's old jazz colleague Herb Geller (1928–2013), a Los Angeles born alto and soprano sax player with highest credentials from the Billy May Orchestra to Quincy Jones, Chet Baker and scores of others. Herb had, in fact, toured with the Benny Goodman Orchestra, though he was never to return to the States with him. Like Georgie, he often worked with the NDR Big Band in Hamburg. The Big Band here turned out to be augmented by nothing less than the full-blown Swedish Symphony Orchestra.

Renowned swingers like first class pianists Kjell Öhman – the old friend of Georgie's from the Organ Grinders and many tours, who later was to help with *Hymns From Home* in 1997 – supplied icings on cakes, as did drummer Magnus Persson.

They helped record the *In Goodmansland* LP with fresh sounding favourites like "Makin' Whoopee" or "Alexander's Ragtime Band", complemented by a rousing medley featuring "After You've Gone" and "Stomping At The Savoy".

The crucial Benny Goodman clarinet parts were tackled by Sweden's prime player of the instrument, Hans Olof "Putte" Wickman (1924–2006), who actually took Benny Goodman as his role model (apart from Artie Shaw, that is) and had been called Sweden's foremost clarinet player as early as 1945, by Swedish paper *Expressen*. He had led his own Big Band in the Sixties in Stockholm's Gröne Lund, and his nickname Putte came about because he co-owned a club of that name there.

In Goodmansland – track by track:

The album starts with a number actually co-written by Benny Goodman with Eddie DeLange, and primarily Lionel Hampton, who was rumoured to have waited for his flight one night, fidgeting and rather restlessly whistling the melody of "Flying Home", some kind of "the old lounge whistle test", to coin a phrase. Lyrics were supplied by Sid Robin, and Benny Goodman had recorded the song with his sextet in 1939 with solos by Hampton and famous guitarist Charlie Christian. For Georgie & Sylvia's version, these tasks are taken over brilliantly by sax man Herb Geller, pianist Rob Pronk and guitar man Jan Schaffer. A true Jazz classic, the number certainly satisfied Fame's early Rock'n'Roll leanings when it featured the then only 18-year old sax player Illinois

Jacquet honking away in the Hampton Orchestra, while big shoes were left behind for Sylvia Vrethammar – none other than Ella Fitzgerald recorded the song in 1979.

"Makin' Whoopee" became the single off the album – written for the Musical *Whoopee!* in 1928 – with music by Walter Donaldson and lyrics by Gus Kahn. Apart from Benny Goodman, this song, a warning about not getting hitched for marriage, has been recorded by Ella Fitzgerald and Frank Sinatra – with the most significant version that followed Georgie & Sylvia done by Fame's friend Dr John with Rickie Lee Jones

Jelly Roll Morton's "King Porter Stomp" from 1905 is next, a 1920s standard recorded by Jelly Roll and trumpeter King Oliver in 1924, taken over by Benny in 1935.

"Limehouse Blues" had London's old stomping ground Tower Hamlets as its setting. It was still called the Limehouse District when its harbour trading scene became a 1934 film, starring George Raft and Anna Mae Wong. Its alternate title was "East End Chant", telling the rather violent story of a man from New York's Chinatown eliminating London rivals.

The actual song was composed by Philip Braham, with lyrics by Douglas Farber, picked up by Goodman in 1937 and included in the later album *Treasure Chest*. The singer Gertrude Lawrence made it popular, but Fame & Vrethammar had lots of versions to be inspired by, among them Django Reinhardt's, Louis Armstrong's, Tony Bennett's, and of course Count Basie's rousing rendition.

Cole Porter's "Just One Of Those Things" was an absolute standard in the 1930s, with adaptations ranging from Ella Fitzgerald and Billie Holiday on Sylvia's side to Bing Crosby, Frank Sinatra and Nat King Cole on Georgie's. In addition, the self-confessed Fame disciple Jamie Cullum picked up the torch for this number in the new millennium.

Irving Berlin wrote "Alexander's Ragtime Band" when he was only 23, and among its early New York presentations was Oscar Hammerstein's Vaudeville house. It may be more of a march than a real Ragtime vehicle, but it surely re-animated the interest in this rhythm, highlighted in the revue *Watch Your Step*. The 1938 film of the same name is about a boy who shocks his family by opting for Ragtime instead of more classical, "real" music and had Benny Goodman's 1938 Carnegie Hall gig written into the script. Here, the evergreen is only a teaser of one and a half minutes – more would have been welcome.

"Sweet Georgia Brown" may very well have already been in Beatles coach Tony Sheridan's repertoire when he was touring with Georgie Fame in Larry Parnes' *Rock'n'Roll Extravaganza* in 1959. Both young heroes could have heard it as a Jerry Lee Lewis number, long before Sheridan hooked up with the Fabs. With music by Maceo Pinkard, Ben Bernie wrote the lyrics and recorded it with his Hotel Roosevelt Orchestra in 1925. There is a Cab Calloway scat version, while Ethel Waters initially made it popular. And which was the blueprint for Vrethammar? Maybe it was Nancy Sinatra's version.

"You Turned The Tables On Me" from the 1936 Musical film *Sing, Baby Sing*, composed by Louis Alter with lyrics courtesy of Sidney D. Mitchell, was made popular by the Benny Goodman Orchestra when Helen Ward sang it. With Annie

Ross, Mose Allison as well as Count Basie having tackled this tune, what more could Georgie want? He turns in a sensitively realized version with the perfect foil in Vrethammar here.

The 1941 standard "Airmail Special" was actually written by Goodman, with his guitarist Charlie Christian and his tenor saxophonist Jimmy Mundy, who also worked for Count Basie and with the often Fame-quoted Sonny Stitt.

"Memories Of You" is performed by Vrethammar in wonderfully relaxed ballad style, with the strings underlined by Mads Vinding's precise and defined bass work.

"In Goodmansland Medley" combined six further tunes in one rousing five and a half minute tour-de-force, the perfect album advert to be put on the B-side of "Makin' Whoopee". "Let's Dance" comes as a Samba with great flute work, seamlessly leading into Swing for "Stompin' At The Savoy", which Georgie introduces but soon includes Sylvia in. "Rose Room" fits the mood so perfectly that we hardly notice it succeeded "Savoy".

"After You've Gone" is performed to a straight 4/4 beat, but soon the medley is doubling in speed for Louis Prima's "Sing Sing Sing", the penultimate part of the medley, using the lyrics the Italian-American Swing comedian had recorded with his New Orleans Gang in 1936 for Brunswick Records, while Benny Goodman's version of 1937 was an instrumental, "Goodbye".

The Goodman experience led to a lifetime of friendships, first of all to Sweden's musicians – and an ongoing soft spot for Big Bands all over Europe. For the next decade, Georgie was to appear and record with orchestras especially in Scandinavia, like the Danish Radio Big Band, many Swedish outfits like the already mentioned Sandviken Big Band, the Norwegian Per Husby Orchestra, the BBC Big Band and German radio station orchestras The WDR Big Band and the NDR Big Band.

Parallel to the *In Goodmansland* project, Georgie had started to tour with the high octane Hudik Big Band, who among many other virtues had the Count Basie sound down pat. He first worked with them in 1982, and the following year saw him sing there in connection with Sylvia Vrethammar as well. Apart from appearing all over Scandinavia, Fame and the Hudik Big Band toured Poland together in 1984, playing in Lublin, Zamosc and Warsaw.

The charming Sylvia had stiff competition from Lill Lindfors (b. 1940), a Finnish-Swedish star since the 1960s, who had won a second place in the European Song Contest in 1966, would host it in 1985 – with a so-called wardrobe malfunction that was secretly planned as a gag and serves as one of the most memorable Eurovisian cock-ups. Lindfors had several of her TV shows awarded in Montreux. She had appeared with the Hudiks since 1973, and, like Vrethammar, got on with Fame famously.

Other winning combinations happened as well, like a quartet vocal set-up with the Bahamian-Danish Jazz and Gospel queen Etta Cameron (1939–2010), Tommy Körberg and Tim Hagans, or as a duo with Eva-Karin Bengtsson and also Ulrika Beijer.

On record, Georgie got to sing almost the whole of the second side of the album *Live At Montreux Jazz Festival*, recorded on July 11th, 1983. It was a joint effort with the arrangers Ole Kock Hansen and Bengt-Arne Wallin – the former presenting famous bass player Nils-Henning Ørsted-Pederson's (1946–2005) suite "Dancing Girls" comprising a tremendous drum solo by Stig Andersson.

Wallin was responsible for putting his stamp on Duke Ellington's famous "Echoes Of Harlem". After the equally instrumental "Hjartflimmer", it was Fame's turn for another "Bluesology" take, Jimmy Witherspoon's "Times Are Getting Tougher Than Tough" and two of his favourite Vocalese pieces with lyrics by King Pleasure, namely Charlie Parker's "Parker's Mood" and James Moody's "Moody's Mood", both of which he obviously and audibly enjoyed.

"Saturday Night Fish Fry" – Party Flames in the New Romantic 1980s

Tons of synthesizers, Fairlight computers and "Voices electric" ruled the New Romantics Age in the early 1980s in Georgie Fame's England, but he and his Blue Flames seemed to thrive on being seen as an anachronism. They simply carried on in their old style, which included starring in a big open air event in London's Battersea Park in the summer of 1983. Record companies, though, tended to play it safe with tried and tested alleged veterans, and what the Decca label offered was little more than a revamping of old hits. Nevertheless, Georgie rose to the occasion and recorded his # 1 trio "Yeh Yeh", "Getaway", "The Ballad of Bonnie and Clyde" and many R&B pearls like Louis Jordan's "Saturday Night Fish Fry" in the current Blue Flames stage versions, and invited hand-picked friends and career companions like ex Amen Corner and part-time Blue Flame Andy Fairweather Low as well as his Big Roll Band competitor from Soho Flamingo days, Zoot Money. The resulting album, *My Favourite Songs*, remains a reliable party piece.

Zoot Money remembers the sessions: "It was somewhere in Soho, or did we do it in Olympic? I'm not sure where it was done [it was recorded in Old Smithy Studios, Worcester, and PRT Studios in London] and I know it was painless. He said 'We'll just do stuff that you are familiar with. I just want your input on a couple of things'. Of course, Clive comes over as a serious performing artist, but he loves having people in for a kick and a laugh. He does like to have fun while he is recording. That is most important. On gigs, he will come over as soon as you set up on gigs, he'll say 'Why are you so happy?' and you go 'I am actually happy tonight, it's alright'."

The Blue Flames would always remain a solid live attraction during the 1980s – with consistent, high calibre protagonists. They had two first-rate saxophonists in Peter King on the alto and Steve Gregory on tenor saxophone.

Peter King, born 1940, had played Ronnie Scott's Club when he was just nineteen, worked in the Johnny Dankworth Orchestra and showed his chops with Ray Charles and Maynard Ferguson. He is reputed as one of the best alto players in the world, was a member of the Brussels Big Band as well as Charlie Watts' Tentet, who also played Ronnie Scott's. Most impressively for Fame, who had worked with him as early as 1967's *Two Faces Of Fame*, he also collaborated with Vocalese master Jon Hendricks.

Steve Gregory, born 1945, a revered soprano, tenor and alto saxophonist and also an accomplished flute player, had been a member of The Alan Price Set, had worked Alan's "I Put A Spell On You" supplier Screaming Jay Hawkins and for Georgie as well as Geno Washington and the Ram Jam Band, and later famously played with Ginger Baker's Air Force, and subsequently would spend working time in Nigeria with Ginger's buddy Fela Kuti.

His session catalogue includes Screaming Jay Hawkins, Chris Rea, Amazulu, George Michael and the Rolling Stones. During 1983 and 1984, there were quite a few Blue Flames dates that Gregory could not do because of his commitment to playing for the big Animals reunion, which at the time comprised all of the original members, including former boss Alan Price, as well as Zoot Money on organ. Other exciting live commitments by Steve Gregory were with the Funk Big Band Gonzales, which sported many more Blue Flames horns like original saxophonists Mick Eve and Buddy Beadle.

Some signature tunes which feature Steve Gregory are the Rolling Stones' 1969 comeback "Honky Tonk Women", George Michael's "Careless Whisper" and New Wave turned Jazz lady Alison Moyet's "That Ole Devil Called Love".

After leaving the Blue Flames in 1983, Steve Gregory was still busy working in Van Morrison's band, and also started to record his first solo album, the instrumental work *Bushfire,* a Caribbean flavoured affair, produced by Reggae legend Dennis Bovel and crediting British poet Linton Kwesi Johnson. This came as no surprise at all as Gregory had played for the likes of Steel Pulse and Amazulu.

While assistant engineer Henry Holder's synthed keyboards are an acquired taste on *Bushfire*, Robert Ahwai plays a cool guitar throughout, and engineering partner Dennis Blake grooves on drums for Gregory's saxes and flute to shine.

Of special note is Georgie Fame's first appearance on the album's title track: "Bushfire" features three Blue Flames in Gregory, Fame and trumpeter Eddie "Tan Tan" Thornton, while Queen's quiet member John Deacon (his band had employed Gregory for "One Year Of Love") lays down the bass line over John Kpiaye's guitar in order to let Gregory fly. Fame is not credited on this one, but his Hammond off-beat touches are clearly detected.

Georgie does get a credit on the oriental Blue Beat "East Of Aman", where he seems at home like in the old Flamingo days, but as always leaves the limelight to Gregory, before being asked to solo in a short and sweet way. "Oasis" is clearly hypnotic, settling for yet another, very percussive Reggae Funk groove, where Georgie seems to listen but then delivers a lively, fitting solo passage and turns over to the boss in time.

"Work-out" is one of only two non-Steve Gregory compositions, supplied by Linton Kwesi Johnson, maybe the best of Georgie Fame's performances here. Never one to repeat himself, but still always easily detectable, his playing oozes a warmth and sophistication without which this track would be much the poorer.

In his own band, Fame still alternated between Brian Odgers and Ian "B.B." Richardson on bass, and he employed drummer Dave Cutler and Geoff Dunn. On guitar, he had the young Ronnie Johnson from Richmond in Surrey. Johnson had once been discovered by Beatles film director Richard Lester, played in Lional Bart's *Oliver!* and worked at the legendary "Speakeasy" Club in London. When he auditioned for Georgie, he had already played on three Peter Green albums: *In The Skies* (1979), *Little Dreamer* (1980) and *Watcha Gonna Do* (1981).

Ronnie Johnson's history is interestingly related to that of Fame: "I started out playing the flute, but the problem was I wasn't learning chords. So I picked an instrument – I would have liked the piano, but really, that would have cost a lot of money. So the guitar is easy, isn't it, and then the bloody thing took over."

Johnson continues: "I used to have this little group called Seventh Heaven which was instrumental music, two black guys and two white guys. Great fun and we caused a little bit of a stir on the London club scene. We were in the Speakeasy one night, and oddly enough – this is weird synchronicity – two guys from the Van Morrison Band came in and saw us and went back to Warner Brothers the next day and said "ah" – they thought we were great. Bless them, Warner Brothers kind of signed me, so even though we didn't put any records out with my music they kind of signed me to get better, which would never happen in a million years these days. "They nurtured us, and after that I went to America to play with a guy called Paul Williams who used to work with Zoot Money in the Big Roll Band. We went to America, and then I got two more little jobs there which I shouldn't have had, and then I came back from America. I'd had some good jobs there, I played with Stanley Turrentine, been quite lucky around the New York scene a little bit and learnt a lot."

Georgie Fame might have seemed a minor career move from a New York perspective, but the man turned out to be Johnson's saving grace: "When I came home, I couldn't get arrested. So I went on a Tamla Motown tour. And after that tour, a mutual friend of Clive's called Rod Slade, who used to be in Nero & The Gladiators, came to a little gig I used to do with Paul Williams. He got me an audition with Clive in a night club in Windsor, oddly enough, where he was playing. I went to have a play with him, and then Clive gave me some gigs after that."

The first thing that Ronnie Johnson had to learn when he joined in 1982 was the repertoire from Georgie's album with Annie Ross, *In Hoagland 1981*: "He had given me the tapes of that, once I had been to the audition. So that was recorded before I had even anything to do with him. We did a really strange recording – was that done in some sort of Edwardian house, some funny studio? In fact, it was with Andy Fairweather [Low] and Zoot. Also, him and I did some tracks, I don't know if they are ever coming out. They were done in Pye, the old Pye Studios, with just him and me. I would not mind hearing them, sometimes, whatever they were. I can't remember what they were. Then we did a lot of BBC Sessions as well. Some of them are really good."

While the album with just Georgie and Ronnie Johnson never did see the light of day, the "funny studio" was "The Old Smithy" recording "complex" in Kempsey, Worcester – with Colin Owen in charge of the engineering – where Ronnie did indeed share guitar duties with the old Amen Corner and part-time Blue Flame Andy Fairweather Low. Zoot Money provided piano where Georgie played Hammond, and vice versa. Steve Gregory, Dave Cutler and Ian Richardson helped play what was a fair amount of the current live fare of the band, albeit in fresh, often decidedly up-tempo versions:

My Favourite Songs – track by track

Fancy starting an album with the cabaret nugget "Rosetta" from the Fame & Price era – but with the added Hammond touches and ex Alan Price Set member Gregory's imaginative sax work, it is a number not out of place in a typical Blue Flames gig at all. We did not know it was a favourite, but it's certainly executed with panache here!

The proto soundtrack machine-gun noises in "The Ballad of Bonnie and Clyde" have always had their fans – check out Guy Barker elsewhere – but here is the stage version, and the speeded-up arrangement gives it a special edge.

When you have Zoot Money guesting – as he would do again fifteen years later during Georgie's *Birthday Big Band* proceedings – you give him a special spot from his glory days, hence Bobby Parker's "Barefootin'" evergreen from the 1960s, with Steve Gregory especially at home.

"That Old Rock'n'Roll" came from the Island album Georgie Fame and was the B-side of the J.J. Cale tune "Everloving Woman". The dreamy intro of the original is replaced – Georgie's mantra of "Children have eyes" based here on Dave Cutler's drum groove; the Ronnie Johnson solo lives up to the title, as does Georgie's raucous yet elegant singing.

"Getaway" also benefits from a much more streamlined, speeded-up reading, which may be less sophisticated than the original, but lives up to the general party mode here. "Yeh Yeh" is as faithful as it gets here, and the performance is certainly nearer to pride here – Georgie not for one second treating this # 1 smash as going through the motions. Adrenalin runs high, mission accomplished.

Sam Cooke's "Bring It On Home", a firm Animals favourite too, is a prime example of why Zoot Money and Andy Fairweather Low had to be on this album. The way these two complement Georgie's crooning here is exemplary, the harmonies are smooth yet still sound spontaneous.

Louis Jordan often gets plugged by Georgie, especially his not so glamourous times with the Tangerine label during the later 1960s. Here, he digs up one of his biggest hits, "Saturday Night Fish Fry", which topped the US R&B charts for 12 weeks in 1949. Although he had written it, with Ellis Lawrence Walsh, he was not the first to record it – that honour fell to Eddie Williams and his Brown Buddies. According to Chuck Berry, this is the first Rock'n'Roll record ever. Louis Jordan's British biographer, John Chilton of Feetwarmers' fame, points out in *Let The Good Times Roll*

that "Gradually there was a rebirth of interest in Louis's work. The British singer and pianist, Georgie Fame, who had long been a fan, often featured Jordan's songs."

One of Georgie's most interesting choices was "Someday (You'll Want Me To Want You)", a popular Country song written by Jimmie Hodges in 1944. The Mills Brothers had a hit with it in 1949. It had been on Dean Martin's album *Now I'm Swingin'* in 1960, but it is most likely that Fame had heard it via a Ray Charles recording – the ex Florida Cowboy recorded it for *Modern Sounds In Country & Western, Volume Two* in 1962. Fame hero Jerry Lee Lewis recorded it, too, among dozens of others. Georgie and the boys give the old number a definite Rock'n'Roll feeling, first and foremost by the straight and precise piano theme used here.[19]

The album closes with "Lawdy Miss Clawdy", the New Orleans evergreen by New Orleanian Lloyd Price, which has always been dear to Georgie's heart and which he adds to his live set till today, often playing it on his own, sometimes right at the start, sometimes as the final number. This rendition is heartfelt, but at just over two minutes could have been expanded without boring the listener.

Many Sixties fans know the song in the Greater Manchester buddies The Hollies' version, but Lloyd Price's version from 1952 had always been priceless, with Fats Domino on piano and Dave Bartholomew supplying the backing band.

A special significance for Georgie: the term "Lawdy Miss Clawdy" stemmed from Price's radio jingles for Nola's radio station WBOK. A catch phrase by "Okey Dokey" Smith, he used it for adverts like "Lawdy Miss Clawdy, eat Mother's Homemade Pies and drink Maxwell House Coffee!" Listeners liked that slogan so much, Price just had to make a song out of it – and how could Georgie resist, having become a Maxwell House endorser himself in the early 1970s?!

Finally, as a reminder of the old Larry Parnes days, "Lawdy Miss Clawdy" had been recorded by his stable mate Duffy Power together with the Fentones, Duffy having asked specifically for Ginger Baker as the drummer for the session a fact which he regretted during our interview in 2012: "That was a mistake, really, because Ginger was much too heavy, far too heavy for them, but I wanted Ginger to play for me any time. So being greedy and because Ginger was there, I got him. I was used to him via the connection to Graham Bond."

Like Georgie actually, for this kind of material, Duffy would have been much better off with The Fentones' original drummer, Hollies sticks man Bobby Elliott, but: "Bobby Elliott was not with them when I joined them."

From his earliest youth, Fame has always been a natural with the Fats piano triplets, and he handles these eight-bar Blues progressions with absolute ease. Zoot had often played the number with the Animals, Paul McCartney recorded this "R&B Record Of The Year 1952" eight years after Fame's Flames.

The album appeared on CD with almost the same track-listing in 1986 as *Georgie Fame And The Blue Flames* via the German Delta Music label, which had leased the tapes from Decca Records and combined it with four tracks from the *Closing The Gap* Reggae album from 1981, "Lean On Me", "Everything I Own", "Uptight" and "I Love Jamaica". A year later, the UK label K-tel International followed suit issuing *Back*

---

19. See Addendum

Again, but they decided to leave off "Lawdy Miss Clawdy" and replace it with the Lloyd Charmers composition "Give A Little More" from *Closing The Gap*.

Both releases benefitted from the Hamburg producer Volker Spielberg and his careful digital re-mastering, which he honed regularly via several *Non-Stop Disco Dancing* releases as well as interesting projects like the *Live At The Star-Club* album from 1987, which had been recorded live in 1980 with a number of Georgie's one-time Larry Parnes, Star-Club and other tour comrades: Tony Sheridan, Lee Curtis, Cliff Bennett and Screaming Lord Sutch.

For really insistent train spotters – one of Spielberg's first production jobs was 1976's *The Giants Of Rock'n'Roll* by, hold it, Roy Powell & The Shiver Givers. Who would dare ask Georgie if there's a family relation here?!

Georgie Fame's Brother-in-Charms – Steve Gray

When you look at the curriculum vitae of pianist and arranger Steve Gray (1944–2008) a number of similarities to Georgie Fame's own career are immediately apparent.

Born in Middlesbrough in the north of England, less than a year after our man, and brought up in that area, Gray taught himself the piano at 10, just like the young Clive Powell. He played the bassoon in the Middlesbrough Municipal Junior Orchestra, where he met Ron Asprey, future sax man with the fusion trio Back Door – the link to Fame being the trio's endorser – Blues godfather Alexis Korner (1928–1984). Asprey was on the coach to Newcastle with young Gray to experience the great Duke Ellington as 14-year-olds, a real treat "when all you heard was those players from Middlesbrough of the late Fifties. He'd come on, and you'd hear …" – the piano chords to "Take The A-Train", which Gray proceeds to play in the BBC interview with Fame.

The keyboard wizard didn't just love Peggy Lee, just like Georgie did back in 1961 up in Mike O'Neill's flat. Gray actually played with the dame, and he accompanied Sammy Davis Junior and Henry Mancini as well. He started out his London career during the early Sixties in the combo of occasional Blue Flames drummer Phil Seamen. He also worked in many other bands, including The Mike Cotton Sound, who supplied the brass for the Kinks' regular albums and also musicals/soap operas, carrying his own Hammond organ around: "You had to", he told Georgie at the BBC, "if you had a Hammond, you were in demand … you'd split it in half and have somebody to deliver it."

Gray's first self-composed solo album in 1969 was called *A Woman In Love*. By that time, his love of Duke Ellington – again, shared with Fame – had brought him lots of television and film scoring work. Arranging had come ever so early: when he was just 14 years old, he played in a Middlesbrough band, Jimmy Carr and his Orchestra. Carr taught him the rudiments of arranging, as Gray told Georgie in their BBC radio discussion: "Jimmy came up one day and said 'I need an arrangement for Carousel Waltz for next week […] piano players do arrangements […] it's simple: you put the melody on the trumpet, until you think the trumpet has had enough, and then you give it to the saxes [...] And that's the only lesson I've ever had, and a very good one ...!"

Gray could do anything from light Funk to heavy Latin, as shown in his group WASP with ex Shadows and Blue Flames drummer Brian Bennett. Steve helped Olivia Newton-John, Tom Jones, Petula Clark, and he also arranged albums by The Walker Brothers, namely their mid-Seventies comeback collections *No Regrets* and *Lines*.

By 1981, Gray was part of guitarist John Williams' famous Classical/Pop band Sky, and upon leaving them wrote a piece for Williams & Symphony Orchestra. Apart from working on the equally symphonic versions of ambient music pioneer and former Roxy Music member Brian Eno, he found time to work on the musical called *Singer* with his friend Georgie Fame. The story goes like this:

Singer The Musical – Fame's fab lyrics & Steve Gray's great melodies

During 1984, both Gray and Georgie Fame found themselves working in a concert situation for Dutch Radio, fronting the Metropole Orchestra, a fabulous Big Band which the two British artists had dealt with before and hugely admired. The entertainer Edwin Rutten, a very popular public figure in the Netherlands, was also part of the procedure, and one night after long hours of production duties, the trio went out for a meal. As Fame recounts, "Edwin suggested that Steve and I might compose an original work which could be performed with the Metropole Orchestra. We were flattered and a little excited about the prospect, but nothing was discussed."

Fame resumed his versatile gigging schedule, among it one of his tours of down under with the Australian Blue Flames. Playing in Sydney, Steve Gray called in January 1985 and brought the news that the collaboration with the Metropole Orchestra had got the thumbs-up. But there was a catch – the recording had been pencilled in from March 3rd to 6th, mere weeks ahead, and Georgie would only return to the UK in mid February. Not to worry, was Gray's reply, he could always start with his ideas. Needless to say, Fame joined his friend as soon as he had flown back, made easy by the fact that they lived pretty near to one another. Georgie found that Steve had some great melodies down, as well as the main idea for this Musical show – the life story of a lady vocalist.

As a role model of the female *Singer*, who they had in mind for the plot, Gray and Fame asked Madeline Bell if she would impersonate the main protagonist and sing on the project. They could not have approached a more fitting personality.

Originally from Newark, New Jersey, Madeline Bell is one year older than Georgie. She had perfected Barbershop songs on street corners and came to London in 1962 with the Bradford Singers for the fantastic West End Musical *Black Nativity*, as she told Georgie on his BBC Radio series, and Fame uses this fact often when he introduces her in shows like *Birth Of Cool*. She sang backing vocals for just about the whole scene, including early Donna Summer records, for Dusty Springfield, the Small Faces, Humble Pie, Hummingbird with Bernie Holland, Rod Stewart, Elton

John, Pink Floyd, Roger Waters, Ashton, Gardner & Dyke, The Baker Gurvitz Army, Climax Blues Band, Donovan, Chris Farlowe and James Last. There was work for John Lennon, Ringo Starr and George Harrison: "Paul McCartney is the only one of them I did not work with". Bell was also renowned for her work with Blue Mink, with hits like "Banner Man" and "Melting Pot". One interesting kind of work she had in common with Georgie is recording commercials, advertizing jingles. One of hers, for instance, was "Wonderful Gas" for British Gas in 1982. Another "Get Away", maybe belatedly via YouTube?

Madeline Bell happily agreed to work on *Singer*, although it was clear from the outset that it was going to be a symbolic reference, not an autobiographical piece: "It's not based on me. Georgie phoned me when he and Steve got the go-ahead to do this piece. And he said 'Steve and I, we've got this commission from a radio station in Holland. It's not your story, but we would like to "hang" the story on you. Do you mind if we use you as a model in our mind? Because he was writing the lyrics, you see, and he needed somebody that he knew and sort of knew about my story.

"Basically, when you think about it, it applies to just about every female *Singer* you can think of. But it is not my story. This is the thing. They used me as a model, as a mannequin to hang the story on. Then they could build – add more layers to it, as they went on. But because he wrote the lyrics and he knew me so well, it fits. I know so many singers that it applies to, even to the sinking into drugs and everything. This is not me, but I know singers that it has happened to. They started off small, got really big, and then sunk into drug land for a while, but eventually came out of it. So that is what the story is about."

It was a story which Fame and Gray now only had three weeks to develop. Having a dozen songs ready was one thing, but, Fame says, Steve had the added responsibility of writing the scores "for a Big Band and orchestra of over 60 pieces and a 30 piece choir, and we met constantly. I personally made many trips from the bedroom to the music room in the middle of the night, pursuing lyrics and music. I had never been put under such pressure to meet a deadline, but I am eternally grateful to Steve Gray for dragging me out of the lyricist's closet."

Steve wrote down what he had in mind as the storyline, and his description would eventually get on the released album, (all of 29 years later and posthumously), crucial for the understanding of the overall plot:

"Young girl from a small southern USA town, beautiful singer: She sings Gospel in church and Jazz'n'Blues with local bands. Her personality is that she's a nice girl but (on the forbidden fruit principle) a little intrigued by bad men and bad habits and her first love affair hurts her but also makes her realize the she'll accept the pain for the pleasure – not masochism, but a realistic appraisal of the odds. She is also very poor.

"She gets a call to the big city and becomes a star, but by singing novelty music. She relaxes by singing Jazz after hours. Originally she is happy – she is rich, a star and can still satisfy herself musically after hours but the awareness of her sell-out led her to become more and more dependent on the naughties, and eventually her career is in ruins. In the last song she is given a second chance and she asks herself if she will make it? The question is never answered directly, but the music makes it perfectly clear that she doesn't, thus rounding off an extremely exemplary story."

Fame had always worked meticulously on big projects. He had accomplished the high profile Big Band orchestral *Sound Venture* as a very young man, had put a lot of sweat and money into his Hoagy Carmichael tribute *In Hoagland 1981*. But this one was beyond even the scope of these two endeavours.

In the Dutch city of Hilversum, Fame & Gray then met up with the experienced conductor, musician and soundtrack composer Rogier van Otterloo (he wrote for crime movies; his 1978 album *Tin Pan Alley* featured Harold Arlen and George Gershwin music), who would sadly die just three years after the start of this project at only 47 years of age. It was Otterloo's patience and inspiration that helped Georgie – who was still writing lyrics by the time rehearsals had started.

By the time Madeline Bell's invitation to work on the project in Hilversum came about in 1985, she had started a kind of second career in the Netherlands after a spell of six years in The James Last Orchestra – and this special assignment was something she really treasured.

Madeline Bell was full of praise for the amount of dedication Steve Gray and Rogier van Otterloo put into the music for the collection of song lyrics that Georgie Fame had written in their entirety: "[Steve] did all the arrangements, and he was there for the whole original recording. So he and Rogier would gather up the whole time in the studio, and they got it together. And the scores – I remember seeing there was a stack in the control room – of scores, and he had done it all."

The 1985 version was transmitted on the Dutch airwaves but never appeared as a record. But luckily, there was to be a repeat performance two decades later. Fame: "We were all immensely proud to have pulled it off, and the orchestra invited us back 20 years later. Better still: in 2004, we were given the opportunity to present the work in a matinee concert at Tilburg, Holland where Steve Gray was present in the audience. Thanks to the Dutch Radio Authorities we are proud to be able to make the 'live concert' version available to the public on CD." There was another performance in Amsterdam's De La Mar Theatre in 2012, with a slightly reduced line-up.

Georgie Fame also pointed out that, contrary to other conventional Musicals, there are no spoken word scenes in this project. The songs reveal the whole story.

Singer The Musical – track by track

"Prelude (The Game Of Life)" is a kind of overture into the atmosphere and musical riches of this Musical. The melodies get introduced on piano, with brushes and double bass following – lovingly orchestrated by Steve Gray and performed with panache by the Metropole Orchestra.

Electric guitar starts "Small Town", which is custom-made for Georgie Fame, as he grew up in the provincial town of Leigh, Lancashire. "Living in a small town, dreaming of the future" and making it in music, a delightful straight shuffle and a chance for

Steve to let loose with some fine Rock'n'Roll piano, like Fame himself once played it in Butlin's, with Madeline Bell's influences not too far away, considering her Doo-Wop past on New Jersey street corners. Great cello breaks.

"My Second Home" is about praise for the many houses of God which Christians find everywhere as a resort for prayer, contemplation and refuge, and the "Singer" is fulfilled by singing Gospels: "Some days I'm down, trouble in mind. But when Sunday comes round, salvation I find. There is a special place I call my second home. I can feel an inner glow as I walk through the door. I can hold my head high – it's so wonderful to be one big family, safe and warm – Brothers and sisters grateful to be safe and warm in our second home." According to Georgie, "Madeline herself helped out with one line of the song."

Madeline and Georgie were able to perform it together in 2004 and the later performance in 2012, although Bell did the piece solo with a choir on the original radio broadcast in 1985. Only a few months later, in November 1985, Fame recorded the Gospel-Blues ballad piece as a duet with Swedish singer Lena Ericsson, for a project of touring churches in Sweden and the resulting 1986 album *Georgie Fame, Lena Ericsson, Lasse Samuelson*.

"The Singer" – whose theme graces several other songs, is picked up by trumpet and baritone sax, getting delivered in its full melodic glory and lyrical significance for the whole play: "Young and gay, fancy free, now she says, she wants to be a singer. She's got class, naturally, learning fast, she's gonna be a swinger. She can't wait to take the stand, and be out there in music land. She's as game as game can be, reaching out for her destiny" – a convincing, semi-autobiographical story line, sung by Georgie.

The tenor saxophone leads into a great Big Band finale: "She can't cook, she can't sew, what do you know, she wants to be a singer. [Could there be a pun in there? 'Singer' is a well-known – in Britain and Germany at least – brand of sewing machines!] Swinging high, swinging low, there you go, she wants to be a singer." This can also be found on the 1992 *City Life* album, starring Fame & Bell, plus the BBC Big Band, arranged by, who else, Steve Gray.

The main theme of the *Singer* title song leads into "Learning". Madeline sings "Venturing unprepared into the unknown" in this slow, darkly symphonic ballad, with her as the "Singer" about to dare leaving the more bourgeois path of a nine-to-five job and going in for a career in music that may be an existential risk but ultimately an inevitable course to be followed. Then "what's done is done, a new age has begun" – relief about the decision sets in, and the protagonist, Madeline, can proudly say she is gathering experience: "I'm learning".

A great horn theme with exciting metropolis meanderings lead into "Big Town", a kind of prequel to the great original *Singer* number "City Life". "Big Town" is about this scenario: "All the streets and sidewalks will be busy, city people coming to your show, and the orchestra playing the overture right now", a really stunning and exciting musical description of what it must feel like to perform in a huge town for the first time. "The critics loved you every minute", sums up the reaction. The Swing is only interrupted by small slow sections, and again there is a reference to the *Singer* theme, before a Funk pattern is introduced, bringing home the "novelty" factor Gray wrote about.

Consequently, "That's How Hit Records Are Made (The Crap Song)" is first full of orchestral drama, with Madeline Bell: "Welcome to the big time, prime time, glitter time, and goodbye to the grit and grime that used to be." She seems intent on following the part lined out for her by the agent: "Instead of singing the Blues, I'll sing the songs they'll choose for me". The dramatic ballad intro leads into an optimistic old time Swing that states that she has "kissed the Blues goodbye". And now, "Popularity's soaring", she's "learned to love success". "The record producer makes all the decisions, the company calls me an ass in the song!" Adding to Madeline Bell's impact, a gorgeous Hollywood type choir is used very effectively here.

"The Blues And Me" is a perfect early-in-the-morning lament which would become a minor classic for Georgie Fame in the last two decades, even without a proper release of the *Singer* Musical Play. Fame would use it as a title track for his second Go Jazz album *The Blues And Me* in 1992, and the song is also on *City Life*. In the show, Madeline does it mainly: "It's after hours, those wee small hours between night and day. I'm out relaxing, instead of acting my part on the stage. Things I get up to, things I ought not to, nobody's business but mine. The Blues and me, we get along fine."

Another hint at the title theme, and then "Where Do You Go From Here?" has Georgie point out: "You had the world dancing to your tune". He claims that for the *Singer*, "the thrill has gone" now. This turns out as a nicely syncopated up-tempo arrangement with flute interludes. "Where you're at isn't paradise", it says here, and that is exactly what Fame thought during his CBS period 1967–1971, whose atmosphere this song somehow evokes: where do you go from here? Melancholic piano touches end this number and lead into:

"Isn't It Strange", which turns out as another expressive ballad for Madeline Bell: "Isn't it strange, one day you look around, and everything you always wanted, lies forgotten on the floor, you don't want it anymore." – "The morning came, and I had it all", she states, and now what's more important, it seems, is that "I need a dream or two to help me through the day". This has become necessary because of a crucial change: "Isn't it strange how time can catch you unawares and all the friends that you once knew have gone away" is a bitter conclusion to make. The sad flugelhorn performance underlines the message in an exemplary way.

"Be True To Yourself" is what both protagonists can now firmly agree on in this Blues number. "Some people live in a fantasy", Madeline Bell begins, but has found her personal answer: "Be true to yourself, and the truth will come on to you – "truth in yourself". To which Georgie's confirming answer is that "drifting apart from reality, out on the sidelines of life, and the best years of youth are spent searching for some truth, while the truth is left behind!" Madeline and Georgie both get together for the rousing chorus, accompanied by the brass and strings sections of the Metropole Orchestra.

The moving duet about being true to oneself leads into the slow finale "From Now On" about not being afraid anymore – complete with choir, and a kind of open ending: "There will be a lot of changes", but also the reassuring reminder "You have everything you need", "You are safe from danger", and "You take it all in your stride", something which Georgie has been doing for a long time. And now the song gathers pace and develops into a Swing with both *Singers* delivering like hell, taking the brass section and choir with them towards a real climax.

"Epilogue (The Game Of Life)" has some more philosophical insights to offer, set to a slow 8/4 pattern: "We go through life, there's some times in our sadness. We find it hard to face a new day, we count the cost of moments of madness, broken romances, chances been frittered away" – but "In this world we live in today, there's so much left to say, and there's a romance waiting to be played", one has to remember that "The game of life is a game of prediction. The stakes are high, the winner takes all. You must decide between fact and fiction, play with conviction. Learn where you stand – or you'll fall." And with that, the *Singer* theme is repeated for one final time. Georgie re-recorded this as an intimate BBC studio version with Steve Gray on electric piano.

"City Life" is a rousing tribute to the pulsating atmosphere in a big metropolis, and was suitably performed in an up-tempo, high-octane manner: City people know what's happening – city people know what's going on. Get yourself a city agent, city pattern, have some city fun." Of course, there is the old comparison to the alternative and the claim "Say goodbye to country life" can't be avoided. The song was part of the *Singer* concept, but would not end up in the 2004 recording released in April 2014. It was going to be introduced to Fame's record-buying fans via the BBC's 1992 *City Life* CD credited to Georgie Fame, Madeline Bell and the BBC Big Band – with an equally impressive and lavish arrangement, including a fantastic Latin section. A small band arrangement would follow for the Blue Flames album *Relationships* in 2001.

Steve Gray's "post Georgie" work is way too remarkable to neglect for Fame fans, so here's some appetizers: In 1992, he recorded *Survivors* with ex Blue Flames drummer Brian Bennett, NYJO trained bassist Paul Hart, multi-instrumentalist Mo Foster and Clem Clempson on guitar, Clem being a musical partner of Fame's saxophonist Dick Heckstall-Smith in Colosseum.

Gray's collaborations with Dagenham Jazz singer Norma Winstone, MBE, (b. 1941) include the 1993 album *Well Kept Secret* (1993) and *Manhattan In The Rain* (1997). On *Secret*, which was recorded with the legendary American pianist Jimmy Rowles, Norma sings a selection of rare Jazz standards, including Jimmy's famous tune "The Peacocks" – with a Steve Gray arrangement – for which she wrote the lyrics and re-titled it "A Timeless Place". This piece has since been recorded by other artists – Jazz singer Mark Murphy, The Swingle Singers, and the long-standing Blue Flames vibraphone wizard

Anthony Kerr has done a marvelous version of the song on his 1997 solo album *Now Hear This*. So really, it's now up to the readers to convince Georgie to cover it.

In 1996, Steve Gray contributed to the "Swedish Connection" of Georgie's. He joined fellow organist Kjell Öhman for recording a Christian album, *Hymns From Home*, for Fame's own label Three Line Whip, which has a dear place in Georgie's heart indeed.

Then there is Gray's renowned work with two "world class" (Georgie Fame) German radio orchestras: Hamburg's NDR Big Band and Cologne's WDR Big Band. Together with South African pianist Abdullah Ibrahim, Gray created *Ekapa Lodumo* in (2001 NDR), and *Bombella* (2009 WDR). Steve wrote his *Requiem For Choir And Big Band* for the orchestra in 2004, followed by *NDR Big Band plays Piazolla* three years later, and another coop in 2008, *Peter Fessler & The NDR Big Band*.

My Second Home – More Musical Adventures in Sweden

After recording his collaboration with Steve Gray, *Singer*, in Amsterdam, Georgie flew back to his always beloved Sweden for a complete change of scene. Sweden is not only a welcome refuge from the touring schedule, Georgie also loves the people there for their hobbies and habits. An experienced plane pilot and an ardent car buff himself, he likes the Swedish for their meticulous spare time pursuits, as he pointed out in 2009:

Talking about taking good care of his beloved Hammond organ, Fame compared this to vintage automobiles, saying "It's like old cars. I know in Sweden, particularly, there's a lot of people who love the old American cars. They have them in pristine condition, and they work on them and clean them and drive them on the Sunday – they cruise in these fantastic old cars."

On the musical side, Fame first cut a number of tracks with the Norwegian singer Grethe Kausland (1947–2007), a former child star who represented Norway in the Eurovision Song Contest in 1972. Georgie shared duet vocals with Grethe and played organ for late 1984 sessions which eventually surfaced as part of *Jazz My Way* on the tiny Curling Legs label. Fame and Kausland worked together on interesting choices: "The Nearness Of You", then "Two SleepyPeople" from the fairly recent *In Hoagland* project, and "Centerpiece". Two ever so familiar numbers very dear to Georgie's heart were also tackled, "It Could Happen To You" and "I'm In The Mood For Love". Grethe Kausland later reverted to acting and appeared in popular Scandinavian sitcoms, and she sadly died of lung cancer when she was just 60 years old.

Then, in early 1985, one of his best Swedish friends, the now familiar Stockholm, producer, arranger and flugelhorn player Lasse Samuelson, organized a small combo as well as a nine-piece choir which featured the singer Lena Ericsson. Ericsson (b. 11th November 1952) had toured North America with Abba and famously supplied the Swedish voice of the Walt Disney film *Peter and the Dragon*. She was going to record the Georgie Fame related songs "Doodlin'" and "Guess Who I Saw Today" for her album *Doodlin'* in 1991.

The plan was to record tracks for a Gospel album which was going to be toured around Swedish churches. As Lasse Samuelson remembered in 2013, "We did a church concert, and I think we played 40 to 50 churches in Sweden. That was with Georgie and a girl named Lena Ericsson. We had different choirs in every church, so it was just Lena and Georgie and me travelling. I think we did a test tour for 10 days, and then we recorded everything. After a couple of months, we did the big tour. Lena Ericsson lives in Copenhagen now, so I don't see her that much."

The small band behind the trio and the choir alternated between drummers Egil Johanson and Ola Brunkert, as well as the bass men Arne Wilhelmsson and Jan Bergman.

Georgie, Lena and Lasse mixed standards like "Amazing Grace" and "Stormy Weather", Duke Ellington's "Come Sunday" and yet another "Georgia"-version with two recent Fame/Gray songs, "My Second Home" and "Sweet Perfection". There was also an adaptation by England's fine piano romantic Peter Skellern, "O Georgia Moon".

Georgie Fame, Lena Ericsson, Lasse Samuelsson – track by track

"My Second Home" from the Musical *Singer* with its theme of feeling protected and comfortable in a house of God was a perfect opener for an album of faith, Georgie starting out alone on piano and vocals, to be joined by Lena and the band for the second verse, during which the choir would also set in, Fame changing to Hammond organ for the finale. Lena Ericsson would later re-record the song for her own album *Doodlin'*. Lasse Samuelsson was aware that the song was an integral part of the *Singer* Musical, "but it fitted the concept so well, because the "Second Home" is the church. That was the idea. But the Musical he did with Steve Gray was before the church concerts, and at that time he didn't have that much contact in Sweden."

Lasse's trumpet plays the intro for Peter Skellern's "Oh Georgia Moon". Skellern (b. 1947), an old friend of Georgie's from "up north" – i.e. Bury, Lancashire – is known as a singing pianist, like our hero. He had a hit with "You're A Lady" in 1972. Mentioning Skellern seems significant because he has always had songs from the Fame universe in his repertoire, especially with regard to Hoagy Carmichael, having recorded "Two Sleepy People", "Rockin' Chair" and "Stardust" amongst others. Skellern, originally a trombonist, grew up in the tradition of Northern brass bands, which are often

traceable in his arrangements. This waltz gets a real Gospel feeling with the choir. Peter Skellern recorded the tune in 1973 for his album *Not Without A Friend*.

"Runaway" is by George Keller and Philip Antony Kruse, who works as an orchestra leader, trumpeter and composer like Samuelson, and who has written about 2000 numbers. This is a spiritual ballad, sung solo by Lena Ericsson, who also accompanies herself on piano.

The Kurt Weill composition "My Ship" from the 1941 Musical *Lady In The Dark* is performed by Lasse Samuelson and the band, in a tender Ray Conniff Singers style which has pleasant 1950s connotations.

"Let The Rest Of The World Go By", written in 1919 by J. Keirn Brennan and Songwriters Hall of Fame inductee Ernest Roland Ball, is another nostalgic waltz: "With someone like you, a pal good and true, I'd like to leave it all behind. We'll build a sweet little nest somewhere in the west".

The Gospel Swing "Yes Indeed" by American singer, composer, arranger, singer and trumpeter Melvin James "Sy" Oliver (1910–1988) once was a hit for Tommy Dorsey. It brings some real punch into the churches, delivered with panache by Georgie, who conducts a fabulous Call & Response with Lena and the choir, high-pitched vocal kicks and a great Hammond solo included, during which the choir continues and Lena Ericsson sets her piano accents. It has of course been made famous by Fame's idol Ray Charles, who was the first to combine God's tunes with the devil's music, now led back into Christian waters.

Side two of the album begins with the Gospel ballad "Soon And Very Soon", a 1970s hit by The Disciples, featuring the US Christian singer and composer Andraé Crouch. In Church of God in Christ, his first band, Crouch sang with Billy Preston. He also worked with Presley, Quincy Jones and Paul Jones and composed for *Free Willy*, *The Color Purple* and later *The Lion King*.

"Soon And Very Soon" has an Edwin Hawkins Singers/Les Humphries Singers touch, the latter being especially popular presenting Gospel songs in Germany and Holland at the time. One year after the recording of these faithful tunes, 1987, the Andraé Crouch Singers sang on their friend Michael Jackson's "Man In The Mirror" on the *Bad* album. The choir handles most of the vocals, topped by Lena Ericsson and accompanied by the band who prominently features Fame's Hammond – Georgie joining vocals towards the end.

Duke Ellington's "Come Sunday", the spiritual movement of his *Black, Brown & Beige*, is another lead performance for Lasse Samuelson's trumpet, joined by the tenderly vocalizing choir: "Please look down and see my people through". Ellington had introduced this song in his Carnegie Hall concert in January 1943, six months before Georgie was born. Apart from the original, the young Clive Powell knew at least the versions by Mahalia Jackson and his hero Clark Terry, a former Ellington employee.

Georgie had done "Georgia On My Mind" four years before these recordings for his tribute to Hoagy Carmichael, *In Hoagland 1981*, but in this arrangement, a different intro was added from a marching song of the American Civil War, written by Henry Clay Work in 1865: "Marching Through Georgia": "Away, away, the time has come to say..." –

a charming and clever idea which actually adds even more of a Gospel touch to the great Ray Charles stamped evergreen.

"Amazing Grace" appeared as another definite showcase for Lena Ericsson, before a brass intro leads into Georgie Fame and his own composition "Sweet Perfection", the fourth single from his time with Island Records, which was released in 1976. Like the original, the choir plays a major part, although here, Georgie sticks to a straight 4/4 rhythm instead of a first verse in a waltz pattern.

Finally, there is more from the American Songbook with Harold Arlen's "Stormy Weather", which Georgie again has in common Peter Skellern. Unlike most versions, Fame takes the tempo way down for this duet with Lena Ericsson, a measure that makes this classic song all the more emotional and moving.

Of course, working in Sweden with Lasse Samuelson's small combos or several Big Bands like that of Per Husby, meant less work for his England based Blue Flames, but Fame never tired of recommending how they, too, could diversify, and most of them did.

As Ronnie Johnson remembered in 2006, "He kept telling me, 'Stubbs, go to work out of the country!' which was why he encouraged me to go and work in America. He said 'You can't work in England – you've got to be able to travel, and play'. He is bang on it. I was trying to get Zoot [Money] into it, 'Zoot, this is the way to go'.

"He was doing things like coming to Denmark and playing with Per Husby. 'I am going to see Per Husby', that's what he said. And then he went to Australia and played with the Aussie Blue Flames, all sorts of things. He had this idea that he should have a group in every country, which I can completely understand. That is the way to go."

"New York Afternoon" – A new sound door opens

In late 1984, a UK Latin band called Matt Bianco covered Georgie's first hit "Yeh Yeh" and promptly hit the charts. The first impression was that Fame couldn't – or wouldn't – benefit from new interest in an evergreen that would always clearly be linked to his name. Then, during 1985, its success would enable Fame to record a couple of singles with the definite flavour of the year – disco disc manufacturers Stock-Aitken-Waterman who worked with singer Rick Astley and Bananarama, among others!

Luckily, the results they came up with, including Georgie's fine singing and the surprisingly tasteful use of the Jazzman's worst enemy, the drum computer, owed more to the smooth Latin Lounge sounds of Matt Bianco than to the deadened Disco beat of their client Kylie Minogue:

The first release, "New York Afternoon" – a Richard Cole composition issued by Lisson Records in 1986, both as a 7-inch and a 12-inch single just like "Daylight" a decade before – came over as attractively grooving. It was created with the Matt Bianco sound-alike studio group Mondo Kane, with Matt Aitken strumming an acoustic guitar and programming drum computers and keyboards played by Andy Stennett and Mike Stock.

They featured the female singers Dee Lewis and Coral Gordon, with Georgie Fame as their "guest star", "walking through the arts show in Washington Square, heard some

Jazz on the Lower East Side", by all accounts feeling at ease with the Brazilian groove. The maxi single came with a long version as well as the shorter, more bass-heavy "Little Samba Mix". Then there was the B-side's "Nip On Mix" which was sung by the girls only, completed with the instrumental number "Manhattan Morning", played in a Bossa Nova rhythm like the other three tracks. It reached a respectable number #70 in the British charts.

The follow-up was issued by Chrysalis/Warner Brothers, presenting a 7-inch and an over seven minutes long 12-inch version of "Samba (Toda Benina Baiana Mix)", composed by Gilberto Gil with English lyrics by Georgie himself, who sang Portuguese, too, and managed to make this recording as easy-on-the-ear as the predecessor, absolute airplay stuff which reached the top one hundred in the UK, too, peaking at #81.

This time, Georgie had been able to supply his own B-side, his own production of the Candida Lycett Green/Georgie Fame composition "Willow King", which did not have the high-octane two 48-channel dance floor sheen of Mike Stock, Matt Aitken and Pete Waterman, but kept with the lively, whistle-driven Samba idiom of the A-side. Written and recorded in 1982 as a tribute for the cricket player Vivien Richards, the song had originally been part of a bigger concept of portraying masters of special skills, not necessarily in music: *Heroes*.

The Aussie Blue Flames – Touring and recording "down under"

For a number of years, Fame had performed "down under" on an annual basis, and therefore assembled an Australian Blue Flames version, for several tours and album sessions in September 1987 at Albert Studio in Sydney. Their album *No Worries* came out on the Swedish Four Leaf Clover label in 1988. As well as revamping tried and road tested live highlights like Louis Jordan's "Saturday Night Fish Fry", he seemed to have immense fun with the injection of their own enjoyment and expertise in the process.

Especially, having Sri Lankan percussionist Sunil De Silva on congas brings to mind fond memories of old UK Blue Flames cohort Speedy Acquaye. Quite independently of any prevailing nostalgia, however, this tiny percussive detail makes one hell of a difference and begs the question whether Georgie should have filled the conga vacancy on a permanent basis beyond this outfit at the other end of the world. (As an anorak's aside, Sunil De Silva later played Las Vegas with the appropriately named fellow rhythm ace Ron Powell.)

Fame chose to revisit four of his own compositions: "Eros Hotel", "Little Samba" and "Zulu" from the *Right Now!* album and also "Cat's Eyes" from *That's What Friends Are For*. This probably made sense, as Georgie's Pye albums were even more difficult to purchase in Australia eight years after Pye Records/PRT folded, and it also gave Aussie fans a chance to buy the material featured on stage there. Also, such re-workings always contained a dedicated and inspired love of detail. But the album also presented four valuable brand new additions to the Fame canon, as will be revealed in detail below.

No Worries – track by track

"Oh Lady Be Good" shows Georgie on piano and vocals as the great Gershwin lover again, in a song from the 1986 British tour production *Singing on 10th Avenue* in which he co-starred. Fame has always enjoyed digging into the American Songbook, like in this 1924 song which was often introduced in the 1941 Broadway show of the same name, and which was also recorded by Ella Fitzgerald. It has the laconic easy mid-tempo Swing groove which has always suited Georgie best. In contrast, the admired sax legend Ronnie Scott had played the tune both as a very slow late-night ballad and then an up-tempo Swing in one of the first British Bebop recordings, made in London by his Esquire Five in January 1948, almost four decades before this Aussie version. And by co-incidence, Georgie had just started to play Ronnie Scott's Club in Soho, London, with a Jazz quartet featuring Peter King.

Fame plays a piano with a slight honky-tonk Western feel to great effect on "Old Buttermilk Sky", which could be seen as serving as a kind of encore to *In Hoagland 1981*, because this Hoagy Carmichael song, written with Jack Brooks of "That's Amore" fame, was not included in Fame and Annie Ross's tribute album with the Harry South Big Band. Contrary to Hoagy's own lazy, laid-back reading with Lou Bring's Orchestra from 1946, Georgie and the Aussie Blue Flames Brass love their high speed samba here, making for a hilarious, jolly party effect, with Jimmy Doyle's guitar licks announcing the Midnight Special train and also some great trombone playing courtesy of James Greening.

"Eros Hotel" is Georgie's third studio version of the song. After its debut on *Right Now!*, and the quite different Reggae version on *Closing The Gap*, this one has Fame use synthesizer and keyboard strings for the first time since *In Hoagland*, augmented by Col Loughnan on flute. The second part finds Georgie whistling his way into a mellow Reggae section as a little reference to his 1980 version.

"Little Samba" shows that it doesn't take the sophisticated production gimmicks of Stock-Aitken-Waterman from his two 1986 maxi-12"-singles, "New York Afternoon" and "Samba", to achieve a really dance-floor friendly recording. This one really grooved thanks to Greg Lyon's bass and the combined rhythmic power of percussionist Sunil De Silva and drummer Russell Dunlop (1945–2009), a musician, producer and singer who had worked with the band Mental As Anything and the jazzy Hard Rock group Ayers Rock.

Georgie's song "It Ain't Right", a mid-tempo Swing about difficult love life, had been the B-side of his 1965 single "Like We Used To Be": inspired Hammond work, a heartfelt guitar solo by Jimmy Doyle and a precise horn section with Keith Sterling on trumpet, James Greening on trombone and Col Laughnan on sax.

This album's version of the frequently sung favourite, "On A Misty Night", where Fame augmented a Tadd Dameron composition, again features his great Hammond accompaniment. This song showed Georgie's smooth vocals, especially in showcasing his Vocalese talent again. It was originally on *The Prestige Sessions* from 1964, and would give him ideas for a complete tribute to another idol in due course – the album's late but unforgotten star being Chet Baker. Georgie's *Portrait of Chet* would contain another version of this song which clocks in at more than six minutes.

"Cat's Eyes" has guitarist Jimmy Doyle emulate cat-sounds via his wah-wah pedal, and high harmony backing vocals gave the song a different feel from the previous version. "Zulu" became more daring on the percussion front, with De Silva ably assisting drummer Dunlop again.

Georgie also re-visits his all-time cornerstone, Mose Allison's "Parchman Farm". In fact, it seems almost unbelievable, but "Parchman Farm", although often identified with Georgie, had never before been honoured with his own studio version, having previously appeared as live recordings on *Rhythm and Blues at the Flamingo* in 1964 and *Shorty* in 1970. Here, we get the delight of hearing the master's pure art on his Hammond organ, playing and singing unaccompanied and on great form.

Fame's own "Zulu" from *Right Now!* sounds more relaxed here, and was too good to leave out – if only for the much praised Sunny De Silva. Speedy Acquaye, the original Blue Flames conga man, had graced the original studio version, but this one works so well it's just good to have as a "spare" version.

The Louis Jordan chart smash "Saturday Night Fish Fry" had been studio-tested in *My Favourite Songs* only four years before this recording, but its inclusion here is justified, if justification were needed, by the slightly slower reading. That does not detract from the hilarious story of the raid at a New Orleans joint of dubious nature – instead, the lyrics seem to flow more easily and can be followed with even more amusement.

The most interesting collaboration happened with sax-player Dick Heckstall-Smith (1934–2004) of Graham Bond, John Mayall and Colosseum fame, a lifelong friend and – until Fame's country retreat to raise a family 1971 – a London buddy of Fame's. The number was called "Try'Na Get Along With The Blues".

As Georgie told me in 1994, "I was working at Ronnie Scott's [Club] with my own band. In fact, it wasn't the Blue Flames. It was a special Jazz group that I put together: Peter King on the alto, Mike Pine on piano. It was the first time I'd been asked to do something at Ronnie's for a while in a Jazz setting. I didn't want to do it with the Blue Flames, 'cause at the time they weren't playing much Jazz. They were doing a lot of Hard Blues then. I'm at Ronnie's every year now with my own band, and then we play everything – but this was about five or six years ago [around 1987]:

"Dick was playing opposite with a quartet. And the funny thing was – we used to play opposite each other every Friday night in the "Flamingo" in '62, when Ginger [Baker] was on the drums and Jack Bruce was on the bass. Before Alexis Korner's Blues Incorporated, they were the resident quartet every Friday night at the "Flamingo", and there was a different band on the Saturday, but we played Friday and Saturday.

"Anyway, Dick played this thing in "Ronnie's", and I said 'I like that, what's that?' And he said 'I don't know, it's just a Blues, call it what you like!' So I said 'Maybe I'll write some lyrics' and I said 'What do you want it to be about?' And you know what Dick is like, 'I don't know', he said, 'just make it a profound political statement!' I'm not into politics, but anyway, in order to try and accommodate Dick, that's the way the lyric came out, "Politicians lying, populations dying, Flying high in search of some truth". Or how about "People on the left and the right, they're all squaring up and ready to fight." As so often, Fame is just the observer, not revealing his position, just hearing the "sirens wailing in the night". "On a corner", living with his song.

Finally, Fame offered goodtime remakes of two of his biggest hits, "Yeh Yeh" and "Get Away". Nothing revolutionary here, but there is an easy flow, thanks to the road-tested and obviously grooving band members, especially – again – the augmented rhythm section and Col Loughnan's sax wailing.

Georgie has always played the Aussie and Kiwi territories regularly, playing New Zealand in 2007, for instance, back to back with the legendary Kokomo, who had often accompanied both Alexis Korner and Alvin Lee. Fame and his band were announced as follows: "Georgie Fame's career has spanned more than four decades. Apart from being known as one of our finest contemporary jazz vocalists he is also a great keyboard player. He will be accompanied by Brian Smith (Saxophone), Billy Kristian (Bass), Tony Hopkins (Drums) and the Tauranga Big Band."

After Hoagland and Goodmansland – Bakerland: A Portrait of Chet

The singing trumpeter Chet Baker (1929–1988) had become a hero of Georgie's during his early days in London. Fame had started to write lyrics for the cool American's famous trumpet solos more than a decade before this recording, taking up the example of his erstwhile 'Leigh Lancashire Godfather' Mike O'Neill, as he pointed this out in the liner notes to the album: "During the winter of 1962 I was put up by my old friend and fellow Lancastrian Mike O'Neill. The Riverside album *It Could Happen To You* was played constantly and Mike wrote lyrics to some of Chet's solos. I followed his lead."

There was also Georgie's own personal connection to his idol Chet: "At the Castle Hotel in Stockholm I discussed with Chet the possibility of recording together" – which was not to happen because of Baker's untimely yet possibly inevitable death in Amsterdam in 1983 – "and his enthusiasm encouraged me to complete the enclosed dedication."

At the time, from around the mid-1980s, Georgie had been busy working as a lecturer, a professorial vocal coach, in the Netherlands, probably the European nation most dedicated to find resources for the education of a new Jazz generation. He lectured in Utrecht, Den Haag and Groningen:

"I was invited in Holland some years ago to teach Jazz singing. I didn't think I was qualified or capable of doing it, but the directors of the musical university said 'No, we don't want the technical or theory capabilities. We want the experience, the approach – how you approach singing and the experience of living the Jazz singing life'. So I did it, and I enjoyed it, too. I did it in Den Haag, I did it in Utrecht and I did it in Groningen, in the north of Holland. And there were very good singers, very good students. In fact, the concert I did in Holland one month ago in Amsterdam with the Big Band, the other singer was a Jazz singer called Fay Claassen who is now a very successful Jazz singer in Holland, and she was one of my students, fifteen or twenty years ago. It is important to pass on the knowledge."

Another of the numerous students was the Dutch singer/songwriter, guitarist and bass player Arjan van der Linde, whose band Vanderlinde also makes fine use of the Hammond sound, like on their 2011 album *Wind And Rain*. He can recall his tuition with fondness. Arjen van der Linde remembers, "I got the foundation of my vocal training in 1997 at the Conservatorium in Groningen – I enjoyed master classes by the great British Jazz singer Georgie Fame!"

Fame met the then 31-year-old Ellen Helmus, a Dutch Jazz Fusion artist, during the course of their performances at the Loosdrecht Jazz Festival in 1988. There and then, Georgie and the Dutch Ellen Helmus Sextet decided to record *A Portrait of Chet*, another gem of an album which came out on vinyl and CD on Sonet Records in Sweden; thus an import for the rest of Europe. Consequently, it suffered from limited outlets but fans lapped it up as a welcome sign of life.

Ellen Helmus (1957–2011) first started out playing the guitar, then added flute and keyboard, and she performed several times at the famous North Sea Jazz Festival. Trained at the Koninklijk, i.e. Royal Conservatorium in The Hague, she worked with her own band – presenting tender albums like *A Gentle Approach* and *Out of The Blue* – as well as with the Metropole Orchestra, which had provided the music for Fame & Gray's *Singer* Musical. Like Fame, she would go on and lecture at the Utrecht Conservatory, and together, they were invited to the JakJazz Festival in Indonesia.

The cover art work of *A Portrait of Chet* displays a Chet Baker portrait on raw canvas by artist Kristina Bjuhr and its layout was credited to Mike Norriss and Jonathan Pilkington. Just as Georgie never fails to do during all of his live appearances, Eddie Jefferson and King Pleasure are name-checked in the acknowledgements – as they are responsible for the sonic Vocalese design of this album. (Amazingly, in the 2011 re-release of the album's CD version, the two Vocalese pioneers get thanks for the sleeve design: "Cover design by Eddie Jefferson, King Pleasure".)

Kenny Drew and John Surman, who both worked with Chet Baker, gave Georgie advice for the album, as did his Vocalese mentor Jon Hendricks.

Again, Fame was able to present the tracks with the NDR radio orchestra in Hamburg, re-uniting with his friend Herb Geller, an L.A. native saxophonist, composer and arranger (1928–2013) who – starting out in 1946 – worked for the Sinatra-trained Billy May Orchestra, his idol Charlie Parker, Quincy Jones and dozens of other artists. Playing in the Berlin Big Band from 1962 to 1965, he made Hamburg his residence and work place thereafter, connecting the NDR Big Band with artists like Don Byas, Bill Evans, Ray Charles and Chet Baker. It was certainly illustrious company for Fame. The association "Swinging Hamburg" awarded Geller the "Louis Armstrong Memorial Prize (in German: Gedächtnis-Preis)" in 2008.

Fame first tried out some of these numbers in a live setting in November 1986, when he starred in a George Gershwin West End show called *Swingin' On 10th Avenue*, which was then taken on the road through the whole of the UK.

Georgie: "*Swinging On 10th Avenue* was a tour I did with a trumpet player called Keith Smith, and a great English singer called Elaine Delmar. We just did a big tour in England celebrating the music of George Gershwin, which gave me a chance to sing some of the Chet Baker trumpet solos. "But Not For Me" was written by George Gershwin, and "How Long Has This Been Going On?", and so I put lyrics to the Chet Baker trumpet solos."

A Portrait of Chet – Georgie Fame/Ellen Helmus Sextet, track by track

"The More I See You", had been track six on Chet Baker's album *It Could Happen To You*, of which seven tracks were interpreted on this collection. The number had been composed by Mack Gordon and Harry Warren, a mellow Swing piece from 1945 which got famous via the movie *Diamond Horseshoe*, where it was sung by Dick Haymes. From Nat King Cole to the Four Freshman there is a wide palette of singers who tackled it – and for song spotter nerds, Baker had his version out a full eight years before Chris Montez got the hit, which again found film fame, via Roman Polanski's *Frantic* with Harrison Ford.

Georgie gives it a careful, clever but easily floating arrangement, where Ellen Helmus' flute takes prominence. Jo Krause lets his drums groove ever more dynamically during the rendition, and the vibraphone of Frits Landesbergen – who also happens to be Madeline Bell's long time band leader – can be enjoyed especially during a lovely solo. Georgie obviously loves the song, revelling in its melody with panache and comfort and adding his own lyrics for Baker's trumpet solo.

"On A Misty Night", as mentioned from the 1964 Baker *Prestige Sessions*, and *Boppin' With The Chet Baker Quintet*, is much more mellow again than the version which Georgie had presented the previous year on *No Worries*, Landesbergen's vibes and Frans Tunderman's double bass creating a very different and welcome feel. The Vocalese lyrics for the Chet solo are again Fame-made.

Richard Rodgers and Lorenz Hart's "Dancing On The Ceiling" (nothing to do with the 1986 Lionel Richie song and album of the same name) goes back to the popular 1930 Musical *Ever Green* and had been done by Ella Fitzgerald as well as Frank Sinatra in the mid-1950s – the lyrics for Chet Baker's trumpet section on *It Could Happen To You* were created by Georgie himself.

George and Ira Gershwin's "How Long Has This Been Going On?" from 1927 was done by Sarah Vaughn, Julie London, Louis Armstrong with Oscar Peterson – the list is again endless. Here, it's dominated by the warm and pleasant chords of Peter Nieuwerf's guitar – and is therefore a kind of prequel to Fame's 2013 guitar & bass album *Lost In A Lover's Dream*. With solo lyrics again by himself, he and Van Morrison would make this the title song for their joint 1995 album. Georgie created his lyrics for the trumpet solos of this song during a stay in the Portuguese Algarve (south of Portugal). He told our friend António Alfaiate that he was then an ardent golfer – which he dropped "in the meantime" as boring. But in the late 1980s, Fame had come to the Algarve for a week of playing golf. Unfortunately it rained solidly for the whole week, so Georgie chose to stay mainly in his hotel room, where he wrote the lyrics for "But Not For Me".

The Gershwin brothers did "But Not For Me" in 1930 for *Girl Crazy* with Ginger Rogers. Apart from the usual Jazz suspects like Ella & Coltrane on both ends of that vast spectrum, over the years it was performed by Linda Ronstadt, and Elvis Costello was allowed to do it for *The Glory Of Gershwin* in 1994. Georgie loves it because of his own Vocalese contribution and is in great harmony with the Helmus ensemble here, giving Nieuwerf the chance for a sophisticated, subdued guitar solo. He did another deeply felt version on *Poet In New York* in 2000.

With "Do It The Hard Way" it's back to Rodgers and Hart and familiar territory for Georgie – he finished his album *The Two Faces Of Fame* with this song, already using the lyrics which Mike O'Neill had written.

The second but last song on the vintage '67 *Two Faces* album had been Chet Baker's title track, "It Could Happen To You", for which O'Neill's lyrics had also existed at that time. Johnny Burke and Jimmy van Heusen had written the soon popular standard in 1944, and by the time Baker gave it his golden bugle touch, it had already been done by Dinah Washington and the Fame-championed Four Freshmen, with Diana Krall and Robert Palmer to follow later. A firm favourite of Georgie's, this was also too good to leave out of *Poet In New York* eleven years after this – but the instrumentation of the Helmus group remains unique.

A real departure was the lightning fast Swing "Go Go", a Richard Carpenter [20] tune and the second one off *Boppin' With the Chet Baker Quintet*, which the trumpeter had done in 1965 and released two years later. Here, Georgie's lyrics present quite a tremendous tongue-twisting challenge, which the experienced Vocalese champion tackles in a skilled and masterful way, followed syllable by tricky syllable by Landesbergen's vibes, and then followed by a thrilling section with just Jo Krause's skilled drumming for company. Fame repeated the exercise with many a Big Band, too, including a treasured recording on the deleted *Bravissimo II* by the NDR Big Band.

"You're Driving Me Crazy" by Walter Donaldson had been the third track on that Chet Baker *It Could Happen to you – Chet Baker Sings* LP in 1958, and Georgie had first tackled it on his 1967 album *The Two Faces Of Fame* (again track 3). But he gives it a smoother arrangement. The lyrics for the trumpet solo had been supplied by Mike O'Neill, who had first met Chet Baker in Milan in 1959, visited his shows there and was given Baker's mentioned album from the previous year late one night. Chet's favourite, it soon became O'Neill's too. It would inspire him to get lyrical, just as it would get Georgie going later, too. Its repeat performance on *A Portrait of Chet* is very valuable, not least because of the new colours which Ellen Helmus's flute and, again, Fritz Landesbergen's vibraphone manage to add.

"Everything Happens To Me" could be seen as a lyrical continuation of "It Could Happen To You". Georgie had done it with a different intro, using a big orchestra on his under-rated, under-appreciated 1970 album *Georgie Does His Thing with Strings*, following the drama up here with this more intimate line-up. Mike O'Neill's famous Vocalese quote about one of the things "happening" being the protagonist "trying to join Sgt Pepper's Club band, couldn't get in" did not get used then – there was still a trumpet solo, just like it had been on Chet Baker's Riverside album.

For the finale, Georgie wrote his own "Lament For Chet", performing alone behind the piano: "The way that you played, the statements that you made, the beauty you created as you walked that hallowed ground, drifting as you did from town to town. How we miss you and your warm and gentle sound ... blessed to be in earshot of your horn, where truth and love and melodies were born. Farewell dear friend, creative to the end, the legacy you leave as can be heard all over town, echoing for miles and miles around ... Mr Chet, we miss your warm and gentle sound."

20. See Addendum

Chapter 8

The longest-serving band in Fame history: The Vintage 1990 Blue Flames

In order to present the album *Portrait Of Chet* on stage beyond the Netherlands appropriately, Fame started to re-shape his Blue Flames in 1989. It turned out that this was going to be the band with the least fluctuation of all the line-ups he has ever fronted. For band members serving for such a long time, it is certainly worthwhile looking at their background more intensely, and it makes sense doing it right here rather than taking the latter day left-handed approach via your touch screen.

Guy Barker – "Bugler" Extraordinaire

As Eddie Thornton had now left the Blue Flames, Georgie thought of a young trumpet player whom he had wanted to hire before: Islington native Guy Barker, born in 1957 and so 32 at the time. Barker's connection to Georgie Fame and his music had come early in life, before he started to play the trumpet at 12:

"I was a kid in the Sixties, and I grew up listening to the Beatles and stuff like that. My dad was an actor and a stuntman, and my mother was an actress. They were always encouraging of music. I think the thing that got me into Jazz was actually *The Jungle Book* by Walt Disney. I loved it! I love all of that, and I loved going to the music with my dad. So music was always around the house in various forms. But I heard Georgie singing "The Ballad of Bonnie and Clyde" on the radio. And initially, as a kid, the bit that I thought was amazing was – there were all the gun shots at the end of the thing. Then I listened to it again, and it just became my favourite thing, and my favourite song, I suppose.

"So it was coming up for Christmas, and you write your letter with all the things you want. There was a whole lot of things I wanted, but that was number one! That was what I wanted. I remember when it arrived: Father Christmas brought it, and I played it loads of times on Christmas Day. And it was not until many years later that I realized that what it was – I found his voice really infectious. There was something about the sound of his voice. And I always remember hearing my Aunt Tan, my dad's sister. She used to talk about Georgie Fame a lot. I heard his name mentioned in the house a lot. And I think I saw him on the TV as well, so that record was something that got to me."

Fame has always maintained strong connections to the Jazz fraternity, starting out with watching the veterans in the Flamingo Club, using older legends like Tubby

Hayes and Ronnie Scott in his *Sound Venture* venture, and now, with his two sons Tristan and James almost ready to join the proceedings, he was getting onto the next generation. Therefore, and because he has been a member for almost a quarter of a century, a look at Guy Barker's career deserves a lot of detail:

"What happened was, I joined the school brass band, and I really found something that I wanted to do – which was playing the cornet. Then my dad came home, and gave me two records: one was of Louis Armstrong in the 30s and 40s, and the other one was a record called "The Golden Era of Dixieland Jazz", and it featured Rex Stewart on trumpet. Rex Stewart [1907–1967] made sounds on the instrument I couldn't believe were possible. I used to sit on the sofa, I had my school cornet next to me, and I'd have this record on, and I'd be listening and looking at the cornet, listening and looking at the speakers – wondering how on earth he was able to do this. And then it became quite an obsession."

Guy Barker in Jazz Café Camden, 2004

"So I joined a local Jazz orchestra, which was the Harrow Youth Jazz Orchestra, which funnily enough I joined at the same time as the guitar player in that band, who was Martin Taylor. Martin was a year older than me, and I was 13 or 14, and there I was, with all the other kids, struggling, trying to play music and it sounded terrible. But in the corner, there was this guy just playing amazing music, and it was Martin. His father brought him along. His dad played bass, because there weren't many kids who played the bass. Martin was amazing. We did our first gig together then, and we played 'Lil' Darlin', and Martin and I recorded it together years and years later."

"I was practicing obsessively with the cornet [which has piston valves, unlike the modern trumpet's revolving valves, and is mellower in tone]. I played the trumpet all day. It was a Sunday I think it was, and there was a rehearsal. The National Youth Jazz Orchestra were going to have a rehearsal the following day, and the guy that led the band, Bill Ashton [the one-time NYJO leader Bill Ashton is the father of sound engineer Miles Ashton] lived just round the corner. So he knew that there was a Harrow Youth Jazz Orchestra, and he knew me when I was a kid trying to fit in. He turned up and said 'We have got a rehearsal tomorrow and one of the trumpet players can't make it. Why don't you come and do it?' I said 'Great', but I got the call after practicing for about four hours. And I had smashed my chops up, I had nothing left. I went round the house, and he said 'Let me see how you can play.' So I played and I couldn't play, I had nothing left. So Bill said 'In a couple of years, we will see, maybe faster.' I went 'Damn!'"

In the end, Barker did get in, though: "Then I was invited into this Jazz course. Maynard Ferguson was one of the tutors on it. I remember what happened was that by then I hadn't been playing all day, and I sat down in the section and I played a lot. There were two trumpet players there. One was Henry Lowther, and the other one was George Chisholm, the trumpet player who moved to New Zealand. And they were both very encouraging to me. As a result, Bill said 'You can come and join the band now'. So I had gone through that bit and I joined the band and I played there for seven years."

In 1976, Barker got lessons by Georgie's big idol Clark Terry: "Clark taught me; I was 16 and at that time. One of my ambitions was to go to New York and get lessons from Clark Terry, because I just thought he was the most incredible player. People had told me he was an incredible teacher and he played perfectly. I hear stories – somebody told me a story that during the Fifties or Sixties in the New York studios, Phil Woods used to get up really early. A 10 o'clock session, he used to try and get into the session like about 8.30 in the morning, an hour and a half or two hours before, to practice. As he opened the studio door, he'd hear Clark Terry already practicing. You could never beat Clark, and that's why Clark Terry was so amazing.

"Clark – I was introduced to him backstage in the Royal Festival Hall. I was playing with the National Youth Jazz Orchestra in 1976, doing a concert in celebration of Louis Armstrong. What happened was, the bandleader knew that my ambition was to be taught by Clark Terry, and playing on the bill that night was Wild Bill Davison, the trumpet player [1906–1989, then 70]. The bandleader said to me 'Come backstage, I've got somebody really important I want you to meet.' I was frightened, you see, because I had a solo part and I had to do a duet with Humphrey Lyttelton (1921–2008). So I got taken backstage, looked at the dressing room door and it said 'Wild Bill Davison'. I thought 'Great, I'm going to meet Wild Bill Davison, fantastic.' They opened the door, and sitting in the corner, there was Clark Terry. I was just speechless!

"They said 'Guy, this is Clark Terry'. And he stood up and shook my hand. I was just, mouth open, and I couldn't say anything. I was completely star struck. So the bandleader [Bill Ashton] said 'This is Guy, it's always been his ambition to come and be taught by you in New York.' He said 'Really? Here's my card.' He took me to Ronnie Scott's. He called me up on stage, and I sat in with him. In those days I used to squash up my bottom leg and and play with a very bad embouchure. Clark saw me doing that. Then, when Ernie Wilkins was playing his tenor solo, he came up to me and said 'How long have you been playing like that?' I said 'Since I first started'. He said 'You're not playing like that anymore – get backstage.' And Clark gave me lessons. Since then he wrote me letters. I even called him Uncle Clark. Clark was a huge, huge inspiration. So, Georgie did know all those stories. So Clark changed my embouchure. He taught me how to play with a more correct embouchure, and he taught me how to do circular breathing."

The first professional contact with Georgie Fame was one that rather makes Guy Barker shiver until today: "Then I was at the Royal College of Music. I was about 19 or 20, and we were all sitting round the dining table, at my parents'. The phone rang, and my dad came in. He said 'Guy, it's Georgie Fame on the phone.' I said 'What?' And we all looked up. I spoke to him and he had a gig. Obviously, he had heard about me from somewhere, because I was still in the National Youth Jazz Orchestra. I was still at college. He said 'I have got a gig and was wondering if you could do it.'

"I was thrilled and I looked in my diary, and I had already got a concert at college. In the concert I think I had to play the trumpet solo that appears in the second movement of the Gershwin Piano Concerto. That was my first year at college, I think. So there was no way I could get out of it. So I had to say to Georgie 'I'm sorry I'm busy.' And I came back in and I sat down. My parents just said 'What happened?' I said 'Well, he asked me to do a gig and I can't do it, I'm at college.' I was really disappointed, and my mum said 'He'll call you again one day, I'm sure". So that was that really."

And then, as Barker's mother had predicted, Georgie Fame did call up again, even if it was after more than a decade: "The next time I worked with him, I think it was the Jack Sharp Big Band. We did something with Jack Sharp's band, which was a band that was made up of various guys who were around. But before that, I started to work with Alan Skidmore and Pete King and various people like that. There was a long time before I actually became an official Blue Flame. In fact, I can tell you the date. It would have been 1989."

With other bandleaders, private matters like the following incidents would seem out of place. Barker: "What happened was: I got married and I had a daughter, and within seconds we were getting divorced. It wasn't the right thing to do, but the thing that was great about it was, I've got a great daughter, who is going to be 23 on Sunday [born September 1988]. I wasn't doing very well, and I had moved out of the house and was living back with my parents. I lost a lot of things and had nowhere to live, except my parents' which was fine. So it was a bad time, and there was a gig happening at the Grosvenor House Hotel. It was a big band that was put together. I think it might have been Georgie who put it together. It was some company, and I know they wanted Ronnie Scott. Ronnie was in the band, so I played with Jack Sharp's Band plus a variety of other people."

The reason why we go into Guy Barker's fate here is that the reaction to it says a lot about Georgie Fame as a sensitive, caring human being. It was certainly an aspect which warmed Barker to his new bandleader: "I remember that night, I was talking to Georgie. He said to me 'Are you alright? Somebody told me you have been through a lot of shit.' I said 'I have actually'. He said 'Do you want to talk about it?' So I said 'Yeah, alright'. They had given him a suite at the hotel. He pointed at the mini bar and said 'There you go, help yourself, and tell me what happened.' I told him everything, how I had met this woman, that she got pregnant, we got married, and how it all went wrong. I felt this was a special person. He bothered to take time out to talk to me, which he did not have to do. After that, he called me and said that he was thinking of putting a band together to recreate an album as a tribute to Chet Baker."

Would Fame expect Barker to play like Chet Baker? Or maybe blow his horn a bit like the veteran Eddie "Tan Tan" Thornton? Guy soon found out another quality in Georgie's way of working: "Georgie did give me free reign. He knew that I know what he likes as far as what we do. It is like when I get the trumpet out and do a lick that was Clark Terry's. There is a kind of familiarity there. He knew that I was up to lots of different things. That is the thing about Georgie: he never tells you to change your own personality, your own stamp. You just have to be yourself. That's what he likes. That is why his soloists, somebody like Alan Skidmore – Skid sounds like Skid, and plays like Skid, and Pete King. That's what he has in all his bands – the American bands, the Norwegian bands. He would never say 'Can't you play it like this?' Because the reason you are there, I believe, is because he wants you to sound like you."

So in the end, mother Barker had been right – it seemed that somehow this encounter was meant to happen, even if it was going to take an extremely long time indeed: "More than 10 years, yeah – it was one of those things. I was working, doing a lot of studio work with a variety of people. Then this situation turned up. As soon as we started it, that was it – I'm still in the band now! There were times when it was busier than it is now, but there was always something, and I was always available for the gigs." Plus, almost a quarter of a century after joining the Blue Flames, Barker would get to literally arrange Fame's 70th birthday – not the buffet, but the Big Band and orchestra charts.

Outside of the band context, Georgie and Barker performed "Always True To You In My Fashion" for a project called *JazzVoice*. It belongs to a shortlist, or rather a long list of numbers which fans would love to own in a Georgie Fame version, but as the trumpeter explained in 2011, sometimes things are neither easy nor impossible in this music business:

"What that is: For the past four years, my life has changed as I've spent most of my time writing and arranging, there is a thing called *JazzVoice – The Century of Song*. And there is a concert: we have a 42 piece orchestra. We have eight or nine singers from all walks of the industry, if you like, for want of a better word. I do all the arrangements and conduct the band. All songs are chosen because they have to have an anniversary of some sort, basically through the decades. So I start with a 100 years: It can be a song or a composer, it can be a film. It could be a play, where this features. It can be 50 years, 60 years, 70 – so I told Georgie.

"To be honest, as a trumpet player, it was one thing. But as an arranger and a writer – I know that Georgie spent years and years with the great Steve Gray, who is one of the great, great arrangers. In my heart, once I started writing, one day I wanted to write some arrangements for Georgie. There's a couple of charts I've written for other people, but I was thinking of Georgie while I was doing them. When this opportunity came up, I said to them 'Please, can we get Georgie?' And the great thing was that there was an anniversary that meant we could do "Everything Happens To Me", which was great. But the reason for the 'Always treat it in the fashion' was because Peggy Lee had some sort of anniversary last year [2010]. It is that album *Beauty And The Beat* which Georgie refers to a lot. That has that song on it. So I did an arrangement of that, using the George Shearing riff as a basis for the whole arrangement.

"It was on as a radio broadcast, so I have got it. A lot of these things exist, they all exist now. But for example, a long time ago, in the Forties and Fifties, through to the Sixties, there were regular Jazz concerts at the original 'Feldman Swing Club' that was the '100 Club'. The deal was to be able to make it financially possible. The union said to the team 'Okay, you can do these as broadcasts, but they can't be recorded, they just go straight out. If they are not recorded, you only have to pay a much cheaper rate and then we can do it.' So everybody knew about all these broadcasts.

"There is a famous story of them doing a *Tribute to Louis Armstrong* and asking Humphrey Lyttelton to play the 'West End Blues'. So he was terrified, and in between the sound check and the gig, he actually walked out to Piccadilly Circus and was trying to work out – look out to see the furthest possible place to go to and hide. In the end he came back. But he said in an interview – the thing was, he always knew that nobody would ever hear it again because they weren't allowed to record them.

"And at last year's Cheltenham Jazz Festival, there was a library that had almost every one of those shows, because there was a drummer, who was a fanatic: Carlos Cromer. He had recorded everything, off the radio, and the British Library was invited round to his place. And they opened the garage up, and there were piles of tapes and acetate things and watt cylinders and everything. And there was every one of his broadcasts, hundreds of them, thousands of hours, like Tubby Hayes, loads of it. So there's loads and loads of stuff, any number of broadcasts."

Alan Skidmore – still in the Blue Flames

The second "horn" of the Vintage 1990 Blue Flames was old cohort Alan Skidmore, a genius tenor sax player who Georgie had collaborated with since 1969, "using" him in his US touring band Shorty, and subsequently incorporating him in many different Flames line-ups, and also guesting with him in his own Alan Skidmore Quartet. The sax man has always appreciated their time together, including some easy-going Fame type humour:

Skidmore had taken turns or worked together with long-time Blue Flames member Steve Gregory, whose flute work – which was also needed on the album Georgie wanted to promote with the new Blue Flames, *A Portrait of Chet* – sounded as stunning as his

Skid in Jazz Café Camden

saxophone skills. Gregory and Peter King were still often on the shortlist for the Blowing Blue Flames. Both Gregory and King got portrayed in the 1980s band portfolio and would follow Georgie in playing for the Van Morrison Band.

As somebody who has been in the Sixties Blue Flames as well as the one starting to evolve in 1990, he has a unique perspective, one which includes the new generation of Fames/Powells: "When Eddie Thornton left the band it was Guy [Barker] who came along. And by then, of course, James and Tristan – they had been learning to do what they did, under the guidance of Clive. Of course, I have known Tristan and James since before they were born, the whole family, when Nico was pregnant with Tristan. And then they've grown up and they've learned their trade, and I would imagine Clive is very proud of them.

Alan Skidmore's transcription of the solo of "It Happened To Me" played on the *Invisible Jazz* video

The bass player was also going back to the Shorty days: Brian "Badger" Odgers. But his days in the trade, after almost two decades, were numbered, as especially Alan Skidmore regretted: "Brian Odgers was our bass guitarist, although originally a very fine double bass player. He was tremendous; he was a lovely man, fantastic. He was doing so many sessions a day. He decided to take up the bass guitar, and he did very well. But I'm afraid he has since packed it in altogether. Sadly he is not playing anymore. There is a really good recording with John McLaughlin, *Extrapolation*, that is with Brian Odgers on bass: Tony Oxley is on drums."

"Aaaaaaa-Anthony Kerr" – Wizard on the Vibraphone

A Portrait of Chet also included a vibraphone, courtesy of the already mentioned Dutchman Frits Landesbergen. So the search was out for a flexible and likeable vibes player. Guy Barker remembers how they found one: "We did some gigs, and Peter King was on it. Georgie calls him "The Pied Piper". He wrote the words to one of his tunes. And it was Georgie who said to me 'I'd like to have a vibes player, but I'm not sure who to get.' I had just seen Anthony Kerr playing a gig at the Pizza Express – people had told me about him. I spoke to Georgie and said 'I've got your vibes player. He is fantastic.' I think actually Anthony joined the band only a year or two after I did."

Anthony Kerr, a Northern Irishman, may be the most inspiring vibraphone player working in Jazz today. The man from Belfast has also worked with the BBC Big Band, Rolling Stones drummer/swinger Charlie Watts, Jacqueline Dankworth and Kathryn Williams, to name but a few.

Kerr had first met Georgie in Dublin: "He played with the Cork Jazz Fest. I went down there one year before I even moved to Dublin, about 1984. We went down in one of those VW camper vans, fantastic old things. We slept in that for the weekend and saw as many gigs as we could. The reason I sort of felt I had to go was because Milt Jackson was playing there. Georgie's band was on there as well, in the Metropole Hotel. There was one hotel which had lots of gigs going on all the time. And I had seen him on TV as well. He did not have a vibraphone in his band then, but he wanted one for a tribute to Chet Baker project."

"He wanted to re-create that project, *Portrait of Chet*, in London, with a UK based band, and he called me. How he knew me, it may have been Guy [Barker ...] – Guy has certainly put my name forward to a lot of people in my time and helped me a lot in that way. I came home, and there was a message on my answering machine. I had actually been away in Portugal for 10 days, and hadn't checked my messages. He was probably quite surprised I didn't call him back. I heard the message and he wanted me to do one night at the "Bull's Head as a sort of warm-up gig, and then a week at Ronnie Scott's. It was a fantastic message to hear. I thought it was going to be eight dates, it was going to last for eight days. And now it's 23 years [in 2013]" and counting.

With such a long run in the Flames, Anthony Kerr qualifies to tell us more about his musical background and on how he became a disciple of the vibes: "Disciple is a good word actually. I played drums and percussion. As orchestral percussion was perceived, I was taking lessons in three categories: snare drum, timpani, tuned percussion, and in order to study percussion at the [City of Belfast] School of Music – for evening lessons when you're at [normal] school [during the day] – you study all three of those. And I was much more leaning towards the tuned percussion side. Otherwise, I was playing the drum kit and timpani as well."

"I was listening to Jazz. I was in a little school entertainment group, I played in old people's homes, things like this: a good way not to play Rugby on a Wednesday afternoon. There was a saxophone player by the name of Dermot Holland, who knew lots and lots of standards. He had listened to Zoot Sims, and he played me an old Milt

Jackson recording. And that overlapped with my known musical world at that time, insofar as I was already playing around with chords on the piano, and I was holding mallets and playing things. Here I was hearing that beautiful sound. I didn't know what it was, and I was told it was a vibraphone, or vibes. There weren't too many of these around in Belfast at the time, but I played a few notes on one of them in the School of Music. I instantly liked it, much more than I'd liked any other instrument I had played before. So it is just that feeling, I suppose – like you put a pair of shoes on that fit perfectly. It is that sort of a feeling."

For Georgie Fame, Jerry Lee Lewis had been the initial role model; for Kerr, "Milt Jackson was the first one. Milt Jackson I listened to with the Modern Jazz Quartet, got their recordings. It was much harder to get hold of music then, in pre-internet days, and there were no actual Jazz record shops as such in Belfast. There were a few records in the library, and the rest was just what people had. People made tapes for each other. It was like that when I moved to Dublin as well. If anyone went off to New York, they'd come back with a whole load of vinyl records – and the inaccessibility of it made it even more precious. We did some mail orders, too, but you had to know what to order. There was a big list of names to discover. It wasn't that scarce but there was a much lower chance of someone chancing upon it in those formative years."

Like Fame, Morrison and literally whole pre-Internet generations, Kerr was informed by radio, too: "There were some Jazz programs in the BBC. There was the *Sounds of Jazz* broadcast, which later became *Jazz Parade* on Sunday nights, from Maida Vale Studios, and *Big Band Special* was going in those days as well. It went all over the UK, but it was more difficult to receive in the Republic of Ireland because they didn't have any transmitters there. It was like 'Can they hear it from the westernmost part of Wales?'"

But it takes a lot of patience and luck to develop from an enthusiast to somebody who is discovered for the actual Jazz scene, and certainly "it was not like getting signed up for Manchester United, seeing you in the street. But the first opportunity that got me out of the small world of Belfast – there was formed an Irish Youth Jazz Orchestra. The Belfast Jazz scene was very small. There were only a couple of people that everybody wanted to play with, and you ended up playing with the same people all the time, and there was not much cross-pollination of ideas. Now, this saxophone friend of mine, Dermot Holland, he called me up and said 'Do you know they are holding auditions in the outskirts of the building right now?' I hadn't booked in an audition or anything, but I just rang them up and said 'Can I come?' and they said 'Oh yes, you can'."

"They were forming a Big Band, and would be basing it in Dublin. And I got my vibes up there, and they said 'Oh yes, come down.' That was run by Bobby Lamb. Working with Bobby Lamb I learned some of the Big Band repertoire and got into that music. That was the first time that I thought of music as something that can take me beyond this one little place. From that perspective, Dublin was a big city. Bigger than Belfast, more going on, meeting new people. It's what musicians need, as we know."

Still, it turned out to be a long and winding road from even the capital of the Republic to London, UK – and that road went via America for Kerr: "When I moved, I had gone off to university, and basically found myself in a course that didn't fit me. I wasn't sure what to do with myself, and I moved on to Dublin just intending to spend the summer there, before I did something. When I got there, I decided I wanted to be a professional musician." So the move to the UK mainland "was via New York, haha. I met a good friend of mine at the time in Dublin, a drummer called Stephen Kjell. He now lives in Spain. He was telling me how New York was a great place to go. I had already become accustomed to the idea of moving away to a bigger place, and found that to be a rewarding, enriching thing to do. And so I thought 'Why not go even further, why not go to where it really counts – where it's really going on? The centre!' Everybody was telling me New York was the centre of the Jazz world. So I thought 'OK, I'm going to be away from home anyway. I might as well pick that one.' And I went off there. That was in the spring of 1986.

"I stayed there for slightly under two years. I studied with David Friedman, the vibraphone player, Kenny Werner, a wonderful pianist, and met numerous big name musicians, and played with lots and lots of wonderful musicians. The thing about the Jazz scene in New York I suppose is that for every big name musician, there's a hundred or several hundred wonderful musicians who don't have a name. They don't get the career, the vast majority don't. But they can play – just as I think the vast majority of sports people aren't superstars. There's only room in people's minds for a certain number of names on each instrument, and there's only a certain number of nights per week people can go out and hear music, only a certain number of records they can buy. If they're in love with a CD, they're going to play it lots and lots of times, and there isn't enough time for the Jazz fan, however keen, to become familiar with anything other than a tiny fraction of the number of musicians who they could appreciate and cherish."

Anthony Kerr has certainly come to appreciate his work inside the Blue Flames. He grins about Georgie's way of announcing him as "Aaaaaanthony Kerr!" And loves to talk about the musical benefits his band membership has. Introducing a new number, "we will just play with it, see what works. The vibes part floats around different roles, more than some of the other instruments do. For example, an arrangement will typically have some horn lines, either in unison or harmonizing with the trumpet or saxophone. Sometimes, I'll play those lines with them, sometimes – if it's not moving very quickly, I'll play both their notes, – or sometimes, I won't play with them at all. Sometimes I play in complement with them and blend more with the guitar, as a texture, a texture instrument. Sometimes I'll be playing in unison with the organ. I've always got freedom just to play with it all, that's one of the many nice things about the gigs. If [Georgie] likes something, he says it, and if he wants something else, he'll say. It's all very quick, it's just like – if we haven't played together for ages, and then we get a gig, we don't have to sort of rehearse for days. We don't generally rehearse until the time of the sound check. He'll bring out a couple of new things. The old stuff is well in the memory by now. It is like the band has been together for so long that it doesn't take long to get it in fine shape for the music."

And if something should not be in fine shape yet, it may still be adventurous, edgy or interesting enough to present it to an audience at an early stage, and Fame actually says to the audience "Thanks for the public rehearsal" from time to time. Kerr can see the benefit of that: "Yeah, people like that. They like a little peep – it's like a little peep backstage, isn't it? If it's a fairly new thing, we always make it take off, as long as it gets to the end."

Georgie was still a vocal coach in Groningen in the Netherlands, and Anthony also "had started to teach the odd lesson, and I was teaching percussion as well. We did discuss teaching, and I think we both agreed that it wasn't good doing too much of it. There is a balance to be had between gigs and coaching. If you're not doing any gigs, your teaching isn't fresh. If you're doing gigs, it's a nice approach. When you're coming off a gig the night before, it's all fresh. The issues are fresh in your mind and it's not hard to find them. I think I remember us talking about the balance. If I had the opportunity to do a wonderful gig, five or six nights a week, I would, and other things would take a back seat. But that is not on the table at this time. Small gigs in small places, Jazz club type sizes, those are becoming fewer for quite a long way, even before the current economic problems." Kerr is teaching at the Birmingham Conservatoire.

About involving Georgie in an Anthony Kerr solo project, he says "We've talked about it, and it's some way away now, but I'd love to do something with this marimba and these vibes. Some of those – but there are no plans at present for that. It takes a fraction of a second to have an idea, good or bad, and it takes a lot longer to put it into practice. A lot of things are spoken about and agreed in post-gig chatting, but it hasn't happened as yet. It'd be lovely to do something. I see James from time to time in the West End."

"Guy Barker: "Funnily enough, when Anthony Kerr is around, when he walks in now, all the musicians in London go 'Aaaaaanthony Kerr!' Even people who aren't in the band; anyway, I've done it for 23 years now. It's amazing

James and Tristan Powell join their father's band

But the two most remarkable members of the Last Blue Flames came from a very different kind of Fame Jazz School – his own family. Tristan (b. 1969) had been in a school band with Alan Price's daughter Elizabeth and graduated in the mid-1980s. He then divided his time producing and playing guitar in the mid-1980s, while James (b. 1972) was busy in various school bands and found himself drumming full time at the end of the Eighties. Georgie slowly proceeded to get his sons into the band between 1989 and the early 1990s, but not before warning them about the dangers and unpredictability of choosing a lifetime career in music, pointing out that income could never be taken for granted:

"They are very good musicians, and we enjoy playing together. I'm very proud of them, and I am happy that they enjoy playing my kind of music, which they do. I let them develop, and then we used to jam, do jam sessions together in the home. They did it themselves. I encouraged them to enjoy music and learn the music. I didn't encourage them to become professional musicians as a career, because there is no guarantee that you can earn a decent living as a professional musician. But they decided to do it, and they are both very accomplished musicians, and still do", he said in 2009, and this still holds true in 2014.

First and foremost, a subliminal influence on the two sons must have been the fact that musicians came to their house regularly, in spite of the fact that Fame had made a point of leaving London in order to raise his family in the picturesque countryside of Devon.

Apart from Alan Skidmore and Ronnie Johnson, who had been regulars in the house, Tristan says "I remember Don Weller, always, because he was usually horizontal somewhere with a saxophone in his mouth. Mose Allison I remember particularly, because there was a bit of a buzz going round the house when he visited. And I think my dad and him just disappeared off on one of those long country walks in the summer. I remember him."

"But most of all, I remember – not really a musician, but someone who was great fun and slightly anarchic – it was Malcolm, Malcolm McDowell. He used to hang out."

Malcolm McDowell is also a link to Alan Price because of the man's soundtrack work for films starring McDowell: "Yes, *Lucky Man* and *If*. *Lucky Man* was a great film I remember from my childhood. I'm sure it was '18' [rated], but I think I managed to watch it. It was on late one night on the telly."

"Also, I remember we were on holiday in the Bahamas once, and we were staying with relatives. We bumped into Paul and Linda [McCartney] and ended up going over to their house for dinner."

Both can remember vividly what it was it like for them to see their father on stage for the first time. Tristan, the older son, reminisces that it he was "around six or eight years old. The most impressionable early gig that I saw was in Bournemouth. I sat with Mum in the back of the auditorium, because I was probably too young to go to a concert in those days. I remember being very impressed with the two guitar players, Ronnie Johnson and Bernie Holland. I think that's the earliest time", around 1977.

His brother James remembers "seeing him with a Big Band somewhere in London. There was a rehearsal for a gig. He was looking after me at the time, and I was quite young, probably eight or 10 or something".

There comes a time when you realize that not only don't you have a 9-to-5 dad, but you got a father who performs as a popular, in some quarters a famous, artist. Tristan Powell:

"I think it was third hand. I was at a charity cricket match, which my Dad was playing in, and one of the children came up to me saying 'Your Dad is Georgie Fame!' That didn't quite compute, because my name was Powell, and it was all a bit confusing. That was my first recollection that he was a musician and well-known. It was just bowling and maiden over and watching the match. There were loads of other musicians. Julian Bream was there I think …"

James: "I was having a wee in school. It was my primary school, so I must have been less than seven, six at the oldest. Somebody was in there with me. I think he said 'Is it true your Dad is Georgie Fame?' or something like that, I can't remember exactly. But I remember thinking here was somebody asking me whether something was true. For some reason I knew that it was true, but it surprised me that he was famous."

"Brother Tristan on guitar"

This is how the proud father announces his guitar playing son. Tristan may have been very impressed with Bernie Holland and Ronnie Johnson, but choosing the guitar was by no means an early calling: "I think that came much later. At the time I was struggling with piano lessons. Those didn't last very long at all. I had a reasonably strict and unimaginative piano teacher in my primary school. And then later on, when I was about 11 or 12, I started playing the violin, and I had a really good teacher called Simon Skinner, who encouraged me to do all sorts of weird and wonderful things like plugging my violin trough a wah-wah pedal and amp, which in those days was sacrilegious. I got to grade six with the violin and took it as far as I could go thanks to my teacher Simon Skinner. Then I got interested in the guitar when I was about 14."

The wah-wah pedal could well have led Tristan to the then famous Frank Zappa violin cohort Jean-Luc Ponty: "I wish I had listened to him then, because I think I might have stuck to the violin. But I didn't. I have only just really started listening to Django [Reinhardt] and Stephane Grappelli – great. My younger daughter plays violin very well, she gets a much better tone than I did when I was her age. So maybe she will carry the mantle for the old scratch machine as I tend to call it."

Instead, the guitar had started to beckon: "At the time, when I was at school, some of the more sophisticated listeners in my age group were listening to people like early Eric Clapton and Hendrix. And I think just the whole approach to his guitar playing and the sounds that he was getting inspired me to go and think 'Wow, I'd like to at least try and learn how to play like that.' So I think the influence really came from sounds in the corridors at school. There was one particular student and friend of mine who was really into Hendrix and the *Band Of Gypsys* album, which was a live concert in 1969 in New Years Eve, a very special recording. That really caught my ear. And then I started learning things like 'The Wind Cries Mary' or the intro to 'Hey Joe'. If I could just muster the first couple of lines – I thought, ah, I'm getting somewhere (laughs). [Tristan has done a very credible version of 'Red House' on stage with Fame & Sons since 2008.]

Tristan Powell and Anthony Kerr, Jazz Café Camden

Discovering Jimi Hendrix and probably talking about it at home, his father must have told Tristan that he had jammed with the great guitar god and also shared an apartment with his drummer Mitch Mitchell: "Mitch, yeah, I think he did, but it went over my head. He [Georgie] is so modest with his achievements. And having been surrounded with such luminaries, it was always mentioned just in passing, and literally, if you were not paying attention, you would have missed it – a nugget, so to speak. For instance, I only recently found out – he never told us this – only about five years ago, that Blossom Dearie had written "Sweet Georgie Fame", and it had been covered by Tony Bennett and Emily Remner."

Like virtually all musicians including his dad and brother, Tristan made his first steps with like-minded mates he had met in the school environment: "I remember Alan [Price] and his daughter, who is roughly the same age as me, Elizabeth. We probably hung out and played a little bit, indeed, after school. I met a bunch of people at school who were a little bit older than me, and we formed a band and then did gigs and things like that. Elizabeth joined us after we left school, and for about two years we played "Moles" in Bath, and Bristol, and a few gigs up north, and even went to France to some skiing resort, for a paid holiday. It was a good little band. We learnt quite a lot together, playing all sorts of funky numbers, Hendrix of course and then some more obscure stuff. But yes, and I still speak to Elizabeth every now and then."

His brother James remembers the Elizabeth Price Band, too: "That was after school, but there is a school connection, because there was a guy – when Tristan was about 15 or something – who would crank up his amp in the old music school, and our boarding school where we were both quite miserable, and he was playing. A guy who was a year above him, who was doing his A-levels, probably around 17, happened to hear it and came in. This guy's name was Jerry, and he heard Tris, his playing, so he would pick up the guitar. And within about a year, he had pretty much overtaken Tris by becoming this incredible guitar player. I think he was a flautist before, he was obviously a very good musician. And he is still very busy playing, as a guitar player in Bristol. He teaches a lot, plays a lot of Bebop and stuff. So Jerry and Tris had a band with a bass player and a drummer, which was like a school-based Rock band. Then after school, they carried it on a bit, there was still Jerry and Tris, and I played with them, and it was kind of a Bristol-based Funk band. It was quite a few years after school, he would come down and stay with us and we'd have jams in the afternoons in the barn. Elizabeth [Price] was part of that. She sang in that band for a bit. So it was not really a school thing. We were never at school together; it was the remnants of a school band. We did do a couple of recordings but 'amateur' is being polite, they're shit really. There is a couple somewhere, they must be on cassette."

What Tristan could bring to the table was some tuition by a member of his dad's Blue Flames. He benefitted "not very much – bits and pieces: Bernie [Holland] didn't show me anything, but Ronnie Johnson did, and I ended up buying a guitar from Ronnie, which had a rather interesting history behind it. Whether it is mythological or real, I am not sure. I think there is a certain amount of truth in it. But Ronnie was a bit of a gear head. So he used to mess around with delays and choruses and things like that. And I think I copied him a little bit on a Roland digital delay which I occasionally wheel out for the odd gig. But Ronnie's style is very different – comes from the Allan Holdsworth school. So it is very atonal, very melodic as well, but less bluesy."

"So I tried to learn a little bit from him, but as soon as I try to compute more than five notes I get lost. He had a very great band called First Light. He did an album with them, and I was blown away with some of the solos he played – again, in that Holdsworth thing. Ronnie has got an incredible technique. He'll fly around the neck and it sounds in a way like tapping. But it's not. It is actual proper picking, and hammering and stuff. I still keep in contact with him every now and then."

Still, when it comes to defining his main direction in guitar playing, Tristan is one for "the more bluesier ones, Stevie Ray Vaughan, Ry Cooder, Eric Clapton – more or less that sort of thing, the simple Blues touch, not a hundred notes a second."

So when there came the time to join his father's Blue Flames, what every son must dread is making his predecessor lose his job because of the family connection. But this did not seem to happen directly in Tristan's case: "I am not quite sure how that came about. I think initially there was a dual guitar player role for a bit, where we would do a few gigs together. Then, I guess, as my comping got a little bit better, I guess the natural progression was then just to revert back to one. And I think, in the early days we were doing the odd trio gig, and it seemed to work fine as a three-piece. It seemed to stand up on its own, so maybe two guitarists was surplus to requirements."

"Brother James on the drums"

James Powell has been in the band longer than his guitar playing *and* producing brother Tristan. We can imagine the young kid listening in to plenty of jam sessions in the Fame household, but "I don't think there was much of that. I do remember once at our house, there was some documentary about him being made, and the whole band were there. So it was kind of a day of filming, and they were all hanging around. An exciting day; I must have been around five, I guess, late Seventies."

This was when the renowned veteran Tony Crombie was in the Blue Flames. Still, as Jamie remembers "I don't think I knew who Tony was until much later. I didn't really know him very much, actually; I didn't hear him. I do recall the house where we lived at the time. I have got some extraordinary pictures of what it is like right now – I downloaded a brochure of it, a quite nostalgic brochure.

"Broadly speaking, my childhood was not really about music, it was about running around in the garden and getting muddy, and playing on motor-bikes and shooting air rifles, making model aero planes, things that kids do. It was a very big place, and I grew up feeling like some sort of a prince really. It was a very peaceful house, and there were quite large areas that were not developed. It was just too big for us, in fact.

"There wasn't really much music around. It wasn't like guys [were] coming round. Childhood really was childhood – we had a nanny living with us, who was quite severe. So it was more of a quite traditional parent thing. We were at school – before we were at boarding school – we would come home from day school and play in the garden. We wouldn't be
hanging out with our parents. I suppose Dad would be working, or be away quite long. He wouldn't bring any gigs back with him, he wouldn't bring any musicians back. There really was no playing that went on. I remember very well what we called the Green Room at that house. There was beautiful, this cozy stuff that we had, a cozy little sitting room with a piano, this upright piano. He played that, and that's where the record player was, so we would hear music there."

That said, it did not take too long for James to discover his first drum kit: "There was what seemed like warehouse sized rooms for a kid, which were dusty and grey and full of cobwebs and storage boxes. And in one of these there were two toms. They had a mother of pearl finish, Ludwig or something. They must have been [Tony] Crombie's, and I don't know why they were there in this dusty old room with no lights in it. And there was a pair of sticks that must have been Crombie's, [with] really thin, kind of nylon tips which I still have somewhere. I remember we left the house at 10, and I remember I must have been five or six. And discovering these drums, I must have been banging around them a little bit. I think that's my first memory of having any drums. It was two toms, no stands, and I just bashed them, like a kid would sort of thing."

It wasn't long before his dad Georgie Fame took him to concerts, and one day in 1983, he was sure to pick a world famous drummer for the occasion: "There was a time when he took me to see Buddy Rich at some big theatre in Bournemouth. I think it's a mythologized story. I was maybe 10 or 11, and he took me down to this gig, and the only thing I knew was that Buddy Rich was obviously a big man. He [dad] said that I fell asleep, and then, "ping" – awake, I came alive, when the 20 minute drum solo came – I was totally animated by it. And did we meet the man afterwards? We might have met him. Anyway, he made a big impression on me."

Back home, James came face to face with another, bigger drum-kit: "There was a time in his office, which was always very shambolic: singles and posters all falling out of each other all over the place, lots of stuff in this crammed kind of office next to the kitchen at that house, One day, his roadie at the time, Robert Walker, came and set up this Sonor kit, which became the first kit I ever owned. I think it must have been

Dad's kit. It was a kind of green Sonor kit. It was the first time I ever saw a big kit set up and thought it was very exciting. I was probably about nine or 10, banging. They were just set up for a few days, and then it went away."

So James' awareness of the drums came in sequenced steps, and he was – and is – acutely aware of it: "The fact that I do remember very clearly this guy saying to me at school 'Is your dad a pop star?'... and suddenly knowing the answer was yes, without having thought about it before. Then finding these tom-toms in this storage room, and playing them for a few days – I was very young and I do remember that kit being set up, and being fascinated by it. I think those were all big spikes in my interest which then prepared me for being truly engaged when the opportunity came along, which was actually at my school when I was 11 or 12, a year before leaving my prep school."

So finally, there was some kind of tuition in rhythm for James: "There was an afternoon at the music school. I was walking by, and every Monday or whatever, there would be this thing called Percussion Workshop. There was this guy in my year or a year older than me, called Adam Shriber, and he was deaf. And he was kind of a friend of mine. He played drums quite well. It seemed to me he was playing them quite well. And there would be two or three other people playing roto-toms or whatever percussive instruments. It was run by this really cool guy. He was called John Parish. He had this very avant-garde Punk band, quite locally, called Automatic Dlamini. An early singer, an early member of the group was Polly Harvey, P.J. Harvey, and he produced all of her records. He had a real kind of edgy pedigree. This guy was a really good musician. He was really a guitar player, more than a drummer. But he played nice, clean kind of Rock drums.

"I just came in and sat in on this percussion workshop one day. People would take it in turns, sit down and try to hold down that basic kind of Rock rhythm, including the bass and hi-hat. They would take everybody for 20 minutes, including me, and I really loved it, and I wanted to learn. So I would have drum lessons with him for the next year or two, once or twice a week, at school, as part of the curriculum. Those one-on-one drum-lessons, that's the only education I got, in terms of anything formal, more or less. He had a nice feel. We had the school band with him. We played 'Alright Now' at the school concert, by Free, with a big guitar player. So that was kind of Rock'n'Roll. That was when I first really started getting into it. It was rather from that than from Dad. There was a range of subjects at school, you choose six subjects when you are 15. So I did get a bit of music theory as well. But generally speaking I am self-taught, certainly with drums. It is imagination, really. Like most, I had a most serious Dave Weckl phase when I was about 17. I became very Weckl-centric around that time."

Brother Tristan had mentioned the guitar chops of Jimi Hendrix that impressed him early on. For Brother Tristan, the link could hardly be the guitar, but the fact that his own dad had not only employed Hendrix's drummer, Mitch Mitchell, but had shared an apartment with him while they were in the Blue Flames together:

"That is not something I knew until probably a few years ago when we started to do a lot more trio gigs. The numbers are different and the atmosphere is different. So are the announcements. Dad would invite Tris[tan] to sing that Hendrix tune, he does "Red House" when we play as a trio. And he presents that number with Mitch Mitchell anecdotes. Tris told me that story about when he met Mitch Mitchell – very funny. It was probably about eight years ago. Tris met him somewhere, and he kind of introduced himself, told him who his dad was. And he went 'Oh yeah, I remember your dad'. And he did a one-word imitation of him to Tris: he kind of shrugged his shoulders a little bit and put his fingers in a keyboard position. He hunched his shoulders a bit and put on this angry face. He then shot his head sideways and growled the word 'Hi-Hat'! And it was a very faithful reproduction of the real thing."

So how did it come about that James actually join the Blue Flames as a permanent member? Did he actually signal to his dad 'I'm ready for your current drummer giving his notice and me stepping in'? James: "I remember being much more passive on my part than ever. I don't remember ever setting [out] to get that job. It was much more a case of 'Well if you're playing the drums, why don't you come?' The first thing I did was when Geoff Dunn [now in Procol Harum] was in the band at the time, and I was 12. There was a school concert. It was at some school that was related to my school; it wasn't where I was. It was a senior school to my prep school or something. Dad was supposed to play a dance or something. Geoff was on drums, and Dad wanted me to play snare drum for the finale or whatever. I would stand next to Geoff and play along. And it was his idea. I almost couldn't sleep the night before. I was terrified the whole day. I had this horrible feeling in my stomach, the first time I ever performed, and it was terrifying."

"And then there was another time at my school dance. He was supposed to do that. Then I did – not the whole thing, maybe five numbers on a second drum kit. I got pictures of that, it's quite funny.

And so James slowly settled into the band: "There was a series of concerts for a year or so, two years, where Geoff [Dunn] would play the drums and I would come guesting. Terrific drummer – Geoff was fantastic, and I am not sure how much he had done with Dad. It wasn't like he had been there for years. It was all slack a little bit, so it wasn't like somebody had to get fired to make way. And then it was a case of doing one or two gigs on my own with him on the holidays from school, instead of getting pocket money. I never got pocket money, but a cheque for the gigs, and that would last me until the next holidays or whatever. So that's how that went really."

"Having left school, then I started doing more. Whenever he had gigs, he would ask me to do them. But it was kind of rubbish back then – I mean the playing was a bit shitty, and it took a while to get it together. You're saying very nice things about the playing which I understand is good as it is, it's what it should be for that gig. I've done it for 20 years. You get a feeling very quickly for what is appropriate and what isn't. In the early days, the steering from him was quite brutal, on and off stage: 'More backbeat', 'Less backbeat', 'On the snare', 'Sticks!', 'Brushes!', 'Ride!', 'Hi-hat!' [like Mitch Mitchell's memories] – you know, instructions, a lot of that, and the audience could hear it. That was quite hard to tolerate a lot of the time, but it was a very good education! And eventually, that all stopped – I suppose he was happy about what was going on. Now, if he finds something that is not right, then he wants to correct it, and he can at times – [if] he wants it faster or slower, he'll get it. But it is no big deal. He probably doesn't feel he is dragging a beat like a sack of coals behind him anymore."

"Working For The Van" – The Van Morrison Connection
"As much as I can do with him, I enjoy it very much." Georgie Fame 1994

Since 1989, Georgie Fame had added yet another hat to his numerous roles in the world of music. Apart from Big Band front man and Blue Flames boss, he was now back to his Larry Parnes *Extravaganza* role as a revered sideman, albeit with a much better standing and legendary reputation, for the Van Morrison Band. "Not as his musical director, Van doesn't need one", he would often insist though. Georgie's work here, via his warm and versatile Hammond sound, managed to 'encourage' a welcome return for Morrison to hearty R&B – and a beautiful addition, sometimes a contrast, to Van's Celtic world. Apart from numerous world tours, Fame left his valuable and subtle imprints on Morrison albums.

The two veterans also had much more in common than the Flamingo Club, and their love of Blues, R&B and Jazz. Both suffered from being typecast by fans and especially critics. Morrison was Rock when he wanted to be Folk or Jazz, and Fame was even put into the Easy Listening category once he was deemed to "mature" for Pop. While Fame often managed to shrug this off with his "Didn't bother me, never has done, never will", Morrison tended to suffer, as Johnny Rogan pointed out in *Van Morrison: No Surrender*:

"Walk into almost any record shops and you will find his albums under the label 'Rock'. In music encyclopaedias Morrison can be found under Rock or Pop, while his name is conspicuously absent from the Jazz, Folk or Blues volumes. Such categorization is understandable. Folk music followers regard him as too commercial or insufficiently authentic; jazz publications realize that his playing ability and technique are rudimentary compared to the greats;"

Replace a few labels, and this could be about Georgie Fame, too – while there was less of a danger of seeing him on Rock shelves, the Easy Listening section threatened. Plus of course: The only person to accuse Fame of limited playing ability has always been Fame himself; he remains a fantastic Hammond player, inventive pianist and competent guitarist on top of his unique singing.

As Rogan continues, "finally, the rude person who derided him [Van] at Montreux with the suggestion 'only back men' can sing or play the Blues summed up a prejudicial but still commonly held viewpoint. Morrison may not like the term Rock musician but for most of the world that is what he is and is likely to remain. It is only in recent years that he has mounted a serious and convincing challenge to this classification, largely thanks to a number of collaborations with Georgie Fame, John Lee Hooker, Mose Allison, Lonnie Donegan and Linda Gail Lewis."

Well then, if Van raised his credibility thermometer via Georgie, we can be sure that, including Fame's view, the Morrison connection solidified our man's standing as well. And so, sharing immature categorizations and benefitting from each other, there was a solid bond between the two strong and gifted characters which remains intact.

The collaboration started with *Avalon Sunset* in 1989. Fame was invited to Morrison's studios in Bath, where the "Belfast Cowboy" wanted some relaxed Hammond backing for a number of his songs, including the Jazz shuffle "I'd Love To Write Another Song" – where Van wrote about his temporary inability to create: The ballad of writer's block. Georgie tinkered away while listening to the already recorded parts of the backing track. When he felt comfortable with his organ lines, he said "Yep, we can do it now I think". To which a satisfied and amused Van would chuckle and answer "It's already been done" – the kind of spontaneity that Bob Dylan, for instance, is also renowned for.

Fame was not part of the sessions for Morrison's duet with Cliff Richard, "Whenever God Shines His Light", where Van had to fight of the press's amusement about working with yet another Pop artist: "You're joking, right?" he replied according to Rogan, reminding the credibility police that Richard hadn't been in the business for decades by being amateurish: "I grew up with the man!"

In order to promote the album *Avalon Sunset*, Van Morrison took Fame and the assorted Flames on the road to America, something Georgie had not experienced for a number of years. The first gig that he did backing Van was on the 6th May 1989 at the Municipal Auditorium in New Orleans.

As Van's manager Stephen Pillster told Johnny Rogan: "Here was a guy that Van idolized and respected as a musician. Georgie has a pretty light-hearted approach to everything. One big change I noticed was hanging out with the guys. Van didn't want to travel with them so much. They'd be in the bus and he'd be in the car but after the show he'd say, 'Where's the band? Which room are they in?' Prior to that, when the American band was there, he wasn't that comfortable. It was more like he'd step into their dressing room a few minutes before and maybe after the show. But he genuinely liked the camaraderie of the English band. He got back more into touring and did a lot of dates" – thanks surely because of Georgie's "vibes".

Come the album *Enlightenment* (in September 1990), Georgie supplied electric piano and back-up vocals, too. He also led a number of active US-hardened and ex Blue Flames into Morrison's band: saxophonist Steve Gregory, bass player Brian Odgers, Henry Lowther on trumpet and Bernie Holland on guitar. On the album, Morrison chose to visit the East Belfast of his childhood and teenage years, and Georgie was able to contribute most significantly to one of these reminiscent Van songs: "In The Days Of Rock'n'Roll", as Johnny Rogan describes, calling the number "the album's eccentric highlight":

"Co-written and narrated by Trinity College writer-in-residence Paul Duncan, "In The Days Of Rock'n'Roll" was a powerful distillation of all that Morrison had been attempting to achieve in his own songwriting. [...] They found common ground in their approach to performance, sharing a strong emphasis on accentuation and rhythm. Duncan's strange, hypnotic voice luxuriated in every syllable of his poetry, bringing dramatic life to his writings. Like Morrison, he relied on repetition for effect, creating a droning chant. This effect worked spectacularly well on "In The Days Of Rock'n'Roll" with its references to searching for Radio Luxembourg on an old Telefunken, a theme which recalled '*Wavelength*'."

So where was Fame, himself a poet of considerable strength and imagination, in all this creating process? His contributions may have been mainly on the Hammond organ, but that didn't mean he couldn't come up with poetry. Or could it?

Rogan: "Georgie Fame's musical contribution was in turn inspired by Duncan's evocative lyricism. 'I didn't know what to play on that', he recalls, 'then I thought about the waveband, so I played a signal on the organ which is the Morse code, three dots, three dashes, three dots [the SOS signal]. You always used to get that Morse code interference on the radio when you'd be trying to tune it in. You'd pick up the ships. It was all completely out of time, but if fitted."

It was certainly dear to Georgie's heart that Morrison indulged in a long and memory tweaking series of "name dropping". As Fame would put it, "Thank you for" – Van's and his own first hero Fats Domino, then Elvis Presley, Lightnin' Hopkins, Sonny Terry, Muddy Waters, John Lee Hooker (soon to be touring with them), Ray Charles, Jerry Lee Lewis, Little Richard.

Fame's input was even more prominent on the ambitious Van double album *Hymns To The Silence* in1991, where his warm and tender vocal sound – to use the kind words he had for Chet Baker – echoed quite a few of Van Morrison's lines. As secret musical director, Georgie contributed great little organ themes for Gospel tunes, for instance "See Me Through (Just A Closer Walk With Thee)", "By His Grace", or the almost 10-minute-long title track, where he shared the organ stool with Belfast singer and pianist Eddie Friel* for some haunting, dreamy sounds: "Hymns To The Silence" picked up on the notion of listening to Radio Luxembourg late at night from "In The Days Before Rock'Roll", and even used that very same line, but did not use the Morse code from that number.

The R&B material – like Mose Allison's "All Saints Day" – positively sounded like an equal billing of the two, graced also by National Youth Jazz Orchestra trained Carol Kenyon, (who also sang for Pink Floyd and Roger Waters.) But with all his input, Fame knew restraint when he heard it, and his Hammond sounded all the more attractive when contrasted with Neil Drinkwater's piano touches. On the other hand, he got to handle both the organ and piano tasks on "Quality Street" and "I Need Your Kind Of Loving", which featured the imaginative flute playing of then Blue Flame Steve Gregory.

Too Long In Exile followed in 1993, and right from the title track, Georgie's backing voice and Hammond left their mark clearly and were now seemingly indispensible. Van Morrison was right on the button on one of his longest and most inspired albums. On "Big Time Operators", he angrily raged against the music business and politician thugs, recalling days when he was about to be deported from New York. The way he attacked his guitar, you'd be forgiven to think it was John Lee Hooker himself doing the honours, but that was Hooker indeed sharing lead vocals on "Wasted Years", where John Allair took over the Hammond and the rhythm section was borrowed from Robert

---

* Train spotters: Edward Joseph 'Eddie' Friel (b. 1965) represented Northern Ireland in the 1995 Eurovision Song Contest. He registered at # 14 with "Dreamin'"

Cray: Richard Cousins and Kevin Hayes served on bass and drums. With "Moody's Mood For Love", Van made sure there was a song out of Georgie's standard repertoire included, an obvious compliment and laudable gesture on his behalf.

At the same time, the band captured their stage magic on the double-CD *A Night In San Francisco,* where Morrison once more gave Fame ample room to present his talents on Hammond and backing vocals, not least by getting the chance to introduce the second set with a lead vocal on "Jumpin' With Symphony Sid" from his then current album *The Blues And Me.* By now, Flames guitarist Ronnie Johnson officially served as musical director, and Fame saw himself among a number of stars: John Lee Hooker, who could even remember the date he and Georgie met at the Flamingo, more Blues giants in Jimmy Witherspoon and Junior Wells. Dutch saxophonist Candy Dulfer – familiar from the *Hymns To The Silence* and *Too Long In Exile* sessions, was part of the magic night, as was Van's daughter Shana Morrison.

A lot of live adventures were to be had, as Fame told the BBC on air: "I do remember that gig with Van. It was one of the first gigs that the new band that we put together did. Part of the magic of working with Van is – he keeps you on your toes."

Much has been said about Van Morrison's unpredictable nature and behaviour, certainly behind scenes, but also on the actual stages of this world. A specialty of Morrison's on-stage grumpiness seems to be the fight for a perfect saxophone sound, and many roadies may know the odd anecdote here. But more than the other "boys in the band", Georgie and Van always seemed to get on famously. There was never a bad word from Fame's side about Morrison, or vice versa.

Rather than commenting on the Morrison troubles with the old horn, Georgie would prefer to recall his own struggles with the old and trusted Hammond organ, as in this story from July 1994:

"Let me think! Yes, it was last month. It didn't actually happen in public, but it was before a Van Morrison concert somewhere in England. I didn't use my own organ – they rented a very good Hammond for me, a C3. We went to the sound check, and there were a lot of roadies.

"Everything is all set. Van walks on and we start to play. I started to play with the band – they were playing in A, and I was playing in A on the organ, but I was in the key of D! Half an octave up! Something had happened with the organ generator – it wasn't playing in the true pitch. That's never happened to me before! Occasionally it's been slightly out, like a semi-tone or half a semi-tone.

"So it was 'What the fuck's going on? We're in A?' We stopped and I said 'Just play an A on the guitar.' Ronnie Johnson played, I did an A on the organ – and it was D! Anyway, we took the back off and what had happened? A roadie hadn't switched it on properly. It was very simple: I switched it off, and on again correctly, and it was a great relief – we'd thought it was a major problem!"

Apart from Ronnie Johnson, another Blue Flames guitarist doubled as a Morrison man, Bernie Holland, who has vivid memories of joining Van Morrison's band in connection with Georgie:

"Georgie Fame is a very kind person, and so he is the complete opposite of Van Morrison. Fame & Morrison, they are two completely opposite people in their character. I don't mean musically, the music was good to do […]"

"We did several trips to America and most of the European festivals. This was 1988 to 1990. We did the Glastonbury Festival, we were top of the bill at Glastonbury, which was a big gig. What happened was, when the Van Morrison gig came up, it was just me on guitar. Well, Van Morrison played guitar as well a bit, sometimes, but I was the guitarist."

As for some bitter comments, these are understandable on Bernie Holland's part, but they are not so important with regard to the impressive rapport the two leaders had in this band.

Likewise, bass player Geoff Gascoyne sometimes found it hard to work for the two, according to a demon found in hundreds of biographies all over the music world. Gascoyne remembered in 2012, "When I was playing with him with Van Morrison, those were the kind of big drinking days. Van Morrison especially was drinking a lot, and they would spark each other off. I actually did a few gigs with Van Morrison as well when Clive was doing it, and there was one memorable moment. I think it was a gig in Wales with Van and Clive. The pair of them were so drunk, I have never seen them like that before. Clive was on the floor, it was so bad."

From 1990, Ronnie Johnson was the only guitarist in the band, and at least two of many live documents pay homage to the successful blend of characters.

On the extraordinary bootleg *Steppin' On A Dream*, of true "soundboard quality" and released in 1996 on the Luxembourg imprint Moontunes, Morrison would start the traditional "Homeboy" and hand over the lead vocals to Georgie after a couple of minutes. Fame would improvise the 12-bar Blues, singing about "going To Kansas City" and taking turns with Guy Barker, Hammond and trumpet letting rip and being followed by exceptional sax solos, courtesy of Alan Skidmore and Pee Wee Ellis. "Jelly Jelly Jelly" was next, and Lester Young's "Jumpin' With Symphony Sid" was also presented, including – as always – the additional Vocalese lyrics Georgie had written for the tune popularized by Louis Jordan. Again, his Hammond playing was as delightful as the truly inspired velvet tone singing. The version on Van's *A Night In San Francisco* double on Exile/Polydor from 1993 is almost as satisfying as this marvellous recording.

There would be two studio collections where Georgie Fame was to achieve almost equal billing to Van Morrison, see the Ronnie Scott chapter.

The last gig that Fame would play as an official member of the Van Morrison Band took place on the 12th of March 1998 at the Apollo in Manchester. Of course, after that, Georgie has occasionally joined several Van gigs, as was the case at the Larmer Tree Gardens in Tollard Royal – near where Georgie lived then – on the July 5th 2001 and on the July 11th 2003. Most recently, Fame appeared at the concert broadcast by the BBC at the St. Luke's Church in London on the 10th February 2008.

Proof that Van really likes and misses Georgie can be found in Van's song "Don't Go To Nightclubs Anymore" on the album *Keep It Simple*, also from 2008, where Van sings "Don't see my old friend Mose, I don't run into Mr. Clive, I cut out all that off the wall jive, I don't go to nightclubs anymore."

Chapter 9

The Go Jazz Years – "The Blues And Him"

When Georgie Fame appeared on German NDR television in the winter of 1990, in a quartet situation with his son James on drums and brother Tristan Powell on guitar, he proudly announced that a new album of his own was in the can. When he namechecked "Will Lee, Will Lee" during a particularly attractive bass line that was actually played on TV by B. B. Richardson, it became clear that Fame was reminiscing about the recent recording process.

Indeed, the term "a new album" marked a severe and modest understatement. His American blood brother Ben Sidran, Chicago's Jazz professor, and also a dedicated Mose'n'Fame fan, had assembled an illustrious gang of studio "cats" in New York: drummer Steve Gadd, bass player Will Lee and pianist Richard Tee had served as a congenial rhythm section for champions as diverse as Joe Cocker and Paul Simon. The guitarist Robben Ford dropped in, and so did their mutual Chicago friend Boz Scaggs, with whom Sidran had played on the first couple of Steve Miller Band albums.

To top it all, Georgie's mentor Jon Hendricks as well as his "part-time employer" Van Morrison joined the proceedings. The repertoire of *Cool Cat Blues* is jazzy and inspired and contains seven new additions to the Fame repertoire as well as six Blue Flames favourites. With Georgie, "alternative versions" are never a sign of repertoire shortages – it is the eternal strive to make a good performance even better or give it an extra texture. There is nothing sensational about attempts like that, although the results often are. So, instead of pretending to hit profound new depths, he seems to be always striving for perfection, and thus sees his beloved numbers as work in progress. A case in point is "Yeh Yeh", with Steve Gadd's Reggae groove, which he will be remembered for just as much as for "Fifty Ways To Leave Your Lover" for Paul Simon in 1975 – a magic groove that could also be called "50 Ways To Move Your Brushes".

Cool Cat Blues – The first Ben Sidran directed album

Fame's last couple of albums had slipped out virtually unnoticed, albeit critically acclaimed by those who came across these collections – the 1986 Swedish collaboration with Lena Ericsson, the *No Worries* LP (out on vinyl as well as on CD in 1987) with The Australian Blue Flames, and *A Portrait Of Chet* with the Ellen Helmus Quintet 1989, all of those on the Sonet label.

The British low budget label *Music Collector* had closed the gap by issuing the label crossing collection *The First Thirty Years* in 1990, an album which Fame had the chance to compile himself (see discography).

But soon there was a chance to reach a wider audience again – one which had recently read his name in music papers and the small print of CDs as a musical companion of Van Morrison, whose albums *Avalon Sunset* and *Enlightenment* he had recently graced with his Hammond organ and electric piano, taking along the Blue Flames members Steve Gregory, Bernie Holland and Brian Odgers for the second one.

Now Fame's American Mose-tinged Jazz counterpart, Wisconsin music buff Ben Sidran, offered Fame a contract on his newly founded Go Jazz label. And at the end of a US tour during which Georgie had accompanied Van Morrison, in spring 1991, Ben Sidran proceeded to assemble a studio line-up which Georgie proudly announced during an appearance on German television with the regular Blue Flames.

These New York City Honorary Blue Flames would have been anybody's dream – well, everybody who had half a mind for contemporary music – and for Fame it was a highly satisfying team as well. Steve Gadd, then 45, was on drums – the session animal whom none could forget due to his exquisite grooves and who was lauded by Chick Corea for his "orchestral thinking". Then there was Richard Tee (1943–1993), another studio pro, whose piano style Fame always had immense praise for and who is often honoured by Georgie's in-gig name dropping. Tee had been in The Gadd Gang with Steve, as well as the band Stuff, who recorded on their own and backed Joe Cocker in 1976.

Said Will Lee on bass was a Jazz musician from San Antonio, then 38, who heard Be-Bop as a toddler and who had gained his reputation via Randy Brecker, Billy Joel, Frank Sinatra and Mick Jagger, and served on *The Late Show* with David Letterman. Guitarist Robben Ford, who had served in Tom Scott's LA Express as a teenager and got name-checked by Joni Mitchell on her *Miles Of Aisles* live double in 1974, and played on George Harrison's *Dark Horse* the same year, was also on board. On saxophone, the team had Bobby Malach, who as a solo artist was also on the Go Jazz roster. He formed part of a complete horn section together with Lawrence Feldman and Ronnie Cuber.

This line-up was certainly mouth-watering on its own, but then Sidran and Fame added vocal partners as a bonus: Jon Hendricks, Georgie's Vocalese guru of all time; Boz Scaggs, a fine R&B and jazz singer whom Ben Sidran had come to appreciate and befriend during their mutual days in The Steve Miller Band. Boz and Sidran had played together on the first two Steve Miller Band albums, and Georgie had already covered the song "We Were Always Sweethearts" on the UK version of the *Georgie Fame* Island LP."And last but not least Fame's part-time boss, Van Morrison.

Ben Sidran had first heard his brother in charms when both were on tour in Australia during 1986, via the Sydney promoter Barry Ward, as he recounts in his book *A Life In The Music*: "[Barry Ward, the promoter] put on a tape of a swinging Big Band featuring a very hip singer. I said 'Who's that?' and he said, 'Georgie Fame'. I made Barry play it three times in a row as the sun set behind Bondi Beach. It was a name I wouldn't forget."

Sidran actually met Georgie in 1990, at a venue of the Perth Jazz Festival: "As I walked into the lobby, I heard a great Jazz singer working with a tight horn band. It was Georgie Fame, the voice I had heard on the tape at Barry Ward's office a couple of years before. That night, Georgie and I got as tight as only a couple of Jazz fiends from different corners of the world can get, huddled together at the end of the earth, drinking fine wine and exchanging classic lyrics from the past. By the time we said goodbye, Georgie had agreed to join [saxophonist] Bob Malach and me as the third Go Jazz artist."

Cool Cat Blues – Track by Track

Georgie's own title song "Cool Cat Blues" had been recorded immaculately as early as 1976 for the never properly-released *Daylight* album, and would eventually see the light of day, i.e. daylight, 23 years after the event, on the boxed set *The In-Crowd*. But these New York sessions presented a welcome opportunity to create a fresh version and, with Georgie nonchalantly introducing his inimitable vocals to a wider audience again, augmented by a great horn arrangement by Ronnie Cuber, Lawrence Feldman and Bobby Malach.

Apart from the two recordings, the song had found its way into the live set of the Blue Flames. As Ronnie Johnson remembers, its sophistication made him think twice of getting bored with the Blues: "With Clive, I wasn't going from F to B flat – I was going from F to B seventh, and even in the very early days when I played with him, he had tunes like 'Cool Cat Blues'. I love that kind of sophistication in Blues music. For me it was 'Ah, what?' If you were playing Blues like this, with these chord changes, I could go for it. I don't want to hear 'dum, de-dum, de-dum'. Sometimes we would play 'Cool' on a BBC session. I think the key to that tune being 'Cool' was when that guy, the drummer, Steve Gadd played on it. The meter was so good on it when he did that album *Cool Cat Blues*. At the time, we all thought we were rushing it a bit. I would anyway, because I was playing in front of the beat, but there you go.

"Every Knock Is A Boost" is a composition by one of Fame's main heroes, the great Louis Jordan.[21] Due to his wife's lyrics it was credited to Jordan/Waters. But how come there is a Fame credit as well? Ben Sidran tells us via his liner notes: "I sent the tapes of this song to Georgie a few weeks before the session, and he told me he was working on some origi-

21. See Addendum

nal words to Jordan's saxophone solo, much in the tradition of Jon Hendricks", who Sidran admired just as much as Fame had always done – their mutual Vocalese guru of all time.

Ben again: "When we got into the studio, he whipped out this piece of ruled paper, and proceeded to sing the extraordinary verses that herein so lyrically capture the state of the world today. Even better was when several days later, we were listening to the playback of the song and Jon Hendricks was in the room. Half way into the solo, Georgie slyly sidled up to Jon and whispered 'I got you this time, Jon, I finally got you.' The thus genially revamped number gets a vocal introduction by Ben Sidran, who then formally announces Georgie as if he was the compère and vocal partner in a live situation – the master's Hammond organ forming a perfect back drop for the Fender Rhodes piano of Richard Tee, whom Fame had as a keyboard partner. Sidran quotes "Sweet Georgie Fame", the title stemming from that great Blossom Dearie tribute song of 1965. In his *A Life In The Music*, Sidran adds that "while the song introduced his name to thousands of Jazz fans, many of them, to this day, still have no idea whether 'Georgie Fame' is a man or a myth. But in New York, all the musicians knew his work and everybody dug recording with him." Well, you can hear that here in every groove!

"Moondance" from 1970 had always been one of Fame's favourite Van Morrison compositions – and for this elaborate version, Georgie gets the chance to swop vocals with the composer himself, with great harmony singing of both. As if that was not enough, Jon Hendricks again adds a great vocal solo after a spectacular guitar solo by Robben Ford, which, by the way, Georgie mirrors with his organ.

Georgie greets his Chicago sparring partner in true Big Apple style, "Hey, Boz Scaggs, my man". And after introductions have been made on top of Gadd, Lee & Tee's rhythmic groove, the whole clearly inspired and comfortable band slips into the old Memphis Curtis 'Rap'-Jive, recorded in 1954 as one of the first Atlantic sessions by Ray Charles, "It Should Have Been Me". They decided to change Brother Ray's "chicks"-devouring vocals to their own taste and generally wailing in a great atmosphere – and in particular excellence, the way drummer Steve Gadd anticipates and prepares the typical syncopations of the number is a sheer delight.

Every Georgie Fame fan has heard "Yeh Yeh" a million times, on the radio and in their record collections. Does that mean the man is going to get away with neglecting it when it is time to introduce his art to a new generation? Even the Matt Bianco[22] version was history by this time, while admittedly very pleasant history. So what does Georgie do with the situation? He slows down the original tempo, applies a sophisticated Reggae pattern to it all and calls the thing "Yeah Yeah". Robben Ford takes turns again with Georgie's Hammond inflections, and that great combo of Gadd, Lee & Tee is assisted percussively in fine style by Ralph McDonald, who adds great touches to an already impeccable performance.

Willie Dixon's celebration of his life's perspective and principle, "I Love The Life I Live", has always been a favourite of Georgie's which he shared with the great idol Mose Allison: "It was always Mose's version that inspired me." Fame had included a Hammond-laden, groove-heavy and tabla-backed version on his album *Fame At Last* in 1965. So why not make use of a driving Robben Ford arrangement which makes

22. See Addendum

great use of the Malach-Feldman-Cuber-Horns? But this was done only after throwing one of his truly explosive Hammond solos into the mix.

Some loose but focused Funk is next, adding a new flavour to Mose Allison's always up-to-date spy spoof "Big Brother" – who is of course watching you. Steve Gadd's open-and-close hi-hat groove is certainly something to write home about – the wailing horn sheets were prepared by Bobby Malach himself this time. "Don't tell anybody you're having fun, easy – walk don't run!" Right. Mose's vocals could be a tongue-in-cheek hint on how to play this tune.

It is debatable whether Georgie could ever top his reading of "Georgia On My Mind" from his *In Hoagland 1981* tribute to Hoagy Carmichael, but he keeps trying. Fame certainly adds lovely details every time he records it again, like adding a daring gospel intro on the album *Georgie Fame – Lena Ericsson – Lasse Samuelson* in Sweden in 1985. Five years later, this may seem like a subdued version in comparison, but the small combo of Robben Ford's guitar, piano and the Gadd/Lee rhythm section make Fame's vocals come over all the more intense, augmented by his totally harmonious Hammond work – and the old battleship seems to play itself here.

Fame's own composition "Cat's Eyes" was a lost number, although it already had been released – on the always hard to find *That's What Friends Are For* album in 1979. So this new attempt seems entirely justified – and successful, with more Soul than Latin this time, which works thanks in part to that great horn trio that was assembled for this album, Ronnie Cuber, Lawrence Feldman and Bob Malach. It was arranged by Fame & Malach – and what a chart they created! It could soon be found making way for quieter passages where Georgie sings harmony with himself again wonderfully. And please note, any number you may already possess, you will need again anyway, because of Steve Gadd's groove.

Georgie first heard "You Came A Long Way From St. Louis", a Brooks, Russell & Harrison composition, on Peggy Lee's album *The Beauty And The Beat* with George Shearing when he was biding his time in his Leigh Lancashire friend Mike O'Neill's London flat in 1962, and the number has stayed with him and his repertoire ever since this album. Relaxed, assured, performed here by the small combo, plus some great sax soloing by Bobby Malach. There is also a warm and intimate recording of this song by Georgie with just his two sons, recorded for a BBC programme in the late 90s: "The trio sometimes referred to as Three Line Whip", Fame added at the time.

Hidden away on his 1974 Island album *Georgie Fame*, the dramatic as well as sarcastic Fame-Ryan plea for a more responsible treatment of our planet, "Survival", had been way ahead of its time. Its truths and tribunal even more relevant at the beginning of the 1990s, the sextet – Fame & rhythm with Ford, Malach & Tee, equip this 12-bar Blues with admirable dynamics. In the end, after a quick count-in, the finale is executed as a fast Swing, even more urgently it seems than on the original version.

For "Little Pony", Georgie was in "Hendricks Heaven" again, as Ben Sidran once again revealed in his comments in the CD booklet: "As the two of them were about to sing 'Little Pony', I asked Georgie on the studio talk-back if he felt alright. He said 'Of course I do. I'm with the master.'"

"Rocking Chair" goes back nine years to *In Hoagland 1981*, and this time Georgie gets to sing it himself, having wisely left the rendition to its author at the end of 1980. As a mutual tour had been planned at the time, featuring Annie Ross also, it could hardly have been anticipated that this was Hoagy's last ever vocal performance. Reminiscing, Georgie "just" sings, revelling in Richard Tee's genius piano strokes, Robben Ford's tender licks – and that miraculous rhythm section subdued and subtle.

For Fame's son Tristan, the way these sessions ran seemed to be a unique moment when everything was perfect: "The only time I have witnessed it was when I was on the other side of the glass: that was when the *Cool Cat Blues* album was being recorded in New York, with Steve Gadd, Robben Ford, Richard Tee. That was an amazing bunch of musicians, who literally just turned up in the evenings from 8 till midnight over four or five nights, so they had very little time to rehearse. And I remember being in the studio when they did one take of 'I Love The Life I Live', and Robben took a guitar solo that was burning, and that moment was reached at the end of the take. Everybody in the recording studio – there weren't many of us – was on their feet, everybody just stood up, halfway through the song. That's always a good sign, I think. That doesn't happen very often.

"*Cool Cat Blues* is one of my favourites, great sound, great vibe, all done live in the same room, fresh as a daisy, very little rehearsing, amazing when you think that these guys hadn't really played together. And they just got together and made the whole album in less than 24 hours, from scratch, and I think it's one hell of an achievement. I think it's one of his best, but I also love the stuff that Denny Cordell produced, like 'Funny How Time Slips Away', the kind of Chicago version, the funkier one, production with a capital P.

"The word 'production' is in some respects a dirty word for him [Georgie], nowadays. As you get older, you care less about those elements, because they require patience and planning and, as you know, Clive is quite impulsive and not-fussed about how things are delivered, as long as they are delivered reasonably well."

Tristan's brother James, again, totally agrees: "I have [a favourite] actually, and it is the only one I really listen to, *Cool Cat Blues*: a great band with Steve Gadd and Robben Ford, amazing. I was backing up a little tour with it as well after it, for about a week's worth of gigs in the UK. And he got the whole band that were on that record, apart from Gadd, because Gadd was too expensive. They couldn't stretch to Gadd, so you could say to keep in the fashion, they asked myself to take it. I had just turned 20, and it was Will Lee, Robben Ford and me, hah, hah. It was beautiful, I loved doing it. It is still the highpoint, I think, of my career. Playing like a dream really."

Go Jazz All-Stars Live in Japan – A "pitch black studio" and enthusiastic crowds

Fame would soon reap rave reviews and solid sales for the spring 1991 release of his first album with Ben Sidran's Go Jazz label, and he toured Japan in April with the Go Jazz All-Stars: He and Sidran took Bob Malach and Ricky Peterson there with the latter's brother Billy on bass and the Steve Miller Band's drummer Gordy Knudtson. Apart from some high octane club gigs, the band met around 5 p.m. in a "pitch black studio" on the outskirts of Tokyo immortalized on *Live In Japan* in 1992, and proceeded to re-record some tracks from their respective albums. Georgie got in with the *Cool* Reggae version of "Yeah Yeah" – different spelling notifying style change again – as well as the R&B classics Allison style "It Should Have Been Me" and "I Love The Life I Live", topped off with "Georgia", which included the Civil War section "Marching Through

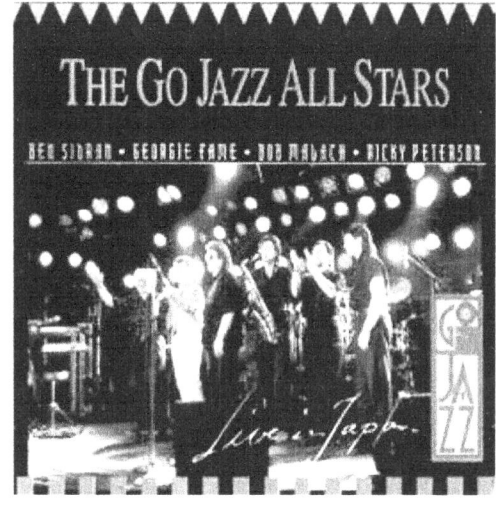

Georgia" from 1865 that Fame had used on the Swedish album *Georgie Fame, Lena Ericsson, Lasse Samuelson*, this time added as the coda. There were some Ben Sidran items like the clever opener "Lip Service". Light Funk included "Let's Make A Deal", and Sidran had a favourite in that department:

"The band was totally relaxed, even as ten camera operators dressed like ninjas circled us relentlessly; Bob Malach's 'Mood Swing' was the last thing recorded that day and remains my favorite moment of that particular Go Jazz Allstar tour." *Live In Japan*, which came out as a CD and video cassette, keeps all the promises about a relaxed yet cooking show and is available till today on Ben's website.

Georgie has always loved touring Japan, quipping "When you arrive at a hotel, there's at least three guys waiting: One to welcome you, the next one to enquire about your menu wishes, and a third one to ask you whether you want any trousers pressed!"

The *Cool Cat Blues* follow-up, *The Blues And Me*, would come exactly a year later. Most of the team was about to return, although on drums there was now another Paul Simon rhythm rattler, Grady Tate, taking turns with Chris Parker. A legendary duet partner this time was Dr John, for Percy Mayfield's "Maybe It's Because Of Love".

Georgie On My Mind – Live In Zagreb hot on the heels of Japan

It is hard to believe, but the cover states the date: The Tokyo plane carrying the Go Jazz All Stars could hardly have touched the ground in Heathrow, when Georgie flew out again, this time heading for Croatia – with only Peter King in tow – to work at the BP Club of his long-standing friend Boško Petrović [the Zagreb Jazz artist, 1935 – 2011], a renowned Croatian violinist, accordionist, drummer, vibraphonist and producer. He worked at the Montreux Jazz Festival with Oliver Nelson in 1971, visited the Berlin

Jazz Fest the same year, and among his legendary guests who were "cut" at his own Zagreb B.P. Club, he counted guitarist Joe Pass.

The British "delegation" was accompanied by a trio of local jazz buffs comprised of bass player Krešimir Remeta, drummer Silvicje Glojnarić, a member of Petrović's Zagreb Jazz Quartet, and guitar legend Damir Dičić (1938–2005).

It was to be a series of three relaxed evenings, starting on April 25th. B.P. Club owner and fellow musician Boško Petrović recorded the last evening – featuring ace trumpeter Guy Barker "depping" for a pre-booked Peter King – on good equipment. Certainly, the great vibes, and also maybe four songs you could not get anywhere else were the reason for him to make a proper live album out of this, issued on his own Jazzette label. It was never authorized by Georgie – "I never gave my permission to get this out! Round the end of 1990, Bosko Petrovic of the *BP Club* in Zagreb asked me whether I could get him one of these new DAT recorders. Well, on my next trip to Croatia I brought him one of these things and, lo and behold, the very first thing he recorded on that machine was my gig down at the club on the 27th April 1991.

"It came out as a bootleg in 1991, *Georgie On My Mind*, and I had not even been aware that the tapes were rolling."

Fame was not able to fly his Hammond organ in and had to stick to piano for his three dates to the Zagreb venue, which has been immortalized as "At The BP Club" on Georgie's 2009 album *Tone Wheels-A-Turnin'*. But this limitation is exactly where the surprise is hidden: Whereas Fame often states that his piano playing is nothing to write home about, the whole set proves his modesty wrong. His performance is so much more than a mere tinkling of the ivories; he sounds inspired throughout, especially on the sophisticated jazz tunes like "Everything Happens To Me".

It was an amazing adventure as a whole, as described by Guy Barker, who happened to replace King for the last night, in a detailed account: "We didn't know that was recorded. What happened was that Pete King was doing it, but he couldn't do the last two nights, and he asked me to do it. I remember it was when the Yugoslavian airlines hadn't paid their tax or their landing fees, which is ridiculous.

"So they weren't allowed to land at Zagreb airport, which is a bit like BA [British Airways] not being allowed to land at Heathrow. So I remember there was a lot of weird stuff, and it took me ages to get there. This is very typical of Georgie: I got to the airport, and he was there, waiting for me. Not the club owner, not a cab. He was there!

"'You're alright? Come on, then. There you go.' That's the thing with Georgie: He never *tells* you to do anything. He would always *ask* you, even phoning for a gig. He would never say 'Right, here's this gig, it's on such and such.' He would always say 'What do you think? Do you fancy doing this?'

"The thing I remember about that gig: It was me and him and Boško Petrović. There was a guitarist and a drummer. It was only a small club. You could barely see the back door for the smoke. Every one of the forty was smoking. And it was like a thick piece of fog, of smoke."

The fact that people were allowed to smoke was something Georgie appreciated, and it was part of the charm of the place that made him create a song out of the experiences there: "At The B.P. Club" from *Tone Wheels 'A'-Turnin'*. Feeling at ease himself, he had the task to get people's minds away from the hassles of the Civil War that was raging.

Guy Barker: "To be honest, at the time, I didn't even realize that anything was going on. I just remember being with a lot of wild and crazy people. We went out for these lunches and ended up drinking quite a lot. There was a lot of good feeling. I didn't really notice that kind of thing – but I did notice that the response to what we did was great."

So what did they do? The accidental yet accomplished quintet kick-started their set with a little drum solo by Glojnarić, with Georgie – audibly in an excellent mood, shouting the melody of "Yeh Yeh", leading into two long workouts from the *Portrait Of Chet* album, "But Not For Me" and "Everything Happens To Me", which was dedicated "to Chet".

He then gave the audience and "Kolya Petrović" his big hit "Yeh Yeh", with good-hearted quotes from Ray Charles' "What'd I Say" – "see the girl with the red dress on!" It was followed by Charles' Hoagy-Carmichael-adopted "Georgia On My Mind", which Georgie soon changes to "Zagreb in my mind", with British good time Jazz original "George Melly on my mind" quoted as well.

The new album *Cool Cat Blues* was featured via the Peggy Lee *Beauty And The Beat* chestnut "You Came A Long Way From St. Louis". Then a jolly version of "Lady Be Good" harked back to the 1987 *No Worries* LP and was ended with quick references to "Jumping With Symphony Sid".

But interestingly, there were some Petrović-tape-tempting numbers (it was a digital recording actually) which you couldn't yet collect with Georgie: Mose Allison's "The Fool's Paradise" with Georgie performing a beloved song alone on the piano which he used to do with Alan Price during their TV days in 1969.

For the long encore, Fame came back for Harold Arlen's "One For My Baby", with a story for "my friend Bosko". He announced "one more for Guy Barker and one more for the road", singing about "putting another Dinar in the machine". "You may never know it, but G.F. is a kid of poet, and he's got a lot of things to say and when I'm gloomy, you simply got to listen to me". "Boško, I know you're getting anxious to close", he continues, "thanks for the beers", but he remains utterly focused and attentive to every detail of his cool yet emotional performance, whereas he tackled the last three songs on his own, in true late night club style:

Benny Goodman's "Don't Be That Way" displayed a groovy left bass hand, and finally Hoagy Carmichael's "Memphis In June", which also included some rare Scat singing.

Unlike "Georgia On My Mind", it was not included in Fame's Carmichael tribute *In Hoagland*, and ended a mesmerizing set in a most tender fashion: "Nothing's half as nice as Zagreb in June!"

Guy Barker: "The audience was fantastic! Everybody was really high with the whole thing. It was very, very enjoyable. I remember it taking ages to get home, because we didn't finish till God knows what time. We didn't get back to the hotel until the sun was coming up ["Dawn Yawn" all over again]. Then we went into a taxi. It was just Georgie and me going home. Then we got to the airport, Zagreb airport, and then we had to fly to Belgrade.

"Then we had a six-hour wait-over. We were both exhausted, and we walked in. Georgie was just tired, but still in high spirits. He put his passport down, he looked up and said 'Hello. My name is Georgie Fame. This is my musical director. His name is Guy Barker'. He says 'I'd like a suite and a bottle of Dom Perignon immediately!'

"So we went up, it was a great big room. Georgie opened up this bottle of Dom Perignon. And we drank this, you know – we just sat and talked until it was time to get on the plane. I remember when I got home – I was living in Finchley Road at the time – the lady I was living with at the time just looked at me and said 'Have you …?'

"I realized that it was now night, and the night before I had been playing in Zagreb and I realized I was wearing a suit. I was wearing the same suit I'd been wearing on the gig, because we hadn't had the chance to even get home. We had just been travelling all the way, going through all this madness. I think I survived pretty well, I think I lost a button off the jacket, that was the only thing. It was very funny."

The Blues And Me – The second Ben Sidran produced album

By this time, Georgie Fame had enjoyed his most respected and at the same time best distributed album in years with *Cool Cat Blues* – one which was actually in the shops all over Europe and partly in the United States. Producer and Go Jazz label boss Ben Sidran wasted no time in arranging sessions for a follow-up, *The Blues And Me*, at "The Power Station" in New York City.

Crucial crew members remained in Will Lee on bass and Bobby Malach on tenor saxophone, who arranged the album's horn sections with his 'brother Ray', a word play that must have amused Georgie. For Robben Ford, there was now Hugh McCracken on guitar, a New Yorker who had served both Paul McCartney (on *Ram*) and John Lennon (on *Double Fantasy*) and so had stories to swap with the Beatles-buddy Fame. Rhythm responsibilities with Grady Tate happened for two tracks this time. As with Steve Gadd on the previous album, the drummer had the great distinction of having played with Paul Simon, a fitting match for Fame's own sensitivity and sensibility when it comes to meticulous recording. On the remaining 11 tracks, Chris Parker played the drums – a New Yorker known to many as Steve Gadd's predecessor in the band Stuff. His session ABC included Ashford & Simpson, the Brecker Brothers and Cher.

Having put himself on the map again with the *Cool Cat Blues* album and an almost inevitable re-vamp of his greatest hit "Yeh Yeh", Fame resisted the notion to re-record more biggies, but instead presented four of his own songs on *The Blues And Me*, mixed with old and new favourites which, with the exception of "Bluesology" and "Passed Me By", had not been committed to tape or hard-disc by Georgie before.

The album's title track opener, "The Blues And Me", is a romantic tune Fame wrote with his friend and arranger Steve Gray, the highly gifted and well-regarded Big Band specialist who died all too early in 2009, and it was also a part of their mutual Musical *Singer*. The late night, honky-tonk type piano sounds were provided by Paul Shaffer, the TV personality from *The David Letterman Show*. Shaffer pointed out "We will be The Blue Flames for a night". His piano work is complemented by Fame's own delicate Fender Rhodes touches, to which he sings "It's after hours, those wee small hours between night and day. I'm out relaxing instead of acting my part on the stage." Bobby Malach's tenor sax is assisted by Phil Woods on alto, the man Georgie name-checked on "Jimmy McGroove". At home, Fame had relied on his vibraphone master Anthony Kerr supplying mellow tones. He made sure he had similar dab hands here in Mike Mainieri. By the time *The Blues And Me* came out, Gray had been instrumental in arranging the BBC Radio Big Band album project with Georgie Fame and Madeline Bell, *City Life*, which featured this song in a more opulent, highly exciting version and which Ben Sidran called "an upcoming musical play". "Nobody's business but mine – The Blues and me, we get along fine", Georgie repeatedly sings in the chorus, and apart from the notion that Fame is summarizing his career attitude here, this album was going to prove this again, in the literal sense of the phrase.

No Georgie Fame album seems complete without digging into the Ray Charles catalogue – after all the great Floridian Cowboy was indirectly "responsible" for getting Fame kicked out of the Billy Fury team (which he then hi-jacked, you know the story). So here is a rousing version of Ray Charles' composition "I Want To Know", with an infectious call-and-response chorus and Bobby Malach part of a lively, theme-introducing horn section that also features Alan Rubin on trumpet and Keith O'Quinn on trombone. Breaks are sharp, and the swing is irresistible – Fame happy behind his Hammond, but Malach gets the solo!

Fame had great vocal sparring partners on *Cool Cat Blues* in Boz Scaggs and his part-time band boss Van Morrison, so how was he going to top that? How about having Dr John, the ex "Night Tripper" Mac Rebennack stroll into the studio? Georgie on Hammond, and the good doctor on his rolling New Orleans piano, they both croon through Percy Mayfield's "Maybe It's Because Of Love", a highly amusing and satisfying rendition, probably the best there is, with Mac telling Georgie why "his goose pimples pimple" when he is all alone with his loved one. You can't get more relaxed than those two here, and a complete duo album can still happen at the time of writing.

The music of George Gershwin and the lyrics of his brother Ira have always been dear to Fame's heart, and it is still hard to grasp even more than 20 years after the event why Georgie had not been asked to be part of the big tribute arranged around harp player Larry Adler around 1992. Still, here he was with a studio version of the stage favourite

"How Long Has This Been Going On?", using McCracken's well placed chords, Phil Woods' perfect alto touches and the Parker/Lee rhythm section while letting his Hammond linked Leslie cabinet swirl, and overdubbing his Fender Rhodes later. As Ben Sidran pointed out in his sophisticated comment, it should be noted that Fame not only sings custom-made lyrics for Chet Baker's trumpet solo here, but also puts his inspired Vocalese touches on Kenny Drew's piano solo for the number's Baker take. Three years on, he would re-record this standard with Van Morrison.

On top of Georgie's role of celebrated sideman in Van's band – and denying he had been employed as musical director – Fame had his own support slot in Morrison's shows for the last three years, and he often got audiences all over the United States into the swing of the night by the amusing "Jumpin' With Symphony Sid", written by Lester Young and King Pleasure and a favourite both of Fame and his hero Louis Jordan which Joe Jackson had rescued from obscurity ten years previously in 1982 with his album *Jumpin' Jive*. Symphony Sid Tories a.k.a. Sidney Turnopol was a New York Jazz DJ (1909–1984) renowned for his great taste in music, who had started out in a record shop by Symphony Records, hence the nickname. Note Chris Parker's tricky syncopation without missing a beat, or the Swing groove for that matter. Again, Fame's Hammond and Malach's tenor are a match made in Jazz heaven, as Georgie croons "Symphony Sid is swinging, that radio is ringin". "The dial set right there close to eighty on the dot" was a hint on where on the old radio scale the DeeJay was to be found in those pre-digital days.

More Ray Charles, and more Dr John. This time, in "Roll With My Baby", Georgie and Mac's roles are reversed, with the latter taking over Hammond duties and Fame handling the piano. Pure joy by the horn section again, which "Fathead" Newman led in Charles' band – here fittingly "replaced" by Bobby Malach directing trombonist Keith O'Quinn and trumpeter Alan Rubin. Great electric guitar licks and solo work by Hugh McCracken, uncredited here but probably his best moment on the album.

Georgie Fame had flown to the United States on his own, but he still had to have his "favourite saxophone player" (as Ben Sidran pointed out), Peter King, on their joint composition "The Woodshed". As Peter King explained in a BBC radio programme with Georgie, the tune had a long history: Charlie Watts' book *Ode To A High Flying Bird* about Charlie "Bird" Parker was re-released with an album, *From One Charlie* (1993) on Continuum Records. The first of the seven tracks, which Peter King supplied, was "Practicing, Practicing, Just Great". It developed into "The Woodshed". The tune was in itself based on Bird's "Exercise" which quoted the classical saxophonist Marcel Mule. King asked Georgie Fame to supply lyrics for "Practising", and Georgie of course "kindly accepted". Grady Tate provides a fantastic drum groove. King's part was added at the famous Abbey Road Studios in London, with Fame's son, guitarist and engineer Tristan Powell at the multi-channel board.

"Bluesology" had a long history for Fame, but was probably too good to miss in this high-class collection and re-definition of sound for a younger generation. As mentioned, the Milt Jackson and Mel Lewis composition – with additional lyrics by Georgie and his old friend Mike O'Neill – had been part of the 1970 US tour that was documented on the album *Shorty ft Georgie Fame*. No horns here, just like on Georgie's Prague version with Jon Hiseman on drums, which is notorious on YouTube these days.

A straight Blues is called for next, "Everybody's Cryin' Mercy"[23] penned by Fame's Mississippian role model Mose Allison. Tenor sax veteran Stanley "The Sugar Man" Turrentine (1934–2000), is the star here. "Mr T" had worked with Milt Jackson and Richard Tee. Here, Georgie reverentially accompanies him on Hammond, aided by the Cracken-Parker-Lee engine room on this relaxed yet intensive reading, which at one point leaves the impression of going half-time like "Survival" on *Cool Cat Blues*, only to pick up the 6/8 pattern after a little breather break.

In the opening section of "Blues For Ann-Marie", Georgie welcomes his listeners to New York City, in Swedish. This Swing number contains some great Hammond Jazz standard quotes and narrates 10-year-old Ann-Marie's love of scatting "just like Ella", name-checking band members Bobby Malach and Paul Shaffer in the process. Vocal assistance for Georgie was provided by a veritable studio choir of Katherine Miller, Ben Sidran and Bobby Malach. A year later, the song appeared on *Endangered Species* with the Danish Radio Big Band, where Fame presented this joint composition with fellow organist and Stockholm friend Kjell Öhman as an instrumental. Now he was revealing it as a tribute: The music composer, Hammond partner and Dynamite Brass veteran had asked Georgie to write special lyrics for this melody, dedicated to Kjell's daughter.

Ivory Joe Hunter's "Almost Lost My Mind" enjoys the most minimal arrangement of all here – highly effective and impressive, though: in very slow tempo, Fame performs it with just Hugh McCracken's lovely slide guitar and Will Lee's vocal backing, supplying the bass himself on Hammond organ. It is an inspired and interesting choice, especially in the light of an Alan Price version which came out on Polydor in 1978 on the little known album *Two Of A Kind*, which Price recorded in the Netherlands with singing pianist Rob Hoeke. Price & Hoeke, at the time, had opted for a similarly slow reading.

"Passed Me By" was one of Fame's own compositions again, debuted on the album *All Me Own Work* from 1972 and a tribute to his very first musical hero Fats Domino, without whom, as Ben Sidran reminds us in the booklet, Georgie had pointed out "I wouldn't be a professional musician today." There had to be a step up from his 1964 EP *Fats For Fame*, though, as Chris Parker especially was going to notice: Georgie set his composition in 11/8 time, theoretically making his drummer take turns in counting 6/8 (Blues) and 5/4 (Brubeck "Take Five" time) – only jokingly of course, because Chris Parker had that in his blood anyway.

23. See Addendum

More traditional Blues, more traditional song material for the finale – Duke Ellington's "I Ain't Got Nothing But The Blues" is a great reminder of Fame's late 1980s revue *Music From 10th Avenue*, where Ellington's music had been celebrated – unfortunately without being recorded. This is a valuable teaser though, with Malach, Lee and McCracken shining and an inimitable pattern laid down by drum legend Grady Tate for a second time during the sessions.

Apart from the aforementioned London Abbey Road overdubs, some of the tracks had been added to at New York's Skyline Studios, where the album was eventually mixed by recording engineer James Farber. No cost was spared when Ben Sidran then decided to have the 13 excellent tracks mixed by the famous George Marino at the Big Apple's renowned Sterling Sound.

If there should ever be a re-release of *The Blues And Me* with bonus tracks, then "Easy Street", which was made for the film *Glengarry Glen Ross*, starring Jack Lemmon and Al Pacino, should be considered, although it did not make the final cut of that movie. The Arlen/Mercer composition was also produced by Ben Sidran, and featured the great musicians Jim Rowls on piano, John Patitucci on bass and Jeff Hamilton on drums, with a great sax solo by Jeff Clayton, all of this arranged by the legendary Benny Golson. He later wrote Georgie a very charming and praising letter, more of which later.

The Blues And Me was promoted with the Go Jazz All Stars, featuring Sidran & Fame, saxophonist Bobby Malach, keyboard player Ricky Peterson and the rhythm section of Gordy Knudtson and Billy Peterson. Six weeks of clubs all through the United States, but in spite of a lot of fun, success and musical magic, at the end they could have felt worse than Joe Cocker in *Mad Dog & Englishmen*. Sidran in *A Life In The Music*: "We eventually landed in San Diego, more than $10,000 in debt and with a pile of excuses from club owners, promoters and the record distributor as to why it hadn't gone better." Money for Jazz musicians seemed to be only in festivals.

A bitter lesson for Sidran maybe, but Georgie does not share his sentiment. He has gorgeous memories of the outing, and still feels there is nothing wrong with it – "a very pleasant experience".

Back home in Britain, Georgie Fame's old Flamingo friend and 1970s Blue Flame Dick Heckstall-Smith had fallen ill in 1991, and he was in bad need of intensive as well as extremely expensive care. A benefit concert was arranged at the London "100 Club" in Oxford Street on 2nd June 1992, and Bob Brunning, long-standing bass player in the Brunning Sunflower Blues Band and one-time original Fleetwood Mac member, saw "a long-standing wish to play with Georgie" come true. Art Themen, Zoot Money, Paul Jones, John Etheridge, Dick Morrissey and also Chris Farlowe were part of the huge gig, a six-hour-spectacular which was filmed for an 8-part video concept, which was also shown as "in-flight entertainment" by British Airways.

Heckstall-Smith did get that treatment, he did recover, and two years later he was fully able to join the big Colosseum reunion in Germany with Chris Farlowe, Clem Clempson, Mark Clarke, Dave Greenslade and Jon Hiseman. He died in Hampstead Hospital on December 17th, 2004, after he had enjoyed the Colosseum revamp and also happy times in the Hamburg Blues Band for a full decade. Dick's most ambitious album ever, *Celtic Steppes*, has been produced by Tristan Powell, incidentally.

In early 1994, Georgie and his sons, Tristan and James, would present "Roll With My Baby" on German television. Georgie: "That was on *Schmidteinander*, a regular TV spot by comedian Harald Schmidt." Viewers on the continent could hardly tell that, only days previously, a horrendous tragedy had been endured by the family – and had not been publicised by the German media either."

Three Line Whip – The Family Trio as the Blue Flames nucleus

Between the second and the third Go Jazz albums, there was a long gap. The friendship between Georgie Fame and Ben Sidran endured – how could it not? But then professional and private events led to different paths for a six year period. In 1993, shortly after the Japanese tour with the Go Jazz roster, Fame went on one of his many tours with the Van Morrison Band. It was then that tragedy struck: his wife Nico committed suicide at Severn Bridge in Bristol on August 13th, 1993.

The news devastated Fame. It has been the author's policy of never asking Georgie about this very private matter. Van Morrison's, and also The Blue Flames' former guitarist, Ronnie Johnson, was with Georgie, and he reminisced how he had come to feel, and grieve, like he was a family member himself: "When I was on my own, before I got married, I saw a lot of the boys. I would go down there and he would put up with me. I still think of the boys like I am their uncle. I watched them grow up, and we are mates now. To be around them gave me a tremendous education for having my own sons. That was very interesting and great. He clearly knew I was trying to find my feet. I got a lot of time for Clive. I love him dearly, him and the boys."

Rather than return to New York City for more Go Jazz sessions or resume his touring schedule, Fame decided to work at mourning one day at a time by doing what he had always known best, turning to his family and the music for comfort.

Independently of the tragic events, he and his sons, Brother Tristan on guitar and Brother James on drums, as he always lovingly announces them on stage, would from now on not only be the nucleus of The Blue Flames, "plus Guy Barker on trumpet, Alan Skidmore on tenor saxophone and Brian Odgers on the bass." They would also form a trio, both for studio work and live – Three Line Whip. Did the three of them bond for this, or was it Georgie's idea?

Tristan Powell: "I think Dad had the idea, because taking a leaf out of his manager's book, 'You halve the overheads, and double the profits', especially when there is family involved. You've seen that outfit, it's a tight little unit, we do everything from humping the gear to driving the wagon around. So it is a very low maintenance gig and relatively easy to fill all sizes of theatres, small and large. So, it all works out quite well, and I think we started that from about the early Nineties onwards."

As the actual term for the trio, *Three Line Whip*, came about with the album of the same name. Somehow it had seemed that the trio thing started to get the three of them closer together after the tragic passing of Tristan and James's mother. Tristan: "That's a very good point. We started around that time as a rallying around to put something together. It must have been 1993/94."

James sees practical points: "It is all his idea, anyway. The thing about the trio, it's just lower maintenance. He doesn't like things complicated, and he gets in a terrible twist with loads of charts and logistics, loads of people. And he feels he has to provide all the answers for everybody all the time. He generally is a lot happier, more amenable and amiable on trio gigs, where there's just two other people to worry about. We are able to look after ourselves. It is easier-going for him, and it's more about the logistics being easier, the end result being better. He pays out more, and he feels better about doing that, about helping us out more. The trio gig has a very high power per night ratio, which is very pleasing. I think he feels good about doing that, and he doesn't have to worry about where Alan Skidmore is going to park or whatever. He doesn't have to worry about the program or what numbers to play, the repertoire is not set."

"And it is more of a challenge for him playing-wise, which is probably a good thing. And it keeps him busy. He runs the whole thing, because he is playing left-handed: he is completely in command, more than he is with a bass player in the front line. It's rough on the other guys. All the gigs that he ever did, he used to call everybody to go out with gigs. And now that band only gets out when we do Ronnie [Scott]'s really, or when someone especially asks for it. Most people who book him these days in the UK or somewhere, they get the trio. If they don't specify what they want, they get the trio."

The idea of playing with just a trio had occurred to Georgie generally – about principally working with a three-piece line-up, Georgie remarked: "I met John McLaughlin in Finland, and he is doing the same thing, with Joey DeFrancesco and Dennis Chambers on drums. They are going round as a Hammond organ trio. [At least this band, The Free Spirits, was active during 1993–94]. I'm not a very good bass player with my left hand. Also I'm not very good at soloing and playing bass at the same time. But it works well with my boys, because we keep it simple."

A few weeks after the passing of their mother, Tristan and James Powell joined their father in Barefoot Studios in London to record a very special studio album, a more than worthy follow-up to *The Blues And Me* in one respect, but a one-off in terms of melancholy and intimacy, too.

As Alan Skidmore remembers, "That was a very tough album for him to do. He found that quite hard – he was in an emotional place and he did a very good job, under the circumstances. I can remember us doing the recordings. That episode was very, very heavy for Clive, but it affected all of us, also because I knew Nico very well, and so did my wife, Kay. We all knew her very well. So it affected us as well, although not as much as him, of course. It must have been a dreadful time. It was a very tragic period. And it would be nice if you could put it like I just said – that it did actually affect the guys in his band as well. We were all very upset by the whole thing. They weren't just colleagues, they were friends. We were all very close friends."

Anthony Kerr agrees, "It's hard for anybody who has been bereaved, getting back to normal and doing your thing again. I'll never forget watching the news, and the view of the next morning's papers! It wasn't just a tragedy for our boss and bandleader, there were three of them! He lost his wife, and they lost their Mum!"

When this author told Tristan Powell that the tragic passing of his mother could not really be left out of this book completely, his reply was, "No, I'd been very surprised if you did. You are in an interesting situation as the author.

"I wouldn't want to wish it on anybody, but it happened. My philosophy has been: if you can turn something that is potentially incredibly damaging, the negative, into the positive, it certainly makes you value things more. Having lost [someone] in such tragic circumstances, it makes you realize how valuable your life is. You know, James and I have children. I think we would never – even if things got really tough – we would never leave our children in the same way. I think it puts a very, very high price on life. And we would never want our kids to go through the same things.

"It sounds very odd, but you learn things in life. If you don't, then you don't. But if you do, your life is richer for it. Sometimes a loss can mean a gain. And I don't think anybody has the answer for it, but I think it's just very tragic that people lose their self-respect or self-worth to that extent that they think that life isn't worth living anymore. I don't know what the answer is for that. I'm not convinced the answer is medication, it's a much more subtle thing that needs to be addressed.

Three Line Whip – the family album

How do you conceive an album which combines coming to terms with a painful loss and the joys of music? Theoretically, the only possible way seems to follow the path of a "New Orleans Jazz funeral", the slow march to the grave, which follows Spanish and French martial traditions and mixes them with Afro-American and Indian customs, with dirges and hymns played by the Jazz band. When the body is "cut loose", the music is allowed to become faster, rougher, and some "second line" dancing is allowed, as a cathartic way to find one's way into life again. This is exactly how *Three Line Whip* seems to have been composed, weaving mournful ballads like "You Are There" and Fame's own beautiful "A Declaration of Love" with more upbeat material like "Kan Tsukete" or the nostalgic cry for "Vinyl" records in the age of the CD.

Tristan Powell has the first word about the conception of the album: "I think we set it in a number of different studios, and I think it was a good thing and not such a good thing, obviously because of the tragic circumstances under which our mother, Nico died. We – I guess – sought some sort of solace in doing an album together as a core unit, but I don't really have any vivid images, or memories of it."

About the *Three Line Whip* sessions, Tristan remembers "I think it was very moving when Dad did a take of "It Happened To You". I think he was a little watery-eyed after his first run-through. But it was sort of put together in quite an odd way, because I think some of it was constructed first with the drums and then playing keyboards and guitar or vice versa. And I think our strength is when we all play live together and it just happens instantaneously.

"I can't remember what the exact circumstances were, but, you know, it was just a difficult time. Some people can find solace by diverting their energy into other things. I haven't really heard that album for a very long time. I remember Steve Gray being around, who was a wonderful arranger and brilliant musician. He popped up for a number of things and put some overdubs on. I guess that might have been the beginning of *Three Line Whip*."

Guy Barker also remembers the period very well, because he was close when it happened and played a key role in the recording of the album. "That was a horrible, horrible thing. I don't really want to go into it. I was staying there with them, at the time, when all that happened. It is an awfully huge thing to deal with, and I do think that one of the things that Georgie did was – how can you say it? He might have recorded that album anyway. But we all did end up in the studio, and I remember that there were times when it was really, really difficult for him, and then there were other times when it was okay. I remember a lot of what we did during that period afterwards was very, very hard. It was tough."

One of the things they did around the same time to get the healing done and escape the time for too many dark thoughts was going to Hong Kong together, which is reflected in the ballad "Since I Fell For You". Barker again: "For example, we went to play in Hong Kong together, and both Tristan and James came out as well. Everybody was incredibly supportive of each other. Also, the trip to Hong Kong was always very special, because that was a very special place to us – I had played there in 1989, with Clark Tracey's Quintet, and it was a fabulous little club. It was tiny, and it was run by people who just loved it and wanted to make this Jazz club happen. Anita O'Day played there, lots of people. Anyway, we finished – and on the last night with Clark Tracy's Quintet, the guy who booked it, a guy called Rick Halsted, a British expat, he took me in the backroom: 'We are thinking of getting Georgie Fame'" – more of that later.

Georgie on one of the peculiarities: "On the *Three Line Whip* album, even though I got one of the best electric bass players in the world, Brian Odgers – who – Brian only plays about sixteen bars [on the track "It Happened To Me"], the rest of it is all my left hand bass, either on Hammond or the digital piano."

James Powell remembers the procedure of recording this album as principally like a lot of other albums to follow, but recalls its special conditions in these hard times: "Recording with him is generally very hard. The background is that it has never been easy, except if it's live, because I think he wants to do it cheaply, so as he is paying for it, that's understandable. That means he wants to do it quickly. Usually it's pretty uncomfortable. I never have any parts, so I have to get a feel for it. It's quite hard to do that when I'm hearing him, but by hearing it a couple of times at least, at the end I can have a go at it. It is a very uncomfortable vibe recording with him normally, because he wants to get it done very quickly, and he is very tense and irritable. And there is always a little bit of shouting, usually before the red light goes on."

"So that recording [of *Three Line Whip*] was no exception. That was tense and irritable and up against the clock. In addition there was this horrible feeling that we were all going through. It was very hard. [As far as a cathartic experience is concerned], perhaps it was something that was in the diary already, and something that perhaps should have been cancelled or postponed. But it is very much like him to just carry on. I think that was probably the purpose of it. I think it is not just catharsis but showing the world and therefore showing oneself that you are carrying on and marching through this crap. If you are going to do that by recording or working, then you're telling yourself you're ok. I think that's it.

"We did a gig in Germany, I think that was in Baden-Baden, and it was probably three days after Mum died. It was really, really close – and nobody knew about it. That was very hard, and something that probably should have been cancelled. The band were there, and it wasn't yet widely known, I don't think they knew about it. And I think he didn't want to tell them until afterwards. It was kind of the burden of secrecy. I mean, this is probably inappropriate and very personal, but it could be a back-up of what I was saying about showing the world that you can carry on. On that gig – it is not often that he would do that – he would usually do as an encore one of his ones.

"And he went out, having got through this gig, and the band didn't know about it. I wasn't supposed to say. He did an encore, and he did 'One For My Baby', 'and one more for the road', whatever that thing is: he did that alone at the piano. I was at the back, listening to it, thinking, how can he do that?

"And I remember thinking how could he really manage to sing it and not collapse? What I mean is nobody was asking him to be that brave. You are setting the scene that you can be that brave, as a way of coping. That is my theory about it. There was no need to do any recording. There was no deadline with any company or anything. It was a personal project that could have been delayed or cancelled or whatever."

Three Line Whip – Track by Track

The sedate, melancholic "It Happened To Me" with its hymn-like theme of piano, sax and trumpet can be seen as kind of a lyrical sequel to "Everything Happens To Me" by Tom Adair and Matt Dennis, which the Tommy Dorsey Orchestra did with Frank Sinatra, followed by hundreds of versions, of which Chet Baker did the relevant one here on *Chet Baker Sings*, with Georgie following suit in 1970 on *Georgie Does His Thing With Strings*. Here, after the slow first part, the solo-imitating Vocalese lyrics by Mike O'Neill are sung thoughtfully by Georgie to Fender Rhodes and the sons' Swing accompaniment before he is followed by Barker and Skidmore with fine trumpet and saxophone solo work.

"Kan Tsukete" was written in and about the famous Japanese Bullet trains, which Georgie enjoyed on his way from Tokyo to Osaka (and back) when he went there first with Go Jazz, warmly greeted with Sake spirits, which you have to "make hot", i.e. "Kan Tsukete". Georgie is again on a Fender Rhodes, with female Japanese voices in the background, and an alluring intermittent theme thrown in by horn and sax. James Powell lays a great Rock groove here – quite unusual for a Georgie Fame record – and Tristan

 supplies a fitting wah-wah guitar solo to "reflect the feel of the Bullet train", as Georgie comments.

"Vinyl" is a fast Swing about Fame's love of "real" records, from *Ray's Record Store* in London. Georgie took the melody from his ongoing work in the world of commercials music, which he still did "occasionally, if I have the time I'll do it. I wrote a piece of music last year for an industrial video. It's always fun to do that. Actually, this is a funny story:

"The song 'Vinyl' – the idea for that song was from Hong Kong two years ago at a Jazz Club I worked in with Guy Barker. One of the original Troggs, Alan Grindley, was in Hong Kong – I'm going to see him on Sunday, we're doing some charity things with the Troggs, with my boys – Alan had a film company. He was travelling the world making a documentary film about Hilton hotels, Conrad & Hilton hotels. Alan suggested that I might want to write some music that he could use in the film. So I thought – fantastic!

"So I wrote this song which is now 'Vinyl', a little slower, and I did a demo disc with machines, I didn't use a band, and I wrote all these fantastic lyrics about the joys of staying in Hilton hotels, thinking this would be great if Hilton used this. If they liked this film and if they used this song in the hotels in every elevator, every restaurant, every hotel room, the royalties could be phenomenal! Like 10 number one records! But I didn't hear back from him. I don't think he has completed the film. He has sent a tape to California and we didn't hear anything.

"And then I was in Japan last year [1993] with Ben Sidran, Phil Upchurch and Bobby Malach, as the 'Go Jazz All Stars', and when we were backstage in Tokyo, all these young Japanese kids were coming backstage for autographs. They were carrying vinyl – and I've always liked vinyl anyway! So I thought 'This is a good song, and if Hilton don't want it, I'll just change the lyrics'. But if Hilton hear it and they like it, they can use it in the future, because they have their own lyrics, so it could work both ways – like 'Get Away': 'Get Away' was written as a commercial for a gasoline company. They had a promotion going and wanted a little song that they could give away in a gas station on floppy disc as part of the promotion campaign. But because it didn't mention the name of the company, we released it as a single. I got paid twice. So 'Vinyl' is similar to that. It's always interesting to be asked to do something like that, because you have to think quickly and throw in the kitchen sink in 30 seconds." Great Hammond work, and a fantastic solo by Alan Skidmore, too.

"Mercy Mercy Mercy" was written by Joe Zawinul for Cannonball Adderley, as early as 1966 and long before Zawinul's band Weather Report came about. This one took shape at a time when the Fender Rhodes was still revolutionary, having been introduced to the public first and foremost by Ray Charles. Fame uses it ever so well and combines the instrumental with Van Morrison's "Vanlose Stairway" from the collaborator's 1982 LP *Beautiful Vision*. The Irish heartbreaker had written this composition about his Danish girlfriend, Ulla Munch, who lived in the Copenhagen district of Vanlose, in an apartment block without a lift. A roomy snare sound and groove is laid down by James Powell, and there is some gorgeous vibraphone work by Anthony Kerr, underlined by Tristan Powell's delicate dobro slide work and muted licks by Guy Barker's trumpet.

Buddy Johnson's 1945 ballad "Since I Fell For You" is a rare duo performance featuring "just" Georgie on Hammond organ and vocals, his dreamy melody lines being followed telepathically by Guy Barker on his trumpet, recalling their mutual days at the Hong Kong Jazz Club where Barker had suggested the tune in 1990. Stanley Turrentine as well as The Rascals were some of the many artists to cover it, and the Fame partners Van Morrison and Dr John did it, too, on *Pure Bootleg* (which is actually a true bootleg) and *Going Back to New Orleans* respectively.

"Zavolo" had a very special place in Georgie's heart, as he revealed in one of his BBC programmes: "One of my favourite cities is Capetown in South Africa. Five years ago I spent a wonderful Christmas there with the family, and we were invited by a group of musicians on New Year's Day, at a special festival that was being held down there. The group that opened up the concert [was] Winston Mankuku [1943–2009] on tenor saxophone, Mike Perry on Yamaha grand piano, Richard Pigott on drums, and Mike Campbell on bass.

"The tune they opened up their set with was a thing called 'Zavolo'. I fell in love with that, and we play it regularly with The Blue Flames." Completely understandable, because it has got an attractive melody and most infectious groove, which James does not attempt to copy, but rather deduces its essentials, as if his dad had shouted "Dave Mattacks", the one-time Fame studio drummer (1977) who is famous for his economic yet magic playing. Lovely long vibes break by Anthony Kerr, too.

"You Are There" by Georgie Fame and the Blue Flames saxophonist at the time, Steve Gregory, is a Jazz fusion tune that would not be out of place on a Morrissey-Mullen LP by two Fame cohorts, Dick Morrissey and Jim Mullen. "Are you there to save me from despair" sounds like some kind of longing mantra, very appropriately assisted by Gregory's own flute playing.

"A Declaration Of Love", an original Fame composition that apparently wrote itself, was originally conceived as a Big Band Ballad, as Georgie had shown on *Endangered Species* with The Danish Radio Big Band the previous year, but this time he indulged himself by re-interpreting it as a Swing Waltz, as arranged by Steve Gray. Sensitive brush work by James helps both Anthony Kerr on vibes and Georgie himself on his Hammond organ to really shine here.

"Will Carling": Here was another famous person who Georgie sang about, as he loves to do. I asked him to elaborate about it in 1994, and he happily consented: "Of course. Will Carling is the captain of the English Rugby team. It sounds like a drink, Carling Black Label, and the irony is: the song really has nothing to do with Will

Carling himself, except – it's a composition by Steve Gray, who plays the keyboard on that track, he's one of my great friends.

"Steve and I collaborated a lot, he lives near me. He did all the arrangements for the BBC [Radio Big Band] album *City Life*, with Madeline Bell. So Steve sent me a cassette – which I have in my bag, I'm gonna give it to the English trombone player for tonight – of his composition which he called 'Will Carling', because it reminded him of the Count Basie tune 'Little Darling'. So this is his musical sense of humour – 'Little Darling – Will Carling'. So he asked me to consider writing some lyrics for it, so I rang him up and said 'Steve, are you serious? Will Carling, the English Rugby player?' He said 'Yeah, well, see what you think.'

"So I did think about it, and I'm very happy with it. It's one of the best lyrics I've written, it's also one of the funniest I've done, although it's the most romantic piece of music. And the lyrics are very romantic until you get to the punch line. Because the punch line is 'I suddenly awake and wipe my sleepy eye, as Will Carling scores another try!' When you score points in Rugby, when you reach the line and put the ball down, that's called a 'Try'.

"So, not many people outside of England, or other Rugby playing countries, like New Zealand, South Africa, Australia, maybe Japan, would understand this meaning. A 'try' is not an attempt to do something, you score three points! So in order to accommodate the name of Will Carling in the title – although I do admire Will Carling, he's a great player – I use my imagination. Because the song is so warm, and it's a beautiful morning, and you set this wonderful scene. But the crux of the piece is really that I as the singer have fallen asleep in front of the television while the English Rugby is playing, and I'm having this wonderful romantic dream. And then I wake up, and the dream is shattered as 'Will Carling scores a try'."

With Georgie's contract to Ben Sidran's Go Jazz Records seemingly on hold, the new album came out under Fame's own label of the same name as the album, Three Line Whip (picked up by Hypertension in Germany). Apparently, Fame wanted it for current and future releases as well as for his back catalogue as far as he owns it:

"I've only just formed 'Three Line Whip' as my label – it's a family affair, it's just something for me and my two sons to be involved with. There are two or three other albums which I own completely, which have never been released around Europe, maybe on import: I did a Chet Baker dedication album, *A Portrait of Chet*. I recorded that in Holland, and I own that one [now]. But that has only been distributed in Scandinavia through a friend of mine in Stockholm [Lasse Samuelson]. I could put that on Three Line Whip and distribute it generally. And there's an album I did in Australia with the Australian Blue Flames, as we call it, *No Worries*, I own that one too. There's also a Reggae album which I do which has been released around Germany through a guy Volker Spielberg, who is not a very nice man. I own that one, too." Fame was talking about the German Decca release of *Closing The Gap* (1980) as *I Love Jamaica* in 1983.

It was shortly after the release of *Three Line Whip* that Fame spoke about his relationship to Alan Price again: "[I see him] occasionally; we speak to each other quite a lot. I don't see him much, because we're both busy working. He has Zoot Money in his band [on keyboards, plus Bob Tench on guitar, ex Jeff Beck Group and The Streetwalkers]. I spoke to Zoot last night, because my sons are involved in a new band that Zoot Money is in. And Alan Price's daughter Elizabeth was singing in a band with my boys last year, they put something together. Alan works live around England most of the time, because of his fear of flying."

This nucleus of the Blue Flames, soon called Georgie Fame & Sons instead of Three Line Whip, which remains the name of Georgie's label, has developed into a tight trio in its own right over the years, which has slowly been proceeding to working more than the actual band, but they had not got round to releasing an album as of 2014:

"The only thing that has not been documented is this band, the Family Trio, which is rather unique, I can't think of another band. I know that Dave Brubeck's sons all play – I saw a TV documentary of them many years ago, and he was playing with his three or four sons. They are all musicians. But as a working unit, it is kind of unique. And it hasn't been recorded. We keep saying – Tristan has taped a few gigs – but we should go into the studio and do it properly. And then that would be it, I think. Although I've got about three new compositions, songs, and I don't know if they will ever get recorded, or if I get someone else to sing them – I don't know. I'll just take it as it comes."

One of the most pleasant ever GF & Sons gigs this author has witnessed ever happened at The Castle, Finchley Road, Golders Green in 2011:

"There are people here from Portugal, from Croatia and from Germany. Because that's what music does", Fame stated as he took a seat behind his old trusted Hammond organ, while landlord Denis Cook quipped "and I've come all the way from Muswell Hill!" Seriously though, with all the promising air of fun at this new music pub, there is always a feel of authentic 60s Flamingo flair when Georgie & Sons perform, starting with "I Got A Woman" – "Eddie Cochran being responsible for bringing the music of Ray Charles to the masses in this country."

Aided by the charming swing of "Brother James" on drums and the deadpan, groovy guitar licks of "Brother Tristan", they glided easily into the old Willie Dixon warhorse "Spoonful" along the way, before "You Came a Long Way From St. Louis" celebrated the Blues according to Miss Peggy Lee, a teenage sweetheart for Georgie, at least on record.

At sixteen, Fame was smitten with Fats Domino – related in hilarious anecdotes from Butlin's Holiday Camps – but soon became a disciple of Mose Allison, whose "If You Live" got a relaxed, philosophical rendition by the trio. Spotlight on drummer James Powell – after Fame had told us how he himself lost that family name due to svengali Larry Parnes fatherly blackmailing – for "Big Easy Meat", an impressive course on New Orleans second lining and general partying. Melancholic sojourn for some Texan country with his sibling Tristan, who gave Jim Reeves' "He'll Have To Go" the Ry Cooder treatment and related a gorgeous sense of melody, picked up by Daddy Clive via some tasty harmony singing. "Don't Send Me Flowers", "when I'm in the graveyard – cause baby, I can't smell a thing", wisdoms like these sound like Louis Jordan, and indeed this was has always been one of Georgie's B-side favourites, punters then moving merrily to its famous A-side, "The Point Of No Return".

Georgie & Sons returned, after an intermission to say hello to scores of relatives and friends from all parts of Britain as well as the mentioned European delegations, with Booker T's evergreen "Green Onions". The infectious Leslie sound was applied for the Slow Blues "Help Me" in the process, Sonny Boy Williamson territory flown in via Ten Years After, who Georgie shared the Albert Hall with in 1969. "Get Away" came next, and the familiar but highly amusing tale of how a National Benzole commercial could get airplay on the BBC and rise to No. 1 had the sold-out venue in stitches.

Fame's memoirs then harked back to the break-up of his first Blue Flames band and the lucky transfer of his drummer cum flat mate, the late Mitch Mitchell, to the Jimi Hendrix Experience – show time for Tristan again, who not only sang "Red House" in his very own laconic style not unlike Matt Taylor, but also remembered Jimi with wah-wah attacks that never lost his care for structure, tunefulness and, ultimately, drama.

A bopping Ska rhythm got everybody back into party mode: Nobody had ever heard "The Ballad of Bonnie and Clyde" treated to Jamaican Blue Beat, but Fame was only joking, of course, changing gear for "Humpty Dumpty" from his famous *R&B at the Flamingo* live LP debut 1964. "Yeh Yeh", which a year later became his first of three number ones, was what everybody got into.

The pace was kept for "Get On The Right Track, Baby", and that one had two pint-armed granddads nod their white heads in unison – Muppets-Stadler-and-Waldorf style. We all believed Georgie when he quoted Willie Dixon in song: "I Love The Life I Live". He does, and he did on the night, shuffling Jimmy Smith's "Back at The Chicken Shack" and his old chestnut "Pink Champagne" into the beat. He left us on a philosophical note on mortality by his peer Mose Allison, "Was". Hey, Allison is 83, Fame just 67. Let's hope we get at least sixteen more years of spellbinding nights like this one in the Castle. Long live Georgie Fame."

Set 1: 21.0 –21.50	Set 2: 22.50–23.40
I Got A Woman/Spoonful	Green Onions/Help Me
You Came A Long Way from St Louis	Funny How Time Slips Away
If You Live	Getaway
Big Easy Meat (shuffle James Powell)	Red House (sung by Tristan Powell)
He'll Have To Go (voc TristanPowell)	Humpty Dumpty (w. Bonnie & Clyde)
Don't Send Me Flowers	Yeh Yeh
Point Of No Return	Get On The Right Track, Baby
	I Love The Life I Live (w. Back At
	The Chicken Shack/Pink Champagne)
	Was

Geoff Gascoyne – the ace bass player who followed the incredible Brian Odgers

Brian Odgers could have played in the Blue Flames forever, but decided not to. Geoff Gascoyne (b. 1963) had been a member of the band Everything But The Girl from 1990. He also worked with Welsh Jazz singer and pianist Ian Shaw, and in late 1993, he first met Georgie on tour: "I obviously knew the hits. I had heard of him before. It all came about when I first met him in Germany. We did a festival, and I was playing with Jim Mullen, the great English [Scottish, actually] guitar player, and [Fame] was the guest. He asked me to do a few concerts after that. Georgie obviously had a reputation. Also at that time, it was not that long after his wife died. So he was not the easiest guy to get along with at first. He was going through a lot of stuff, and the boys were there. I think I met the boys shortly after that. He called me into the band after playing with him just one time, which was amazing."

Gascoyne, having joined during a difficult period, saw Georgie coming to terms with the most challenging period of his life: "Clive is very loyal. He can be quite stroppy. I know what he is like, but I have seen him be very rude to sound guys and get fairly agitated very easily. He is not as bad as that, but in the early days, he would be very agitated by one bad sound in the P.A. or in the monitors. You would be on egg shells, if you like, and be very wary of what he would say next."

Tristan Powell, engineer and record producer

"It started very early. When I was at school I was always fascinated with what was – in those days – modern technology: a cassette studio." This led to Tristan's engineer's and producer's interests: "So when I was about 13 or 14, I got into recording, messing around with tape recorders and things. I was just fascinated by how it all worked and took it from there and was very luckily given a trial at Abbey Road after I left school. I went for an informal interview with Ken Townsend, who was the manager of the studio. Ken had worked with the Beatles and was instrumental in developing ADT, artificial double tracking. They put me on a trial for six months, and it kind of worked out. I was there for five years and learnt a lot about microphone techniques and generally how to record things. Ken was very supportive of my endeavors."

"I got a reputation of being a Jazz man, as I knew lots of Jazz artists and they were all looking to record in those days, but they only had small budgets. So I would get them a deal in the small penthouse studio, which was in the roof. We couldn't afford multi-track taping, because it was £130 a reel, and that would only last for twenty minutes. So I said 'Look, we can make an album, but it will be live to 2-track.' And we would do a whole album in two days over an eight-hour session, which was a cheap recording deal. Basically, I had to make sure you had a good balance in the studio and what you heard, there and then, was your finished product. So it was just like in the old days really, when they recorded live."

"Because of that, I was lucky enough to get given the responsibility of re-mixing a whole load of the Roulette session tapes, which included artists like Count Basie [coming full circle with his Dad], Sarah Vaughan, Ella Fitzgerald, Joe Williams, Tony Bennett – a whole load of incredible multi-tracks. I was only 19 at the time, so I was very young, quite naïve.

"Certainly, the first of those live sessions that I did up there in the penthouse were very rewarding, because we all got on well, and it did sound pretty good. I think the second album I did was with Martin Taylor, and the first was a very good pianist called David Newton, with Clark Tracey on the drums, and Dave Green on bass. So we did loads of albums with those guys, just good days. I did Claire Martin's first album, *The Waiting Game*, and two more after that which were good fun, loads with Tina May. Both the Guy Barker's *Into The Blue* and Stan Tracey's *Portraits Plus* got Mercury nominations. So that was good, getting involved with mixing and recording an album that gets a Mercury nomination."

Tristan Powell also worked with his father's Sixties friend and colleague Elkie Brooks on her album *Inspiration* during 1993: "I got Paul Stacey, a friend of mine. He is a great guitar player. And a very interesting producer, Greg Walsh [with Trevor Jordan and Pip Williams], was producing Elkie's album. He said 'We need a guitar player.' I said 'I know this friend of mine called Paul Stacey.' Paul turned up within an hour, with tons of gear and racks and loads of guitars and really impressed Greg. We did a really good couple of days work with him, and Paul ended up being the guitar player in Elkie's band. He replaced Zal Cleminson, he was in the Sensational] Alex Harvey Band: a really good guitar player, very unpredictable. Paul ended up filling his shoes in Elkie's band. – I just made a call. It's funny how it works." Fifteen years after the Elkie Brooks sessions, Paul Stacey appeared in the picture again – that's him playing guitar on "The Burdee Song", the lightning speed Swing on Georgie's album *Tone Wheels-A-Turnin'* in 2008.

His dad's footsteps were everywhere, for instance when Tristan engineered for an old Flamingo cohort and part-time Blue Flame – Graham Bond and Colosseum sax man Dick Heckstall-Smith: "That came about through [Cream and Jack Bruce lyricist] Pete Brown. I might have come across Pete at Abbey Road, and he may have come in to do some overdubs. Then he rang me after I left Abbey Road and said 'Would you come and do some sessions?' I worked with Pete about four times. Pete was actually producing the Dick Heckstall-Smith thing, I was just the engineer, brought in to mix it, *Celtic Steppes*. Pete wanted it mixed and I said yeah, sure."

"I didn't know about Dick Heckstall-Smith conncection, but during the session, Dick would reminisce a little bit about this and that, when they had a minute. They were fast and furious sessions, because they had to do a lot in very little time, very big line-up. And I think I had two or three days to mix the album. There were some inevitable overdubs while we were mixing as well. But he was great to work with, affable, and very funny and very intelligent. He knew a lot about everything. Interested in politics, and a wordsmith, very clued up about the origins of just about everything you can ever think of. So he was good and it was a pleasure working with Dick."

And then there is the Holy Grail, certainly for every British engineer: "When I was at Abbey Road, I was assistant engineer on the [Pink Floyd] double live album, *The Delicate Sound Of Thunder* (1988). That was very hard work, but very, very rewarding. I learnt a lot about tape machine offsets and things. We had to take solos from other nights and make them work in the existing night by nudging a tape machine by frames, and then dropping in, and then nudging it a few more frames and then dropping in. This was in the days before digital recording, cut and paste. You were actually dealing with up to three tape machines at different speeds."

The young Powell's interest in recording and producing also came from a connection to his father's session work, although at home Georgie Fame apparently refrained from name dropping (*Name Droppin'* would become a future album) almost completely. Tristan: "When I was about 12 or 13, he gave me a Walkman, when [the] Walkman had just been launched onto the market. He gave me two tapes with the Walkman, one was Jimmy Smith *Organ Grinders Swing*, and the other one was Joan Armatrading's *Show Some Emotion*. I was really impressed that he had just been playing on that session – the album had just been released. He gave me the tape, and said as an aside 'Here is something I have been involved in. Have a listen'. I love that album. Also the Jimmy Smith album, with a great guitarist Kenny Burrell, and there's a guitar player on that *Joan Armatrading* album called Jerry Donahue, a great player, Country and Blues licks and things. I was really impressed that he had been playing on that session.

"Of course, *Show Some Emotion* was produced by Glyn Johns, who is a great producer – very simple. A recording engineer, who keeps it very simple but gets a big, natural sound. Three mikes on a drum kit! Glyn recorded the first live album *Rhythm and Blues at the Flamingo*, which was actually a second take, as there was something wrong with the the tape recorder. So they had to do it again."

Tristan Powell is always well aware that he is an engineer and also a guitarist, and he can never shed one hat completely: "When you're in the studio, and when you are doing it, I'm always very conscious having this sort of schizophrenic existence of being an engineer and a musician when you are actually doing it. You are either in one place or in another, and I don't think I have ever been completely in the zone, or never completely blown away. I remember working with Cat Stevens and I found that he was incredibly focused, very interesting to work with and very, very driven. He knew exactly what he wanted and was very charming and vibey and tended to get very good takes out of people."

In that line of work, you are sometimes witness to rare magic: "Hearing Dave Gilmour play a solo through a Gaelian Kruger amp on a record I was tape-op-ing for at Abbey Road, that was a kind off seminal moment for me cause I thought – it's not an amazing amp, the Kruger, it's a tiny portable thing, and when he plugged it in, he got a huge sound. He's one of my favourite guitar players; such a distinctive sound and lyrical phrasing."

Chapter 10

"Chat as much as you like" – The Ronnie Scott's Club live residencies

It is amazing to watch in what musical state Georgie Fame & The Blue Flames arrive at their traditional Soho playground, often enough after they haven't played together for quite a while, due to Fame's trio, Big Band and solo work with other small ensembles.

One the one hand, there is so much to choose from, on the other hand the set is often about last-minute second thoughts, spontaneous additions and brand new songs which the band members have sometimes never heard about. So the atmosphere backstage can be ever so tense – with "shush" and "go away" signs aplenty as soon as you open the door. Guy Barker has his observations about the process:

"Everybody has their own personality, and everybody has their own way of working. The thing about Georgie is – we never would have full rehearsals as such. What he would do was, when we had a new session – a season at Ronnie's, for example – at the sound check, he would always say, 'I've got something new. Let's try this out.' That's where we would try out new songs. He would always write out the parts for us, everything, and he would come up with these tunes. A lot of the times, it would be very easy to play the same repertoire, because everybody likes it."

While Guy Barker was able to take this way of working in his stride, having known Georgie for half a decade now, things were a little more awkward for the "new boy" on bass, Geoff Gascoyne: "We always used to play at Ronnie Scott's for a couple of weeks in the old days while Ronnie was around. The first night was always a trial, because we didn't know what was going to happen. And of course, there is the drinking as well."

Barker continues: "But Georgie was always doing that to keep himself active, and to keep us active as well, to try and make sure that there was new material. Inevitably, we were always going to do 'Yeh Yeh'. There are certain things you just have to do. But there were also these things that were interesting – what would happen was that Georgie would turn up with a tune or an idea of something, and he would start it one way. As the weeks and months progressed, the tune would end up going into another direction altogether. Things would develop from that, a bit like how the intro to 'Moondance' got stuck on [the intro then became a song of its own, "I.E.O.K.O" on the *Charlestons* album, inspired by the movie *Sanders Of The River* starring Paul Robeson.]

"He will always say 'Right, we will try these things out'. It means that he will come out with a line and will always say to the audience, 'If you'll forgive us, we will have a public rehearsal'. And at the end, he will say 'Thanks for the public rehearsal', but he would keep saying it even when we got it right anyhow. Part of it means that you know when he stops saying that, we have all got it right. When you have done that, you will never hear those words again. Right, we've obviously got it.

"So I think the thing with Georgie was always 'Try and keep everybody active', and it is also entertaining for the audience. Even though Georgie has done his thing all his life, he has never gone away from the fact that an audience has to be entertained. So he will tell the stories, even though sometimes he will tell the stories, like the introduction to "Yeh Yeh", that he has told every night for years and years and years.

"Sometimes, he will get fed up with it and just do it very quickly, and then, as he said one night to me – and I took it on board, because I realized that – he said 'It doesn't matter how many times we are up there doing it – you are playing to an audience and for a lot of those people, this may be the first time they have come to the gig.' So you have to do that thing, which is part of the whole element of that."

Even people who heard that "Yeh Yeh" story three dozen times, like this author for a start, seem to whisper along, almost like a prayer. Guy Barker agrees: "Oh yeah, there's a couple of guys that I often see when we do Ronnie's, who are always there, every time. And they say 'Oh, we love the stories'.

"So many people said to me that when they go to see Georgie do the show, particularly in Soho. It's a bit like now when you go to "Ronnie's" – you can't get a ticket, it's sold out. It is completely rammed. Because now, not only is it 'Ronnie's' and not only is it Georgie, but Georgie has become this figure that will sing great songs, play great Hammond organ, give you new songs, give you the old songs. But also, what he's doing is – he is a link with those days of Soho. It's like now you can get people who are half his age turning up saying 'We never experienced that thing – stories that become legendary: he is our link.' So they will go there for that, and you do feel that. I feel that when I am walking to Ronnie's and I see Georgie, he looks up and smiles and says 'How are you doing?' You just think 'Here we go, it's that magic thing.'"

The Story of Ronnie Scott and his Club

With "the old Flamingo" Club long gone, Ronnie Scott's Club – always held in awe by Fame during all those decades – has almost come to replace his original 1960s London hunting ground, and the fact calls for another detour to chronicle the club's history and impact.

"You got a reservation, Sir?" This would certainly always help during the weekends. On Saturdays and Sundays, it has never been too easy to get beyond the black-clad "bouncers" who tend to guard this Jazz establishment in the heart of London's entertainment district: Soho. More often than not, they'd ask you this question even as you're preparing to wait in the queue along Frith Street – with or without an umbrella – with Soho Square, a miniature green created during the 1670s, behind you, and facing Chinatown. If you turned your head to the right, there'd be the four hundred year-old *Dog & Duck* pub – where Ronnie Scott would sit in a cozy corner with a pint of real ale between sets.

Reservation in fact means that you have booked a table very well in advance and are prepared to eat as well. It also means that you react on the spot once you learn about a gig, and this certainly goes for Georgie Fame, whether he plays for one week like these days, or for a full three weeks like he and The Blue Flames used to in the 1990s. Tables can be gone in days or sometimes minutes – via the phone or net.

The security suits aren't the only items in black – as soon as you are led to your table by an elegant lady, you realize immediately that all the walls are black, too: displaying the rich history of the place with black & white photography from Miles Davis to Ginger Baker, and there are little table lamps like the Cotton Club had 90 years ago. Cocktail prices can be as high as the risotto amount on your plate is low, but the music tends to be fantastic.

There are Soho music venues which are legendary because they're extinct. There used to be the Blues-rocky Marquee Club where The Who and The Small Faces started, and where Georgie accompanied Alexis Korner in 1983, shortly before the Blues father's sad and early demise, or Fame's "own" Flamingo Club. Ronnie Scott's seems to stay.

Tenor sax man Ronnie Scott (1927–1996), born Ronald Schatt into a Jewish family in Aldgate, London, counts as the first British musician who was influenced by Charlie Parker. As early as the 1940s, the young Londoner whose father, Jock Scott, was a renowned dance band saxophonist, worked on the salon stages of the *Queen Mary* in order to hear his beloved Jazz first hand in the United States. He had an especially soft spot for the Jazz clubs of Manhattan's 52nd Street. His experience of listening to his heroes remained unforgettable for him: "We'd usually arrive in New York in the morning and leave the evening of the following day", Ronnie writes in *Some Of My Best Friends Are Blues*, "which gave us a full night to do the Jazz rounds. I'll never forget the night I heard the quintet of the great Charlie Parker with Miles Davis at The Three Deuces. And next door, incredibly, was Dizzy Gillespie's band."

"Unrelenting Jazz" was on his mind, but commercial paid the rent, so Scott had an idea: "A group of us got together in January 1949 and rented a rehearsal room at 41, Great Windmill Street, which we ran cooperatively as the Club Eleven. There were ten musicians – Leon Calvert, Hank Shaw, Lennie Bush, Joe Muddel, Bernie Fenton, Tommy Pollard, Tony Crombie, Laurie Morgan, Johnny Rogers and myself – and a manager; hence the Club Eleven."

Club life became addictive: and so working the Atlantic Ocean route in conventional dance bands, mostly with much older musicians, soon bored the young sax star. He invented a sick-note to cop-out: "I buttonholed Ray Feather, the tenor player in one of the *Queen Mary* bands, and persuaded him that he'd like nothing better than a round-the-world-cruise. Then I called my mother and got her to send me a telegram that my grandmother was very ill and I should return home immediately [...] I got back to England on 17 January 1950, and I went down to the Club Eleven and played like Charlie Parker, Lester Young, Don Byas, Dexter Gordon, Lucky Thompson and Coleman Hawkins all rolled into one."

The 11-piece joint had given Ronnie ideas: Apart from playing true Jazz, owning his own establishment became Scott's foremost ambition, while on the other side of the

Atlantic Ocean, they predicted a great career for his sax skills. Parallel to his excellent live and studio work, for instance for Ted Heath Band and the Johnny Dankworth Orchestra, Scott prevailed and opened his place thanks to a 1000 pound loan by his stepfather.

On Friday, 30th October 1959, he opened his club in a partnership with Pete King (1929–2009), another tenor sax man and, like Scott, in the Jazz Couriers with Tubby Hayes. Called "Ronnie Scott's", rather than Scott & King, it was housed in the basement of 39, Gerrard Street – slap bang in the middle of Chinatown.

The "basement" – well-known amongst many musicians as a taxi waiting area and a tea room – was meant as a jamming venue. The first real live guests was, of course, The Tubby Hayes Quartet, joined by the Eddie Thompson Trio. From the very beginnings of Ronnie Scott's to the present day, there has always been a renowned house band. Initially, the ensemble guaranteed that US stars were able to play in spite of being forced by the British Musician's Union to travel without their own bands. On the other hand, the infamous American Federation of Musicians had to get motivated to let American Jazzers honour performances in the Kingdom in the first place – Pete King was able to get this going.

The Scott-King team deserves a lot of honour in pioneering a "transatlantic exchange" between the United States and the United Kingdom, where swapping the stars meant nobody was going to lose out on working opportunities. In 1961, Zoot Sims was the first US celebrity who managed to reach – and preach at – Ronnie Scott's. In exchange, the Tubby Hayes Quartet was allowed to appear at New York's *Half Note*: this was in November 1961. Ronnie Scott went over to the *Half Note* in 1963, with Jimmy Deuchar and Ronnie Ross. There, they worked with a classical and pianist from Massachusetts, Roger Kellaway. Once the Beatles had started a States conquering "British Invasion" that same year, it was of course much easier for the Jazz stars to come over.

The house band featured the legendary Phil Seamen, a part-time Blue Flame, whose tremendous skills made him probably the greatest drummer in British Jazz, remembered also as the Flamingo Club regular (pianist James Pearson runs Ronnie Scott's All Stars.), Stan Getz, Benny Golson – who was to become a Georgie Fame admirer in due course – and Wes Montgomery belonged to the numerous legends who were about to follow Zoot Sims.

After six years, the club had been successful in such a continuous and stable way that moving in equally dark, but more spacious premises made sense: They got 47 Frith Street. Made idealistic sense, that is; financially sound it wasn't. Those 35,000 pounds which Ronnie Scott borrowed from concert promoter Harold Davison would calculate at about a quarter of a million quid these days. Instead of cashing in properly, the powers that be let the lease of "The Old Place", the former establishment in Gerrard Street, just continue for two years, in order to give young talent a chance – musical gain spelling financial loss! The year was 1959, and saxophonist Peter King, eight years before he graced *The Two Faces Of Fame*, opened the Frith Street Ronnie's.

Ronnie Scott himself was renowned as a compère and told the most daft, dubious, if strangely addictive jokes, as our Blue Flame Guy Barker attests: "When we used to go and see Ronnie Scott, and saw Ronnie tell his jokes, he would tell the same joke every night for years and years and years. I don't know how long I had heard them. As soon as Ronnie was on, I'd run round and stand at the back. I wouldn't go to the dressing room. I wanted to listen to the jokes – again!"

But Scott always kept mouth, hands and powerful lungs in check for the music. That is how he played the sax on the Beatles session for "Lady Madonna" in 1968 – and was appalled how little of it ended up on the actual single mix. That same year, yet another building was added to the enterprise. There was now a talent club on the first floor, and downstairs there was enough seating for 250, and a proper bar was installed – with a further one, "Upstairs at Ronnie's", available today.

The Beatles experience led Scott into opening his club for Rock music: The Who introduced the world to their *Tommy* Rock opera in spring 1969, and the "super group" of fellow mod Steve Marriott and future fellow Rhythm King Peter Frampton, Humble Pie, played their debut here later that same year – their inspired 20-minute workout of Dr John's "Walk On Guilded Splinters" turned out to be worthy of a Jazz club, being miles above their current chart run with "Natural Born Bugie".

At the same time, Georgie Fame's Jazz quartet and later The Blue Flames have to be counted among those who played the club then and now, and who managed to sell out three weeks of concerts in one go during the 1980s and the 1990s – profits that were always needed so badly. As John Fordham records in *Jazz Man: The Amazing Story of Ronnie Scott and his Club*, Georgie was also part of the 30-year celebrations in 1978, and they were in damn good company, too: "The BBC sent in a documentary team from its *Omnibus* arts programme to share in the fun, and the result was an ironic, touching and revealing sixty-minute tribute to the club and its founders. Dizzy Gillespie, Sonny Rollins, Johnny Dankworth and Georgie Fame appeared to tip their hats to the lugubrious pioneers."

One of the Ronnie Scott's highlights for Fame's tenor sax man Alan Skidmore – apart from the annual Blue Flames bashes – was a special project which Swing fan, Charlie Parker fan and Rolling Stones drummer Charlie Watts put up at the club, his own Big Band: Don Weller, John Surman and Tony Oxley were part of it just as new sensations Courtney Pine on clarinet, flute and more, plus baritone saxophone man Gail Thompson. Apparently, The Jazz Warriors started that night. It is not known if Watts became a mortgage worrier, because the whole event cost him 30.000 pounds, and he told enquirers with his poker face: "I had to buy the club to put this on!"

How broadly you can define the term Jazz became clear when Elkie Brooks, Eric Burdon or Peter Green's Splinter Group got a chance to appear at Ronnie's – Green actually appearing in top form compared to later performances. In 1981, Ronnie Scott received the OBE (Order of the British Empire) from Queen Elizabeth for his "Services to Jazz".

There was another expansion of the club in 1989, and by 1991, a second Ronnie Scott's Club opened its doors in Birmingham. It almost didn't happen, because Scott, with his 52nd Street Manhattan club taste hated the first interior design. Once that was fixed, the quietly swinging Charlie Watts struck again and was able to open the place in the autumn, accompanied for his Charlie Parker mixes Classical & Jazz musings by

Peter King and trumpeter Gerard Presencer. Scott just about lived to see the opening of yet another club branch in the German Ruhr area town of Oberhausen near Düsseldorf. Georgie Fame and The Blue Flames were one of the first acts there, wooing the twice sold-out place but hating the surroundings of the futuristic "Centro" shopping centre even more than Ronnie Scott had hated the initial Birmingham design.

Guy Barker couldn't make the gig, but Alan Skidmore, Brothers James & Tristan as well as Geoff Gascoyne on bass and the wonderfully fluent vibraphone wizard Anthony Kerr were there, the latter presenting a refined alternative to sticky keyboard sounds that were still de rigeur in the 1990s, including Jazz outfits. "I Love The Life I Live" opened the proceedings, and quickly the audience seemed to have forgotten about the plastic Las Vegas all around them and could mentally stroll to Frith Street.

For "Yeh Yeh", Georgie promised the German version for the next sojourn. Mose Allison's mellow and morbid philosophical leanings in "If You Live" and "Was" were contrasted with Ray Charles' up-tempo shuffle "Roll With Me Baby". The mood was positively African with "Zulu", and "The New Symphony Sid" kept the mood jolly. The second half began full of nostalgia with the slow ballad "A Decleation Of Love", but then a British delegation had audibly used the intermission for some liquid lunch, and Georgie reacted amiably by stating "I can hear it's Rock'n'Roll from now on: 'Lawdy Miss Clawdy'.

What followed was the equally dance-friendly and single release compatible Swing about the good old black "Vinyl" records – the ailing Ronnie back home in Soho would have approved. With Duke Ellington's "I Ain't Got Nothing But The Blues" it was back to the American Rhythm & Jazz Songbook. The prolonged Blues medley featuring the original Louis Jordan composition "Jumping With Symphony Sid" led to a real party final, which the boss of the band had sweetened by deliverance of fine Whiskeys.

Towards the end of 1996, after a thrombosis, a subsequent leg operation and heavy dental treatment, whose success is crucial for any sax player, Ronnie Scott mixed painkillers with brandy – a lethal cocktail for him! Pete King continued to run the club for a further nine years, before it got sold to the theatre manageress Sally Green, who had been introduced to the place as a child. These days, Leo Green, another sax player (Jerry Lee Lewis, Van Morrison, Bob Dylan) runs the club. You want Billy Cobham? Terry Reid? Van Morrison? Georgie Fame & The Blue Flames? Book early.

Like Ronnie Scott, Fame's old saxophonist Mick Eve had always been torn between two professions – that of booking agent and of course a musician at heart. That way, he was able to look at the proceedings of the club from more than one angle: "I was still doubling in between Gonzales. It was the only thing I could do really – people would always want me to get back to an agency, get on the phone and talk to the promoters I had known for years. So that would create a little circuit where people would go on playing, including Gonzales of course, I was looking after that. But at the end of the day, there were a lot of other nice bands around, like Kokomo, and Average White Band, and F.B.I. The music was changing around, but I was still obliged to do the bookings – well, not obliged to, I needed to make a living. I finished up being at Ronnie Scott's as an agent. And then of course, every so often, there'd come the word

from downstairs, "Oh, can you bring the band in next week to support Bill Evans?" There were marvelous acts we supported."

"But I had nothing to do with Georgie Fame at that point. I would go to Ronnie's any time he was down there, and usually, he used to bring a tremendous Big Band down there. This was while Ronnie was still alive; the club has all changed now, beyond any recognition. It just had a very good atmosphere – like the world that I knew in the Sixties. It was more like that in there, because all the people that went, they went because they loved the music. It would be a few people who paid full price tickets and maybe wouldn't quite know the way to react, but they were cool tapping it."

All the more, Eve has been aware of the changes: "Whereas now you go in there and it is sort of gold credit card, only on one side – it's just a very strange atmosphere. People are doing as little as they can to participate. The spirit has gone from the place."

According to Eve, once there was "that feeling that the audience is there principally to listen to the music. They used to make jokes about the food and the drinks not being particularly appetizing. It didn't matter, the place was a nice place to be, friendly faces and knowledgeable people. With all these listed staff on this, people were talking all through Bill Evans's piano solo, and we would be going "Shhh" around the place, and it had a great effect. Ronnie used to make announcements, "If you really wanna speak, you needn't spend 20 pounds for coming in, you could have been talking on the street. It's weird, people coming there and they start yapping, cause it's a bass solo or a delicate pianist."

These days, staff still tend to go round saying "Please keep your conversations to a minimum". But then, as it happened in 2013, Georgie turns up saying that "Actually, you can chat as much as you like"!

Mick Eve has an explanation for this, too, "Well, haha, he knows that they've done a lot to kill the atmosphere that used to exist down there. You didn't have to encourage people, it was a good time – if you felt like dancing, you could do it where you were sitting. That has vanished. Anyway, I only went back twice in the last three years. One was for Maceo Parker, who always tries to liven people up. But he found it pretty impossible. And Fred Wesley, he's great."

The constant "rabbiting" in Ronnie Scott's Club was by no means just a later phenomenon. There is a lovely cartoon in Scott's own 1977 memoirs *Some Of My Best Friends Are Blues*, "The band is so loud, I can't hear what you're saying" and as John McLaughlin had told Mick Brown in the Rock magazine *Sounds* in 1975, "I certainly don't identify with a 'rock culture'. A rock audience, if it's good they don't care what it's called or who's doing it – as long as it's for real. I discovered this many years ago. I'd play Ronnie Scott's and get one kind of feeling, and then play Middle Earth and get a whole other feeling ... I'd take the Rock audience any time over the Jazz audience."

For Georgie, the club isn't what it used to be. More than once, he related to his eagerly and amusedly listening audience how young staff when politely asked for a glass of water will react with an enquiring 'Who are you?', only to be led to the big poster with the "Sold Out" sticker right outside in the hustle and bustle of Frith Street. "That's me, I'm only the guy who makes the place run for this week."

And Georgie has a point, too, because in Ronnie Scott's day and age, or Pete King's for that matter, all the staff would have easily known the prime movers and groovers of the place as well as their nearest and dearest – and spoilt them lovingly in the process.

Ronnie Scott – portrait glimpses of the man and the club

Of course, playing in Ronnie Scott's Club triggers more vivid memories of the man who started it all, Ronnie Scott – especially those musicians who not only met him in person but actually worked with him.

When you sit in the legendary club-adjoining 16th century public house, the *Dog & Duck*, out for an intermission pint with Scott's lifelong friend Alan Skidmore, and Skid raises his glass and goes "This bench is where Ronnie always used to sit", you can positively feel his ghost still around somewhere between Soho Square and Chinatown.

How does a veteran like Alan Skidmore remember Scott the club owner, celebrated saxophonist and ladies' man? Skidmore: "Ronnie Scott once said to my then 18 year old daughter, Alice: 'Alice', he said, 'if I were 20 years younger, I'd be wishing I was 20 years younger!' He was a great guy. I miss him! I still miss him, to this day. We had some great times together. I probably knew a slightly different guy, because we worked together there. I was younger than him, of course, but at the same time, I was fortunate enough to do quintet gigs with him and with two tenors. We did a bit of touring, and I used to go up to the club in the afternoon and practice with him. And then eventually he would say "Well, that's enough of that, let's go to the *Dog & Duck*, and get happy!"

Ronnie Scott and Georgie Fame must have been on good terms, as Skidmore confirms: "Sure they were, absolutely. They were friends. Georgie/Clive always fills the place, doesn't he? It doesn't mat-

Ronnie Scott 1948

ter how many nights he is there." Which Anthony Kerr can add to: "He fills the place with nice people. The staff always likes them. They are nice. They are polite. They tip the staff, a nicer crowd than some of the other people who pack the club."

Guy Barker's memories of the club are directly related to Fame: "Georgie was somebody who – I didn't see him [perform] there, but he was one of the first people I saw when I went to Ronnie Scott's. I went there when I was about 15 or 16. I saw Roland Kirk, and I then became just completely fascinated by the music. I used to go to Ronnie Scott's as often as I could. I saw Dizzy Gillespie, this and that. And I can't remember, I was a teenager though. I suppose I was about 17 or 18, and I went to Ronnie's one night and stood at the back, and I remember Georgie was wearing a green jumpsuit of some sort [a pilot's jump suit which he had still got in 2011, as witnessed by this author]. He was on stage in this jumpsuit, all the band were there. I just loved it. I just found it a fantastic night, and I just loved the music, and I loved his voice. Of course I was reminded of how I got the record. He was somebody that was always there, and around somehow."

Apparently, old Ronald was such a winner with the ladies that ex-Fame drummer Jon Hiseman wouldn't have him receive lessons from his wife Barbara Thompson:

"By the way, when Barbara was 25, Ronnie Scott wanted her to give him flute lessons. And I said 'Barbara, you can do whatever you want with your life, but as your husband I'm telling you now: you're not going to give Ronnie Scott flute lessons.' And Ronnie and I laughed about this for the next 30 years: because he was a killer with the women!"

On the strictly professional side, James Powell recalls how the procedures for a week at Ronnie Scott's Club would suddenly change during the year 2013: "There was a breakthrough a couple of weeks ago. Before Ronnie's, we actually did two days' rehearsal at the Bull's Head [the Jazz club in Barnes, London]. So by the time we played on Monday night at Ronnie's, we had already played some of his tunes at least two or three times. And we were getting more of a feel about it.

"Usually what would happen is we'd arrive at the sound check for the first day at Ronnie's, and he'd shout at everybody. He'd spend 30 seconds off each new tune. You have to give these things time in order to be comfortable, so this was a very good development that he spent the time and the money to have a couple of days rehearsal with us, which we are eventually going to record. When we get into the studio, we might feel more comfortable."

"Jeannine" – Ronnie Scott's Club live specials over the years

The thrill of attending the annual Ronnie Scott's gigs by Georgie, now mostly in the spring time, is not only the ritual of comparing notes on the word-by-word anecdotal introductions to songs, and enjoying nuances in the performances of numbers that some of the hard core fans have heard hundreds of times, but of enjoying Georgie as the great explorer, the Jazz geologist.

21 years ago, Georgie received an ultimate and well-worded compliment from eye-witness journalist Phil Johnson, among whose praises was the following:

"Although he'll be 50 this year, Georgie Fame still looks and sounds like his *Ready Steady Go* incarnation of 1964 [...] The hair is greyer and the bags under the eyes more pronounced, but everything else is gloriously intact; deep, languid voice, effortlessly hip demeanor, a Hammond organ grown old in the service and a repertoire of jazz, blues and soul tunes culled from the Soho record-shop import racks of 30 years ago. As the ultimate badge of credible continuity, he even has his original conga player, Speedy, slapping out the backbeats. Lest we forget, 'Yeh Yeh' was kept back as far as the second number in the set. It would be difficult to think of any other artist who, over such a long time-span, has kept faith with his original influences so assiduously and yet managed to avoid slipping into self-parody or nostalgia. This is at least partly because of the sense of responsibility Fame feels towards those who have traditionally provided his material: the songs may come via King Pleasure, Ray Charles, Mose Allison or Chet Baker [...] Opening the first set with King Pleasure's 'Red Top', and standing at front of stage, Fame showed how skilled and sophisticated a vocalist he is. Moving the hand- mike up and down to modulate the volume of his voice, trembling his jawbone to bend a note and alternating baritone, tenor and even falsetto registers, he sounded quite masterly. "

About 2003, Fame would re-introduce a driving, melodious standard popularized in the early Sixties called "Jeannine". For Blue Flames archivists, this number goes back to their 1966 sets:

There was a BBC radio show show called *Jazzbeat*, presented by George Melly. It used to be transmitted on late Saturday afternoons. One time Georgie Fame and the Blue Flames were invited there, it was for a 30-minute gig, which featured the great horn section of Peter Coe, Glenn Hughes and Eddie Thornton. Hughes' piece de resistance was "Jeannine" by Hard Bop and Soul Jazz pianist Duke Pearson (1939–1980). Duke Ellington admirer Pearson had composed the thing around 1960, and Cannonball Adderley had covered it on one of Georgie's favourite albums, *Them Dirty Blues*, before Oscar Brown Jr. got his hands on it and Jon Hendricks added more lyrics. Glenn Hughes played a marvelous baritone sax. He had played it at an All-nighter as well. Fame had Guy Barker and Alan Skidmore play rousing solos for his own rendition.

In 2004, five years in advance, although he surely wasn't aware of the delay, Georgie started to introduce songs from his forthcoming album *Tone Wheels 'A' Turnin'*, delivering the fast shuffle "The Burdee Song" and his wry observation "Guantanamo-by-the-Sea" about waiting for visa documents in a London government office. He also re-introduced his remarkable 1974 environmental Blues plea "Survival", which would find its way onto the new CD in a third, epic and stunning version. Finally, there was room for some African type Calypso: Alan Skidmore and his composition "Enkosi Dumisani" from his work with South-African band Amampondo, *Ubizo*. Fame presented another African tune during his 2011 series, "Uncle Ezra".

Georgie dedicated "Jeannine" to Eddie Jefferson and mentioned the legendary album *King Pleasure Sings/Annie Ross Sings* which came out in 1954 on Prestige Records, one of his most influential treasures where "Jumpin' With Symphony Sid", "Red Top", "This Is Always", "I'm In The Mood For Love" and "Parker's Mood" can be found.

Another prime example was "No, Not Much", a composition by Robert Allen with lyrics by Al Stillman. Georgie had assumed that no one knew it and no one had a clue where it came from: "It is just a nice tune. King Pleasure didn't write it, but he is the only guy that I heard sing it. And it was in my memory box, somewhere. And it just pulled itself out one day, while I was sitting at the piano. It is just a good tune, good nice little simple swing tune. And then, somebody – it wasn't you, was it? – told me that Robert Palmer had recorded it a number of years ago", he wondered, smoking another cigarette in front of Ronnie Scott's in Frith Street. Asked whether we could hope for a studio recording of it one of these days, he wondered, "Maybe. I play it with the trio, and I do it with the band, of course. Well, it doesn't matter. I only ever heard King Pleasure sing it. It is one of those not well known songs."

In 2007, Fame added from the stage, "I heard this was already covered by Robert Palmer, he probably ruined it completely!" Palmer had designated it as "unknown" in origin, but in fact it had been recorded by The Four Lads, a vocal group in the vein of The Four Freshman, in 1956. Anyway, Georgie often did his wonderful version at the club, and it is a prime contender for a recording wish list in this author's "book".

Also in 2007, Fame sang a fairly rare (for him) excerpt from the American Songbook, presenting "It Ain't Necessarily So" with a "Thank you for all the afore mentioned" – name-dropping has he always is during his performances – and especially Clifford Brown".

A firm favourite over the last decade has been Fame's rendition of the Brill Building classic "The Point Of No Return", written by Carol King and her 60s husband, Jerry Goffin. At the Ronnie Scott shows, he always pointed out that the couple had most probably written this thing immediately pre-divorce.

Georgie said frequently that he based his version of the song, which he had originally recorded for his first studio album *Fame At Last* in 1964, on the Louis Jordan version on the 1963 single 45-TRC-933 which came out on the rather short-lived Ray Charles led Tangerine label, and he performed that number with relish and panache, with the Blue Flames enjoying it every time.

"Don't Send Me Flowers When I'm In The Graveyard" had been the B-side, and Georgie loved this song as much as his old mate Brian Auger, because it always raises a chuckle with the audience. As our man pointed out, it is usually dedicated "to composer Floyd Dixon to George Melly, stolen by Sonny Boy Williamson!" Over many years, Tristan Powell has had them under his spell, too, with a finely crafted guitar solo which gets more refined each and every year. Tristan was also responsible for picking the old Jim Reeves ballad "He'll Have To Go", which is also regularly featured in the Thee Line Whip/Georgie & Sons repertoire. Tristan preferred the version on Ry Cooder's acclaimed 1976 album *Chicken Skin Music*, which he delivered with his own, pleasant singing.

For a long period of time, Georgie had announced during his gigs that he would exchange his Equitable Life pension scheme with someone who could give him a mint copy of that single. So one day, his Portuguese friend and ardent follower António Alfaiate, always flying in from Lisbon, gave him a mint copy, and Georgie was delighted.

But alas, he managed to break it during the gig at Ronnie Scott's that very same day when he accidentally crashed it against his Hammond organ! He said then, in the middle of the gig: "António you've got to find another copy for me because I just broke the one you gave me!"

Georgie sang on Ben Sidran's album *Dylan Different*, delivering a truly cool version of "Rainy Day Woman # 12 and 35". At Ronnie Scott's, Fame paid his friend Ben the compliment of delivering the first incident where he was able to understand any of Bob Dylan's lyrics. But it was kind of typical that he did not choose to sing his contribution to the collection, but opted for "Everything Is Broken", which he complemented with some audience participation. The guests were asked to watch out for the break in the band's deliverance and then shout, "It's all fucked up, man!" Not your typical Jazz club behavior maybe, but tons of fun for the bandleader – and others, proved by lots of grins all round.

It is always a joy to hear Fame present "the fine composition" by his ex Blue Flames member Andy Fairweather Low, "Wide-Eyed And Legless", which he had on his album *Charlestons* and digs out again from time to time, much to the listeners' joy and the composer's pride; Andy still considers himself first and foremost a fan, in spite of having worked in the Flames and the Rhythm Kings.

While 2014 had seen a pretty standard but highly enjoyable set of classics, the April gigs of the year before had been full of pleasant and brand new nuggets. "Another year has gone", Fame started to sing, introducing his "Diary Blues" from a forthcoming album, which is about "dining with the aristocracy: caviar filled my plates", with a "Parchman Farm" type of ending. We got a cleverly worded, relaxed homage to "Mose Knows" Allison. There was an unheard, finger-snapping Calypso in "The Caribbean Way", we got the new ballad "This World/Love Has Brought Me Here", and Georgie's moving tribute to his good friend Mike O'Neill, "My Ship (Is Coming In)". Little did he know in April that half a year later, on October 10th, he would sing the song again in Copenhagen as a farewell to the just deceased "other man from Leigh".

How Long Has This Been Going On – The Morrison & Fame Ronnie Scott's album

Six years after first working together with Georgie Fame, Morrison decided to make a spontaneous album of standards and some of his own numbers, and thereby actually giving credit to Georgie on the front cover. The recording was done in the in the daytime at Ronnie Scott's Club, with no audience present, on the 3rd May, 1995. Fame junior, Blue Flames guitarist Tristan, was hired as their engineer, credited here as Tristan "Beenz" Powell, a little amusing windbreaker moniker he is rather hesitant to discuss these days.

Van Morrison's own Swing "I Will Be There" starts the proceedings. It looked as if each artist had brought half of his own band, but they were all used to working live together anyway: Georgie's Guy Barker and Alan Skidmore were in both groups; Van had Ralph Salmins on drums, Alec Dankworth on double bass, Robin Aspland

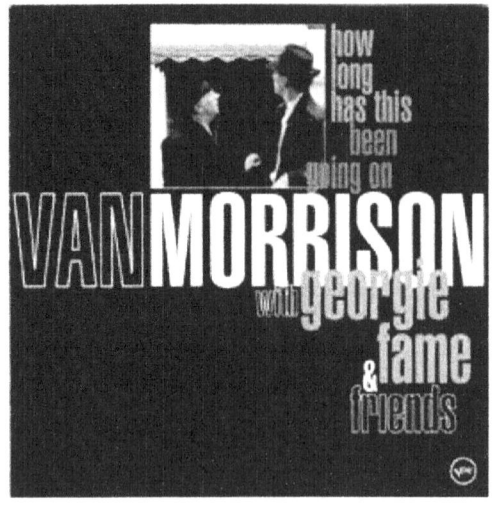

on piano; and guest star Pee Wee Ellis was on saxophones, who 18 years later would join Ginger Baker's Confusion with Alec Dankworth in tow.

"The New Symphony Sid" is a sequel to the Lester Young composition with King Pleasure lyrics, "Jumpin' With Symphony Sid", which Georgie did on Van Morrison's *A Night In San Francisco*, also on the fine Morrison-Fame bootleg *Stepping On A Dream*, recorded at the Bournemouth I.E.C. on September 16th, 1995. Finally, he cut it in 2000 as a studio recording on *Poet in New York*. Georgie loves sequels – "It Could Happen To You" from *The Two Faces of Fame* just had to be followed by "Everything Happens To Me" on *Georgie Does His Thing With Strings*, for instance. For "The New Symphony Sid", Fame had added new lyrics and a different melody to the King Pleasure and Lester Young tune about the famous New York City Jazz radio personality Sidney Tarnopol a.k.a. "Symphony" Sid Torin (1909–1984). It was all about his grooving and a whole house being moving with tales on what Sid was putting down – playing his Swing as a greatest and latest Dee Jay: Fame's organ touches are sparse compared to Asplund's pearly piano runs.

Swing Waltz is next – re-arranging the famous Louis Jordan tune "Early In The Morning" that was a Calypso originally. Call and response between Van and Georgie before the latter lets his Hammond really do the talking here.

"Who Can I Turn To?", a well-known Blues ballad by singer and actor Anthony Newley and the musical lyricist Leslie Bricusse, is mainly sung by Morrison, with Fame throwing in the chorus line and repeating lines like "I'll find what I'm after". Van's main man Pee Wee Ellis arranged the horns and supplied some great saxophone, taking turns with Guy Barker in soloing.

A firm live favourite, "Sack O'Woe" was arranged by Georgie Fame here – hardly a surprise because Jon Hendricks had written the classic together with Julian Cannonball Adderley as typically early 60s R&B. As cleverly syncopated Swing, this works ever so effortlessly, with Morrison and Fame trading vocals with obvious fun, Barker and Ellis again shining brightly during their solos.

Another attempt at Van's classic "Moondance" is always welcome, and it grooves along inspiringly here, but in the author's estimation, this cannot touch the version Georgie had delivered on his *Cool Cat Blues* five years previously. Both could top their respective versions during nine magic minutes, again on *Stepping On A Dream*. A highlight must be Alec Dankworth's fluent, warm and elegant double bass solo – he would play this number often enough after joining the Blue Flames as a successor to Geoff Gascoyne. Barker's trumpet is set next to Ellis' sax work with Leo Green, and some pleasant scat singing by Van.

Jon Hendricks wrote his legendary "Centerpiece" in connection with Harry Edison, and must have been delighted to listen to Messrs Morrison and Fame doing a "Lambert, Hendricks & Ross" – from *The Hottest New Group In Jazz*, 1960, where it was followed by Georgie's Sixties chestnut "Gimme That Wine" from *Fame At Last* – with his number: featuring as they did the wonderful Annie Ross, who came over from New York having just finished her new album *Music Is Forever*. "Centerpiece" includes a quotation from Frank Foster's "Blues Backstage".

Fame's Hammond leads into the title track, George Gershwin's "How Long Has This Been Going On". Morrison does the singing, assisted by Guy Barker's trumpet interludes. This time, Van's version can be treated as a valid take on a par with Georgie's version on *Walking Wounded*, the second Ronnie Scott's live volume recorded a few months later. Fame's studio organ solo here is a lesson in sensitive understatement.

There is a story Georgie tells audiences, as he did at the 'Jazzens' in Vasteras, Sweden: At Ronnie's, Van refused to record "How Long Has This Been Going On" unless the name-dropping of "Columbus" went: "A Norwegian discovered America!" Fame: "I'm producing this record. The clock is ticking, and so are my royalties! He won't sing the song." Since nobody in the club had a clue who the hell the Viking was, the Belfast explorer reminded Georgie about his Scandinavian ties. So at a late hour, Fame frantically phoned friends to find the sailor's identity, like Big Band boss Per Husby. "I had one more number: Karin Krog (see next chapter): She was down under, in Aussie. 'Karen, it's me, Georgie! Listen, I'm in the studio with Van Morrison; he won't sing this song! What's the name of this Norsk explorer who came to America in 1100 or so, way way before Christopher Columbus!' She says 'Oh (mock Swedish) it's Leif Eriksson. I tell Van and he goes 'Put on the red light, I'll sing it'. He sang about Leif Eriksson". They were damn lucky the Gershwin heirs didn't sue them!

Next, in the recording of Mose's treasures is "Your Mind Is On Vacation" – the title track of his 1976 album. Morrison does an inspired reading of this, and when you listen to Allison's lyrics about people who talk too much without giving it too much thought, you can't help but believe this is an attitude which both Van and Mose loath. A small band with Ellis, Barker, Salmins and Dankworth, highlighted by Robin Aspland, delivers just the right groove.

Fame was allotted the task to arrange, play a lot of Hammond and sing his bit on Morrison's "All Saints Day", realized here as a rousing Swing with ever-inventive brass work thrown in by the usual suspects. Compare this to the night club 1991 version Van did on his double album *Hymns To The Silence*, where Carol Kenyon sang backing vocals with Georgie, and his organ was nicely offset with an elegant Neil Drinkwater piano solo: Due to the horn section, Fame's solo vocal lines and the accelerated tempo, you get even more of a Blue Flames feeling here, although Van's *Hymns To The Silence* version of the Allison song is ultimately more controlled and deep.

The 1941 Harold Arlen song "Blues in the Night (My Mama Done Done Tol Me)" with lyrics by Johnny Mercer got arranged by Georgie with Pee Wee Ellis. His sax collaboration with Alan Skidmore is especially convincing here, with the warmth of the track once again guaranteed via the unobtrusive organ work. The original from the film

Blues In The Night was sung from a prison cell, and what's the betting Ronnie Scott's Club was just as dark during the recording.

More Mose – via Allison's "Don't Worry 'Bout A Thing", and Georgie was included: playing his old tone wheels as well as arranging, and making sure Guy Barker could put his magic touches between Morrison's verses.

Another standard – Van Morrison often performs Dean Kay and Kelly Gordon's "That's Life" in concerts, a brave choice with regard to the famous Frank Sinatra version from *That's Life* in 1966 and Aretha Franklin's rousing version year later. Van and his band, including Georgie, did it for *Later With Jools Holland* on BBC television. Here, the Blues sounds correspondingly well rehearsed and tight, with possibly Pee Wee Ellis's best sax solo here, succeeded by Barker, Morrison belting it less harshly here, with the benefit of a more harmonious sound picture.

Fame and Morrison sing the finale "Heathrow Shuffle" together here – Van's song celebrating many an hour in the VIP lounge of London's huge "hub" (as Georgie tends to call airports), but not before they have given ample time to some Hammond, trumpet and sax excursions. This time, it is Alan Skidmore who went out to lunch, leaving the saxophones to Ellis – and now Van Morrison himself, so that he has the last blow and vocal job this way.

Guy Barker recalls the sessions with ever so positive vibes: "I really enjoyed the one we did at Ronnie Scott's. Van wanted to record an album, and he wanted to get the atmosphere, so we recorded it in Ronnie Scott's in the afternoon. Annie Ross came in. The rhythm section was set up on the stage, and they cleared the tables, and the horns, we were on the floor where the audience sat. We recorded it in an afternoon. I enjoyed that: It was a nice gig with different people who dropped by, and I think when Annie Ross walked in, it was like 'Wow, this is fun!'

Tristan Powell remembers the sessions with good feelings: "There was the one with Van done at Ronnie Scott's, *How Long Has This Been Going On*. That was done very quickly. I don't think he was difficult to work with. It depends how you perceive people like that. If you treat them just like anyone else, and don't get wrapped up in the occasional whirlwind, it's fine. The night before the sessions, I had a £50 bet with him that we would record 12 songs. At the end of the day's recording session, we had recorded 12 songs. I won the bet."

His brother James actually got a rare chance to work with Van live shortly after: "I did play drums with Van on three occasions only. It was during the tenure of my great friend Ralph Salmins, who is a terrific drummer. He played on that Ronnie Scott's record, [*How Long Has This Been Going On?*]. He was booked to do a load of dates with Van, and there were a couple that he needed to get out of, so I depped for Ralph at one or two theatres round the south coast. And the first thing we did was a live TV thing in Hammersmith. There used to be a show called *TFI Friday*, which is a live music show, until presenter Chris Evans said 'fuck' live on air [it was Shaun Ryder of the Happy Mondays actually] and then it was no longer live. This was the last live one.

"It was Van's band, but it included Dad and me. Tris was not on it. We played 'Moondance'. I did a couple of theatre gigs, and Ralph had done these incredible charts. I love

Van, but there are so many hundreds of songs, and often quite similar harmonically. So he wrote me about two live charts, about twenty numbers per page, a kind of book to flick through, to help me. I remember it very fondly, and I'd love to do it again, as I am much more mature now. As a musician I have grown, I'd do a great job now. I had done a lot of homework, too. I had that ambition. It was a big deal for me. I must have been probably in my mid 20s, maybe early 20s. I might get another opportunity."

Chatting with Ben Sidran in the Chicago man's *Talking Jazz, An Oral History*, Mose Allison paid Van Morrison a huge compliment, reprinted in the album's liner notes: "I really admire Van. He writes good songs. And he does it from a musician's approach [...] And he doesn't have any of the mannerisms that you would associate with some of the more outrageous musical acts that are doing real good in the music business." Van knows: A mutual, true admiration society.

Ronnie Scott's Club and the first Blue Flames live album for 33 years

Looking back on The Blue Flames' Ronnie Scott's Club performances of the year 1994, Georgie commented about the possibility of recording there a few weeks after the event: "We could do that any time. I think the next time I'll play at Ronnie Scott's with my own band – we're doing two weeks at the club in Birmingham in January 1995, and I think we should record it. We played for two weeks at Ronnie Scott's in London at the end of April 1994, and everybody said it felt fantastic every night – we should have recorded that every night. So I think next time at Ronnie's I'll record it!"

It didn't happen in January, but it did happen in the autumn of 1995: Two sets were played and would eventually lead to two albums' worth of material. A year later, the CD *Name Droppin'* appeared on the market, or rather slid into some specialist shops, as the third release on Georgie's own high profile, low visibility label TLW (Three Line Whip).

Avid readers of the booklet's small print noted that the album was co-produced by Fame with his older son, Tristan Powell, who – as shown – had developed an interest in the other side of the recording process since he was very young.

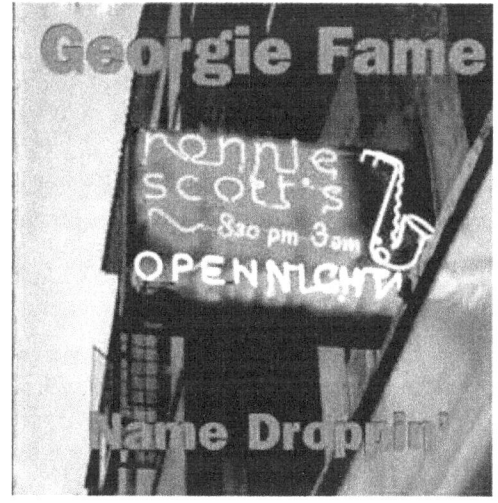

When *Name Droppin'* came out in the autumn of 1996, almost a year after having been recorded and in time for the opening of Ronnie Scott's Oberhausen in Germany, there was no real hint that it was a first volume, other than the fact that there were no real hits on it. Still, it was a relentless tour-de-force of great material which the Blue Flames performed with obvious pride and joy.

Name Droppin': Live At Ronnie Scott's – track by track

With "Jimmy McGroove" proceedings started by Georgie "getting ready to play", "warming up": introducing a new number, which immediately "dropped" two names for a fitting Hammond tribute – homages to Jimmy Smith, Jimmy McGriff and Richard "Groove" Holmes.

He announces "a self-deprecating Blues" – "Cool Cat Blues", which had been the title track of his 1990 studio "comeback" and also still lingered in the Island vaults in its first 1970s incarnation. This version runs more than six minutes – characterized by Brother James' and Geoff Gascoyne's easy patterns. The melodic ground work of Alan Skidmore's tenor sax and Anthony Kerr's vibes lead to a short but ecstatic Guy Barker solo, Georgie enjoying himself with tasty licks and joyful squeaking.

The tempo goes up again for Ray Charles and Percy Mayfield's "Tell Me How Do You Feel" from *The Blues And Me*. The name dropping by no means ending with Charles: Georgie dedicated this number to "Eddie Cochran, who had introduced the masses of this country to Ray", the audience mumbling the words with Georgie for the hundredth time as if saying the Lord's Prayer – and happy with it. The rendition has such an easy flow thanks to all involved that Alan Skidmore's solo seems to play itself, before Fame takes over on Hammond and quotes John Lee Hooker's "How How How".

Georgie's own "Zulu" had been in the repertoire for almost 20 years by 1995, a steady party piece in the set that he finally recorded in 1978 for *Right Now!* Comprising virtually all the numbers on a typical Ronnie Scott's night, there is a generous running time – our man starts alone on the piano and dedicates this to Niimoi "Speedy" Acquaye, his original conga player, who deeply deserves this name dropping and often played it himself when he was still in the Blue Flames. James's drum work, alternating on toms and cymbals, is nothing short of exquisite; Gascoyne slaps and Kerr can let go on the vibes.

Mose Allison's "Was" had already been pencilled in for Georgie's tribute album to him with Van Morrison and Ben Sidran, *Tell Me Something*, a philosophical reflection about our life on this earth being limited. Fame does the wonderful melody, the thoughtful lyrics and "Mose's kind of sound" full justice in this quiet reading, whose Hammond touches are complemented by quiet vibes and subdued bass and brush work.

Next, alto saxophonist Peter King is welcomed on stage as "The Pied Piper", for Fame's composition "Vinyl" which he dedicated to *Ray's Record Shop* again, like on the *Three Line Whip* studio version. Once more, the live version has an easier flow, organ and vibes in happy unison. How Georgie manages to get those mean and dirty sounds out of his Hammond and sing the nostalgic lyrics so well simultaneously is quite an achievement. King solos all around.

The medley of the standard "Mercy Mercy Mercy" and Van's "Vanlose Stairway", also from *Three Line Whip*, had been long and varied in its studio incarnation, but in spite of the faithful rendition, it sounds even more natural and complete in this comfortable club environment – one can see the three horns gather their steam for the great climaxes, before Fame takes the band down to a more intimate level again. Tristan's wah

wah is an inspired departure from the studio workout, as is Brother James's steady groove.

At almost 20 minutes, the following "Blues Medley" was a very special delight, because not only did it combine four top notch compositions – it also presented a part of the Blue Flames repertoire which to date has still not been graced with studio recordings and is therefore unique to this document. First was Richard Holmes "Groove's Groove" which shows where his nickname comes from. Then came Lionel Hampton's "Red Top": Georgie sings part of it in falsetto – delivering the basic melody first – announcing Peter King again as "The Pied Piper", and after King, it's "Aaaaaanthony Kerr" and as Kerr mentioned, some of his friends even greet him the way Georgie announces him on stage.

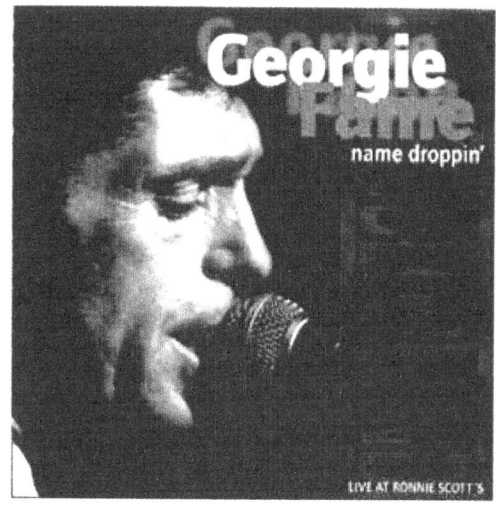

"Guy Barker" is announced in the same way for his solo spot, before the singer gets into some pretty breathtaking Vocalese and Alan Skidmore takes over on tenor: "El Skid"! Next comes Harold Edison's "Centrepiece", and the finale, Stan Getz's "Don't Getz Scared", with Vocalese words by King Pleasure. All that calls for more *Name Droppin'* – "Gene Ammons, the great saxophonist from Chicago, King Pleasure [of course], Harold Edison from Count Basie's Orchestra, with Lambert, Hendricks & Ross".

By anyone's standards, this would have been the end of a wonderfully varied and atmospheric live album, and that's the way it seemed when this slipped out in the autumn of 1996. Okay, no "Yeh Yeh", but you can't have everything, and what was presented was certainly a fine selection, pristinely presented.

How can this burning band have been ill? – Walking Wounded

But then GoJazz Records picked *Name Droppin'* up in 1997, and followed it up with what had been Set 2 of that same November 1995 night all along. Paying dues to the fact that basically the whole band had been down with the flu and other ailments during the night picked for recording – including Set 1, of course – that second part of the night was duly called *Walking Wounded*. Well, a lot of artists would have been proud to deliver sets like these when they were on top form and in the best of health, but this lot was really suffering.

The stories accompanying the ailing ensemble are manifold. Obviously, the most precious item that could be "wounded" during a live recording is always the singer's throat and voice. But what we can hear over and over again is fine even for a completely healthy singer. Plus, as Alan Skidmore recalls, "actually, over the years, I think it's got better. He always complains and coughs, but once he's on stage, he's right on it. I've never ever heard him goof, he's always smack on."

At the time, though, getting into the club after the winter recess could mean hitting a time of virus infections. Vibraphone man Anthony Kerr: "We all have – this was done with the *Walking Wounded* album. Remember, there were three weeks at Ronnie Scott's, and we used to call it "the health farm" in a sarcastic humour. It always came when the cold virus had started to get the winning hand against the human defense system. The weather is changing. Suddenly we are up late into the night, up till 3 a.m. every night, for three weeks solid. And the band room wasn't the most hygienic. It was very, very crowded. There were leaking pipes and things. Suddenly there is the most unhealthy lifestyle you can imagine, just at the time of year when it's getting at you. The easiest part was always on the stage – everything else was verging on the intolerable. Am I dragging myself into the West End again?"

Alan Skidmore confirms this: "I'm the same! The times over the years we have done three weeks. That is tough – to do three weeks at Ronnie Scott's with the old regime. The original regime which was Pete King – who was a great guy, by the way, and Ronnie was a sweetheart, fabulous, and a great saxophone player [Pete King not to be confused with the twelve years younger Peter King, who played here in The Blue Flames] – it used to start late and finish late, didn't it, whereas now it starts early and finishes early, apart from Friday and Saturday.

Anthony Kerr: "They do it New York style and double. But it used to be like we didn't go onstage until a quarter to 11 on a Saturday nights. We would go to Soho, buy the Sunday newspaper on the street which was on sale from half nine or something. And you would be reading the Sunday paper before you started to work on Saturday. Some days, it took its toll. But the music was the medicine!"

Tristan Powell as the haunted man at the guitar *and* the soundboard: "I remember that for *Walking Wounded*, I didn't tell the band that we were recording, and that kind of worked out quite well. I told them afterwards, so they had no idea, and they didn't think about it. It's always a good thing when they don't know."

Anthony Kerr can also recount a completely different problem: "The thing I remember, once he [Georgie] fell over a sheep. Then he turned up at Ronnie Scott's and had pulled his muscles because – at that time he lived in the countryside the west of England, in Wiltshire. The night before he was due to come up to London, he got a call from his neighbour, saying a sheep was loose, had escaped. So he ended up picking up this sheep and ripping all sorts of muscles in his shoulder. And he turned up to the gig in severe pain."

Walking Wounded: Live At Ronnie Scott's Part 2 – track by track

Fame opened Set 2 of the club evening with "Eros Hotel": Fran Landesman's Soho poem about a "rainy day in London" had been a long-time favourite of Georgie's. Alone at the piano, he lets his romantic feelings slowly take momentum. But this number works no matter what he does – even the Reggae arrangement in *Closing The Gap* hit the spot in 1980. Here, the protagonist is completely on his own, whistling one verse in true Hoagy Carmichael style.

"This is one of Mose's old cotton sack songs", this was how Fame introduced one of the vintage Allison numbers he has always loved: "If You Live", "your time will come". This version had not been released on the Allison tribute *Tell Me Something* when *Walking Wounded* was being recorded, but even so it was a nice plug of an album in the pipeline. Heartfelt Hammond work gets nicely enhanced by exquisite guitar chords courtesy of Tristan Powell, wah wah licks to follow suit. Brother James locks in with Geoff Gascoyne for a finger-snipping groove.

Guy Barker and Alan Skidmore get welcomed back to the bandstand, and Fame gives us "Georgie Fame & The Walking Wounded" the way that Ronnie Scott himself used to announce the artists – it is rare indeed that Georgie utters his own stage name. Without the famous "Roger Moore was in first class" intro about first arriving in Sweden with "Yeh Yeh" in tow, the Flames go straight into that first #1 – relatively close to the original recording from 1964.

The Hammond groove of "Moondance" is instantly recognizable, but it is woven into the theme of the old "Blue Moon" evergreen – then Georgie goes straight into this famous Van Morrison song which he recorded himself for *Cool Cat Blues*. Gascoyne's double bass lines are especially effective here, as are the horns, Alan Skidmore cooking up an adventurous solo, the start of a whole series with marvellous ideas from Georgie himself, Anthony Kerr on vibraphone and an ecstatic climax by Guy Barker that has Georgie shout and squeak his encouragement. More name dropping as promised via the title of the first volume – here it's the constant mantra "John Coltrane", and a daring kind of ending that only Fame seems to be able to come up with.

"The inimitable Peter King" is welcomed back for George Gershwin's "How Long Has This Been Going On". It had been on the same 1991album, but it was also the title track of Georgie's recent col-

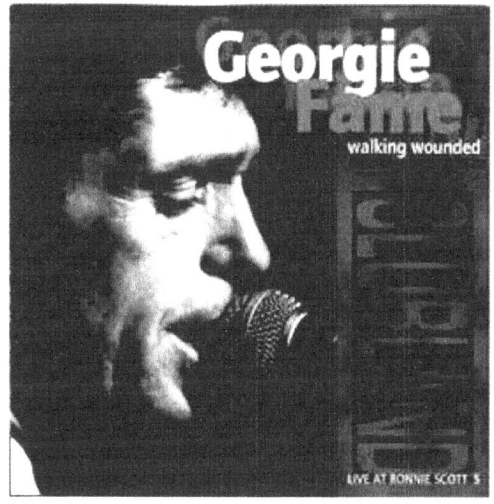

laboration with Van on a mutual Verve album of the same name, where this number had actually been recorded in the same room. A comparison shows that – perfect renditions on both occasions aside – the presence of an audience does give a band that special edge and extra adrenalin to truly come up with a performance that American Jazz musicians once called "in the pocket". All this gets topped – again – by the wonderful Vocalese section and Peter King's ideas. King meets Georgie's sentiments and humour by mixing Cool Jazz, romance and a tongue-in-cheek quote of the standard "Tico Tico". There's room for Anthony Kerr and his vibes, picked up in turn by Georgie's organ – and back to Peter King, before Georgie muses that he knows "how Leif Erickson felt when he discovered a whole new world".

There were two numbers introduced which weren't – and still aren't – included on any studio work of Fame's. First we get his own "Cape Cuckoo", featuring breaks with a lovely and unforgettable trumpet theme to grab listeners' attention and put them in a party mood. "Ngcukana, Ngcukana, Ngcukana", Georgie starts another mantra about a favourite Capetown saxophonist, and gives enough rope to Gascoyne and Kerr's playfulness, while the three Fames cum Flames provide the marvellous rhythm section, which leaps into a jolly march for the surprise ending.

The hymn-like instrumental "Abide With Me" by Thelonius Monk makes for a complete contrast to the African joyfulness, and leads into Peter King's alto reflections of Charlie Parker, building on the way his recording was "flown in" to New York City for *The Blues And Me*: "The Woodshed Intro", which soon gets counted into "The Woodshed" proper, King's Charlie Parker adaptation linked with Georgie's own lyrics about "When I'm in the woodshed I feel just great – here's an example from a man who spent a lot of time in his own woods, just like Phil Woods", all at breakneck speed and following the saxophone lines ever so precisely: "Don't forget your horn, you can't go on your own!"

The ballad "It Happened To Me" with Guy Barker's heart-breakingly sad trumpet intro had been the opener of *Three Line Whip* from late 1993, which while in the club was still the latest Fame album. It segues into a Swing section and is coupled with the popular 1922 song by Walter Donaldson and Gus Kahn, "My Buddy", whose takers read like a *Who's Who* of Georgie's heroes: Doris Day (1951), Chet Baker (1953), Count Basie (1947), Dr John (1989), to name but a few.

"Zavolo", also from the *Three Line Whip* album, harks back to Fame's South African adventures, and Georgie announces: "I'm staying home for Christmas, but I wanna go to Capetown!" There is more name dropping – "Brotherhood of Breath, Chris McGregor, Chris McGregor!" plugging the South-African pianist and bandleader from Somerset West (1936–1990) and his Big Band Brotherhood of Breath with Alan Skidmore, Marc Charig, John Surman, Harry Beckett, Elton Dean – virtually half of the Big Blue Flames of 1974!

Then the catchy horn theme is introduced, "Radio Belfast" gets plugged by Georgie, and James Powell presents one of his best ever snare patterns. When he reverts to some quiet rim shots, his engine room partner Geoff Gascoyne impresses with a sensitive bass solo. Gascoyne reminisced about the club scene in a pleasant chat 2012:

"It was just a great experience for me, because I got to play at Ronnie's for instance. We were at Ronnie Scott's all the time, and just being there was inspiration enough. And I led my own band through all those years as well, so I would always put a quartet of my own into Ronnie's as well. Because I was there such a lot, I was hanging out with Ronnie Scott and Pete King. We had some amazing times at Ronnie's – we used to do two or three weeks, straight through.

"We did a few live albums from there which are great. One of them was called *Walking Wounded* I remember, because we were working so hard, and we were all so knackered that he got the guys upstairs to record the gig and he didn't tell us. He only told us the following week after we had recorded it. And he called it *Walking Wounded* because we were all falling ill. But it was still amazing because we were so used to playing at Ronnie's at the time.

"By the way, the album title *Walking Wounded* by Everything But The Girl is probably due to the fact that Ben Watt from Everything But was very ill. In fact he almost died, he lost part of his intestines through some [auto-immune] disease, and I guess that's why the album was called *Walking Wounded*. Just a coincidence."

Praise and satisfaction with *Name Droppin'* and *Walking Wounded* also came from Alan Skidmore: "They were both really good albums: When you listen to them, that's how long it took to record them, cause they are live. Somebody said 'How long did it take you to record that?' and you say 'Well, how long did it take you to listen to it?' That's how long it took."

So there is nothing doctored or replaced, is there? "Not in my field, not in my life. If I do a live recording with my quartet, or Ubizo or anything, it's all completely live." For Alan, music and family go together as far as inspiration is concerned: "As far as creating music, by the way, my wife, Kay, has been a constant source of inspiration and help to me."

Some of his part-time boss's *Name Droppin'* rings a very pleasant bell for him, especially as Georgie frequently calls out "John Coltrane", for instance in "Moondance": "My daughter's name is Alice, who was named after John Coltrane's second wife, and my daughter's daughter, who is my granddaughter and who's beautiful, her name is Naima, which is John Coltrane's first wife. There's also a most beautiful tune called "Naima"."

About working at Ronnie's over the years, Guy says "It's funny, because now that everybody has done it for so long, you turn up and get on the bandstand, and it's like we have never been away. It starts, and you go 'Here we are again'. Because of the nature of the whole thing, and because you've got these elements that some things can work and some things can't work – so there's times when the atmosphere is better than others, but then there is huge humor around all the time. The thing is, as soon as we all see each other – I have always had a great time. Skid and I will joke with each other, and Anthony Kerr and I will joke with each other, come out with stuff. It's another corny word, but it feels like family! It's when I arrive after something like not being at a gig for a while, and we're setting up at Ronnie's: When I look at Georgie, there's a way – sometimes, he will be looking down, and then he'll look up, and there's a smile that he gives me, and it's that moment – and you know he's going 'Here we fucking are again' [laughs] – and you know, here we go.

"In the earlier days, we used to do two weeks, and then one time, we did three weeks – seems they did four weeks before. We did the Big Band the third week. Hence the title of the album *Walking Wounded*, where everybody had a cold."

And even with a cold, Georgie is going to give it his utmost: "It's almost like – sometimes when he's doing "How Long Has This Been Going On", or one of these ballads, and there is a swoop up to this note. Sometimes you can see where he is going with this. He's going with this with full voice up there, and he's going to get it!"

Anthony Kerr: "I really enjoyed the live album we recorded at Ronnie's, *Walking Wounded*. I think the band were either injured or ill through the whole time, and we had a bit of a triumph over adversity, and so we called it *Walking Wounded*. As for studio albums, I don't remember any tracks that didn't end up on the albums. If you have a working band that has done a lot of gigs, you can be a little bit more sure as to how things are going to sound, and less needs to sort of cushion the CD plan with a few spare tracks which may or may not go on there. It is much easier to see it as a gig. A gig is such and such a number of minutes long, and this number of tunes, and this sort of variety, it's all sort of worked out.

"To be honest, if I had to put money on it, I'd say that everything made it to the CDs. Ronnie's of course, they record everything. You know, like the live album, they just record the lot, and then I'm sure there were songs that were never intended to go on. But they just leave the tape going, and then cut it up later. But it does happen – if you ask people who've been working for say 40 years, if you ask them what have they ever done, a lot of the times you just can't remember every day's work.

Tell Me Something:
The Morrison/Fame/Sidran tribute to Mose Allison

A year after the relaxed Ronnie-Scott's-without-an-audience album *How Long Has This Been Going On* – the Morrison & Fame collaboration with half their respective bands, a complete Mose Allison tribute was cooked up by Van and Georgie, but Fame wanted a good friend and colleague from across the Atlantic in. As Ben Sidran writes in his memoirs *A Life In The Music*, Georgie called and said "Just pick your favourite Mose tunes, you know, maybe some of the 'cotton sack' stuff he won't sing any more, and you'll do a few and I'll do a few and Van will do a few." It did sound easy, but it wasn't – Sidran is such a fan that he wasn't able to limit himself in his choices – 10 or 12 songs remained absolutely indispensible for him. So with a heavy heart, he took his plane to England in order to work in Morrison's studio in Bath – and actually found he hit the shortlist jackpot: nobody else had bothered to make any choices, so they accepted his favourites.

Morrison's studio complex is a historical stone-walled hall from the days of the sheep trade, beautifully refurbished, and Sidran – enjoying the gorgeous surroundings, began to write out arrangements for the songs, keeping Van's idiosyncrasies in mind. With a co-production credit of Van with Georgie and Ben Sidran, who were all going to sing and incorporate Mose himself, they went to work the next day, using the same band members they had on the Ronnie's "studio" album. Tristan Powell was engineering and mixing the proceedings, with a little help from his mate Richard Manwaring.

But Morrison himself still hadn't even arrived, so just like they did at Ronnie Scott's, and like The Band had done for their *Basement Tapes* with and without Dylan 30 years previously, Georgie on Hammond, Ben on piano, Ralph Salmins on drums and Alec

Dankworth on bass set up in a circle and rehearsed the songs. And when Van did finally arrived, he called the shots, decided on who-sings-what on the spot and they managed to record 10 of the 13 songs in one day, as live as live could be.

Presenting 13 tracks sounded fine, but at a running time of just 36 minutes, this fell well below the body of work all these artists would normally present individually – and the huge body of work that Allison's canon presents – and a number of fans had hoped for a few more numbers.

For some listeners, there was another catch: both Georgie Fame and Ben Sidran had always been ardent fans and aficionados of Allison's repertoire and therefore knew how to handle his material sensitively and with a nonchalant air. And all that was expected of Mose of course was to be Mose.

That left the man who had top billing on the cover of *Tell Me Something: The Songs of Mose Allison*: Van the man. How would he tackle the easy-going ways of Mose? Some critics felt it was a little bit like casting Tom Jones to pay tribute to J.J. Cale, or asking Jools Holland to fill in for "Whispering" Bob Harris. Excited and motivated, Morrison truly threw himself into interpreting Allison's lyrics in his own inimitable way, showing his excitement for Mose's music in giving it all of his power. Didn't he have it in him to show a little restraint?

A look at Morrison's past reveals that this couldn't be further from the truth. Van could impersonate any singer he put his mind to, like his and Georgie's childhood idol Paul Robeson, for instance. Likewise, it would have been easy to assume the part of Mose Allison. But what would have been the point? Have a fourth Mose? Mose is Mose, Fame is a natural at this, "the boy can't help it". Neither can Ben Sidran.

So the Belfast belter's chance was to take on the persona he does best: Van Morrison as Van Morrison. And he was in good company with that intensive approach when one thinks back to Roger Daltrey and Pete Townshend's famously enthusiastic take on Allison's "Young Man Blues" on The Who's *Live At Leeds* in 1970.

So the approach to his interpretations was surprising, but certainly calculated. As the young lead singer in his second band Them, he had impressed fans and media with first-rate, quieter performances as well, and fairly recently, like on *Hymns To The Silence*, Van had confirmed his ability to use his vocal chords with warm feeling and precise dynamics from whispers to screams. And what's more, Mose liked what he heard, so Van must have been on the right track.

Tell Me Something: The Songs of Mose Allison – Track by Track

"One Of These Days" serves as the initial case in point for both aspects – the joyful Van shouts his way in, kind of announcing his trademark. It's just a Blues though, and the other players realize this – with Sidran honky-tonking to Fame's Hammond organ, Ralph Salmins and Alec Dankworth providing the 12-bar rhythm. Guy Barker, who can switch on his adrenalin supply at the snap of a finger, gets his trumpet contribution in just perfectly.

"You Can Count On Me (To Do My Part)" immediately comes over as a good-hearted, finger-snipping shuffle, and Van plays an exciting harmonica intro over Georgie's organ licks, and then he really rips into Allison's lyrics and lets his genuine excitement do the talking. Pee Wee Ellis supplies an exquisite horn arrangement, with solo spots by Leo Green on tenor and "bugler" Barker.

"If You Live" works still better: Georgie often sang this live and enjoys his warm and tender oiling of the Hammond tone wheels, but Morrison lets Sidran handle the vocals here, which he does with literal ease and expertise, virtually born to sing these laconic, philosophical lyrics about patience. Ben's piano solo is faded out. Maybe Tristan Powell should have left it running for a while.

Another stage favourite of Georgie's, he gets to sing the peacefully morbid "Was" himself here, wondering what will happen "when I become was and we become were", often stating that his beloved Hammond organ will certainly survive him. A welcome guest here is keyboarder Robin Aspland, who adds Wurlitzer electric piano to Salmins' inventive strokes on the snare with his brushes.

We hear more snare bristling and some fantastic stride piano for Ben Sidran's take on "Look Here", like "One Of These Days" from *The Word Of Mose Allison* (1964) which he performs with gorgeous panache and obvious enjoyment, revelling in Mose's grooves and sarcasms. Short and sweet, this is one of the best tracks, but again it seems over too soon.

"City Home" is Georgie's second solo spot. Like several of his self-written compositions, it is about the love of both town and country again. This way, he can be found making Allison's musings his own again. A sparse and extremely effective arrangement, this is like Fame & Sons with Sidran's indispensible piano icing on the R&B cake, for whom this song has a philosophical significance, because it was "the song that first got me out of Racine [his small home town] so many years before." Only Tristan & James's part is played by Salmins & Dankworth.

"No Trouble Livin'" picks up the "Was" topic of death, and it is Ben Sidran's turn to make the most of it, and we believe his thoughts about fearing death much more than any trouble the dangers of life could ever give him. Again, just a little quartet performance, and quite rightly so, these vignettes never need anything else.

The same principle works for the second 12-bar Blues, "Benediction", Morrison can be heard choosing a subdued beginning, but then soon enough, he puts his powerful vocals in an interesting contrast to Fame & Sidran, who add their responses to Van's wild calls with their unfazed calm.

"Back On The Corner" swings infectiously, but Georgie doesn't let this carry him away, his vocals delivered ever so understated yet assured, his organ providing the sonic carpet for some joyful Sidran piano before he lets his own mini solo rip. Here, the Pee Wee Ellis horn colouring comes in again, with his tenor sax and Guy Barker's trumpet.

Yet another Blues, "Tell Me Something" is the title track of this collection, very proficiently executed, with gold dust via Pee Wee's tenor sax taking over from Morrison's well paced reading. Ben Sidran's piano and Georgie's organ do their bit, in a faultless way.

On "I Don't Want Much" Mose Allison leads Dankworth and Salmins through the modesty preaching Swing about some people never seeming to get enough, and Van adjusts well to Allison's phrasing and pacing, thus making for an amusing and rounded number.

"News Nightclub" is overall of a little wilder character, and can use a little temperament, so Morrison handles this kind of a second line dance groove with ease, Ellis and Barker having a ball with the horns, before – once more – it is all over far too quickly.

"Perfect Moment" happened when Georgie Fame and Ben Sidran were out to lunch, but admittedly, this finale is heartfelt because Van & Mose really sing to one another here, obviously performing the song spontaneously, because their contributions are not in sync, while having the desired effect of a live reading. This track is a little short again; one wonders if longer takes wouldn't have given the listener a more intensive experience.

Chapter 11

"Strike Up The Band" – More Big Band adventures

When Georgie Fame started to record his *Sound Venture* album with the renowned British Big Band of Harry South in 1964, he could hardly have guessed that only three years later, in 1967, he would get the chance to work with the world famous Count Basie Orchestra. But even then – his emotional exclamation "Welcome to my dreams" having been cited in many a paper – little could he have known about his status of singing with dozens of Big Bands on an international level and with an impeccable and impressive reputation throughout – taking in the whole of Scandinavia, Britain and the Republic of Ireland, The Netherlands and Germany, to name a few.

As a lovely gesture, he acted as godchild and godfather in 1990: godchild of the great *Sound Venture* mentor, and godfather for the Big Band which had started the career of many of his peers, including that of trumpeter Guy Barker.

Georgie wrote and sang for an album by the National Youth Jazz Orchestra, the NYJO, called *Portraits – NYJO plays The Music of Harry South*. He performed a special new Harry South arrangement of "The Point Of No Return", featuring Nigel Crane with some impressive baritone sax work.

And Fame specially composed the tribute "Blues At The Bull" – with the long-running Jazz Venue The Barnes Bull's Head in Barnes, London in mind – which Harry South also wrote the charts for, already ailing and passing on soon after, in Lambeth, at the relatively young age of 60. Here, Martin Shaw plays a muted trumpet, the trombone being supplied by Pat Hartley.

Fame often raves about his Big Band work all over the world: "Yeah. The thing is: it keeps me fresh, because I'm not doing the same thing all the time, and it's always great to sing songs with this noise – this band and the orchestra."

At the time of this praise, 1994, we were both sitting in front of Bielefeld's Oetkerhalle, with its famous acoustics, talking about the Wuppertal Symphony Orchestra on top of the WDR Big Band. "It is fantastic. Jerry van Rooyen has done an arrangement of one of my compositions for this concert, which for me is a great honour, "Declaration Of Love". It is on the Big Band album [*City Life*] with Madeline Bell, a ballad I wrote three years ago, and it's an instrumental on *Three Line Whip*, as a waltz, so we did it two different ways. Jerry's done a big orchestral arrangement of the waltz version which I'll sing tonight, so things just keep going! I'm still learning."

Ever since the early 1980s, Georgie has been free to make his choices, to work whichever way he feels best, while towards the end of 1966, his manager Rik Gunnell had persuaded him to "go solo" – "so that *he* could make more money!" Fame shuddered at the thought and talked enthusiastically about his multitasking:

"Now I do both, I mix between the two all the time. It's always fantastic to be able to work with people like Jerry van Rooyen, and his WDR band is one of the best Big Bands in the world, all the musicians in the band are my friends. But I still work with my own band: next week, we will play two concerts at festivals in Scotland, with my sons Tristan and James. In Holland on Saturday I'm working with a Dutch

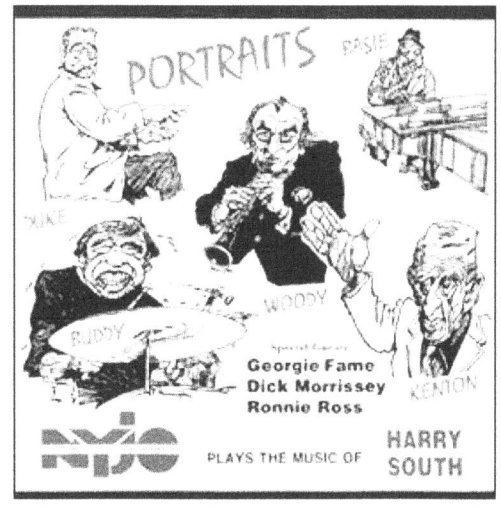

Big Band in Rotterdam, and then I go to Eindhoven the same night to play a Jazz Festival with the Dolph deFries Trio and Ellen Helmus, the flute player [and collaborator on *A Portrait For Chet* in 1989]. So I'm moving all the time." In 1992 – one of many more examples – Georgie toured Scotland, the BBC Big Band and favourite female duet partner Madeline Bell in tow.

Due to this winning combination, Georgie had "fresh product" for the Big Band side of things as well at the time – the already mentioned fabulous studio collaboration *City Life*, where he and Bell fronted the 18-piece prime selection of British Broadcasting Corporation Jazz champions during a single studio day in November 1992, celebrating the music of George Gershwin, some choice self-written numbers, excerpts from their Musical *Singer*, and especially five treasured Duke Ellington standards. The charts had been provided by none other than Steve Gray, *Singer* co-creator and soon-to-be Jazz professor in Berlin.

City Life – track by track

"Strike Up The Band" starts proceedings, remembering the famous Gershwin Musical from 1927. As that work's message was anti-war and also a spoof on militaristic marching music, it is fitting to introduce it with a rousing snare pattern, courtesy of Mike Smith, a drummer Fame had known via Johnny Dankworth. It leads into some pure George Gershwin hard Swing. Guitarist Graham Atha and trombonist Clive Hitchcock on alto saxophone help Georgie enjoy the melody, the lyrics and his backing even more.

Fancy getting a rare single track next: "I Still Care About Us", the B-side of "Go For It", theme song for Granada TV's series *El C.I.D.* from 1989. Getting the pace down from the opener, Gray wrote a romantically charged arrangement, in which Georgie shares the starlight with (muted) trumpeter Paul Eshelsby, a veteran of the BBC Scottish

Radio Big Band, who is now Director of the National Youth Jazz Orchestra, and also leads his own Big Band. At the time of this wonderfully dreamy score, he had already worked with Ella Fitzgerald, Freddie Mercury & Queen, George Benson and Tony Bennett – quite a CV.

Over to Madeline Bell for this collection's introduction to Duke Ellington, via his legendary "I've Got It Bad And That Ain't Good", for which Paul Francis Webster supplied the famous lyrics in 1941. The piano intro has Andy Vinter "do the Duke", but Steve Gray wrote these bars for Bell with strings originally. Madeline had Ella, Etta (James) and Shirley Horn for competition, but what she does here is peerless – first rate. So is Graham Atha on guitar licks.

Gershwin's "But Not For Me" must be Georgie's most recorded number, but this arrangement is especially rewarding. The softer Big Band Swing is led nicely by Atha's rhythmic strumming, and the Vocalese singing so apparently effortless, but the truth is that Fame worked and worked this to perfection over many years since 1967. Paul Eshelby changes to Flugelhorn, and we enjoy the tenor saxophone of Vic Ash, 52 at the time, who played with Frank Sinatra, Hoagy Carmichael and once started out with Blue Flames famed Tubby Hayes in 1951 – credentials that surely made Georgie smile his broadest smile.

It shows no mean feat to complement the American Songbook with a British made item, but Fame and Steve Gray pulled it off – with the main piece for their joint Musical *Singer*, for which Madeline Bell was chosen as the main, if not autobiographical, protagonist. Debuted in the mid Eighties on Dutch radio, this was the first time the composition was presented on a record.

"The Singer" is sung here as a duet between Georgie and Madeline, and the booklet rightly points to the three Big Band members who play the lengthy, memorable intro and outro here: Bill Turner with his trumpet; Vic Ash; and Bernie George. Then Fame & Bell pick up the Swing, and the solo is reserved for fellow saxophonist Barry Robinson.

Clever yet so harmonic – what a great idea to combine two great songs in a most sophisticated way: not as a medley, but sung side by side. The two singers are taking turns with each and every line of two numbers. Madeline and Georgie did that here with a pair of Duke Ellington standards. "I Let A Song Go Out Of My Heart" was the earlier hit – pole position for Duke in 1938, with lyrics by Irving Mills. Dinah Washington sang it, too, and Martha Tilton performed it in Benny Goodman's band. Crucially for Fame, Thelonious Monk covered it in 1955 for *Thelonious Monk plays The Music Of Duke Ellington*.

The interwoven second song, "Don't Get Around Much Anymore", came out in 1940, originally as "Never No Lament"; two years later, Bob Russell's lyrics were added. Both Ellington and The Ink Spots scored R&B chart #1's with it in 1943. Soon, Mose Allison recorded it twice, with dozens of other versions ranging from Etta James to B.B. King.

"Cotton Tail" (spelt "Cottontail" here) is presented as a pure instrumental, showing off the Big Band in a gorgeously fast groove, carried by Iain Dixon's tenor solo, but locked tightly by the experienced bass lines of Centipede and Soft Machine veteran Roy Babbington (b. 1940), who also worked for Mose Allison. In Babbington's year of birth, the number had started out as a Duke instrumental, actually, before Ellington added lyrics. Independently – and here's the obvious link to Georgie – Jon Hendricks created his own words, for the recording of the song on *Everybody's Boppin'* in 1959 by his fantastic Vocalese trio Lambert, Hendricks & Ross.

This is followed by Fame's own ballad "A Declaration Of Love" which was to find its way onto *Three Line Whip* a year later, and which Georgie had been so proud of in his interview in Bielefeld. Apparently, he was "visited by a third force", which was his way of describing his true inspiration for Robin Sedgely's liner notes.

Duke Ellington's 1933 "Drop Me Off In Harlem" seems custom-made for Madeline Bell as well as the Fame/Gray Musical *Singer's* storyline. In order to reserve the spotlight for her, and also to enhance the nostalgic 1930s style of Georgie's *The Third Face Of Fame* album, the trumpets of Eddie Nigel Carter and Bill Turner get muted here, as does Bill Lorkin's trombone. The way the lyrics came about is legendary – apparently, writer Nick Kenny had offered to share a taxi with Ellington, asking "Where to, Duke?" The song's title was the famous answer. If you've ever been told – in Manhattan – to take the A-train, you will know that this anecdote holds true.

Georgie had once detected "When My Dreamboat Comes Home", written by Cliff Friend and Dave Franklin, on Mose Allison's 1982 *Middle Class White Boy*, and he makes the most of Steve Gray's arrangement here in opting for a long and dramatic slow introduction – an exemplary exercise in good old New Orleans call and response with trumpeter Brian Rankine, before the whole 18-strong bunch attack the Swing part with gusto and madness.

In complete contrast, the reeds provide the romantic yet dark background for Madeline, who wails in Screaming Jay Hawkins' "I Put A Spell On You". While Alan Price's version was a long-standing favourite, Bell's reading sounds even more convincing than Nina Simone to these ears. This is partly due to a special challenge for Madeline – the key which Steve Gray had in mind when putting pen to chart was perfect for Georgie. While we knew how well Ms Bell can always handle the higher registers, here she goes well down, which would have amused the composer no end. In any case, Bell's tender reading is a far cry from the original, which Screaming Jay Hawkins recorded completely sozzled after his producer "brought in ribs and chicken and got everybody drunk".

The horns go full blast, and Georgie hails "Taxi" – referring back to the "Drop Me Off In Harlem" history? – before he goes into the best studio version of this composition made for announcing the *Singer* Musical. The way saxophones and trumpets echo on another, the sounds of a huge metropolis are portrayed perfectly by Gray, and Georgie makes the most of adding to this atmosphere, "City people know what's going on", animal noises for a Funk interlude included, before jumping behind his Hammond organ, confirming "I'll never go back to Georgia" and "Thank you for Thelonius Sphere Monk".

"The Blues And Me" is from the same Musical, and is also the title track of Fame's album in the year of this Big Band recording. Steve Gray's original idea here is to have the reeds precede Georgie's melody line, whose piano duties are performed by Andy Vinter. The call and response partner here is Bernie George, while the great tenor sax solo belongs to Iain Dixon.

"It Don't Mean A Thing If It Ain't Got That Swing" from 1931 triumphs as the Duke Ellington finale, starting in a Charleston mood with the famous words – again by Irving Mills – which make clear that the music is nothing without good words, and a good mood. Thelonious Monk tackled the song as well as Ella Fitzgerald and Tony Bennett, but neither Steve Gray nor Fame & Bell need any role models here. The way Madeline and Georgie handle the vocals, on their own and in harmony, is exemplary, and Gray leads the Big Band from the 1930s to war-time hard Swing on a matter of just over three minutes.

The Danish Radio Big Band

For the casual CD browser, it must have seemed as if Georgie's *City Life* with Madeline Bell, Steve Gray and the BBC Big Band came out at exactly the same time as its Scandinavian counterpart with The Danish Radio Big Band, while it was in fact recorded exactly half a year later, in June 1993, during only one single day in the DR building of the Danish Broadcasting Corporation, with the exception of "A Declaration Of Love", which had been cut in the Scanticon Theatre in Kolding, Denmark on October 18th, 1992.

The general manager of the Danish Radio Big Band, Peter H. Larsen, explains the album's title *Endangered Species* in his liner notes – "capable Jazz singers are so rare that they should be included under international legislation for the protection of endangered species". He also uses a metaphor that must please the soccer fan Fame no end:

"The good Jazz singer lets the rhythm do the work, just as the good footballer lets the ball do the work. Georgie Fame has this talent. Even though we know him largely from his 30-year career in European R&B and Soul music, he is also a great aficionado of Jazz – and also football for that matter. Fame's phrasing and timing show his understanding of the fact that Jazz singing is a question of organic tension between soloist and accompaniment, and here in DRBB, we are proud to be part of this exciting interchange."

It's hardly possible to put it in a nutshell in any better way, and the resulting 50 minutes never leave a doubt that, even next to *City Life*, this parallel album *Endangered*

Species is indispensible. What's more, there were only four doubles – "I Still Care About You", a longer version of "City Life", Fame's ballad "A Declaration Of Love", and the now not so rare B-side "I Still Care About You".

Endangered Species: Danish Radio Big Band/Georgie Fame track by track

"Blues For Ann-Marie" was the tribute to fellow organist Kjell Öhman's daughter from the Fame album *The Blues And Me*, presented instrumentally here, with the full blast of the Danish brass hitting us thanks to their prowess and Steve Gray's imaginative arrangement, and sophisticated soloing by tenor sax man Hans Ulrik and trumpeter Henrik Bolberg Pedersen. Also a renowned flugelhorn player, Pederson played with US Jazz pianist Tommy Flanagan and also the ex Johnny Dankworth and *The Two Faces Of Fame* percussionist Tony Coe.

Pedersen gets the spotlight for Georgie's 1989 B-side as well – his reflective Swing "I Still Care About You" is played out in a brighter way here compared to the *City Life* version, and has more Vocalese.

Toots Thielemans (b.1922), the legendary Belgian harmonica player, guitarist, whistler and Benny Goodman and Quincy Jones sidekick, contracted Fame to write a tribute to his wife, and Georgie took the request "For My Lady" literally, and composed this very melancholic, moving piece.

For "Drip Drop" from Georgie Fame and Annie Ross's Hoagy Carmichael tribute *In Hoagland 1981*, arranger Alan Deak knew he had to come up with something spectacular, in order to follow in the big footsteps of Harry South, for whose Famous Flamingo Orchestra the top London musicians had been gathered – but thanks to an inventive score with more reed and brass action behind the vocals and Georgie's own piano work, this is one hell of an alternative version to enjoy.

"Little Samba" from *Right Now!*, custom-made by Fame for Latin American markets, gets its first Big Band treatment here thanks to Rob Pronk, after having graced *No Worries* in another small group version. A little library music written by Steve Gray follows, featuring pianist and Oscar Peterson Award winter Nikolaj Bentzon (b. 1964) prominently. It takes a little bit of 1940s Hollywood, and has connotations to "The Blues And Me", too.

Georgie often had to be persuaded to perform his big gangster hit "The Ballad of Bonnie and Clyde" over the years. But this arrangement by Count

Basie's favourite arranger Chico O'Farrell made all the difference right from the start, as it takes the – to some ears – corny elements out and puts real drama in albeit in a still slightly tongue-in-cheek manner. "And now he likes it", as Paul Jones sings with his Blues Band.

Madeline Bell did "I Put A Spell On You" on *City Life*, Fame makes it his own here, treating it as if the Screaming Jay Hawkins number had always been pure Jazz. Steve Gray and L.A. guitar grandmaster Robben Ford provided the arrangement, and Danish Radio axe man Anders "Chico" Lindvall (the second Chico here) really has us believe it is Ford working his fret board here – what he does is not only a joy to listen to, but also little short of a stunning impersonation. Georgie himself gets the "Spell" across without ever going over the top, replacing the original's shock horror with elegance and subtlety.

As compensation, Fame gets the chance to really let loose in a rousing version of "City Life" which lasts more than seven minutes. Another "Taxi, taxi!" cry and he is really in the Swing, while drummer Jonas Johansen gets some valid assistance via Ethan Weisgard on Latin percussion. Together with Thomas Ovesen's walking bass, they provide a perfect magic carpet for some wild yet thoughtful soloing. Tenor man Uffe Markussen and trumpeter Henrik Bolberg Pedersen are soon followed by fabulous trombonist Kjeld Ipsen, and pianist Bentzon covers the rear end of the solo section, before Georgie cuts back in and changes his lyrics in the sympathetic line "Next time we're in Copenhagen, come on down and listen while we blow".

Towards the end, things get more subdued again: "A Declaration Of Love" has even more of a hymnal vibe than the version on *City Life*, while it follows the same arrangement. The piano solo by Nikilaj Bentzon is something to treasure.

"One For My Baby" by Harold Arlen and Johnny Mercer is often presented by Fame as an after-hours finale at "a quarter to three", sitting alone at the piano, and it seemed to help him get over hard times, even when an audience was present. Consequently, he does the moving standard here on his own as well. It was one of Frank Sinatra's absolute favourites – he recorded it at least six times between 1947 and 1993, parallel to this session in fact, so Georgie can do quite a few more himself. Lyricist Johnny Mercer is getting name-checked here by Fame with "One more for Johnny Mercer."

On Saturday, July 14th, 2007, amongst countless other occasions, there was a remarkable event at PLÆNEN – "The Lawn", in Copenhagen's Tivoli. The concert featured Georgie Fame and Gary Brooker, the Procol Harum leader and one-time colleague of Georgie's in Bill Wyman's Rhythm Kings, together with the Tivoli Big Band, which was conducted by Peter Kragerup.

The orchestra started the concert with one of their own compositions, more than 20 musicians of obviously brilliant sophistication. Then Georgie came in with his big hits "Yeh Yeh" and "The Ballad of Bonnie and Clyde". As a third number of his first spot, he chose "I Put A Spell On You".

Georgie in 2009: "At the time, Screaming Jay Hawkins was only known with some purists. I never heard Screaming Jay Hawkins until late 1966. I heard him by listening to the Nina Simone version. But Nina always said that it came from Screaming Jay Hawkins. We knew where it came from, but we didn't hear the original." On this night, he presented an arrangement by Steve Gray.

Gary Brooker was next, presenting R&B material from his Paramounts days, sitting at the Hammond for "I Got News For You", the catchy "No More Fear Of Flying" from his first solo album of the same name (with the Fame-experienced Dave Mattacks on drums) and, from the piano, Rhythm Kings repertoire with Ray Charles' "Hit The Road, Jack".

Georgie came back, taking over the Hammond organ for "City Life" and a related original song, "Copenhagen Life". This was followed by the fantastic arrangement of "Papa's Got A Brand New Bag", which he had fought so hard for during the sessions for *Sound Venture* in 1966. For Count Basie, he then sang his own "A Declaration of Love".

Would Brooker and Fame perform together? They would, and with obvious fun, too: "I Keep Forgetting" was first – it had once featured in Procol Harum's set, and after the final "A Whiter Shade Of Pale", where the Tivoli keyboarder handled the Hammond, Georgie and Gary got back together as Rhythm Kings for the literal audience reminder "Let The Good Times Roll" and "Shake, Rattle And Roll".

A magic evening from 10 to midnight which should get a worldwide DVD release!

Sweden & Denmark, where else in Scandinavia? "S/S Norway"!

Apart from being a household name between Stockholm, Gothenburg, Malmø and the latter's neighbouring city over the bridge, Copenhagen, Georgie had also worked in Norway regularly since the 1980s.

Two key personalities, and soon his good friends as well, were the renowned Jazz singer Karen Krog (b. 1937) and pianist/composer Per Husby (b. 1949). Krog, 77 and counting, is still considered one of the best Jazz singers in the whole of Norway. Her link to Georgie is having worked with the adored Dexter Gordon – and Karen had a hit in the Sixties with her R&B band Public Enemies, singing "Sunny".

Husby was educated at the Music Conservatory in Oslo, and later became an acoustics expert at the Norwegian Institute of Technology, which seems always good to have for a musician, but he never worked in that field. Intensive Jazz studies in Boston followed at Berklee, and soon Husby led quintets and sextets. His chops as a Big Band leader were honed by 20 years of working with the Norwegian Broadcasting Corporation, and what better reference could there be for Georgie than having worked with a mutual colleague on the trumpet, Kenny Wheeler from *The Two Faces Of Fame* – and a trio of Fame heroes: James Moody, Chet Baker, Clark Terry.

When Husby started the 13-strong Per Husby Orchestra in 1984, Karen Krog as well as Georgie Fame were soon taken on board as guest vocalists. The album *Dedications*, recorded in Oslo's Rainbow Studios in January 1985, actually starts with Georgie and the Tadd Dameron number "Accentuate The Bass", in which he feels his way into this Big Band very well, and shares the attention with Stein Erik Tafjords tuba work as well as Martin Drover's trumpet, a London Jazz regular he would later work with again in Bill Wyman's Rhythm Kings. Frode Thingnaes is on trombone – Georgie would meet him again in the Kampen Janitsjar Orkester.

Fame shares the Dameron & Count Basie Medley of "Good Bait"/"Ladybird" with Karin Krog, and after some great instrumental Mingus workouts, the duo get another solo spot for Tadd Dameron's "That's The Way It Goes" – again presenting his custom-made and truly sophisticated Vocalese chops.

Regular live appearances followed in the coming years, and also, a decade after *Dedications* – another record project, this time in New York City's Clinton Studios. Per Husby arranged and conducted an all-star album called *If You Could See Me Now*, with an impressive cast of seasoned session musicians, where Georgie was able to work again with Grady Tate, who had played on *The Blues And Me* four years earlier. On guitar, Husby had Annie Ross's long-standing club partner Bucky Pizzarelli, and his vocal sparring partner was – again – Karen Krog.

The two of them shared the often recorded "On A Misty Night" – Husby's clear hero Tadd Dameron once again – with Fame's tried and tested Vocalese lyrics for the 1965 Chet Baker solo. It is a very distinctively traditional take which lasts over seven minutes and gives room to quiet passages for Georgie and also classy solos by Frank Wess's tenor and Jim Pugh on trumpet. Then there's another Dameron number for the two, the faster, absolutely joyful Swing "Dig It" which Fame may have recorded nowhere else, where Krog does some Scat singing.

Fame leads the Per Husby and Chan Parker composition "Seasons Change", along with an intro by Ted Rosenthal's piano, then accompanied by the hymnal brass backing which makes the song so melancholic, and the suitable tenor solo by Frank Wess. Instrumental prowess aside, Georgie gives the song its life and soul.

Towards the end, Georgie also handles the lengthy, 10 minute long "Blues Medley", yet another Dameron based work. The American legend and Husby certainly have in common that they started out with bourgeois jobs in (parents') mind. In Tadd Dameron's case it was medicine – and, yes, they share their eventually lucky fate with the "lawyer" Hoagy Carmichael.

The one-time Judy Garland, Frank Sinatra and Sting bassist Jay Leonhart (b. 1940) from Baltimore starts the Blues with his elegant lines. Then Chris Potter from Chicago (b. 1971), courtesy of The Mingus Big Band, James Moody and Steely Dan, takes the first solo on his alto sax, after which Georgie comes in with "There's No More Blue Time". Jim Pugh (b. 1950), the Woody Herman man who also played for Steely Dan, gets his trombone spot, and Fame goes into "Breezin' All The Way". Having enjoyed these Big Band treatments of the two Dameron pieces, Georgie would combine these again 17 years later in a very intimate setting, only accompanied by guitar and bass, on *Lost In A Lover's Dream* in 2012.

There were also numerous appearances and unofficial recordings with the Sandviken Big Band, and the Bohuslän Big Band, with both of whom Georgie was able to realize a lot of his Big Band material on a regular basis.

Another welcome and interesting stop on Georgie's numerous Scandinavian sojourns was the equally Norwegian based Kampen Janitsjar Orkester, by whom he was invited to Oslo's Rainbow Studios again, the venue for *Dedications*. In May and June 1990, he joined the more traditional Brass Band with a weakness for the lighter side of orchestral music there, in order to record three familiar tunes, albeit in completely fresh and therefore attention grabbing arrangements. They have the reputation of taking "light music seriously", and this could often be said of Georgie during his long career.

"Georgia On My Mind" has rarely sounded more celebratory and reverential, and it seems only fitting that Georgie uses the old coda about heading back to Dixie here. Gershwin's "How Long Has This Been Going On" is sung along to tender Fender Rhodes guiding – both numbers benefit from Erling Andersen's tenor sax. Best of the lot is "Sunny", performed here at a really fast pace and with an imaginative brass arrangement.

Interestingly, the other vocal soloist here is Wencke Myhre (b. 1949), an Oslo native resident in Germany, and much more popular there in Schlager circles, ringing a bell for Georgie's "Bonnie & Clyde"-side. The way she sings "I'm A Brass Band" here in honour of Kampen Janitsjar's Orchestra, she displays her tremendous humour, which is reminiscent of Fame's stage persona.

The 55th Birthday Big Band

"After such a marathon I don't think I ever have to enter a studio again", the eternally humorous master had grinned at the time. As early as 1998, for Georgie Fame's 55th birthday, this Rhythm & Swing Revue had been celebrated and swiftly recorded. "It cost me a fortune, but it was worth every minute of it", he had quipped, but could hardly have predicted that until this double party package could be released, the host, at the age of 61, would have done half a dozen albums with Bill Wyman and his Rhythm Kings and three of his own studio works, *Poet In New York* in 2000, *Relationships* in 2001 und *Charlestons* 2003 – apart from side projects in Scandinavia.

Fame summarized the project's outline looking back in 2009: I put my own Big Band together some years ago for the album *The Birthday Big Band*, which contained all the great players, people I've worked with for forty, fifty years. They were in that Big Band. And they are still playing great: Derek Watkins is still the best lead trumpet player, and he's my age. So I just called all my friends, who I knew were the best players, and put them all together in my own Big Band.

"But there are very few Big Bands in England working now. There is the BBC Radio Big Band, and I have an invitation to play with them, as soon as I can. But I don't have any time until at least next May, 2010. I'm working in Sweden on Friday, I have a Big Band concert with a very fine Big Band. They have copies of my arrangements in their office permanently. So we just go "Programme", do do do, I turn up, do the sound check, and that's it. I have been working with Big Bands since 1964, 1965. But I have been a professional musician for fifty years, from 1959. So you have a potted history of the Georgie Fame Big Band repertoire here, on *The Birthday Big Band*.

Georgie's Go Jazz label boss and stylistically related friend Ben Sidran acted as the charming compère, slicker than John Gunnell in the Flamingo, and soon it became obvious that such a "This Is Your Life" gala was not able to make do without the old hits. But the evergreen "Yeh Yeh" showed right away that there had been rehearsals with meticulous attention to detail. The fabulous gimmick of having every phrase like "Every evening" and "I call my baby" followed by horn response makes sure that there is much more than a nostalgia value on the move.

Ben Sidran had his awakening to this Fabulous Fame Orchestra the day before, as Guy Barker vividly recalls: "One of the most amazing gigs was when we did *The Birthday Big Band*. Georgie decided, as he was going to be recorded, we should have a rehearsal. So he booked the Bull's Head in Barnes, and we just did a night, and then went in the next day. We played the Tubby Hayes arrangement of 'Yeh Yeh', which just starts with this powerhouse Big Band stuff, and Ben Sidran walked in, and was standing at the side. The band started, and he literally seemed to be flung backwards. His mouth remained open until the chart was almost over. He was just going 'Oh my god!', because the band sounded amazing. It was almost like 'Ok, this is the one chance, let's try to get this right before we record it tomorrow!' And off it went, unbelievable."

The love-hate relationship the birthday boy had for "The Ballad of Bonnie and Clyde" got solved once again in the first rate live version of the early 1968 mega hit in the refined Count Basie treatment – and this is not only due to the fact that he was allowed to work the UK with the Basie Band shortly after the song hit the hit parade. Comparing the historic studio recording with the 1992 (*City Life BBC*), 1993 (*Danish Radio Big Band*) and this 1998 live version proves an exemplary point: the art of phrasing this vocalist is capable of has risen over those three decades, and his power of delivery is miraculously intact. Thirteen horn and reed blowers, among them trumpeters Guy Barker and Derek Watkins, four trombone players and a bunch of saxophonists – Peter King, Alan Skidmore and Art Themen – guarantee precise, uplifting attacks.

Georgie remembered Art Themen from his early days with Larry Parnes, and had called on him to play on his album *Seventh Son*. "And of course, later on he played in my Big Band. He spent a lot of his professional career playing with Stan Tracey. But he had a wonderfully successful career as a doctor – and he's got Ferraris in his garage, and he's got houses all over the place.

"But he still does a regular monthly residency at the Bull's Head pub in Barnes. [He and Dick Heckstall-Smith] played with Alexis together. And when Alan Skidmore was sick during one of our Ronnie Scott's residencies, Art came in at five minutes' notice and played with the band for a couple of nights. He reads music and I had some parts. There's not a commercial recording of it, but I do have a tape of my Big Band at Ronnie Scott's with Art and Skid.

"And on Steve Gray's arrangement of "Singing Horn", he plays one of the best solos you will ever hear from anybody. I sent a copy of that to Bobby Malach and said 'You've got to hear this!'

"Steve Gray also did a great Big Band arrangement for 'Anthem For A Band'. And the Big Band loves playing it. So, as Jimmy Scott used to say 'Obladi Oblada, life goes on'. Paul McCartney borrowed that from him. Unfortunately, Jim had got pneumonia, I think. He died of pneumonia some years ago, on a flight back from New York. He caught a cold on the flight, and it's turned into pneumonia, the air con on the plane, and he died."

The rhythm section on *The Birthday Big Band* was made up out of the then Blue Flames regular Geoff Gascoyne on bass, Ralph Salmins on drums, Robin Aspland on piano and Dave Cliff on guitar, while old cohorts Alan Price and Colin Green were welcome party guests but didn't join the already busy stage proceedings. Green: "We could have done, but we weren't invited."

A guitarist who did jump up on stage was Jim Mullen, electrifying a great version of "I Put A Spell On You", while vibraphone wizard Anthony Kerr, as always, made sure that his trademark vibraphone got in some more mellow, if inspired softer colours.

The virtually indestructible and forever young Blue Mink Lady Madeline Bell then enriched three titles of the Jazz Opera *Singer* which Steve Gray had composed using Georgie Fame's lyrics, the often mentioned masterpiece that so far had only been performed for Dutch radio.

Zoot Money excitedly took over "Papa's Got A Brand New Bag", because Fame was fully occupied doing the conducting for the diverse stops and starts of his Big Band for the night, like Harry South had done on *Sound Venture*. Right after finishing

that Soul anthem, the two quarreled good-heartedly over who had the best Flamingo-days Soho band at the time. Zoot contradicted Georgie's Big Roll Band endorsement with a heartfelt "No, he had the best!"

What followed was "Vinyl", Fame's tribute to the good old-fashioned plastic platter, and the tour de force "Dawn Yawn", from *Sound Venture*, about the Flamingo Club era of the early Sixties. Georgie had re-recorded this in 1991 for *The Blues And Me*, but it would only get released, finally, in 2008 on a Japanese only compilation, *Every Knock Is A Boost – The Go Jazz Years*.

There were gems galore beyond the well known chart successes: "Little Samba" had once been written by Fame for an international Song Festival in Brazil. "Jimmy McGroove" developed under the influence of the three fellow Hammond masters – Jimmy Smith, Jimmy McGriff and Richard "Groove" Holmes – and the ballad "My Lady" – called "For My Lady" on *Endangered Species* in 1993, was an assignment for the unforgotten Toots Thielemanns as a tribute to his wife. Even though the celebration ended with the rather melancholic "Declaration Of Love", it remained a real Jazz fireworks first and foremost.

Geoff Gascoyne remembers the magic night of the Birthday Bash: "We did a memorable concert in The Forum in Kentish Town in London. It was his 55th birthday, and that was recorded for a double CD. That was a really memorable night. The [Big] Band was just a killing band. It was just amazing. Jim Mullen was there, and Guy [Barker] was playing – everyone was playing! Madeline Bell was playing – lots of guests. Just the sound of the band was amazing. You can hear it on the record, on the intro, when he starts with that Latin version of 'Yeh Yeh', I think it's the Tubby Hayes arrangement. Just the power – it was a memorable night. Ben Sidran was there on the night of the 55th birthday concert. He introduced it. I worked with Ben before."

"Brass Damage" – continued Big Band bashes

As mentioned, Georgie has sung with the best, like the WDR Big Band in Cologne, or the often Steve Gray led NDR Big Band in Hamburg.

"I worked with the best radio orchestras in Deutschland, I worked with them all, WDR, NDR, Rias before it closed, in Berlin. I have an invitation from the Südwestdeutscher Rundfunk to play with them next year [which was for 2010], and the one in Frankfurt, Hessischer Rundfunk Big Band, I played with those guys. There is a very fine Jazz Orchestra in Amsterdam, Holland, where I played one month ago. The conductor is a friend of mine. Whenever the opportunity comes – I have the music. It is expensive to put together, which is why most of the best orchestras are sponsored by radio or state. To do it yourself is very very expensive.

"Even Quincy Jones with his first Big Band was stranded in Paris with no money, and he had to find a way to get the musicians back to the United States. It has always been a financial burden, putting a Big Band together, and keeping it. But there is nothing quite like that sound."

But Fame was by no means inclined to just stick to the big names: "There are quite a lot of amateur Big Bands that I worked with. There is one called Blechschaden Big Band in Lüneburg, Germany".

They played with Georgie in the summer of 2007 ("Blechschaden" being the German term for material damages in traffic accidents, roughly translated as "car body damage", or, in musical terms, as "brass damage") They appeared in the "Kultur Forum" of Lüneburg, a Northern German town set between Hamburg and Hannover.

Excerpts from a newspaper review in the local "Lüneburger Landeszeitung" attests to the respect he commanded again: "'Oh how the time passes' – Georgie Fame grins, shakes his head: 'Next year, I will be 65'. Neither is the hit he just sang a spring chicken: 'Yeh Yeh' entered the British charts in December of 1964 and reached the pole position. Today, Georgie Fame may sport his hair as well as the light summer suit in a whitish grey, but as a musician he is ageless. Together with the Big Band 'Blechschaden', he presented Blues, Swing, Evergreens and less well known songs in the well attended concert barn of the Kultur Forum Gut Wienebuettel – and the audience enjoyed a chapter of lively Jazz history ... He had a similar success to 'Yeh Yeh' in 1967 with "Bonnie & Clyde" and this number could not be left out in Lüneburg – but it was by no means the last one before the encores began, as is so often the custom.

"Georgie Fame has performed with numerous orchestras and Big Bands, and started groups he called 'The Blue Flames' again and again. And now he is with 'Blechschaden'. The Hamburg-Lüneburg ensemble celebrates a long past with this Fame appearance, they clock up an impressive 30 years. Full of routine and with the precious talent of being able to listen to one another, the musicians celebrate classics like 'Cool Cat Blues', 'Jimmy McGroove' or 'Georgia On My Mind'. In the process, Georgie Fame took to the piano from time to time and was accompanied by the rhythm section of the Big Band.

"Apart from that he concentrated on being the singer – his prime instrument had once been the Hammond organ. Instead, the guest had fun with the "Hänschen-Klein" interlude [a German 'Volkslied', a folk traditional] and finally played pieces he called 'pack music' – Rock'n'Roll piano by Fats Domino for instance, during which the members of 'Blechschaden' did in fact pack their instruments. It was a first class concert – versatile, full of virtuosity, relaxed, sophisticated, and accompanied by an obviously expert audience. 'We played Nienburg, and now Lüneburg', 'Blechschaden' boss Detlef Shult mused. At least in the case of Lüneburg – Mr Fame will keep it in good memory."

Another example is from Southend. The local newspaper *The Essex Chronicle* reported about the Southend Jazz Festival in 2004, with the headline "GEORGIE'S FAME VERY MUCH ALIVE":

Welcome cake in Gütersloh

"Nearly 40 years on from taking jazz to the top of the pop charts with 'Yeh Yeh', Georgie Fame is still singing the music he loves. His Southend Jazz Festival show at the Palace Theatre, as guest star with the Hefty Jazz All-Stars, allowed him a nostalgic wallow in classic songs by the likes of Hoagy Carmichael, Cole Porter and George Gershwin. This was Fame in middle of the road mode. His singing was great but fans of his trademark Hammond organ may have been disappointed he played the piano instead. The band, led by trumpeter Keith Smith, switched smoothly between traditional and mainstream styles. The first half of the show celebrated the music of the New Orleans, with a swinging 'Jambalaya', a bluesy 'Don't Send Me Flowers' and a great version of 'Rocking Chair', performed by Fame alone at the keyboards. Things got very schmaltzy in the second half, which featured Broadway show tunes. You don't often hear 'When You Wish Upon a Star' in a Jazz set! This was not the most challenging sessions of Southend's eight days of Jazz, but it was good to hear a master vocalist at work and playing to a full theatre."

One particularly satisfying Big Band venture happened in the summer of 2009 in the author's hometown of Bielefeld, the 320.000 strong Westfalian metropolis where Fame had worked before in 1994, touring with the WDR Big Band. This time, the idea had been to combine the University Big Band with Georgie.

They were good, dedicated semi-pros, but Georgie did not hesitate, but kindly and immediately agreed to get into his old tuition territory. Three months before the show at the "Festival of the Small Arts" in nearby Gütersloh, the adventure began, recalled by reporter Matthias Gans in *Die Glocke* after the event:

"Those were the happy times in the Sixties, when artists like Georgie Fame could romp in Jazz or R&B – and simultaneously conquer the charts with Pop songs. The singer, composer and master of the Hammond B3 surely survived through the highs and lows of an artist's life, but the 66-year-old can enjoy the fruits of his work and doesn't have a problem working with laymen, especially when the present themselves as well prepared as the Uni-Bigband Bielefeld led by Hans-Hermann Rösch.

"Uli Twelker, the Cultural Society's link to the British music scene, had made sure to travel to London especially [well, and also to enjoy a couple of nights at the annual Ronnie Scott's ritual there] in order to receive a suitcase full of Big Band arrangements; sheet music which the Count Basie Orchestra had used [in 1967 and 1968]."

Rehersing the Bielefeld Big Band, 2009

Georgie then flew in a day in advance, duly driven to the campus site, and he spent a whole evening monitoring and coaching the young persons' orchestra, patient, charming, conducting with all of his intuition and power. The students loved it, loved *him* – and even those who had to be told by their parents to what extent they could feel privileged simply felt that this was damn special.

During the afternoon of the show, Fame remembered the rehearsal night with real pleasure: "I mean, today there are musicians here from the University of Bielefeld, who are amateurs. But you have to start somewhere. You *must* start somewhere. You cannot just go from being nothing to a super musician. I gave them some difficult arrangements to play, so it helps them to learn their craft. I'm trying to help them with my experience and make them feel comfortable, so they can enjoy the music – and learn from the music. That is the most important thing."

Remembering his short Count Basie era, he continued: "I did one concert in London in the Royal Albert Hall in 1967. In fact, the arrangement of "Bonnie & Clyde" which I will sing tonight, the arrangement was made for me by Count Basie's arranger at the time, Chico O'Farrill. It was written for that first concert. And the next year, in 1968, we did a long tour of the United Kingdom, and we also played in Frankfurt, and we played in Hamburg, and we played in Den Haag in Holland.

"And it was a fantastic experience, learning, education. I had great help and encouragement from the musicians in the band, and from Count Basie himself. What better university?! So now I am comfortable singing with any Big Band in the world. I have the music to go with it, my own personal collection. Richard Boone, the trombone player in the [Count Basie] Band, was a great singer, a unique singer – he used to sing a couple of tunes, a couple of Blues things, and Boone became a great friend, until he died maybe five or six years ago, in Copenhagen [Based in Copenhagen from 1970, Boone was also a member of the Danish Radio Big Band, like Georgie, from 1973.] So these people were

Soundcheck in Gütersloh

my mentors, and I was working with them. Now I am trying to pass on my knowledge to these students tonight."

He also explained about one of his choices "I Put A Spell On You": "When we were young, we heard the Nina Simone version, of course, and then my colleague Alan Price did a great version with The Animals, Eric Burdon sang it, but Alan Price was the musical director and the leader of the Animals, and they did a great version of "I Put A Spell On You" [as Alan did with the Alan Price Set].

"And when I was recording in New York with Ben Sidran, one of the albums on the *GoJazz* label was by the saxophonist Bobby Malach, who is a great friend of mine and one of the best tenor players in the world. He played on my New York recordings. But he did his own album [*Mood Swing* from 1995], and on that album Dr John sang a great version of "I Put A Spell On You", which was arranged by the guitar player, Robben Ford. Robben played on the album; he played on my albums. I heard this version via Dr John, and I gave it to my friend Steve Gray, who is the best arranger in England, and I said "Make a Big Band version of this version! Blow it up for the Big Band." So that's what you'll get tonight. And Robben is a great musician!"

On the night, Georgie appeared in his Humphrey Bogart gear, as promised: "Tonight I am going to wear my Harry James jacket. I've never worn a white jacket, I don't think in my life, and I bought a white linen jacket in London, which I will wear tonight for the first time. Everything is in black and white tonight. No color!"

And then he truly delivered: as the *Neue Westfälische* wrote under the heading "With Charme & Energy", their competing dailies *Die Glocke* and *Westfalen Blatt* titled their articles "Dreiecksplatz [the open air venue, something like "Triangle Square"] makes dreams come true" and "Georgie Fame remains unforgettable", where Gans picks up the story: "And Georgie Fame didn't have to be asked twice, but served his classics right at the beginning, 'Yeh Yeh' and 'The Ballad of Bonnie & Clyde' or 'Papa's Got a Brand New Bag'.

"Elegantly clad in a white jacket and black shirt, the 66-year old gave the part of the stage animal, animated his colleagues towards artistic heights and rewarded them by presenting them, calling out their names (by heart) one by one: A man who showed true greatness in every aspect during this evening."

Fame is quite rightly proud of all the Big Band arrangements he owns and of course, he *uses* all the time. There must have been thoughts about recording another big band album, studio or live, 15 years after the *Birthday Big Band* album was taped in 1998.

Asked once again in April 2013 whether there was a chance for some more orchestral recordings, Georgie doubted that another Big Band album was on the cards, explaining

G.F. in Gütersloh with the Uni Big Band Bielefeld

in 2009 that "I've got loads of tapes and things from a lot of concerts, radio concerts I have done. You know, I think the live one was enough. That concert (the *55th Birthday Concert*) was not going to be recorded in the first place. It was just at the last minute that I thought 'Oh shit, I might as well record it.'"

Asked about where he gets his arrangements, his answer is "I commission. In the last ten to fifteen years, I only wanted Steve Gray to do my arrangements. Now Steve is sadly dead, so I don't know. But I have maybe well over one hundred arrangements in my own personal library – good Big Band arrangements. The original arrangements that Harry South did for me in 1964/1965 – I still have those, plus everything that I've asked or commissioned to do since. I kept all the old stuff I've done, stuff I did with Sylvia Vrethammar in Sweden. Very rarely [do I make changes], because I am working with people that I know and I respect.

"Make my voice part of the orchestra", Georgie had told him, and Gray duly did, making all the sophisticated brass and reed used sound ever so effortless.

"With Steve Gray, I would go to his house and I would play the song on the piano, and say 'Put my voice in the band. Don't put my voice here, with the band here, and I sing something, they play something. I want to be in the band.' So my voice is part of the saxophone section, or the trumpet section, or the trombone section. I'm singing as a member of the band, not the singer in the band, and that is the way I do it. He was such a wonderful arranger. I have about 10 or 12 of Steve's arrangements in my library. And now I'm kind of lost. Who do I go to, to do new arrangements? I don't know. I have enough Big Band arrangements.

"And what is going to happen to them after I'm dead and gone? I don't know. I was talking to the boys about it. Maybe they should go into an archive. So I do not plan to do another Big Band album. I think I've done it, really, with all the recordings."

Meanwhile, Georgie's "collection of Big Bands he worked with all over the world" continues. On April 6th, 2014, he joined the outfit The Lumberjackers in Germany's federal state of Baden-Württemberg in the city of Göppingen, taking along his precious Count Basie/Chico O'Farrell and Steve Gray arrangements to be conducted by Alexander Eissele.

Bogart-Fame with the Uni Big Band Bielefeld

Working For A Stone: The Bill Wyman's Rhythm Kings membership

Chapter 12

Rolling Stones bass player Bill Wyman and Georgie Fame go back a very long time, as Georgie remembered in February 2000: "I think we first met at what used to be an all-night café – what do you call those places? It was in the Earl's Court Road, and it was one of the all-night places in London. It must have been around 1961/62 – "Egg", "The Golden Egg" or something they used to call it. That was the only place you could go to after you finished work. I had a little room in Earl's Court at the time. I was living with a couple of prostitutes actually, in Concord Road. I had finished at the Flamingo Club one night, I think, and I went in there, and Bill was in there with the rest of the lads."

Bill Wyman adds: "Right when we started, we went to the Flamingo Jazz Club, where he was established. Georgie Fame played Cool Jazz, jazzy Blues. It was the cool thing. It was all that Mose Allison sort of thing. I really liked what he did then, because I love Mose Allison. And he kind of looked on us as – kind of upstarts, but in a nice way! He never had a bad thing to say of us, which many people did in those days."

Georgie picks up the story: "The Stones played the Flamingo on a couple of Thursdays, or was it Tuesdays? The Tuesdays and Thursdays sessions were kind of open. And the Stones did play a couple of times in 1962 or 1963. It wasn't quite their scene, the Flamingo, I think. They were very popular in Richmond and Ealing and even the Marquee, but the Flamingo was kind of a totally different world. Not many people turned up, but I was there. I really enjoyed them very much, and it was the first time I actually heard the band play properly."

In the meantime, the two remained good friends, and actually, Georgie worked for Bill Wyman before in the 1980s, albeit extremely briefly: "I played with Andy Fairweather Low on one of Bill's weddings":

Presenting good time remakes of songs was certainly the given task when Georgie was, touring all over the world as usual in 1989, was asked to perform a "private function" of a very special nature – an event which the tabloid press had a field day portraying. Fame's old Flamingo cohort Bill Wyman, still a Rolling Stone then, was getting "hitched" again. (He had been married to Diane Wyman for a decade, and had a relationship with Swedish lady Astrid Lundström for 16 years).

This time, on June 2nd, 1989, Bill married 18-year old Mandy Smith. Both the Rolling Stones and Georgie had once sung "My Girl" – but whatever, Wyman would state in his memoirs *Stone Alone* that "Keith and Patti, Mick and Jerry, Charlie and

Shirley and Ronnie and Jo all came to the party for 400 guests that afternoon at the Grosvenor House Hotel. Andy Fairweather-Low, Gary Brooker and Georgie Fame provided great music."

Andy had been a Blue Flame from time to time anyway, Brookers pre-Procol band The Paramounts had shared ballrooms with the Stones and Andy's Amen Corner, and to top it all, Andy, Gary and Bill had all performed in that loose conglomerate Willy & The Poor Boys, too, for assorted gigs and a live and studio album each.

In a relaxed interview in 1997, Bill Wyman took time out to explain why and how his regular collaboration with Georgie came about:

"For our rapport with audiences all over Europe, we have to establish some sort of contact, and Gary [Brooker] as well as Georgie are the perfect people for that, cracking jokes and so on. That's how a concert becomes more like a party and isn't so serious. And this is how music started in the first place; entertaining people. That's what it was like in medieval times with the court jesters. People were supposed to laugh and feel good. But when you listen to the music of the last two decades, it's all so damn serious. They all think of their image and are afraid to change their style."

Remembering the Flamingo Club days in the early 1960s, Bill confirmed that Georgie had always been very friendly, but "I didn't see him very often in those days, this was only at some concerts. But eventually we did something together in Soho – it was the 25th jubilee of the Marquee Club. Apart from the two of us, Alexis Korner and Andy Fairweather Low had been invited. Then we did the Alexis Korner tribute together when he died. When I started this project [The Rhythm Kings] I was too shy to call him. It's because he is like a saint for me, someone very special. And he never got the recognition and the success that he deserves. I picture him on a pedestal, just like Albert Lee actually.

"Even for someone like me it turns out to be difficult to contact these people. Eric Clapton, on the other hand, I know very well, because after all I play cricket with him, and we drink tea together. George Harrison or Ringo Starr I can just give a call. It's also pretty easy with Jeff Beck or Jimmy Page. Then again, I don't know Mark Knopfler so well. So that's how even somebody like me can't get in touch with everybody, and I was reluctant to give Georgie a ring. Andy Fairweather Low encouraged me and said 'Just give him a ring' but then he offered to do it for me. And Georgie was excited immediately!"

Bill, who had become used to working almost 100% with Jagger/Richards material over the previous three decades, describes the Rhythm (Kings) Method: "Every time I hear something on an old album or CD, it grabs me: I've known those songs for a long time. I put them all on cassette and then decide which are worth doing with the people I've got and give them a shot."

Georgie confirms this method: "Bill is very thorough about what he wants to do musically. He covers such a wide range of music from Fats Waller to Nellie Lutcher through to a really obscure mixture of 1940s R&B and Swing things, coupled with all the famous John Lee Hooker, Howlin' Wolf Blues type of things."

Wyman believes that good music is utterly timeless: "If somebody wrote a song in 1910, it's still a great song in 1999", or 2014, for that matter. "'Stardust' and 'Georgia

On My Mind', they're classic songs." – "Stardust" and "Georgia" are perfect vehicles for Fame of course, because he sang them many times, not least for his *In Hoagland 1981* album, recorded with Annie Ross.

Struttin' Our Stuff + Anyway The Wind Blows + Groovin' = 1 Fame album

Before the old Stones bass man actually released the first Bill Wyman's Rhythm Kings album *Struttin' Our Stuff* in 1997 on his Ripple Records, he had about four albums' worth of material in the can, including not only classic songs from the Swing and R&B catalogues, but also his own compositions, jointly created with his long-term mate, The End and Tucky Buzzard guitarist Terry Taylor. Wyman confirmed to me that "People just come in and just have a good time, enjoy it. You rehearse the song two or three times and then we just cut it and take one, or take two. Maximum take three. We can do three or four songs every day. It works for this band. They're so talented, they know their styles and they know what to do on the songs."

If we concentrate on the numbers that Fame dominates with his Hammond and vocal work, instead of just accompanying the band, we end up with 12 songs – enough for an imaginary first Georgie Fame's Rhythm Kings album:

On *Struttin' Our Stuff*, Georgie and the charming Soul lady Beverly Skeete, ex-Eurythmics and lured away from the Annie Lennox touring band, tackled the bluesy "Melody" which Stones fans remember from their first album with Ronnie Wood, *Black And Blue*. The way they interpret it with subtlety and wit, it sounds as if it was written more for their duo act than for a Rock'n'Roll band, in spite of Eric Clapton's delicate guitar licks. "Motorvatin' Mama" is a Wyman/Taylor Swing composition in the J.J. Cale vernacular, and "Hole In My Soul" by Sascha Buriand gets kick-started by Fame with a Hammond figure not unlike "Parchman Farm" – in a kind of Swing waltz rhythm. With its fabulous stops and starts, tongue twisting vocal delivery on the definition of Soul music and a horny horn section of Martin Drover, Frank Mead and part-time Blue Flame Nick Payn, Fame sounds as if he's leading his own group, and it could be the highlight of any GF album.

Anyway The Wind Blows from 1999 features Georgie prominently on the J.J. Cale title track, where he alternates with Peter Frampton's tasty guitar licks. You can feel that the two performed together on the debut tour of the Rhythm Kings two years earlier. Part of the vocal choir was a young lady called Keeley Smith (but no, she is *not* the then 67-year old Jazz legend associated with Frank Sinatra and Louis Prima).

"Walking One And Only" by the American Cowboy Folk and Bluegrass swinger Dan Hicks is a lightning speed tour-de-force for Fame & Skeete, where the organ work is lovingly complemented by Dave Hartley's stride piano work. Bill Wyman: "Dave is our jazz guy who covered all those areas. Dave isn't really a Boogie Woogie player or a Blues player, but he can play any kind of Jazz or popular stuff. With Mose Allison's "Days Like This", Fame was firmly on home ground, and so this is, like the lyric says, more like "a calculated risk".

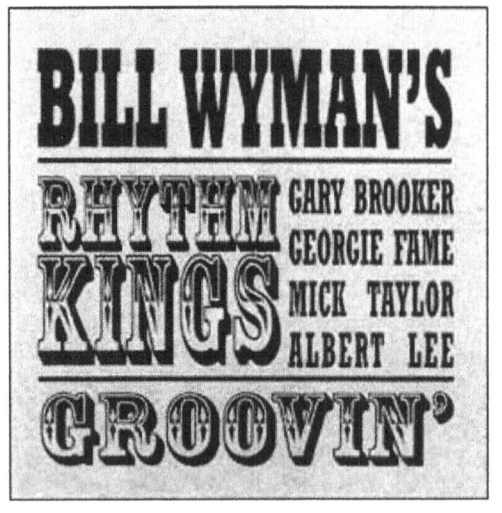

"Gee Baby Ain't I Good To You" by Dan Redman and Andy Razaf presents another 32-bar Blues, where once again the Fame Hammond is augmented by Dave Hartley's stride piano as well as Georgie and Bill's friend Eric Clapton.

Groovin' came out in 2000. The album completed Wyman's promised album trilogy of Thirties, Forties and Fifties music, as well as Fame's first batch of album-sized contributions: "We had enough material for the third one more than a year ago, but Bill kept summoning us to the studio, and we've recorded a tremendous amount since, some of which crept on the *Groovin'* collection at the last minute. So, I would say there's enough songs for at least two more albums."

Wyman felt there was no harm done in letting the Rhythm Kings members write songs for their repertoire, and Fame is a case in point, because in 1999, he wrote a song on the road which became a kind of anthem for this band: "Rhythm King". Firmly set in a JJ Cale groove, Fame would later record his composition for the solo album *Relationships*.

The old Stone kept his ears open for more contributions by other Rhythm Kings members: "They are very welcome to. If they come up with anything, I'm quite happy – this is not an ego trip. I am quite willing to listen, and if it's going to fit, then we could use it. But they don't seem to be so interested to do that. They are more interested in the things that I usually do, because lots of the things they haven't heard before and they like them. They like the style of it. I have in my archives of Rhythm Kings about 30 songs not used. Sometimes we go back to them and think 'Oh, this one will work with the new album'. Me and Terry [Taylor] would write various songs which we haven't used over the years, or that we had the basic song of, but I wasn't happy with my lyrics. Then I'd change them and then it works. So there is always a big collection of tracks and ideas and finished masters in the cupboard. That's what the Stones would do."

Of the Bill Wyman or Wyman & Taylor compositions on *Groovin'*, no less than three were sung and played by Fame: the nice Soul Twist "Rough Cut Diamond" with the lovely film line quote "Diamonds are a girl's best friend", custom-made for Georgie and graced by a slide solo by Australian guitar champ Tommy Emmanuel. In the cool Swing "Tomorrow Night", Fame worked out a lovely call-and-response routine with Beverly Skeete and Janice Hoyte, and was allowed to bring his own vibraphone man, Anthony Kerr, for some delicate solo work, with Martin Taylor and Dave Hartley joining in for excellent lead guitar and stride piano respectively. Again, a real Fame number, made to order by Wyman, Stone Alone, that could grace any of his own releases.

"Streamline Woman" praises a Hot Rod car the way you would normally rave over a young lady – lead guitar supplied by Rhythm King regular Albert Lee and well bedded in Fame's Hammond grooves.

Georgie also fronted "Can't Get My Rest At Night" by J. David Ray, which featured two ex-Stones, Bill on bass and Mick Taylor on a magic slide guitar that put character into a Mississippi Delta type Blues that is a real departure for Fame – a task which he mastered admirably. But apart from his own contributions, Georgie always finds a compliment for the other choices and performances: "On the new album *Groovin'*, we spent about three days, here and there, in the studios in December, and did some great numbers. I can remember we did Nina Simone's "I Put A Spell On You", and there's a great version of "Groovin'", the 1960s hit by The Young Rascals."

"I'm A Qualified Rhythm King" – touring with Bill Wyman

Theoretically, touring was out of the question, as Wyman made clear in 1997: "I really didn't want to do gigs anymore. I was fed up with all the travelling, and that's why I left the band, left the Stones. I'd had enough of hotels, soundchecks, the worries about the right chord changes and effective arrangements. But I soon realized that if you want to sell an album, you have to do some promotion, and that's why we are here [in Hamburg]. And if you have this type of musician around you, this is a lot of fun – so I don't mind at all! We're laughing, we're having fun, so it's like a massive ball."

But there were hang-ups as well, and the 1997 example can stand for many similar situations over the years: "Andy [Fairweather Low] was supposed to be part of the tour, but he's touring Japan with Eric Clapton. He was very sorry, 'I would have loved to be part of it', I could hear him moaning, but with Eric he's paid so much better. With such a short tour on this level, a lot of money gets spent for hotels and travelling, so I had to ask the record company to chip in with something. Nevertheless, there's not a lot left for the musicians. I called Albert Lee, for example, 'Can you do these ten days – four days of rehearsals and six gigs- for just three or four thousand quid?' I somehow dreaded his reply: 'Impossible'. Because that is how much he earns in one day if he does overdubs in an American studio. But then Albert said 'I will be there', and I thought 'Almost there – I've got Albert!' then on to Gary [Brooker] and Georgie."

Asked about the possibility to offer the lads a better paid tour of the United States – which they eventually did visit – Wyman was very reluctant: "No, cause first of all, I don't fly, and you can't drive to America, swimming there isn't possible, and I don't go by ship either. Instead, we're going to film parts of this show for a special. Apart from that, it would be impossible to get people of this calibre for a longer period of time. Gary Brooker wasn't even there for the first day of the rehearsals, because he was busy with a classical choir and orchestra, something which he does all the time. That very night, Beverly Skeete appeared at the London Palladium, that's why she wasn't there for the first rehearsal. The moment we stop playing, Georgie Fame will immediately fly to Ireland in order to work with Van Morrison. Albert Lee, Peter Frampton – they're just gone, I just had these ten or eleven days with all of them. After this success here in Hamburg, we could have done Paris too, Brussels and so on, but – impossible. It's a shame, but everybody had their fun."

After *Struttin' Our Stuff* and *Anyway The Wind Blows*, Bill Wyman's Rhythm Kings toured the 1999 album *Groovin'* extensively during the year 2000, and Bill was once more in a position to bring a lot of the players and singers who appeared on *Groovin'*:

"The people in my band cancel other shows and other tours to play with the Rhythm Kings. Beverly Skeete in her time worked with the Eurythmics and Annie Lennox. Annie asked her to do this summer with her. And Beverly, she has just cancelled, said she wanted to be with the Rhythm Kings. She makes much more money with Annie Lennox, of course, because they play big stadiums. But she loves to play with the Rhythm Kings, so she turned it down. So I have to find some decent money for her. The same applies to people like Georgie Fame, Andy Fairweather Low, people like that. They can get good money from other people, so they sometimes sacrifice it to play with the Rhythm Kings, which I think is very nice of them."

Wyman & Co came to Germany during spring of 2000. Was this a case of "Fame At The Races" on the 14th April near Duesseldorf? Georgie betting on the horses? Not quite: Bill Wyman's Rhythm Kings played the "Galopprennbahn" (the gallop race track) in Krefeld. Its quaint, pompous 1930s building must have housed huge banquets – and Georgie was delighted: The chef had turned out to be an ex-Londoner/Hungarian exile whom our "Godfather of Flamingo Club One-Nighters" knew from their mutual Soho days. What an encounter. For the third European Rhythm Kings tour, Fame acted as a secret MD for the Ex-Rolling Stones man's returned All-Star Band, which amongst its ten-piece line-up featured, again, Honorary Everly Brother Albert Lee, Procol Harum's Gary Brooker, Jazz-Django Martin Taylor and Soul Dame Beverly Skeete.

People always admire the relaxed way the Rhythm Kings perform and obviously enjoy themselves on stage, and the fans marveled at the fact that Fame and Martin Taylor actually got round to sharing a joke while in the process of playing. Georgie: "There is a very nice new song on the *Groovin'* album, 'Mood Swing', written by Irish guys [Nial Toner with Wendy Buckner and Keith Sewell]. I'm not playing on the record of that song, but there is a Cajun accordion player, it's not Nick Payn, I don't know who it is [Chris Hall], so Bill said 'Maybe you can take a little solo', and I'm trying to get a kind of accordion effect, 'waco waco', on the organ."

One of Georgie's specialties is laying down a Hammond groove and then singing in unison with a soloist. Georgie laughed and said "That was in Martin Taylor's solo – 'tadadada, tadadada'. I do that sometimes, because he plays that lick quite often, just to let him know that I can hear it. But tonight I went through the whole chorus with it. Nick Payn, the saxophone and harmonica player, came off at the end and said 'That was great', riding the wave of the lick. There is a lot of that spontaneity, even though we have a set – it's like the Blue Flames, we have a set programme of songs, but every night there's different licks going on."

Coming backstage after the show, Georgie noted that "tonight I had a little sound problem. I pulled out all the draw bars, and started to play something. I thought 'Shit, this is the wrong sound', and after I played my little solo, I went up to Martin and I said, 'That sounds like Robin Richmond, an old English theatre organ player'. In fact I meant to say it is this other guy in Blackpool Tower, so we had a little joke."

This showed how much Georgie has always loved playing with this band, and although he often said "I need a break from the Rhythm Kings", he always tends to be back on track with them, and at the time of writing, 2013, was booked solid with them until the end of the year. Georgie: "It's all music – it's all part of the same musical tree. But there are various branches on this wonderful musical tree, but if you retune with the roots and the trunk, you can just wander off on any of these branches and enjoy it."

Double Bill & Just For A Thrill – the 2nd Fame Rhythm Kings "album"

Meanwhile, during the second half of 2000, it was back in the studios for them. Bill Wyman got the band back into the studios, and at the same time "we took some things that we had from previous recordings, which were now suitable with the new songs, and which were not suitable for the last album. That happens: it happens with the Stones, it happens with everybody. You do songs and sometimes they don't fit, or there's too many ballads, or too many songs in the same key, in the same rhythm. So you save some and you can use them later. We don't sit in the studios for months and months, like I used to, and like many bands do. Some artists, they spend a week doing the vocal, line by line, don't they? We don't do that." This time, what appeared was actually two CDs with the lovely pun *Double Bill*, released in April 2001.

Georgie played the Hammond organ on many of the tracks, perhaps most remarkably on "Hot Foot Blues" by Marc Benno, who brought pleasant memories from his home town of Austin, Texas. Fame recorded a lot of the tracks for his Island albums in Texas, and in fact chose two Marc Benno compositions for the *Georgie Fame* album in 1974, the contemplative "Donut Man" and the delightfully swingy "Hall St. Jive".

Fame fronted the Rhythm Kings on seven *Double Bill* tracks, opening with the great Nat King Cole classic "Hit That Jive, Jack" by John Alston and Skeets Tolbert, which was also covered by Diana Krall.

He sang and played "I Can't Dance" by Charence Williams and Charlie Gains, which Wyman always had a very soft spot for: "I just came in and I said 'There's this song, it's from 1934, and it's by this girl called Valaida Snow, who you've never heard of, and it's called "I Can't Dance, I've Got Ants In My Pants". It is quite catchy, because my kids sing along to it, and they just love it. And I give a copy to everybody before we start. Then we run through it a couple of times for the arrangement." Quite an appropriate Jump Jive choice for Fame, who would come to love *Charlestons* a lot for his next solo album in 2003, graced here by a stunning Martin Taylor guitar solo.

Wyman feels the way you work with the American Songbook is fairly similar: "Most of these songs from the past are two minutes, two and a quarter or three. You have to put another solo in it, another verse or a bridge or whatever it is. So you work the arrangements out, some of the guys write chords out, and we run through it two or three times, getting the parts right, 'No, you shouldn't play there', all that bit, music bits. And then we just cut it, take one, done!"

This is how Bill worked with Georgie on Nelly Lutcher's "Do You Or Don't You", pointing out in his liner notes of *Double Bill* how much he adored Lutcher, and allowing Georgie to combine this 1940s classic with his own "I Wanna Know".

Another specialty is the medley of "Snap Your Fingers" (Martin/Zanetis) and the Gospel standard "What A Friend We Have In Jesus", a traditional arranged by Wyman and Fame. Interestingly, Fame's ex-partner Alan Price had used the traditional melody for his song "Changes", which had done massive wonders for VW and was cheekily credited to himself on the album *Liberty* in 1989.

Bill Wyman recalls how it came about to link this song to the well-known Gospel melody: "You have to listen closely, because it's very subtle. When 'Snap Your Fingers' is going on, in the background you can hear the organ theme of 'What A Friend We Have In Jesus' playing at the same time because it's the same chord structure. You hear that very faintly. We didn't put it right out front and make it too obvious. Georgie Fame suddenly discovered it was the same chord structure and while we were doing it in the studio, he was singing it in the background. I am glad you noticed."

Firmly in 1930s Jump Jive mood again comes Fats Waller's "The Joint Is Jumping" – here, the horn blowers Frank Mead and Nick Payn are joined by third sax player Nick Pentelow, who played for everybody between Roger Chapman, the Steve Gibbons Band and Rhythm King/Blue Flame Andy Fairweather Low – another collaborator on *Double Bill* – Georgie and AFL both enjoying Louis Jordan's "Boogie Woogie All Night Long" for instance.

"Where Is The Money", like "Walking One & Only" from *Anyway The Wind Blows*, is from the catalogue of Mills Brothers and Bing Crosby fan Dan Hicks from Little Rock, Arkansas, who delighted both Wyman and Fame with his Hot Licks in the Sixties, and just released a live album from his 70th birthday. This funny dance tune is from the 1971 Dan Hicks & Hot Licks album of the same name.

Back to Gospel country for the traditional "Jealous Girl" which Bill Wyman and Terry Taylor arranged, not to be confused with the Lana Del Ray song. This is a pleasant Blues in 6/8 time with great background vocals by an all-girl ensemble led by the two "road chicks" Beverly Skeete and Janice Hoyte.

Fame's final vocal contribution for *Double Bill* was the snappy Wyman/Taylor number "Keep On Truckin'", a nice enough shuffle that serves as perfect dance floor material: "Don't you lose the rhythm 'cause it gives this man the Blues", he pleads with Wyman's lyrics, before Terry Taylor sees to guitar duties. And finally, Melanie Redmond, Sonia Jones and that young lady with the famous name of Keeley Smith – the original Keely Smith (b. 1928 or 1932) worked with Louis Prima, Frank Sinatra and, hey, rocked with Kid Rock in 2008! – get the backing choir going.

The final Bill Wyman & The Rhythm Kings album so far was 2004's *Just For A Thrill*, which, like the debut with "Melody", is another collection to feature a Fame-sung song with a Rolling Stones connection, "Down Home Girl". As Wyman explained to me in 2004, "it's not a Stones number, but the Stones did it. We did one on the album *Groovin'*, 'Oh Baby (We Got A Good Thing Going)'.

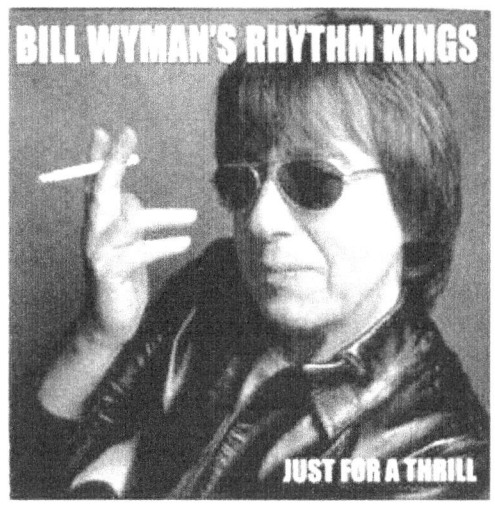

"The point of doing 'Down Home Girl' was: I've always liked the song, I think it has got great lyrics, which is a bit difficult for foreign listeners, but sometimes they understand. But the originals had horns and an R&B feel. The Stones made it more kind of Rock'n'Roll, and they didn't have horns, or girls singing or anything. Keith just did that "d-ding, d-ding" on the guitar. We could do it like the original horns, and backing vocals, girls, that's why I liked it. We could do it in a different way, but it's still a great song."

Georgie sang and played on the swinging "Cadillac Woman", which according to Wyman's liner notes was "chosen in honour of the great early piano player 'Archibald' who influenced every piano player that came after him in New Orleans". With Fame busy on his trusted Hammond, German Boogie Woogie wonder Axel Zwingenberger did the honours on the old 'Joana'. Our hero's final stint in the ballad *Just For A Thrill* was the title track, a Ray Charles number that Wyman always loved. Charles had revived the original in 1959 – it was composed by Lil Hardin Armstrong, Old Louis Armstrong's second wife.

As Georgie sums up the proceedings, "Bill looks at the big picture. He has got a great taste and a very wide taste in music, so he decides basically what we are actually going to record."

Wyman adds that "I love the recordings the most, which is opposite to the Stones, where I liked the touring best, because the recording was always hard work, whereas touring was whack, whack, whack. Now I like the recording best, because I can be more creative and more inventive, and I can be in control. I am not a control freak as such, but the end of the line is me.

"If my ideas work, fine, and if not, I can take ideas from the others around me. If they suggested 'Maybe that horn line isn't quite right' and they come up with something – I might say 'right'. I am not a dictator. But I have the final say in everything: what songs are chosen, what songs we use on a particular album. We have got 40 songs as finished masters for this album and we will probably take 14 of them. There's about three albums there, it just depends what fits with what."

Georgie: "I think we are all cogs in the same wheel. Bill is very much in charge in the studio. He gets me to sing the way he wants the performance on a particular song to sound, which I am very happy with. On stage, Bill does what he knows best, which is probably what he did all his life with the Stones, which is sit in the back and play fantastic bass and lay down a solid bass beat, with the drummer, which everybody can take advantage of. I think it is the same for me as a band leader in my own band. It's not that different, but it is a different band. But I surround myself with the best musicians I can have, and I always make sure that they are very good friends of me, like family. By surrounding yourself with great musicians, you can just lay it down. For instance, when I play with my band, I just lay the Hammond organ down and allow all those other people to play around what I'm playing. It's probably fair to say that Bill does the same with the Rhythm Kings, he plays that wonderful bass in the background and allows everybody to colour it around him."

Bill: "But we get on stage, you see, and then I am not the boss anymore. They all want me to be, but I'm not that sort of person on stage: I'm Mr Stand-at-the-back, like your favourite undertaker. I am the bass player. So I got two people, Georgie Fame and Gary Brooker on keyboards [who was later replaced by Mike Sanchez and then Geraint Watkins], on organ and piano, who are my MDs, musical directors.

Georgie experienced many guest stars during the tours with Bill Wyman, among them Maria Muldaur and Mary Wells on a 2013 British sojourn which he partly had to cancel due to health reasons, and it is a pity that there weren't more lucky fans who could hear Georgie Fame & Mary Wells' wonderful rendition of the Koehler/Arlen standard "Stormy Weather". It should be recorded and used to introduce TV weather reports all over the world.

From an earlier European tour with American Soul legend Eddie Floyd, Nick Payn, the Rhythm Kings' saxophone and flute player who also works for the Blue Flames from time to time, had this funny anecdote from the tour bus:

"It is always one of the benefits of the journey to talk to other musicians. But most of the time, Floyd would be sitting on his own, a pair of huge head-phones on his ears, and listen to world-wide cover versions of his world-wide hit 'Knock On Wood'." Of course, among them would not only be the one by part-time Rhythm King Eric Clapton, but also Georgie's own from 1966.

Two out of a thousand gigs – Osnabrück and Düsseldorf

Two of this author's most enjoyable concerts with the Rhythm Kings took place in Osnabrück in 2011 and Düsseldorf in October 2012:

Round one: January 28th at the Osnabrück Stadthalle: Will this show become comedy? Georgie Fame begins with the BeeGees and dedicates their song "to US president Barak Obama", because his motto seems to be "'Words' are all I have". Laughter is guaranteed – then the following Gospel touch changes the mood, before dirty Hammond sounds lead into "I Got A Woman".

Of course this is *all* comedy, but it's a Rhythm & Blues Revue first and foremost. That is guaranteed by the agile Rhythm Section of Bill Wyman with Graham Broad, who served the drum part for Stones mentor Alexis Korner more than 30 years before this event.

In front of these two, one swinging nugget follows another: "Jump, Jive & Wail" by Honorary Everly Brother Albert Lee and his Nashville style picking, "Sweet Soul Music" with "our Rhythm Queen Beverly Skeete" (Wyman) and the precise good vibes horn men Frank Mead and Bill Payn.

Via the Boogie "All Nite Long", piano boy Geraint Watkins from the Thames Delta establishes vocal contact with the packed crowd which seems in danger of comfortable complacency via the soft theatre chairs. Very soon, Madame Skeete grabs Geraint Watkins' ex-Dominators partner – and ex Blue Flame! – Andy Fairweather Low for a duet of the once Stones-tackled "Harlem Shuffle", which has Wyman grin uninhibitedly: this version is better than the Jagger-helmed single, for sure.

Bass boss Bill and Georgie Fame continue by enjoying Creedence Clearwater Revival and their old chestnut "Run Through The Jungle", and Beverly Skeete threatens "I Put A Spell On You", which Georgie and also partner Alan Price used to interpret with comparable gusto.

Beverly's spell seems to have hit Welshman Watkins, because the strength he displays in "Out Demons Out", vocally and with sheer piano power, is pure exorcism and so near to madness that it would make the Pope shiver. Apart from tried and tested toe tappers like "Route 66", "I Just Wanna Make Love To You" and "Honky Tonk Women" – Fairweather and Beverly sing the old Stones classics – there is also time for contemplation.

"Just For A Thrill" gets tenderly performed by Georgie Fame, Dylan's "I'll Be Your Baby Tonight" follows by a romantically inclined Andy, and the Everlies evergreen "Crying In The Rain" comes in heart-melting fashion by Ms Skeete, only accompanied by Albert Lee on the piano.

The encores cover the spectrum between philosophy and euphoria: With Mose Allison's "Days Like This", Georgie Fame characterizes that the then 82 year-old Mississippi master is still alive and kicking and a role model for everybody, and Albert Lee's "Tear It Up" shows the Osnabrück punters that after such a two-hour knees-up, the only way to continue is to celebrate someplace else with – what else – Rhythm Kings records grooving "all nite long".

Round two: October 12th, 2012 in Düsseldorf's nicely retro Savoy Theatre: The Old Stone's Rhythm Kings without their fast fingers fretboard king Albert Lee on guitar – that's a very rare occasion, but the Country lover is busy touring with his Hogan's Heroes. Regrettable as this is, it offers chances too – for some band members as well as those dedicated regulars who have come into the sold-out Savoy.

Rhythm Kings founder member Terry Taylor is the guitar governour for the night and – this becomes clear immediately – he does a brilliant job, via unobstrusive rhythm work, an impressive slide guitar and some finely crafted solos.

Bill Wyman's band introduction shows how many capable singing voices remain in the nine-piece Rhythm Kings even without Lee: The sweet dreadlock Soul Sister Beverly Skeete puts us under a magic spell with Etta James "Tell Mama", thrills us to pieces with James Brown's "It's A Mans Mans World" and takes the Memphis classic "Sweet Soul Music" into the present.

Andy Fairweather Low, GF, Beverly Skeete, Bill Wyman, Graham Broad, Albert Lee

Geraint Watkins – apart from dry Welsh humour – presents New Orleans' best via Allen Toussaint's "It's Raining" and, working his accordion, lets us enjoy Chuck Berry's Cajun cracker "You Never Can Tell". In Watkins' reading, the catchy "Man Smart, Women Smarter" was originally "by the famous Chicago Blues man Harry Belafonte", and he has a point – many only know him as the Calypso King.

Even Frank Mead out of the enternal Rhythm Kings sax tandem with part-time Blue Flame Nick Payn – the duo frequently stealing the show courtesy of brilliantly set horn accents, solo sensations and Las Vegas compatible dance steps – gets a chance to croon two Boogie numbers by his famous Blues Harp hero Little Walter, and he delivers with panache.

Meanwhile, blowing partner Nick Payn hits the dance floor with Miss Skeete, in a mixture of choreography and comedy, and Bill Wyman himself gets a rare glimpse of the limelight in celebrating "Honky Tonk Women" with Beverly, which has the audience jump out of their theatre seats, again.

But the loudest applause – even as he strolls in casually – is reserved for Georgie Fame. After a another cheeky intro of the BeeGees' "Words" which had at one point had the chance of a "Bonnie and Clyde" follow-up, he grooves into Ray Charles' "I Got A Woman", sways with old Louis Armstrong's "Just For A Thrill" from the 2004 Rhythm Kings album, and honours the Rolling Stones with "Route 66".

Fame has lots of fun with Wyman's never-ending, descending bass line for "Hit The Road Jack", cheekily calling out "This is also your only chance of a bass solo tonight, so make the most of it!" Beverly joins the vocals, and they combine the Ray Charles Swing with Louis Jordan's Jump Jive "Is You Is Or Is You Ain't My Baby".

This starts, in Georgie's own words, "a real Karaoke party – because I always see such a lot of Japanese guys in the streets of Düsseldorf", which happens to be the main German community for the people from Nippon. With a few Japanese expressions thrown in, Georgie seems their man. Bill Wyman's 76th birthday is going to happen a fortnight after this musical celebration. Let's hope that he and Georgie will follow the old Blues man's lead – Pinetop Perkins recorded his last album at age 97 and bopped till he dropped, on Caribbean cruise ships!

For fans: don't forget to buy The Bootleg Kings!

Chapter 13

Poet In New York – adventures in the new millennium

After the second Go Jazz studio album *The Blues And Me* that Georgie recorded and issued in 1992, it would take seven long years before he worked in a New York studio again. All the while, Fame fans had not been short of releases – the album introducing his sons, *Three Line Whip*, a couple of live albums and Big Band radio albums each, and a high profile Mose Allison tribute with Ben Sidran, Van Morrison and Mose himself, *Tell Me Something*, had made the rest of the 1990s a prolific, fruitful era.

A first look at the repertoire could have an initially sobering effect: many numbers had been tried, tested and tackled on previous collections, five of them for instance on *A Portrait of Chet*, a project very dear to Fame's heart. As he told Gudrun Endress for the German *Jazz Podium* magazine,

"When I work with my own band, or with other musicians, it is important to inform the audience where the story of the song comes from." He went on that in interpreting other people's material, hopefully with a new dimension added, "There are reference points to the performers, or even the virtuosos who sang or played these songs before. For instance, if I sing a Chet Baker trumpet solo, I am attempting my own interpretation, and it is possible that I let quotes in there sound like a Lester Young solo."

So there would always be room at the top to refine and perfect staples of the repertoire, and what's more, the afore mentioned *A Portrait Of Chet* had come out on the tiny Swedish label Four Leaf Clover, not exactly a household name with distributors worldwide and a sales success mainly to Georgie Fame's hard core audience. For the same reason, Fame included his heart-breaking ballad "A Declaration Of My Love" in this small combo context – it had been part of his *Three Line Whip* album as well as his vast Big Band catalogue.

Georgie further explained his renewed collaboration with Ben during a relaxed chat in Krefeld, Germany, around the time of its release: "After not doing an album with him for quite a few years – but of course, my own albums go through his company – we thought it was time to do another one. The original concept for this album: we talked in New York a couple of years ago."

Originally, the album had been conceived as a collaboration with the great Jazz legend Benny Golson, as Georgie explained: "I don't know if you know this: a few years ago Ben took me to California and I sang a song which came out on CD: songs associated with the *Glengary Glen Ross* movie. I sang a song called 'Easy Street'. The musical director for this was Benny Golson, and he was conducting the band at that session. Benny is a wonderful Jazz legend, and he wrote me a letter, congratulating me and complementing me on the recording that we did.

"One of Benny's favourite words is "coscort", which I had to look up in the dictionary, and it means kind of "sparkly". So I started to sit down at the piano and started to write a song. But I didn't realize I was composing a song. It turned out to be the song really inspired by my girl friend, disguised as tuning into the radio, or tuning into whatever, it is called 'Tuned Into You'".

But another time, in a BBC programme hosted by himself, Fame hinted on that radio connection, "tuning into AFN, American Forces Network, back in the old days of shortwave radio, when the only chance of hearing Jazz on the radio was perhaps American Forces Radio, when Willis Conover beamed *The Jazz Hour* from Washington DC."

"Tuned Into You" became the first song on the album, recounting the encounter with Golson:

"And on the strength of Benny Golson's letter to me, I wrote this original solo, and the text of the solo is all about Benny Golson writing to me, and saying 'Hey man, it was great.' That is how the song came to be completed. So Ben and I decided to approach Benny Golson with doing a special kind of Jazz album, using a lot of Benny Golson's great compositions, some of which already had lyrics to them, like 'I Remember Clifford' for Clifford Brown, or 'The Gypsy', 'Whisper Not' and 'Blues March'. And there were others, which Ben and I were going to write lyrics to."

The song "Tuned Into You" was re-recorded with The Blue Flames for BBC Radio, featuring Anthony Kerr on vibraphone, Alan Skidmore and Guy Barker on their respective horns and the sons on drums & guitar.

This author recalls Georgie raving about this, at the "Docks" venue on the notorious Hamburg Reeperbahn, during the 1998 Rhythm Kings tour. "Benny said 'Yes, great idea!' And then a few weeks later Benny came back and said 'Ah, I've decided to do something else, blah, blah, blah …', so that killed that idea."

And so Ben Sidran wanted to come to the rescue. "But also, before we did this album – I was talking with Ben about it – I didn't want to make my own album. I thought I'd have enough of recording my own albums for a while. I wanted to make as many duets as possible with Ben. But the way we worked so fast – we had one rehearsal one afternoon, and Peter Washington, the bass player, couldn't even make the rehearsal. So he just turned up at the studio instead – the only duets on the album are 'Doodlin'' with Ben, and 'Girl Talk', which is [with] Ben's lyrics also. And it was all over in two days!"

This was also due to working with a very small combo: Sidran selected the musicians for this project. There was Bobby Malach on tenor, one of Georgie's favourite saxophone players, who had been with Georgie on the two previous sets *Cool Cat Blues* and *The Blues And Me*. Drummer Louis Hayes had also been one of Fame's idols, ever since he listened to him with Cannonball Adderley's group.

New Yorker Bebop man David Hazeltine (b. 1958) and his wonderful piano touches, universally known via his work with Jon Hendricks, prompted Fame to concentrate on "just" singing and leaving the ivories to the master. Continuously being too modest about his own playing Georgie didn't play piano or Hammond organ this time, because "we had this fantastic piano player called David Hazeltine, who I'd never met before. He is a very talented musician. The only thing I knew he had done was he had worked sometimes with the Mingus Big Band, you know, the new Mingus Big Band. And he is a very versatile and sympathetic player. He can play like Cedar Walton [the American hard bop jazz pianist of 1934 vintage] one minute, and then he can play like Kenny Drew the next minute. So he is a great player, and I was very happy to let him play. I gave him a couple of ideas on the arrangements at the rehearsal, but I just left it to him. So I was just wearing my Jazz singer's hat, standing there with Bobby Malach."

"I also spoke to Ben about suddenly realizing when we were recording that I don't know whether Peter Washington, the wonderful bass player, is from Philadelphia. But Bobby Malach certainly is from there. And then I realized that the CD had a lot of connections with Philadelphia. 'Tadd' Dameron [1917–1965] is from Philadelphia. Clifford Brown [1930–1956] is [too]."

"There's the story of Clifford dying in a car crash on my birthday, when I was 10 years old I think [13 actually], on the 26th June. And Clifford Brown's first Rhythm & Blues group, the band he played with in Philadelphia in the early Fifties, maybe late Forties, was called Chris Powell & The Blue Flames." Mind-boggling – as Georgie's real name is of course Clive Powell. "So I said to Ben there was an awful lot of Philadelphians."

Georgie felt at home with Ben Sidran's musicians, because they reminded him of his adopted second home Sweden, as he recalled in 2009: "But if you go to Minnesota in America and places like that, or to Canada, there's a lot of people called Johanson, there's a lot of Scandinavians in that part of the USA. Ben Sidran's friends and colleagues, Billy Peterson plays bass, and his brother Ricky Peterson, they are from Minneapolis and they are Scandinavian heritage. Their drummer was Gordy Knudtson, which is a Norwegian name – a great drummer [he was with the Steve Miller Band]. Leo, his son, plays with him of course."

The album *Poet In New York* not only gave Georgie the opportunity to focus his Vocalese chops, but also a chance to chat about his idols in that department, something he has always enjoyed, on stage as much as in our conversations. Apart from King Pleasure, Eddie Jefferson and "Yeh Yeh" master lyricist Jon Hendricks, he has always adored:

"Oscar Brown Jr., who is a true poet, just like Mose Allison, who has a most distinctive sound on top of his lyrical talent. I mainly listened to musicians who sing, rather than many singers, only Ray Charles and Betty Carter really. I would much rather go for musicians' singing. That is why I sing Jazz, because I use my voice as an instrument. On *Poet In New York*, I sing some melodies along with Bobby Malach's saxophone voice, even some solos, so it sounds like a Jazz quintet.

"Ben and I had decided to do a kind of Jazz album in the way we were thinking already, and that's the result now: *Poet In New York*, which includes some of my own compositions, which I'm very glad that they enjoy, and of course there's a couple of Chet Baker things."

The method of creating his own songs is reflected in what Georgie told Gudrun Endress in 2000 in the German *Jazz Podium*: "When I play something I realize what I have found, and play it again in the complete form, and then it stays in my memory.

Then I call a musician and say 'Please write that down for me', or I secure it on tape. With my songs like 'Tuned Into You" or "Declaration Of My Love", I had the feeling as if a different power was guiding me." For "Declaration Of My Love", I wrote the melody and the text, and only then did I decide to write a solo for myself which I could sing. I don't like to sing Scat, I prefer to sing things which sound like improvised solos, but they become a structured piece of music for which I write lyrics."

Poet In New York – track by track

The album naturally starts with Fame's own "Tuned Into You", which kick-started the original project. Here, in his typical modesty, Georgie points out that for writing valuable, poetic lyrics, he depends on a good melody, like the kind that Benny Golson composes. He celebrates the letter of praise which he got after the two of them worked on the soundtrack of the film *Glengarry Glen Ross* in 1992.

Apart from vocal contributions by Dr John and Al Jarreau, Georgie contributed Harold Arlen and Johnny Mercer's "Easy Street", crediting Golson in "Tuned In To You" for his subsequent letter of praise: "Benny Golson wrote to me, I treasure what he said, talking 'bout the music, his wisdom was clear and good for my ear." The music develops slowly with sparse piano touches by David Hazeltine, then rolls along easily in an effortless Swing provided by Washington & Hayes, with Bobby Malach's sax not unlike Dick Morrissey's mellow tones on *Hoagland*.

Bass player Geoff Gascoyne was not part of the sessions, but has a lot of praise for this song in 2012: "And even his original music – he writes such great music. One tune of his is called 'Tuned Into You'. He has written what is actually like a Vocalese on one of his own tunes. He is brilliant. I remember I was in New York on tour with Jamie: and I happened to see that Clive was on at the Blue Note. So I went down to see him do

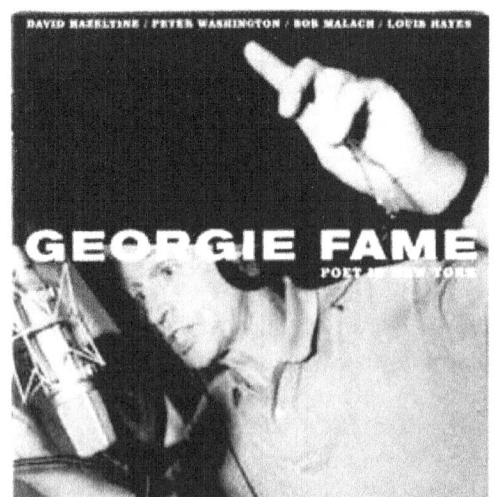

the *Poet In New York* album, which is amazing. Again, he wasn't playing, he was singing, he was with David Hazeltine on piano. It was just a quartet, and it was a fantastic gig.

The second track starts with Georgie's mouth percussion, echoed by Louis Hayes' sensitive strokes on brushes, then Hazeltine chimes in, charmingly re-creating London's "Big Ben" melody on piano for the Brit vocalist. Fame had this to say for the song he also did on *A Portrait of Chet*: "There's 'But Not For Me', the George Gershwin thing with the Chet Baker trumpet solo", which the boys in his band actually used to discuss his vocal prowess. Anthony Kerr: "He doesn't have to change the key to fit into a more narrow range." Alan Skidmore: "Yes, like most vocalists, singers do. That is why most of the musicians call vocalists 'the enemy'. But we don't refer to Clive as the enemy, because he can actually sing, like, 'But Not For Me' in E flat, which is the original, correct key. Doesn't matter what it is, there's not many singers around that will do that. He's got a huge range, from bass right up to falsetto."

"Doodlin'", a duet with Ben Sidran, is straight from the Lambert, Hendricks & Ross songbook, another showcase yet for Vocalese, where Georgie sings a piano solo by Horace Silver, using wonderful lyrics created by Jon Hendricks. As Georgie told me in Recklinghausen before a gig with Bill Wyman's Rhythm Kings when this album was just out, this tune had not been recorded in the most perfect key for him: "It sounds more like a baritone sax solo, and I almost felt like Pepper Adams!"

"Declaration Of My Love" seemed like an old friend when it appeared on *Poet In New York*: Georgie had sung it with the WDR Big Band in the summer of 1994 and this author will always connect his heartfelt, sad ballad with that live rendition – it had first come out on *City Life* in 1993 with the BBC Big Band and also graced *Endangered Species* with the Danish Radio Big Band. Georgie told *Jazz Podium* that there is a line in 'Declaration Of My Love' that goes 'I threw away my dictionary, 'cause I'm looking for a phrase, one not overused, one that's not abused, maybe just a word or two, something for my muse …' and at the same time, I had the feeling that I *was* kissed by my muse …"

"I wished somebody would sing 'Declaration Of My Love', but not so many people have heard it yet. I have a wonderful Big Band arrangement of it by Steve Gray, which I have performed with the WDR Big Band and the HR Big Band, but not recorded yet. Jerry van Rooyen [WDR] thinks it is one of the most wonderful pieces he has ever heard. He wrote a string arrangement for it. I would love it if a few female singers picked it up. My songs are also meant for other vocalists to hear and other instrumentalists to play. It would be a great honour for me if I heard a good musician with one of my compositions."

As Ben Sidran puts it into thrilling historical context in his liner notes, "With 'Symphony Sid' we are harking back to the radio in 1953, Georgie singing King Pleasure's lyrics to Lester Young's theme, and then his own lyrics to both Charlie Fergusson's tenor solo and Eddie Lewis's trumpet choruses from that original King Pleasure version." Fame loved to open Van Morrison's shows with this animating party piece.

"On A Misty Night" is one of three numbers here by the well known Bebop and hard bop arranger and composer Tadley Ewing Peake Tadd Dameron, and as Fame recalls, "Dizzy Gillespie's Big Band recorded a lot of his tunes." For this one Georgie supplied the lyrics: "'On A Misty Night' is another great Dameron tune where I wrote the text to the melody, and the lyrics to Chet's trumpet solo on his recording with George Coleman." Fame must love this number, as he included it on both his Australian album *No Worries* in 1988 and the collection *Portrait Of Chet* 1989.

"And there is also a beautiful ballad by Tadd Dameron called 'That's The Way It Goes' which I wrote lyrics to maybe 12 or 15 years ago." "That's The Way It Goes" is a medium Swing where Fame sings about feeling blue due to losing a lady. There were tender memories of Ginger & Fred, "It might have been better if only I'd tried, but I went and blew it like Bonnie and Clyde". It was her who had the man "like a puppet on a string – I couldn't do a thing".

The best line comes right at the beginning, where, after "I can't understand why I'm feeling so blue", Georgie brought in the clever alliteration "I thought that the melody mellowed you, too". And before there is a short change to half time, he even quotes the beginning of "Moody's Mood For Love", going "There I go, there I go, there I go" – it's all awesomely inspired.

"Do It The Hard Way" by Richard Rogers & Lorenz Hart is an old chestnut of Fame's, but gets the most elegant Fame reading yet – in spite of Georgie's voice sounding a touch rougher – after decent versions on *The Two Faces Of Fame* from 1967 and *A Portrait Of Chet* in 1989. The first reading had a similar line-up, with Peter King on tenor sax.

As Georgie mentioned about "It Could Happen To You": "Again another Chet Baker trumpet solo, which Mike O'Neill wrote – Nero and The Gladiators – that's Mike's lyrics there. So it is a historical jazz thing."

This Burke/Van Heusen composition also got kick-started on *The Two Faces Of Fame* by Georgie, and, obviously a firm favourite, it again got refined on *A Portrait Of Chet*. Fame aficionados know, though, that every remake is an adventure with him: Here it is the "Wandering Star" ending courtesy of Lee Marvin which he loves to do on stage. Georgie: "It's a bit like 'Everything Happens To Me'. I wrote the text to the melody, and also the solo that I sing on that is my own solo, it's an original solo with text."

Ben Sidran had received Bobby Troup's outspoken consent to write additional lyrics to "Girl Talk", which the "Route 66" creator had done with Neil Hefti, "some twenty years ago, after I sang them to him over a long distance phone line." So both Sidran and Fame had recorded the song before they performed it live in the studio for this collection, Fame on his controversially discussed LP *Georgie Does His Thing With Strings* in 1969, then of course without Sidran's fine contribution. The way they ad-lib in the final section, talking about a girl from the previous night they fantasized about is just gorgeously effortless.

"Accentuate The Bass" is not a tribute to a particular bass player, but a speedy swing seminar about what a fellow can do when he always comes second – spend some time in the bass/basement and keep a low profile, apparently, sung by Georgie in a very low 'Wandering Star' register once more. Fame's bass player here, Peter Washington, deserves and gets a high profile here. Again, everybody's playing is a pure delight, the rapport between the musicians a dream. That includes the human instrument that Georgie plays – his remarkable voice.

Billy Strayhorn's "Lush Life" had been part of Linda Ronstadt's highly successful sojourns into Swing and Big Band territory. On her three Jazz albums, she also did "But Not For Me" and "Someone To Watch Over Me".

Fame raved over this choice, too: "And of course Billy Strayhorn's 'Lush Life', which is one of the most overwhelming compositions in Jazz. I sang that for the first time. It is one of those songs that singers always avoid, unless you're a real good singer. It's a very difficult song to sing if you don't know it. Again, Ben said 'Come on. You can do it', and it was another first take, "let's try and sing this song".

As a radio DJ for Saarländischer Rundfunk in the German state of Saarland, Thomas Kreutzer, remarked on the occasion of Fame's 70th birthday: "If you don't get every note and nuance right in a sophisticated number like "Lush Life', it's all crap. Georgie Fame gets it right here to an extent that wipes the floor with all the young Jazz prima donnas who want to force their success by wearing negligees on their record covers."

This kind of praise was reflected within his band, too. As Alan Skidmore said, "he can actually sing in any key! He can sing a tune in the written key. For instance, if he were to sing 'Body & Soul', he would do it in D flat. Well I'll tell you what is a very good example – 'Lush Life'. He sings that in D flat, which is the written key, which is great. He has got such an incredible range."

Fame continues to talk about the collaboration with Sidran: "Then there's Ben's lyrics to 'Ask Me Now', which is a wonderful old Thelonious Monk composition. It was on the list of things to consider, but we never got round to doing that. I knew it from one of the first albums I heard Ben Sidran do. So there is a great historical connection between not only my relationship with Ben Sidran, but in the whole material that is on the album. I would call it a straight ahead Jazz album, done with paying due respect to people like Chet Baker, Clifford Brown, Billy Strayhorn, Thelonious Monk etc. and 'Song For My Father', Horace Silver, 'Doodlin'', all that sort of stuff."

"When you're working with such wonderful musicians and we had James Farber engineering again – James is one of the top engineers in the world! James also paid us a great compliment – because we recorded straight to two-track: balanced up and done like a gig. James Farber said that it's in the top 'Top 5' albums that he has ever engineered. And he has done everything."

Everything means Madonna, Al Jarreau, The Thompson Twins – even the famous *No Nukes* triple album featuring Crosby Stills & Nash and Bonnie Raitt is on Farber's CV.

"I think it's fair to say that it's a fairly true, very representative documentation of where I stand as a Jazz singer, which is why immediately I've gone into the studio with my own band to record material which will counter that album, to give the other side of me, apart from work I do with Bill Wyman and everybody else – [*Relationships*, released in 2001].

"Because you know me, I don't want to be known as just a Jazz singer, and I don't want to be known as just a Hammond organ player or a Rhythm & Blues singer. So the next album with The Blue Flames will contain a little bit more mixed material. But that's a very nice, straight Jazz album – and I am very happy with it."

The first Blue Flames studio album for seven years – Relationships

By the year 2000, Georgie Fame was well-established in Bill Wyman's all-star Rhythm Kings, serving – like he had in the Van Morrison Band – as a secret musical director, and writing on the road with renewed vigor. The result was the first studio album

Georgie and Flames as youngsters and in 2000, spot the members.

in seven years – since *Three Line Whip* – to feature the eternal Blue Flames, who by that time had been stable since Geoff Gascoyne followed the renowned Brian Odgers in 1994.

You can measure how happy Georgie was with the Blue Flames by the fact that when he was offered a series of six programmes on BBC Radio 2, he took the whole band with him to the studios, recording many of his current as well as historical tunes "the way it used to be" in the BBC, and in the process providing some significant one-off connections as well.

His first guest during the "shows" was old Flamingo cohort Zoot Money, and after a lot of reminiscing about Zoot taking over the Flamingo residency slowly but surely, Georgie would go and offer the unique chance "My band is your band", resulting in Zoot Money and The Blue Flames performing a version of the rare Ray Charles tune "Hide Nor Hare" on the spot. George Bruno Money knew that this was "the usual story: the girl runs away and leaves him the sickbed", but really, he just loved the tune – consequently, he and the Flames were obviously having a ball, with Georgie joining in on the Hammond! In the same programme, Zoot takes over Boz Scaggs' part in "It Should Have Been Me", high time for the British Broadcasting Corporation to get these precious jewels on the market before everyone involved turns 80!

Other guests in that series were Peter King, Claire Martin, Bill Wyman, Steve Gray and Madeline Bell. The inclusion of King in this illustrious "guest list" is all the more significant, it has to be repeated, because he was found not even mentioning his and Georgie's frequent collaborations in his autobiography, *Flying High – A Jazz Life and beyond*.

The long player was recorded in the studios of drummer Ralph Salmins in Welwyn Garden City near London during March and then November 2000. Salmins had served as Fame's drummer for *The Birthday Concert* in 1998, and supplied percussion during the sessions. The album was called *Relationships* – its cover depicting a traditional family

photo album made of leather, with a six-year-old Georgie in a black and white pic, by the seaside with his mother by his hand.

Inside photographs – in a lovely layout provided by bass player Geoff Gascoyne and artist Gareth White, show childhood snaps with his father and sister, the teenage Georgie in Butlins piano mode, his sons Tristan and James in younger, pre Blue Flames child and teenage days, as well as the band members, sax men Alan Skidmore, trumpeter Guy Barker, vibraphonist Anthony Kerr, Ralph Salmins, Geoff Gascoyne. And we spot Peter King, again. *Relationships* showcased 11 Fame compositions, two of which had been co-written. Partners were, again, famous Bebop man Tadd Dameron (1917–1965, so Georgie became his "partner" posthumously) and lyricist Candida Lycett Green, as well as a Henry Mancini tune to which Georgie's old friend Mike O'Neill had added his own lyrics, "This Is A Gas".

Relationships – Track by Track

"Rhythm King", which Georgie originally wrote in honour of Billy Wyman's Rhythm Kings, opens the album in much the same mode as he once honoured J.J. Cale's "Everloving Woman". It had kick started the Island album *Georgie Fame* in 1974, when 26 years previously, Carl Radle on bass, Tommy Triplehorne on guitar and Jamie Oldaker pretended they were The Blue Flames.

This time, the Jamie on drums is called Powell and his fast Rumba groove is executed with panache. "Just to be a good Rhythm King is the most important thing – old Rock'n'Roll to satisfy my soul, when I sing the Blues, I try to spread the news", and, "every night, you set the scene alight". You've got to believe Georgie the way he wails in the message and works his Hammond excitingly, the sax players answering on cue. "Feeling good to know you're a Rhythm King" indeed, because "even drummers have been known to sing".

"They say that life's a lesson" – Fame's philosophically quite challenging thoughts in "Everybody's Guessin'" come packed into a lazily simmering Swing where Guy Barker and Anthony Kerr get the chance for their wonderfully contemplative solo work. After making clear that nobody has a real recipe for life, he states that the "post-war Fifties weren't depressing, but there was no time for guessin'", lashing out at modern day plagues like bureaucracy and blaming others for your fate. Lines like "Adversity a blessing, sounds to me like window dressing" – contain strong words indeed, and are certainly on a par with the great Mose Allison. It is the longest track on the album.

The rocky number "F.N.G. (Mr Nobody)" successfully invades Kink Ray Davies' territory – the way Georgie describes the pest of a man whose voice "has that familiar tone, he tries to come on slick, he has one hand on his mobile phone and one hand on his dick" is highly amusing. He shines on both Fender Rhodes and Hammond, with Tristan Powell's underlying guitar chops and great breaks by trumpet and saxophones. Gascoyne's walking bass is delight. FNG is American slang for "Fucking New Guy", and according to Georgie "I think it came out of the Vietnam War: a new guy that had been brought into a military unit to replace someone that had been killed. I used it to refer to another person – completely different, nothing to do with Vietnam, who shall remain secret."

"Mars & Venus" is a slow Swing Waltz that continues the great tradition of Fame ballads. The acting character's (autobiographical) stars may not be aligning, he may be on the decline, but he is confident he will find his way out of all this loneliness and confusion: "If she calls and I should answer, it would take my breath away." Geoff Gascoyne supplies a gorgeous, truly moving double bass solo in the middle. Especially attractive is the way Georgie sings harmony with himself towards the finale – again making it sound like Fame & Price.

The swingy medley of "There's No More Blue Time"/"Breezin' All The Way" was written for a composition by Tadd Dameron. Initially, the protagonist is again heading for a blue time because "she" has left him, alone and undecided, "in no condition to play my part, ever since you left and broke my heart, my position is decidedly unsure", but, following sound advice, he then feels great in a new neighbourhood after another blue interim. There is a beautiful sax solo by Alan Skidmore. The two saxes here follow Fame's vocal lead softly.

The soft Funk groove "It" contains some fantastic percussion work courtesy of Ralph Salmins and inspired Fame to really let loose on his Hammond organ, picking up the theme of "Woodshed" from *The Blues And Me* for his solo. This time the harmony singing continues through the complete number, to great effect, complemented by another well-executed solo by Guy Barker assisted by E-piano and James's great groove: "Let's call it IT instead of "we": When simple things are overlapping, and every moment ideal, we can be sure that IT is happening, this thing called IT must be for real!"

Georgie's musical idea: "If you wanted to categorize it at all, I would try and categorize it as something like a mellow Bill Withers groove."

"You", once created with Candida Lycett Green for Georgie Fame's 1979 album *That's What Friends Are For*, gets a new, welcome arrangement, less Reggae-fied but more in "Moondance" swing mode – Ralph Salmins's conga work is reminiscent of the unforgettable percussion man from Ghana, Speedy Acquaye. "You black out the blue in me" remains a heartfelt way of expressing love.

"Say When", a slow Swing, serves as ballad number two on this album, the lover never knowing "when to say when" with his lady of choice: "We don't need an old magic potion sprinkled inside our gin." Anthony Kerr adds some melancholic vibes before Fame repeats "Be my guiding light, take me to the heights and then let's do it all over again."

More lively Swing comes via "The Wolf Gang". "They say the best defense is to launch an all-out attack", citing "Little Red Ridinghood" the way a Louis Jordan would have done – a tradition worth following in the 21st century. This time, the sax solo is supplied by Peter King, while Guy Barker supplies the great fills in between Georgie's vocal gymnastics.

"The Keeper Of The Blues", a delightfully lazy two-bar Blues, is defined by Tristan Powell's inspired slide guitar work: "When you're hurtin', feeling sad, down and dirty, good and bad, there's a marvelous playground, full of indigo hues, welcome to the land of the Blues" indeed, he Blue Flames can do a Blues more elegantly than most bands who specialize in the genre – in fact they could do this in their sleep but prefer to stay alert and sensitive all the way. Tristan's poignant solo is followed by Guy Barker, before Georgie name-checks Ray Charles and Percy Mayfield as keepers of the Blues.

"Extra, extra, read all about it": "City Life". Fame: "It was from another time. That was written by me and it was added to the repertoire of *Singer*, the Musical, in what was going to be the extended version. The reason these things were recorded, like "City Life" and the song "The Blues And Me" – which had been written for Madeline in the original version which I sang on my album – was that Ben Sidran was to try and get exposure to the world with this Musical. That is why they were recorded." "City Life" had its first product debut on Fame's album project *City Life* with Madeline Bell and the BBC Big Band – an urgent, hot-blooded Swing that works extremely well in the Blue Flames context, too. The main man's often quoted favourite theme of describing and comparing the atmosphere and living conditions in urban as opposed to rural settings is picked up yet again – collecting all his statements with regard to that topic could result in a highly thrilling concept album compilation.

"City contacts open all the doors, say goodbye to country living …" – "day and night the tempos never slow" – let's assume that Georgie likes it both ways. Both Alan

Skidmore and Peter King wail their cans admiringly, and Georgie & Sons throw in some great Cuban patterns, all underpinned by Gascoyne's elastic bass lines and Salmins's "Speedy" congas.

"This Is A Gas" started life as a Henry "Pink Panther" Mancini instrumental, before Mike O'Neill, he of the Nero and The Gladiators history. This really is, as O'Neill writes and Georgie sings with silken voice, "a touch of class, a quiet gas, like a quiet afternoon in Surrey, no hurry, no rush, everything is hunky dory – in fact the age of reason is in season" – again, city life is followed by ample praise of the rural pleasures of this world, in slow Swing mode the Blue Flames know to execute to perfection. The icing on the cake is the sophisticated touch of Vocalese, before Barker & Kerr act especially softly in the procedures.

When *Relationships* came out in 2001 on Georgie's Three Line Whip label, not too many fans beyond the Ronnie Scott's Jazz Club and Rhythm Kings audiences became aware of it, and while it has been out of print for a while at the time of writing in 2014, it is at least possible to purchase it as a download. Bless the entrepreneur who suggests a re-release on vinyl and CD with a solid distribution deal.

Relationships was to be the last Georgie Fame album to feature saxophonist Peter King – it had been almost 33 years of working together. Geoff Gascoyne is the man who knows both musicians very well, and he is aware that King does not mention Fame & Flames in his memoir *Flying High*:

"I know. In fact, I am now a member of Pete's band. I've played with him for a couple of years now. I am not sure why. There was something that went on with the last Big Band with Clive. Peter King was on it, and then one thing led to another and Peter wasn't on it. Something went on, I am not sure. Whenever you mention it to Pete – about Clive – he always has a bit of a moan. So I think there is something in the past."

On the heels of Relationships – the Blue Flames album Charlestons

While *Relationships* had been the first real band studio album since 1993's *Three Line Whip* – albeit bridging a gap of eight years – his follow-up was started, again at Ralph Salmins's studio in Welwyn Garden City, only one and a half years after *Relationships* quietly slipped on the "market". It contained eight new Fame compositions, two covers and another collaboration with Candida Lycett Green, "Wogan's Air" about the well-known British radio and TV personality Terry Wogan, which had been waiting for public airing for more than two decades.

For the Blue Flames, who – unlike the original combo during the Swinging Sixties – had been almost without fluctuation since 1991, Georgie Fame wrote an "Anthem For A Band". It tells the story of this band which he lovingly tends to call "The Last Blue Flames" because there will be no line-up after this one (see Georgie's comment for *Tone Wheels-A-Turnin*). Based on its unmistakable succession of trioles, James Powell's understated, then urgent groove, plus a reflective horn theme, Fame tells us about "the family that you extend" that "sings your song all night long" and about "when you missed your last train home and a mugger took your phone". Almost invariably, this composition remains in the Blue Flames' live set – in 2012, for instance, Fame played it during his traditional Ronnie Scott's week and also at the Gronau Jazz Fest in Germany.

Swing time for the "Charleston Walk". The reason Georgie calls this finger-snapping rhythm *Charlestons* is pointed out in his liner notes for this album: "In 1991, during a recording session in New York City I was going through an arrangement with Paul Shaffer (compère of *Saturday Night Live*) who had kindly agreed to play keyboards on a couple of tracks – making him a Blue Flame for the day! Looking at a couple of bars of music signified by a dotted crotchet followed by a quaver, Paul nonchalantly commented 'Oh yeah, those are Charlestons'". Bingo!

The Swing Waltz "Preach and Teach" had once been on the B-side of "Yeh Yeh" and makes a welcome return in this line-up, enriched by a fantastic double bass solo courtesy of Geoff Gascoyne which winds itself around Georgie's own Fender Rhodes colouring and James Powell's tenderly brushed cymbal strokes.

"How Blue" is a pleasant slow swinging Blues about, well, having the Blues: "How blue can blue get to be?" "Hibernation is a choice, you can put to bed your voice" is something that Fame tried for himself, using some "down time" in Sweden, maybe also "having a good time feeling really bad".

This, in its nonchalant form here, is unthinkable without the vibraphone charm of Anthony Kerr, who had just released his own trio album *Too Marvellous For Words* with Hammond man Jim Watson and, according to commentator Dave Gelly, "tasteful, swinging and listening drummer" Steve Brown. The swinging on this recording is supplied by Jamie and Geoff Gascoyne. Fame would later re-visit this number on his guitar-and bass-only exercise *Lost In A Lover's Dream* in 2012. Oh, and the recipe against the Blues: "Gotta get yourself a date, gotta make a rendezvous with fate, singing 'Kansas City here I come', climb into your little hole, play a little Nat King Cole, till the winter winds have been and gone."

"Flamingo Allnighter" tells the story and, even more importantly, name-checks all the important players, actors, posers and movers of that night-club scene in the 1960s Soho scene. As an invaluable companion piece to "Anthem For A Band", "The Flamingo Allnighter" recalls the story for all the folks that come to Ronnie Scott's Club each year in order to secretly remember the Flamingo Club just round the corner:

"When I was a young lad in 1962, London was buzzing, and I was buzzing, too. Flamingo Allnighter was where we played. We were living and learning, and getting paid. It started off round midnight, lots of happy feet, now and then a big fight, turning up the heat. But we never stopped groovin', until the dawn. We had to keep on moving on and on and on. I'm talking about the old Flamingo, what a crazy scene, way down the old 'A-Go-Go', you know what I mean, Rik Gunnell, Al Watson, and Mike O'Neill, Zoot Money, Big Roll Band, no better deal. Good Ganja, sweet Bourbon, and a Purple Heart, no egos, and no hassles, just playing our part."

Guy Barker remembers that the melody of "Flamingo" had overseas origins: "There was one tune that started life as an instrumental, inspired by a guy in South Africa, and the same song ended up becoming a song about all his days in the Flamingo Club. It's called 'The Flamingo', but it started life as something else."

Georgie would then slip into his old habit of slipping into Afro-American baritone Paul Robeson's old "I.E.O.K.O." from "The Canoe Song" out of the old movie *Sanders of the River* which he had loved as a child, and which he normally employs for his reading of Van Morrison's "Moondance". This is really an extra tale which he has often loved to tell at gigs before leaping into "Moondance":

"I was once in an unlikely place called Ronnie Scott's Club Oberhausen, near Düsseldorf [the third, if short-lived Ronnie's Club after Soho and Birmingham] when the phone rang and I heard the familiar voice going [belting in an Irish accent]: 'Wherre arrre ya?' I told Van I was in Oberhausen, in this bleak club built into a shopping centre, and chatting, I got the idea of putting "I.E.O.K.O" from "The Canoe Song" into Van's tune as an intro."

Picking up the story of the "Allnighters", Georgie continues with "The boss man was a gangster, he would bawl and shout: 'Hot dogs, hamburgers, Coke with or without'. A young man named Cassius dropped in to say hi. He was on his way to Highbury, Henry Cooper in five. 'I told you I was the greatest!' Yankee man was in town, super cool G.I., buttoned down, light-skin brown, looking to get high. Big Roy was dancing, and talking loud, all our minds enhancing, it was quiet in the crowd."

Georgie then even name-checks the US military air bases in the UK where the G.I. audience hailed from: "From Chicksands, Brize Norton, Newbury, too, Alconbury, and Fairford, all paying dues. These guys came from South Ruislip and High Wycombe and Weathersfield, all weekend in Soho, looking to get healed."

Apart from the Air Force fans, gangsters, VIPS and then idols would be included in the "name dropping", Georgie's art form which he had made into an album title for his first of two Ronnie Scott's live albums: "Big Wes, George Conley, Slick and D.Q., Count Suckle, Prince Buster, Speedy, Geno too. Gene Ammons, Dexter Gordon, yeah, and Sonny Stitt, Christine Keeler, Lucky Gordon, and Johnny Shit! We had King Pleasure, Jon Hendricks, Eddie Vinson (Clean), Babs Gonsalves, Johnny Griffin, and Stanley Turrentine. Louis Jordan, Percy Mayfield, yeah, and Brother Ray. Count Basie with Joe Williams, singing 'Every Day I Have The Blues'."

And Count Basie gets attention for the finale, too: "Dig Count Basie blow those Blues away!" he sings twice, before the "I.E.O.K.O." sees the song peter out.

Rendered in a pleasant Swing rhythm – too slow to dance the Charleston to it, folks – it chuggles along attractively with a horn theme where, for once, easy listening is not a dirty word. Georgie's long-time friends and musical partners Madeline Bell and Zoot Money joined him for this eight-minute rendition.

"Wide-Eyed And Legless" goes back a long while for Georgie. He once played keyboard on an ITV television's *Supersonic* presentation in early 1976, lead by its composer, singer and one-time part-time Blue Flames member, Andy Fairweather Low. The renowned guitar wizard, erstwhile Amen Corner front man, long-time Eric Clapton and Roger Waters cohort, and also an occasional Bill Wyman Rhythm King, had a hit with this song in 1975, and included it on his album *La Booga Rooga*. AFL turned out to be immensely proud and full of praise with regard to Fame's cover version, which was suitably transported from its original falsetto key to Fame's comfortable – and richly wide – range.

Georgie: "When I played with Andy Fairweather Low on 'Wide-Eyed and Legless', he did it in B natural, not in F sharp: One of those horrible keys for piano players, if you're not an accomplished pianist, which I'm not. And I had terrible problems, trying to make it sound right, playing the right inversions, because you don't play in this key. Not like Jack de Johnette, who is a fantastic musician. Jack de Johnette had to make the decision, when he was younger, whether to become a drummer or a piano player. He is just as good on the piano as he is on the drums! And he says in the book, you know, he used to practice all the tunes in all the keys. So you learn to play a tune, and then you learn to play that tune in every key. And we are talking about tunes, good tunes, not Blues, not twelve bar Blues. I mean here I am, having problems with Muddy Waters!"

Here, Georgie is referring to his session work for Muddy, where he was too shy to ask the Mississippi-born Chicago man for a key change, told in Fame For A Price – The Session Man in the 60s and 70s.

Fame continues: "'Wide-Eyed and Legless' is one of the great tunes that have ever been written, by anybody. That particular song, everybody loves that song, and it's not as well known as it should be. Some of the more popular and bigger American artists could do great versions of that tune. Diana Krall could do a great version. We have to give it more exposure. We are always looking for material to sing, and we're looking for tunes that not everybody does. Where are all these great tunes that people haven't heard?"

Talking of wide – wide-eyed and legless – both Andy and Georgie could well have been during the original sessions in the Seventies: cue "I can't find my way to San José" towards the end of this fine version, which was not going to be Fame's last. Fairweather Low's comment on including "San José" was "Why didn't I think of this?!" Fame did Andy's song again with guitarist Primoz Grasic and bass man Mario Mavrin for *Lost In A Lover's Dream*.

"Your Face" is another easy Swing about love at first sight where "all the elements were right", but he could not find the lady again, even his laptop was no help, which gets Fame's romanticism firmly into the 21st century. A great Guy Barker trumpet solo takes up the mid-section, before his pal Anthony Kerr takes over for his magnificent vibes. Meanwhile, Georgie is "short of cancelling the show", all because of the lady he had "just seen for a minute, but felt for a long long time".

The "Medley: Skiing Blues"/"I Lost My Sugar In Salt Lake City" is about Georgie "not getting the drift" after an accidental lack of concentration, "acting like a clown" and "losing control", before he went "tumbling down the mountain side". He then realizes that life "ain't good without your girl". Fame combines this confessional song with "I Lost My Sugar in Salt Lake City" by Leon Rene and Johnny Lange, which Peggy Lee had sung in 1959 on one of Georgie's favourite albums of all times, *Beauty and the Beat*. "Me and Pat Boone, me and the Osmond Brothers", he croons while his son Tristan adds some great slide guitar patches.

"Wogan's Air" had been written by Georgie Fame with Candida Lycett Green for one of the leading broadcasting idols in the United Kingdom: "Tell me where would he be, without the BBC?" is a fitting question for this Irish media veteran (b. 1938), son of a grocer in Limerick who had worked for the British Broadcasting Corporation since the late 1960s.

Wogan hosted the family orientated comedy game show *Blankety Blank* from 1979 to 1990, which Fame's generation is well aware of. He had eight million listeners for *Wake Up To Wogan*, starting the day for his British radio audience with his BBC breakfast programme for many years, until he retired from that immensely popular format in 2009, aged 70, but continued to work in other formats. Wogan's link to the music scene is as the long-time presenter of the Eurovision Song Contest, both preliminary run-ups and the actual shows.

Georgie could easily have called his tribute "Wogan's on the air", as this is what he actually sings in the song's chorus. The fact that he doesn't – and asking Georgie would only spoil it – this poet could just have opted, with a wink and a smile, to use his little omission of "on the" as a reminder that "on the" head of the man is normally nothing but "air", or the Cockneys' way of saying "'air", meaning a wig.

As Fame remembers, "Yeah, we did it many many years ago. I mean, he is still very popular on the radio. He still has his radio show. I had this tune, this song, which I thought should be about Terry Wogan. And in those days I couldn't write lyrics, so I had a good friend, Candida Lycett-Green, who is a very good poet. And she likes writing lyrics to tunes, and we wrote some good tunes together. She wrote lyrics to my melodies. And that was one of them, and she wrote a very witty lyric. She did the research on Wogan, where he started in Dublin. I thought it had the possibilities of being one of these novelty hits, and I gave it to the BBC, to maybe get their corporation and release it through the BBC as a commercial. The BBC Commercial Department didn't see the joke. That was about thirty years ago, probably around 1979, 1980."

"Charleston Walk", including stride pianist James P. Johnston's "The Charleston" from 1923, which was one of the key tunes in the Roaring Twenties. Jimmy Johnson (1894–1955) has taught or influenced many greats from Fats Waller to Count Basie. Georgie did not use the lyrics that Chubby Checker song on his 1961 version, but stuck to his own "Charleston Walk" text which also has autobiographical elements:

"I mean, "Charleston Walk" from the *Charlestons* album, that was basically written while I was walking in the country lanes with Suzie [his girl friend], and I'm thinking this is great. Like Johnny Mercer said, "You can write a song about anything, anywhere, anytime, if you use your imagination". And it doesn't have to be personal. It just so happens that somebody some time has personal connotations, and they are not always sad, and not always bluesy. Like Mose Allison said "You don't have to get up in the morning and it will come tumbling down." Jon Hendricks said, and he is a master of that: "The Blues can be really happy, shouting, joyful affairs."

"Hymn For Him" is a deeply religious instrumental, reminiscent in style of the organ CD *Hymns From Home* from 1996. But it was a new piece, "it hadn't been composed when the *Hymns From Home* album was produced", which Georgie directed in England but did not play on: "The two organists on the album were Steve Gray and Kjell Öhman." It is a thoughtful and moving finale to another great album by the man. "That is just a reference to my church Sundays when I was going home. In fact if it was written for anybody, it was written for my Uncle Jack, either him or for God himself."

A man like Georgie Fame just doesn't do something like promotion. But in a way, the sojourn which followed the release of Charlestons was some kind of advertizing for *Charlestons*, simply because it was there.

The Go Jazz All Stars live in Worpswede, Germany, 9th May, 2003:
A band name for insiders mostly, which was why posters promoted the names of their two main protagonists in bold letters: Ben Sidran & Georgie Fame. Those billboards, put up in the painters' resort of Worpswede – a kind of North-German Woodstock – served their purpose: The town's "Music Hall", a cozy 400-seater fitted like a huge Midwest bar, was filled to the rafters.

"The kind of music we present is now played and heard all over the world", pianist and jazz researcher Ben Sidran mused as the show took off, "it's called Bebop." Introducing long-serving bass player Billy Peterson, Copenhagen-based saxophonist Bob Rockwell and his son Leo Sidran on drums, he lead the four-piece to play just that: cleverly and sensitively interwoven rhythmic patterns between Peterson's warm and precise, fretless five-string bass and Sidran junior's tender groundwork, changing between brushes/rods and sticks – clever, nonchalant.

His Dad and saxman Rockwell set this base off with their melodies, ranging from the quirky to the beautiful. Composers like the (too) obscure Alec Wilder manage to merge both these ends of the spectrum, as "Walk Pretty" proved: the title track of a recent album the Sidran/Rockwell Quartet dedicated to the half forgotten master and sung with an easy charm by Ben. Another highlight was "Sonny Clarke", where, for once, jazz was not a never-to-be-repeated improptu composition, but an exquisite piece that had been painstakingly written down to honour a Hard Bop champion. Bob Rockwell was especially impressive when he changed from saxophone to flute in mid-song.

Then it was time to call the man up who, according to many, including compère Ben Sidran, "needs no introduction" – "the forever young Georgie Fame" – flattery which the great man behind the curtains answered with a wry "I'll be 60 in June, man". Cheers greeted Fame when he grabbed the mike to pay tribute to one of his own heroes, "Jumpin' With Symphony Sid". And jump he did in good humour, before "How Long

Has This Been Going On" saw him at a small Hammond. The equally romantic "It Could Happen To You" put everyone in a dreamy mood, followed by admiration as the singer/writer gave Chet Baker's famous solo its lyrical content. Then a huge smile when Georgie ended it with a spoof on Lee Marvin's low-register "Wandrin' Star". Instrumental Bebop promised yet more to come.

The second part of the show was dedicated to Blues and Soul, and who better to join the hot proceedings than Clyde Stubblefield, James Brown's legendary drummer from the Sixties onwards, and a Sidran sideman ever since 1972. The way he sang and rhythmically felt his way through "Georgia On My Mind" was mind-boggling, he didn't so much play the drums as make love to the toms, cymbals, snare and bass. Meanwhile, Leo Sidran was by no means out of work – the stunned audience watching him change with ease to an expertly used electric guitar, and listening to the young talent with pleasure. Georgie Fame then told us the story of an unrehearsed Jon Hendricks joining Terry Clarke at the Newport Festival in 1962 to present "Yeh Yeh", the Mongo Santamaria tune which became a Fame-Smash '65 with its lyrics provided by Hendricks. Fame led the All Stars into a groove which had the auditorium jumping again.

The singing Hammond champion (according to Sidran "the world's leading Jazz singer – unsung!") followed it with Mose Allison's cool yet simmering "I Love the Life I Live". The mood was perfectly picked up by the Sidran-side with "I Wanna Talk To You/Silver Lining" and "Trouble Spot". Georgie Fame had no trouble soothing the latter into a medley with Stevie Wonder's "Don't You Worry 'Bout A Thing", which he had recorded himself in 1978 with one of his many Blue Flames line-ups. Ray Charles' "It Should Have Been Me" had Ben & Georgie duetting and left the fans shout for more – a request Sidran & Stubblefield answered with the heartfelt "Looky Here", before Fame tackled the old rock'n'boogie "Lawdy Miss Clawdy" solo from the piano, making it the perfect goodbye for the night when he sang its "down the road *I* go". Two lessons in Jazz and fun, six musos, and *all* stars.

The last Blue Flame (so far) – Alec Dankworth

For quite a while after the release of *Charlestons*, bass player Geoff Gascoyne did not see himself in a position to keep up regular work with The Blue Flames and simultaneously back the build-up career work for his young and gifted protégé, the then 24-year-old Essex pianist/guitarist/drummer/singer/songwriter Jamie Cullum, whose album *Twentysomething* began to make waves, including glimpses of the American Songbook in "I Get A Kick Out Of You" and also Jimi Hendrix in a stunning reading of "The Wind Cries Mary". Increasingly writing his own material, the young Cullum had always seen himself as a huge Georgie Fame fan, sitting quietly in Ronnie Scott's Club and going "Shush, I'm in class". So Gascoyne, helping kind of a younger generation Fame up the ladder, had finally decided in 2005 – as Georgie always put it half jokingly – to accept the "Cullum shilling", and leave the Blue Flames. Did he give his notice then?

Geoff in 2012: It wasn't really like that – it was a gradual thing. I gradually got more and more busy, and there were more and more gigs I couldn't do, so I wasn't really giving my notice. In this business, it is very rare that you work with one person exclusively.

"I worked with Clive for twelve years, and he is still very loyal. He still stays in touch, and I still get a lot of work from him. I have been in touch with him, and I've done a few things, as well as doing the occasional gig. – It was unfortunate, I couldn't really do both when I was playing a lot with Jamie Cullum, so a few other gigs had to go, you know, because I had to compare: I just had to work with one person. Unfortunately, I worked with Clive. – I mean, he had gigs and I couldn't make them, so he asked Alec Dankworth to step in. And because Clive is so loyal, he feels like he can't let Alec down now. That is the way he is.

"I'd like to be in a band with him again, but I can't expect to walk into it again. And Clive is not really working as much as he used to. He doesn't work in the UK half as much as he used to. They were certainly great days. – I mean Alec doesn't really play electric bass very much now. So when he came into the band, it was more acoustic bass the whole way. But I would always play half and half – half electric bass and half acoustic. So I would always get the intro on "Moondance" – now that was my feature on electric bass. I'd have a big roar-up, as he would say. He would always give me those solo moments, you know."

So who was this Alec Dankworth (b. 1960)? The name rings a bell, because of his famous father, orchestra leader and Ronnie Scott's legend Johnny Dankworth (1927–2010). But his mother is just as famous; Dame Cleo Laine, the renowned Jazz singer (b. 1927), who many British fans remember from appearing with Frank Sinatra at the Royal Albert Hall in 1992. Alec has well-known strong ties to his mother, and when he was – for once! – late for gig at Ronnie Scott's, Georgie teased him about "dinner with mum".

Fame fans knew him from many projects like the Mose Allison homage *Tell Me Something* – he had often worked with Georgie and was a natural choice, not least because he had worked with Fame cohort Dick Morrissey in the 1980s *and* with Mose Allison in the 1990s, the blueprint of a perfect Blue Flames CV.

About his beginnings, Alec told this author in 2013: "I started on the clarinet probably and started learning the saxophone at school when I was 12 or something. I didn't start the bass guitar till around 16, and then I went to the Berkeley College of Music at 17 – but double bass not until 19.

It wasn't a Eureka moment, as many musicians do get. My family – as you know – is very much involved in music, so it was in the household from an early age. In the early days, I had a Rock band, but then I started playing Jazz on electric bass – and from there it was a natural move to double bass. I was playing double bass music on electric bass eventually.

"I would say my father was a factor in me playing the bass, because he was also interested in bass guitar, and he had bought a bass guitar, which was lying about the house. His interest in the bass probably is one reason that led me to playing the bass. He had the bass just to purely learn how it worked in order to write for it. He didn't play the instrument – he played the clarinet and saxophone. There were plenty of those lying around the house, that's for sure.

I didn't have any Rock bass idols. Early on it might have been Ray Brown and Oscar Pettiford in the Jazz world. Probably a bit before that maybe it was Stanley Clarke, on the electric side of things – more fusion playing – Jaco Pastorius I guess. Then after that Eddie Gomez and Rich Davis, those people come to mind immediately.

"Wanting to become professional came early on really, because my family was so involved in music."

Dankworth shares an interest in African music with Georgie – he toured South Africa and Europe with Abdullah Ibrahim, and lately he joined Ginger Baker's Jazz Confusion, with Pee Wee Ellis on sax and Abass Dodoo on percussion, also appearing on the notoriously difficult, but magic drummer's latest album *Why?*

Add to that stints with Anita O'Day and Clark Terry, Van Morrison and Martin Taylor, and Georgie would be hard pushed to find a better-suited bass player, apart from the one standing in the wings after the Cullum shilling: Geoff Gascoyne. He told this author in 2012:

"I played with Jamie for seven years, and we got to the end of the last tour, and we were all exhausted, because we had been touring constantly for a couple of years. So Jamie decided to take a year off, and that turned into 18 months. Then after two years, he decided to start working with some other musicians. So I was back to becoming a freelance musician again. I have known Guy [Barker] for a long time. In fact I played with Guy on the Queen's Jubilee celebrations. He had a Big Band on one of the boats on the River Thames. It was good, but it was very rainy that day, so it could have been much better."

"Closing Another Gap" – The Imaginary Swing Album

There was to be no Fame studio album between 2003 and 2009 – a pretty long gap even by modern standards where artists let two to three years pass between new releases. But on the other hand, Georgie had been so productive recording songs for stray projects that it would be easy – artistically, though not necessarily in terms of label diplomacy, to put another very good studio album together from what had been put on tapes and hard disks between 1994 and the early Noughties. Such a compilation would be "something for the boys to do", Georgie would often say to such thoughts, most certainly handing over such duties to Tristan and James Powell and limiting himself to actual performing.

In 1995, the Swedish singer and keyboard player Ulf Rådelius, worked on an album of Beatles tributes, *From Me To You*, and Georgie got the chance to play organ and share lead vocals with Rådelius, including beautiful close harmonies, on a Swing version of "Paperback Writer" – for train spotters that's 26 years after including "When I'm Sixty-Four" on *The Third Face of Fame*. Clearly Fame's had fun, too, by the sound of this version!

Ulf wrote and recorded a song more recently with the title "Mr. Nice and Cool" as his "hommage to Georgie Fame one of my musical inspirations in life". The song can be heard on YouTube and the lyrics are the following:

"Hey there Mr. Nice and Cool, swinging from your piano stool
Singing out your heart and soul, R'n'B to Rock'n'Roll
Man, you showed me the jazzy bluesy way
And you moved me and showed me other spaces
Singing out your heart and soul R'n'B to Rock'n'Roll
Hey there Mr. Nice and Cool

And there'll be no one else around, music is your only rule
Never been nobody's fool, voice and hands in your control
Man, you showed me the jazzy bluesy way
And you moved me and showed me other spaces
Music is your only rule, never been nobody's fool
Hey there Mr. Nice and Cool and there'll be no one else around

Hey there Mr. Good and Bad, what a time you must have had
Spreading all your songs of joy I was just a younger boy
Man, you showed me the jazzy bluesy way
And you moved me and showed me other spaces
What a time you must have had spreading all your songs of joy
I was just a younger boy
and there'll be no one else around, and there'll be no one else around"

And so, many years after the song "Sweet Georgie Fame" by Blossom Dearie, Fame is honoured by another dedication praising his music qualities.

Fame was invited to collaborate with vocalist, composer and reed player Kate St John, who had worked in The Dream Academy and who he had met while working with Van Morrison, to appear on her 1995 album *Indescribable Night*. "Green Park Blues" features Georgie on piano and vocals, shared with Kate, who is also heard on cor anglais and oboe. Fame's stage mates Ralph Salmins on drums and Alec Dankworth on double bass find Georgie on familiar ground.

For a 1999 soundtrack which was to accompany – and actually feature in – the movie *Swing*, British singer Lisa Stansfield asked Georgie to sing two songs which she had written with her husband Ian Devaney and Stockport singer-songwriter Richard Darbyshire, who had composed for The Temptations and with Tessa Niles, among others. The first one, "Got To Get On This Train", was a fast Swing which fit Georgie like a glove, and he sounds so comfortable here that it makes the track a must for one of his own collections.

Stansfield herself sang Swing standards apart from her own numbers, like "Mack The Knife" and "There Ain't Nobody Here But Us Chickens", and gives Fame a really relaxed number in a similar vein, "I Thought That's What You Liked About Me", which he also performed with audible joy.

Also during the last year of the old millennium, Fame – often active in The Netherlands as a vocal coach as well as performer, got an offer from a musical community called New Cool Collective. On their Big Band album *Big – Soul Jazz Latin Flavours Big Band Vibes* Georgie contributed his own "Miss Bitch" as a kind of high octane Big Band Ska, with precision and zest. The baritone sax is supplied by David Queksilber. Fame also sang on the Bill Cook song "You Can Have Her", where he is joined on vocals by Vera van der Poel. This one starts as a kind of Crime Jazz number, and soon takes on Techno patterns as well, highly sophisticated Big Band Modern Jazz. Benjamin Herman leads on sax, David Rockefeller shines on trumpet. You can certainly tell that this collective features three percussionists.

Georgie then joined The New Gary Husband Trio of the highly talented drummer and keyboardist for one number, "Deep In A Dream" – "The smoke of my cigarette climbs through the air", this is a perfect torch song for Fame, for the early hours of the morning – a sensitive performance to be treasured. End of millenium.

Since the year 2000, Georgie has been involved in a number of remarkable sessions again. The wife of his long-time bass player Geoff Gascoyne, Trudy Kerr, invited Fame to sing on her album *My Old Flame – Tribute To Chet Baker* in 2001. The album could well be taken as a hommage to his own Vocalese efforts, including tracks like "Do It The Hard Way" or "But Not For Me", and Georgie duly sang two duets with her. "You Make Me Feel So Young" comes as a pleasant Swing by Myron and Gordon, with the singing couple obviously enjoying one another's company, a bit like Annie Ross and Fame during the *In Hoagland* sessions in 1981.

Then there was Rodgers & Hart's "My Heart Stood Still", where Georgie actually starts ballad style with "memories of sweethearts he's laughed at during schooldays", Kerr then sharing similar sentiments before the couple leaps into perfect harmonies in the swinging chorus. Both of these songs contain Vocalese passages of Chet's solos which Fame wrote. He handled the section on "My Heart Stood Still" in his inimitable way before Dick Pearce took over "bugle" duties, while Miss Kerr sings her Vocalese lines in unison with Steve Melling's piano. What a remarkable invitation, as Kerr's husband Geoff remembers:

Clive had used this song with Trudy, in a duet on one of her albums, [and also "You Make Me Feel So Young"] when Trudy recorded her tribute to Chet Baker. And Trudy in fact sings some of the Vocalese, some of the instrumental solos Clive has written lyrics for, things like "Do It The Hard Way" and "But Not For Me", the classic Chet Baker things that Clive does. They have been an influence for Trudy, just as Clive is still an inspiration for Trudy as well. Clive is a big influence because he is such a great singer. And the way he learns those solos – he doesn't just learn them, they are really inside him. They are really part of him.

"And he has been good enough to sing on one of my albums": Georgie tackled his own "I'll Sing You" and Mose Allison's "Somebody's Gotta Move" on Geoff's *Keep It To Yourself* album from 2005.

That same year, the German veteran Jazz pianist and singer Paul Kuhn (1928–2013) invited Georgie to participate in the tribute album in a Big Band line-up: *Remember When – Paul Kuhn meets Bert Kaempfert*. Kaempfert had been the Hamburg based "thinking man's James Last", and Kuhn had loved the post-war Jazz scene and was a Count Basie disciple just like Georgie. Side-tracked into some Jazz Schlager hits like "There Is No Beer On Hawaii" – recorded both in English and German, Kuhn had been an orchestra leader all his life, when budget cuts in Berlin's SFB Big Band forced him to re-think his career in 1981. He started his own orchestra and worked with smaller outfits again since the late 1990s, which gave him the rather welcome excuse to play nothing but Jazz. On this album, Georgie got to sing the immensely catchy "L.O.V.E.", and took part in the big finale "Danke Schön".

As Georgie recalled in 2009, "Paul Kuhn, yeah, he is a friend of mine. Paul phoned me and said he wanted to do this album, and the band comprised of most of the members of the WDR Big Band, who are all friends of mine, and I made some marvelous productions with them, and I said yeah. I flew to Köln and I did my little piece. Paul is a very nice man, a very talented musician – I love the way he plays piano and sings, and I didn't know until I met him that he was a very successful band leader for many many years. But we have been involved in different productions together over the years, with WDR, NDR and so many good friends. And that's the way I like to work. If somebody asks me to do something, and I like the idea, like I said, there is nobody to stop me. I trust my own judgement. And you don't do it for the money. Sometimes there is no money involved at all! It is part of what we do!"

Add to this Georgie's drum machine driven but still very amusing and catchy "Summertime In The Park", recorded for the Dutch "Floriade" flower exhibition 2002 – rather stiff competition for Mungo Jerry – and you have 12 tracks: a versatile, enjoyable compilation album, to assemble from the stray sources mentioned.

Touring with the Blue Flames – More adventures on stage

There is the old world-weary legend that the late Alvin Lee of Ten Years After fame would often enough neither know the time of day, the day of the week nor the actual city they were touring. This was not due to a surfeit of tipple; Alvin, with Hammond ace Chick Churchill in tow, was just doggedly belting out his set between "Good Morning Little School Girl" and "I'm Going Home" night after night for months on end.

This could never happen to Georgie Fame. Always working hard – as his Swedish friend Lasse Samuelson says: "I don't know anybody who works as hard as Georgie! He has versatile engagements all over the world, with and without the Blue Flames, but certainly the environment, the local culture and certainly its people play a crucial role in the whole proceedings, and that makes it more fun for the band members, too."

At the same time, neither Georgie Fame nor the accompanying Flames could ever forget that the true, and best, adventures often happen on stage.

As Anthony Kerr remembers with regard to mixing the good time with the serious, the R&B with the Jazz, "I think it's a very balanced set. I have learned a lot from being a sideman with Georgie. He will play "Yeh Yeh" on every gig for example, and in doing so, he earns a lot of attention. He gets the audience on his side a lot, and then he'll use that to introduce something that's new and different – and so it's a balanced set, and it has got history and it's why he'll talk a little bit about the history."

"Like anyone who's had a hit, or has had hits, it's a blessing and a curse. The blessing is, it opens doors, it brings audiences in, brings in a following etcetera. The curse is you have to keep playing them over and over again, just as Duke Ellington had to play 'Satin Doll' every night. So Georgie is very much like that. He plays these hits, and the presence of those hits in people's memory and their desire to hear them again and again, and to be honest, I've never quite understood why they want to hear those things played in the same way. If I were a follower of a musician to the extent that I would go and hear their gig every year, I would feel a little bit short-changed if they always did the same.

"And it's not always the same, but I would not necessarily want to hear the hits. But the fact of those hits being there means that people come in, and he has used it as an opportunity to play some of the other music he loves. And people have been exposed to that kind of music and they wouldn't have ever heard it. They wouldn't have heard 'How Long Has This Been Going On', they wouldn't have heard 'Jeanniné' [covered from Oscar Brown Jr.], if it hadn't been for 'Yeh Yeh'". Surely, it is a ritual for the audience to hear 'Yeh Yeh', and it's a ritual to hear the stories just like he relates them every single time.

For the audience as much as the band and certainly Georgie himself, his beloved Hammond is another key element in the range of on-stage adventures, as Anthony Kerr confirms:

"The Hammond organ is such a vast instrument in terms of variety. The vibraphone is one sound, and it is three octaves long, it is one sound. Well, you might try harder mallets or softer mallets. The Hammond organ is not like that. It can sound very whispering and gentle, a bedding of sound. Or it can sound like twenty brass players all unanimously blasting in. It can sound very big and very gentle, all sorts of sounds. And Georgie is a master of knowing which of these control slides to use, and he does it very quickly – snap them into a different sound. It's a bit like a whole load of trumpet players all whacking in mutes off the centre, and the whole eight brass section goes from full on, loud, open sound, down to muted, soft, gentle, quiet sounds. A Hammond organ can do this with flicking a switch, changing a sound. The Hammond organ has so many moods. It is part of a bandleader's skill. It's sort of an arranger's skill as well. It's what an arranger does, saying 'Yeah, I'll put the mutes in here'."

Another reason why playing with the Blue Flames is great for Anthony Kerr is: "I like variety, I like diversity. How important, as a chunk of the overall, working with Georgie has been, I would say it has been very, very important. I have learned a lot from playing that music, from playing with Georgie. It has been a very big influence, of course. Some of it is exactly right in the middle of what I want to do, and some of it is a little more like an away game. Cannonball Adderley stuff and things like that, I love playing those tunes. I enjoy the gig, I enjoy the fact that it has variety

G.F. and Guy Barker at the Camden Jazz Café in 2004

and I want to do different things. I enjoy the fact that someday I might play a solo piece on the vibraphone, or a duet – vibes and bass, vibes and guitar. Another day it is a Big Band, small group and different styles. I just like the variety, it needs to be fresh. It needs to be different. I don't want to play the same thing all the time. He is a master of so much. A singer standing in front of a band, just singing, not playing – he doesn't have anything like the control at his disposal that Georgie does behind the Hammond organ."

Alan Skidmore appreciates Georgie's humour on stage: "We were doing a quartet gig, my quartet plus Clive, playing some really nice stuff, Chet Baker stuff, some nice standards, nice tunes. We were in the Berlin Philharmonic Hall, and we were doing the sound check in the afternoon. It was not going too well. The monitors weren't quite right, the sound wasn't quite right. So Clive, he looked up at the engineers in the first tier where they are, and he gets the microphone and he says: "Look, this is a bit 'Vorsprung *duff* technique'!" – You know, Audi – which really made us laugh! The engineers were fine with it, there was no problem. It was just Clive being Clive. And then it did get better. But I thought that was very quick-witted to think of that. There have been some funny times. On the whole, it's always been good music, and it's been enjoyable – well, I'm saying *been*, it *is* enjoyable!

Geoff Gascoyne: "What I always did enjoy: I love his Hammond playing, and I love playing in the band, but it was always great when he got up from the Hammond and he just sang. I always felt that he sang much freer. I always enjoyed those moments when he would get up from the Hammond. It's not that I am complaining that I don't like the Hammond, because I love the Hammond. But I think he sounds freer without playing – that's an obvious thing to say."

Tristan Powell also has his favourite stage capers: visiting Capetown and playing with local musicians. "Dad thought it would be good to augment the trio with a saxophonist.

G.F. presents the German "Yeh Yeh" lyrics in Gütersloh

We met a great saxophonist called Ezra Ngcukana. This lovely guy Ezra would turn up, like a big gentle giant, played beautiful saxophone, a tenor."

"Some of the little gigs are probably the best gigs, where you connect with the audience on another level, where it is very intimate and small. That is usually when it's best. There had been many of those, where you can see the whites of the audience's eyes. When it's good it's really good. Ronnie's is sometimes like that, as you know, that is also a small gig, because it's intimate.

There have been gigs where we've sort of turned up late, under pressure, because the traffic has been bad and we were literally throwing the gear on stage with no sound check and just done it. They have been very rewarding. You know, some people spend hours sound checking – we never spend more than about 15 minutes, if that."

"Playing at Glastonbury was a good one. Finishing Glastonbury a couple of years ago [2010] on the acoustic stage, which is a big, big tent that holds about five thousand people. We played on a Sunday night, and that was good fun, with The Blue Flames. There is a whole mix across the board at Glastonbury really – families, young and old. That was nice, reaching out to all of them."

James Powell remembers a memorable open air appearance by the trio: "There was this gig when we came to your town, [Gütersloh, Germany] and we were playing in this square ['Triangle Square', which is Dreiecksplatz in German]. He decided to bring with him the lyrics of 'Yeh Yeh' in German. He was clutching the paper in his hands. The piece of paper with the lyrics in German, and was kind of holding them aloft while introducing 'Yeh Yeh', saying he had recorded it in the Sixties and so on. And as he was getting towards the end of the introduction of 'Yeh Yeh', he said 'I have here in my hand this piece of paper', just like Prime Minister Neville Chamberlain who had said these famous words in 1938 when he came back from visiting Hitler, and he goes on that Hitler had signed it, an agreement about the Sudetenland or whatever it was. And when he said 'I have here in my hand this piece of paper', I thought 'Oh fuck, don't say it, don't say it.' And then he said 'Oh, I sounded like Neville Chamberlain in 1938 when he was with Hitler'. People are coming to his show, and he can't resist, he'd wind them up."

Touring with the Blue Flames – Adventures off stage

Tristan Powell reminisces about the time in 1994 when the South African saxophonist Ezra Ncgukana asked the Blue Flames to come into his home:

"He invited us to his house, which was in Gugulethu, the township outside Capetown. We turned up, and it was very humbling, because he lived in a corrugated iron house, which was called a double decker, as it comprised of two floors, which was considered luxury in the middle of this township, where there was very little running water. It was a very humbling experience, going for a drink in his house and meeting his family, who lived, literally, in a corrugated iron shack, in the heart of Gugulethu Township.

"I'll never forget that – that was one of the highlights of being on tour and meeting people, seeing that even in very hard conditions, people are still happy enough and passionate enough to play music. It is a universal language. Also, it was very shortly after Nico had died, so we had gone out to Cape Town to sort of escape the winter and had a very magical time there."

"Going to Thailand to play for the King at one of his Royal Jazz Festivals, and being surrounded by people like McCoy Tyner and Roy Hargrove, Ahmad Jamal and James Moody. It was just a great five day tour around Thailand with some incredible musicians. The whole country re-united, because let's say they're royalists, they have a lot of respect for their king. And he is a Jazz fan. The leader of their country plays saxophone and records. He is a Jazz saxophonist, a big, big fan, he loves Jazz and has a Royal Jazz Festival every year, in his honour."

James Powell has less favourable memories of playing in Arab places: "We even did a gig in Saudi. The gig was good, but it was one of the most unpleasant destinations I've been to, because of the culture. Live music is illegal – all forms of entertainment are totally Hãram, you're not allowed to take music there, and it was only because we were in some school. It was a diplomatic thing for expats. I think it was probably on some diplomatic property rather than actually theirs, so you could get round the rules. You know, some struggling Jazz Society that operates within the diplomatic community in Riad. You step out the door and you're – in trouble. You can't wear shorts, it's unbelievable!"

Anthony Kerr loves meeting other musicians: Touring with the Blue Flames abroad also brought a lot of inspiration for him, for instance "Stockholm was good, listening to Toots Thielemans, and then playing. Toots was on stage at the same festival. Really, the festivals have been the best. Many of the most memorable trips were going off to Jazz festivals, because spontaneous things happen. You sit in with people, they sit in with the band – so you hear other great musicians. In one way, a gig is a gig, it's always the same, and the greater part of the day is just avoiding some mishap that will make the gig not go ahead, like missing your plane. There is the journey, and then the setting-up, making sure that it's okay. And once you are on stage, then that's the most comfortable bit, because that's when you're immune from all that other stuff. And then everybody goes out to eat, drink and be merry for a while, and go home."

"We did a tour of the UK, as part of a concert called *The Best of British Rhythm & Blues*, which was Georgie Fame & The Blue Flames as the last band to go on, with Cliff Bennett & The Rebel Rousers, and The Animals were on that. We were only playing one set, and there were 35 gigs, which is quite a lot. It was the biggest tour we've done. When music has a chance to bed in like that, through repetition, that's I think when the most remarkable things happen musically, which is why we've done Ronnie Scott's, of course. After the first night, you don't have to think about [things like] what's the sound like? Can I hear this, or that? Is something too loud, is something too quiet? What are we playing? Where do I park? All of that is gone. And there is something that wants to be a little bit different each night, you hear things a bit differently, and you don't play it exactly the same – it has a chance to grow. It's quite rare, it is very rare."

Trumpeter Guy Barker has fond memories of Hong Kong: "A friend there said 'We've had bands here, but a lot of the times we just can't afford to have whole bands here, so we have single people come and play with a local rhythm section. Would you be interested in coming over and play?' I said I would love to. And then he said to me 'We want to try and get some more people to come over', and mentioned to me and said 'We are thinking of getting Georgie Fame – do you know him?' I said 'Yeah, of course I know him.' So he said 'Well, would you be able to see if he was interested in doing it?' And then he said 'How about this: Would you be able to do maybe a week on your own, and maybe guest with Georgie for a couple of nights and then go back and he'll stay on?' And I said 'Yeah, I'm sure that will be fine.' And that's how it was all set up.

"I called Georgie and he said "Yeah, alright, I'll do it.' The first time they had Georgie go in for a few nights, and then they had me join in for a couple of nights, and then do my own week. Then they said 'No no, why don't you come and do the whole lot with Georgie, and then do your week afterwards?' As a result, it went down really well, and so we did it every year for about ten years. It was really, really great. We had lots of good friends there. There was a wonderful guy there called Peter Thompson. He would regularly take us out – he had this fantastic boat. We used to have Sunday lunches on his boat. There were some real magical nights there at that club. It really was fantastic. For the people in Hong Kong, it was like they would go to Soho again.

"I could tell you humorous stories about being on a boat in Hong Kong, and we're having this trip, having a bit of a good time, a bit of a laugh, and there was one of these massive hornets. Georgie actually sat down, and this hornet stung him in the arse. And it was the most painful thing, he said, that he ever felt. Years later, he could still feel it. I don't know if we did a gig that night, but I remember that being a ridiculous thing that happened."

Guy again: "I remember we went to have lunch at one of the supporters of the club's place in Hong Kong, and there was a piano there. We'd all had a few drinks and Georgie had a few drinks. And I remember one of the promoter's little daughters was there, looking at him. And he sat down at the piano and he sang to her. The atmosphere that he can create – it sounds corny, it's not the right thing to say, but it is kind of magical! I think some of the most magical things that I have experienced has been off the bandstand, has been afterwards, it's been, you know, 'I'm alright, let's do it.'

"And it was all because of little things that happen in this life. I think that's the thing with Georgie. There's been times where, like in Hong Kong, it would be – the gig's over, he's gone back to sing one more song, and he's told a story, and he sat there, and just an atmosphere has been created.

"There was a thing in – we did this gig in Cheltenham, and there was a club thing afterwards, and we would all go there afterwards, and they were hoping Georgie might play. When we arrived, there were a couple of young people on the door, who didn't know who Georgie was. They looked at him and Martin Taylor and said 'Oh, it's a private event, you can't come in' – and these were the guests. So we went back to the hotel and of course the people came running back, and they were mortified about this mistake, and said 'Would you come back in'. And Georgie said 'I don't think so'. So we sat down and we had a bite to eat, and we had a glass of wine, and we had another glass of wine. The promoter had been going off.

"There is a thing inside him that happens in all those situations: He looked up and said 'How far is this place again? That we were going to play?' So this was after all this, after it was all over. I said 'It's just round the corner.' And he looks at me and he says 'Do you fancy it?' – 'I said 'Shall we do it, it could be fun for *you*. It's a good reason.' He said 'Yeah, we could, couldn't we? Come on then.' He walks in and he sits down, and he says 'Hello, everybody', and then sings. There have been moments like that – that special sort of intimate thing.

"Once he had a birthday party. What he wanted to do was have a load of musicians, and he wanted them all to play. But he thought, it's a birthday party. So what he did was, he decided he would book everybody as a gig and pay them. So everybody turned up, and there are their instruments, and they all brought their own voices, and they all got paid, and they all had a great time, and we had a jam session. But he made it feel like we were just having a good time."

Guy Barker also remembers: "He did that [album, *A Potrait Of Chet*] with the Ellen Helmus Quintet, and I think she died recently [at 53 on March 26th, 2011]. She is a flute player, and died tragically. Georgie and the boys and me, and Ellen Helmus played in Indonesia, we did a gig I remember, in the Nineties. We went out from Hong Kong, and that was an adventurous journey. Ask James and Tristan about the journey through Indonesia when we drove home from a gig. We saw the sun come up, and it was the most terrifying thing we have ever done. There were cars coming head on all the time. It was really scary. There were just two lanes, and there were cars in front, overtaking – and they were doing it so close to us: it was really, really scary.

Sessions in the new millennium – Georgie much in demand

One of the most publicly remarkable sessions Georgie did was playing on Pink Floyd taskmaster David Gilmour's 2005 album *From The Island*. Again, Mr Hammond himself would be too modest to mention it much, but the brothers remember it for the mercurial circumstances, with a smile on their faces. James:

"I know he went to Dave Gilmour, and Andy Newmark was playing drums on it. He is a good friend of mine. I told Andy Newmark the story and he said it made sense. He [Georgie] was invited down to his ship and he played on the track and, you know, a fair fee for going there and recording the thing would be kind of 500 quid, bearing in mind Gilmour invited him down to do this, because he admired him from years ago."

"They finished the session, and he said to him at the end 'Oh God, I can't believe you've come here, taking the time to come and play on my record. You've been such a big influence on me: I remember we used to hitch-hike down from Cambridge to see you at the Flamingo in the Sixties. So you have been a seminal influence on me on what I wanted to do as a musician etcetera. Then he said 'What shall we give you for today?' And he said 500 quid, but he could have said 15 grand. I mean talk about selling yourself cheap."

"And then I told Newmark the story, and he said 'Ah, that figures', because he was told off by the management for asking for too much. He said some of the stars he was having, to collaborate on this, were only doing it for such and such. I don't think they could pay the drummer a thousand pounds a day. So he could have got 10 times as much, not that it is about money. Bearing in mind this man had just said 'I really appreciate this – you're one of my heroes.' He could have acted like a hero and said 'Give me a few grand or whatever.'" One thing is for sure: David Gilmour wouldn't have got Graham Nash or David Crosby to sing even one note for that kind of money.

"It's symptomatic that he doesn't do the fellow stuff. Actually, that's what happened, something like reverse tracking. Dad said something like 'Well, 500 quid', and Gilmour said (laughs) 'Let's make it 750!' He actually rounded it up! Apart from Gilmour, the guy should know what he's worth and ask for it."

Other significant projects included yet another tribute – this time to Fame's Billy Fury emancipation hero Ray Charles. Swedish singer Claes Janson used an all-star Big Band for his 2009 *The Best Of Ray Charles* on Gazell Records and let Georgie guest on "Let The Good Times Roll" and "Busted", which he did with aplomb and audible enjoyment.

The same can be said about Fame's reunion with Ben Sidran, also in 2009, on the – for him – unusual project of a Bob Dylan tribute. "This is the first time that I am actually able to understand any of the lyrics of the man", was Georgie's way of summarizing the attraction this invitation had for him. Laconic and to the point, he graced "Rainy Day Woman #12 & 35", the famous *Blonde on Blonde* anthem where Dylan was heard with an endless litany of "They stone you when …", with all his session guys having to swap instruments. Georgie, on *Dylan Different*, was allowed to stay with his Hammond, and loved the idea of this set so much that he included another number in his live repertoire: the opener "Everything Is Broken".

In 2012, Fame teamed up with Nigel Mooney again, the Irish guitarist and singer he had met during the Lisa Stansfield sessions in 1999. "He asked me to sing 'How Blue Can You Get', and as I happened to be in Ireland, I could do it", Georgie remembered doing his own number from *Charlestons* again, which had originally just been called "How Blue". But at the same time, it didn't go down too well that *Jazz Alley* radio presenter Donald Helme had claimed in his liner notes that the song had been "written a decade ago especially for Nigel by his friend and conspirator Georgie Fame." There had never been such a dedication, Fame pointed out. The other song he recorded with Mooney was Freddie Green's "Down For Double".

TV in the new millennium – Georgie and The Birth of Cool

No, this is not about Miles Davis, although Guy Barker, Alan Skidmore and Georgie himself are great admirers. It's all about a special, unheard-of series of concerts by musicians from all over the globe. Georgie Fame appeared at the LSO St Luke's in London, and it was all documented for posterity by BBC 4's TV camera men – who could give their best having been assured these tapes, or rather hard disks, would not be wiped to make room for next week's flavor.

For April 4th, 2005, the British Broadcasting Corporation promised "Cocktail Jazz" (the term was still on their website in 2014), "Rhythm & Blues", and, wait, "some original members of his first band The Blue Flames." Tex Makins and Colin Green are indeed still alive, as is their first trumpeter Eddie "Tan Tan" Thornton. Makins and Green couldn't make it, but Tan Tan was there!

Especially for all the good people who phone Ronnie Scott's Club in Soho as soon as they find out about the actual gigs, only to hear – or see on the website – that Georgie again sold out within hours, this was like a night out on the club, only more festive, and with guests!

The complete Blue Flames were there of course: British trumpet impresario Guy Barker and Fame's sons James and Tristan were part of the proceedings, so were sax legend Alan 'El Skid' Skidmore and Anthony Kerr on the vibes.

But to start the evening off, Georgie – looking smart in shirt & tie, snappy vest – sat behind the grand Steinway piano first: smiling, mumbling "Eat your heart out, Jools Holland" and reminding all and sundry of his Fats Domino obsession as a youngster via "Lawdy Miss Clawdy". Fame shares this craze with TV presenter and ex-Squeeze pianist Holland, who had invited him to his Later … with Jools Holland more than once, not least for a marvelous rendition of "Enjoy Yourself (It's Later Than You Think)" featuring Madness and slide trombonist Rico.

He gave his TV audience his now well-known history in a nutshell, for all of us to mutter along to: "In 1959, I was saddled with the name Georgie Fame, and when I protested 'What's wrong with my real name?', he said [putting on stiff upper lip Oxford accent] "If you won't use my name, I won't put you in my show, and I needed the gig. Back in 1960, Larry Parnes brought over two great Rock'n'Rollers, Gene Vincent and

Eddie Cochran. I was a 16-year-old piano player. The other band was Nero and The Gladiators."

The camera transferred to a guest of honour in the audience: Mike "Nero" O'Neill, the other man from Leigh, Lancashire who had inspired and helped Georgie on his way. More words heard a hundred times by many but welcome eternally:

"Eddie Cochran was tragically killed after we just did a weekend at the Bristol Hippodrome, and I have always said that Eddie Cochran was singularly responsible" – here we go again, and love it – "for introducing the masses of this country to the music of Ray Charles".

End of chat, start of Swing, and Georgie almost whispers "The line is so busy, I'm feeling so dizzy, I'm weeping and wailing, and I'm ready", which leads into "Get On The Right Track Baby", which he sings with a very young man's voice yet with all his expertise, interrupted by a really dedicated Hammond solo.

More familiar history snippets followed: "At the end of 1961, we were out of work for a while, and I was put up in Mike O'Neill's flat in Old Compton Street for several weeks." But Fame's eternal gratefulness to Mike O'Neill was also in guiding him "round the corner to Wardour Street to an agent who later became my manager. His name was Rik Gunnell."

"One of the first people", he reminisced, "I met at the Flamingo was a man by the name of Niimoi Speedy Acquaye from Ghana, who would introduce me to West African music". Sitting at the Steinway again, Fame declaimed:

"An upstairs room in Princess Square, along the Moscow Road, Alexis lived round the Korner, at the time we didn't know", leading into "Zulu" from *Three Line Whip*.

"The clientele at the Flamingo was fanastic" – we know Georgie, but will never get tired of hearing it again – "West Indians, pimps, prostitutes, night people who worked until three and came to our place until six o'clock when we stopped playing – lots of G.I.s who were here with the US Air Force. A lot of them would get up and sing with the band – people like Ronnie Jones. But the most famous of them, stationed at Bentwaters, is here tonight" – and he surely was – Geno Washington!"

And his disciples could recite easily what had to come next: "Thanks to the West Indian contingent, I got to hear a lot of Ska, as it was called then. I'd like to introduce you to two of my oldest Jamaican friends to 'play de ting' with me: Eddie Thornton – 'Tan Tan' – and Rico Rodriguez!"

Then Georgie sang the Ska version of "Humpty Dumpty", inserting verses like "Once there was an old lady who lived in a shoe, she had so many children, she didn't know what to do", happily egging Rico and Tan Tan on: "Play de ting, play de ting", and thankfully ignoring any politically correct, boring notions of not applying Patois or any other accents – after all, his very own Lancastrian vernacular has been made fun of often enough.

Fame announced "Yeh Yeh" with the reminder that "our recording of that tune got us out of the Flamingo, basically, and it allowed another band to come in and take over the residency", introducing Zoot Money, who promptly had his own dedication to make.

Money simply whispered "For Alexis" and went into a moving rendition of "Will The Circle Be Unbroken", reminding us that "too many people have gone, but remember the good stuff they left you, really good stuff: Ronnie Scott, Alexis Korner, Nina Simone, Robert Palmer, Tony Ashton, Tommy Eyre [the unforgotten one time John Mayall pianist] and Peter Bardens. Alexis and Pops Staples gave me this and told me to remember everybody. You can just tune into them whenever you like", to which Georgie echoed "in the sky" and said "that falsetto, I don't know where he gets it!"

After performing Gerry Goffin & Carol King's "The Point Of No Return", Georgie enjoyed singing the praises of Count Suckle, who was also present at *Birth Of Cool*, as the gentleman from Jamaica who had the best record collection of anybody he knew and was the best disc jockey he ever heard.

"Get Away" was next, with the hilarious story about how a British Petroleum advert could lead to a pole position chart smash, and then Fame introduced another invited companion, very dear to his heart, onto the stage:

"Back in 1962, just about when we started to play at the Flamingo, my next guest came to these shores, and she had a part in a Musical. It played in the West End of London for many many weeks, and it was called *Black Nativity*. And to our great joy she stayed and she carved out a wonderful career for herself. She was a number one call as a session singer for many many years, and she was the co-leader of the very successful band in the 1960s and 70s called Blue Mink. And she's going to sing a song composed by Steve Gray and myself especially for her. I'm delighted – one of our most fantastic singers and entertainers.

"Ladies and gentlemen – Miss Madeline Bell!" A late-night organ solo lead into the magic words "It's after hours, those wee small hours between night and day. I'm out relaxing, instead of acting my part on the stage. Things I get up to, things I ought not to" – "The Blues And Me", from Georgie's album of the same name and also originally composed for the Singer *Musical*.

Final words of praise filtered into the many revealing verses of Georgie's great anthem "Flamingo Allnighter" from his album *Charlestons*, where the same two great singers had already sung as they did on this night: Madeline and Zoot.

Chapter 14

The Last Blue Flames

For his 2009 album *Tone Wheels 'A'Turnin'*, Georgie Fame put the group name The Last Blue Flames on the cover finally: not because it would be "my last LP", as he sighed one night at Ronnie Scott's in 2007, but because after these Blue Flames, there would not be another one: "I called the album 'The Last Blue Flames', not because it is going to be the last of anything, but I just wanted to separate the current band from all the other compilations that you see around, because there have been so many of Georgie Fame & The Blue Flames: which Blue Flames, you know? Different ones, from Sixties recordings, and I don't own those recordings. This combination of the Blue Flames has been together for over 16, 17 years [22 in 2014] with no personnel changes, except one on bass, Geoff Gascoyne and Alex, so longer than any other Blue Flames."

"This is the best Blue Flames! This is The Blue Flames as they are now. That is why I put the *Last* Blue Flames on there. It will be the last form of The Blue Flames. Alan Skidmore on saxophone has been in incarnations of my band since 1969. He is also a very successful and important individual modern jazz saxophone player with his own band, and he has played all over the world in other units. My two sons are in the band – they've been in the band I forget how many years, since they left school – dates are not important really."

"And I want people to see the difference – this is not another compilation record by Georgie Fame & The Blue Flames. So that's why I call it The Last Blue Flames, not because it will be the last CD, but it is kind of onerous, because perhaps, the way the business is – is it worth making another CD? I contemplated that myself about this CD, but then I had the songs and I thought they should be documented."

Explaining the title, he continued, "the album is *Tone Wheels 'A' Turnin'*: the tone wheels are inside the Hammond organ, which makes the original magic sound from the original Hammond organ, which they stopped making in 1972. That's got tone wheels, and that's what creates the magic sound of the Hammond organ. So it's also dedicated to the Hammond organ.

"The album's material had been in the can for a while at that time, but the numbers ended up being recorded only in January 2008. Most of it was live. The way we set it up, I just wanted it to be like a gig, and so that's how it turned out. But it is about as live as you can get. I maybe overdubbed a couple of vocals. But then, mixing got postponed towards the end of that year: "If Tristan does not get round to it soon, I will find another way", he pointed out during the autumn, and the work actually got done soon after.

When *Tone Wheels 'A' Turnin'* appeared in the spring of 2009, it was so solid and versatile that it almost sounded like a "Greatest Hits 2" – all the typical ingredients a Fame *Best Of* has to carry were there – trumpet, sax, vibraphone, Samba & Swing rhythms galore, and above all Fame's warm timbre, underlined by those Leslie-twirled, hot-running "Tone Wheels" of his Hammond A100. (Georgie: "The M102 was only the second Hammond I bought, which was still a small spinet model.") But these were new, self-composed songs – grown during long nights at home in England or on the road and in London's Ronnie Scott's Club. As a result, the band proceeded to cook in the studio as if they were still in the club, performing. (Fame had tried the best of both those worlds, of course, when the album *How Long Has This Been Going On* was recorded at Ronnie Scott's Frith Street premises during the day, without an audience being present.)

Tone Wheels 'A' Turnin' – track by track

There was the Bert Kaempfert-esque "All I Know", speed Swing in "The Burdee Song" with tongue twisting rhymes and exotic tenor sax courtesy of Alan Skidmore, who adds African colourings to his own "Enkosi Dumisani". There are soft touches like "I'll Sing You", biting political "observations in the treacherously finger-snipping "Guantanamo By The Sea", dangerous New Orleans grooves for "Big Easy Meat" and a 12-minute, all previous versions eclipsing version of Fame's 1974 environmental plea, "Survival". These Last Blue Flames have been working in their steady line-up since 1993, apart from Alec Dankworth, who had succeeded Geoff Gascoyne in 2005. They were still featuring Fame's sons, brothers James on drums and Tristan Powell on guitar, trumpeter Guy Barker and pleasantly sound-defining Anthony Kerr on vibraphone.

As engineer and producer, "Brother Tristan" captured Georgie's voice perfectly in all its variable facets – and apart from the wonderful melodies every track has a completely different rhythm pattern – something you do not find on many other contenders' musical statements so easily. Plus, of course, Fame cognoscenti were able to find plenty of organ sounds on the collection: "I wanted a Hammond on all the tunes. Obviously, on the last couple of studio albums I did, I played another keyboard as well as a Hammond, because I like that kind of Rhodes sound from the digital piano.

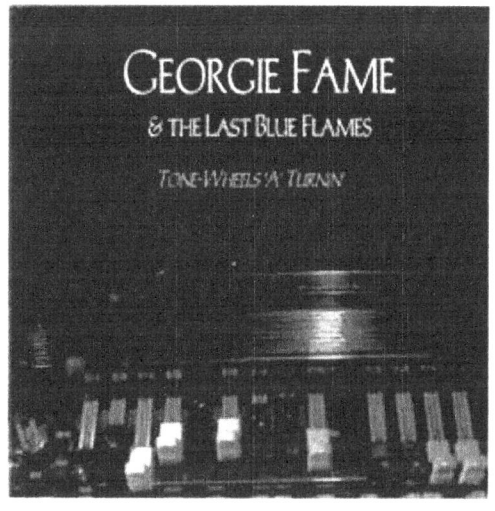

Perhaps I might have played piano on a couple. Most of the tunes required a Hammond to be fairly dominant."

Starting with "All I Know", the Rumba rhythm may be easy-going and relaxed, his words tongue in cheek, but the message is clear. Old age will eventually claim all of us, first and foremost many folks in Georgie's generation. Where have coordination and, with it, concentration gone? "Because it happens to everybody, it is happening to me. That's why I wrote the song. I am at the age now where you start to forget things. It happens to all of us at a certain age. And I saw this wonderful one man show on video in America: Bill Cosby, which is why I mention Bill Cosby in the song. And he did this one man show, and it was Bill Cosby at 50. So it must have been like a good 15 years ago, 20 years ago perhaps, when he actually did it in a theatre. And it was the funniest thing I have ever seen. It was brilliant; he was just talking, and describing what happens when you get up from the chair and you're going to the next room to get something, and by the time you get there you have forgotten what you went into the room to get, and you have to go back to the chair again and sit before you remember. So that happens to us all. It's a whimsical song, it is not sad at all. It's not meant to be sad. That's why there is the line "I gaze into the mirror, and I watch the whiskers' growth", because they are growing out of your nose and your ears. So it's a funny song really, it is an observation of what happens."

So the comedian Bill Crosby had him "rolling round in stitches" when he pointed out to his kids that "This will all be yours one day" pointing at his brain. – A memorable sax theme and a cool organ solo add to the impact.

As Georgie is also a huge fan of Tommy Lee Jones (b. 1946), the Sheriff Tom Bell in *No Country For Old Men*, and the detective Dave Robicheaux in the James Lee Burke film adaptation of one of his Louisiana novels *The Electric Mist With Confederate Dead*, we can possibly expect songs about Bill Cosby *and* Tommy Lee Jones – extra tracks for an excavated *Heroes* album maybe.

"The Burdee Song" is certainly as swingy as The Last Blue Flames will ever get. It is here that the album gets its title, the "tone wheels a-turnin'" referring to the mechanics of Georgie's trusted Hammond: "The "Burdee Song" is basically just a dedication – I love that groove. I wrote the song with that lick – da-da-daaaaa, bedada-dap! Then, through a couple of years I used that lick as a kind of intermission piece and started to sing "Jambalaya and the crawfish pie": "Goodbye Joe, we gotta go" – very close to Jambalaya. But I wanted to write my own piece, and I decided to write some lyrics and a melody dedicated to the great Swing artists I listened to, which is why I mentioned Louis Jordan, Slim [Gaillard] & Slam [Stewart], Dizzy Gillespie, Cab Calloway. Dizzy Gillespie sang this with his own Big Band on a live recording in Greece in 1956. They did a version of "School Days". So that is just a fun Rock'n'Roll piece. I mean one of my favourite Rock'n'Roll records is Dizzy Gillespie's Big Band in Greece in 1956 when they did a version of Louis Jordan's number "School Days" [not to be confused with the equally rock'n'rolling number by Chuck Berry]. That is one of the best Rock'n'Roll recordings you will ever hear. And so that's what "Burdee Burdee" is all about: just a fun piece with two chords, celebrating that early groove of the 40s and 50s.

With "Louis Jordan Slim & Slam", the solo passage here is unusually long, with Alan Skidmore's sax getting several truly inspired turns before the man himself takes over for a highly charged solo: With "gimme five, in the hood they're talking jive" it goes on, until Fame calls "Let's go home" and finishes after more than five minutes. The one Blue Flame who does not get to play is Tristan Powell. Fame: "Yeah, that's right, and he actually overdubbed guitar on a couple of things, because he was in the sound booth, playing, sometimes live – but on a couple of tracks where he had to actually be engineering, he had to overdub the guitar."

"Then there was this friend of his, Paul Stacey, [the long-time guitarist in Elkie Brooks' band] who has a studio where they mixed it. While they were mixing it, I was not there. Tristan suggested to Paul "You better play a bit of guitar", which he did do, and which kind of surprised me. And if I had been there, I probably wouldn't have sanctioned it, or I would have asked them to play it differently. Paul is a very good guitar player, and I liked the idea. I wanted Tristan to play guitar, it needed guitar on it anyway. But for some reason, maybe Paul suggested that he wanted to kind of play on it. And he turned it into a bit more of a Gene Vincent bag, because the song really is about the real good swinging Fifties. You got the Dizzy Gillespie Big Band and a bit of Louis Jordan on that. The guitar sound took it out of that bag and put it somewhere else. And I just said that I'll take the view that Humphrey Lyttelton did when he first heard the mix of "Bad Penny Blues", and he hated it. And he said he wouldn't have put it out, if he had the control, because he didn't like the mix, the sound of the piano. And that was one of the most influential records of all time. So I said I'll take Humph's view on the 'Burdee' because I was not there to prevent it happening, but there's nothing wrong with it. It is just slightly taken out of the bag I envisioned the song in the performance to be. So I think of 'Bad Penny Blues' and it's perfectly alright. So I am happy with it."

Even a hardened Vocalese pro like Georgie must be admired for getting the amount of lyrics across without getting short of breath or succumbing to potential tongue twisters – the number is really that crazy and speedy: "Is it fast? I mean the album was done so quickly anyway. I think the tempo of the actual recording is slightly faster than it should be, but it's just one of those things. We could make it swing at that tempo. It feels fine, but it was perhaps meant to be a touch slower. But everything was working so fast, and we had a lot of technical problems, for the first few hours. So we were late in actually starting the recording. So it was all done a bit under pressure. But, yeah, I can remember – I can just about remember the lyrics for "Burdee". I will be singing it with the band next week, anyway, so. Once you've done it a few times, it goes in the memory box. That's the only thing I would start to get concerned about. It is okay to forget little things, but if I ever came to the stage actually forgetting the lyrics to songs, then I know I would be in trouble."

A man his age could be forgiven to use lyric sheets or tele-prompters, but Fame is adamant here: "I could never do that. Bill Wyman uses computer screens for the routines for all the songs, and you get to rely on them. It becomes a crutch. I don't like it, and I refuse to use it, cause you have to exercise your brain."

The slightly Funk-orientated "Vanguard Road" takes its thematic cue from the cat calls of the *Walking Wounded* live shows at Ronnie Scott's: "It kind of started as a slow hymn. There was kind of a hymn feeling to it, a church hymn feeling. It is basically about a musician's career. You have ridden in the vanguard, which is at the front. You've done it – you've been all over the world, you've coped with the situations, and some of your friends have fallen by the wayside. You have survived, and – it had a kind of Van Morrison feeling to it – when I was composing it, it reminded me of him.

"I wanted to put it in that Van Morrison groove anyway, like "Vanlose Stairway". It is my kind of dedication to that kind of Van Morrison composition [that he performed as well], and "Vanlose" is one of my favourite Van Morrison tunes. In fact he used to insist that I sing it some nights. So that is where it came in. And then, when it actually came to thinking of how to arrange it and record it, I thought it was too melancholic. So I decided to up the tempo and throw in the Van Morrison licks, 'dada, dadada-dada' [Woody-Woodpecker-like] and all that. So it becomes a dedication to *Van* Morrison, rather than *Van*guard Road.

"So that is where the secret ingredient is. The Vanguard Road is the reference to being on the road with Van Morrison. I rode in the Vanguard. I played in Van Morrison's band. I don't think he has heard it, I'm going to send him a copy, and I'm alright if he'll like it. I think he will. I did tell him that I'd write it, that I'd got this song about us, and I told him that I was going to throw in those 'dada, dadada-dada', which are his trademark licks, and I hope that he didn't sue me! (Laughs) No, there is no copyright on licks, and we knew that. So it was a joke. I will send him a copy and I hope he likes it, because it is basically Van.

"And I was quite flattered, because on his last album, *Keep It Simple*, there is a Blues that he sings which he refers to Mose Allison and me, so he's kind of repaying the compliment." [Fame is in that exclusive circle of people who Van genuinely likes.] "And I feel the same about him. I think he is an extraordinary artist and a great poet. In the vein of Dylan, he writes his poetry and sets his poetry to music. And the music doesn't have to be complicated, but the poetry is quite intense. That is very important – I think he is one of the great poets, comes from that long line of great Irish poets – hence, that's Vanguard Road. That is the secret."

"B.P. Club After Midnight" had often been "second home" to Georgie, for "sharing a joke" as well as for "having a smoke" (though alas not at the time the CD came out, due to EU regulations). The Zagreb Jazz venue "B.P. Jazz Club" stands for Boško Petrović, the Croatian vibraphonist and producer who, 17 years prior to this recording, had taped a concert of Georgie's at the B.P. Club, *Georgie On My Mind*. At the time of this loving dedication, Petrović was still alive – he died in 2011 shortly before his 76th birthday.

"Enkosi Dumisani" is a composition by Alan Skidmore, done as an infectious Calypso, which Georgie put lyrics to: He manages to name-check half the geographical landscape of many vinyards from Bulgaria to Switzerland, from Argentina to Peru and Africa as well. James Powell decides to work first as his true self and also includes the part of the legendary Speedy Acquaye, with inventive drum and percussion contributions, helped along by Alex Dankworth's double bass and a great trumpet showcase by Guy Barker. But the crunch is the saxophone of composer Skidmore.

Fame: "It is from Alan's work with the South African band Ubizu. He made two or three CDs with these guys, it's a drum band of South African drummers. "Dumisani" was one of his compositions from one of those albums, and it actually means "praise" in the local Xhosa language in South Africa. I've heard it played with his band, and we started to play it in our band. Then I said maybe I should write some lyrics. Well, he actually suggested that. Then I said 'What is Dumisani?' And he said it means praise, and it is also coincidentally the name of a very fine South African wine, Dumisani. And I didn't know what to write the lyrics about really. Then, when

Alan Skidmore in Camden's Jazz Café

he told me about the wine, I took a jokey, light-hearted look at it and thought – I will just write a song about all the wine growing areas of the world."

Georgie frequently refers to the African Community and African influences. This is partly down to Alan's influence, via Ubizo, as Skidmore confirms:

"It is an inherent part of our musical history. We both draw – all of us really draw from the African historical rhythms. The story of the slave trades who went from Africa to Brazil, so that we would not have known any Brazilian music or West Indian music without the slave trade that came from Africa. I was fortunate enough to go to South Africa and record with a group of great drummers called Amampondo, which was my first album with Ubizo. And I composed a thing called "Enkosi Dumisani" which was on the second album I did – which was named after a great bottle of wine. It just so happened that the tune is very influenced by, shall we say, Sonny Rollins and Calypso, which obviously originally comes from Africa, in the grand scheme of things.

"I played it to Clive, and he really liked it. It was him who suggested would I like it if he put some lyrics to it, which is what he did. And I think he is a great lyricist. He is so fast if he wants to write lyrics to a tune. He can tell it just like this. He talks about the great Jon Hendricks as being his hero, but I think Clive is just as good. I think Clive can do those wonderful lyrics just as good himself – he is a great lyricist, a great brain. When it comes to writing lyrics, he is probably very intelligent."

The next number on the album came about while Fame was waiting for his papers at the London Embassy: 'Guantanamo By The Sea' is something entirely different. That was composed as a poem first, and then I put it to music the next day. And the poem was composed in the visa section of the United States embassy in Grosvenor Square, London, when I was sweating over my work permit to go to New York and open up the "Blue Note", to play with Bob Malach and David Hazeltine and the guys from the *Poet In New York* CD. We had two nights at the "Blue Note" in New York, and two nights up in "Scholars" in Boston. After the 9/11 thing, it became more and more difficult, and the authorities had had all my details for three months, and I still didn't have my visa. I had to sit in the embassy for several hours with other refugees, waiting for the visa, so I could fly to New York the next day and open up the "Blue Note". So it was quite stressful. The vending machine didn't work. There was no water. So I just sat there. After I had done the 'Telegraph' crossword, there was nothing to do. I was looking around at my fellow visa people and I wrote the poem."

The great Latin touch works well as a basis for the lyrics as well as the Hammond and trumpet solos: "Then I set it to music, which was quite easy. The musical side of it tended a little towards Mose Allison, originally. And when I got to the 'Blue Note', at the end of the concert I sang it, because I was still under pressure, stressed out from the experience. But the important thing about Guantanamo is that it is not Anti-American, because some of my best friends are American, and I'm not sniping at America in general. It is just an observation. It was an observation. I was sitting in the visa section for several hours, sweating on whether I was going to get my work permit to catch the plane. And I understand the problems that the bureaucracy has, that life has changed, globally. It could be read or interpreted as anti-American, but it's not. When I came back to England, I decided to give it the Cuban setting, because the anomaly of Guantanamo being on Cuban territory. The USA have no relations with Cuba since the Bay of Pigs disaster, yet they still have this territory on the island of Cuba. So that is why I set it in the Cuban musical vein. And it is humorous. You have to have a sense of humour, otherwise you go crazy."

"I'll Sing You" is another Swing, softer this time, and concerns itself with our communication mad times, with Georgie preferring a hearty singing message to anything like E-mails or text messages: "Technology's not for me", he observes, "I'll meet you at the coda!" Georgie: ""I'll Sing You" is just a kind of traditional Jazz melody. It has got a little Thelonious Monk in there somewhere, a little Johnny Griffin, some of my heroes. Lyrically, it is an amusing lyric about the difficulty in communications between men and women, and how some of the problems occur with communication. How we are not on the same wavelength, which is a natural genetic thing, and historically, always will be. And so I thought, well ok, the best way I can communicate with you is by singing you. It's like I'm meant to write a letter, an e-mail or a text or two, I went and found a better and hipper way of reaching you.

"So the lyric is quite amusing – I think it's a good lyric. I am quite pleased with it. And I have a nice Big Band arrangement of that tune which has been done for me by one of my Swedish friends, who works with a very good Big Band in Gothenburg, called Mikael Carlsson. I've got it in my library, I've sung it, and in fact I'll sing it on Friday with another Swedish Big Band. I wanted to keep it short and sweet. It is one of those tunes that Jazz musicians can play all night long. It could have lasted 30, 40 minutes on my CD, I would kind of like Guy Barker and Anthony Kerr and Alan Skidmore to take solos I think – one of those things where you play chorus after chorus after chorus of solos. But I wanted to keep it short and sweet, so I gave Alec the bass solo and came back immediately in the bridge."

"Singing Horn" is an extremely slow ballad, in the mood of Georgie's *Three Line Whip* album 16 years before this one. Again, there is an interesting story to this number: "After I left America – after working with Bobby Malach, who is one of my favorite people and one of my favorite saxophone players, we have been working together on my Go-Jazz-CDs, particularly *Poet in New York*. He played a very important part on that *Poet in New York* album. And I had the pleasure to share the bandstand with him all over the United States and Tokyo and around Japan – and as I was leaving America to come back to Europe, we gave each other the big hug, the usual thing, and he said, "Hey man, go write a tune for me!" Hm, now him being such a wonderful musician, it was kind of a – I thought about it. What is it going to be? And finally, I settled on a ballad, and I wrote "Singing Horn", because his horn sings, and he has a singing horn, so the tune is for Bobby. 'Singing Horn' is surrounded by your singing horn on the same bandstand. I think you've heard it at Ronnie Scott's. There is also a wonderful Big Band arrangement by Steve Gray of that tune, which I sent to Bobby. No, I sent him a copy of *Tone Wheels 'A'-Turnin'*, saying here it is. It is finally out. Your tune is finally out, in the ether. So "Singing Horn" is for Bobby."

If Dr John heard "Big Easy Meat" with James Powell's really powerful New Orleans toe-tapping second line groove, he would not hesitate one minute in trying to lure the still youngish British family man to either Louisiana or the many clubs of Manhattan – such is the power of his pattern here. The second longest track on this album, there is more pleasing Hammond work here. Asked about his son James's fantastic drumming here, Georgie said "No, I don't know where he picked it up from. He probably just learnt it himself and practiced it. He is very good on that, plays a great second line." And James would be too modest to mention his achievements here.

"The Blues thing is 'Rollin' Blue'. Basically, I was singing Blues, but as you know, Blues doesn't have to be sad all the time. But with this, there is a particularly kind of sad lyric to it. But I wanted to put it into – the first Jimmy Smith thing I ever heard was 'Midnight Special', with Stanley Turrentine on the tenor saxophone, one of my favourite tenor players, of course. And I wanted to do something with that kind of tempo, that kind of feel to it, like with Grady Tate on the drums. The basic feel of 'Rollin' Blue' is based on Jimmy Smith's 'Midnight Special', although the structure is completely different. But the intention and the inspiration came from that and I wanted to have that thing. And then the horn arrangement, I wanted to keep it simple. On one of my Go Jazz albums, Bobby Malach wrote the horn arrangements for *The Blues And Me*, all in a Benny Carter kind of voicing. And I use the same kind of voicing for the horns. We overdubbed the horns, so there are two saxophones and two trumpets, to get that Benny Carter small Big Band feel to it. But basically it belongs to Grady Tate and Jimmy Smith. And it is just a Blues with a different kind of structure to it. And it is a reference to Duke Ellington's 'Jeep's Blues' in the solo section, which is from that great recording *Ellington at Newport* from 1956. Paul Gonsalves played his choruses over 'Diminuendo and Crescendo in Blue', and there is also a great version on 'Jeep's Blues', by his lead alto player, known as the 'Rabbit'.

"Second Honeymoon" was designed as a happy celebration of a, well – second honeymoon. I got the inspiration when my son James got married and went off on a honeymoon. And I was hoping for a second honeymoon with my own relationship – Suzi [Doscher] and I were still living together at the time, and I was hoping for a second honeymoon, but it didn't happen. But there is still a possibility that it will, and I tried to make it jolly. I didn't want it to be sad. Actually, you get married, or you have a special relationship, and things can go wrong during the relationships – and they do, generally. But there is always a possibility of a second honeymoon, or without separation, of actually rejuvenating the relationship as it was before material things got in the way.

"So that's what "Second Honeymoon" was about, and of course, with my love of Brazilian music, from my experience in Rio De Janeiro in the Sixties, I decided to set it into – it's probably played on the album a little faster than it was intended to be, but that was because of the pressure of time while recording, we were running out of time. We had a lot of technical problems, and it was becoming expensive. We probably played it a little faster than it would have been." Suzi Doscher has heard it, "of course. There are a lot of songs that I composed in the last 10 years that have references to relationships with loved ones, not necessarily your own partner, with other loved ones in your circle."

"'Survival' of course was a composition by Jeff Ryan, the poet, and myself. The first recording was in 1974 in Tulsa, Oklahoma, with Jamie Oldaker on drums. I remember that Carl Radle, the bass player said "This is the slowest Blues I've ever played in my life". And then Ben Sidran liked it, and he put it on *Cool Cat Blues*. So we did it with Steve Gadd in New York in 1990. And here we are in 2009, and I've done it again, because the lyrics and the feel are very poignant. And they seem to be more relevant now than they were when it was composed 35 years ago. It's now 15 minutes long, whatever, but it's there. And the coda, when the tempo changes and it goes into this optimistic celebration, like looking on the brighter side, that could go on forever in its own entity. And as you know, recently, in the last couple of years, I have been using it as the last number of a gig. I think it's a great way to end a gig. It starts with the slow bit and goes on for 11 minutes as a slow bit, and reminds people of the problems – if they need to be reminded – and the mistakes that have been made, and the possibilities of rectifying those mistakes for the future generations. So it's quite a heavy statement to make, and yet we did.

"If Steve Gray was still alive – bless him – I would have him do a Big Band arrangement of it. It's nigh on impossible to replace him, but then I have so many Big Band arrangements anyway. They will become the property of my sons. But what will they do with them? Where are the Big Bands to play them? I don't know – I think they should be held in an archive, and bands can buy them for a modest fee. There is a place in New York where you can buy Quincy Jones arrangements for a hundred dollars. [I will continue to work] there is no question of that. You bop till you drop. As long as you have your health and you are capable of doing it, there is nothing else to do. It does keep you alive. It's just that some of us are fortunate enough, or unfortunate enough, to choose it as a profession." [As Oscar Wilde would see it, there are two ways of disappointment, choosing music as a profession and not choosing it.]

Alan Skidmore remembers that for lyrics, "he had Mike O'Neill and Jeff Ryan [and also Fran Landesman]. Plus of course, he composes great tunes. On top of that, he puts great lyrics on *them*. 'Survival' is a tremendous tune. This album was made in a very short time – two and a half days, something like that."

At 65 minutes, in old-fashioned terms this would count as a double-LP, about one minute less in running time than The Rolling Stones' celebrated *Exile On Main St.* – and although it presents "just" a dozen songs, none of these outstays its welcome.

The clever, moving liner notes of the new CD were written by Kunle Mwanga, the Fame fan from the Flamingo days, whom Georgie met again during the sessions for a solo album by the female singer Sandi Russell. Mwanga went to the West Village in 1970 and became involved in producing Anthony Braxton. Fame is still in touch with him, regularly. "His Christian name was George Conley, and he used to come down to the Flamingo. I met him in the United States when he was living in New York and he had left Chicago, cause he did a lot of work on the musical scene in America, on the Jazz scene, he is a well respected figure. He worked with Anthony Braxton of course, and the Chicago Art Ensemble. He toured around with them as a kind of tour manager, and he organized a memorial concert for the great Jazz drummer Billy Higgins, who died a few years ago. So he is operative in the States on the Jazz scene. And he is the only G.I. – apart from Geno Washington and Ronnie Jones, who was also a singer, who now lives in Italy – but Conley is the only G.I. I stayed in touch with, out of all those Black American Jazz musicians that we met."

Singer Reloaded: the Fame/Gray/Bell Musical back on stage – and record

In May 2012, Fame and Madeline Bell got together once again in order to perform the Musical that Georgie had written with Steve Gray. This time, it was going to be performed with a full Dutch Big Band, the Jazz Orchestra of the Concertgebouw, in connection with the Vocal Ensemble o.l.v. Eva Baggerman: the Choir of the Conservatorium of Amsterdam. The excellent compositions had often been feared a lost cause for the two singers, but now they were excited again.

Up until this time, they had enjoyed staging it on three different occasions, as Madeline Bell remembered in 2012: "I really enjoyed that. Have you ever heard the [1985] original or the second recording of *Singer?* With the full Metropole Orchestra, that was such a pleasure to do. We had one performance of it in Tilburg in 2004/2005, and Steve Gray was there. And no one in the orchestra – there we had the full Metropole Orchestra as well – no one in the orchestra knew that Steve was there, until the very end, when we were all bowing and everything, and Georgie went to the microphone and said 'Ladies and gentlemen, will you please say thank you to Steve Gray', and he made Steve come up on the stage. And the whole orchestra was in awe of him! He stayed in the background. When we did the original, he didn't conduct that either. That was Rogier van Otterloo. You mention his name to musicians, especially the older musicians, they all go the same way you do and say 'Wow!' Rogier was the greatest conductor for Holland" – and tragically he would die very suddenly three years after the premiere, in 1988.

The praise for Steve Gray has always been shared by Georgie, and as for the great mix of lyrics and melodies that makes up *Singer*, Fame has never given up hope that it should and could come out as an album one of these days. In 1994, he assured me, "We hope so, yeah, we should do it: Madeline (Bell) and I are always talking about it. It was written for Madeline, really: Madeline is the centre piece of it, and when we did the first version in Holland with the Metropole Orchestra, it was only 50 minutes long. But then we took it to some other people in London, and they suggested that we extend it in order to maybe put it in the theatre. We did do that about three or four years ago. It's now 90 minutes long [bootleg documented], and it's still very good."

As Miss Bell reminded us: "There's a lot of great songs in it: 'City Life', that BBC CD title track is from that Musical as well." Fame: "We tried to get people interested in producing it for the theatre. If nothing happens in the next few years – I mean we didn't have to do it with a huge orchestra, we could do it in a small work-shop setting. There's only four characters in it, Madeline and me and two others, and you only need a good small band – with synthesizers for the strings. There is a workshop theatre in Sweden that's very interested in doing it. Otherwise it would make a very good double album, 90 minutes long and it's a great story. And I think there's not one spoken word in it – the whole thing is told through song."

By the time it came to the second public performance of *Singer* in May 2012 – the "premiere" in 1985 had been merely a radio broadcast – Steve Gray had passed away four years previously. So the task of re-arranging the whole Musical score from a big symphonic palette to that of an 18-piece plus choir fell to the current conductor and arranger, Henk Meutgeert. He literally worked day and night to get it done, which led to an extreme shortage of rehearsal time, a fact that both Georgie "Yes, it was great. All the mistakes included" – and Madeline Bell took in their stride: "I think Henk Meutgeert did a good job in condensing it from a full orchestra to the Big Band. That was a lot – 'cause I know every piece of that music. I know all of Georgie's music, all of the solos, everything. He had a lot of work to do."

That evening of May 25th, 2012 in the De La Mar Theatre in Amsterdam really delighted 'Miss Bell': "When you are standing on the stage, and you've got 18 musicians blowing at the back of your head, and blowing from their hearts, because all of those guys really enjoyed doing it, to the point that we had such a long rehearsal for *Singer* that we didn't have time to rehearse the second set. So that was totally unrehearsed. The last time I performed the songs that I did with the band was in October. I don't know when Georgie had done his – and I don't think they had ever played one or two of his pieces." That is another reason why finally getting a chance to record that dedicated work *Singer* in the studio "would be nice" as a reward for all the efforts. "We should really do some gigs as a memory of Steve, because it is such a beautiful piece, and musicians need to hear it! I always call Steve Gray 'My Gershwin'. We mentioned 'My Second Home' – I had to sing that at Steve Gray's funeral, and I sang to his family to the sound recording of a demo of Steve playing piano, and Georgie playing organ, and that's all there was on it – and that's what I used for his funeral, just Georgie and Steve. It was amazing!"

That tune Madeline Bell mentioned appeared on a 1996 album called *Hymns From Home* (on Three Line Whip), which features Georgie Fame only in spirit and contains spiritual music performed by Steve Gray in collaboration with Swedish organ master Kjell Öhman, among them the *Singer* tune "My Second Home" as an instrumental.

An official recording of the entire *Singer* is now available in 2014. Until then, Dutch radio listeners as well as bootleggers worldwide would have good copies. But help was on the way, as Fame explained in 2012, and it is left in here to show how hard it was to get the record, any record of it, out to the public:

"I had a meeting with people from the Dutch broadcasting in Amsterdam. We are looking into the possibility of releasing a live concert that we did in Tilburg for this thing, with the orchestra. I had forgotten we did it. So I got a copy of it and it sounds rather good. So I was looking to negotiate with these people. And the negotiation went quite well, to release *a* version of *Singer*. Whether we can get the original takes from the original recording in 1983/84, or whether we will use the second studio version from 2003 – which I don't think is as good as the first – or we'll release the live concert version which was in Holland in 2004."

"The live recording is surprisingly good. I think *that* will probably be the release if we can do it. But the negotiations seem to be ok. And I'll continue, but there is no hurry with that. It might come out next year, or I might wait until 2014, which would be the 30th anniversary of the first performance. It's such a pure thing from start to finish in its entirety, so I wouldn't want to combine a studio and a live version. We will either do the live one – on which the conductor did a fantastic job with the montage thing at the end – or we will use the original recording. But it's a case of the Dutch being able to clear it with the orchestra and the choir, and there doesn't seem to be any major obstacles in that at the moment. I would have to finance the manufacturing and all that."

In the end, it was decided to release a CD of the live recording from 2004 in April 2014, and as Fame pointed out, "this will be the 30th anniversary of the first performance."

"Keep It Simple": The acoustic trio album Lost In A Lover's Dream

An unexpected, pleasant bridge between albums with original compositions, Georgie Fame delivered an acoustic delight in the summer of 2012, playing down its brilliant execution with typical modesty: "Well, it was just an idea. I just thought about it, as I had been working with the guitar player Primaz Grašič, and the bass player Mario

Mavrin with Boško Petrović for many years, 15 years or more, since the war in Croatia, 20 years. So we knew each other. And Boško died, one and a half years ago. They have a Jazz camp outside of Ljubljana, every year where I go and help. We make one concert and I do some teaching. There's a good Austrian Jazz singer who does the vocal teaching, Ines Eggburg – anyway, they have good teachers."

So – no Hammond organ this time? No drums or "singing horns"? There was no need to worry, because Georgie's long-time friends from Zagreb made sure that the melodic and rhythmic background appeared as clear as spring water, but as full-bodied as a Californian Chablis at the same time. Vocals and subdued acoustic guitars appear in your face, so they seem nearer than your front room. This works even when Primaz Grašič lets Mario Mavrin do a bass solo, or the former relies on Mario's six bottom-end strings to let loose on his fine acoustic Yamaha guitars:

"I just thought these are fantastic musicians. Boško's trio had no drums, and I joined them every year for a tour in Croatia and Slovenia, and we didn't have any drums. It was great. So I just had to choose material that I thought was going to sound good with the three of us, and that's why I didn't play. I just wanted to keep it simple, because Primaz is a marvelous guitar player, and Mario is a fantastic bass player. He plays a six-string bongo bass. So you just choose material that you think is suitable. I tried to get a good balance. And then of course, when you try to put it in the final order, you have to try and work the order out – how it is going to sound when you listen to it."

It was Georgie who actually benefited from this expertise. His voice always reigns centre stage here, story-telling. It represents the third – or no, in reality it is the first instrument in this remarkable trio. At almost 70, Fame's voice was still oozing all the warmth, dynamic power, tenderness, tonal range and humorous interludes of his younger years, while actually continuing to improve in terms of his very own, inexplicable richness in delivery and precision.

And the man clearly loves these songs and their tales.

"I thought it would be a nice idea just to sing some ballads, and there is nobody to tell me that I cannot do it: 'Don't do it 'cause it's not a good idea!' It was difficult – well, it wasn't easy. But we did it in two days, because we knew each other, some of the songs we had played together – and some of them we hadn't played at all! But they are very good musicians. And I just thought I'd like to sing an album of good ballads, and maybe some slow Blues. Some of the Blues things didn't quite work the way I wanted them to do, but there's no point in spending more time. So I just did it, in January 2012, and it was fun, just another thing to do."

With six compositions from albums Fame did about a decade previously, and one old nugget from 40 years ago, namely his tribute to "Blossom" Dearie, why look back this way, one wondered: "One, I was looking at some of my older compositions. The thing when you are producing an album of course is you have to decide on the material first and what is going to be suitable for the unit that you are using. And I didn't want the whole album to be one ballad after another. Otherwise it gets boring, except when you listen to John Coltrane playing ballads – but even then it is one ballad after the other. So I tried to find a couple of tunes that had a little bit of tempo, and "Blossom" we had played together once before and I said 'It's a nice little up-tempo waltz', although it's very short. So that is why we did it. I was looking at songs that had a romantic bent to them."

Lost In A Lover's Dream – Track by Track

In the opener "Wide-Eyed And Legless", Fame can be found treating his pal Andy Fairweather Low's famous liquor lament to an attractive Bossa Nova arrangement. Georgie had done the song before on 2003's *Charlestons*, and he could also be watched presenting the original AFL version on British television in 1975.

"My Foolish Heart", a 1949 standard by Victor Young with lyrics by Ned Washington and a new one in the Fame oeuvre, was sung by Martha Mears for the film of the same name, and Georgie's whole family of idols and friends have tackled it. Sinatra and Tony Bennett, also the Blues Flames' early guitarist John McLaughlin, the sister of Flames bass player Alec, Jacqui Dankworth and Georgie's ex pal Elkie Brooks. Starting with Grašič's mellow electric guitar, the mini band are a perfect foil for this exquisite vocal performance, and the solo passage sounds full-bodied like a complete combo.

Georgie was also in good company in terms of his own musical peers. As Colin Harper points out in his John McLaughlin biography, "John would feature 'My Foolish Heart' – an Oscar-nominated song, published in 1949, describing the beguiling force of romantic passion, with an invocation to 'beware, my foolish heart!' – as a solo piece during late period concerts by the second Mahavishnu Orchestra, after the failure of his third marriage, and would record it in this form on *Electric Guitarist* (1978). 'The lyrics have a special meaning for me', he said", and he certainly shares this sentiment with his erstwhile employer Georgie.

"Skiing Blues" is the second of four songs taken from *Charlestons* – this one about domestic quarrels abroad had originally been written by Georgie in the year 2000. At the time, he had combined this with "I Lost My Sugar In Salt Lake City" by Johnny Lange and Leon René, here it's a stand-alone composition with more verses, a favourite line being "On the roof of this old worl(d), ain't no good without your girl: feeling cold, got everything to lose!" – Nice dynamics with the staccato chords in the bridge which make this Swing all the more vivid. "I'm going downhill with the Mormons," our man adds at the end.

"Blossom" re-visits Fame's homage-replying tribute to "Blossom" Dearie which had originally appeared on the 1969 *Seventh Son* album, delivered here as a short and sweet, delicate Swing Waltz. The tiny but giant American Jazz singer and pianist had shown a soft sport not only for London but for Georgie especially when she dedicated "Sweet Georgie Fame" to him in 1966.

"Say When" is again from Fame's 2001 Blue Flames album *Relationships*. Before Georgie tells about his emotional wrangles, guitarist Primaz Grašič gets into a conversation with himself, answering his licks with gorgeous chords – no overdubs. Fame's diction is crystal clear to a T here when he sings "be my guiding light", as he will explain in the next song.

"Don't Blame Me" – "It's all your fault": "You mean the diction. I had to be careful, because some of those old American songs like "Don't Blame Me" and "My Foolish Heart", things like that. They have to be sung correctly. Frank Sinatra always had very good diction when he sang. But I didn't want them to sound pretentious, and I just wanted to sound natural. But I was not in the best of health when I did it, because I had an accident. But I don't want to talk about that, because otherwise it will go all over the world." In "Don't Blame Me" Fame allows himself to stretch his voice and also makes it go raw for a split second to prove his personal dedication, to great impact. The song is by Boston pianist and composer Jimmy McHugh, with a lyric by Dorothy Fields, the same partnership that wrote "On The Sunny Side Of The Street" and "I Can't Give You Anything But Love". Georgie's choice "Don't Blame Me" was part of the Chicago revue *Clowns In Clover* in 1932. [For train spotters, McHugh wrote another song for namesake Jane Powell in 1948: "It's A Most Unusual Day", which she still performed 60 years later …]

"Medley: There's No More Blue Time"/"Breezin' All The Way" is also from the album *Relationships*. Instead of a sax solo by Alan Skidmore, the Croatian mini Big Band of Grasic and Mavrin swing ever so well after Georgie again showed his skills in talking his way through a song, like only he (and maybe Ben Sidran) can.

"Singing Horn" is the third choice from *Charlestons* and Georgie's musical tribute to US tenor saxophone player Bobby Malach. The solo here belongs Mario Mavrin, cleverly juxtaposed by his guitarist mate – and Georgie, with this sparse arrangement, sounds all the more dedicated and unfiltered.

Another standard follows via "Cry Me A River", the vintage Julie London evergreen by Arthur Hamilton which Georgie could have heard first as a 12 year old, actually played in the same line-up in 1955, with Barney Kessel on guitar and Ray Leatherwood on bass. The fact that the song was part of the influential movie *The Girl Can't Help It* may have whetted Young Clive's appetite in Rock'n'Roll and Torch at the very same time.

For the George Gershwin standard "I Can't Get Started (With You)", there is Fame's re-write of some lines, in order to get rid of its Wall Street Crash connotations. "I listened to a couple of versions of that song. One was sung by Jamie Cullum, and the other one was by a good American singer, I can't remember, not Anita O'Day. And they always change the lyrics, because the Ira Gershwin lyric in that song was written in 1930:

"In 1929 I sold short" – that was like the Crash of 1929. So that was when he wrote the song. And since then, other singers have changed the lyric to update it to wherever it is. And I just had this idea and thought 1929 was too far back. So I just quickly thought "What can I sing?" So I mentioned being on the road with Van, also working with Basie, and it fitted." This is how he applied some auto-biographical observations: "I toured with Basie's band for a while, and Tony Bennett sketched my profile – with Van The Man I spent halcyon days, from Benny Golson I had high praise, yet you got me down-hearted, I can't get started with you." Anyway, "Superman turned out to be a Flash in the Pan" – and consequently Fame never aspired to be one.

"How Blue" is the fourth and final selection from *Charlestons* – a great R&B number praising the joys of hibernation, and proving that this kind of a swinging Blues works perfectly well in this limited/unlimited setting.

Finally, the title track "Lost In A Lover's Dream" works in the tradition of Fame's own ballads like "A Declaration Of My Love". This one is about a solitary man with no plans, who is coming to terms with the loss of a partner, the dreams of her taking him nowhere. Also, he reveals, "I tried but failed at schmoozing, alas now we're no longer a team." This is delivered with painful honesty, touchingly so – and in the process one of the best vocal performances of Georgie's career.

Tristan Powell, Blue Flames engineer on and off since the *Three Line Whip* album in 1993, knows what he is talking about when, after 20 years in the band, he suggests to put the Fame studio side in (even) more professional hands:

"The word production is in some respects a dirty word for him, nowadays. As you get older, you care less about those elements, because they require patience and planning, and as you know, Clive is quite impulsive, and non-fuss about how things are delivered, as long as they are delivered reasonably well, someone who's not precious about pushing someone out of the comfort zone. Sometimes that can produce really, really good results."

"I've mentioned the word producer a couple of times, and I have fallen on deaf ears. But there is a chance that we will get someone in maybe for the next record. He tends to follow his own nose. He listens to other people's advice, but at the same time follows his own instinct. Sometimes that is a good thing, sometimes not so good. I think people who have been doing it that long and have had that extensive a career, that spans many generations and many styles of music, they kind of know what they want, and he always has, and therefore he will always be the one that calls the shots. I would like to see him doing something along the lines of what Johnny Cash did."

Cash of course was one of the forgotten artists who benefitted from the Rick Rubin purifying treatment – stripping the sound down to the, how would Baloo the bear say – "Bare Necessities". Tristan Powell agrees. "Slightly out of his comfort zone, but it has to be a comfortable environment, and there has to be a mutual respect, and I think maybe he can only achieve that with Ben Sidran, because Ben Sidran has always been an accomplished musician obviously, and a great producer, and a very knowledgeable one. I think there is a mutual respect because of Ben's history, his extensive knowledge, and again being a musician and an engineer/producer."

"I would like to do a proper production of that track "Lost In A Lover's Dream". It is a great song. It's a really well written ballad. I would like to hear strings on it, just something more unusual, modern but also derivative of the old days."

The dreamy artwork for the album, based on a colour shot of clouds, was supplied by an old Blue Flame, Geoff Gascoyne: "In fact, I just finished the art work for his new CD [*Lost In A Lover's Dream*]. He recently made a new CD in Slovenia, with two Slovenian musicians, and he asked me to do design the cover for the CD."

Friday Night Is Music Night – Honouring Georgie's 70th at Cheltenham

While Georgie's attitude to his upcoming 70th birthday certainly seemed to be a mixture of gratefulness, and a cool, calm and collected "Keep on working and learning" attitude, the "scene" and the media were certainly aware of the "old music master's" jubilee, as Georgie noted in October 2012:

"People are asking. I am going to try and find some time to do something. I know that Ronnie Scott's want to do a special concert, probably not in a club, but in a hall. And I've been invited – Guy Barker rang me; Guy is very successful at the moment with his own orchestra at the BBC. We're going to do an evening with the BBC Orchestra and Big Band. So I have to think about that. We will see how it goes. That's going to be a big concert in Cheltenham, in May. There's all kinds of possibilities. But at the moment, I am too busy with thinking what I'm playing tonight."

"The BBC equivalent of a gong!", Georgie called it on the air at BBC Radio when it was announced that in the series *Friday Night Is Music Night*, the man was going to be honoured with a full Big Band, orchestra and guests, who he announced, sitting in the bar of the London Bloomsbury hotel in April 2013, as "Alan Price and Zoot Money and Madeline Bell, three of my favourite people, and three artists that I have done some of my best work with."

Fame and his trumpeter for more than 20 years, Guy Barker, were to be responsible for the great night: "He's graduated to the school of carving", he told the BBC, "which is arranging and conducting to you. He was in the right place at the right time to suggest, as I was turning 70 this year, why don't we do a kind of career retrospective. I had the idea to start with a brief version of Jerry Lee Lewis's 'High School Confidential', which is really the song – and the performance – that got me my first professional gig. Then it will be almost chronological: we're going through the Flamingo Club, where I was resident for three years, and there were West Indian influences, and great songs like 'Sunny', the Bobby Hebb tune. My hits of course, and I've got the guests."

The just-quoted Guy Barker led the orchestra into his own, wonderfully arranged eight-minute overture of Georgie's Sixties hits like "The Point Of No Return", "Lil' Pony", "Sitting In The Park" and, but of course, "Yeh Yeh" too. All this impressed not least because Baker let Swing and ballads, Big Band and strings, take turns for dramatic effect.

"Ladies and gentlemen, please welcome Georgie Fame" was the obvious announcement just like in Flamingo Club days, and the man, as promised, got into "High School Confidential", albeit all too brief, and remembered the crucial moment in 1959, before he welcomed Madeline Bell, Alan Price and Zoot Money onto the stage for "What'd I Say", with all three of them taking verses before the Hammond led into strings and brass the way Brother Ray would have liked it, with enough looseness involved to avoid a slick showbiz impression. "Excuse the false intro", Fame quipped before he dedicated the song to the late Eddie Cochran the way he always does.

The following medley was a tribute to Charlie Parker and Lester Young, "Going To Kansas City"/"Jumpin' With Symphony Sid" with some of his great Vocalese exercises involved. Saxophone duties supplied, as so often was the case in the last 45 years, by Alan Skidmore.

Then Georgie repeated the exercise of his *Birthday Big Band* live double album recorded in 1998, pronouncing Zoot Money's Big Roll Band as the Flamingo Club's finest, this time Zoot keeping his mouth shut about Fame having the best. Instead, they both joked about the friendly competition with a "Me, me, me, me, me" contest and went straight into "It Should Have Been Me" which both recorded over the years but which Money had introduced to British fans.

"Zoot took over my residency at the Flamingo", Fame reminded his audience, and the reminisced how 'one of my oldest friends – we grew up in Lancashire about three miles apart and both played piano in various pubs and clubs around our neighbourhood', got him the club job in the first place: "Mike O'Neill: he was about four years older than me and about 50 years hipper. We both played piano in various pubs and clubs around our neighbourhood." Of course, O'Neill also introduced Fame to the Vocalese technique, and his first attempt was the Mac Dennis number "Everything Happens To Me", and first recorded by Fame on the *Georgie Does His Thing With Strings* album.

The Soho club era tales are kept up with "Flamingo All-nighter" from 2003 *Charlestons* album, telling the story "from March 1962 to the Profumo affair" and mentioning many names of the era, not least Christine Keeler and Cassius Clay, and Count Suckle. No wonder, Madeline Bell and Zoot Money hit their stride alongside Fame here – they took part in the studio recording, too. Well padded by the wonderful orchestra, Georgie remembers how they got home to Earls Court on early Sunday morning after the All-nighters, the "working girls" he shared the flat with busy in the kitchen, "getting no sleep and getting up in the early afternoon to do it all over again."

Next, as the fans surely expected him to, the main protagonist related the story of how Roger Moore "stole his show" on arrival at Stockholm airport in the wake of the next number in the concert: giant hit "Yeh Yeh" and documented earlier, done here with a gorgeous Count Basie style intro. Later, his rendition culminated in a tremendous sax solo by Alan Skidmore.

Bobby Hebb's "Sitting In The Park" was next, and Georgie reminded us that there were actually three versions of this song in the 1966 charts – apart from Hebb's own ("I don't know whether he wrote anything else, but he probably didn't have to") and his own there was Cher's version. Golden memories again: "When I was in New York in 1967, he came to my hotel and we had a very pleasurable evening up in Harlem. Hebb took me to the Apollo Theatre where we saw Jackie Wilson. We had a ball. And I haven't seen him since." Barker arranged the beginning with lush strings in ballad form, a bit like "Eros Hotel", and it's only with the second verse that a light Latin rhythm comes a little closer to the original, which gradually takes shape with fitting flutes and saxes.

"This is just a simple Blues by the great Blues composer and bass player Willie Dixon", Fame pointed out, "put into a different time signature because of its title": "Seventh Son" in 7/4 time. His version of the song, (and the parent album *Seventh Son*), he added, had been produced by one of his guests for the evening, Alan Price. Not for the last time, Guy Barker excellently takes the opportunity for an opulent Big Band arrangement, where tympani stress the sophisticated time.

"Bring on the producer", Fame quips, and immediately, a Sixties movie music style orchestral intro leads into the former duo's chart smash "Rosetta", often criticized as family cabaret but a lot of fun here, again, audibly, for both unfazed heroes of *Fame & Price/Price & Fame Together*.

After a mini documentary by Ron McCrate about the Flamingo Club history, Madeline Bell introduced the tribute song which the American pianist and singer Blossom Dearie wrote about Georgie – fittingly singing it herself to the audience – and explaining how the lady preferred him and the Blue Flames to the pop music of the day. The late Dearie would have loved Guy Barker's tender arrangement here.

Low down and dirty piano tunes start "The Ballad of Bonnie and Clyde", for a change, but the orchestra mostly sticks to the lovely treatment which Count Basie's arranger once attached to Georgie's third big hit, which remained unloved until these charts convinced him there was something in it.

For the following medley, Fame praises great lyricists he worked with during his career before writing them on his own: Candida Lycett Green, Jeff Ryan and "the late Fran Landesman": with "Entertaining Mr Sloane" from the film of the same name, and "Eros Hotel" from the album *Right Now!*

Next, and very proudly now its release had finally been secured, Madeline Bell and Georgie leapt into the title song of their joint Musical show *Singer* with the late Steve Gray. This show had been aired in Holland for the first time in 1985, and the BBC first issued "The Singer" in 1992 with Fame, Bell & The BBC Big Band as *City Life*.

Steve Gray, the unforgotten collaborator and friend, also wrote the charts for Hoagy Carmichael's "The Old Music Master", which Georgie recorded with Annie Ross in 1981 and which Madeline Bell performs here with Fame, violins opening the song and Guy Barker secures a gripping solo before the saxophones take over.

"Doesn't matter how you sing, boy", Fame remembers Hoagy Carmichael saying to him, "my songs will always make you sound good", and – again with Madeline, he segues into "The Nearness of You".

From orchestral backing to the trio format – Georgie's sons Tristan on guitar and James on drums join him "on what can only be described as a commercial break": his British Petroleum jingle cum chart hit from 1966.

Big Band and strings are back for Georgie's JJ Cale style composition about being a qualified "Rhythm King", written on the road "somewhere between Leipzig and Copenhagen on the back of an envelope, on the back of a bus" with Rolling Stone Bill Wyman's swell band of the same name – and fittingly, there are quotes about Eddie Floyd knocking on wood, and even "Satisfaction", and Fame rattles off the styles they play, starting with that "good old Rock'n'Roll", just like his own career began.

"Running short of time, there's a composition by the great Texan Willie Nelson", but Georgie "never heard the original version, but Little Joe Hinton": "Funny How Time Slips Away", which he had recorded for his Harry South Big Band christening *Sound Venture*, and again on *Right Now!* The line "I've got to go now" seems fitting, because the show is about to close – and more "name dropping" is on the cards: "calling Denny Cordell, calling Curtis Mayfield, calling Major Lance, calling Phil Upchurch, calling George Benson, and calling Quincy Jones."

Shortly before the end, Georgie declares "Victory because we all went past 70", and thanks his guests, all the musicians, the BBC as well as his bugle player, Guy Barker, for arranging all this so adeptly.

It has been an opener of his gigs before, but it makes for a great finale as well: Louis Jordan's "Saturday Night Fish Fry" closes a great homage, with Alan Price and Madeline Bell taking over a welcome verse before all three guests join in on the chorus.

Georgie had just praised his "older, but hipper friend Mike O'Neill at the Cheltenham celebration. It was only five months later in Copenhagen – shortly before an appearance in the "Jazzhus Monmartre" on October 10, 2013 – when Fame found out that O'Neill had died of liver cancer. That night, Georgie was performing with the Danish version of the Blue Flames who featured Bob Rockwell on sax, Jacob Christoffersen on piano, the legendary Mads Vinding on double bass and Morten Lund on drums.

Georgie announced that Mike had died that morning, describing the crucial part his big friend Mike had in helping his career get on its feet. Then dedicated one of his most consistent repertoire pearls, "It Could Happen to You", to O'Neill, with sections of "My Buddy" and "Stranger in the Paradise" fitted in. It was a very touching and special moment. Witness António Alfaiate reckons that "My Buddy" has never seen a rendition by Georgie that was so truly heartfelt and caring as during that night. Georgie's homage to Mike, "My Ship (Is Coming In)", will appear on CD in 2015.

During the last few years, the Danish Blue Flames have been playing at least annual gigs at "The Jazzhus Montmarte" in Copenhagen.

Anthems For a Band Leader

Fame was barely 18 when he grasped the opportunity to claim Billy Fury's Blue Flames as his own band. Opportunity that reads responsibility – one which he took ever so well for four years, and then interrupted for about "six minutes", when his manager Rik Gunnell told him to go solo. Whether it was The Georgie Fame Band that took shape only weeks after the disbanding of The "Flamingo" Blue Flames, whether it was the band "Shorty" in 1971 or the numerous incarnations of the band until The Last Blue Flames of the recent decade, Fame has always been a great man at the helm, while he obviously enjoys being away from the driving wheel by moonlighting for Van Morrison or Bill Wyman's Rhythm Kings. This comes as no surprise, because running a band, as many will attest, can be a ticket to madness.

Fame's attitude towards the running of a band is, and always has been, caring. His musicians' attitude towards working for him is characterized by respect, admiration and comfort, very much in contrast to leaders who command respect and reap fear and resentment in the process – including personalities admired by Georgie, from Ray Charles to James Brown.

Let's take selected Blue Flames' word for it. Here are some "Anthems for their band leader":

Sax man Alan Skidmore, a Blue Flame on and off since 1969, i.e. over a 45-year period, knew in 2011 that "when you are a bandleader, the logistics can be an absolute nightmare and nothing goes according to plan. This might – and I'm not saying it does – have something to do with the fact that Clive feels like he does, about the logistics of getting a gig together, and a tour together."

Skidmore continues: "You go along and you take your instrument, you take the appropriate attire: you take a suit depending on what type of gig it is, and you turn up and you do it. And it's always good! There is never a big drama, there is never a big deal about it. We just come straight after a year or two years, and it sounds like we played the night before. Even if he has a completely new piece or two new pieces that we have never seen before, we normally get it together pretty quick; you just go along with it. –

"A couple of years ago we did Glastonbury. Although it took forever to get in and forever to get out, the actual gig was no big deal: it's always the easy bit. We just went on stage and played. The Blue Flames, which is easy. And it was a success."

Skidmore has been working for dozens of bandleaders, plus he has been one himself for decades, so we can trust him when he compares Van and Georgie in a very subdued but still revealing way: "I did not work for Van Morrison for too long. I certainly did my time with him, and this was because Georgie wanted us. He suggested to Van that Guy [Barker] and myself were to maybe do the horns for a while, and it was a nice experience while it lasted. But the list of bandleaders and people that I have played for – we'd be here for another fortnight. You are talking about Blues. What I have always enjoyed with Clive is that it's never really much of a problem.

"For me it's over *forty* years! There have been periods where we had a break for several years. He's been doing things and we do our own thing, but it is well over forty years."

In this author's scrapbook, Skid's first 1980s gig with Georgie Fame was at The Torrington Club in London in the autumn of 1985. "That's very true. It was probably where we kind of re-joined forces and then the rest of it came along as it did. It's 21 years since this band [The Last Blue Flames] came together.

"I would just like to say: all the years that I've worked with Clive, it really has been a pleasure. There have been one of two sticky moments, like – well, it's something like a marriage. There isn't a marriage that runs smoothly. Clive is not the best guy to be around first thing in the morning at the airport. There have been one or two sparks flying, you know. Not with us, but with the people you have to deal with. But by and large, it's been a great experience. I really want to say about Clive, and that is, I really do think that he is a supreme Jazz musician. It has been a joy working for him over the years, because he is such a great musician. It's not like working with a vocalist. It's not like working with a singer. He's a front line musician, for the record."

As vibraphonist Anthony Kerr put it in 2011, "I think what I learned in Clive's band, more than from anyone else: In that band, Modern Jazz really got back to the Blues. And the remarkable thing is how long the band has been going. We could probably go for a year, we could probably go for ten years without a gig, take out the instruments and play. It's because the style is not something we haven't seen before – the style is so much ingrained, so much of a home game, as it were. You just instinctively know where the horns go, when it's their time together, then with Tristan we have little things that we are doing. It's like you're having friends you meet up with and chat with happily and you have been doing this over a long period of time. If you introduced a new subject to talk about, "Let's not talk about football tonight, let's talk about motor racing", it wouldn't be difficult to talk about it with those same people. You have a rapport! And *we* have a 21 year old rapport.

"You are much more stressed when you are the bandleader, we all are. We have done gigs as sidemen, and we have done gigs as bandleaders. If you're a sideman: 'What time is it? Where is it?' Everything else around it is a tough one, like the bus, the roadies. What sort of intruments, what sort of equipment would wait for you at the other end. There's got to be somebody making the calls and placing the advertisements.

"As a sideman, you just turn up and say 'Do I need to look at it beforehand or not?' Everything you are looking at a couple of months in the future. And you are looking at a chunk of time, and you're saying 'Do I want to make a million phone calls and deal with all this stress', or do I just want to say 'Yes' to somebody and get on the bus?"

"It's easy because you know you are going to get the direction you need from him. You're going round and round, and you think is it the ending now, or do we go round again? You are never in any doubt. He always looks at you, makes the signal at exactly the right moment. You're feeling completely free. You're just keeping an eye on him: the signal may come or may not come."

Alan Skidmore could not agree more: "Absolutely: He will always guide you wherever you have to go. Maybe it would be a little difficult for someone who's coming in, doing the gig for the first time, but because we have all been together for so long, we've done it and done it and done it, we know the slightest little nod and wink: exactly what's going on. And in that sense he is a joy to work with, absolutely. It's not like working with a bandleader as such. It's just like working with another guy in the band. He is the singer, and he is the Hammond organ player. And the other thing which is good: he always makes the programme before we go on. He could skip one or he changes …"

Anthony Kerr: "… but you're never in any doubt. You are never going to be hung up dry. You're never going to be scrambling for a part or wondering what's going on, thinking you might look like an idiot. You are always guided, and the structure of the gig is clear enough, and you can enjoy the music."

Kerr gets even more specific: "He is a very good bandleader. I learned a lot from him. He has very good instincts, as to which tune to pull out next. He can read the audience that way very well. He also is very clear and simple in his communication. You don't have this anxious feeling of 'I don't know what's coming up'. Is it the ending or isn't it? It is because his tunes are flexible. Sometimes they can be longer, and sometimes they can be shorter. You might have an option to do an extra solo or not, and he gives signals on stage very very clearly. I am always at the opposite side of the stage, for all these years I have always been on the other side. The Hammond organ goes on that side, the horns in the middle, the drums and bass at the back, and I'm by the guitar. I am always looking right across to him. But it is very easy to play with someone who gives a clear signal. Takes all the doubt, you are on solid ground and all the doubt's gone. You can just get on with it and play and enjoy the music, instead of having uncertainty."

Guy Barker, Fame's trumpeter/"bugler" for the last 25 years, knows that "the similarity with Georgie and other bandleaders I worked with is: there's certain things you see them do, and you realize that they are in the process. They are actually harder on themselves than they are on anybody else. Sometimes people will talk about certain well-known bandleaders, asking 'Why are we rehearsing for so long when we know the stuff?' Most of the time, they are doing it for themselves, because it is a totally different thing being the bandleader than being the sideman. You play totally differently. You are carrying the weight of it all. You are the person whose name is on the ticket. So it immediately becomes different. It is a different thing. Georgie was just the same, and I'm sure that a lot of the time I see him and hear him trying things out, and if it wasn't working, I'd hear him sort of shout at the piano and all get upset, because he would just be hard on himself."

Guy goes on to explain that both efficiency and impatience may rule in the studio, but inside this spectrum Fame eventually gets things done: "If things are working, if you spend all your time practicing your stuff, like Georgie has – doing the Flamingo every night, trying to get all this stuff together, you know what I mean – and he has been on the toad, and he has worked with the Basie band, and he has worked with lots of different people – so when you go into a situation, and things aren't together, then of course you are going to get pissed off. So of course there have been times in the studio, we have got all this 'Let's get this done.' There are some musicians out there – apparently Ronnie Scott was a bit like that – they didn't really enjoy going in the studio and doing that, because I suppose there is a kind of 'Committing something is forever'. When you do a gig, it goes out into the air, and that's it.

"I remember there was one song we did, where in the studio, it just took forever to get things together. You thought 'We could have made an album in this time.' Of course, the atmosphere isn't going to be great when you've got that kind of thing going. *Charlestons* I think it was, not the most recent one. Everything took forever to set up. I think probably the way Georgie would like to do it is to be able to walk into a room, we're all in there, together, we are not separated, and we'll just play, like we're on a gig. Stand there, and then I think it would be perfect." But striving for perfect moments is also what a good leader of a band is all about, so there is a point.

Geoff Gascoyne, Blue Flame bass player for almost a decade, complements the praise for Georgie: "He is very much a musician's musician. He is part of the rhythm section. I played with a lot of different bands, where you are [just] hired. With Everything But The Girl, I was just a session musician. I was told what to play. That's very different, but I played in so many different situations. But it is definitely more fun playing with someone like Clive, because he is such a great musician. There is a lot more improvising going down. Obviously, we were still working within his boundaries, and we were playing his music, but basically I could play what I liked, totally. It was very giving.

"That's the good thing about him: He never says anything about the music. He doesn't need to – and to be honest, I probably know what's required anyway, but he has never given me any instructions. Occasionally, he might say 'Could you play in two, or in four on this section?' or something, but very minimal instructions. I have also done a lot of arranging for him. I arranged the horns for the *Relationships* album, and a couple of other ones as well. So I have done a lot of that stuff for him as well. He obviously trusts me as a musician. I don't need any instructions, and he gets what he wants to hear."

Colin Green, Fame's first long-term guitarist, realizes that he learnt a lot of things from Georgie, "some quite musical things actually: he instinctively voices things in a very unique way. The way he played the changes on the piano – there was a freedom to it. It was what he heard rather than what he knew. And it took me an awful long time to free myself up if you like from being too constrained and too logical in what I was doing. To be able to say "Ok, just play what you hear", rather than what you know."

Jon Hiseman played drums behind Georgie between 1967 and 1968, and his praise is typically concise: "Georgie ran a really friendly but tight ship. He was clear about what he wanted, he was clear about what he didn't want, and he required you to be on time, and in good shape. Please give Clive my regards."

Guitarist Bernie Holland, who was with him from 1972 to 1979 and then again in the Van Morrison Band, remembered in 2013 that "I find it strange calling him Georgie, you see. We, the band, never called him Georgie, but of course everybody else did, his fans and people who used to come to the gigs. I never actually asked him, because it might be too personal – I wonder if he wished he hadn't been called Georgie Fame, whether he would appreciate being called Clive Powell. The name Georgie Fame does suggest, I mean he was a pop star, but he wasn't a pop star in the sense of some lesser quality artistes that go by the name of pop stars. He never did anything that he didn't believe in, he never did things just because it might be a quick buck. He always did stuff that he liked doing and that he felt a connection to. I always considered him more of a Jazz musician than a pop musician. Having said that, he had some hits and they were good records. Of course he had 'Yeh Yeh' and hit albums.

"There were a lot of songs he had that weren't hits. The situation for Clive was: he didn't want to have people who didn't know what they were doing, messing his life up. He wanted to do things his way. A lot of these industry people, they don't know anything. When it comes to artistry and integrity, they don't know anything; I'm talking about the 1970s. He didn't want to play their game, and consequently things didn't get pushed as much as they might have been. That is maybe why he didn't have so many hits.

"Anyway, I liked the bands with all the horns in – great – and he's had some fantastic sax players. All the musicians who ever played with him, you are talking about the best musicians available. That is a reflection on him, because he needed people who could do that standard as players, to work with him. Unlike the pop stars of the day – there were other people who had hit records, but they weren't too bothered about the standard of musicians, because they only had to play a few hits that weren't particularly demanding to play.

"He is still working. Other people have finished, they're not playing anymore and are forgotten. He's still out there, playing. It is a lifestyle, a way of life, no retirement for him. His family is music and his sons are music. When he gets people involved who are not interested in music, just interested in business and bullshit, then he walks away from them. I don't blame him at all for that. Even if it has meant that he has not been as successful as Elton John or whoever else, he will carry on. He is his own man. It's like his song 'Gimme That Wine' – that's what he is. He is the wine, and as the years go by, the wine gets better.

"Georgie Fame is very much like Les Paul in character. Georgie Fame, he would play for anyone. If only three people turned up for a gig, he would play for these three people as if there were three hundred thousand there. I saw a tribute program to Les Paul on the television: he was in an old folks' home in New York somewhere. All these 80 and 90 year old people and he entertained them for an hour. That's the sort of thing Fame would do.

"I'll say that in fairness to Clive as well: he was a very democratic person. Ok, it was his band, Georgie Fame & The Blue Flames, but he made sure everybody was treated fairly. He would ring me up and say "Sorry, those gigs I gave you are off, they got cancelled, but I'll pay you." It's your livelihood, and he had respect for the livelihood of his musicians."

The praise is confirmed by part time Blue Flame Andy Fairweather Low: "We need to make use and be aware, too, that this Georgie Fame is a rare thing that we got – in that he is alive and he is playing *now*. We need to cherish it and go out and see it more, because he is on the top of his game. It is a treat to watch. I was brought up listening to Georgie Fame, and I have never lost that. When I meet him, I am the guy who listens to him. I am not the guy who might have written a song that he is playing on the album. I'm still the guy that was at home or who drove up to London to the Flamingo [24] to see him. I am still that person, I'm nothing else!"

Ronnie Johnson, Blue Flames guitarist from 1982 to 1993, states that "One of the things that I really admire about Fame: sometimes he will move away from his original desire, but then he always knew when to come back to the original idea that

---

24. See Addendum

he had in the first place. And one of the major problems why Zoot [Money] doesn't have the kudos of Clive, although he does as a musician, is the fact that Zoot, instead of just saying 'I'm gonna get on with what I do', he will change it. When you change from your original idea, you may be out of fashion for a little while, but it doesn't last long, in my view.

"I was always really encouraging him to go with this Jazz thing, because it seemed to me that would have a lot of success in that area. I don't see Clive as an improvising musician – he would probably kick me in the shins about this. And (his repertoire) works so well. And he brings improvising musicians into the scene, but he's playing his thing, he will play his solo, work on his solo, which I really admire within what he does. I think the fact that he doesn't get moved from the initial desire – this is what makes people timeless."

Finally, Georgie Fame's loyalty and reliability have to be pointed out over and over again. When his long-term bass player Geoff Gascoyne left amicably to join Jamie Cullum's band, effectively concentrating on monitoring the young Jazz man's career, Georgie gave the slot to Alec Dankworth – as a permanent replacement. When the Gascoyne-Cullum collaboration came to an end, Geoff would have loved the job back as much as Georgie still rated his former band member. But his loyalty to the Dankworth handshake weighed stronger, which says something about Fame's stability in a fickle business.

Anthems For A Great Singer

There are other bandleaders, and there are other Hammond players, starting from Fame's heroes Jimmy Smith and Booker T. and never ending with unsung heroes like Chick Churchill from Ten Years After and Dieter Reith, or bigger names like Brian Auger, Joey deFrancesco, Larry Goldings, Munich's Barbara Dennerlein or the British James Taylor, Mick Weaver a.k.a Wynder K. Frog, Ian McLagan, Charles Earland, Ingfried Hofmann, the list is endless. With Jazz singers, in many experienced people's mind the world champion's shortlist is a very short one indeed, and a lot of experts seem to wonder why Fame is on it but not so visible!

Alan Skidmore is mystified: "Probably the only person who can answer that is Clive. I have always been baffled why Clive isn't a bigger name in America. I think he should be world famous. But nobody knows what goes on inside Clive's head. That is a big secret to all of us, how he thinks about things."

Colin Green gets more specific: "About Georgie not being as famous as he is, I think there was a bit of bad management. How much Clive had to do with that, I don't know, but I think he could have been huge. He should have been! He upset a lot of people. He got a bit drunk on a couple of occasions, or whatever, upset the bosses of one or two places. He is very much Jekyll & Hyde. He is sweet person, if you keep him away from the bottle. And he knows it. I think there is an element of truth in saying that whether he prefers to play in small venues, there is an intimacy with the audience that you don't get in a stadium, but financially and career wise, you don't want to be that type of artist."

Fame certainly doesn't want fame. His son Tristan reckons "that's a bit ironic, given his given name, his adopted surname, but he is anything but that insidious culture of stardom, and probably even then, back in the Sixties, he never forgot who he was and where he is from and always kept it real. And even now, when we turn up to gigs, he loads in the wagon. He might even drive or hump the organ to the stage and lift it up himself, plug it in. He still keeps very real, and that's a great thing."

Guy Barker passes on a compliment: "Do you know a trombone player called Mark Nightingale [born in 1967, NYJO, BBC Big Band, Sting]. To give you an idea of the respect that musicians have for Georgie Fame: I was getting a lift somewhere, and Mark Nightingale said to me 'So what are you doing tonight?' I said 'I'm going on a little tour with Georgie Fame'. 'Georgie Fame's voice? The perfect Jazz instrument' - that was what Mark said to me. Everybody talks about Sinatra's phrasing. But there is something about the way that Georgie sings a song, and also being in that Jazz world, because he doesn't scat. Although he doesn't really like it, I have heard him do it. And he *can* do it, but his thing is Vocalese, just singing a song. It's just glorious. And the swing is still there! That was one of the things that we used to say, Anthony Kerr said that to me about the gig with Georgie: You turn up there, get on the stage, do it, and all you have to do is just swing as hard as you can, and stay right in the pocket, that's it.

And there's more from Guy's book of praise: "Take Vocalese for instance, on the Chet Baker solos: Sometimes, when he finishes, the roar of the audience can be quite amazing. I remember looking over to him, and even he looked taken aback by it.

"There was once a well-known actor who was doing the announcement of the gig: Dougray Scott. I worked with him in a film, and there was a lovely thing on a broadcast I heard, and at the end, when he finished, this guy was reading from a script, and on the broadcast, you can hear him say, quieter, because the applause is going down, you just hear him saying: 'I love Georgie Fame.'

"One thing I always wanted to do, because I do think it would work, is: I want to hear Sting and Georgie sing together. I think there is a blend there that could be really interesting. My dream is to do 'Seventh Son' with the two of them in harmony. I mentioned it to Georgie, and he seemed to think that it's a good idea. We did Ronnie's and I remember Sting came to see us once. He admired Georgie, and I remember he was knocked out with James's drumming."

Guy Barker knows another young admirer: "When we were at Ronnie's with the Big Band, Jamie Cullum came in to hear it. I've known Jamie since he started, and then we sat down. And in the interval, Jamie was on the table in the corner, where the bar used to be, looking at the band. I went there during the interval, and he sat there alone. I said 'How are you doing, Jamie?' And he looked at me and said 'I'm in class.' He was just sitting there alone, and maybe it was that moment, maybe he had people with him and they had gone, they weren't there now, but all I remember is him sitting there in the interval by himself, saying 'I'm in class." I said 'He's good, isn't he?' And he said 'My God! It really is quite something what he does!' As this author witnessed, Jamie Cullum has been at Ronnie's much more than once. Apart from interviewing him, he always returns, and quietly takes it all in. [25]

"There's nothing else to do" – Clive on Georgie

There have been so many fan letters, blogs and concert break conversations about why and how come Georgie Fame is not a worldwide sensation. Try Tom Jones for reference, as long as he was a Las Vegas sensation, he recorded albums that proceeded to grace the cut-out bins and CD surplus racks – stuff the Welsh belter wouldn't much listen to himself, being much happier catering for an audience interested in Blues & Roots. The same can be claimed for Georgie.

Check his CBS years from 1967 to 1971, when they wanted to make him "a British Andy Williams". You can't help but like a lot of the middle-of-the-road ballads and toe-tappers he recorded for albums like *Going Home*, because they bring back wonderful memories and were done with professional care and dedication, but the protagonist did suffer. So he had been there, done that. And when the intended big comeback via Chris Blackwell's Island Records did not work out – half-hearted label politics were to blame entirely – the man they call Georgie Fame decided he was going to live as he pleased, and only work for friends, as he patiently explained time and again, including a lovely long backstage conversation in Gütersloh, Germany in the summer of 2009:

"I mean if I wanted to live in a city, I would live in Manhattan. I'd live slap bang in the middle of Manhattan, which is great. It is a great city, New York. But if you want to live in a city, you have got to live right in the middle. As a place to live, maybe not all the year – half a year or whatever – I would rather live in central Manhattan, or anywhere on Manhattan Island, basically, than anywhere in London. London has lost its charm. The British Museum has lost its charm. The whole of London has lost its charm.

"But that is just a personal thing. I have been on the road for fifty years. So I am becoming quite particular in what I want to do and where I want to do it, and where I want to live and reside. But I am in a position to do that, which is also true with the jobs I do. I only work – I only do the jobs that I want to do. I don't do jobs that I don't want to do, and I don't have anybody behind me telling me I must do this job. I am my own boss, and it's cool. It is great. It is freedom. And I enjoy my work. Two weeks down I will be in Japan with my family, playing to packed houses."

The examples Georgie gave for 2009/2012 are exemplary of the routine he goes through every single year of his career: "And then I am on the road with Bill Wyman's Rhythm Kings for 33 concerts in the UK. My diary is full. I work with Big Bands, small bands. Some are as big as your head. But I am working with friends, and I have been fortunate enough to be successful enough to travel the world and make great friends, soul mates, through the music – with no language barrier. So I can go to Hong Kong, I can go to Japan, I can go to New Zealand, I can go to Australia, I can go to the United States if I want to. I can go anywhere in Europe, and I can play with friends and enjoy

25. See Addendum

music. And as long as there is a public that is willing to come and share this experience and listen to it, then I won't quit, because there is no reason to quit. If the public stopped coming to listen, then I'll play alone at home."

Georgie has every right to keep his home life away from the public, so it is a rare chance to get a tiny glimpse of it in conversations with him:

"I have a bicycle. I ride my bicycle every morning, maybe sort of four kilometers. I have a secret house in Scandinavian countries, where I go to, to relax. I have a boat, and I row the boat every morning, after I've been on the bicycle. I work in the garden. I do normal things – being together with nature. I do preparing for my garden.

"I have a concert in Scandinavia on Friday, next Friday, with a Big Band, so I will spend a couple of days in my house. They always have been great. Traditionally, Scandinavia, Sweden in particular, like Paris/France in the Fifties, were the great Jazz havens for visiting American Jazz musicians, and then of course, and very important and not to forget, the Americans here in Deutschland. One of the most influential radio programs, Jazz radio programs, was "The Voice of America: Jazz Hour" with Willis Conover, which actually came from Washington, D.C. but they beamed it from Frankfurt. And we could get it in England. (Whispers) "How's that? American Jazz on the radio! Wow!"

"I'm not a great virtuoso as a player", he told *Jazz Podium*, "I can sing Jazz better than I can play it. That's why I like to stand in front of other bands and sing. This gives me the chance to let my voice develop. As a player I consider myself in the medium range, especially from a Jazz perspective. In my band, I allow the band members to let loose and express themselves. We simply play good music which we have fun with. That's why there are a lot of references in my solos to the solo performances of other musicians, quotes and so on. There is a phrase in "Rhythm King" which is steeped in Rhythm & Blues, a phrase which I added a text to, which is from a piano solo by Horace Silver in "Filthy McNasty", taken from the live version at the Village Gate.

"'Labour Of Love' means that other people have fun with it. That is my recompensation. It's not the financial benefit that counts, but the satisfaction you get from appearing publicly, that's why I am first and foremost a live performer. I sing and I play to earn my living, this makes me stay active. When I'm in the recording studio, I have the feeling I have to get out of there as quickly as possible [...] We play as if we are together in a club or a concert hall. The spontaneous feeling is there for a short time, and gone again.

"All this repeating and overdubbing, I can't do it. I don't want to produce music as if I was in a music factory."

"Lost In A Collector's Dream" – Possible Future Releases

Five years after announcing in wonderfully quaint or ironic words that he was going to release "my last LP", namely *Tone Wheels A-Turning*, there is enough in the pipeline for an ongoing recording career, although Fame might very well leave a lot of fine-tuning and certainly all kinds of re-releases and compilations to the next generation: "There is no hurry. This Slovenian album [*Lost In A Lover's Dream*] is [the Three Line Whip label's] 009. I've got the rights to the Chet Baker album [*A Portrait of Chet*], I own that. It was not on Three Line Whip originally, as you know. But I've got all that, so that would be TLW 010. There is 50 percent of the Australian album [*No Worries*] that I did.

"There's certainly ten albums, at least ten, and you can make a good compilation. You can make many compilations. I think that's the boys' department, after I'm dead and gone, or when I'll stop working, when I can't work anymore, and I stop writing, which is probably after I've done this album next year, because I don't see myself writing any great tunes anymore. Then I'll start thinking of the compilations. I'm tired, I'm very tired. This tour [the Rhythm Kings Tour of 2012, just like the one in 2013] is hard and long, with the travelling. But as long as I am capable of doing anything – and my diary is always full, and I only do things that I enjoy, so ... as long as that keeps going, God willing, I'll keep doing it. When I stop doing that – that will be the time to think: 'What can I put out?' But I think my legacy and my archive – stuff that I own – is up to the boys to do whatever they want to do."

One album that is still not out on CD is *In Goodmansland*, Georgie's album with Sylvia Vrethammar, Georgie's kind of follow-up to the tribute album *In Hoagland*, this time honouring Benny Goodman, of course, "which I have no interest in. It's not in my interest. It is a good album, but it's got nothing to do with me. I'll ring Dagen, the record company. He sold the record company, but I'll call him, they might put it out on CD."

In the can for a long time has been the possibility of documenting the marvellous work that Georgie Fame & Sons have done over the past two decades: "There is a live recording which is mixed. We are not entirely happy with it, but I think 70 percent of it is good. There is probably enough for an album. We recorded a live gig in London at a Blues festival, and it's rough and ready, but it sounds pretty good. That is in the can, but we haven't done anything about it."

James on a trio album: "I don't know, I'd like to do one. We have some crappy recordings from different theatres and places around, but I never heard them, but Tristan says they are not good enough. But he's got very high standards, so I think they probably *are* good enough and sound right. We did do one a year or two ago, and there were some problems with the check-up and it was a little bit stressful. Going with hall mikes is not ideal, but it sounds quite good. I think we should do trio records, they might be more relaxed."

Then – and this is always the ultimate motivation for Georgie – there is the urge to get brand new numbers out into the world: "There is the fact that I found that I've got about 10 new compositions which have never been recorded. And there's also a very nice song by Mike O'Neill who always keeps creeping back into my life, and I thought perhaps if I had the energy and the money, I would do one more album with the Blue Flames. I've already asked Madeline Bell to sing on a couple of songs, because there is one tribute song that I wrote for Steve Gray, which I think Madeline and I should do together, and I've asked Jim Mullen to play guitar on a couple of tracks."

The songs he talks about from time to time are "Drinking and Thinking" with the music supplied by Bob Rockwell, for which he created the lyrics himself. We will get

"Moanin'", where he wrote the text and the music is supplied by Bobby Timmons. There is a lovely previewed Calypso number, which he played at Ronnie Scott's in 2013, called "The Caribbean Way" and his equally Scott's tested "Mose Knows". Then we can hope for his version of the title track of a recent Ben Sidran album called "Don't Cry For No Hipster" and also "Hooglin'" which Sidran composed to lyrics by Georgie.

Shortly after having talked about getting tired, Georgie got ill for a while. But the new year, 2014, saw him up and playing again, and we can be almost sure that the creative juices will also be visiting him again. After all, even more than seven years ago he said that the album that would eventually surface in 2009 would be "my last LP!" Long may he be playing – and release long-players!!

The World Wide Star or The World Wide Friend

As one of this globe's leading Jazz singers, stage personality and Hammond hero, the questions that remains over five decades now as to why Georgie isn't a worldwide mega star. Well, first of all, Fame has surely been operating worldwide ever since "Yeh Yeh": working all over Scandinavia, central and also southern Europe, Canada, the USA, Brazil, Australia, Hong Kong, Saudi Arabia, Japan, you name them.

But frankly, the notion of an enormous American 40-date stadium tour, no matter how many hits and smash albums could have been amassed, seems downright ludicrous: Because it wouldn't fit the man's personality. Time and time again, Georgie has pointed out to every enquirer that he's only "working for friends now", and the term "now" has rung true for at least thirty years. He is much more comfortable in a Copenhagen or Croatian club than in a stadium, would rather see eye to eye with 50 dedicated listeners than an anonymous crowd.

Besides, he has had enough big halls with Van Morrison's band, The Rhythm Kings and Big Bands to last him a lifetime of a spontaneous, purely hypothetical hunger for the masses. Of course, Georgie could have retaliated when Matt Bianco hit with a new version of "Yeh Yeh" in 1984, starting a massive campaign to get his version back in. Naturally, he could have built on that prestigious *Prix Billie Holiday* which he got from Paris in the year 2000 for *Poet In New York*, could have undertaken a long French tour. As late as this year 2014, why not properly promote the wonderful Musical *Singer*, organize ads, mention it at gigs, work it into the repertoire?

"Our books are full" he grinned when he recently saluted Chris Farlowe on sharing the bill in Germany, and for the autumn of 2014, this means romantic gigs like the Ropetackle Arts Centre in Shoreham-By-Sea and big do's like the Royal Albert Hall *Blues Fest* where Georgie Fame and The Blue Flames will collaborate with *Sound Venturer* Elvis Costello. Georgie loves what he's doing, always has done. He is travelling the world, he is combining all the eclectic musical styles which he values. He thrives as the eternal storyteller. Georgie can be so charming, and you might hear a song you got seven versions of – you'll want his particular reading. An organized career plan would mean he'd lose that independence of the worldwide musical ambassador who can board another plane on a whim.

And so, is this all? By no means – this book could have five volumes, if you really dig deep into the archives, and if you let Fame carry the Flame(s) on for a while longer, on record and on stage, too. After all, John Mayall finished his current tour as an 80 year old, and asked why he sets up amps and drums himself, was found quipping: "Why sit around and pay someone else to do it?" That's the Fame spirit, too, and as far as many of us know the man, he will pick up the phone, agree to do the gig and tell you his modest conditions.

Let's keep Georgie keeping on – there's nothing else, and nothing better, to do!

Acknowledgements

My sincere thanks go to Georgie Fame a.k.a. Clive Powell – the man himself. Ever since 1982, Georgie – as he prefers to be called by me – has always patiently answered my questions: from the stage, backstage, in hotels, pubs, on the fringe of open-air venues and during long car journeys to and fro one of his "favourite hubs", Düsseldorf Airport, and in our garden, too. He never ever gave me the feeling of "Oh no, not him again", (though I certainly would not have blamed him), and he duly read the manuscript of an earlier draft and spent hours going through details. Any cock-ups now will be entirely my fault, whose else?

Tristan Powell – "Brother Tristan on the guitar" – as well as James Powell – "Brother James on the drums" – have been ever so helpful as well as charming and informative interview partners, giving accounts of their childhood as well as Blue Flames comradeship, always showing a deep affection and understanding of their multi-faceted dad. Ever so much obliged, fellows, even though you call me "Oxford" ☺.

Long, enjoyable, and also unforgettable pub sessions were spent with Fame's Flames Alan Skidmore (tenor sax) and Anthony Kerr (vibraphone) at *The Mops & Blooms* pub in Borehamwood, North London. At different times, Guy Barker ("bugler") and Nick Payn (sax, flute) as well as the guitarists Ronnie Johnson, gave me generous chunks of their time. Thanks for many comments that really matter.

My good friends Andy Fairweather Low and Zoot Money also had all the time in the world for Georgie and me, while they could well have asked why it wasn't time for their own biographies to take shape. Madeline Bell and, more than a decade ago now, the late Dick Heckstall-Smith contributed valuable insights. I am grateful to them as well.

Jon Hiseman, on the other hand, just had his own history out of the way via *Playing The Band* (see bibliography), but he still had the patience to be my backstage storyteller, too, on a Colosseum tour, just like my dear old Hamburg Blues Band friend Chris Farlowe. And let's not forget firm Fame admirer Bill Wyman. Interesting aspects were added by the Ronnie Scott's Club soundman and renowned studio engineer, Miles Ashton, who happens to be the son of the legendary National Youth Jazz Orchestra leader, Bill Ashton. Thanks a bundle.

Long and informative telephone calls were spent with Georgie's singing partner Annie Ross, Blue Flames bass players Geoff Gascoyne and Alec Dankworth, drummer Jamie Oldaker, guitarist Colin Green, legendary horn blowers Mick Eve and Art Themen, and, about a year before his recent passing, Georgie's Larry Parnes partner Duffy Power – who would remember getting introduced to "the wrong kind of woman" even half a century after the rendezvous, just like John Mayall realized on the phone that Georgie had been the only artist to ever solicit a song from him. Thanks to all of you.

Several letters were written to Alan Price for an interview. Alan is known as a very private and often shy character, and I duly respect this, of course.

Instead of a therapeutic coach, I have to be very thankful to my good friend and GF buff António Alfaiate – for going "How's your book coming along?" for years and years and supplying me with copies of rare stuff, for instance Swedish Big Band LPs. His calls for discipline were all the more severe because, first of all, he was right about my resistance to put the lid on quotes and get on with it, but I have also suspected him to know more about Georgie Fame than I do. He duly read my book, opened his archive of Bill Wyman-esque dimensions and came up with numerous helpful remarks.

My friend and music journalist, guitarist and singer Alan Tepper read the text as well, using up about thirty red felt pens in order to suggest a lot of invaluable changes, additions and streamlining.

Fellow writer, and before long a good friend, too, Colin Harper, author of the fabulous 2014 biography *Bathed In Lightning – John McLaughlin, the 60s and the Emerald beyond*, and many others, scrutinized the way I happen to use the English language, and in the process came up with valuable suggestions.

Danke schön to my lay-outer and true comrade Thomas Auer, for invaluable aesthetic advice, constant and patient e-mail assistance – he's the man with the eternally impeccable taste, a cool eye and the clear view.

A grateful thank you to cartoon artist and painter Johannes Saurer for his skills and sensitivity to come up with the wonderful cartoon of the "Nicotine & Tar" singing Georgie – what a Single cover that would have been for the lost Island Records song!

Welcome assistance, appraisal and advice have come from my long-standing, brilliant and reliable New York agent, Barbara Jacobs, the lady with the knack for confidence and contacts. I am obliged to my co-writer of the 1990s, Roland Schmitt from Eschringen, Saarland, for pointing out the Mod and Small Faces quotes from his part of our mutual *Happy Boys Happy – The Story of the Small Faces*.

Thanks to Michael Ackermann from Wuppertal, ardent follower of both Georgie Fame and Alan Price's careers ever since the late 1960s, who supplied some thrilling paraphernalia – like private snapshots and Fan Club brochures, which added colour to times in Georgie's life when I already listened, but was too young to have been around "the scene".

I am also obliged for assistance and attention to detail to Fame followers on the net, including Alan Ladlow for sonic nuggets, Syd Kreft and Michael Bedford, Gavin Paterson, Nick Rossi, Mike Masterton and Alan Durrant for corrections, insights and additions. To Andy Fairweather Low's and Joe Brown's manager John Taylor for contacts, my bass player Roger Clarke-Johnson for Bluesville Memories, Harry Shapiro for kind advice, Good Times main man Fabian Leibfried and former boss and founder Peter Seeger and Westfalen Blatt's Wolli Wotke for rare photo material

Who is that strange man typing away, glued to his monitor, on the phone at night, on the road to gigs, making Georgie Fame a part of the family by having him crawl out of every loudspeaker and screen in house, garden and cars?

Warm and grateful thanks to my wife and best friend Senta for not only keeping up with all this research and rewriting, but encouraging a potentially never-ending story via endless cups of tea, gentle pats on the back, phone calls and stylistic suggestions.

Interviewees A-Z

Miles Ashton
Guy Barker
Madeline Bell
Alec Dankworth
Mick Eve
Andy Fairweather Low
Chris Farlowe
Geoff Gascoyne
Colin Green
Dick Heckstall-Smith (+)
Jon Hiseman
Bernie Holland
Ronnie Johnson
Anthony Kerr
John Mayall
Ian McLagan
Zoot Money
Jamie Oldaker
Nick Payn
Clive Powell (Georgie Fame)
James Powell
Tristan Powell
Duffy Power (+)
Annie Ross
Lasse Samuelsson
Alan Skidmore
Art Themen
Geno Washington
Bill Wyman

Discography

SINGLES

Baby Baby (Don't You Worry)/Prince Of Fools (1962 Decca 11497) The Blue Flames join Perry Ford & The Sapphires, UK

Change Of Plan/Little Gloria (1963 R&B JB 113) The Blue Flames join Clive & Gloria UK

Orange Street/J.A. Blues (October 1963 R&B JB 114) The Blue Flames, UK

Stop Right Here/Rik's Tune (December 1963 R&B JB 126) The Blue Flames, UK

Shake Some Time/Comin' Home (1963 R&B JB127) The Blue Flames with Ronnie Gordon UK

Do The Dog/Shop Around (January 1964 Columbia DB 7193), UK

Do Re Mi/Green Onions (April 1964 Columbia DB 7255) UK (B-side F: **Let The Sunshine In**)

Bend A Little/I'm In Love With You (July 1964 Columbia DB 7328) UK

Yeh Yeh/Preach And Teach (December 1964 Columbia DB 7428) UK #1 (N, S, D picture sleeves, Swedish B-side **Baby Please Don't Go**, no sax-solo in US Yeh Yeh)

Yeh Yeh (German language version)/Humpty Dumpty (German language version) (1964 Columbia C 22 909) Germany, picture sleeve, also *The In-Crowd Box* Set (Verve Universal)

In The Meantime/Telegram (February 1965, Columbia DB 7494) UK #22, picture sl NL, N, S, DK

Like We Used To Be *(Powell)*/**It Ain't Right** *(Powell)* (July 1965 Columbia DB 7633) UK #33

Blue Monday/Like We Used To Be *(Powell)* (1965 Columbia CH 3100) NL picture sleeve
(US Imperial 66125, Blue Monday is B-side)

Something/Outrage (October 1965 Columbia DB 7727) UK #23

Getaway *(Powell)*/**El Bandido** *(Powell)* (June 1966 Columbia DB 7946) UK #1 NL picture sleeve (Turkish B-side **Ride Your Pony**)

Sunny/Don't Make Promises (September 1966 Columbia DB 8015) U K #13, picture sleeve NL, S

Sitting In The Park/Many Happy Returns (December 1966 Columbia DB 8096) UK #12
picture sleeves NL, S, N, also India, AUS, South Africa

Sweet Thing/Last Night (1966 Columbia DB 2315) Sweden

Last Night/Funny How Time Slips Away (1967 Imperial 66299) US

Because I Love You *(Powell)*/**Bidin' My Time** ('Cos I Love You) *(Powell)* (March 1967 CBS 20 2587) UK #15 picture sleeve, also in D, N, F, NL, no pic US, CAN, AUS, NZ

Knock On Wood/Roadrunner (1967 CBS 2781) picture sleeve D, NL, F (promo only in UK CBS 5946 backed with **Didn't Want to Have To Do It**

Try My World *(Powell/Landesman)*/**No Thanks** *(Powell/Colton)* (August 1967 CBS 2945) U K #37 picture sleeve NL, DK, F, N

Nel Tuo Mondo (Try My World – Italian language version) *(Powell/Landesman)*/**No Thanks** *(Powell/Colton)* (1967 CBS) Italy

Celebration/Try My World *(Powell/Landesman)* (1967 CBS 33529) Brazil

The Mini Mob (Instrumental by The Mino Mob)/**Words** (August 1967 Lyntone LYN 1402) UK promo acetate

Knock On Wood/Roadrunner (August 1967 CBS 2781) D, NL, F

The Ballad Of Bonnie And Clyde/Beware Of The Dog *(Powell)* (December 1967 CBS 3124) UK (#1) also US, CAN, picture sleeves D, F, NL, DK, E, PT, J

The Ballad Of Bonnie And Clyde/Nel Tuo Mondo (Try My World sung in Italian) *(Powell/ Landesman)* (1968 CBS 3254) I, picture sleeve also **La Ballata Di Bonnie E Clyde/Try My World**, (1968 CBS 3307), again with a picture sleeve. (Later, the Italian A-side came backed with "Come Mai" by James Royal (1968 CBS ODJBH 72)

Bullets Laverne/St. James Infirmary (1968 CBS 3495) D picture sleeve

By The Time I Get To Phoenix/For Your Pleasure *(Powell)* (CBS 3526) UK; picture sleeves F, DK

Cuando Vuelva A Phoenix (By The Time I Get To Phoenix)/**Lado A Lado** (Side By Side) (1968 CBS 21939) Argentina picture sleeve at 33 rpm (CBS 90 020) Chile picture sleeve

Hideaway/Kentucky Child (Epic 5 10347) U. S. & Canada, S, N picture sleeves

Kentucky (Kentucky Child, Italian language version)/**La Donna Che Sogno** (Hideaway, Italian language version) (1968 CBS 3582) I, picture sleeve

Chica De Kentucky (Kentucky Child)/**Escondite** (Hideaway) (1968 CBS 21978) Argentina

Peaceful/Hideaway (June 1969 CBS 4295) UK #16; D, POR, NL, N picture sleeves

Someone To Watch Over Me/For Your Pleasure *(Powell)* (1969 Epic 5 10402) US

Down Along The Cove/I'll Be Your Baby Tonight (1969 Epic 5 10477) US & Canada

Seventh Son/Fully Booked *(Powell/Ryan)* (November 1969 CBS 4659) UK #25; DK, D, F, N, NL, P & E picture sleeves

Somebody Stole My Thunder/Entertaining Mr. Sloane *(Powell/Ryan)*(May 1970 CBS 5035)UK

Fire And Rain/Someday Man (August 1970 CBS 5131) UK, US B-side **The Movie Star Song** (Epic 5 10640)

Knock On Wood/Didn't Want To Have To Do It (February 1971 CBS 5946) UK

Rosetta/John And Mary Georgie Fame and Alan Price (1971 CBS 7108) UK #11 NL, D, PORT, N, AUS picture sleeves

Follow Me/Sergeant Jobsworth *(Powell)* Georgie Fame and Alan Price (1971 CBS 7602) UK; NL, DK, YU, E picture sleeves

Hey Baby (I'm Getting Ready) *(Fame)*/**City Hicker** *(Fame)* (July 1972 Reprise K 14191) UK

Don't Hit Me When I'm Down *(Fame)*/**Street Lights** Georgie Fame and Alan Price (1973 Reprise K 14230) UK; NL picture sleeve

Everlovin' Woman/That Ol' Rock And Roll *(Fame/Ryan)* (September 1974 Island WIP 6213) UK, D (Island 13618 AT) D picture sleeve (US B-side "**Ozone**")

The Ali Shuffle *(Fame/Ryan)*/**Round Two** *(Fame)* (December 1974 Island WIP 6218) U K
NL picture sleeve

Yes Honestly *(Fame/Ryan)*/**Lily** *(Fame/Ryan)* (September 1976 Island WIP 6279) UK

Sweet Perfection *(Fame/Ryan)*/**Thanking Heaven** *(Fame/Ryan)* (June 1976 Island WIP 6311) UK

Daylight/Three Legged Mule *(Fame)* (1977 Island WIP 6384 and 1 DJ 25) UK 7" and 12"

A Different Dream *(Fame/Landesman)*/**Ollie's Party** *(Fame)* (March 1979 Pye 7N46184) UK

Maybe Tomorrow/Cat's Eyes *(Fame)* (September 1979 Pye 7P/12P139) UK

Give A Little More/Give A Little More (Dub Version) (1980 PRT 7P 194 and PRT 12P 194) UK 7" and 12"

Red Arrows Theme *(Powell)* Famous Flamingo Orchestra/**Talkback** (1980 Rif Raf RAF 1) UK picture sleeve

Drip Drop *(Carmichael/Gilbert/Fame)*/**One Morning In May** The Famous Flamingo Orchestra (January 1981 Bald Eagle BEE 181) UK

Hong Kong Blues/The Old Music Master, Georgie Fame & Annie Ross (July 1981 Bald Eagle BEE 182) UK

The Hurricane *(Fame)*/**The Hurricane Part 2** *(Fame)* (1982 My Records MY 001 UK RCA Victor PB 60002 Sweden) picture sleeves

Makin' Whoopee/In Goodmansland Medley: Let's Dance/Stompin' At The Savoy/Rose Room/After You've Gone/Sing, Sing, Sing/Goodbye, with Sylvia Vrethammar (1983 Sonet 12T 10113) Sweden

I Love Jamaica/Everything I Own (1983 Telefunken 6 13710) D picture sleeve

Swinging On A Star/I Feel Like Loving You (with Patti Boulaye) (1984 Hollywood Records HWD 016)

Samba (Toda Menina Baiana Mix) *(Gilberto/Fame)*/**Samba** (Toda Menina Baiana 7" Edit) *(Gilberto/Fame)*/**Willow King** *(Fame/Lycett Green)* (1986 Chrysalis/Ensign ENYX 605) UK picture sleeve 7" and picture sleeve 12" (Samba also as "Ipanema Beach Party" remix)

Go For It/I Still Care About Us *(Fame)* (1989 Food For Thought YUM 119) UK picture sl

Moondance (edited version 4:52)/**Yeah Yeah** (edited version 4:05)/**Georgia** (1992 Go Jazz vBr 2043 8) CD single, D

The Blues And Me/unknown further track(s) (1992 Go Jazz CD single) D

Maybe It's Because Of Love/How Long Has This Been Going On/Roll With Me Baby (1992 Go Jazz GoJ/vBr 2104 8) D CD single

Summertime In The Park (2002 EMI 7243 5507902 2) NL one track CD single

Selected rarities:
In 1966, there was an unreleased acetate of **Funky Mama** by Georgie Fame, backed with "Things We Said Today" by The Sandpipers on Emidisc BBC X103/YLP117 in the UK.

There was an odd release in 1967 of **By The Time I Get To Phoenix**, backed with "Sounds Of Silence" by Simon And Garfunkel (CBS Special Product WB 732) UK

EPs (EXTENDED PLAY 45'S, 2 SONGS EACH SIDE)
(EPs with identical titles are listed more than once only if the track listing differs)

Rhythm & Bluebeat (April 1964 Columbia SEG 8334) 1980 UK reissue **Blue Beat** (RSO 2252 136) Madness/Tom Hark Goes Blue Beat/Humpty Dumpty/One Whole Year Baby

Rhythm And Blues At The Flamingo (November 1964 Columbia SEG 8382) UK #8
Night Train/Parchman Farm/Work Song/Baby Please Don't Go

Do The Dog (1964 Columbia ESRF 1516) France
Do The Dog/Let The Good Times Roll/Shop Around/Baby Please Don't Go

Fame At Last (March 1964 Columbia SEG 8393) U. K.
Get On The Right Track, Baby/Point Of No Return/I Love The Life I Live/Gimme That Wine

Yeh Yeh (1964 Columbia ESRF 1618) France
Yeh Yeh/Preach And Teach/Do Re Mi/Let The Sunshine In

Yeh Yeh – different track listing (1965 EMI/HMV La Voz EPL 14 146) Spain
Yeh Yeh/Preach And Teach/I'm In Love With You/Bend A Little

In The Meantime (1965 Columbia ERSF 1645) France
In The Meantime/Get On The Right Track, Baby/Telegram/Pride And Joy

Fats For Fame (May 1965 Columbia SEG 8406) UK #15
No No/Blue Monday/So Long/Sick And Tired

Like We Used To Be (1965 Columbia ERSF 1706) France
Like We Used To Be *(Powell)*/It Ain't Right *(Powell)*/Monkeying Around/The Monkey Time

Move It On Over (October 1965 Columbia SEG 8454) UK: Move It On Over/Walking The Dog/Hi Heel Sneakers/Rockin' Pneumonia And The Boogie Woogie Flu

Something (1965 Columbia ERSF 1751) France
Something/Walking The Dog/Outrage/High Heel Sneakers

Getaway (December 1966 Columbia SEG 8518) UK #7
Getaway *(Powell)*/See Saw/Ride Your Pony/Sitting In The Park

Get Away (1966 Columbia ERSF 1796) France
Getaway *(Powell)*/Music Talk/Dr. Kitch/El Bandido *(Powell)*

Get Away (1966 Columbia EPOC 40008) Israel
Getaway *(Powell)*/El Bandido *(Powell)*/Something/Outrage

Get Away (1966 Columbia SLEM 2250) Portugal
Get Away *(Powell)*/El Bandido *(Powell)*/My Girl/Sweet Thing

Sunny (1966 EMI/HMV La Voz EPL 14 301) Spain
Sunny Don't Make Promises/Getaway *(Powell)*/El Bandido *(Powell)*

Sitting In The Park (1966 Columbia ERSF 1751) F
Sitting In The Park/Sweet Thing/Ride Your Pony/The World Is Round

Sitting In The Park (1967 EMI/HMV La Voz EPL 14 335) E
Sitting In The Park/Ride Your Pony/Many Happy Returns/See Saw

Georgie Fame (1967 CBS EP 6363) UK #2, P
Knock On Wood/All I'm Asking *(Powell)*/Close The Door/Didn't Want To Have To Do It

By The Time I Get To Phoenix (1967 CBS 6509) P
By The Time I Get To Phoenix/For Your Pleasure *(Powell)*/Kentucky Child/Hideaway

The Ballad Of Bonnie And Clyde (1967 CBS 6449) P
The Ballad Of Bonnie And Clyde/Beware Of The Dog *(Powell)*/Try My World *(Powell/Landesman)*/No Thanks *(Powell/Colton)*

Georgie Fame Sings The Ballad Of Bonnie And Clyde (1967 CBS – BG 465040) NZ
The Ballad Of Bonnie And Clyde/River's Invitation/You're Driving Me Crazy/It Could Happen To You

The Ballad Of Bonnie And Clyde (1967 CBS 6442, 33 rpm) IL
The Ballad Of Bonnie And Clyde/Beware Of The Dog *(Powell)*/Because I Love You *(Powell)*/Bidin' My Time *(Powell)*

La Balada De Bonnie Y Clyde (1968 CBS EPC 806) MEX
La Balada De Bonnie Y Clyde (The Ballad Of Bonnie And Clyde)/Esperando Que Me Quieras (Bidin' My Time) *(Powell)*/Porque Te Amo (Because I Love You) *(Powell)*/Cuidadao Con El Perro (Beware Of The Dog) *(Powell)*

The Ballad Of Bonnie And Clyde (1968 Epic 5 26368) US 7" 33 rpm (For jukeboxes only)
The Ballad Of Bonnie And Clyde/Ask Me Nice/Exactly Like You/Someone To Watch Over Me/Blue Prelude/Side By Side

Seventh Son (Sétimo Filho) (1970 Epic 22035, 7", 33rpm) Brazil
Seventh Son (Sétimo Filho)/Inside Story (A História Verdadeira) *(Fame/Ryan)*/Fully Booked (Lotado) *(Fame/Ryan)*/Ho Ho Ho *(Fame / Coppes)*

GEORGIE FAME SUNG SONGS A–Z

Abide With Me	*Walking Wounded*
Accentuate The Bass	*Poet in NY, Husby Dedications*
A Different Dream	Single A-side, *Right Now!*
A House Is Not A Home	*Georgie Does His Thing With Strings*
After You've Gone (in Medley)	*In Goodmansland*
Airmail Special	*In Goodmansland*
Alexander's Ragtime Band	*In Goodmansland*
All About My Girl	*Fame At Last*
All I Know	*Tone Wheels A Turnin'*
Am I Wasting My Time?	*Seventh Son*
And I Love Her	*Georgie Does His Thing With Strings*
Anthem For A Band	*Charlestons*, Concertgebouw Orchestra
Any Way The Wind Blows	Rhythm Kings *Any Way*
Ask Me Nice	*Third Face of Fame*
Baby Please Don't Go	*Flamingo*
Back On The Corner	*Tell Me Something*
Ballad Of Billy Joe	Fame & Price *Together*
Barefootin'	*My Favourite Songs, In-Crowd3*
Because I Love You	Single A-side
Bend A Little	*Flamingo+*
Benediction	*Tell Me Something*
Be True To Yourself	*Singer*
Beware Of The Dog	Single B-side *(Ballad of Bonnie and Clyde)*
Bidin' My Time	Single B-side *(Because I Love You)*
Big Brother	*Cool Cat Blues*
Big Easy Meat	*Tone Wheels A Turnin*
Big Town	*Singer*
Bird In A World Of People	*Seventh Son*
Black Head Chinaman	*In-Crowd3, Island Years*
Blue Condition	Fame & Price *Together*
Blue Monday	Single A-side, *Fats For Fame EP*
Blue Prelude	*Third Face of Fame*
Blues At The Bull	*Harry South Portraits, Birthday Big Band*
Blues For Ann-Marie	*Blues&Me, Endangered Species, Birthday BB*
Bluesology	*Two Faces of Fame, Shorty, Blues&Me,* etc
Blossom	*Seventh Son, Lost In A Lovers Dream*
Bouden Buck	*In-Crowd3*
BP Club After Midnight	*Tone Wheels A Turnin'*
Breezin' All The Way	*Relationships, Lost In A Lover's Dream*
Bring Back My Love	*Closing The Gap*
Bring It On Home	*My Favourite Songs*
Bullets Laverne	Single A-side, *Third Face of Fame*
Busted	Claes Janson *Best of Ray Charles*
But Not For Me	*Chet, Georgie On My Mind, Poet in NY,*
By The Time I Get To Phoenix	Single A-side
Cadillac Woman	Rhythm Kings *Just For A Thrill*
Call Up The Devil	*In-Crowd3, Island Years*
California Girl	*In-Crowd2, Island Years*
Can't Get My Rest At Night	Rhythm Kings *Groovin'*
Cat's Eyes	Single B-side *(Maybe Tomorrow) Friends* , etc
Celebration	Single A-side
Centerpiece	Grethe Kausland *Jazz My Way*
C'est La Vie	*Two Faces of Fame*
Charleston Proposition/The Charleston	*Charlestons*
Charleston Walk	*Charlestons*
Children Of My Mind	*Going Home*
City Hicker	Single B-side *(Hey Baby), All Me Own Work*
City Home	*Tell Me Something*
City Life	*City Life, Relationships, Birthday Big Band*
Cloud Cuckoo	*Walking Wounded*
Cool Cat Blues	*In-Crowd3, Cool Cat Blues, Name Droppin', Birthday*
Country Girl	*Right Now!*
Country Morning	*Georgie Fame*
Cross A Lazy Afternoon	*Right Now!*
Cry Me A River	*Lost In A Lover's Dream*
Dancing On The Ceiling	*Portrait Of Chet*
Dankeschön	Paul Kuhn Meets Bert Kaempfert
Dawn Yawn	*Sound Venture, Birthday, In-Crowd2*
Daylight	Single A-side, *In-Crowd2, First 30 Years*
Days Like This	Rhythm Kings *Any Way, On The Road Again*
Declaration Of My Love	*City Life, Three Line Whip, Poet in NY, Birthday*
Deep In A Dream	*Gary Husband From The Heart*
Didn't Want To Have To Do It	Single B-side *(Knock On Wood)*
Dig It	*Husby You Could See Me Now*
Do I Love You	*In-Crowd2*
Do It The Hard Way	*Two Faces, Portrait Of Chet, Poet in NY*
Don't Be That Way	*Georgie On My Mind*
Don't Hit Me When I'm Down	Single A-side/Price & Fame, *Friends*
Don't Make Promises	Single B-side *(Sunny)*
Don't Send Me Flowers	Live only so far
Don't You Worry 'Bout A Thing	*Right Now!*
Do Re Mi	Single A-side, *Hall Of Fame*
Do The Dog	Single, *Flamingo*
Do You Or Don't You/I Wanna Know	Rhythm Kings *Double Bill*
Don't Be That Way	*In Goodmansland*
Don't Blame Me	*Lost In A Lovers Dream*
Don't Getz Scared	*Name Droppin'*
Don't Try	*Two Faces of Fame*
Don't 'B' Movie Me	*Georgie Fame, In-Crowd2*
Don't Get Around Much Anymore	*City Life* (coupled with *I Let A Song*)
Donut Man	*Georgie Fame*
Doodlin'	*Poet In NY*
Down Along The Cove	Single A-side
Down For Double	Nigel Mooney *The Bohemian Mooney*
Down Home Girl	Rhythm Kings *Just For A Thrill*
Down For The Count	*Sound Venture*
Dream Pony	*All Me Own Work*
Dr. Kitch	*Sweet Things, In-Crowd3*
Drinking And Thinking	Live only so far
Drip Drop	Single A-side, *In Hoagland, Endangered*
Early In The Morning	*How Long Has This Been Going On*
Easy Lovin'	*Going Home*
Easy Street	Soundtrack *Glengary Glen Ross*
El Bandido	Single B-side *(Get Away)*
El Pussycat	*Two Faces of Fame*
Enkosi Dumisani	*Tone Wheels A Turnin'*
Entertaining Mr Sloane	Single B-side *(Somebody Stole My Thunder)*
Epilogue (The Game Of Life)	*Singer*
Eros Hotel	*Right Now!, Closing The Gap, No Worries* etc
Eso Beso	*Flamingo, In-Crowd1, Ricky Tick*
Every Knock Is A Boost	*Cool Cat Blues*
Everybody's Cryin' Mercy	*Blues &Me*
Everybody's Guessin'	*Relationships*
Everlovin' Woman	Single A-side, *Georgie Fame, In-Crowd2*
Everything Happens To Me	*Georgie Does His Thing With Strings, Chet.*
Everything I Own	Single B-side *(I Love Jamaica), Closing The Gap*
Everything Is Broken	Live only so far
Exactly Like You	*Third Face*
Feed Me	*Sound Venture*
Feet On The Ground	Sandi Russell *Sweet Thunder*
Fever	Rhythm Kings *Europe*
Fire And Rain	Single A-side
Flamingo Allnighter	*Charlestons*
Flying Home	*In Goodmansland*
FNG (Mr Nobody)	*Relationships*
Follow Me	Single with Alan Price
Foolish Child	*Going Home*
For My Lady	*Birthday Big Band*
For Your Pleasure	Single B-side *(By The Time I Get To Phoenix)*
From Now On	*Singer*
Fully Booked	Single B-side *(Seventh Son), Seventh Son, Shorty*
Funny How Time Slips Away	*Sweet Things, Sound Venture, Right Now!*
Gee Baby Ain't I Good For You	Rhythm Kings *Any Way*
Georgia On My Mind	*Hoagland, Fame-Ericsson-Samuelson, Cool Cat Blues*
Get Away	Single A-side, *My Favourite Songs, No Worries*
Get On The Right Track, Baby	*Fame AtLast, Hall Of Fame, In-Crowd1*
Gimme That Wine	*Fame At Last*
Girl Talk	*Georgie Does His Thing With Strings, Poet In NY*
Give A Little More	Single A-side, *Closing The Gap*
Give Him A Hand	*In-Crowd2, Island Years*
Go For It	Single A-side
Go Go	*Portrait Of Chet*, NDR Big Band *Bravissimo*
Good Bait – Ladybird	*Husby Dedications*
Goodbye (Goodmansland Medley)	*In Goodmansland*
Going Home	*Going Home*
Gotta Get On This Train	Lisa Stansfield *Swing*
Green Back Dollar Bill	*Two Faces*
Green Onions	Single B-side *(Do-Re-Mi), Fame At Last*
Green Park Blues	Kate St John *Indescribable Night*
Guantanamo By The Sea	*Tone Wheels A Turnin'*
Guess Who I Saw Today	*Georgie Does His Thing With Strings*
Hall St. Jive	*Georgie Fame, In-Crowd2*
Happiness	*Going Home*
Heathrow Shuffle	*How Long Has This Been Going On*
Here And Now	Fame & Price *Together*
Hey Baby (I'm Getting Ready)	Single A-side, *All Me Own Work*

454

Hideaway	Single A-side	Let The Good Times Roll	Flamingo, Bootleg Kings Europe, Claes Janson Ray
High Heel Sneakers	Something EP	Let The Rest Of The World Go By	Fame-Ericsson-Samuelson
Hit That Jive, Jack	Rhythm Kings Double Bill	Let The Sunshine In	Fame At Last, Ricky Tick, Hall Of Fame, In-Crowd1
Hit The Road, Jack	Rhythm Kings Europe, Travlin' Band	Lily	Single B-side (Yes Honestly)
Hoagland	In Hoagland	Like We Used To Be	Single A-side, Hall Of Fame
Ho Ho Ho	Seventh Son	Lil' Darling	Sound Venture, Hall Of Fame
Hole In My Soul	Rhythm Kings Struttin'	Lil' (Little) Pony	Sound Venture, Cool Cat Blues, Birthday Big Band
Home Is Where Your Heart Is	Fame & Price Together	Limehouse Blues	In Goodmansland
Hong Kong Blues	Single A-side, In Hoagland	L In L.A.	That's What Friends Are For
Hot Stuff	In-Crowd3	Little Samba	Right Now!, No Worries, Endangered Species,
How Blue	Charlestons, Lost In A Lovers Dream		Birthday
How Long Has This Been Going On	Single B-side (Maybe It's)Chet, Blues&Me	Lost In A Lover's Dream	Lost In A Lovers Dream
Humpty Dumpty	Flamingo, Blue Beat EP, Ricky Tick	L.O.V.E.	Paul Kuhn Meets Bert Kaempfert
Humpty Dumpty German	Single B-side (Yeh-Yeh D), In-Crowd3	Lovely Day	That's What Friends Are For
Hymn For Him	Charlestons	Lovey Dovey	Sound Venture
		Lush Life	Poet in NY
I Ain't Got Nothing But The Blues	Blues &Me		
I Almost Lost My Mind	Blues &Me	Madness	BlueBeat EP, In-Crowd3
I Am Missing You	Sound Venture	Makin' Whoopee	Single A-side, Goodmansland, Rhythm Kings
I Believe In Love	Going Home		Travlin'
I Can't Dance	Rhythm Kings Double Bill	Many Happy Returns	Single B-side (Sitting In The Park), Sound Venture
I Can't Get Started With You	Lost In A Lover's Dream	Mars & Venus	Relationships
I Can't Take It Much Longer	Fame & Price Together	Maybe In The Spring Again	Georgie Does His Thing With Strings
I Don't Care Who I Dance With	That's What Friends Are For	Maybe It's Because Of Love	Single A-side, Blues &Me
I Feel Like Loving You	Single B-side (Swinging On A Star)	Maybe Tomorrow	Single A-side, That's What Friends Are For
If I Didn't Mean You Well	That's What Friends Are For	Mellow Yellow	Third Face of Fame
If You Live	Walking Wounded, Nights Of The Blues Table	Melody	Rhythm Kings Struttin', Just For A Thrill
I Let A Song Go Out Of My Heart	City Life (coupled with Don't Get Around)	Memphis In June	Georgie On My Mind
I Lost My Sugar In Salt Lake City	Charlestons	Mercy Mercy Mercy/Vanlose Stairway	Three Line Whip, Name Droppin'
I Love Jamaica	Single A-side, Closing The Gap	Miss Bitch	Big Cool Collective
I Love The Life I Live	Fame At Last, Cool Cat Blues	Moanin'	Live only so far
I'll Sing You	Tone Wheels A Turnin'	Money (That's What I Want)	In-Crowd1
I'm A Gambler	In-Crowd3	Monkeying Around	Fame At Last, Ricky Tick
I'm In Love With You	Flamingo+	Moody's Mood For Love	Ricky Tick, Hudik Montreux
I'm In Love With Ya Baby	Right Now!	Moondance (+ Blue Moon)	Single A-side, Cool Cat Blues, Walking Wounded
I'm In The Mood For Love	Fame At Last, Grethe Kausland Jazz My Way	Mose Knows	Live only so far
In Goodmansland Medley	Single B-side, In Goodmansland	Motorvatin'Mama	Rhythm Kings Struttin'
Inside Story	Seventh Son, Shorty	Move It On Over	EP Move It On Over, Ricky Tick
In The Meantime	Single A-side, Ricky Tick, Hall Of Fame	Music Talk	Sweet Things
I Put A Spell On You	Birthday Big Band	My Buddy	Walking Wounded
I Still Care About Us/You	Single B-side (Go For It), Endangered Species, City Life	My Foolish Heart	Lost In A Lovers Dream
In The Wee Small Hours	Georgie Does His Thing With Strings	My Heart Stood Still	Trudy Kerr My Old Flame
I Thought That's What You Like About Me	Lisa Stansfield Swing	My Girl	Sweet Things
I Want To Know	Blues &Me, Rhythm Kings Double Bill	My Resistance Is Low	In Hoagland
I'll Be Your Baby Tonight	Single B-side (Down Along The Cove)	My Second Home	Fame-Ericsson-Samuelson, Singer (Bell)
I'll Sing You	Geoff Gascoyne Keep It To Yourself	Mystery Train	Rhythm Kings Europe, Ride Again
Is It Really the Same	Seventh Son, Shorty		
It Ain't Right	Single A-side, No Worries	Narcolepsy	All Me Own Work
It	Relationships	Need Your Love So Bad	Georgie Does His Thing With Strings
It Could Happen To You	Two Faces of Fame, Portrait Of Chet, Poet In NY	Nel Tuo Mundo	Single A-side
It Don't Mean A Thing (If It Ain't Got...)	City Life	Nocitine And Tar	In-Crowd3, Island Years
It Happened To Me	Three Line Whip, Walking Wounded	Night Train	Flamingo
It Should Have Been Me	Cool Cat Blues, Birthday Big Band	No No	Fats For Fame EP
It's For Love The Petals Fall	Sound Venture	No, Not Much	Live only so far
It's Not Supposed To Be That Way	In-Crowd3	No Thanks	Single B-side (Try My World)
It Won't Hurt To Try	Going Home		
		Oh Georgia Moon	Fame-Ericsson-Samuelson
Jealous Girl	Rhythm Kings Double Bill	Oh Lady Be Good	No Worries, Georgie On My Mind
Jeannine	Live only so far	Ole Buttermilk Sky	No Worries
Jelly Jelly	Fame At Last+	Oliver's Gone	Shorty
Jimmy McGroove	Name Droppin', Birthday Big Band	Ollie's Party	Single B-side (Ollie's Party), Right Now!
John And Mary	Single B-side (Rosetta), Fame & Price	On A Misty Night	No Worries, Portrait Of Chet, Poet In NY
Johnny Too Bad	Georgie Fame, In-Crowd2	One For My Baby	Georgie On My Mind, Endangered Species
Jumpin' With Symphony Sid	Blues &Me, Van Night In San Francisco	One Room Country Shack	Shorty
Just For A Thrill	Rhythm Kings Just For A Thrill	One Whole Year Baby	Blue Beat EP, Fame AtLast+
Just One Of Those Things	In Goodmansland	Outrage	Single B-side (Something), Something EP
		Ozone	Georgie Fame
Kan Tsukete	Three Line Whip		
Keep Your Big Mouth Shut	Two Faces of Fame	Papa's Got A Brand New Bag	Sound Venture, Birthday Big Band
Kentucky Child	Single B-side (Hideaway)	Paperback Writer	Radelius From Me To You
Kentucky (Italian)	Single A-side	Parchman Farm	Flamingo, Shorty, No Worries
King Porter Stomp	In Goodmansland	Parker's Mood	Flamingo+, In-Crowd1, Hudik Montreux
Knock On Wood	Single A-side	Passed Me By	All Me Own Work, Blues&Me
		Pass It Around	Going Home
La Donna Che Sogno	Single B-side (Kentucky)	Peaceful	Single A-side, Going Home
Lady Be Good	No Worries	Pink Champagne	Fame At Last
Lament For Chet	Portrait Of Chet	Point Of No Return	Fame At Last, Hall Of Fame, Harry South Portraits
Last Night	Single A-side, Ricky Tick, Sweet Things	Preach'n'Teach	Single B-side (Yeh Yeh), Charlestons, In-Crowd
Last Song	Right Now!	Pride And Joy	Fame At Last
Lawdy Miss Clawdy	My Favourite Songs		
Lay Me Down	Going Home	Rainy Day Woman # 12 & 35	Ben Sidran Dylan Different
Lean On Me	Closing The Gap	Rhythm King	Relationships, Rhythm Kings Groovin'
Leaving The City Behind	Georgie Fame	Red Top	Name Droppin'
Let's Dance (Goodmansland Medley)	In Goodmansland	Ride Your Pony	Single B-side (Get Away), Sweet Things

River's Invitation	*Two Faces of Fame*
Roadrunner	Single B-side *(Knock On Wood)*
Rocking Chair	*In Hoagland, Cool Cat Blues*
Roll With My Baby	Single B-side *(Roll With My Baby) Blues&Me*
Rollin' Blue	*Tone Wheels A Turnin'*
Rosetta	Single A-side, *Fame & Price, My Favourite Songs*
Rough Cut Diamond	*Rhythm Kings Groovin'*
Round Two	Single B-side *(The Ali Shuffle)*
Run Away With Me	*Closing The Gap*
Sack O'Woe/Centerpiece Blues Package	*How Long Has This Been Going On*
Samba	Single A-side
Sasketchewan Sunrise	*Shorty*
Saturday Night Fish Fry	*My Favourite Songs, No Worries*
Say When	*Relationships, Lost In A Lovers Dream*
Sea Of Heartbreak	*In-Crowd3, Island Years*
Seasons Change	*Husky If You Could See Me Now*
Second Honeymoon	*Tone Wheels A Turnin'*
See Saw	*Sweet Things*
Sergeant Jobsworth	Single B-side *(Follow Me)* with Alan Price
Seven Power	*All Me Own Work*, In-Crowd3
Seventh Son	Single A-side, *Seventh Son, Shorty*
Shop Around	Single B-side *(Do The Dog), Flamingo*
Sick And Tired	*Fats For Fame EP*
Side By Side	*Third Face of Fame*
Since I Fell For You	*Three Line Whip*
Sing Sing Sing (Goodmansland Medley)	*In Goodmansland*
Singer	*Singer, Birthday Big Band*
Singing Horn	*Tone Wheels, Lost In A Lover's Dream*
Sister Jane	*Going Home*
Sitting In The Park	Single A-side, *Sweet Things, That's What Friends Are For*
Skiing Blues	*Charlestons, Lost In A Lovers Dream*
Small Fry	*In Hoagland*
Small Town	*Singer*
So Long	*Fats For Fame EP*
Somebody's Gotta Move	*Geoff Gascoyne Keep It To Yourself*
Somebody Stole My Thunder	Single A-side, *Seventh Son, Shorty*
Some Day	*My Favourite Songs*
Someday Man	Single B-side *(Fire And Rain)*
Someone To Watch Over Me	Single A-side, *Third Face*
Something	Single A-side, *Something EP, Hall Of Fame, In-Crowd3*
Soon And Very Soon	*Fame-Ericson-Samuelson*
Soul Stomp	*Ricky Tick,* In-Crowd3
Stardust	*In Hoagland*
St. James Infirmary	Single B-side *(Bullets Laverne), Third Face*
Stompin' At The Savoy (Medley)	*In Goodmansland*
Stormy	*Going Home*
Stormy Weather	*Fame-Ericson-Samuelson*
Streamline Woman	*Rhythm Kings Groovin'*
Street Lights	Single B-side *(Don't Hit Me) w. Alan Price*
Strike Up The Band	*City Life, Birthday Big Band*
Summertime In The Park	Single 1-track
Sunny	Single A-side
Super Road	*All Me Own Work,* In-Crowd3
Survival	*Georgie Fame, Cool Cat Blues, Tone Wheels*
Sweet Georgia Brown	*In Goodmansland*
Sweet Perfection	Single A-side, *Fame-Ericsson-Samuelson, In-Crowd3*
Sweet Thing	Single A-side, *Sweet Things, Hall Of Fame*
Swinging On A Star	Single A-side (with Patti Boulaye)
Symphony Sid	*Poet in NY*
Telegram	Single B-side *(Meantime), FameAt Last*
Tell Me How Do You Feel	*Name Droppin'*
Tequila	*Seventh Son*
Thanking Heaven	Single B-side *(Sweet Perfection), In-Crowd2*
That Ol' Rock'n'Roll	Single B-side *(Everlovin' Woman), Georgie Fame.. Favourite*
That's How Strong My Love Is	*Fame & Price Together*
That's The Way It Goes	*Poet in NY, Hudik Dedications*
That's What Friends Are For	*That's What Friends Are For*
The Ali Shuffle	Single A-side, *In-Crowd2, First 30 Years*
The Ballad of Bonnie and Clyde	Single A-side, *Third Face, My Favourite Songs, Birthday*
The Blues And Me	*Blues & Me*
The Burdee Song	*Tone Wheels A Turnin'*
The Caribbean Way	Live only so far
The Dole Song	*Fame & Price Together*
The Fool's Paradise	*Georgie On My Mind*
The Hurricane	Single A-side, *First 30 Years*
The In Crowd	*Sweet Things,* In-Crowd1
The Joint Is Jumping/Keep On Truckin'	*Rhythm Kings Double Bill*
The Keeper Of The Blues	*Relationships, Birthday Big Band*
The Monkey Time	*Fame At Last*
The More I See You	*Portrait Of Chet*
The Movie-Star Song	Single B-side *(Fire And Rain)*
The Nearness Of You	*Grethe Kausland Jazz My Way*
The New Symphony Sid	*How Long Has This Been Going On*
The Old Music Master	Single B-side *(Hong Kong Blues),Hoagland*
The Preacher And The Bear	*In-Crowd2*
The Way You Do The Things You Do	*In-Crowd2*
The Whole World's Shaking	*Sweet Things*
The Wolf Gang	*Relationships*
The Woodshed	*Blues & Me, Walking Wounded*
The World Is Round	*Sweet Things*
There's No More Blue Time	*Relationships*
Things Ain't What They Used To Be	*Two Faces of Fame*
This Guy's In Love With You	*Georgie Does His Thing With Strings*
This Is A Gas	*Relationships*
This Is Always	*Third Face of Fame*
Three Blind Mice	*Sound Venture*
Three-Legged Mule	Single B-side *(Daylight), In-Crowd2*
Time I Moved On	*Fame & Price Together*
Times Are Getting Tougher Than Tough	*Hudik Montreux*
Tom Hark Goes Blue Beat 1964	*Blue Beat EP*
Tomorrow Night	*Rhythm Kings Groovin'*
Too Good To Be True	*All Me Own Work*
Too Shy To Say	*Right Now!*
Train	*All Me Own Work*
Try My World	Single A-side
Try'na Get Along With The Blues	*No Worries*
Tuned Into You	*Poet in NY, Birthday Big Band, Critchinson Scott Tribute*
Two Sleepy People	*In Hoagland, Grethe Kausland Jazz My Way*
Up A Lazy River	*In Hoagland*
Up Tight	*Closing The Gap*
Vanguard Road	*Tone Wheels A Turnin'*
Vinyl	*Three Line Whip, Name Droppin', Birthday Big Band*
Walking One And Only	*Rhythm Kings Travlin' Band*
Walking The Dog	*Something EP*
Was	*Tell Me Something, Name Droppin'*
We Were Always Sweethearts	*Georgie Fame*
What's New	*Georgie Does His Thing With Strings*
What You're Doing I Can Do	In-Crowd3
When I'm Sixty-Four	*Third Face of Fame*
When My Dreamboat Comes Home	*City Life*
Where Do You Go From Here?	*Singer*
Where's The Money?	*Rhythm Kings Double Bill*
Who's Kissing you Blues	*Georgie Does His Thing With Strings*
Wide-Eyed And Legless	*Charlestons, Lost In A Lovers Dream*
Will Carling	*Three Line Whip*
Willow King	Single B-side *(Samba)*
With My Eyes	Soundtrack: *To Kill A Clown*
Woe Is Me	*Georgie Does His Thing With Strings*
Wogan's Air	*Charlestons*
Words	Promo Acetate
Work Song	*Flamingo*
Yeh Yeh	Single A-side, *My Favourite Songs, No Worries, Cool Cat*
Yeh Yeh (German)	Single, *In-Crowd3*
Yellow Man	*Fame & Price Together*
Yes Honestly	Single A-side
Yes Indeed	*Fame-Ericsson-Samuelson*
You	*That's What Friends Are For, Relationships*
You Are There	*Three Line Whip*
You Came A Long Way From St. Louis	*Cool Cat Blues, Georgie On My Mind*
You Can Have Her	*Big Cool Collective*
You Can't Sit Down	*Flamingo*
You Make Me Feel So Young	*Trudy Kerr My Old Flame*
Your Face	*Charlestons*
You're Driving Me Crazy	*Two Faces oof Fame, Portrait Of Chet*
Your Mind Is On Vacation	*How Long Has This Been Going On*
You Turned The Tables On Me	*In Goodmansland*
Zavolo	*Three Line Whip, Walking Wounded*
Zulu	*Right Now!, No Worries, Name Droppin'*

ALBUMS (LPS AND CDS)
(Compilations are only selectively listed, after the regular albums. For the first thirty years of Compact Discs, copyright holders chose not to reissue any of the original early Georgie Fame albums – outside of Jaoan, anyway – before the era of CBS. Bootleggers jumped in and issued them all with bonus tracks. With respect to Georgie's legal body of work, these "re-issues" (disguised as "promo discs") are not featured here. On the other hand, those bona fide releases which Fame did not actively license either, but did not choose to go and fight actively, like the Croatian (HR) release *Georgie On My Mind* on Jazzette Records, got onto this selective list.) [26]

Rhythm and Blues at the Flamingo
LP (February 1964 Columbia 33SX 1599) LP reissue (1984 RSO SPELP 80) UK (Polydor CD UICY 93169) J
Night Train/Let The Good Times Roll/Do The Dog/Eso Beso/Work Song/Parchman Farm/ You Can't Sit Down/ Humpty Dumpty/Shop Around/Baby Please Don't Go

Rhythm and Blues at the Ricky Tick
LP (recorded 1965, R&B Records 1, released April 2014) Not a vintage release, but designed as one, exclusively presenting vintage material: live recordings and early studio Single tracks:
Let The Sunshine In/Monkeying Around/Eso Beso/Moody's Mood/Soul Stomp/In The Meantime/Move It On Over/Humpty Dumpty/Last Night//Orange Street (The Blue Flames)/ J.A. Blues (The Blue Flames)/Shake Some Time (Ronnie Gordon)/Rick's Tune (The Blue Flames)/Stop Right There (The Blue Flames)/Baby Baby (Perry Ford And The Sapphires)/ Little Gloria (Clive & Gloria)/Prince Of Fools (Perry Ford & The Sapphires)

Fame At Last
LP (September 1964 Columbia UK 33SX 1638, Columbia AUS OEX 9459) (UK #15) (Polydor CD UICY 93170) J
Get On The Right Track, Baby/Let The Sunshine In/Monkey Time/All About My Girl/ Point Of No Return/Gimme That Wine/Pink Champagne/Monkeying Around/Pride And Joy/Green Onions/I Love The Life I Live/I'm In The Mood For Love (Moody's Mood For Love) (CAN LP Capitol T 6122 and US Imperial LP-9282 (Stereo LP-12282) *Yeh Yeh* featured Yeh Yeh, no Green Onions, no All About My Girl (stereo re-issue 1969 as *Georgie Fame And The Blue Flames*) (Regal/Starline SRS 5002)

Sweet Things
LP (May 1966 Columbia SX 6043) UK (#4) (Polydor CD UICY 93171) J
Sweet Thing/See Saw/Ride Your Pony/Funny How Time Slips Away/Sitting In The Park/Dr. Kitch/My Girl/Music Talk/The In Crowd/The World Is Round/The Whole World's Shaking/ Last Night

26. See Addendum

Sound Venture
LP (October 1966 Columbia SX 6076) UK (#9), CD (Polydor UICY 93172) J, with the Harry South Big Band
Many Happy Returns/Down For The Count/It's For Love The Petals Fall/I Am Missing You *(Powell)*/Funny How Time Slips Away/Lil' Pony/Lovey Dovey/Lil' Darlin'/Three Blind Mice/ Dawn Yawn *(Powell)*/Feed Me/Papa's Got A Brand New Bag

Hall Of Fame
LP (Greatest Hits 1967 Columbia SX 6120) UK #12; AUS, Odeon ROU
Yeh Yeh/Sunny/Point Of No Return/Like We Used To Be *(Powell)*/Get On The Right Track, Baby/Outrage/Let The Sunshine In/Getaway *(Powell)*/Sitting In The Park/In The Meantime/ Something/Do Re Mi/Sweet Thing/Lil' Darlin'

The Two Faces Of Fame
LP (June 1967 CBS BPG 63018) mono (CBS SBPG 63018) stereo / CD (Columbia Rewind 477850 2) 1994 UK (#22), CD (Sony MHCP1253) J
Green Back Dollar/Things Ain't What They Used To Be/River's Invitation/Bluesology/ Don't Try/Keep Your Big Mouth Shut/You're Driving Me Crazy/C'est La Vie/Pussy Cat/It Could Happen To You/Do It the Hard Way

The Third Face Of Fame
LP (April 1968 CBS BPG 63293) mono (CBS SBPG 63293) UK (Sony CD MHCP1254) J
The Ballad Of Bonnie and Clyde/When I'm Sixty-Four/Ask Me Nice/Exactly Like You/ Someone To Watch Over Me/Blue Prelude/Bullets Laverne/This Is Always/Side By Side/St. James Infirmary/Mellow Yellow, also as:
The Ballad Of Bonnie And Clyde (1968 Epic LN 24368) Mono (Epic BN 26368) Stereo US
and Canada, and as Anni Ruggenti, E Altre Canzoni Dell'epoca – LP (CBS S 63293) Italy
La Balada De Bonnie Y Clyde (1968, CBS 8851) AR, with the song "Celebration"
Two Faces and Third Face came out on one CD (2006 Beat Goes On BGOCD708) UK

Seventh Son
LP (November 1969 CBS 63786) UK (CBS SBP 233775) AUS, CD (Sony MHCP1255) J
Seventh Son/Blossom *(Fame/Ryan)*/Inside Story *(Fame/Ryan)*/Am I Wasting My Time/ Is It Really The Same/Somebody Stole My Thunder/Ho Ho Ho *(Powell/Coppes)*/Bird In A World Of People/Fully Booked *(Fame / Ryan)*/Tequila

Georgie Does His Thing With Strings
LP (February 1970, recorded in 1969, CBS LP 63650) UK, CD (Sony MH CP1256) J
And I Love Her / Maybe In The Spring Again / In The Wee Small Hours / What's New

/ Woe Is Me / A House Is Not A Home / This Guy's In Love With You / Girl Talk / Who's Kissing You Blues *(Fame / Ryan)* / Everything Happens To Me / Guess Who I Saw Today / Need Your Love So Bad (1970 as Georgie Fame in Poland (Pronit XL 0993) mono (Pronit SXL 0993) stereo

Shorty featuring Georgie Fame
LP (1970 Epic BN 26563) US, CAN, NL, D (CD Sony MHCP1257) J
Oliver's Gone *(Fame)*/Bluesology/Saskatchewan Sunrise/Parchman Farm/Is It Really The Same/Seventh Son/Somebody Stole My Thunder/Inside Story *(Fame/Ryan)*/One Room Country Shack/Fully Booked *(Fame/Ryan)*

Going Home
LP (May 1971 CBS 64350) UK (2001 CD 1st World ESCA7849) (Sony MHCP986) J
I Believe In Love/It Won't Hurt To Try It/Going Home/Foolish Child/Sister Jane/ Peaceful/ Happiness/Children Of My Mind/Lay Me Down/Easy Lovin'/Pass It Around/ Stormy

Fame And Price/Price And Fame/Together Georgie Fame and Alan Price
LP (1972 LP CBS 64392) (1985 CBS Nice Price LP 32509) (1995 Columbia/Sony Rewind CD 480972 2) (Sony CD MHCP1258) J
Rosetta/Yellow Man/The Dole Song/Time I Moved On *(Powell)*/John And Mary/Here And Now/Home Is Where Your Heart Is/Ballad Of Billy Joe/That's How Strong My Love Is/Blue Condition I Can't Take It Much Longer

All Me Own Work
LP (August 1972 Reprise LP K 44183) UK (REP LP 44183) D
Super Road *(Fame)*/Too Good To Be True *(Fame)*/ Train *(Fame)*/Seven Power *(Fame)*/ City Hicker *(Fame)*/Narcolepsy *(Fame)*/Passed Me By *(Fame)*/Hey Baby (We're Getting Ready) *(Fame)*/Dream Pony *(Fame Ireland/Stewart)*

Georgie Fame
LP (August 1974 Island LP ILPS9293) UK (Island 88 335) D, NL (Island ILPS 9293) US
Everlovin' Woman/Don't "B" Movie Me *(Fame/Ryan)*/Donut Man/Ozone *(Fame/Ryan)*/ Leaving the City Behind *(Fame/Ryan)*/Country Morning/We Were Always Sweethearts/ Hall St. Jive/That Ol' Rock and Roll *(Fame/Ryan)*/Survival *(Fame/Ryan)*
(for US & CAN Johnny Too Bad instead of We Were Always Sweethearts/Hall St. Jive)

Right Now!
LP (March 1979, recorded in 1978, Pye LP NSPL 18600) UK, CAN (Pye PYC 6076) ZA (BMG CD BVCM 37868) J
A Different Dream *(Fame / Landesman)* / Funny How Time Slips Away / Little Samba *(Fame)* / I'm In Love With Ya Baby *(Fame)* / Ollie's Party *(Fame)* / Eros Hotel *(Fame*

/ *Landesman*) / 'Cross A Lazy Afternoon *(Fame / Lycett-Green)* / Country Girl *(Fame)* / Don't You Worry 'Bout A Thing / Too Shy To Say / Zulu *(Fame)* / Last Song *(Fame / Landesman)*

That's What Friends Are For
LP (October 1979 Pye LP N11) UK (Astor SPLP 1575) AUS, (BMG CD BVCM 37869) J
Maybe Tomorrow/Lovely Day/L In L.A. *(Fame)*/You *(Fame/Lycett-Green)*/I Don't Care Who I Dance With *(Fame/Lycett-Green)*/That's What Friends Are For/Don't Hit Me When I'm Down *(Fame)*/Sitting In The Park/If I Didn't Mean You Well/Cat's Eyes *(Fame)*

Closing The Gap with The Reggae Philharmonic Orchestra
LP (September 1980 Piccadilly LP N 137) UK, (BMG CD BVCM 37870) J
Give A Little More/Run Away With Me/I Love Jamaica/Eros Hotel *(Fame/Landesman)*/Everything I Own/Lean On Me/Up Tight/Bring Back My Love/Give A Little More (Dub Version) The album features Eddie "Tan Tan" Thornton as a special guest

In Hoagland '81 with Annie Ross & Hoagy Carmichael
LP (July 1981 Bald Eagle LP BELP 181) UK (DRG CDSL 5197) US (DRG CDSL 5197) 1987 A
The Old Music Master (with Annie Ross)/Hong Kong Blues (with Annie Ross)/Georgia On My Mind/One Morning In May (Famous Flamingo Orchestra)/My Resistance Is Low (with Annie Ross)/I Get Alone Without You Very Well (Annie Ross)/ Rockin' Chair (Hoagy Carmichael)/Drip Drop *(Carmichael/Gilbert/Fame)*/Stardust (with Annie Ross)/Up A Lazy River (with Annie Ross)/Small Fry (with Annie Ross)/Two Sleepy People (with Annie Ross)/ Hoagy's Help (Hoagy Carmichael)/Hoagland *(Fame)*

In Goodmansland with Sylvia Vrethammar
LP (1983 Sonet LP SNTF 908) UK (Powderworks LP POW 6071) AUS
Flying Home/Makin' Whoopee/King Porter Stomp/Limehouse Blues/Just One of Those Things/Don't Be That Way/Alexander's Ragtime Band/Sweet Georgia Brown/You Turned The Tables On Me/Airmail Special/Memories Of You/In Goodmansland Medley: Let's Dance, Stompin' At The Savoy, Rose Room, After You've Gone, Sing Sing Sing, Good-Bye

My Favourite Songs! featuring Zoot Money & Andy Fairweather Low
LP (1983 Teldec LP 6 25646) D, CD as **Back Again** (1987 K-tel NCD 5143)
Rosetta/The Ballad Of Bonnie And Clyde/Barefootin'/That Ol' Rock And Roll *(Fame/Ryan)*/ Getaway *(Powell)*/Yeh Yeh/Bring It On Home To Me/Saturday Night Fish Fry/Some Day/ Lawdy Miss Clawdy

Georgie Fame/Lena Ericsson/Lasse Samuelson
LP (1986 Four Leaf Clover LP FLC 5091) S (also available as a legal download)
My Second Home *(Fame/Gray)* GF/Oh Georgia Moon, GF/Runaway, Lena Ericsson/ My Ship, Lasse Samuelson/Let The Rest Of The World Go By GF/Yes Indeed, GF/ Soon And Very Soon GF & Choir/Come Sunday, Lasse Samuelson & Choir/ Georgia On My Mind GF/ Amazing Grace, Lena Ericsson/Sweet Perfection *(Fame / Ryan)* GF/ Stormy Weather GF & Lena Ericsson

No Worries Georgie Fame & The Aussie Blue Flames
LP (1988 CBS 4668682) AUS (Four Leaf Clover FLC 5099, Four Leaf Clover FLC-CD 5099)
Lady Be Good/Ole Buttermilk Sky/Eros Hotel *(Fame/Landesman)*/Little Samba *(Fame)*/ It Ain't Right *(Powell)*/On A Misty Night *(Dameron/Fame)*/Cat's Eyes *(Fame)*/Parchman Farm/ Zulu *(Fame)*/Saturday Night Fish Fry/Try'na Get Along With The Blues/ Yeh Yeh/Getaway *(Powell)*

A Portrait Of Chet
LP (1989 Four Leaf Clover LP FLC 5108) S, CD (FLC CD 108) S
The More I See You/On A Misty Night *(Dameron/Fame)*/Dancing On The Ceiling/ How Long Has This Been Going On/But Not For Me/Do It The Hard Way/It Could Happen To You/Go Go *(Carpenter/Bruce/Fame)*/You're Driving Me Crazy/Everything Happens To Me/Lament For Chet *(Fame)*

Cool Cat Blues
CD (1990 Blue Moon/Go Jazz R2 79352) US (Go Jazz vBR 20432) D (Polystar PSCS 1003)J
Cool Cat Blues *(Fame/Ryan)*/Every Knock Is A Boost *(Jordan/Waters/Fame)*/Moondance/It Should Have Been Me/Yeah Yeah/I Love The Life I Live/Big Brother/Georgia (not in Japan) /Cat's Eyes *(Fame)* /You Came A Long Way From St. Louis/ Survival *(Fame Ryan)*/Little Pony/Rocking Chair

Georgie On My Mind – Live In B. P. Club
CD (1991 Jazzette BPCD 009) HR
But Not For Me/Everything Happens To Me/Yeh Yeh/Georgia On My Mind/You Came A Long Way To St. Louis/The Fool's Paradise/Lady Be Good/One For My Baby/Don't Be That Way/Memphis In June

The Blues And Me
CD (1992 Go Jazz vBr CD 2104 2) D (Go Jazz GJ0105) JAP (Go Jazz GOJ 6005 2) US
The Blues And Me *(Fame/Gray)*/I Want To Know/Maybe It's Because Of Love/How Long Has This Been Going On/Jumpin' With Symphony Sid/Roll With My Baby/Woodshed *(Fame /King)*/Bluesology/Everybody Cryin' Mercy/Blues For Ann-Marie *(Fame/Ohman)*/I Almost Lost My Mind/Passed Me By *(Fame)*/I Ain't Got Nothin' But The Blues

Endangered Species Georgie Fame & The Danish Radio Big Band
CD (1993 Music Mecca 1040 2) S, DK
Blues For Ann-Marie *(Fame/Ohman)*/I Still Care About You *(Fame)*/For My Lady/Drip Drop / Little Samba *(Fame)*/Angel Dust/The Ballad Of Bonnie And Clyde/I Put A Spell On You/ City Life *(Fame, Gray)*/A Declaration Of Love*(Fame)*/One For My Baby

City Life The BBC Big Band with Georgie Fame and Madeline Bell
CD (1993 RBB CD 003) UK
Strike Up The Band/I Still Care About Us *(Fame)*/I Got It Bad And That Ain't Good/ But Not For Me/The Singer *(Fame/Gray)*/I Let A Song Go Out Of My Heart, Don't Get Around Much Anymore/Cottontail/A Declaration Of Love *(Fame)*/Drop Me Off In Harlem/When My Dreamboat Comes Home/I Put A Spell On You/City Life *(Fame)*/ The Blues And Me *(Fame/ Gray)*/It Don't Mean A Thing If It Ain't Got That Swing

Three Line Whip
CD (1993 Three Line Whip TLWCD 001) UK (1995 BMG/Hypertention Music 295 157) D
It Happened To Me *(Fame)*/Kan Tsukete *(Fame)*/Vinyl *(Fame)*/Mercy, Mercy, Mercy – Vanlose Stairway/Since I Fell For You/ Zavolo/You Are There *(Fame/Gregory)*/A Declaration Of Love *(Fame)*/Will Carling *(Fame/Gray)*/It Happened To Me *(Fame)* (Reprise)

How Long Has This Been Going On - Van Morrison, **Georgie Fame** And Friends – LP (1995 Verve 314 529 136) CD (Verve 314 529 136 2) UK (Exile/Verve 529 136 2) D I Will Be There (org)/The New Symphony Sid *(Pleasure/Young/Fame)* (org, voc+Van) /Early In The Morning (org, voc+Van)/Who Can I Turn To (org, bv)/Sack O' Woe (org, voc)/Moondance (org)/ Centerpiece-Blues Backstage (org, voc GF+Van+Ross)/How Long Has This Been Going On (org)/Your Mind Is On Vacation/All Saints Day (org, voc+Van)/ Blues In The Night (My Mama Done Tol' Me)(org)/Don't Worry About A Thing (org)/That's Life (org)/Heathrow Shuffle (org, voc+Van)

Songs Of Mose Allison: Tell Me Something – Van Morrison, **Georgie Fame**, Mose Allison, Ben Sidran - LP (1996 Verve 314 533 203)/ CD (Verve 314 533 203 2) U. K. / (Exile/Verve 533 203 2) Germany
One Of These Days (org)/You Can Count On Me (To Do My Part) (org) / If You Live (org)/ Was (voc, org)/ Look Here (org)/City Home (voc, org)/ No Trouble Livin' (org)/ Benediction (org, voc + Van+ Sidran)/ Back On The Corner (voc, org)/Tell Me Something (org)/I Don't Want Much/News Nightclub (org)/Perfect Moment G.F.- voc + org Was, City Home/Back On The Corner; org + voc (with Van & Ben Sidran)

Name Droppin'
CD (1996 Three Line Whip TLWCD 003 & 1997 GoJazz 6021-2) UK Jimmy McGroove *(Fame)*/Cool Cat Blues *(Fame/Ryan)*/Tell Me How Do You Feel/Zulu *(Fame)*/ Was/Vinyl *(Fame)*/Mercy, Mercy, Mercy - Vanlose Stairway/Blues Medley: Groove's Groove - Red Top - Centerpiece – Don't Getz Scared

Walking Wounded
CD (1997 Three Line Whip TLWCD 004 & 1998 GoJazz 6036-2) U. K. Eros Hotel *(Fame/Landesman)*/If You Live/Yeh Yeh/Moondance - Blue Moon/How Long Has This Been Going On/Cape Cuckoo *(Fame)*/Abide With Me/Woodshed Intro/Woodshed *(Fame/King)*/It Happened To Me *(Fame)* - My Buddy *(Fame)*/Zavolo (both re-released in one cardboard box in 1998 as (Go Jazz GO6040 2) D

Poet In New York
CD (March 2000 CD Go Jazz Go 6044 2) US
Tuned In To You *(Fame)*/But Not For Me/Doodlin'/Declaration Of My Love *(Fame)*/Symphony Sid/On A Misty Night *(Dameron/Fame)*/That's The Way It Goes *(Dameron/Fame)* /Do It The Hard Way/Girl Talk/It Could Happen To You/Accentuate The Bass *(Dameron Fame)*/Lush Life

Relationships
CD (June 2001 Three Line Whip TLWCD 005) UK
Rhythm King *(Fame)*/Everybody's Guessin' *(Fame)*/E.N.G. (Mr. Nobody) *(Fame)*/Mars And Venus *(Fame)*/There's No More Blue Time – Breezin' All The Way (Medley) *(Dameron/ Fame)* /It *(Fame)*/You *(Fame/Lycett-Green)*/Say When *(Fame)*/The Wolf Gang *(Fame)*/The Keeper Of The Blues *(Fame)*/City Life *(Fame)*/This Is A Gas *(Fame)*

Charlestons
CD (May 2003 Three Line Whip TLWCD 006) UK
Anthem For A Band *(Fame)*/Charleston Walk *(Fame)*/Preach 'N' Teach/How Blue *(Fame)*/ Flamingo Allnighter *(Fame)*/Wide Eyed And Legless/Your Face *(Fame)*/Skiing Blues *(Fame)* – I Lost My Sugar in Salt Lake City/Wogan's Air *(Lycett-Green/Fame)*/Charleston Proposition *(Fame)* – The Charleston/Hymn For Him *(Fame)*

The Birthday Big Band
2-CD (recorded 1998 London Forum/released August 2004 Three Line Whip TLW007) UK
Yeh Yeh/The Ballad Of Bonnie And Clyde/Keeper of the Blues *(Fame)*/Strike Up The Band/ But Not For Me/Will Carling *(Fame/Gray)*/Tuned Into You *(Fame)*/Little Samba *(Fame)*/ Dawn Yawn *(Powell)*/Blues At The Bull (with Jim Mullen)/I Put A Spell On You (with Jim Mullen)/Vinyl *(Fame)*/Lil' Pony/Papa's Got a Brand New Bag (with Zoot Money)/Cool Cat Blues *(Fame/Ryan)*/City Life *(Fame)*/The Singer *(Fame/Gray)*/ The Blues And Me (with Madeline Bell) *(Fame/Gray)*/Jimmy McGroove *(Fame)*/For My Lady/It Should Have Been Me (with Ben Sidran)/Blues For Anne-Marie *(Fame/ Ohman)*/A Declaration of Love *(Fame)*

Tone Wheels 'A'-Turnin'
CD (May 2009 Three Line Whip TLWCD 008) UK
All I Know *(Fame)*/The Burdee Song *(Fame)*/Vanguard Road *(Fame)*/BP Club After

Midnight *(Fame/Tomislav Urbic)*/Enkosi Dumisani *(Fame/Alan Skidmore)*/Guantanamo By The Sea *(Fame)*/I'll Sing You *(Fame)*/Singing Horn *(Fame)*/Big Easy Meat *(Fame)*/Rollin' Blue *(Fame)*/Second Honeymoon *(Fame)*/Survival *(Fame/Jeff Ryan)*

Lost In A Lover's Dream
CD (September 2012 Three Line Whip TLWCD 009) UK
Wide-Eyed And Legless/My Foolish Heart/Skiing Blues *(Fame)*/Blossom *(Jeff Ryan/Fame)*/ Say When *(Fame)*/Don't Blame Me/Medley: There's No More Blue Time *(Dameron/Fame)* – Breezin' All The Way *(Fame)*/Singing Horn *(Fame)*/Cry Me A River/I Can't Get Started (With You)/How Blue *(Fame)*/Lost In A Lover's Dream *(Fame)*

Singer – The Musical featuring Madeline Bell
CD (April 2014 Proper Records, recorded 2004) UK, NL, D
Prelude (The Game Of Life) *(Steve Gray/Fame)*/Small Town *(Steve Gray/Fame)*/My Second Home *(Steve Gray/Fame)*/Singer *(Steve Gray/Fame)*/Learning *(Steve Gray/Fame)*/Big Town *(Steve Gray/Fame)*/That's How Hit Records Are Made (The Crap Song) *(Steve Gray/Fame)*/ The Blues And Me *(Steve Gray/Fame)*/Where Do You Go From Here? *(Steve Gray/Fame)*/ Isn't It Strange? *(Steve Gray/Fame)*/Be True To Yourself *(Steve Gray/Fame)*/From Now On *(Steve Gray/Fame)*/Epilogue (The Game Of Life) *(Steve Gray/Fame)*

SOME INTERESTING COMPILATIONS:

Getaway (1966 Imperial LP 9331) * mono / (Imperial LP 12331) * stereo US
Getaway *(Powell)*/Sweet Thing/Ride Your Pony/Funny How Time Slips Away/Sitting In The Park/See Saw/Music Talk/It's Got The Whole World Shakin'/El Bandido *(Powell)*/The World Is Round/The "In" Crowd (*stereo pressing is rechanneled or 'fake' stereo U. S.

Get Away ... (1966 Capitol LP T 6197) Canada
Get Away *(Powell)*/Sweet Thing/See Saw/Ride Your Pony/Funny How Time Slips Away/ Sitting In The Park/Sunny/My Girl/Music Talk/The World Is Round/The Whole World's Shaking/Last Night

Georgie Fame And The Blue Flames (1966 Columbia LP CTX 40 377) France
Getaway *(Powell)*/Something/Ride Your Pony/Do Re Mi/Like We Used To Be *(Powell)*/Monkeying Around/Sunny/Dr. Kitch/See Saw/It Ain't Right *(Powell)*/Rockin' Pneumonia and The Boogie Woogie Flu/No No/Walkin' The Dog/Yeh Yeh

Bonnie And Clyde (1973 CBS LP Embassy EMB 31033, Showcase SHLP 149) UK
The Ballad Of Bonnie And Clyde/Peaceful/I'm A Drifter (previously unreleased)/It Could Happen To You/Somebody Stole My Thunder/Going Home/Stormy/Someone To Watch Over Me/Tequila/When I'm 64/You're Driving Me Crazy/Seventh Son

The First Thirty Years (1989 LP & & MC & CD Connoisseur Collection VSOP 144) UK
Do The Dog/Do Re Mi/Yeh Yeh/Like We Used To Be (alternate take) *(Powell)*/Getaway *(Powell)*/Sunny/The Ballad Of Bonnie And Clyde/Seventh Son/Rosetta (with Alan Price)/ The Ali Shuffle *(Fame/Ryan)*/Daylight/The Hurricane *(Fame)*/Samba (Toda Menina Baiana) *(Gilberto/Fame)*/Moody's Mood For Love/The In Crowd/Dawn Yawn *(Powell)*/C'est La Vie/ Mellow Yellow/Fully Booked *(Fame / Ryan)*/Woe Is Me/That Ol' Rock'n'Roll *(Fame/Ryan)*/ Funny How Time Slips Away/Sitting In The Park/The Old Music Master (with Annie Ross)

The In Crowd (1998 Motor Collector 3-CD 555 509 2) D
Disc 1: Preach And Teach/Parker's Mood/Money/Eso Beso/Get On The Right Track, Baby/ Let The Sunshine In/Point Of No Return/Monkeying Around/I'm In The Mood For Love (Moody's Mood For Love)/Jelly Jelly/Red Number Nine/This Is Always, This Isn't Sometimes/Yeh Yeh/ In The Meantime/Like We Used To Be *(Powell)*/Blue Monday/ Getaway *(Powell)*/El Bandido *(Powell)*/Last Night/The In Crowd/Lil' Darlin'/Papa's Got A Brand New Bag/Dawn Yawn *(Powell)*
Disc 2: Daylight/Everlovin' Woman/Ozone *(Fame/Ryan)*/Hall St. Jive/Don't "B" Movie Me *(Fame/Ryan)*/Give Him A Hand/The Preacher And The Bear/Ali Shuffle *(Fame/ Ryan)*/Do I Love You *(Fame)*/Johnny Too Bad/Thanking Heaven *(Fame/Ryan)*/For Chrysler's Sake/Yes Honestly *(Fame / Ryan)*/The Way You Do The Things You Do/ California Girl/Three Legged Mule *(Fame)*/Cool Cat Blues *(Fame/Ryan)*
Disc 3: Nicotine And Tar *(Fame/Ryan)*/Yeh Yeh (German language)/Black Head Chinaman/ Hot Stuff/Tan Tan's Tune/I'm A Gambler/What You're Doing I Can Do *(Fame)*/ Boudon Buck/Seven Power *(Fame)*/Super Road *(Fame)*/Getaway (II) *(Powell)*/It's Not Supposed To Be That Way/Humpty Dumpty (German language)/Barefootin'/Soul Stomp/Bernie's Tune/ Round Two *(Fame)*/Sweet Perfection *(Fame/Ryan)*/Call Up The Devil *(Fame/Ryan)*/Sea Of Heartbreak/Madness/Something/Dr Kitch

Master Series (1999 Polydor CD 559 968 2) EEC
Getaway *(Powell)*/See Saw/The In Crowd/Ride Your Pony/Green Onions/Get On The Right Track, Baby/My Girl/Sunny/I Love The Life I Live/ Let The Sunshine In/Hi-Heel Sneakers/ Walking The Dog/Blue Monday/Barefootin'/Money (That's What I Want) prev. unreleased studio track/Let The Good Times Roll/Rockin' Pneumonia And The Boggie Woogie Flu/ Sitting In The Park

The Go Jazz Anthology (2003 CD Go Jazz go 6058 2/go 6058 5) D
Disc 1: I Want To Know/But Not For Me/Cool Cat Blues *(Fame/Ryan)*/Maybe It's Because Of Love/I Love The Life I Live/Doodlin'/The Blues And Me *(Fame/Gray)*/It Should Have Been Me/Tuned In To You *(Fame)*/How Long Has This Been Going On/ Every Knock Is A Boost *(Jordan/Waters/Fame)*/Symphony Sid
Disc 2: Music 2 DVD – Audio tracks as in disc 1 – Video tracks: Interview with Georgie Fame (2002)/Yeh Yeh (live with Go Jazz Allstars, Tokyo, March 20, 1991)

On the Right Track: Beat, Blues and Ballads – a Complete Hit Collection 1964–1971 (2004 Raven RVCD-176) AUS
Work Song/Get On The Right Track Baby/Yeh Yeh/In The Meantime/Telegram/Like We Used To Be *(Powell)*/Something/Get Away *(Powell)*/Sunny/Sitting In The Park/Sweet Thing/ Bluesology/Because I Love You *(Powell)*/Try My World *(Powell/Landesman)*/The Ballad Of Bonnie And Clyde/Bullets Laverne/Kentucky Child/Need Your Love So Bad/Seventh Son/ Somebody Stole My Thunder/Blossom/Peaceful/I'm A Drifter/Down Along The Cove/I'll Be Your Baby Tonight/Stormy/Happiness/Rosetta (with Alan Price)

Somebody Stole My Thunder: Jazz-Soul Grooves 1967–1971 (2007 Sony BMG 2-CD 88697 106802) U. K.
Somebody Stole My Thunder/No Thanks *(Powell/Colton)*/Seventh Son/Knock On Wood/El Pussy Cat/Bidin' My Time ('Cos I Love You) *(Powell)*/Oliver's Gone *(Fame)*/Beware Of The Dog *(Powell)*/Down Along The Cove/Peaceful/Because I Love You *(Powell)*/Try My World *(Powell / Landesman)*/I Believe In Love/Fully Booked *(Fame/Ryan)*/Roadrunner/Close The Door/I'll Be Your Baby Tonight/Is It Really The Same/Inside Story *(Fame/Ryan)*/Ask Me Nice/Do It The Hard Way/River's Invitation/Keep Your Big Mouth Shut/Parchman Farm
This double album/CD is highly recommended by the artist formerly known as Clive Powell!

"FAME FOR A PRICE": SESSION MAN & BAND MEMBER (SELECTION)

Gene Vincent: Anna Annabelle/**Pistol Packin' Mama** (Capitol F 4442) US
PPM also on **E.P. Collection Volume 2** (1956–1962/1998 See For Miles SEECD 492)
G.F. plays piano on the 1960 single B-side and EP track Pistol Packing Mama

Gene Vincent: The Crazy Beat Of Gene Vincent (1963 LP Capitol T20453) UK
G.F. plays piano on the LP track **Weeping Willow**

Johnny Hallyday: Salut Les Copains! (recorded September 1961)
Nous Quand On S'embrace/Toi Qui Regrettes/Viens Danser Le Twist/Let's Twist Again/ Douce Violence/Tu Peux La Prendre/Avec Une Poignée De Terre/Il Faut Saisir Sa Chance Johnny and G.F. worked with Joe Moretti (lead guitar), Big Jim Sullivan (rhythm guitar), Brian Locking (bass), Andy White (drums) and Jean Tosan (saxophone).

Derrick Morgan: Telephone/Life Is Tough (1963 Blue Beat BB 196) UK
G.F. organ and backing vocals on the single A-side Telephone

Prince Buster: Wash All Troubles Away (Wash Wash)/Reco & His Blues Band: Soul Of Africa (1963 Blue Beat single BB 200 & 210) UK
G.F. organd and backing vocals on the single A-side Wash All Troubles Away

Prince Buster: I Feel The Spirit (1963 Blue Beat BBLP 802 & diff. LP FAB MS2) UK
G.F. organ and backing vocals on Wash All Troubles Away (Wash Wash), organ on the first Blue Beat LP's Beggars Are No Choosers (maybe also the London recordings Don't Make Me Cry/Jealous/Just You)

Prince Buster And Hazel: The Lion Roars/World Peace (1963 single Dice CC18) UK
G.F. organ on The Lion Roars

Soundtrack: Boom! (1968 MCA LP 3600) U. K.
G. F. lead vocals on Hideaway (all other tracks are instrumentals by John Barry)

Soundtrack: In Search Of Gregory (1969) G.F. lead vocals on Close and Dreams

Soundtrack: Entertaining Mr. Sloane (1969) G.F. lead vocals on Entertaining Mr. Sloane *(Fame/Ryan)*

Soundtrack: To Kill A Clown (1972) G.F. lead vocals on With My Eyes *(Fame)*

Muddy Waters: The London Muddy Waters Sessions (LP 1972 MCA Chess CH-60013, CD 1989 Chess CHD-9298)
G. F. Appeared as "Georgie Fortune": piano and organ Blind Man Blues/Young Fashioned Ways/Who's Gonna Be Your Sweet Man When I'm Gone/I'm Ready /I Don't Know Why

Andy Fairweather Low: La Booga Rooga LP (1975 A&M AMLH 68238)
G.F. piano Halfway To Everything/Champagne Melody, organ on Inner City Highway Man
(The Blue Flames Steve Gregory & Eddie "Tan Tan" Thornton play on several tracks)

Andy Fairweather Low: Be Bop'N'Holla (1976 A&M AMLH 64602)
G. F. piano on "Rhythm'n'Jazz"
(The Blue Flames members Steve Gregory & Eddie "Tan Tan" Thornton on several tracks)

Eric Clapton: No Reason To Cry (1976 RSO 2394 172)
G.F. organ on Double Trouble, organ and piano on several non-issued tracks (according to Fame it is hard to remember who played what for all concerned because of "the ongoing party atmosphere in Shangri-La Studios")

Joan Armatrading: Show Some Emotion (1977 A&M 68433 A&M 394663-2 CD)
G. F. Fender Rhodes E-piano on Show Some Emotion/Warm Love/Never Is Too Late/Peace In Mind/Mama Mercy/Willow

Various Artists: Zvjezdana Prasina (Stardust) (1982 2-LP Jugoton LSY-65033) YU
G.F. lead vocals on This Is Always/Little Pony (rec. 12–16 October 1981 at 3rd Zagreb Jazz Festival in Kulusic Music Hall ft. Clark Terry, Ray Brown, Bud Shank, Laurindo Almeida, Pete King

Patti Boulaye & Georgie Fame: Swinging On A Star/I Feel Like Loving You (1984 single Hollywood HWD 016) F, G.F. vocal duets with Patti Boulaye

Grethe Kausland: Jazz My Way (1984/2008, Curling Legs CLP CD 110) N
G.F. sings and plays organ on The Nearness of You/Two Sleepy People/Centerpiece/It Could Happen To You/I'm In The Mood For Love

The Hudik Big Band/Georgie Fame/Bengt-Arne Wallin: Live At Montreux Jazz Festival
LP (1983 Dragon DRLP 59) Sweden
Dancing Girls/Echoes of Harlem/Hjartflimmer/Bluesology *(Lewis/Fame/O'Neill)* G.F./Parker's Mood G.F./Times Getting Tougher Than Tough G.F./Moody's Mood G.F.

The Per Husby Orchestra ft. Georgie Fame: Dedications
LP (1985 Affinity LP AFF 136) UK (1990 Hot Club Records HCRCD 21) N
Accentuate The Bass *(Dameron/Fame)* G.F./I'm Never Happy Anymore/Prima Vera-Lasse/ Good Bait-Ladybird G.F. & Karin Krog/A Song You'll Never Sing/Chan's Sorta Mingus Blues/That's The Way It Goes *(Dameron/Fame)* voc, p G.F., voc Karin Krog

Van Morrison: Avalon Sunset (1989 Polydor-CD 839 262–2)
G.F. Hammond organ on several tracks

Van Morrison: Enlightenment (1989 Polydor-CD 847 100–2)
G.F. organ, electric piano and back-up vocals on several tracks, album features Blue Flames Bernie Holland (g), Steve Gregory (sax), Brian Odgers (b) and G.F. cohorts Henry Lowther (tr) and Malcolm Griffiths (tromb), Frank Ricotti (vibes)

National Youth Jazz Orchestra: Portraits. NYJO Plays The Music Of Harry South (1990 Hothouse-CD HHCD 1007) G.F. vocals on Blues At The Bull/Point Of No Return

Kampen Janitsjar Orkester: Sing As We Go! CD (1990 CD KampCD1) N
G. F. lead vocals on Georgia On My Mind/How Long Has This Been Going On/Sunny (LP also features Norwegian/German pop star Wencke Myhre)

Van Morrison: Hymns To The Silence (1991 2-CD Polydor 849026 ½)
G.F. organ, electric piano, back-up vocals on Part I: I'm Not Feling It Anymore/Ordinary Life/ Some Peace Of Mind/So Complicated/I Can't Stop Loving You/Why Must

I Always Explain? /See Me Through, Part II: Take Me Back/By His Grace/All Saints Day/Hymns To The Silence/Green Mansions/Quality Street/It Must Be You/I Need Your Kind Of Loving

The Go Jazz All Stars: Live In Japan (1992 Go Jazz vBR 2086 2
G.F. organ on all tracks, lead vocals on It Should Have Been Me/Yeah Yeah/Georgia/I Love The Life I Live

Soundtrack/Various Artists: Glengarry Glen Ross (1992 Elektra/Warner 7559–61384–2) US, G.F. organ and vocals on Easy Street, collaboration with Benny Golson

Starclub: Starclub (1993CD Island 514 320) UK
G.F. organ on Forever/The Question

Motoharu Sano: The Circle (1993 CD Epic/Sony ESCB 1456) J
G.F. backing vocals, organ on Angel, organ on Kimi Wo Tsurete Yuku/Atarashii Shirts

Van Morrison: Too Long In Exile (1993 Polydor/Exile-CD 519 219–2)
G.F. Hammond organ and backing vocals on Too Long In Exile/Bigtime Operators/Lonely Avenue/Good Morning Little Schoolgirl/The Lonesome Road/Moody's Mood For Love/ Before The World Was Made/I'll Take Care Of You/Instrumental/Tell Me What You Want

Van Morrison: A Night In San Francisco (1994 Polydor/Exile-2CD 521290–2)
G.F. Hammond and backing vocals on all tracks, lead vocals on Jumpin' With Symphony Sid, features Blue Flames guitarist Ronnie Johnson as Musical Director

Steve Gregory: Bushfire (1994 CD (LKJ Records LKJ CD 011) UK
G.F. organ on East Of Aman/Shrine/Paradise

Alexis Korner: The BBC Radio Sessions (1983/1994 Music Club MCCD 179) UK
G.F. organ, backing vocals on Money Honey

Ulf Rådelius: From Me To You (1994 CD (dB Productions dB CD 13) S
Beatles covers, G.F. lead vocals (with Ulf Rådelius) and keyboards on Paperback Writer

Kate St John: Indescribable Night (CD 1995 All Saints Records UK ASCD 25)
G.F. Vocals and piano on "Green Park Blues"

Per Husby/Georgie Fame: If You Could See Me Now (1996 Gemini Records GMCD 89) N
On A Misty Night *(Dameron/Fame)* GF & Karin Krog/Dig It GF & Karin Krog/Seasons Change GF/Never Been In Love/Blues Medley GF/The Happy Heart

Van Morrison: The Healing Game (CD 1997 Polydor/Exile 537 101–2)
G.F. Hammond organ and backing vocals on Fire In The Belly/This Weight/It Once Was My Life/Sometimes We Cry/The Healing Game

Various Artists: Knights Of The Blues Table (1997 Viceroy/Bellaphon 290.25.001)
G.F. Vocals and organ, and Blue Flames members Tristan Powell, guitar, and James Powell, drums, on If You Live

Bill Wyman's Rhythm Kings: Struttin' Our Stuff (1997 BMG 74321 51441 2, Velvel VEL-79708–2)
G.F. Vocals and organ on Melody, vocals on Motorvatin' Mama/Hole In My Soul

Bill Wyman's Rhythm Kings: Anyway The Wind Blows (1998 BMG 74321 59523 2)
G.F. Vocals and organ on Any Way The Wind Blows/Walkin' One And Only/Days Like This/Gee Baby Ain't I Good to You, organ on Spooky/Ring My Bell/He's A Real Gone Guy/A True Romance/When Hollywood Goes Black And Tan/Crazy He Calls Me/Struttin' Our Stuff

NDR Big Band: Bravissimo, Vol II/50 Years of NDR Big Band (1998 CD Act 9259 2) UK
G.F. lead vocals on Go

The John Critchinson Quartet: Excuse Me, Do I Know You? A Tribute to Ronnie Scott (1998 CD (Jazz House JHCD 056) UK
G.F. lead vocals on Tuned Into You *(Fame)*

Big Cool Collective: Big (1999 CD A Records AL 73164) UK
G.F. lead vocals on Miss Bitch *(Herman/Herman/Fame/Fleurine)* and on You Can Have Her

Lisa Stansfield – Original Motion Picture Soundtrack: Swing (1999 BMG RCA/Victor 09026–63541–2
G.F. vocals on I Thought That's What You Liked About Me/Gotta Get On This Train (Blue Flames member Geoff Gascoyne plays bass)

The Blues Band: Brassed Up (1999 CD Hypertension 9185) UK/D
G.F. organ on What You Wanted/Stubborn Kind Of Fellow/2k Shuffle/Velocity & Love

The New Gary Husband Trio: From The Heart (1999 2-CD Jazzizit JITCD 9918) UK
G.F. lead vocals on Deep In A Dream

Bootleg Kings: Live In Europe (CD 1999 Ripple Records RIPCD 001)
G.F. trio vocals (with Gary Brooker and Beverly Skeete) and Hammond organ on Let

The Good Times Roll/Hit The Road Jack-Fever, lead vocals and Hammond on Mystery Train, lead vocals on Georgia On My Mind, Hammond organ on Stagger Lee/Rockin' Pneumonia & The Boogie Woogie Flu/Land Of 1000 Dances-Tequila/Good Golly Miss Molly/Tear It Up

Bill Wyman's Rhythm Kings: Groovin' (2000 CD Roadrunner/Ripple/Papillon RR 8544-2
G.F. Vocals and organ on Rough Cut Diamond/Tomorrow Night/Rhythm King, vocals on Can't Get My Rest At Night/Streamline Woman, organ on Groovin', piano on Hole In The Wall/I Put A Spell On You/Daydream/Oh Baby

Bill Wyman's Rhythm Kings: Double Bill (2001 CD Papillon Records BTFLYCD 015) UK
G.F. lead vocals, organ on Hit That Jive Jack/I Can't Dance/Medley Do You Or Don't You – I Wanna Know *(Lutcher)(Fame)*/Where's The Money/Jealous Girl; lead vocals on The Joint Is Jumping/Keep On Truckin', organ on Long Walk To DC/Hot Foot Blues/Love Letters/Love's Down The Drain/Medley Snap Your Fingers – What A Friend We Have In Jesus/Boogie Woogie All Night Long/Trust In Me/Turn On Your Lovelight/Lonely Boy Blue/Bye Bye Blues/Breakin' Up The House

Trudy Kerr: My Old Flame: Tribute To Chet Baker (2001 CD Jazzizit JITCD 24795) UK
G.F. duets with Trudy Kerr on You Make Me Feel So Young/My Heart Stood Still

Bootleg Kings: Ride Again (2001 CD Ripple Records RIPCD 002) UK
G.F. duet vocals (with Gary Brooker) and Hammond organ on Mystery Train, lead vocals on Georgia, Hammond organ on I'm Ready/Lead Me To The Water/Baby Workout/Jump Jive & Wail/I'll Be Satisfied/Hello Little Boy/Baby You Got What It Takes

Bootleg Kings: Travlin' Band (2002 CD Ripple Records RIPCD 003) UK
G.F. lead vocals and Hammond organ on Walking One And Only, duet vocals and Hammond organ on Hit The Road Jack/Makin' Whoopie/Cat's Eyes *(Fame)* (all with Beverley Skeete), duet vocals only (also with Beverly Skeete) on alternative version of Makin' Whoopie (with Martin Taylor on guitar instead of organ), Hammond organ on Chicken Shack Boogie/ Jitterbug Boogie/ This Little Girl's Got Rocking/I Put A Spell On You/Tell You A Secret

Bootleg Kings: On The Road Again (2003 CD Ripple Records RIPCD 004) UK
G.F. lead vocals and Hammond organ on SOS/Days Like This, duet vocals (with Beverly Skeete) and Hammond organ on Melody, Hammond organ on Down In The Bottom/Too Late/Trust In Me/Jump Jive & Wail/He's A Real Gone Guy/Kiddio/Midnight Special/Lights Out/Chantilly Lace/Frankie & Johnny

Paul Kuhn Meets Bert Kaempfert: Remember When (2003 CD Content/Edsel 0151582 CTT) D
G.F. lead vocals on L.O.V.E., duet vocals on Dankeschön

Bill Wyman's Rhythm Kings: Just For A Thrill (CD 2004 R & M RAMCD007) UK, (CD 2004 Roadrunner International 21227) J
G.F. lead vocals, Hammond organ on Down Home Girl/Cadillac Woman/Just For a Thrill/ Melody* (*Japan only) and Hammond organ on all tracks

Geoff Gascoyne: Keep It To Yourself (CD 2005 Candid CCD 79798) UK
G.F. vocals on I'll Sing You/Somebody's Gotta Move, James Powell, drums on I'll Sing You

David Gilmour: On An Island (CD 2006 EMI 0946 3 55695 2 0) UK
G.F. Hammond organ on This Heaven

Dolf de Vries: Another Touch (2007 Dolf de Vries Musics CD NW2U 881), NL
G.F. sings "Sunny"

Jazz Orchestra of the Concertgebow & Various Artists: 10 Jaar 1999–2009 (CD 2008 JOC JR 109 with book "Een heel behoorlijk orkest", see bibliography)
G.F. vocals on Anthem For A Band *(Fame)* 6th September 2008 at Laren Jazz Festival with an arrangement by Steve Gray, Solo: Simon Rigter tenor saxophone

Sandi Russell: Sweet Thunder (2009 CD, 33 Jazz 165) UK
G.F. vocals on Feet On The Ground, album features Blue Flames Alan Skidmore (sax), Guy Barker (tr) and G.F. collaborator Jim Mullen

Claes Janson: The Best Of Ray Charles (2009 Gazell GAFCD-1102 EAN7393775110221)
Big Band live in the studio, G.F. on Let The Good Times Roll/Busted

Ben Sidran: Dylan Different (CD 2009 Bonsa BON 091101)
G.F. duet vocals and organ on Rainy Day Woman # 12 & 35

The Independent Jazzwerkstatt Orchestra: Jazzwerkstatt (2010 CD Jazzwerkstatt Records)
G.F. vocals on Jumpin' With Symphony Sid/Yeh Yeh

Nigel Mooney: The Bohemian Mooney (CD 2013 Lyte Records LR 018)
G.F. vocals on Down For Double/How Blue Can You Get *(Fame)*

N.B. I count the *How Long Has This Been Going On* album as a collaboration between Van Morrison and G.F., and *Tell Me Something* as a coop of G.F., Van, Ben Sidran and Mose Allison, hence their inclusion in the section **Albums (LPs and CDs)**.

SOME SPECIAL ISSUES:

Warsaw Jazz Jamboree 67 Vol. 2 (Polskie LP Nagrania/Muza XL 0444) Poland featuring Try My World live *(Powell/Landesman)* and Yeh Yeh live by Georgie Fame as an instrumental

The Go Jazz All Stars – Live In Japan ft. Georgie Fame (1992 Go Jazz CD vBr 2086 2) D
Lip Service (Ben Sidran)/Mood Swing (Bob Malach)/**It Should Have Been Me (GF** with Ben Sidran)/**Yeah Yeah GF**/Let's Make A Deal (Ben Sidran)/Good Bye (Ricky Peterson)/ Language Of The Blues (Ben Sidran)/Too Hot To Touch (Ben Sidran)/ **Georgia GF/ I Love The Life I Live** GF (live in the studio)

Knights Of The Blues Table (1997 Viceroy/Lightyear 54189) US
K.C. Moan – Cyril Davies/Send For Me – Jack Bruce & Dave "Clem" Clempson/**If You Live – Georgie Fame** (unique recording)/Go Down, Sunshine – Duffy Power/ Racketeer's Blues – Chris Jagger & Mick Jagger/Rocks In My Bed – Peter Brown, Phil Ryan And Dick Heckstall-Smith/Don't Let Me Be Misunderstood – Miller Anderson/ Blind Man – Maggie Bell & Jim Sullivan/Traveling Riverside Blues – Peter Green & Nigel Watson / Drop Down Mama – Tony "TS" McPhee / I've Got News For You – Dave "Clem" Clempson & Jack Bruce / Nine Below Zero – Nine Below Zero/Judgement Day – The Pretty Things/Play On Little Girl-T-Bone Shuffle – Paul Jones And Otis Grand/One More Mile – Mick Clarke & Lou Martin/You Shook Me – Mick Taylor & Max Middleton

DVDs (SMALL SELECTION)

Feature Film: Entertaining Mr Sloane: starring Beryl Reid, Harry Andrews, Peter McEnery
(2013/1970 DVD StudioCanal) UK, Soundtrack by Georgie Fame/Colin Green, title song "Entertaining Mr Sloane" composed and performed in the film by Georgie Fame

Georgie Fame & The Blue Flames: Cool Cat Blues – Live In Concert
(2008/1991 DVD Delta 94902) D, Live at Theaterhaus Stuttgart, Germany, ft. Guy Barker (tr), Steve Gregory (sax), Dave Cliff (g), Brian Odgers (b), James Powell (dr) Rockin' Chair/You Came A Long Way From St Louis/Big Brother/Cool Cat Blues/ Moondance/Jumpin' With Symphony Sid/Parchman Farm/Yeh Yeh/Cat's Eyes/I Love The Life I Live/How Long Has This Been Going On?

Go Jazz All-Stars: In Concert (2003/June 30th, 1998 DVD inak/Inakustik) D
ft. Georgie Fame (voc, org), Ben Sidran (voc, p), Charlie Wood (voc, org), Bob Rockwell (sax), Gege Telesforo (voc), Keith Copeland (dr)

Mr P's Shuffle/It Ain't Necessarily/Cool Cat Blues *(Fame)*/Parchman Farm/One Kind Word/ That Note Costs A Dollar/Hit The Road Jack/Man And Machine/Mumbles/ Blues Medley

Martin Scorcese Presents The Blues: Red White & Blues (DVD 2004 Snapper/ McOne) Mike Figgis' film about British Blues has Georgie Fame and Pete King talk shop together with Van Morrison, Flamingo pals Chris Farlowe and Eric Burdon, Humphrey Lyttelton, George Melly, Tom Jones and many more

Bibliography (Selections)

Baker, Ginger *Hellraiser: The Autobiography Of The World's Greatest Drummer* (John Blake, 2010)
Berkenstadt, Jim: *The Beatle Who Vanished* [the first historical account of Jimmie Nicol], (Rock And Roll Detective Publishing, 2013)
Bilyeu, Melinda, Cook, Hector and Hughes, Andrew Môn Hughes, *The BeeGees – Tales of The Brothers Gibb* (Omnibus Press, 2001)
Boyd, Joe *White Bicycles: Making Music In The 1960s* (Serpent's Tail, 2005)
Brooks, Elkie *Finding My Voice – My Autobiography*, (The Robson Press 2012)
Brown, Joe *Brown Sauce*: The Life and Times of Joe Brown (Willow Books Collins 1986)
Brunning, Bob *Blues: The British Connection* (Blandford, 1995)
Carson, Annette *Jeff Beck: Crazy Fingers* (Backbeat, 2001)
Chilton, John, *Let The Good Times Roll: The Story Of Louis Jordan And His Music*, (Quartet Books 1994)
Clayson, Alan, *Charlie Watts* (Sanctuary, 2004)
Clayson, Alan, *Ringo Starr – Straight Man Or Joker?* (Sidgwick & Jackson 1991)
Cohn, Nik *Alopbopaloobop Alopbamboom: Pop From The Beginning* (1969, Pimlico, 2004 edition)
Frame, Pete *Even More Rock Family Trees* (Omnibus Press, 2011)
Frame, Pete The Beatles Some And Other Guys: Rock Family Trees Of The Early Sixties (Omnibus Press, 1997)
Frame, Pete *The Restless Generation* (Rogan House, 2007)
Gambaccini, Paul & Rice, Tim & Rice, Jonathan *The Guinness Book Of British Hit Albums 7th edition* (Guinness Publishing 1996)
Goldsmith, Lady Annabel, *Annabel – An Unconventional Life: The Memoirs Of Lady Annabel Goldsmith*, (Weidenfeld & Nicolson, 2004)
Hanson, Martyn *Playing The Band – The Musical Life of Jon Hiseman* (Temple Music, 2010)
Harper, Colin *Bathed in Lightning – John McLaughlin, the 60s and the Emerald Beyond* (Jawbone Books, 2014)

Heckstall-Smith, Dick & Pete Grant *Blowing The Blues: fifty years playing the British Blues*, including Heckstall-Smith, Dick *The Safest Place In The World*, (Quartet Books, 1989 Clear Books, 2004)

Heining, Duncan *Trad Dads, Dirty Boppers and Free Fusioneers: British Jazz 1960–1975* (Equinox 2012)

Johns, Glyn*: Sound Man – A Life recording hits with the Rolling Stones, the Who, Led Zeppelin, the Eagles, Eric Clapton, the Faces…* [and Georgie Fame] (Blue Rider Press/Penguin Group, 2014)

Kaaij, Jorg & Martinez, Juan (compilers) *10 Jaar Jazz Orchestra of the Concertgebouw 1999–2009: Een heel behoorlijk orkest*, (Stichting Jazz Orchestra of the Concertgebouw, AKD Prinsen Van Wijmen, 2009)

Keeler, Christine, with Thompson, Douglas, *The Truth at Last – My Story*, (Sidgwick & Jackson, 2001)

Levy, Shawn *Ready, Steady, Go: Swinging London and the invention of Cool* (Fourth Estate, 2002)

O'Farrell, John *An Utterly Exasperated History Of Modern Britain* (Transworld Books, 2009)

Rogan, Johnny, *Van Morrison – No Surrender*, (Vintage Books 2005)

Scheinfeld, John *Georgie Fame* (Private Publication, Los Angeles, 1989)

Shapiro, Harry *Alexis Korner: The Biography* (1996, Bloomsbury, 1997 edition)

Shapiro, Harry *Graham Bond: The Mighty Shadow* (1992, Crossroads Press, 2005 edition)

Shapiro, Harry *Jack Bruce: Composing Himself* (Jawbone, 2010)

Sidran, Ben, *A Life in Music* (Taylor Trade Publishing, 2003)

Sidran, Ben, *Talking Jazz – An Oral History* (Da Capo Press, 1992)

Twelker, Uli and Schmitt, Roland *Happy Boys Happy! A Rock History of The Small Faces & Humble Pie* (Sanctuary, 1997)

Wyman, Bill with Coleman, Ray *Stone Alone* (Penguin, 1990)

The Blue Flames pre Fame-lead (bandleaders in fat print)

GF/ year	Singer	bass	Drums	Lead guitar	Piano	Rhythm
Nov 1958 March 59	**Clay Nicholls***		Alan 'Al Allison	Anthony "Tony" Harvey	Mike O'Neill	
June 1959 Aug 1959	**Clay Nicholls**	Peter Wharton	Johnny Watson	Joe Brown		Rick Hardy
Aug 1959 Sept 59	**Clay Nicholls**	Peter Wharton	Johnny Watson	Tony Harvey		
Dec 1959	**Billy Fury****	Bobby Gregg	Clem Cattini	Joe Brown	Clive *** Powell	Kenny Packwood
June 1961	**Clay Nicholls**	Tex Makins	Red Reece	Colin Green	Georgie Fame	
June 61 Dec 61	**Billy Fury**	Tex Makins	Red Reece	Colin Green	Georgie Fame	
Sep 1963 R&B LP	**Earl Watson**	Tex Makins	Red Reece	Colin Green	Georgie Fame	

* A.k.a. Vincente Tartaglia ** a.k.a. Ronald William Whycherley *** soon Georgie Fame

Georgie Fame & The Blue Flames (Era I: 1962–1966)

GF/ year	Guitar	bass	drums	tenor sax	alto sax	trumpet	Congas	Vibes
March 1962	Colin Green	Tex Makins	Red Reece					
April 1962	Joe Moretti	Tex Makins	Red Reece	Al "Earl" Watson				
May 1962 June 1962	Joe Moretti	Tex Makins	Red Reece	Mick Eve			Speedy Acquaye	
July 1962	John Mc Laughlin	Tex Makins	Red Reece	Mick Eve			Speedy Acquaye	
July- Oct 1962	John Mc Laughlin	Tex Makins	Red Reece	Mick Eve		Tony Coe (JulyAug)	Speedy Acquaye	
Oct 1962 -April 63	John Mc Laughlin	Boots Slade	Red Reece	Mick Eve		Johnny Marshall	Speedy Acquaye	
April 1963 -Oct 1963		Boots Slade	Red Reece	Mick Eve		Johnny Marshall	Speedy Acquaye	
Sep 1963 R&B LP	Big Jim Sullivan	Boots Slade	Red Reece	Mick Eve		Johnny Marshall	Tommy Thomas	
Oct 1963 -Dec 1963		Tex Makins	Red Reece	Mick Eve		Johnny Marshall	Eddie * Thornton	Speedy Acquaye	* guest

476

Jan 1964 F. At Last		Tex Makins	Tommy Frost *	Mick Eve	Johnny Marshall	Eddie Thornton	Speedy Acquaye	* or Roy Mills
Jan 1964 - April 64		Tex Makins	Red Reece	Mick Eve	Johnny Marshall	Eddie * Thornton	Speedy Acquaye	* guest
April-May 1964		Tex Makins	Jimmy Nicol	Mick Eve	Peter Coe		Speedy Acquaye	
May-July 1964		Tex Makins	Phil Seamen	Mick Eve	Peter Coe		Speedy Acquaye	
July-September 1964		Tex Makins	Phil Seamen*		Peter Coe Alto, tn		Speedy Acquaye	* Mickey Waller if P.S. absent
Sept-Oct 1964		Tex Makins	Bill Eyden	Peter Coe			Speedy Acquaye	
Oct-Nov 1964	Colin Green	Tex Makins	Bill Eyden	Peter Coe			Speedy Acquaye	
Nov 1964-March 65	Colin Green	Tex Makins	Bill Eyden	Peter Coe	Glenn Hughes	Eddie Thornton	Speedy Acquaye	
Mach 65 – Dec 1965	Colin Green	Tex Makins	Bill Eyden	Peter Coe	Glenn Hughes		Speedy Acquaye	
Dec1965-July 1966	Colin Green	Cliff Barton	Mitch Mitchell	Peter Coe	Glenn Hughes	Eddie Thornton	Speedy Acquaye	
July1966-Oct2 1966	Colin Green	"Ricky" Brown	Mitch Mitchell	Peter Coe	Glenn Hughes	Eddie Thornton	Speedy Acquaye	

Georgie Fame Band (1967–1973)

GF/ year	Guitar	bass	drums	tenor sax	baritone sax	trumpet	Congas	Vibes
1967 G.F. Band	Georgie Fame	Rik Brown	Hughie Flint	Lyn Dobson	Johnny Marshall	Eddie Thornton	J. Scott	Derek (trb) Wardsworth
1968 G.F. Band	John Mc Laughlin	Rik Brown	Jon Hiseman	Lyn Dobson				
1969	Colin Green	Brian Odgers	Harvey Burns	Johnny Marshall	Peter King ArtThemen	Chris Pyne	Frank Ricotti	Pete Aherne
1970 SHORTY	Colin Green	Brian Odgers	Harvey Burns	Alan Skidmore				
1972	Colin Green	Brian Odgers	Brian Bennett	Dick Heckstall-Smith				
1973	Bernie Holland	Brian Odgers	Brian Bennett	Dick Heckstall-Smith				

Georgie Fame & Alan Price (1971–1973)

1971–1973	Colin Green	Dave Markee	Clive Thacker	Steve Gregory				Alan Price (piano, voc)

Georgie Fame & The Blue Flames (Era II: 1974–1989)

GF/ year	Guitar	Bass	drums	tenor sax	alto sax	trumpet	Congas	Baritone sax
March 1974 The Huge Blue Flames	Colin Green	Brian Odgers	Brian Bennett & Mitch Mitchell	Alan Skidmore & Elton Dean	Buddy Beadle & Steve Gregory	Eddie Thornton & Marc Charig	Speedy Acquaye	Stan Sultsman & Lennox Langton
February 1975	Bernie Holland	Brian Odgers	Tony Crombie	Alan Skidmore		Eddie Thornton	Speedy Acquaye	
August 1976	Bernie Holland	Brian Odgers	Tony Crombie	Steve Gregory	Buddy Beadle	Eddie Thornton	Speedy Acquaye	
February 1977	Bernie Holland	Brian Odgers	Tony Crombie	Steve Gregory	Buddy Beadle	Eddie Thornton	Speedy Acquaye	
March 1978	Bernie Holland	Brian Odgers	Tony Crombie	Steve Gregory		Malcolm Griffiths*	Speedy Acquaye	*trombone
August 1979	Bernie Holland	Brian Odgers	Tony Crombie	Dick Morrissey		Eddie Thornton	Speedy Acquaye	
July 1981	Ronnie Johnson	Brian Odgers	Barry Morgan	Dick Morrissey	Peter King		Tommy Thomas	
March 1983	Andy FairLow	Ian BB Richardson	Dave Cutler	Steve Gregory	Buddy Beadle	Eddie * Thornton	Speedy Acquaye	* guest
September 1983	Ronnie Johnson	Ian BB Richardson	Dave Cutler	Steve Gregory	Buddy Beadle	Eddie * Thornton	Speedy Acquaye	* guest
July 1985	Ronnie Johnson	Brian Odgers	Geoff Dunn	Dick Morrissey	Peter King		Tommy Thomas	
September 1988	Ronnie Johnson	Ian BB Richardson	Dave Cutler	Steve Gregory	Peter King	Eddie * Thornton	Speedy Acquaye	* guest
February 1989	Ronnie Johnson	Ian BB Richardson	Dave Cutler	Alan Skidmore	Peter King*		Speedy Acquaye	*

Georgie Fame & The Aussie Blue Flames (e.g. 1987, 2008)

GF/ year	Guitar	Bass	Drums	tenor sax	flute/ tenor sax	trumpet	trombone	percussion
September 1987	Jimmy Doyle	Greg Lyon	Russell Dunlop		Col Loughnan	Keith Sterling	James Greening	Sunil D'Silva
September 2008		Billy Christian	Tony Hopkins	Brian Smith				

Georgie Fame & The Last Blue Flames (Era III 1990–2014)

GF/ year	Guitar	Bass	drums	tenor sax	baritone/ alto sax	trumpet	Various	Vibes
March 1990	Ronnie Johnson	Brian Odgers	James Powell	Steve Gregory	Peter King			
March 1991	Ronnie Johnson	Brian Odgers	James Powell	Steve Gregory	Peter King	Guy Barker		
July 1991	Tristan Powell	Brian Odgers	James Powell	Alan Skidmore	Peter King	Guy Barker		Anthony Kerr
September 1993	Tristan Powell	Brian Odgers	James Powell	Alan Skidmore	Peter King	Guy Barker	Steve Gregory	Anthony Kerr
April 1995	Tristan Powell	Geoff Gascoyne	James Powell	Alan Skidmore	Peter King	Guy Barker		Anthony Kerr
March 2003	Tristan Powell	Alec Dankworth	James Powell	Alan Skidmore		Guy Barker		Anthony Kerr
Mar-May 2012	Tristan Powell	Alec Dankworth	James Powell	Alan Skidmore	Nick Payn	Guy Barker		Anthony Kerr
April 2013–2014	Tristan Powell	Alec Dankworth	James Powell	Alan Skidmore		Guy Barker		Anthony Kerr

Index

A

Acquaye, Speedy 5, 11, 49, 50, 52, 70, 82, 91, 100, 103, 104, 108, 123, 130, 145, 171, 206, 213, 215, 220, 221, 222, 226, 227, 265, 266, 338, 389, 410, 416, 476, 477, 478
Adair, George 161
Adair, Tom 313
Adderley, Cannonball 314, 331, 334, 380, 402
Adderley, Julian "Cannonball" 72
Adderley, Nat 72
Adler, Larry 305
Aherne, Pete 155, 478
Alexander, Arthur 83, 106, 156, 160, 161, 162, 167, 187, 209, 210, 213, 240, 245, 246, 460
Alfaiate, António 158, 198, 270, 332
Allen, Colin 139, 243
Allison, Mose 8, 29, 35, 46, 56, 63, 70, 72, 73, 80, 94, 97, 102, 125, 141, 146, 149, 155, 167, 169, 173, 174, 177, 193, 200, 209, 240, 247, 266, 283, 290, 292, 298, 299, 303, 307, 317, 318, 327, 331, 337, 338, 344, 345, 347, 351, 367, 369, 377, 379, 381, 388, 395, 397, 400, 416, 418, 472
Alpert, Herb 161
Amazulu 249
Amen Corner 143, 216, 248, 250, 368, 393
Ammons, Gene 43, 339, 392
Anders, Christian 92
Andersson, Stig 248
Animals 15, 51, 63, 73, 89, 102, 110, 114, 124, 139, 145, 147, 153, 173, 174, 175, 176, 249, 251, 252, 364, 406
Anka, Paul 72
Arlen, Harold 256, 263, 303, 335, 354, 382
Armatrading, Joan 218, 226, 321, 467
Armstrong, Louis 95, 131, 147, 231, 233, 236, 238, 246, 269, 270, 273, 274, 375, 378
Art Of Noise 60
Ashton, Bill 273, 274, 444
Ashton, Miles 273, 444, 446
Ashton, Tony 155, 411
Ash, Vic 350
Aspland, Robin 333, 335, 346, 359
Asprey, Ron 253
Astley, Rick 222, 263
Asylum Choir 200, 203

Atha, Graham 349, 350
Atkins, Chet 160
Atlanta Rhythm Section 171
Atomic Rooster 112
Auger, Brian 42, 43, 45, 48, 53, 55, 77, 84, 164, 171, 177, 198, 332, 437
Automatic Dlamini 288
Average White Band 225, 327

B

Babbington, Roy 351
Back Door 253
Baker, Chet 35, 37, 39, 125, 131, 132, 136, 146, 161, 234, 245, 266, 268, 269, 270, 271, 275, 276, 279, 292, 306, 313, 316, 331, 342, 356, 379, 381, 382, 384, 385, 400, 403, 441, 471
Baker, Ginger 11, 39, 48, 66, 87, 137, 164, 190, 249, 252, 324, 334, 398
Baldry, Long John 53, 80, 84, 87, 91, 110, 141, 151, 181, 190, 196, 219, 223
Band, The 8, 46, 137, 166, 168, 217, 344, 348, 349, 444, 462, 463, 475
Barber, Chris 53, 54, 237
Barclay James Harvest 112
Barker, Guy 7, 141, 223, 251, 272, 273, 275, 278, 294, 302, 303, 304, 309, 312, 314, 315, 320, 322, 323, 325, 327, 330, 331, 333, 334, 335, 336, 338, 339, 341, 342, 345, 347, 348, 359, 380, 387, 388, 389, 392, 393, 409, 413, 417, 419, 428, 430, 431, 434, 444, 446, 472, 473, 479
Barnes, Ricky 47, 85, 114, 115, 123, 154, 330, 348, 359
Barnet, Charlie 117, 182
Bartholomew, Dave 18, 91, 92, 99, 252
Bart, Lionel 22
Barton, Cliff 84, 103, 108, 111, 477
Basie, Count 6, 11, 13, 87, 96, 115, 117, 118, 133, 134, 140, 142, 147, 148, 149, 150, 159, 160, 233, 244, 246, 247, 316, 319, 339, 342, 348, 354, 355, 359, 362, 363, 366, 392, 394, 401, 429, 430
Bassey, Shirley 83, 144, 205, 220
Bates, Phil 114, 131, 143, 146
Bavan, Yolande 96
BBC Big Band 99, 112, 114, 149, 247, 257, 259, 279, 349, 352, 383, 389, 430, 462
Beach Boys 51

Beadle, Buddy 88, 204, 205, 217, 249, 478, 479
Beat Boys 25, 27, 28, 29, 33, 36, 84, 101
Beatles 15, 24, 30, 47, 51, 56, 64, 65, 68, 69, 74, 78, 85, 86, 88, 89, 93, 97, 98, 101, 102, 105, 120, 124, 125, 128, 135, 139, 140, 143, 144, 145, 148, 158, 159, 170, 175, 187, 198, 199, 222, 231, 246, 249, 272, 304, 319, 325, 326, 398, 469, 474
Beckett, Harry 154, 342
Beck, Gordon 129, 132, 146
Beck, Jeff 51, 84, 86, 111, 156, 169, 198, 317, 368, 474
Beijer, Ulrika 247
Belcher, Tony 47
Bell, Madeline 14, 26, 83, 88, 151, 170, 178, 198, 220, 254, 256, 257, 258, 259, 270, 305, 316, 348, 349, 350, 351, 352, 354, 359, 360, 386, 389, 393, 411, 421, 422, 423, 428, 429, 430, 431, 441, 444, 446, 462, 463, 464
Bell, William 94
Bengtsson, Eva-Karin 247
Bennett, Brian 28, 47, 83, 164, 189, 191, 193, 197, 198, 204, 205, 214, 254, 259, 478
Bennett, Cliff 101, 105, 120, 192, 253, 406
Bennett, Tony 133, 148, 161, 246, 285, 319, 350, 352, 425, 427
Benno, Marc 200, 201, 202, 373
Benson, Gary 169
Bentzon, Nikolaj 353
Bergman, Jan 261
Berlin, Irving 246
Berry, Chuck 46, 48, 55, 56, 227, 251, 378, 414
Big Roll Band 11, 78, 79, 80, 81, 90, 113, 138, 174, 243, 248, 250, 360, 392, 429
Black, Cilla 68, 87, 139, 151, 170
Blackmore, Ritchie 83
Blackwell, Chris 52, 103, 199, 203, 204, 209, 210, 211, 223, 224, 226, 439
Blackwell, Rory 19, 20, 21, 22, 23
Blakey, Art 118
Bland, Bobby 106, 147
Blechschaden Big Band 361
Blind Faith 156, 175, 216
Blood, Sweat & Tears 155
Blue Mink 26, 205, 220, 359, 411
Blues Incorporated 39, 49, 52, 66, 82, 86, 267
Bohuslän Big Band 357
Bolan, Bolan 194
Bond, Graham 11, 39, 42, 43, 48, 49, 50, 53, 66, 78, 84, 90, 98, 118, 136, 138, 147, 152, 153, 190, 192, 197, 252, 267, 320, 475
Bonoff, Karla 116
Booker T 43, 65, 66, 91, 94, 100, 104, 105, 108, 124, 191, 210, 212, 318, 437
Boone, Richard B. 133
Boothe, Ken 230
Bostic, Earl 36, 41
Bowen, Greg 131, 144
Bowie, David 39, 104
Boyd, Joe 60, 91
Bramlett, Bonnie 179
Branscombe, Alan 114, 120, 131
Brooker, Gary 354, 355, 368, 371, 372, 376, 470, 471

Brooks, Elkie 53, 68, 81, 89, 320, 326, 415, 425
Brotherhood of Breath 205, 342
Brotherhood of Man 180, 224
Brown, Charles 70
Brown, Clifford 27, 116, 332, 380, 381, 385
Brown, James 35, 45, 46, 71, 74, 78, 94, 116, 118, 119, 157, 191, 227, 355, 432
Brown, Joe 23, 24, 25, 26, 27, 28, 31, 33, 49, 68, 445, 476
Brown, Oscar Jr. 45, 56, 72, 102, 193, 331, 381, 402
Brown, Rik 123, 130, 137, 140, 478
Brown, Steve 391
Bruce, Jack 11, 39, 48, 66, 103, 164, 190, 267, 320, 473, 475
Brunkert, Ola 261
Buchanan, Roy 156
Burch, Johnny 39, 42, 49, 98
Burdon, Eric 114, 139, 173, 174, 326, 364, 474
Burns, Harvey 154, 156, 160, 165, 167, 478
Buster, Prince 45, 63, 64, 73, 75, 107, 216, 227, 228, 392, 466, 467
Byas, Don 244, 269, 324

C

Cale, J.J. 70, 167, 199, 200, 203, 208, 212, 345, 387
Callander, Peter 139
Calloway, Cab 146, 147, 246, 414
Calvert, Eddie 28, 47, 48, 83
Cameron, Etta 247
Campbell, Mike 315
Capers, Bobby 132
Carling, Will 315, 316, 462, 463
Carmichael, Hoagy 6, 7, 27, 219, 231, 233, 236, 237, 238, 239, 240, 256, 261, 262, 266, 299, 303, 341, 350, 353, 357, 362, 430, 460
Carrack, Paul 154
Carr, Ian 234
Carr, Ronnie 24, 101
Carter, Nigel 351
Cash, Johnny 113, 211, 213, 427
Cattini, Clem 26, 33, 111, 476
Centipede 351
Chambers, Dennis 310
Chapman, Roger 154, 173, 207, 374
Chapman, Tony 54
Charig, Marc 196, 205, 342, 478
Charles Lloyd Quartet 156
Charles, Ray 30, 31, 33, 34, 46, 53, 56, 70, 71, 74, 90, 92, 100, 105, 117, 125, 130, 143, 235, 241, 248, 252, 262, 263, 269, 292, 298, 303, 305, 306, 315, 317, 327, 331, 332, 338, 355, 375, 378, 381, 386, 389, 408, 410, 432, 472
Charmers, Lloyd 228, 230, 253
Chas'n'Dave 32
Cheynes 53
Chisholm, George 274
Christie, Keith 114, 131
Christoffersen, Jacob 431
Churchill, Chick 401, 437

Clapton, Eric 11, 51, 55, 69, 72, 123, 164, 175, 179, 200, 203, 208, 212, 217, 223, 226, 284, 286, 368, 369, 370, 371, 376, 393, 467
Clarke, Allan 15, 16, 83, 169
Clarke, Frank 144
Clarke-Johnson, Roger 47, 80, 111, 445
Clark, Petula 83, 254
Clayton, Jeff 308
Cliff Bennett & The Rebel Rousers 101, 105, 120, 406
Climax Blues Band 155, 173
Clyne, Jeff 129, 130, 132
Coasters 117
Cochran, Eddie 25, 30, 31, 32, 33, 34, 90, 105, 143, 144, 317, 338, 410, 429
Cocker, Joe 126, 147, 295, 296, 308
Coe, Peter 65, 88, 97, 98, 103, 104, 108, 112, 120, 331, 477
Coe, Tony 87, 130, 131, 143, 146, 153, 164, 353, 476
Cole, Nat King 70, 95, 118, 132, 237, 246, 269, 373, 391
Collier, Graham 234
Collins, Jackie 20
Collins, Joan 60
Colosseum 123, 152, 153, 190, 192, 259, 267, 308, 320, 444
Colton, Tony 32, 128, 196, 197
Coltrane, John 72, 116, 164, 341, 343, 424
Colyer, Ken 110
Condon, Les 131, 143, 153, 214
Conover, Willis 380, 440
Conway, Russ 27
Cooder, Ry 116, 286, 317, 332
Cooke, Sam 56, 68, 95, 108, 251
Cooper, Colin 155
Cordell, Denny 103, 105, 106, 109, 124, 126, 130, 140, 199, 210, 217, 300, 431
Corea, Chick 296
Coryell, Larry 84
Cosby, Bill 95, 414
Costello, Elvis 93, 115, 118, 223, 224, 226, 270, 442
Coulter, Phil 128
Covay, Don 105, 106
Cream 94, 112, 113, 320
Creedence Clearwater Revival 377
Crombie, Tony 38, 39, 40, 214, 215, 223, 227, 286, 324, 478
Cropper, Steve 91, 94, 105, 108, 210
Crosby, David 408
Cuber, Ronnie 296, 297, 299
Cullum, Jamie 128, 160, 246, 396, 397, 426, 437
Curry, Earl & His Orchestra 76
Curtis jr, Memphis Edward "Eddie" 117
Cutler, Dave 249, 250, 251, 478, 479

D

d'Abo, Mike 140, 148
Dale, Dick 117
Dameron, Tadd 266, 356, 357, 383, 387, 388
Danger Mouse 159
Danish Radio Big Band 8, 133, 142, 247, 307, 315, 352, 353, 359, 363, 383, 462
Dankworth, Alec 8, 151, 333, 334, 345, 396, 397, 399, 413, 437, 444, 446, 479

Dankworth, Jacqueline 279
Dankworth, Johnny 38, 39, 42, 87, 114, 143, 151, 248, 325, 349, 353, 397
Dantalian's Chariot 139
Dave Clark Five 86, 140
Davies, Cyril 79, 84, 473
Davies, Dave 55
Davis, Miles 84, 128, 164, 324, 409
Davison, Harold 101, 182, 325
Dean, Elton 196, 205, 207, 342, 478
Dearie, Blossom 95, 127, 135, 156, 232, 285, 298, 399, 430
Dee, Brian 42
Dee, Dave 30, 143
DeFrancesco, Joey 310, 437
Dekker, Desmond 76
Delaney & Bonnie 175, 179, 199
Dene, Terry 23, 26
Dennis, Matt 161, 313
De Silva, Sunil 265
de Souza, Raul 210
Detroit Emeralds 160
Detroit Spinners 105
Deuchar, Jimmy 114, 325
Dičić, Damir 302
Diddley, Bo 109, 179
Dixon, Willie 70, 94, 131, 155, 167, 298, 317, 318, 430
Dobson, Lyn 123, 131, 132, 136, 137, 140, 154, 478
Dominoes 18, 19, 174
Domino, Fats 18, 19, 26, 46, 56, 91, 92, 95, 99, 104, 105, 106, 120, 125, 143, 192, 194, 206, 252, 292, 307, 317, 362, 409
Donahue, Jerry 321
Donaldson, Pat 139
Donegan, Lonnie 18, 290
Donovan 48, 111, 124, 147, 191
Dorough, Bob 127
Dors, Diana 40
Dorsey, Lee 91, 106, 161, 182, 236, 262, 313
Doyle, Jimmy 266, 479
Drew, Kenny 269, 306, 381
Dr Hook 178
Dr John 147, 155, 246, 301, 305, 306, 315, 326, 342, 364, 382, 419
Drover, Martin 182, 356, 369
Drummond, Don 50, 64
Dunaway, Faye 140
Duncan, Johnny 47
Duncan, Paul 291
Dunlop, Russell 266, 479
Dunn, Duck 108, 210
Dunn, Geoff 289, 479
Dylan, Bob 69, 124, 148, 152, 174, 291, 327, 333, 344, 377, 408, 416, 472

E

Eager, Vince 24, 25, 26, 28, 29, 47
Eagles 69, 199
Easton, Sheena 95

Eddy, Duane 32
Edelhagen, Kurt 114, 244
Edison, Harry 135, 335
Edmunds, Dave 48
Edmunds, Terry 179
Edwin Hawkins Singers 262
Ekberg, Jocke 244
Ellington, Duke 52, 71, 130, 147, 214, 244, 248, 253, 261, 262, 308, 327, 331, 349, 350, 351, 352, 402, 420
Ellington, Ray 87
Elliott, Bobby 103, 111, 252
Ellis, Pee Wee 294, 334, 335, 336, 346, 347, 398
Emerson, Keith 48, 190
Emmanuel, Tommy 370
Emmons, Buddy 208, 212
End, The 110, 112, 369
English, Scott 169, 171
Epstein, Brian 85, 86, 110, 125, 145
Ericsson, Lena 7, 210, 257, 260, 261, 262, 263, 295, 299, 301, 461
Ertegun, Ahmet 70, 117
Eshelby, Paul 350
Evans, Bill 269, 328
Eve, Mick 27, 33, 34, 41, 42, 43, 45, 48, 49, 51, 52, 63, 65, 66, 71, 74, 79, 82, 84, 87, 88, 91, 93, 102, 103, 175, 187, 249, 327, 328, 445, 446, 476, 477
Evennett, Terry 219, 224
Everly Brothers 20, 32
Everly, Phil 83
Everything But The Girl 318, 343, 435
Eyden, Bill 87, 114, 126, 134, 143, 146, 477

F

Faces 6, 41, 45, 128, 129, 130, 133, 137, 143, 144, 148, 149, 150, 154, 161, 166, 167, 201, 206, 234, 248, 271, 325, 334, 353, 356, 384, 458
Fairport Convention 60, 209, 212
Fairweather Low, Andy 14, 69, 143, 213, 216, 226, 248, 250, 251, 333, 367, 368, 372, 374, 377, 393, 425, 436, 444, 460, 467
Faith, Adam 28
Faithful, Marianne 114
Family 7, 22, 90, 114, 154, 170, 173, 196, 216, 309, 317, 474
Famous Flamingo Orchestra 234, 235, 239, 241, 353, 450, 460
Farlowe, Chris 32, 41, 45, 51, 52, 53, 78, 79, 82, 83, 88, 89, 103, 112, 124, 128, 144, 152, 153, 308, 442, 444, 446, 474
Feldman, Lawrence 296, 297, 299
Ferguson, Maynard 182, 248, 274
Fisher, Matthew 74, 75
Fleetwood Mac 162, 179, 225, 308
Flint, Hughie 123, 132, 139, 478
Floyd, Eddie 67, 127, 212, 376, 431
Ford, Robben 295, 296, 298, 299, 300, 304, 354, 364
Foreigner 112
Formby, George 31
Fortune, Lance 24

Four Freshmen 27, 271
Frampton, Peter 39, 54, 111, 155, 326, 369, 372
Franklin, Aretha 95, 336
Frechter, Colin 180
Freddy & The Dreamers 102
Friedman, David 281
Funk Brothers 107
Fury, Billy 23, 25, 27, 28, 29, 33, 34, 35, 36, 55, 83, 140, 171, 193, 207, 305, 408, 431, 476

G

Gadd, Steve 295, 296, 297, 298, 299, 300, 304, 420
Gallagher & Lyle 201, 203, 222
Gallagher, Rory 216
Garfunkel, Art 238
Gascoyne, Geoff 8, 294, 318, 322, 327, 334, 338, 341, 342, 359, 360, 382, 386, 387, 388, 390, 391, 396, 398, 400, 403, 412, 413, 428, 435, 437, 444, 446, 470, 472, 479
Gates, David 230
Gavin, Pete 196
Gaye, Marvin 94, 105, 106, 113
Gayle, Crystal 231
Geller, Herb 245, 269
Gentle, Johnny 24, 28
Georgie Does His Thing With Strings 6, 136, 151, 159, 169, 178, 313, 334, 384, 429, 458
Gershwin, George 146, 256, 269, 305, 335, 341, 349, 362, 382, 426
Gershwin, George 15
Getz, Getz 104, 161, 325, 339
Gillespie, Dizzy 87, 116, 324, 326, 330, 383, 414, 415
Gilmour, David 408, 472
Glojnarić, Silvijce 302
Goffin, Gerry 93, 411
Goins, Herbie 103, 187
Goldie, Ken 114
Golson, Benny 244, 308, 325, 379, 380, 382, 427, 469
Gonzales 66, 72, 88, 201, 249, 327
Good, Jack 25, 27, 28
Goodman, Benny 13, 146, 188, 234, 236, 244, 245, 246, 247, 303, 350, 353, 441
Gordon, Dexter 72, 133, 234, 243, 244, 324, 355, 392
Gordon, Lucky 5, 56, 57, 58, 60, 66, 91, 112, 392
Gordon, Ronnie "Psycho" 52, 56, 66
Gorrell, Stuart 235
Graham, Kenny 38
Grant, Rogers 97
Grašić, Primaz 423
Gray, Steve 7, 26, 86, 159, 220, 253, 254, 255, 256, 257, 259, 260, 261, 305, 312, 315, 316, 349, 350, 351, 352, 353, 354, 355, 359, 360, 364, 365, 366, 386, 395, 411, 419, 420, 421, 422, 423, 430, 441, 464, 472
Grech, Ric 216
Greenbaum, Norman 146
Green, Colin 11, 26, 27, 28, 29, 31, 32, 37, 47, 49, 61, 79, 82, 83, 84, 85, 92, 93, 97, 103, 104, 107, 109, 111, 114, 116, 138, 154, 155, 156, 157, 158, 163, 165, 166, 167, 175, 177, 179, 182, 184, 185, 186, 189, 191, 192,

193, 195, 204, 205, 359, 409, 435, 437, 445, 446, 473, 476, 477, 478
Green, Dave 320
Greening, James 266, 479
Green, Mick 48
Green, Peter 11, 162, 250, 326, 473
Gregory, Steve 14, 88, 174, 184, 201, 204, 205, 210, 217, 220, 226, 227, 248, 249, 250, 251, 277, 291, 292, 296, 315, 467, 468, 469, 473, 478, 479
Griffin, Johnny 234, 243, 392, 418
Griffiths, Malcolm 220, 224, 227, 468
Guardian Angels 229, 230
Gunnell, John 41, 75, 78, 79, 189, 358
Gunnell, Rik 36, 41, 42, 45, 53, 65, 68, 77, 100, 102, 110, 113, 121, 122, 137, 152, 166, 349, 392, 410, 431

H

Haley, Bill 18, 32, 47, 64, 214
Hallyday, Johnny 33, 48, 50, 83, 102, 112, 216, 466
Hamburg Blues Band 308, 444
Hamer, Ian 114, 120, 131, 143, 153, 226, 234, 236, 239
Hamilton, Arthur 426
Hamilton, Jeff 308
Hammer, Tardo 234
Hampton, Lionel 146, 234, 245, 339
Hansen, Ole Kock 247
Hargrove, Roy 405
Harrington, Carey Bell 216
Harriott, Joe 39, 86
Harrison, George 255, 296, 368
Harris, Rolf 49
Harrow Youth Jazz Orchestra 273
Hart, Lorenz 132, 270, 384
Harvey, P.J. 288
Haughey, Bobby 144
Hawkins, Coleman 97, 324
Hawkins, Screaming Jay 174, 249, 351, 354, 355
Haycock, Peter 155
Hayes, Louis 72, 380, 382
Hayes, Tubby 11, 39, 49, 76, 86, 87, 90, 114, 115, 130, 131, 143, 234, 273, 325, 350, 360
Haymes, Dick 132, 269
Hazeltine, David 380, 381, 382, 418
Hazlewood, Lee 243, 244
Heads, Hands & Feet 32, 128, 196
Healey, Derek 143, 153
Hebb, Bobby 124, 428, 429
Heckstall-Smith, Dick 39, 42, 49, 87, 98, 118, 152, 164, 190, 192, 193, 194, 259, 267, 308, 320, 359, 444, 446, 473
Hefti, Neil 117, 161, 384
Heinz 23
Helmus, Ellen 7, 161, 268, 269, 270, 271, 295, 349
Hendricks, Jon 27, 93, 95, 96, 97, 98, 109, 110, 115, 116, 117, 125, 131, 134, 149, 150, 162, 198, 212, 232, 233, 248, 269, 295, 296, 298, 331, 334, 335, 351, 380, 381, 383, 392, 395, 417
Hendrix, Jimi 70, 91, 103, 104, 106, 110, 111, 113, 196, 211, 216, 284, 285, 288, 289, 318, 396

Herman, Benjamin 400
Herman's Hermits 51
Hickox, Douglas 163
Hicks, Tommy 15, 16, 22, 32, 47, 369, 374
Higgins, Alex 156, 240
Hightower, Rosetta 169, 171, 216
Hiller, Tony 180
Hinkley's Heroes 196
Hinkley, Tim 196
Hiseman, Jon 11, 123, 131, 136, 139, 140, 152, 307, 308, 330, 435, 444, 446, 475, 478
Hodges, Chas 32
Hodges, Johnnie 71
Hoeke, Rob 307
Holdsworth, Allan 286
Holiday, Billie 12, 38, 232, 246, 442
Holland, Bernie 69, 179, 196, 197, 198, 204, 205, 206, 208, 212, 213, 214, 215, 220, 221, 223, 227, 283, 284, 291, 293, 294, 296, 435, 446, 468, 478
Holland, Dermot 279, 280
Holland, Jools 64, 75, 336, 345, 409
Hollies, The 15, 16, 83, 87, 103, 111, 124, 152, 169, 179, 252
Hollywood String Quartet 161
Holmes, Richard "Groove" 43, 338, 360
Holt, John 230
Hooker, John Lee 52, 141, 173, 174, 290, 292, 293, 338, 368
Hopkins, Lightnin' 141, 200, 292
Horn, Shirley 95, 160, 350
Houston, Thelma 175
Howe, Steve 83
Hoyte, Janis 370, 374
Hudik Big Band 131, 247, 468
Hughes, Glenn 11, 42, 88, 102, 103, 106, 111, 192, 331
Humble Pie 111, 154, 166, 179, 185, 198, 199, 326, 476
Hunter, Ivy Joe 105
Husband, Gary 400, 470
Husby, Per 247, 263, 335, 355, 356, 468, 469
Hynde, Chrissie 35

I

Impressions 93, 234
Irish Youth Jazz Orchestra 280
Isadore, Reg 198
Isley Brothers 69, 160
Ivy League 32, 102

J

Jack Sharp Big Band 275
Jackson, Al 91, 94, 104
Jackson, Haydon 144
Jackson, Milt 131, 167, 196, 279, 280, 306, 307
Jackson, Totlyn 182
Jagger, Mick 54, 55, 63, 296, 368, 377, 473
Jamal, Ahmad 405
Jamerson, James 107
James, Etta 377
James, Harry 146, 364

Janson, Claes 408, 472
Jarreau, Al 150, 382, 385
Jay, Fred 91
Jazz Couriers 39, 87, 114, 325
Jazz Warriors 326
Jefferson, Eddie 52, 73, 90, 95, 269, 331, 381
Jenkins, Karl 219, 221, 222
Jethro Tull 156, 199
Jody Grind 196
Johansen, Jonas 354
Johanson, Egil 261
John Barry Seven 32
John, Elton 170, 190, 196, 243, 436
John junior, Mertis 162
John, Little Willie 162
Johns, Glyn 68, 69, 73, 123, 199, 200, 201, 202, 203, 209, 216, 217, 226, 321
Johnson, Buddy 315
Johnson, Ronnie 249, 250, 251, 263, 283, 284, 285, 293, 294, 297, 309, 436, 444, 446, 469, 478, 479
Johnston, Bob 152
Jones, Brian "Sax" 31
Jones, Elvin 104
Jones, Kenny 45
Jones, Micky 112
Jones, Paul 11, 55, 72, 87, 88, 148, 243, 262, 308, 354, 473
Jones, Quincy 245, 262, 269, 353, 361, 420, 431
Jones, Rickie Lee 246
Jones, Ronnie 50, 51, 52, 53, 66, 78, 79, 87, 88, 410, 421
Jones, Tom 83, 148, 254, 345, 439, 474
Jordan, Louis 13, 42, 62, 71, 116, 211, 233, 248, 251, 265, 267, 294, 297, 306, 317, 327, 332, 334, 374, 378, 389, 392, 414, 415, 431, 474

K

Kaas, Patricia 205
Karstein, Jimmy 200
Keef Hartley Band 123
Keeler, Christine 5, 56, 57, 58, 59, 60, 61, 63, 77, 91, 112, 392, 429
Keith Jarrett 156
Kennedy, John 22
Kenny Clarke-Francy Boland Big Band 87, 114
Kerr, Anthony 7, 260, 278, 279, 281, 305, 310, 315, 327, 330, 338, 340, 341, 342, 359, 370, 380, 383, 387, 388, 389, 391, 393, 402, 405, 409, 413, 419, 433, 444, 446, 479
Kerr, Trudy 400, 471
King, Albert 94
King, Carol 79, 93, 332, 411
King Crimson 190
King, Earl 91
King, Pete 129, 204, 205, 214, 302, 306, 325, 327, 329, 340, 342, 468, 474
King, Peter 98, 129, 132, 157, 164, 182, 234, 237, 239, 248, 265, 267, 275, 276, 278, 301, 302, 306, 325, 327, 338, 339, 340, 341, 342, 359, 384, 386, 387, 389, 390, 478, 479

King Pleasure 27, 34, 35, 45, 46, 56, 73, 90, 95, 96, 125, 150, 232, 233, 248, 269, 306, 331, 332, 334, 339, 381, 383, 392
Kinks 55, 69, 83, 102, 104, 124, 219, 253
Kinsey, Tony 39
Kirk, Roland 55, 160, 330
Kish, George 144
Kitchener, Lord 78, 107
Kitty, Daisy and Lewis 51
Knopfler, Mark 155, 368
Knox, Buddy 117
Knudtson, Gordy 301, 308
Kokomo 267, 327
Korner, Alexis 11, 24, 39, 42, 43, 48, 49, 52, 53, 55, 66, 79, 80, 82, 84, 86, 87, 111, 114, 118, 154, 164, 165, 166, 188, 205, 220, 253, 267, 324, 368, 376, 411, 469, 475
Kpiaye, John 249
Krall, Diana 146, 271, 373, 393
Krause, Jo 270, 271
Krog, Karin 335, 356, 468, 469
Kruger, Jeff 38, 39, 60
Krupa, Krupa 147, 236
Kuhn, Paul 228, 401, 472

L

Lacy, James 157, 158
Laine, Cleo 151, 397
Lake, Greg 190
Lamb, Bobby 280
Lambe, John 231, 239
Lambert, Dave 96
Lambert, Hendricks & Bavan 95
Lambert, Hendricks & Ross 93, 96, 117, 118, 119, 131, 149, 231, 233, 234, 335, 339, 351, 383
Lamour, Dorothy 132
Lance, Major 93, 431
Landesbergen, Frits 270, 278
Landesman, Fran 127, 128, 220, 221, 222, 340, 421, 430
Lane, Ronnie 45, 79, 123, 148, 153, 201, 206
Langton, Lennox 204, 213, 478
Last, James 83, 180, 243, 256, 401
Led Zeppelin 87, 191
Lee, Albert 26, 27, 32, 82, 128, 196, 368, 371, 372, 377
Lee, Alvin 90, 154, 173, 196, 267, 401
Lee, Brenda 68, 95
Lee, Peggy 131, 237, 253, 299, 303, 317, 394
Lee, Will 295, 296, 300, 304, 307
Lennon, John 69, 72, 93, 139, 160, 175, 304
LeSage, Bill 40, 42
Lewis, Jerry Lee 18, 19, 20, 23, 26, 32, 40, 46, 68, 105, 125, 174, 175, 176, 211, 214, 246, 252, 280, 292, 327, 428
Lewis, John 131
Lewis, Ramsey 108, 160
Ligertwood, Alex 171
Liggins, Jimmy 93
Lindvall, Anders "Chico" 354
Little Richard 18, 27, 46, 68, 104, 105, 214, 215, 292

Little Walter 378
Locking, Brian "Licorice" 33
Locorriere, Dennis 178
London, Julie 95, 160, 161, 270, 426
Lord, Jon 48, 66
Lorkin, Bill 351
Loss, Joe 86, 119, 120
Loughnan, Col 266, 267, 479
Love Affair 140, 159
Lovin' Spoonful, The 127
Lowther, Henry 204, 220, 274, 291, 468
Lulu 153, 175, 176, 182
Lund, Morten 431
Lutcher, Nelly 234, 374
Lycett Green, Candida 221, 224, 226, 264, 387, 389, 390, 394, 430
Lynn, Vera 140
Lyon, Greg 266, 479
Lyttelton, Humphrey 18, 87, 114, 164, 274, 415, 474

M

MacManus, Ross 119, 223
Madness 11, 63, 64, 75, 231, 409, 451, 465
Mahavishnu Orchestra 84, 425
Mainieri, Mike 305
Makins, Ted 28, 29, 32, 33, 36, 66, 84, 409
Makins, Tex 23, 26, 28, 29, 33, 47, 50, 85, 91, 102, 409, 476, 477
Malach, Bob 297, 299, 300, 301, 418, 473
Malach, Bobby 296, 297, 299, 304, 305, 306, 307, 308, 314, 359, 364, 380, 381, 382, 419, 426
Mancini, Henry 253, 387, 390
Manfred Mann 11, 72, 123, 140, 148
Mankuku, Winston 315
Mansfield, Keith 6, 152, 159, 162, 169, 170, 178, 180
Mantovani 140
Markee, Dave 184, 185, 478
Mar-Keys 55, 108
Markussen, Uffe 354
Marley, Bob 60, 199, 228
Marmalade 140, 145, 159
Marriott, Steve 22, 45, 88, 103, 111, 154, 166, 179, 326
Marshall, John 50, 143, 144, 146
Marshall, Johnny 11, 65, 71, 74, 82, 84, 87, 91, 102, 115, 123, 131, 153, 477, 478
Martha & The Vandellas 94, 101, 108
Martin, Bill 128
Martin, George 30, 85, 132, 140, 144, 145, 160
Martyn, John 87, 203
Marvin, Hank 47
Mattacks, Dave 203, 209, 212, 215, 223, 315, 355
Matt Bianco 220, 263, 298, 442
Matthew, Brian 119
Maughan, Susan 49
Mavrin, Mario 393, 423, 424, 426
Mayall, John 11, 41, 51, 52, 53, 70, 72, 76, 82, 89, 90, 100, 111, 114, 123, 124, 139, 152, 164, 168, 220, 243, 267, 411, 445, 446
Mayfield, Curtis 93, 431

Mayfield, Percy 131, 301, 305, 338, 389, 392
McCartney, Paul 90, 92, 105, 120, 145, 147, 158, 159, 170, 175, 183, 192, 198, 252, 304, 359
McClinton, Delbert 117
McCracken, Hugh 304, 306, 307
McDaniels, Gene 93
McDonald, Amy 154
McDonald, Ralph 298
McDowell, Malcolm 185, 283
McDuff, "Brother" Jack 243
McGear, Mike 183
McGriff, Jimmy 56, 90, 93, 99, 230, 338, 360
McLagan, Ian 45, 69, 437
McLaughlin, John 11, 27, 42, 48, 49, 51, 69, 82, 84, 87, 93, 94, 114, 128, 136, 138, 143, 146, 148, 165, 197, 278, 310, 312, 328, 425, 445
McPhatter, Clyde 117
McTell, Blind Willie 147
Mead, Frank 369, 374, 377, 378
Mears, Martha 425
Meehan, Tony 28
Melly, George 24, 39, 119, 207, 303, 331, 332, 474
Memphis Curtis 298
Mercer, Chris 88
Mercer, Johnny 231, 232, 235, 239, 335, 354, 382, 394
Meters 91
Metropole Orchestra 149, 244, 254, 256, 259, 269, 421, 422
Middleton, Max 198, 225, 473
Migil Five 41
Mike Cotton Sound 253
Miller, Steve 117, 199, 200, 202, 295, 296, 301, 381
Millington-Drake, Teddy 224
Mills Brothers 252, 374
Mills, Irving 147, 350, 352
Mingus Big Band 357, 381
Mitchell, Joni 296
Mitchell, Mitch 11, 103, 105, 106, 108, 110, 111, 113, 122, 196, 197, 204, 216, 285, 288, 289, 318, 477, 478
Modern Jazz Quartet 196, 280
Monarchs, The 53
Money, Zoot 11, 14, 51, 53, 78, 79, 80, 81, 82, 88, 90, 113, 119, 131, 138, 139, 174, 177, 213, 243, 248, 249, 250, 251, 308, 316, 317, 359, 386, 392, 393, 410, 428, 429, 444, 446, 460, 463
Monkees 103, 168
Monk, Thelonius 26, 350, 352, 385, 418
Montgomery, Wes 325
Moody Blues 35, 101, 102, 103, 111, 126, 143
Moody, James 94, 234, 248, 356, 357, 405
Mooney, Nigel 409, 425, 472
Moon, Keith 104
Moore, Roger 242, 341, 429
Moore, Scotty 47
Morello, Joe 104
Moretti, Joe 28, 33, 47, 49, 51, 82, 83, 87, 466, 476
Morgan, Barry 205, 220, 221, 224, 226, 234, 237, 478, 479
Morgan, Derrick 216, 466
Morris, Chris 24

486

Morris, Eric 45
Morris, Eric "Monty" 76
Morrison, Van 7, 12, 48, 53, 73, 83, 101, 147, 150, 155, 174, 240, 249, 250, 270, 278, 290, 291, 292, 293, 294, 295, 296, 298, 305, 306, 309, 315, 327, 333, 334, 336, 337, 338, 341, 345, 372, 379, 383, 385, 392, 398, 399, 416, 432, 435, 442, 468, 469, 470, 472, 474, 475
Morrissey, Dick 86, 87, 90, 98, 114, 115, 131, 222, 224, 225, 226, 234, 235, 239, 308, 315, 382, 397, 478, 479
Morrissey Mullen 225
Mott The Hoople 56
Move 5, 35, 39, 47, 68, 100, 103, 295, 400, 452, 457, 472
Muldaur, Maria 376
Muleskinners 45
Mullen, Jim 198, 225, 226, 234, 315, 319, 359, 360, 441, 463, 472
Munro, Matt 40
Murray, Mitch 139
Mwanga, Kunle 52, 421
Myhre, Wencke 357, 468

N

Nash, Graham 15, 16, 408
National Youth Jazz Orchestra 219, 234, 273, 274, 275, 292, 348, 350, 444, 468
NDR Big Band 245, 247, 260, 269, 271, 360, 470
Nelson, Willie 106, 117, 119, 212, 221, 431
Nero and the Gladiators 30, 32, 156, 410
Neville, Aaron 93, 171
Neville, Art 20
New Cool Collective 400
Newley, Anthony 60, 334
Newman, Randy 24, 174, 178, 180
Newmark, Andy 408
New Vaudeville Band, The 143, 151
Ngcukana, Ezra 404
Nice 74, 123, 146, 171, 190, 228, 399, 453, 458, 459, 466
Nicholls, Clay 32, 476
Nicol, Jimmy 29, 47, 76, 85, 86, 477
Nicol, Jimmy & The Shubdubs 76, 85, 86
Night-Timers 51, 82, 87, 88, 103
Noone, Peter 51
Nucleus 7, 219, 234

O

Oberecht, Reggie 91
O'Day, Anita 104, 147, 312, 398, 426
Odgers, Brian 8, 155, 156, 165, 167, 179, 189, 191, 193, 197, 220, 221, 224, 226, 227, 249, 278, 291, 296, 309, 312, 318, 386, 468, 473, 478, 479
O'Farrell, Chico 142, 148, 354, 366
Öhman, Kjell 243, 244, 245, 269, 307, 353, 395, 423
Okin, Earl 170
Oldaker, Jamie 199, 200, 201, 202, 203, 212, 213, 387, 420, 445, 446
Oldham, Andrew Loog 55, 124
Oliver, King 147, 246

O'Neill, Mike 32, 33, 34, 35, 36, 37, 38, 45, 48, 73, 102, 113, 117, 131, 132, 155, 156, 157, 167, 173, 253, 268, 271, 299, 306, 313, 333, 384, 387, 390, 392, 410, 421, 429, 431, 441
O'Quinn, Keith 305, 306
O'Rahilly, Ronan 66, 78
Organ Grinders, The 243, 245, 321
Ørsted-Pederson, Nils-Henning 248
Osbourne, Gary 170
O'Sullivan, Gilbert 182
Oxley, Tony 129, 143, 165, 278

P

Palmer, Carl 190
Palmer, Robert 91, 152, 271, 332, 411
Pan's People 158, 175
Parish, John 288
Parker, Alan 220, 224, 226
Parker, Charlie 74, 128, 129, 157, 161, 248, 269, 324, 326, 342, 429
Parker, Chris 301, 304, 306, 307
Parker, Junior 106
Parker, Maceo 328
Parnes, Larry 5, 22, 23, 24, 25, 26, 27, 28, 29, 30, 31, 32, 33, 34, 42, 47, 48, 49, 70, 80, 83, 105, 220, 236, 246, 252, 253, 290, 317, 359, 410, 445
Patitucci, John 308
Patrick, Pat 97
Patto 196
Patton, John 118
Patton, Robbie 225
Payn, Nick 369, 372, 374, 376, 378, 444, 446, 479
Pearce, Dick 400
Pedersen, Henrik Bolberg 353, 354
Perry, Mike 315
Peterson, Billy 308, 381
Peterson, Ray 64
Peterson, Ricky 300, 308, 473
Pickett, Wilson 112
Pigott, Richard 315
Pike, Vicki 170
Pine, Courtney 326
Pink Floyd 60, 255, 292, 320, 408
Pitney, Gene 135
Pizzarelli, Bucky 233, 234, 356
Platters 40
Playboys 25, 47, 200
Poet in New York 8, 12, 72, 334, 419
Powell, Bud 26
Powell, James 7, 17, 188, 189, 223, 273, 278, 282, 283, 285, 286, 287, 288, 289, 295, 300, 308, 309, 310, 311, 312, 313, 315, 317, 318, 327, 336, 338, 339, 341, 342, 346, 349, 385, 387, 389, 390, 391, 394, 398, 401, 404, 405, 408, 409, 413, 416, 419, 420, 430, 432, 437, 441, 444, 446, 448, 458, 470, 472, 473, 479
Powell, Seldon 216
Powell, Tristan 7, 8, 185, 188, 189, 223, 273, 278, 282, 283, 284, 285, 286, 288, 295, 300, 306, 309, 310, 311, 312, 313, 315, 317, 318, 319, 320, 321, 327, 332, 333,

336, 337, 338, 340, 341, 344, 346, 349, 387, 388, 389, 394, 398, 403, 405, 409, 412, 413, 415, 427, 430, 433, 438, 441, 444, 446, 470, 479
Power, Duffy 24, 26, 28, 29, 49, 55, 84, 252, 445, 446, 473
Preachers 54
Presidents 69
Presley, Elvis 18, 22, 46, 83, 106, 292
Presley, Reg 171
Preston, Billy 175, 262
Pretty Things 104, 473
Price, Alan 15, 17, 18, 51, 84, 89, 103, 105, 118, 123, 147, 151, 153, 154, 155, 156, 157, 158, 167, 173, 174, 175, 176, 177, 178, 179, 180, 182, 183, 184, 185, 186, 189, 190, 191, 192, 195, 204, 207, 216, 219, 220, 227, 249, 251, 282, 283, 303, 307, 316, 317, 351, 359, 364, 374, 377, 428, 429, 430, 431, 445, 449, 459, 465, 466, 478
Price, Elizabeth 285
Price, Lloyd 18, 252
Pride, Dickie 27, 42, 55
Prima, Louis 34, 130, 237, 247, 369, 374
Prince, Viv 104
Procol Harum 74, 87, 103, 126, 289, 354, 355, 372
Purdie, Bernard "Pretty" 198
Pyne, Chris 164, 182, 236, 478

Q

Quant, Mary 78
Quickly, Tommy 76, 85
Quiet Three, The 29, 85

R

Rådelius, Ulf 398
Radle, Carl 180, 199, 200, 201, 203, 212, 387, 420
Ram Jam Band 51, 52, 249
Randazzo, Teddy 93, 170
Rankine, Brian 351
Rankin, Kenny 170, 172
Rascals 232, 315, 371
Ray Davies 110, 388
Ray, Johnny 22, 214
Red Bludd's Bluesicians 66
Redding, Otis 55, 103, 107, 112, 117, 179
Reece, Red 11, 29, 31, 66, 70, 71, 74, 84, 85, 86, 91, 123, 192, 476, 477
Reed, Jimmy 48, 104, 141
Reese, Della 133
Reeves, Reeves 101
Reggae Philharmonic Orchestra 13, 227, 228, 460
Reinhardt, Django 284
Remeta, Krešimir 302
Remo Four 76, 155
Rendell, Don 76, 90
Rhythm Kings 8, 12, 26, 32, 54, 67, 127, 333, 354, 355, 356, 358, 367, 368, 369, 370, 372, 373, 374, 376, 377, 378, 380, 383, 385, 387, 390, 432, 439, 441, 442, 470, 471, 472
Richard, Cliff 20, 23, 24, 34, 47, 68, 72, 95, 180, 291
Richardson, Colin 137

Richardson, Ian 250
Richards, Reynold 130
Rich, Buddy 98, 230, 287
Rich, Charlie 179
Ricotti, Frank 155, 164, 468, 478
Ritenour, Lee 208
Rivers, Johnny 151
Roach, Max 104
Robertson, Robbie 166
Robinson, Barry 350
Robinson, Smokey 73, 95, 107, 212
Robinson, Smokey & The Miracles 73
Rockefeller, David 400
Rockin' Berries 102
Rockwell, Bob 133, 431, 441, 473
Rodriguez, Rico 63, 410
Rogers, Richard 132, 384
Rolling Stones 11, 41, 47, 54, 55, 63, 64, 69, 70, 78, 84, 91, 102, 107, 108, 123, 125, 171, 179, 199, 231, 249, 279, 367, 372, 375, 378, 421
Rollins, Sonny 55, 116, 326, 417
Rösch, Hans-Hermann 362
Rosenberg, Marianne 92
Ross, Annie 7, 27, 95, 96, 149, 150, 214, 231, 232, 233, 234, 235, 236, 237, 247, 250, 266, 300, 331, 335, 353, 356, 369, 400, 430, 444, 446, 450, 460, 465
Ross, Ronnie 39, 325
Route 66 74, 161, 377, 378, 384
Rowls, Jim 308
Royal, Billy Joe 106
Royal Flush Orchestra 147
Roy Coulton Band 50
Rubin, Alan 305
Ruffin, David 107
Runswick, Darryl 234, 236
Russell, Leon 180, 200
Rutten, Edwin 254
Ryan, Jeff 155, 156, 157, 158, 420, 421, 430, 464
Ryan, John 201, 202

S

Salmins, Ralph 333, 336, 344, 345, 359, 386, 387, 388, 389, 399
Sam & Dave 175
Samuelsson, Lasse 7, 210, 242, 257, 260, 261, 262, 263, 301, 401
Samwell, Ian 68, 69, 84, 92, 93, 103, 178, 198
Sandom, Doug 104
Sandviken Big Band 244, 247, 357
Santamaria, Mongo 95
Santana 84, 171, 173, 225
Sarstedt, Peter 236
Sarstedt, Robin 236
Scaffold 148, 183
Scaggs, Boz 202, 295, 296, 298, 305, 386
Scott-Emuakpor, Jimmy 145
Scott, Johnny 130, 132
Scott, Ronnie 8, 38, 39, 49, 55, 70, 86, 87, 107, 114, 120, 129, 130, 131, 134, 135, 143, 146, 153, 157, 159,

163, 164, 168, 183, 184, 198, 204, 214, 220, 221, 235, 248, 265, 267, 273, 274, 275, 279, 322, 323, 324, 325, 326, 327, 328, 329, 330, 332, 333, 335, 336, 337, 338, 340, 341, 342, 344, 359, 362, 390, 391, 392, 396, 397, 406, 409, 411, 412, 413, 416, 419, 428, 442, 444, 470
Seabrooke, Ronnie 144
Seamen, Phil 11, 49, 85, 86, 87, 102, 104, 114, 115, 131, 253, 325, 477
Searchers 83
Sebastian, John 127
Seekers, 102
Seger, Bob 199
Sellers, Peter 60
SFB Big Band 401
Shadows 20, 28, 32, 34, 68, 164, 171, 189, 193, 197, 204, 254
Shaffer, Paul 305, 307, 391
Shapiro, Helen 170
Shaw, Ian 318
Shaw, Sandie 66, 219
Shear, Eernie 144
Sheeley, Sharon 30
Sheridan, Tony 23, 25, 26, 28, 30, 31, 47, 48, 105, 246, 253
Short, Steve 234
Shorty 6, 72, 155, 163, 165, 166, 167, 169, 184, 224, 266, 277, 278, 307, 432, 459
Sidewinders 84
Sidran, Sidran 7, 72, 117, 133, 202, 295, 296, 297, 298, 299, 300, 301, 304, 305, 306, 307, 308, 309, 314, 316, 333, 337, 338, 344, 345, 346, 347, 358, 360, 364, 379, 380, 381, 383, 384, 385, 389, 408, 420, 426, 427, 442, 463, 472, 473
Simon & Garfunkel 151
Simon, Paul 295, 301, 304
Sims, Zoot 80, 279, 325
Sinatra, Frank 40, 95, 116, 117, 146, 148, 149, 152, 160, 161, 170, 231, 233, 236, 246, 269, 270, 296, 313, 336, 350, 354, 357, 369, 374, 397, 425, 426
Skatalites 50, 64, 73
Skeete, Beverly 369, 370, 371, 372, 374, 377, 470, 471
Skellern, Peter 227, 261, 262, 263
Skidmore, Alan 7, 11, 114, 123, 163, 165, 166, 167, 168, 204, 205, 206, 209, 275, 276, 277, 278, 283, 294, 309, 310, 314, 327, 329, 331, 333, 335, 336, 338, 339, 340, 341, 342, 343, 359, 380, 383, 385, 387, 388, 390, 409, 412, 413, 415, 416, 419, 421, 426, 429, 432, 433, 437, 444, 446, 464, 472, 478, 479
Skidmore, Jimmy 164
Skinner, Simon 284
Slade, Boots 32, 50, 66, 71, 74, 84, 156, 174, 477
Slickers 203
Slim Chance 201, 206
Small Faces 45, 51, 78, 108, 120, 123, 124, 153, 154, 193, 199, 206, 324, 476
Smith, Jimmy 43, 44, 147, 318, 321, 338, 360, 419, 437
Smith, Keith 239, 269, 362
Smith, Mike 140, 143, 145, 147, 159, 161, 169, 177, 349
Smith, Terry 143, 146, 222

Snow, Mike 176, 177, 178
Soft Machine 123, 219, 221, 351
Sonny Terry & Brownie McGhee 40
Sounds Incorporated 68, 102
South, Harry 87, 109, 113-116, 118, 122, 125, 129, 130, 131, 133, 134, 143, 144, 146, 167, 214, 224, 231, 234, 235, 239, 266, 348, 353, 359, 365, 431, 458, 468
Specials, The 11, 66, 228
Spencer Davis Group, The 52, 65, 148, 235
Spinetti, Henry 226
Spinners 105
Springfield, Dusty 101, 123, 160
Stacey, Paul 320, 415
Stansfield, Lisa 399, 409, 470
Starr, Ringo 19, 25, 33, 78, 85, 368, 474
Steele, Tommy 22, 32, 47
Steel Pulse 249
Steinberg, Lewie 91
Sterling, Keith 266, 479
Stevens, Cat 123, 125, 154, 198, 321
Stevens, Guy 56
Stevenson, Mickey 105
Stewart, Al 154
Stewart, Billy 106, 124, 226
Stewart, Rex 273
Stewart, Rod 41, 53, 86, 154, 194, 206, 230
Stock-Aitken-Waterman 263
Strayhorn, Billy 384, 385
Streisand, Barbra 95
Stuart, Glen and The Clansmen 28
Stubblefield, Clyde 396
Suckle, Count 51, 62, 63, 78, 90, 392, 411, 429
Sullivan, Big Jim 28, 33, 69, 70, 71, 72, 82, 83, 93, 94, 466, 477
Sultzman, Stan 205
Summers, Andy 82, 139
Supremes 101, 105, 106, 188, 230
Surman, John 165, 269, 312, 342
Sutherland Brothers & Quiver 207
Swedish Symphony Orchestra 245
Sweet Substitute 240
Symphony Sid 61, 244, 293, 294, 303, 306, 327, 331, 334, 383, 429, 461, 463, 465, 469, 472, 473

T

Talmy, Shel 69
Tate, Grady 301, 304, 306, 308, 356, 419
Taupin, Bernie 170, 190
Taylor, James 95, 168, 234, 437
Taylor, Martin 205, 273, 320, 370, 372, 373, 398, 471
Taylor, Mick 11, 371, 473
Taylor, Vince 25, 28, 32, 47
Tee, Richard 295, 296, 298, 300, 307
Temperance Seven 53, 132
Tench, Bobby 198
Ten Years After 90, 154, 173, 318, 401, 437
Terry, Clark 97, 262, 274, 276, 356, 398, 468
Thacker, Clive 175, 177, 182, 184, 185, 186, 214, 478

The Ferris Wheel 178, 179
Themen, Art 31, 159, 308, 359, 445, 446
Thielemans, Toots 353, 405
Thomas, Carla 117
Thomas, Rufus 45, 78, 100, 108
Thomas, Tommy 74, 477, 478, 479
Thompson, Danny 166
Thompson, Gail 326
Thompson, Lucky 324
Thornton, Eddie "Tan Tan" 5, 11, 43, 50, 51, 65, 75, 92, 99, 100, 103, 105, 106, 107, 108, 120, 123, 131, 203, 204, 205, 213, 217, 221, 224, 226, 227, 229, 249, 272, 276, 278, 331, 409, 410, 460, 467, 477, 478, 479
Thunderbirds 45, 52, 79, 82, 89, 103, 124, 128, 153
Tibbs, Jackie 158
Tom Scott's LA Express 296
Tony Knight's Chessmen 53, 81
Top Brass 182
Tornados, The 23, 34, 111
Toussaint, Allen 106, 147, 378
Townsend, Ken 319
Tracey, Stan 87, 114, 115, 164, 214, 223, 320, 359
Tremeloes 88, 139, 140
T. Rex 35
Triplehorne, Tommy 200, 203, 213, 387
Troggs, The 59, 104, 171, 314
Troup, Bobby 161, 384
Troy, Doris 170
Tucky Buzzard 369
Tunderman, Frans 270
Turner, Bill 350, 351
Turner, Joe 47
Turner, Titus 92, 93
Turrentine, Stanley 243, 250, 307, 315, 392, 419
Twitty, Conway 92
Tyner, McCoy 405

U

Ulrik, Hans 353
Undertakers 31
Uni-Bigband Bielefeld 362
Upchurch, Phil 63, 72, 314, 431

V

Vagabonds 25
Valance, Ricky 64
Van Der Graaf Generator 112
van Rooyen, Jerry 244, 348, 349
Vaughan, Billy 65
Vaughan, Sarah 38, 95, 319
Ventures, The 32
Vincent, Gene 25, 30, 31, 32, 48, 68, 105, 215, 216, 410, 415, 466
Vinding, Mads 247, 431
Vin, Duke 62
Vrethammar, Sylvia 128, 244, 246, 247, 365, 441, 450, 460

W

Wadsworth, Derek 123, 143, 144, 146
Wailers 60, 160
Wakelin, Johnny 207
Walker, Junior 127
Walker, Robert 287
Walker, Scott 114, 222
Waller, Fats 96, 368, 374, 394
Wallin, Bengt-Arne 247, 468
Ward, Barry 296, 297
Warleigh, Ray 98, 114, 117, 220, 221, 222, 224
Warwick, Dionne 78, 160
Washington, Geno 50, 51, 52, 53, 55, 81, 249, 410, 421, 446
Washington, Ned 425
Waters, Muddy 6, 74, 216, 292, 393, 467
Watkins, Derek 131, 143, 164, 358, 359
Watkins, Geraint 376, 377, 378
Watson, Earl 36, 37, 41, 113, 391, 392, 473, 476
Watts, Charlie 54, 84, 86, 203, 248, 279, 306, 326, 474
Wayne Fontana & The Mindbenders 102
WDR Big Band 14, 247, 260, 348, 360, 362, 383, 401
Weather Report 96, 314
Webb, Jimmy 151
Weckl, Dave 288
Weisgard, Ethan 354
Weller, Don 283, 326
Wells, Mary 376
Werner, Kenny 281
Wesley, Fred 328
Wet Wet Wet 15
Wheeler, Kenny 114, 115, 131, 143, 356
Whitfield, Norman 94
Who, The 6, 13, 26, 39, 44, 54, 58, 63, 67, 69, 70, 78, 87, 90, 104, 105, 133, 135, 148, 161, 162, 207, 223, 226, 253, 260, 296, 324, 326, 329, 334, 342, 345, 365, 446, 459, 460, 467
Wickman, Hans Olof "Putte" 245
Wild Bill Davison 274
Wilde, Kim 23
Wilde, Marty 5, 22, 23, 24, 26, 28, 32, 33, 49, 83
Wilder, Alec 231, 395
Wilhelmsson, Arne 261
Williams, Andy 125, 126, 150, 151, 172, 439
Williams, Fess 147
Williams, Jerry 243
Williams, Joe 73, 133, 319, 392
Williams, John 254
Williams, Kathryn 279
Williams, Larry 20
Williamson, Sonny Boy 73, 318, 332
Williams, Tony 84
Willis, Chuck 92
Winehouse, Amy 95
Winwood, Steve 44, 156, 170, 216, 103, 148, 235
Withers, Bill 224, 225, 226, 230, 389
Witherspoon, Jimmy 41, 56, 115, 214, 248
Wogan, Terry 156, 240, 390, 394
Womack, Bobby 160, 210, 211

Wonder, Stevie 6, 63, 78, 90, 101, 104, 107, 160, 219, 222, 226, 230
Woodman, Bobby 23, 28
Wright, Geoff 22
Wright, O.V. 179
Wyman, Bill 8, 12, 32, 54, 55, 78, 82, 84, 91, 127, 354, 356, 358, 367, 368, 369, 370, 371, 372, 373, 374, 375, 376, 377, 378, 383, 385, 386, 387, 393, 415, 431, 432, 439, 444, 445, 446, 470, 471, 472, 476

Y

Yardbirds 55, 191
Young, Kenny 171
Young, Lester 294, 306, 324, 334, 379, 383, 429
Young, Roy 40
Young, Victor 425

Z

Zappa, Frank 47, 197, 284
Zawinul, Joe 314
Zombies, The 170
Zwingenberger, Axel 375

About The Author

Uli Twelker (b. 1953) works as a music journalist, singing drummer and English language teacher based in Westfalia/Germany. He has played in Rhythm & Blues, Jazz, Rock'n'Roll and Latin bands all his life, since 2012 in the New Orleans orientated Sazerac Swingers. Apart from contributions for *GoodTimes* magazine, he wrote *Happy Boys Happy – The Small Faces & Other Stories* about the lives and work of the mod midgets, The Faces, Humble Pie, Peter Frampton & Rod Stewart. He lives in Gütersloh, Germany with his wife, Senta.

Addendum

Page 16

1)   GF is not too fond of reading the Alan Freeman quotes, wondering whether Alan Leslie "Fluff" Freeman, MBE (6th July 1927 – 27th November 2006), an Australian born DJ renowned in the world of BBC Radio, really used his genuine interview quotes or just happened to reminisce about things freely from memory. As Freeman cannot be asked for confirmation anymore and never said anything negative about Georgie Fame whatsoever, I have decided to leave his material in the text, for the sake of adding color. Again, GF has always been kind and informative in our many interviews, but with his own book in mind, I was not able to ask him again and again about details from the very early past, which he will probably be able to tell in more detail one of these days, as John Lennon would have said, "in his own write", or rather his ongoing taped recollections directed by Ben Sidran.

Page 29

2)   Here, Georgie Fame pointed out that Duffy Power's memory might not always have served him right, while the singer born as Ray Howard seemed coherent to this writer in our interview, conducted in September 2012. We can't ask him now, because Duffy passed away on February 19th, 2014. Duffy's claim of "having introduced GF to Mose Allison" may not really be scandalous stuff, but does not seem accurate now. As Power didn't say anything disgraceful about Georgie, it was kept in, not forgetting the points Georgie made in March 2015:

> "When we [the Blue Flames] left the Parnes Organization in 1961, Duffy was still contracted to Larry Parnes. It wasn't until the Beatles came along that [the impact of] the Larry Parnes Organization was destroyed" – meaning that Duffy Power was still a Rock'n'Roll singer and not into the Blues yet. Georgie: "We didn't hear anything of him playing the Blues harmonica until he was with Alexis Korner, like a year later. I don't know how he came to claim that he introduced me to Mose Allison! Was it a kind of bitterness? It wasn't until [Alexis Korner's] New Blues Incorporated with Dick Heckstall-Smith that Duffy started to play Blues harmonica. And I never saw him after we left Larry Parnes, apart from a later visit to the club: He did come down to the Flamingo, but by that time I was well on my way of having Mose in my repertoire. It was [the American G.I.] Carl Smith from Grand Rapids, Michigan who introduced me to Mose Allison. And I know that I ripped off Mose Allison's voice, but we've all got to start somewhere."

Page 29

3) Nicol himself preferred the spelling of his Christian name as "Jimmie", for instance on the front skin of his bass drum and in signing autographs, although all his solo singles appeared under the moniker "Jimmy Nicol" which is how it is used in this book. Big Band trained (Rock'n'Jazz Trad Big Band, The Oscar Rabin Band'), Nicol was part of the nucleus of Georgie's Blue Flames in Vince Eager & The Quiet Three, and he shared a love of Blue Beat with Fame even before he joined his band. It's a pity they never recorded together, in spite of Jimmy/Jimmie's inspired studio sophistication.

Page 35

4) In his book *The Beatle Who Vanished* about drummer Jimmy Nicol, Jim Berkenstadt writes that "Little did he [GF] realize that it was Jimmie [he uses the passport spelling] Nicol who had first exposed Mike O'Neill to Jazz. While staying at O'Neill's flat, Fame had an epiphany. He knew that if he could get his own band going, and perform Blues and Jazz for the public, it would catch on."

Page 47

5) Clarke-Johnson was talking about the brothers Freddie and Sammy Irani, who had been the owners of the 2i's until 1955, when Ray Hunter and Paul Lincoln (the Australian wrestler they used to call "Dr Death") took over. On April 22nd, 1956, they opened the actual coffee bar, with Skiffle group The Vipers (featuring Wally Whyton) taking care of the first residency.

Page 51

6) Geno Washington has his chops and skills together still, but not necessarily his Rock history: Mayall had Clapton, Peter Green and future Rolling Stone Mick Taylor – never Jeff Beck! The link between John Mayall & Jeff Beck? Drummer Micky Waller, another one time Blue Flame.

Page 69

7) In his memoir *Sound Man*, Glyn describes the Fame-Talmy encounter: "I had met Georgie several times before when he was the keyboard player with Billy Fury, England's answer to Elvis. So we knew each other and had always got on well. After the show I told him of my new arrangement with IBS and asked if he would care to come one evening with the band and record two or three songs on the understanding that we may be able to get him a record deal […]. When he turned

up, he brought Shel Talmy with him. Shel had evidently approached him, showing interest in producing him, so Georgie decided to kill two birds with one stone. I was not best pleased, to say the least. I had never met Shel and I had no idea who he was. I explained in no uncertain terms that it was my session and I was producing it. Shel remained calm and very politely suggested that, as we were both there, why did we not just get on with it and see how it goes. I begrudgingly agreed and it turned out to be one of the best decisions I ever made. [...] As far as I know, Georgie Fame never used the tapes to get himself a record deal."

Page 70

8) Engineer Glyn Johns disagrees about Samwell "bringing in" a guitarist: "Unfortunately, Johnny McLaughlin and Speedy were not available that night. Johnny was so cool in his sharkskin suit and pencil tie with a button-down shirt. He would lean on the pillar on the left side of the stage, barely moving, while playing the most incredible guitar. So his place was taken at the last minute by Big Jim Sullivan, who, considering that he did not know the material, did a wonderful job.

Page 70

9) Glyn Johns: "Speedy, the conga player in the band, was in jail, having been busted for drugs, so his place was taken by a friend of Georgie and a regular at the Flamingo, Tommy Thomas. He did his best but it was not quite the same. Red Reece and Boots Slade were on drums and bass, and what an incredible rhythm section they were. The snare drum sound that Red got on that stage was certainly one of the best I have ever heard. This is a great record and a fine example of Georgie Fame's extraordinary talent as a musician, bandleader, and singer."

Page 71

10) "Night Train", incidentally, had also been recorded by future Blue Flames drummer Jimmy Nicol as Jimmy Nicol & The Shubdubs. It was the B-side of the familiar tale of the egg-shaped "Humpty Dumpty", whose Caribbean flavor of R&B, Blue Beat and Calypso Nicol also shared with Georgie's live set in the Flamingo, see track 8 of that album.

Page 85

11) According to *The Beatle Who Vanished*, Jim Berkenstadt points out that "over the spring of 1964, Jimmy Nicol occasionally subbed for Red Reece on drums. Fame and [Tex] Makins had played with Nicol over the years, and it was a natural fit for

Jimmy to fill in with the band. Given the band's exhaustive schedule and with Reece's band beginning to falter, the need for an occasional fill-in continued….During the first week of May, 1964, Blue Flames drummer Red Reece became too ill to continue with the band. This left Georgie Fame with a dilemma. Who could he pick up to replace the ailing Reece behind the drum kit of the hottest Jazz and R&B band in London? It was bass player, Tex Makins, who suggested to Georgie that they should hire Jimmy Nicol on a permanent basis", while "permanent" still meant that he was only a regular for about three weeks, before the Fab Four gave him the fateful call for more intense, but even shorter "fame".

Page 86

12) At roughly the same time, Georgie told Jim Berkenstadt that "The [Beatles] tour went to his head. Last time I heard of him, he was in Mexico playing psychedelic music. That was in 1967." This was certainly rubbed in by Berkenstadt: "Starting in Holland and Denmark, and following through the tour, John and Paul would regularly ask Jimmie after each show or press conference, 'How's it going, Jimmie?' Nicol's brief reply was always, 'It's getting better", a phrase that would stick in the back of Paul McCartney's mind and prove useful in the future." So maybe Georgie should have covered "It's Getting Better" from Sgt Pepper instead of "When I'm Sixty-Four"?! - The post-Beatles Nicol had still played in the Blue Flames on and off, when, in September 1965, he was asked to join the Swedish Shadows-type instrumental group The Spotnicks. Jimmie to Berkenstadt: "I had an event at a nightclub in Leeds and some other gigs with Georgie Fame. That's why I hesitated a bit when I got the offer from The Spotnicks.". But by making some well-aimed, flattering compliments, Spotnicks manager Roland Ferneborg managed to lure Nicol in. But after a while, the Mexican scene, including a girl, proved stronger – but that's another story.

Page 92

13) Before Elvis Presley covered "One Night", it had been recorded and performed by Smiley Lewis, as "One Night (Of Sin)".

Page 94

14) To be precise, "The Point Of No Return" only features on the re-issue of *Spike*. It was also a track on the CD single "Baby Plays Around", while it didn't appear on the first *Spike* album release. Actually, Elvis Costello sang "The Point Of No Return" with Georgie at the Royal Albert Hall in London on October 29th, 2014, on the occasion of having invited Fame to his gig, whereupon Georgie persuaded

him to include the full Blue Flames band into the bargain. The performance was a relaxed, swingy affair, with Costello's vocals matched perfectly by our happy protagonists's Hammond wailing, complete with Woody Woodpecker type melody lines and hollering.

Page 170

15) Shortly after achieving his first important cover slot with Georgie Fame, Phil Pickett became a founder member of the group Sailor ("A Glass Of Chanpagne", "Girls Girls Girls"). As a member of Boy George's Culture Club, he co-wrote „Karma Chameleon". His "Don't Send Flowers" was covered by Sheena Easton, for instance, who worked with Fame on the album SWING. Georgie would love the fact that, at age 21, Pickett had a 1967 encounter with Fame hero Duke Ellington, the veteran bringing out a toast in a supper club, advising him to follow his heart in starting a music career back in England.

Page 179

16) Some Charlie Rich buffs claim that this is a sequel to "Don't Take Your Guns to Town" by Johnny Cash. It was composed by Charlie Rich but originally recorded by Fame & Price's hero Jerry Lee Lewis, which explains why Georgie had included it in early, vintage 1960 demos for the legendary and eccentric North London producer Joe Meek, up in his studio/flat in Holloway Road. Neither Georgie nor Alan dare to mention that they're going to hang soon for killing Billy Joe, as composer Rich and cover kid Jerry Lee duly did at the beginning of their respective readings.

Page 201

17) It may be interesting to know that Gallagher & Lyle were also the creative force in McGuinness Flint, contributing to both of their hits, "When I'm Dead And Gone" (1970) and "Malt And Barley Blues" (1971). The duo also initially took part in Slim Chance, the group that fellow Mod and ex-Small Faces bass player Ronnie Lane led in his traveling circus project The Passing Show.

Page 213

18) Georgie's Island Records producer Glyn Johns remembers his own tying of knots in *Sound Man*: "He came and played with Charlie Watts and Eric Clapton at my second wedding. Now that was quite a band."

Page 252

19) Georgie had demoed "Someday" as early as 1960 for London producer Joe Meek, albeit in an instrumental version – maybe a planned vocal never materialized. The rare tracks Fame laid down as a 17 year old also contain Rock'n'Roll material like "High School Hop", "Little Queenie", Lionel Bart's protégé Cliff-Richard's "Livin' Doll". There was the Ritchie Valens ballad "Donna", Ray Charles's Gospel-R&B hybrid "I Got A Woman" and, most interestingly, the traditional shanty "My Bonnie", which became the first Beatles single, led by Georgie Fame's Larry Parnes pal Tony Sheridan.

Page 271

20) On www.jazzportraits.blogspot.de, it is pointed out that the Carpenter in question is "not *that* Richard Carpenter, brother of Karen [in the Pop legends The Carpenters], but rather it's the *other* Richard Carpenter, a noted Jazz shyster, who according to James Gavin [author of *Chet Baker: Deep In A Dream*] ripped off Chet Baker so badly that Chet literally wanted to kill the man". Still, "Go-Go" is credited to Carpenter, together with Bruce-Fame.

Page 297

21) Louis Jordan is believed to have been married five times – the one wife who benefitted most from songwriting credits was Fleecie Moore: in order not to touch a previous publishing deal of her husband. Moore got the writing credit for "Caldonia", for instance.

Page 298

22) Appearing in the German TV concert series *Ohne Filter* with his Blue Flames in 1991, GF announced "Yeh Yeh" in his own deadpan way: "This next song is dedicated to Matt Bianco." Reminiscing about the studio sessions, Georgie then proceeded with some of his famous name-dropping: "Steve Gadd, Will Lee, yeh-ych, yeah-yeah, Robin Ford, Richard Tee". After the Reggae section, continued with a shout of "Old style" in Swing fashion.

Page 307

23) Fame still features this Mose Allison classic in his own live set from time to time, but he also "Fam(e)ously" celebrated the song in a duet with Elvis Costello, who had invited Georgie with his Blues Flames to his concert at London's Royal Albert Hall on October 29th, 2014. Announcing "Everybody's Cryin' Mercy", Costello

informed his audience that "This was written by Mose Allison, and I wouldn't know this man's music if it wasn't for Georgie: He taught me everything I know about Mose." It was a true duet, too, with Elvis and Georgie sharing verses and obviously enjoying every second here.

Page 436

24) Glyn Johns, engineer of the *Flamingo* album and producer of his Island recordings, reckons that "he and Andy Fairweather Low are my two favorite bandleaders. Both have the extraordinary ability to seamlessly take control of a group of musicians without appearing to be bossy or superior in any way and within minutes have them all pointing in the same direction, with remarkable results."

Page 439

25) Producer Glyn Johns adds more praise: "I consider him to be one of the finest musicians I have ever had the pleasure of working with. He is an exceptional Hammond B3 player with a rare complete understanding of the instrument, and I love the sound of his voice, his Jazz roots facilitating the most wonderful phrasing."

Page 457

26) After this book's initial deadline there were a number of new releases:

Rhythm and Blues at the "Camden Theatre" LP (recorded March 1964, R&B Records 33XX/R&B3-180, released April 2015, UK, first published in 1964)

Side 1: "Rhythm And Blues At The Camden Theatre": Night Train/Bright Lights, Big City/ Walking The Dog/Do-Re-Mi/Let The Sunshine In/You're Breaking My Heart

Side 2: "Jazz Club": I'm Gone/Moody's Mood/Fools Paradise/Walking The Dog/Yeh Yeh

The Whole World's Shaking (5-CD Box Set, with four original albums, **Rhythm and Blues at The Flamingo, Fame At Last, Sweet Things, Sound Venture**, plus 18 unreleased tracks, a 48-pages hardcover book, in-depth interview with GF, five postcards, and poster, to be released in October 2015

Photo Credits

p. 009 personal archive of Ian McLagan

p. 121 licenced from Getty Images

p. 142 copyright GoodTimes magazine (permission to use provided)

p. 172 US poster of unknown origin (if provided, copyright will be acknowledged)

p. 183 personal archives of Michael Ackermann, Wuppertal, Germany

p. 215 personal archives of Michael Ackermann, Wuppertal, Germany

p. 273 personal archives of Antonio Alfaiate, Lisbon, Portugal

p. 277 personal archives of Antonio Alfaiate, Lisbon, Portugal

p. 279 personal archives of Anthony Kerr, London, England

p. 284 personal archives of Antonio Alfaiate, Lisbon, Portugal

p. 287 personal archives of James Powell, London, England

p. 362 personal archives of Antonio Alfaiate, Lisbon, Portugal

p. 363 personal archives of Antonio Alfaiate, Lisbon, Portugal

p. 364 personal archives of Antonio Alfaiate, Lisbon, Portugal

p. 365 personal archives of Antonio Alfaiate, Lisbon, Portugal

p. 366 personal archives of Wolfgang Wotke, Gütersloh, Germany

p. 378 licenced from Thomas Osterfeld, Osnabrück, Germany

p. 403 personal archives of Antonio Alfaiate, Lisbon, Portugal

p. 404 personal archives of Antonio Alfaiate, Lisbon, Portugal

p. 417 personal archives of Antonio Alfaiate, Lisbon, Portugal

p. 492 personal archives of Antonio Alfaiate, Lisbon, Portugal

Cover photos - personal archives of Wolfgang Wotke, Gütersloh, Germany

Cover artwork - Johannes Saurer, Moisburg, Germany

MORE 'MERSEY SOUND' BOOKS FROM
www.VelocePress.com

BEAT WAVES 'CROSS THE MERSEY
Manfred Kuhlmann

Originally published as 'The Sound With The Pound', this revised and updated edition includes an additional 142 illustrations and 112 pages. A comprehensive anthology of the 'Merseybeat' era, this book chronicles the complete stories of 164 Merseyside groups, plus an additional 100 line-ups and a list of 344 group names, for a total of 607 groups that were active in Liverpool and the surrounding area in the late 1950's to the end of the Sixties.

SOME OTHER GUYS
Manfred's follow up book

Featuring the complete stories of another 66 Merseyside groups of the 1960's. NONE of these stories are included in 'Beat Waves 'Cross The Mersey' they are all 'new'. Also includes an additional 104 line-ups ~ for a total of 174 groups! These are the 'Some Other Guys' who helped create the Merseysound

THE ABSTRACTS

Liverpool in the 60's was a wondrous place, it was alive with music and the sheer number of local musicians and the depth of the talent pool was mind numbing. Depending on your method of research, you will find that there were between 750 to 950 Liverpool based groups performing at any one time during the early to mid 1960's. So here's a story of one of the not-so-famous groups that's part of that total. While their story will always be overshadowed by those that made the 'big time,' it is an honest and down to earth tale and a fairly typical representation of the many hundreds of other groups that created the 'Mersey Sound' and the real Merseybeat era.

**For more information please visit our website
www.VelocePress.com - Arts & Entertainment**

BLUES AT THE CAVERN
Raymond David

Following in the wake of the Beatles and the remarkable surge of Merseyside groups, there came a memorable resurgence of arguably the greatest grass roots form of music, the 'Blues', not only on Merseyside but throughout the UK. This unique spell in the mid sixties saw the only performances by some of the legendary American bluesmen at the world-renowned original Cavern Club.

Liverpool born Raymond David's book, 'Blues at the Cavern', is a fascinating journey through these times and is a story that has never been told before. If you love the blues, you'll love this book.

In addition, he paints a vivid picture of what it was like to grow up in the suburbs during the post war years with his own humorous recollections that are well worth reading in their own right and give a nostalgic glimpse of that period in an austere Britain.

A mix of wit and pathos, the author tells it as it is, pulling no punches of life in a tough, uncompromising city where the ultimate priority is a sense of humor.

CD's FEATURING THE GROUPS FROM
BEAT WAVES 'CROSS THE MERSEY & SOME OTHER GUYS

Subsequent to the publication of "Beat Waves 'Cross The Mersey" and "Some Other Guys" Manfred produced a series of music CD's that compliment the stories of the groups that are included in those books. They include many previously unreleased recordings, some from the famous Liverpool clubs, all digitally re-mastered. A total of 106 songs on 5 separate CD's this is the ultimate nostalgic collection of 1960's 'Merseybeat' music.

For more information please visit our website
www.VelocePress.com - Arts & Entertainment

Lightning Source UK Ltd.
Milton Keynes UK
UKOW06f2321030616

275580UK00001B/9/P